DATE DUE

CITY CULTURE
AND THE MADRIGAL
AT VENICE

MARTHA FELDMAN

CITY CULTURE
AND THE MADRIGAL
AT VENICE

UNIVERSITY OF CALIFORNIA PRESS

Berkeley   Los Angeles   London

Publication of this book was made possible by generous grants from the National Endowment for the Humanities, the Gladys Krieble Delmas Foundation, the American Musicological Society, the Chicago Humanities Institute, and the General Endowment Fund of the Associates of the University of California Press.

University of California Press
Berkeley and Los Angeles, California

University of California Press, Ltd.
London, England

Library of Congress Cataloging-in-Publication Data

Feldman, Martha.
    City culture and the madrigal at Venice / Martha
Feldman.
        p.   cm.
    Includes bibliographical references (p.   ) and index.
    ISBN 0-520-08314-8 (alk. paper)
    1. Madrigals, Italian—Italy—Venice—History and
criticism. 2. Venice (Italy)—Civilization—To 1797.
I. Title.
ML2633.8.V46F4   1995
782.4'3'094531—dc20   94-31376
                                                  CIP

Printed in the United States of America
9   8   7   6   5   4   3   2   1

FOR MA AND PA

. . . and the rustle of Bybrook

CONTENTS

TABLES AND FIGURES

PLATES

AIM	American Institute of Musicology
B-Bc	Brussels, Bibliothèque du Conservatoire Royal de Musique
BMB	Bibliotheca Musica Bononiensis
Einstein, *The Italian Madrigal*	Alfred Einstein. *The Italian Madrigal*. Trans. Alexander H. Knappe, Roger H. Sessions, and Oliver Strunk. 3 vols. Princeton, 1949. Repr. Princeton, 1971.
Fenlon and Haar, *The Italian Madrigal*	Iain Fenlon and James Haar. *The Italian Madrigal in the Early Sixteenth Century: Sources and Interpretation.* Cambridge, 1988.
GB-Lbm	London, British Library
I-Bc	Bologna, Civico Museo Bibliografico Musicale
I-Fas	Florence, Archivio di Stato
I-Fc	Florence, Biblioteca del Conservatorio Luigi Cherubini
I-Fl	Florence, Biblioteca Medicea-Laurenziana
I-Pc	Padua, Biblioteca Capitolare
I-Rv	Rome, Biblioteca Vallicelliana
I-Rvat	Vatican City, Biblioteca Apostolica Vaticana
I-Vas	Venice, Archivio di Stato
I-Vmc	Venice, Museo Civico Correr, Biblioteca d'Arte e Storia Veneziana
I-Vnm	Venice, Biblioteca Nazionale Marciana

I-Vqs	Venice, Biblioteca della Fondazione Querini-Stampalia
incl.	inclusive
JAMS	*Journal of the American Musicological Society*
mens.	mensuration
m.v.	*modo veneto* (used for sixteenth-century dates falling between January 1 and February 29, since the Venetian Calendar began on March 1)
The New Grove	*The New Grove Dictionary of Music and Musicians.* Ed. Stanley Sadie. 20 vols. London, 1980.
n.s.	new style (refers to modern calendar)
Il nuovo Vogel	Emil Vogel. *Bibliografia della musica italiana profana nuova ed. interamente rifatta e aumentata con gli indici dei musicisti, poeti, cantanti, dedicatari e dei capoversi dei testi letterari.* Rev. ed. François Lesure and Claudio Sartori. 3 vols. Pomezia, 1977.
publ.	publication
RISM	*Répertoire International des Sources Musicales*
RQ	*Renaissance Quarterly*
US-Cn	Chicago, Newberry Library
Vander Straeten, ed., *La musique aux Pays-Bas*	Edmond Vander Straeten, ed. *La musique aux Pays-Bas avant le XIXe siècle: Documents inédits et annotés.* 8 vols. Brussels, 1882. Repr. in 4 vols., with an introduction by Edward E. Lowinsky. New York, 1969.

Venice is a maze. It insists on its own complexity and defies its viewer to resolve the seemingly irresoluble. When I first encountered it I was working on my dissertation, which evolved, at first almost unwittingly, into a study of midcentury Venetian madrigals engaged equally in the play of literary texts and musical ones. Since then I have increasingly tried to understand what singing poetry meant in midcentury Venice by widening my gaze across the city's cultural life. I hope this broadening of perspective is at once a deepening as well, a means to swell the space in which composers' settings of verse are seen to coexist with an array not just of literary texts but of other artworks, forms, events, habits, and personalities.

This book, then, seeks to view madrigals in Venice as specific cultural practices, entangled inextricably with a great variety of other practices. Yet there is a more particular story about it and them, book and madrigals, which emerged from problems that arose along the way. One central, and generative, problem had to do with how to situate madrigals in a city that lacked systematic accounts for their main habitat, the private salon. For unlike many courtly and provincial counterparts, Venetian salons that accommodated madrigals resisted the schemata of chronicles and registers, rules and logs. Refusing to straiten their activities into schedules and preserve them in records, they thwarted the facile discernments of others, the capacity to be known and defined.

I came to these places as removed and inquisitive as the contemporaries they excluded—more so, perhaps. For even as I saw how the city's memory had dispersed and obscured the practices I aimed to grasp, I continued to hone the scholarly tools of documentary discovery and control. Ultimately these tools both failed and enabled my ends: failed in that I quickly had to abandon hopes of recovering the city's memory in a missing document or buried archive; enabled in that the patient, manifold accumulation of data (for which my training had prepared me) was to form the heuristic foundation of a new approach in its several senses of solicitation, access, and direction. In time I came to regard Venice as my ethnographic field and the subject of my study not as Venetian madrigals but madrigals in Venice.

Further, the material amassed on my several "field trips" seemed to carry an irrepressible charge to admit the cacophonous and often contradictory subjectivities and mechanisms that defined madrigals in Venice, even while the city claimed to position sovereign authors in figures like Adrian Willaert, Cipriano de Rore, and Gioseffo Zarlino. (One of my cases in point is a book entitled *Di Cipriano il secondo libro de madregali a cinque voci insieme alcuni di M. Adriano et altri autori a misura comune novamente posti in luce*—a book dedicating less than a third of its space to Rore, the rest to eight named authors and three *anonimi*.) The inalterable necessity to seek out madrigalian practices in fragmentary testaments—scattered dedications, prefaces, dialogues, tracts, letters, occasional and dedicatory poems, handbooks, genealogies, wills, contracts, and more—was thus in the end a liberating constraint. Moreover, as the contexts of Venetian musical life failed to reveal themselves on the cognitive ground on which I was largely trained, they helped remake my ways of knowing according to their own modes and sympathies. The more reflexive spirit of inquiry that has entered musicology had a hand in this in later stages of the book, of course. But that was not all. The image of a unitary musical Venice at midcentury continually broke down on close encounter to divulge not a single fixed reality but particular modes of display that existed in competition with many other ones.

Mine is not primarily a study, then, of musical forms or their numerous manifestations. In developing my thoughts on the subject, moreover, I have not tried to provide anything like an encyclopedic extension of Alfred Einstein's treatment of Venetian madrigals in *The Italian Madrigal*—that is, to account comprehensively for the whole range of composers and madrigal prints that might reasonably be called "Venetian." Readers may find my treatment "selective" but will, I hope, find my selectivity guided by an attempt to construct some compelling, at times provocative, interpretations. By mediating between this complex of relations I hope to make intelligible the place of Venetian madrigals within the particular urban context that engendered them.[1]

We may begin to unravel the skein of questions gathered in this study by starting with a strand from social history. In the year 1550 Bernardino Tomitano, a Paduan teacher of logic, wrote a long, fictitious letter to Francesco Longo enumerating the

1. I appeal here to the kind of history recently described by Edward Muir and Ronald F. E. Weissman, "Social and Symbolic Places in Renaissance Venice and Florence," in *The Power of Place: Bringing Together Geographical and Sociological Imaginations,* ed. John A. Agnew and James S. Duncan (Boston, 1989), pp. 81–103.

attributes necessary to a Venetian nobleman.[2] Despite the casual epistolary pose it struck, his letter masked a dense manifesto of the conduct appropriate to high-placed Venetians. It offered, in effect, a partial Venetian miniature of Baldassare Castiglione's famous *Cortegiano,* defining the boundaries of a Venetian aristocracy with its own special formulas for courtliness. Describing the manners of the patrician politician, for instance, Tomitano exhorted Longo to habits that had long served to clothe Venetians in the public eye: modesty, benevolence, purity and naturalness of speech, sententiousness, gravity, measured orderliness, dignity, and practicality.

> Cede audacity to modesty. Incline toward esteeming yourself less, not more, than your rank. Don't rely on your might. Pay no heed to flatterers. Think in the evening of how benevolent your actions were in the day, how worthy of you, how useful to the common good, especially in managing public concerns. . . . When you come to speak in the [Major] Council, make your speech conform to your age and profession—not rough, for this would not be what is expected of you; nor overtly artful, for this would bring you little praise. Let it then be made up of natural artfulness, pure words, and full of examples and thoughts of your homeland, not sung out but espoused with gravity; not convoluted but disposed with order. Be rich with reason rather than commonplaces. Magnify your case with all diligence and insist on its necessary aspects.[3]

I start with this now obscure text for two reasons. The first is to invoke it as an epigraph for my study, since the ideals it distills might be taken as a standard to which Venetians by turns conformed or resisted. The second is to point up the profoundly Venetian transformations that brought it to print. Tomitano's exhortations found no place in the heavy traffic of Venetian printed words until they were recast

2. Signed "di Padova a xxx d'Agosto M.D.L.," the letter survives in manuscript copies in I-Vnm, MSS Ital. cl. VII, no. 227 (7609), and I-Vmc, Cod. Cic. 770, fols. 90–123. A published edition is extant at I-Vnm entitled *Lettera di M. Bernardino Tomitano al Magnifico M. Francesco Longo del Clarissimo M. Antonio* [n.p., n.d.] (shelf no. Misc. 2765); the Marciana's catalogue gives publication data for this print as "[Venezia: Giov. Antonio Coleti, 17..?]," thus attributing its publication to the author of the preface. Coleti's preface states that the letter was discovered by "Sig. Ab. Jacopo Morelli Custode di questa pubblica Libreria di S. Marco." In addition to the *Dialogo* cited below (see n. 4), at least two other rare editions of the letter exist: Jacopo Morelli, ed., *Operette,* vol. 3 (Venice, 1820), pp. 321–407 (hereafter *Operette*); and *Raccolta ferrarese di opuscoli,* vol. 17 (Venice, 1785), according to the information in the *Inventari dei manoscritti italiani* (I have not seen the latter). I quote here and elsewhere from Morelli's edition, which corresponds in all but modernized orthography to the Marciana manuscript.

Tomitano was born in Padua in 1517 and died there in 1574; for a brief biography see the *Dizionario enciclopedico della letteratura italiana* 5:293 and Chap. 5 n. 17 and passim below. (Note numbers as cross-references direct the reader to the main text in the vicinity of the cited number.)

3. "Ceda l'audacia alla modestia. Pendete nel stimarvi meno, che più del vostro grado. Non vi fidate delle vostre forze. Non ascoltate adulatori. Pensate la sera le operazioni fatte il giorno quanto siano state buone, quanto degne di voi, quanto utili al comune benefizio, spezialmente maneggiando le pubbliche cure. . . . Occorrendovi parlare in [il Maggior] Consiglio, sia la vostra orazione all'età conforme, ed alla professione vostra. Non rozza, chè questo sarebbe fuor d'aspettazione; nè meno d'arte apparente, chè questo vi apporterebbe poca laude. Sia dunque fatta con arte naturale, con parole schiette, e della patria vostra, piena di esempi, e colma di sentenzie; non cantata, ma gravemente esposta; non inviluppata, ma con ordine disposta; sia piuttosto ricca di ragioni, che di luoghi comuni; esagerate con ogni diligenza il caso, ed insistete sopra le parti necessarie" (Tomitano, in *Operette,* p. 366).

in the livelier antiphony of a dialogue between the deceased scholar Triphon Gabriele and an eager youth and published anonymously in 1566. Now part of the vernacular mainstream, they bore the title *Dialogo del gentilhuomo veneziano cioè institutione nella quale si discorre quali hanno a essere i costumi del nobile di questa città, per acquistare gloria & honore* (Dialogue of a Venetian gentleman, that is, treatise in which are discussed the necessary habits of a nobleman of this city in order to attain glory and honor).[4] This made Tomitano's words more palatable to a wide readership than the original would have been, freeing his treatiselike letter from some of its lumbering didacticism. But as a dialogue, the text promoted all the more powerfully his idealized model of Venetian character. In such a form it took as its main target the growing numbers of nonpatrician readers, curious to learn how they might borrow some measure of this "glory and honor" and increasingly able to do so.

The *Dialogo* was adapted by the printer, popular historian, and frequent ghostwriter Francesco Sansovino, son of the famous sculptor.[5] Ironically, but typically, both Tomitano and Sansovino were foreign observers of the Venetian patriciate who assumed the task of codifying already heavily symbolized mores that they themselves could know only as outsiders to the republic and to its highest-ranking classes. For them, as for much of Italy and Europe, Venice functioned as an exemplum among modern states. It represented unmatched constitutional stability, political wisdom, good judgment, and liberty. These virtues were intoned in innumerable public speeches. In his oration for the election of Francesco Donà (or Donato) in 1545, the official state orator Cornelio Frangipane praised the new doge for serenity, gravity, high-mindedness, innocence, justness, prudence, integrity, eloquence, and charity. In the same oration he exalted the city of Venice for its balanced form of government, its rule by many, its liberty, tranquillity, and sagacity, and especially its prudence.[6] Nobleman and city coexisted in a happy synecdoche, both in his own eyes and the eyes of others. The qualities they exemplified had only magnified in the foreign gaze with the repeated invasions of Italy after 1494, culmi-

4. The relationship of the *Dialogo* to Tomitano's letter and identification of the author was first made by Morelli, as recounted in Coleti's preface (see n. 2 above). The *Dialogo* was printed in Venice by Francesco Rampazetto and bears the shelf no. 142.D.197.2 at I-Vnm. As Emmanuele A. Cicogna points out, Triphon Gabriele, who communicated with friends but wrote little, may have been the one who gave Tomitano the ideas included in the letter to Longo. A Venetian patrician resident in Padua, Gabriele's thoughts on the Venetian republic were recorded by the Florentine Donato Giannotti in his *Repubblica de' vinitiani* of 1540. See Cicogna, *Delle inscrizioni veneziane,* 6 vols. (Venice, 1834), 4:82. Cicogna also notes yet another work that appropriated Tomitano's letter "con ben maggiore impudenza," namely Aldo Manuzio il giovane's *Il perfetto gentiluomo* (Venice, 1584), which took not just "i sentimenti, ma quasi anche tutte le parole della detta lettera, e solennemente spacciò l'opera per sua nella dedicazione che ne fa al Principe e alla Repubblica di Venezia."

5. Not a clue was given as to its original author, and its new form carried a dedicatory preface misleadingly signed simply "F. S." Cicogna's account of the work (see n. 4 above) is given under no. 84 of his catalogue of Sansovino's works (*Delle inscrizioni veneziane* 4:81–82). For a biography of Sansovino see Paul F. Grendler, "Francesco Sansovino and Italian Popular History, 1560–1600," *Studies in the Renaissance* 16 (1969): 141–42, and for further bibliography, p. 142 n. 2. See also Chap. 5 n. 23 and passim below.

6. *Saggio di rime e prose di Cornelio Frangipane,* ed. Lorenzo Cosatti (Milan, 1812), pp. 110, 115, and 94–101.

nating in the successive collapses of Florentine republicanism that attended the Medici restorations of 1512 and 1530 and, in 1527, the Sack of Rome. Faced with such perils and failures, both Italy and Europe at large fell increasingly prey to Venetians' myths about themselves.[7]

This too was something of an irony. While Venice's self-image was crystallizing into a doctrine of virtues, its own fortunes had suffered a decline. In 1509 the imperialist republic had been jolted from its confident penetrations of the mainland by the League of Cambrai, which ranged against it all the major forces of Europe. The league's formation represented the shattering moment when Venice's political star began to dim. The city never recovered the full political strength it had exercised at the turn of the century, nor did it regain all of its dominions on the *terraferma*.[8] Venice remained wealthy, but some of the entrepreneurialism that had characterized the older patriciate was gradually becoming the province of citizen merchants, foreign businessmen, and a number of young upstart nobles.[9]

In such a time Venetians might have looked on the imaginative realms of arts and letters with some indifference. But from all that can be deduced, this was generally not so. If the city failed to recoup certain of its land claims, it fortified its assertions of glory after only a brief period of restraint by compensating with redoubled artistic investments. By the mid-sixteenth century the doge's processions, state political iconography, and performances of civic liturgy—all highly visible forms—had assumed unprecedented levels of vigor.[10] They served directly the cause of bolstering civic pride by promoting the city's image and its myths of foundation. They remind us, in turn, that while many of the most famous reinscriptions of Venetian myths came from travelers and onlookers from abroad, these myths started with Venetians themselves. It was partly by these means that Venice continued to maintain its status as the ne plus ultra of republicanism among the Italian city-states.

The mythologizing that marks internal explanations of Venetian history and character, both implicit and explicit, did not just ornament the city's infrastructure, then, but carefully constructed its identity, fostering images of Venetian equilibrium at home while spreading them abroad. Any attempt to reconcile the Venice

7. William J. Bouwsma elaborated such a claim in *Venice and the Defense of Republican Liberty: Renaissance Values in the Age of the Counter Reformation* (Berkeley and Los Angeles, 1968), esp. Chaps. 2–4, and others have expounded the idea since. See, for example, James S. Grubb, "When Myths Lose Power: Four Decades of Venetian Historiography," *Journal of Modern History* 58 (1986): 43–94, and the extensive bibliography cited there.

8. On this see Libby J. Lester, "Venetian History and Political Thought after 1509," *Studies in the Renaissance* 20 (1973): 7–45. See also Bouwsma, *Venice and the Defense of Republican Liberty;* Felix Gilbert, "Venice in the Crisis of the League of Cambrai," in *Renaissance Venice,* ed. John R. Hale (London, 1973), pp. 274–92; and for a summary of relevant literature, Margaret L. King, *Venetian Humanism in an Age of Patrician Dominance* (Princeton, 1986), p. 237 n. 91.

9. See James Cushman Davis, *The Decline of the Venetian Nobility as a Ruling Class* (Baltimore, 1962); Ugo Tucci, "The Psychology of the Venetian Merchant in the Sixteenth Century," in *Renaissance Venice,* ed. Hale, pp. 346–78; and Brian Pullan, "The Occupations and Investments of the Venetian Nobility in the Middle and Late Sixteenth Century," in ibid., pp. 379–408.

10. See Edward Muir, *Civic Ritual in Renaissance Venice* (Princeton, 1981); and Ellen Rosand, "Music in the Myth of Venice," *RQ* 30 (1977): 511–37.

that appears as lived experience with its myths about itself must therefore confront the many paradoxes it engendered. Venice was a town that absorbed and balanced a huge range of divergent views, activities, personalities, social and professional types. It was a necessary part of such an urban fabric that myth should collide with material realities.

Among many spheres in which Venice mediated such contradictions, one that gained new vitality in the sixteenth century was the private drawing room. There, Venetians played out their civic ideals in less systematized and obvious forms than the ritualized ones orchestrated for public ceremonies, but in ways no less implicated in the newly heightened consciousness of civic identity. Private salons could reiterate values of the old order yet still embrace a new diversity of social classes and professional affiliations and a new casualness in intellectual expression. The multiform bands of poets, collectors, polygraphs, singers, and instrumentalists who attended salons probably seemed to descendants of quattrocento Latin humanists too eclectic and dilettantish to be taken seriously. But theirs was a resourceful accommodation of old values to new circumstances—to the intellectual and social mobility promoted by a younger culture and epitomized by its energetic relationship to the press. Ultimately, by accommodating foundational beliefs to a wider, more variable commerce in ideas, Venice's new generations reshaped the ideas of old. Thus, whatever strains of unreality marred the layered myths that compounded the Venetian image, their sum total made for a powerful frame of reference: no one who sought success in Venice, native or foreign, could remain isolated from the insistent demands of the city's mythologies.

Such demands weighed heavily on artists and literati. In many domains—political iconography, music for state occasions, encomiastic verse, and the like—artistic production explicitly articulated the city's self-images, trumpeting its claims to republican success and longevity.[11] Jacopo Sansovino's *giganti,* huge statues of Mercury and Neptune sculpted for the ceremonial threshold of the doge's palace, personified in their powerful bones and muscle the spirit of Venetian civic might (Plate 1).[12] Similarly, the wealth of verse written and set to music in honor of the visit to Venice of Henry III during the summer of 1574 affirmed the city's power, even as it claimed principally to praise the French king.[13] These examples leave little doubt about their impetus and central message. But how are we to understand the interplay of artistic forces and local imaginings in realms less directly allied to state

11. A fundamental article on the topic is David Rosand, "*Venetia figurata:* The Iconography of a Myth," in *Interpretazioni veneziane: studi di storia dell'arte in onore di Michelangelo Muraro,* ed. David Rosand (Venice, 1984), pp. 177–96.

12. See Douglas Lewis, "Jacopo Sansovino, Sculptor of Venice," in *Titian: His World and His Legacy,* ed. David Rosand (New York, 1982), pp. 133–90, esp. pp. 133–36. (Much of the work, it should be noted, was actually done by assistants in Sansovino's workshop, as was the norm in sculpture at the time.)

13. Among the famous settings are those of Andrea Gabrieli, *Hor che suo bel seno* and *Ecco Vinegia bella,* published two years after Andrea's death in the *Concerti di Andrea e di Gio: Gabrieli . . . primo libro e secondo* (Venice, 1587).

1. Jacopo Sansovino, *Mercury and Neptune,* 1554, for the Giants' Staircase by Antonio Rizzo (1484–1501), Palazzo Ducale, Venice. Photo courtesy of Osvaldo Böhm.

machinery—in lyric poetry, pastoral canvases, domestic architecture, or the abstractions of musical style?[14] Still more, how can we hope to comprehend the curious intermixing of foreign habits with local tastes to which a city flooded with *stranieri* in various stages of assimilation was so habituated—and most especially in confronting works with no unilateral relationship to the state?

These are the central questions in my consideration of the city's relationship to one musical genre, the madrigal. Its two most famous exponents from mid-century, Adrian Willaert and Cipriano de Rore, both linked with Venice, were Netherlanders. Even though the repertory of madrigals they developed around 1540 must be understood within the play of things Venetian, much about it that changed the shape of secular music in Italy was decidedly the product of northern music—a network of separate parts woven into a pensive and intricate polyphony. What is more, the most ample and significant contributions to the Venetian repertory were settings of lyrics by a Tuscan poet, Petrarch.

Willaert's one monument of madrigalistic composition was located in his four-, five-, six-, and seven-voice corpus of motets and madrigals called *Musica nova,* published in 1559 but probably written for the most part between the late 1530s and mid-1540s. This collection preserved Willaert's weightiest undertakings in both genres, twenty-seven motets and twenty-five madrigals. It was published in a spectacular format, with its title enclosed in a fantastical illustration representing a storm-swept Venetian sea bordered by mermaids and cupids (Plate 2). A woodcut of the aged Willaert, emanating gerontocratic excellence, appeared on its verso (Plate 3).

The madrigals of the *Musica nova* departed from all previous ones by consistently setting complete sonnets—all but one of them Petrarch's—in the bipartite form of the motet and by adapting a dense counterpoint formerly reserved for sacred music. Like the speech of Tomitano's ideal patrician, these madrigals aspired to a declamation less "sung" than set forth with recitational "gravity." The compositional principle that guided them was above all commitment to an exemplary presentation of Petrarch's words, a principle pursued with all the deliberation, learnedness, and restraint insisted on by guardians of official Venetian character. None of the madrigals Willaert published between 1534 until his death in 1562 in anthologies or other mixed collections echoed the spirit of patrician Venice with the same precision or weight as the *Musica nova;* if anything, they diffused and softened its aims.

Long before the *Musica nova* left its private shelter, Rore made a stunning debut as an apparent unknown with his *Madrigali a cinque voci* of 1542 (later known as the *Libro primo*). Like Willaert's madrigals, many of Rore's set full sonnets by Petrarch,

14. Indeed, David Rosand has argued that Venice essayed a unique sort of iconography designed to thwart single, unambiguous readings, seeking instead multivalent ones. He presented the idea in "Painting in Venice: The Question of Meaning" (paper delivered at the Renaissance Society of America, Annual Conference, New York City, April 1, 1988), and in other forms in "Venereal Hermeneutics: Reading Titian's *Venus of Urbino*," in *Renaissance Society and Culture: Essays in Honor of Eugene F. Rice, Jr.,* ed. John Monfasani and Ronald G. Musto (New York, 1991), pp. 263–80, and "So-and-So Reclining on Her Couch," in *Titian: 500,* ed. Joseph Manca, Studies in the History of Art (Washington, D.C., 1994).

2 . *Musica nova* (Venice, 1559), title page. Photo courtesy of the British Library.

3 .   *Musica nova* (Venice, 1559), portrait of Adrian Willaert. Photo courtesy of the British
Library.

as well as the verse of "high" literary moderns like Luigi Tansillo, Antonio Tebaldeo, and Francesco Maria Molza, and drew the verses along in an opaque polyphony. Yet his madrigals ventured more dramatic and expressive gestures than Willaert's. They contrasted melodies that were sometimes more cantabile than Willaert would invent, at other times rougher and more irregular.

Such biographical fragments as survive about Willaert and Rore might tentatively be related to differences in their music. As a servant to Italian patrons from 1515 or 1516 and chapelmaster of San Marco from 1527, Willaert's connection with the Venetian establishment seems relatively straightforward. Contemporary accounts saw in him the mythological personification of Venice, an embodiment of the modest reserve demanded of its nobles and figured in its stately images. In 1546 his pupil Girolamo Parabosco's comedy *La notte* called him "so kind, gentle, and modest that one could set him as an example of all manner of other virtues."[15] Willaert was hired, in accordance with governmental regulations, by the Procuratori de Supra, but at the express personal initiative of doge Andrea Gritti.[16] Nominally, at least, the *cappella* he administered was the private one of the doge. Willaert was thus an arm of the state whose position demanded unfaltering loyalty to the republic's self-image and its long-standing ideals. The Procuratori approved Willaert's suitability in the record of his appointment with the epithet "circumspectus vir" (a deliberate or cautious man),[17] a characterization on which numerous variations were rung in popular literature during his subsequent tenure. Thus, despite his northern origins—and, as we will see, despite the fact that he enjoyed the private patronage of the elite Florentine nobleman Neri Capponi—Willaert was wholly assimilated to a Venetian image and made instrumental in its representation.

Rore's orientation to Venetian cultural and musical habits is far more ambiguous. His biography remains cratered despite information that he probably resided in Brescia from at least 1542 until possibly 1545 or 1546.[18] From Brescia he seems to have produced freelance compositions for at least two Florentine exiles, Neri Capponi and Capponi's comrade Ruberto Strozzi. It seems doubtful that he ever lived in Venice, except perhaps briefly early in his career and then without a regular appointment.[19] More than this, it is unclear whether Rore was ever really Willaert's student. Only two documents allude to such a relationship between them: one, an

15. "Tanto gentile, & cosi piacevole, & modesto, che si puo porre per uno essempio di tutti queste altre virtute" (as spoken by the character Gerardo, act 3, fol. 32′).

16. On Gritti's dogeship, his military success, his cosmopolitanism, and especially his affinity for the French, see Andrea da Mosto, *I dogi di Venezia nella vita pubblica e privata* (repr.; Florence, 1977), pp. 235–46. For a clarification of Gritti's involvement in Willaert's hiring see Giulio Maria Ongaro, "The Chapel of St. Mark's at the Time of Adrian Willaert (1527–1562): A Documentary Study" (Ph.D. diss., University of North Carolina at Chapel Hill, 1986), pp. 70–81.

17. See Vander Straeten, *La musique aux Pays-Bas* 6:191, and Ongaro, "The Chapel of St. Mark's," p. 75 and Appendix, Document 44.

18. I refer to Richard Agee's discoveries; see Chap. 2 n. 3.

19. It used to be thought, owing to Francesco Caffi's unsupported claim, that Rore had been a member of the chapel under Willaert before transferring to Ferrara; see Chap. 8 below, n. 55. On Rore's trip(s) to Venice, where he delivered compositions to Capponi, see Chap. 2 nn. 35 and 36.

oblique remark in a dedication to Scotto's edition of Rore's *Terzo libro a 5* of 1548 (RISM 1548[9]), referring to Rore, Willaert, and "other disciples of his"; the other, a description of Rore as Willaert's *discepolo* on a title page printed in the following year. But these tell us only in fact that in the late forties some people in Venice had begun to describe Rore as a follower of Willaert's practice.[20] Altogether this is surprisingly scant evidence of a direct Venetian connection for Rore and of a circumstance that would place him in the city for an extended time. It is rather more pointed testimony to an association with Florentine exiles. Yet in their broad contours, if not their idiomatic details, Rore's madrigals of the 1540s embrace a style whose identity is otherwise exclusively the province of composers resident in Venice and the Veneto: Willaert, his students at San Marco—principally Parabosco, Perissone Cambio, and Baldassare Donato—and, beginning in the later 1540s, composers in the Veneto like Giovanni Nasco, Francesco Portinaro, and Vincenzo Ruffo.

Any attempt to explain Venice's effect on the course of secular music through its larger cultural themes, then, will be complicated both by the elusive genealogy of Venetian madrigal writing and by the complex and tacit place its various incarnations occupied in the city's larger cultural patterns.

Among Willaert's protégés even the Italians brought their own training and habits from cities scattered throughout the peninsula. It may be all the more significant, therefore, that one of the few from a Venetian dominion, a native of nearby Chioggia, became the foremost explicator and apologist for the Venetian idiom. Gioseffo Zarlino, theorist, teacher, and later chapelmaster, played a crucial role in clarifying for later generations the aesthetic impulses and compositional habits of contemporaneous Venetian musicians. His first publication, the imposing *Istitutioni harmoniche* of 1558, assumed the daunting task of codifying a style whose constant shifts and irregularities made it all but impossible to systematize. In this his role was unique, for his exegeses of Venetian counterpoint, modes, and text setting were only faintly anticipated by his predecessors and abandoned by his successors. Chief among the former is the Venetian Giovanni del Lago, whose sketchy, derivative writings from around 1538–41 only hint at the new horizons.

Without this written witness we would have virtually nothing from the mouths of musicians themselves. More plentiful explanations of Venetian thinking come from literati, whose accounts complement those of del Lago and Zarlino. Literary figures wrote abundantly on poetics, vernacular style, grammar, imitation, the *questione della lingua,* and genre, and in a wide range of forms: rhetorical handbooks, letters, commentaries, dialogues, and treatises. The large, rapid production of these

---

20. The dedication in RISM 1548[9], written by the flutist Paolo Vergelli to Gottardo Occagna, was taken by Edward E. Lowinsky as evidence that everyone in Venice knew Rore to have been Willaert's pupil; see his "*Calami sonum ferentes:* A New Interpretation," in *Music in the Culture of the Renaissance and Other Essays,* ed. Bonnie J. Blackburn, 2 vols. (Chicago, 1989), 2:602–3. Yet the term used there is *discepolo,* like that in the title page of the 1549 print, *Fantasie, et ricerchari a tre voci* (RISM 1549[34]) (also printed by Girolamo Scotto), a term that often meant "follower" (i.e., of someone's practice) rather than "student." For further discussion of this see below, Chap. 8 n. 56.

texts animated the dynamics of circulation and the creative processes of rejection, reinvention, and revision that were played out in reception. Ultimately, musical and literary writings of mid-cinquecento Venice illuminate one another, both of them translating Ciceronian precepts of style while imposing on them their own idiosyncrasies and formal demands.

In some way, virtually all these theoretical writings were dominated by the Venetian Pietro Bembo's dialogue on the *questione della lingua, Prose della volgar lingua* of 1525, a work whose relevance to secular music has been recognized for some time. Bembo's *Prose* recast Ciceronian rhetorical precepts in the terms of trecento Tuscan literary style. In this study I take Bembo's transformations of Ciceronian canons as central to a tropology of Venice that interconnects civic identity, rhetorical principles, and expressive idioms. Three of these canons were most crucial to Bembo's scheme: first, the separation of styles into three distinct levels: high, middle, and low; second, *variazione,* the varying of each style with a balance of opposed qualities broadly subsumed within the categories of *gravità* and *piacevolezza* (gravity and pleasingness); and third, *decoro* (propriety), the appropriate matching of styles to subjects. I argue that Bembo merged Venetian mythology with ancient rhetoric in a way that made one particular meaning of decorum—that of moderation—the all-embracing, universal principle of his stylistics; and further, that this principle functioned as an inseparable corollary of *variazione,* calling the latter into service as a means of tempering extremes in order to avoid too intense an emphasis on any one style or affect.

In proposing this scheme Bembo claimed Petrarch as his model for the vernacular lyric. Bembo's *Prose* tried to codify and make imitable Petrarch's *rime* for readers whose linguistic style he hoped to shape. Yet Petrarch's lyrics had already come to hold an unequalled appeal for the indigenous society that formed Bembo's most eager audience. Among the aspects of Petrarchan verse that appealed to Bembo and to the rhetorical culture for which he wrote was its delicate interplay of verbal sounds (as Dean Mace has pointed up).[21] In expounding the workings of these sounds according to his principle of variation, Bembo assigned a new importance to sound as an agent of linguistic meaning. This is the facet of his poetics that has commanded the greatest attention of music historians, interested in its effect on contemporaneous madrigalists. Nonetheless, I argue that Petrarch's continual undercutting of verbal utterance through oxymoron and paradox symbolized even more importantly the reserve on which Venetians claimed to insist in other domains. Coupled with its intricate plays of verbal-psychic wit, this poetics, not surprisingly, entranced a society bound by civic habit to discreet emotional display and simultaneously absorbed in a stylized self-presentation. By explicating Petrarch in Ciceronian terms, Bembo implicitly located his lyrics in the performative domain

---

21. Dean T. Mace, "Pietro Bembo and the Literary Origins of the Italian Madrigal," *The Musical Quarterly* 55 (1969): 65–86.

of the orator. So doing he underscored the concerns and biases of his Venetian readers and granted them what must have seemed a deeply satisfying endorsement and an irrefutable authority.

In the succeeding pages I try to enlarge these themes to consider Venice's signal role in steering Italian secular music on a new course. *Enlargement* in this sense means something like the magnification one gets when peering through a lens. For in drawing repeatedly on sources like Tomitano's letter that stand outside the immediate business of making madrigals, I try to picture close up the intricate cultural weave of which madrigals were a part and to reconstruct aspects of its palpable form. My aim is not to find in these far-flung sources exact mirrors of the madrigalists' ideals or the aesthetic structures they built. Rather, it is to develop, figuratively speaking, a colloquy between various players in Venice and to discover in the city's multiple texts a way to contemplate the diverse meanings and eclectic processes that involved madrigals in larger cultural patterns.

On the path to finishing this book I received invaluable help from many institutions and countless friends and colleagues. The groundwork was done with the aid of the Gladys Krieble Delmas Foundation for Research in Venice, the Penfield Scholarship fund of the University of Pennsylvania, and the American Association of University Women. I expanded research in Venice and Florence with help from a Grant-in-Aid from the American Council of Learned Societies and awards from the University of Southern California Faculty Research and Innovative Fund and the American Philosophical Society. A Fellowship for University Teachers from the National Endowment for the Humanities provided me with an indispensable year's leave from teaching, during which most of the writing was done. To all of these I am deeply appreciative. I also wish to thank the American Musicological Society, the Chicago Humanities Institute, the Gladys Krieble Delmas Foundation, the National Endowment for the Humanities, and the Associates of the University of California Press for generous subventions toward publication of this volume.

The *Renaissance Quarterly* kindly granted permission to reprint substantial portions of Chapter 4, which appeared in volume 42 (1991) as "The Academy of Domenico Venier, Music's Literary Muse in Mid-*Cinquecento* Venice."

My work was helped by the staffs of many libraries and archives, of which I would like to acknowledge especially: Sandra Sambo, Michela dal Borgo, and Alessandra Schiavon of the Archivio di Stato di Venezia; Orsola Gori of the Archivio di Stato di Firenze; Paul Gehl and Robert Karrow of the Newberry Library, Chicago; Alice Schreyer of Special Collections at the University of Chicago; and the staffs of the British Library, the Biblioteca Nazionale Marciana, the Museo Civico Correr, the Fondazione Cini, the Folger Shakespeare Library, the Bancroft Library at the University of California at Berkeley, and the University of Pennsylvania Rare Book Room.

At the University of California Press I benefited from the expert skills of my acquisitions editor Doris Kretschmer and project editor Rose Vekony and from astute copyediting by Fronia W. Simpson. I am grateful for helpful comments I received from two readers solicited by the press, James Haar, a longtime source of stimulating dialogue on Italian madrigals, and Dean Mace. I hope I can be forgiven for mentioning just a fraction of the many other people who have helped me along the way: Richard Agee, Tiziana Agostini Nordio, Linda Armao, Jane Bernstein, Lawrence Bernstein, Lorenzo Bianconi, Bonnie Blackburn, David Bryant, David Butchart, Donna Cardamone Jackson, Stefano Castelvecchi, Julie Cumming, Robert Durling, John Freccero, Jonathan Glixon, John Walter Hill, Lynn Hooker, Alvin Johnson, Michael Keller, Victoria Kirkham, Julius Kirshner, Mary Lewis, Anne MacNeil, Paul Martell, Stefano Mengozzi, Robert Morgan, Anthony Newcomb, Giulio Ongaro, Jessie Ann Owens, Claude Palisca, Nino Pirrotta, Harold Powers, Francesco Rizzoli, John Roberts, David Rosand, Ellen Rosand, Shuli Roth, Ingrid Rowland, Marta Tonegutti, Antonio Vassalli, Nancy Vickers, and Elissa Weaver, and all the members of the Petrarchism seminar at the University of Chicago. Many of them are thanked in footnotes where it has been possible to point to a particular debt.

There are several others whose roles I must acknowledge more specially. Tita Rosenthal offered probing comments and copious bibliographical advice on Chapters 1 through 6 and made Venice an altogether richer place for me. Gary Tomlinson, at first the advisor on my dissertation, has since been a continual interlocutor on madrigals and histories. He knows how important our conversations have been to me over many years, for which I could not begin to thank him here. My friend and colleague Howard Mayer Brown gave me many lively conversations and insights on cinquecento music and countless other topics, scholarly and otherwise. Before his sudden death in Venice on 20 February 1993, every page of this book was intended to elicit his sharp reading. At every turn my husband, Thomas Bauman, has contributed his critical acuity as well as his remarkable skills as a writer, linguist, musician, editor, and computer whiz. I have been abashed and touched by his colossal support over all this time. And I have been blessed by the good humor, affection, and patience of Emily and Rebecca Bauman.

Finally a few words about the dedication. I take leave of this project deeply aware that what I have tried to envision in the nexus of people's language, their pictures, their music, and their city had its origins in my parents' house. The example they gave me to imagine worlds beyond our own cannot be measured in words. I dedicate this book to them with the sort of tender appreciation that the frailty of life makes only sweeter.

Chicago, Spring 1993

Part I · PATRONS AND ACADEMIES IN THE CITY

Chapter 1 • FLEXIBILITY IN THE BODY SOCIAL

Mid-sixteenth-century Venice was arrayed in such a way that no single mogul, family, or neighborhood was in a position to monopolize indigenous activity in arts or letters. Venice was a city of dispersal. Laced with waterways, the city took its shape from its natural architecture. The wealthy houses of the large patriciate, scattered throughout the city's many parishes, kept power bases more or less decentralized. Apart from the magnetic force of San Marco—the seat of governmental activities and associated civic ritual—no umbrella structure comparable to that of a princely court brought its people and spaces into a single easily comprehended matrix. As a commercial and maritime city, Venice offered multiplicity in lieu of centralization. It offered rich possibilities for dynamic interchange between the wide assortment of social and professional types that constantly thronged there—patricians, merchants, *popolani,* tourists, students, seamen, exiles, and diplomats. Local patricians contributed to this decentralization by viewing the whole of the lagoon as common territory rather than developing attachments to particular neighborhoods—a quality in which they differed from nobles of many other Italian towns. Since most extended families owned properties in various parishes and *sestieri* (the six large sections into which the city still divides), neighborhoods had only a circumscribed role as bases of power and operation; indeed, it was not uncommon for nuclear families to move from one parish to another.[1]

---

1. See Dennis Romano, *Patricians and "Popolani": The Social Foundations of the Venetian Renaissance State* (Baltimore, 1987), pp. 120ff., esp. p. 123; Stanley Chojnacki, "In Search of the Venetian Patriciate: Families and Factions in the Fourteenth Century," in *Renaissance Venice,* ed. John R. Hale (London, 1973), pp. 47–90; and Edward Muir and Ronald F. E. Weissman, "Social and Symbolic Places in Renaissance Venice and Florence," in *The Power of Place: Bringing Together Geographical and Sociological Imaginations,* ed. John A. Agnew and James S. Duncan (Boston, 1989), pp. 81–103, esp. pp. 85 and 87. The great exception was patrician women. Their lives outside the home were basically restricted to their immediate parishes, at least so long as their nuclear families stayed in a single dwelling (see Romano, pp. 131ff.). In this, Venetian practice reflected generalized sixteenth-century attitudes that tended to keep

We can easily imagine that Venetian salon life profited from the constant circulation of bodies throughout the city, as well as from the correlated factors of metropolitan dispersion and the city's relative freedom from hierarchy. Palaces and other grand dwellings constituted collectively a series of loose social nets, slack enough to comprehend a varied and changeable population. This urban makeup differed from the fixed hierarchy of the court, which pointed (structurally, at least) to a single power center, absolute and invariable, that tried to delimit opportunities for profit and promotion. There, financial entrepreneurialism and social advancement could generally be attempted only within the strict perimeters defined by the prince and the infrastructure that supported him. The lavish festivals, entertainments, and monuments funded by courtly establishments accordingly concentrated, by and large, on the affirmation of princely glory or, at the very least, tended to mirror more directly the monolithic interests of prince and court.[2] Courtly patrons with strong interests in art and literature like Isabella d'Este of Mantua or, later, Vincenzo Gonzaga could infuse great vigor into a court's cultural life, even if the nature of cultural production still tended to be more focused and circumscribed than that of big Italian towns like Venice. With less enthusiastic patrons, like Florence's Cosimo I de' Medici beginning in 1537 (and thus coinciding with the Venetian period I focus on here), centralization and authoritarian control could straitjacket creative production according to the narrowly defined wishes of the ruling elite. In the worst of cases they could suffocate it almost completely.[3]

Structural differences between court and city that made themselves felt in cultural production were thus enmeshed with political ones. In contrast to the courts, the Venetian oligarchy thrived on a broad-based system of rule and, by extension, patronage. Within this system individual inhabitants could achieve success by exploiting the city in the most varied ways—through business, trade, or maritime interests, banking, political offices, academic and artistic activities. Such a pliable setup depended in part on numerous legal mechanisms that, formally at least, safeguarded equality within the patrician rank.[4] The Venetian nobleman's loyalty was in

---

women's social role a domestic one. For a summary of the marriage manuals that defined such a role see Ann Rosalind Jones, *The Currency of Eros: Women's Love Lyric in Europe, 1540–1620* (Indianapolis, 1990), pp. 20–28.

2. Among standard commentaries on this are Lauro Martines, *Power and Imagination: City-States in Renaissance Italy* (New York, 1979), pp. 218ff., 221, 225, and on the courtly penchant for self-reflecting images, pp. 321ff.; idem, "The Gentleman in Renaissance Italy: Strains of Isolation in the Body Politic," in *The Darker Vision of the Renaissance: Beyond the Fields of Reason*, ed. Robert S. Kinsman, UCLA Center for Medieval and Renaissance Studies, Contributions, no. 6 (Berkeley and Los Angeles, 1974), pp. 77–93; and Robert Finlay, *Politics in Renaissance Venice* (London, 1980), pp. 40–41.

3. A single example relevant for present purposes is the patronage of madrigals by Cosimo I in Medicean Florence. Iain Fenlon and James Haar, writing on Cosimo I's effect on madrigalian developments in Florence, propose that the end of republican Florence initiated the degeneration of individual patronage dominated by the family. The Medici restoration, they recall, led to an exodus of painters, sculptors, and musicians from the city (*The Italian Madrigal*, pp. 85–86).

4. On Venetian distrust of factionalism see Finlay, *Politics in Renaissance Venice*, p. 38.

principle to his fellow patricians, rather than to a local prince or foreign royalty, who still commanded the service of many noble courtiers elsewhere. In order to maintain the symmetries of patrician power and an effective system of checks and balances, a large number of magistracies and councils shared the decision-making process, and the vast majority of offices turned over after very brief, often six-month, terms.

This made for a cumbersome, mazelike governmental structure that led many observers to comment wryly on the likeness of topography and statecraft in the city.[5] Yet these same observers often marveled at Venice's success in staying the over-inflated ambitions of potential power-hungry factions or individuals. In the late fifteenth century a complex of attitudes guarding against the perils of self-interest found expression in a series of checks advanced by the ruling group to counter the self-magnifying schemes of several doges—schemes epitomized by the building of triumphal architecture like the Arco Foscari, which verged on representing the doge as divinely ordained.[6] Venice had more than its share of calendrical rituals to militate against the claims of the individual by proclaiming overriding communal values to inhabitants and visitors alike.[7] All of these checks and proclamations were designed to secure an ideal of changeless equilibrium and to foster the spirit of *unanimitas,* of a single shared will, which informed the republic's official ideology.[8]

The patriciate ventured (if hesitantly) to extend these mechanisms to include some nonpatricians. Despite the inequities and stratification that divided nobles from the next rank of residents on the descending social ladder, the *cittadini* (and even more from the still lower *popolani*), the Venetian aristocracy by tradition and a long-standing formula for republican success had accustomed itself to making certain efforts to appease classes excluded from governmental rule.[9] Though without

5. For a review of comments on the deliberate and unwieldy quality of Venetian government, see ibid., pp. 37ff.

6. For an interpretation of this phenomenon see Debra Pincus, *The Arco Foscari: The Building of a Triumphal Gateway in Fifteenth-Century Venice* (New York, 1976). The success achieved by the mid-sixteenth century in checking the doges' schemes is attested by the English translator of Gasparo Contarini's *De magistratibus,* Lewes Lewkenor, who showed astonishment that the patriciate reacted as casually to the death of a doge as to the death of any other patrician: "There is in the Cittie of Venice no greater alteration at the death of their Duke, then at the death of any other private Gentleman" (pp. 156–57)—a translation from the work of another foreigner, Donato Giannotti, his *Libro della repubblica de' vinitiani,* fol. 63', as noted by Edward Muir, *Civic Ritual in Renaissance Venice* (Princeton, 1981), p. 268 n. 53.

7. See Muir, *Civic Ritual in Renaissance Venice,* esp. pp. 74–78.

8. On the concept of *unanimitas* in Venice see Margaret L. King, *Venetian Humanism in an Age of Patrician Dominance* (Princeton, 1986), pp. 174ff. King's interpretation of the interaction of class, culture, and power in quattrocento Venice would argue that the political power of the ruling patrician elite extended far enough into what she calls "the realm of culture"—by which she means the culture of the "humanist group"—as to control them in a unique way (see pp. 190–91, 251). See also Romano, *Patricians and "Popolani,"* pp. 4–11 and passim, on the emphasis Venetians placed on *caritas,* and Tomitano's letter cited in the Preface above, n. 3.

9. On this issue see Finlay, *Politics in Renaissance Venice,* pp. 45ff., and Romano, *Patricians and "Popolani,"* p. 10. On institutions of charity run by citizens and nobles for *popolani* see the classic work of Brian Pullan, *Rich and Poor in Renaissance Venice: The Social Institutions of a Catholic State to 1620* (Oxford, 1971), and on confraternities generally in the period, Christopher F. Black, *Italian Confraternities in the Sixteenth Century* (Cambridge, 1989). For a study that tries to debunk emphases on Venetian traditions

power of votes, for example, *cittadini* could participate in governmental activities through the secretarial offices of the chancelleries. They could ship cargo on state galleys. And they maintained the exclusive right to hold offices in the great lay confraternities, the *scuole grandi*.[10] By sixteenth-century standards the city's embrace was thus relatively broad, and there was considerable play in its social fabric. While many *cittadini,* as well as plebeians and foreigners, were doomed to frustration in their search for power and position, others experienced considerable social and economic success. At the very least many had come to view their circumstances as malleable, there to be negotiated with the right manoeuvres.

The collective self-identity that promoted various attitudes of equality and magnanimity both within and without the patriciate was expressed with considerable fanfare in official postures. Gradually, the underlying ideals had come to be projected in numerous iconic variations on the city's evolving civic mythology. By the fourteenth century, for instance, Venice added to its mythological symbolism the specter of Dea Roma as Justice, seated on a throne of lions and bearing sword and scales in her two hands (Plate 4). By such a ploy the city extended its claim as the new Rome while reminding onlookers of its professed fairness, its balanced constitution, and its domestic harmony.[11]

This conjunction of morality and might was reiterated in a series of bird's-eye maps, the most remarkable of which was Jacopo de' Barbari's famous woodcut of 1500 (Plate 5).[12] Barbari's map surrounded the city with eight extravagant personifications of the winds inspired by Vetruvius's wind heads. Set at the extremities of its central vertical axis are powerful representations of Mercury atop a cloud and Neptune riding a spirited dolphin (Plate 6) — iconography as vital to the city's image as its serpentine slews of buildings and its urban backwaters.

Venice's geography played a real part in encouraging the city's social elasticity. The circuitous structure of the lagoon made for a constant rubbing of elbows between different classes that Venetians seemed to take as a natural part of daily affairs. When the eccentric English traveler Thomas Coryat visited the city in the

---

of charity by stressing patrician corruption and the split between civic ideals and reality see Donald E. Queller, *The Venetian Patriciate: Reality versus Myth* (Urbana and Chicago, 1986). Queller's view seems to me equally problematic in invoking an alternate "reality" as true, rather than traversing the dialectics of various realities and representations.

10. See Finlay, *Politics in Renaissance Venice,* pp. 45ff. On the role of the *cittadini* as members of the secretarial class see Oliver Logan, *Culture and Society in Venice, 1470–1790: The Renaissance and Its Heritage* (New York, 1972), pp. 26ff.

11. David Rosand has written on the connections between Venice and ancient Rome in visual iconography; see *"Venetia figurata:* The Iconography of a Myth," in *Interpretazioni veneziane: studi di storia dell'arte in onore di Michelangelo Muraro,* ed. David Rosand (Venice, 1984), pp. 177–96. See also Deborah Howard, *Jacopo Sansovino: Architecture and Patronage in Renaissance Venice* (New Haven, 1975), pp. 2–7. For a single poetic example in which Venice is linked with Justice, see Chap. 4 n. 79 (and Ex. 2) below on Domenico Venier's *Gloriosa, felic' alma, Vineggia,* as set to music by Baldassare Donato.

12. See Juergen Schulz, "Jacobo de' Barbari's *View of Venice:* Map Making, City Views, and Moralized Geography before the Year 1500," *Art Bulletin* 60, no. 3 (1978): 425–74, and idem, *The Printed Plans and Panoramic Views of Venice (1486–1797),* Saggi e memorie di storia dell'arte, no. 7 (Venice, 1970). I am grateful to Robert Karrow of the Newberry Library for his help with Venetian cartography.

4 . Bartolomeo Buon, Justice seated with sword and scales, fifteenth century, above the Porta della Carta, Palazzo Ducale, Venice. Photo courtesy of Osvaldo Böhm.

5.   Jacopo de' Barbari, woodcut map of Venice, 1500. Photo courtesy of the Newberry Library.

6 . Jacopo de' Barbari, woodcut map of Venice, 1500, detail, lower middle panel. Photo courtesy of the Newberry Library.

early seventeenth century, he observed with astonishment that "their Gentleman and greatest Senators, a man with two millions of duckats, will come into their market, and buy their flesh, fish, fruites, and such other things as are necessary for the maintenance of their family."[13] By Coryat's time, of course, Venice's pragmatic patriciate was less able than ever to afford elitist separatism—hence the increasing number of profitable interclass marriages in the sixteenth century, which represented just one type of business arrangement between nobles and *cittadini,* if one of particular social resonance.

The peculiar habits Coryat observed among the Venetian aristocracy accord with its ideological rejection of showy displays of personal spending (expressly forbidden by strict sumptuary laws)—displays that were de rigueur in court towns like nearby Ferrara and Mantua. Big outlays of cash were supposed to be reserved mainly for public festivals that glorified the Venetian community as a whole. In the private sphere they could be funneled into lasting investments capable of adding to the permanent legacy of an extended family group, but not (in theory) made for more transitory or personal luxuries. Many individual cases of self-glorifying osten-

13. *Coryat's Crudities,* 2 vols. (1611; repr., Glasgow, 1905), 1:396–97.

tation naturally reared their heads all the same. But part of their price was a certain dissonance with established mores, which assigned thrift an emphatic place within the official civic scheme. Coryat himself characterized the idiosyncratic shopping habits of the patriciate—and, we might note, with considerable qualms—as "a token indeed of frugality."[14] This was a frugality located within the patriciate's formalized customs for subordinating individual needs to group concerns. It was one ritualized in any number of ways—to cite a single instance, in the conspicuous insistence on modest burials that one finds repeatedly in Counter-Reformational Venetian wills. Both patricians and nonpatricians acknowledged the custom, as evinced by Willaert's quintessentially Venetian request for a burial "con mancho pompa si possa" (with as little pomp as possible).[15]

All of these factors—decentralization, an institutionalized egalitarianism (in policy if often not in practice), and the substantial presence of foreign exiles, travelers, businessmen, diplomats, and military men—contributed to Venice's prolific artistic and intellectual domestic life. Yet the snug sociological picture of divided authority and pluralistic harmony that we might tend to draw from them tells only part of the story. Personal impulses made strange bedfellows with public ideals, and in Venice the latter took their place as only one set of faiths among many others. Venice was above all a paradoxical city. Among the deepest instances of its divided consciousness was that Venetians of the early to mid-sixteenth century who linked themselves to high culture lived in a peculiarly ambivalent counterpose to the court culture from which their city's paradigm was supposed to depart. As a group they prized and flaunted their ideals of freedom, justice, concord, and modesty, while envying much of the apparent exclusivity, homogeneity, and even absolutism that courtly structures seemed to offer.

———————

This tension tempered the civic, rhetorical, social, and aesthetic domains that I aim to draw together here. Let me begin to explore it by turning briefly to the Venetians' manifesto of literary style, Pietro Bembo's *Prose della volgar lingua*. As I show in Chapter 5, Bembo's *Prose* advanced a smooth, exclusive diction with the same claims to indisputable authority that tend to characterize aspects of sixteenth-century court production. It translated the harmonious heterogeneity idealized in Venice's oligarchy into the terms of literary style. The temptation to read the *Prose* as a conflation of courtly values with Venetian civic ones is encouraged by knowledge of Bembo's upbringing and early adulthood. Although he was inculcated with republican ideals, Bembo's youthful experiences with his father, Bernardo, had been tinged with the court. As a boy in 1478–80 he spent time at the Florentine court of Lorenzo de' Medici, which was attended by the Neoplatonic philosopher

———————

14. Ibid., 1:397. See also Logan, *Culture and Society in Venice,* pp. 17–18.
15. The phrase appears in Willaert's will of 26 March 1558, reprinted in Vander Straeten, ed., *La musique aux Pays-Bas* 6:231, and in the wills of Antonio Zantani and Elena Barozza Zantani (see Appendix, C and D).

Marsilio Ficino and the poet-playwright Angelo Poliziano.[16] His first work of widespread popularity, *Gli asolani* (1505), was a dialogue set in the tiny, lavish court at Asolo of Caterina Cornaro, ex-queen of Cyprus.[17] In *Gli asolani* Bembo inscribed the arcane metaphysical philosophies of Ficino that he had encountered years earlier, and something of the Laurentian world that nurtured them, onto a popularized theory of love. This, and Bembo's subsequent sojourn at the court of Urbino, helped authorize him to appear as central spokesman on Neoplatonic love in the courtly manual par excellence, Castiglione's dialogue *Il cortegiano,* first drafted in 1513–18; by this time Bembo had already written Books 1 and 2 of the *Prose,* and he completed Book 3 while serving as papal secretary at still another court, that of Pope Leo X.[18]

The intersection of Bembo's biography with Castiglione's text suggests yet another way to consider Venice's codification of courtly values. One of the tropes shared by *Il cortegiano* and the *Prose* is that of decorum, which dictates that style should always be modified to suit given occasions and subjects. If their shared commitment to decorum did not lead each author to the same linguistic and lexical norms, with Bembo advocating a formal Tuscan that diverged from the *lingua cortegiana* favored by Castiglione, it nonetheless points to deeper impulses that form a common substratum between them.

Such impulses are expressed in the persona Castiglione urges on the ideal courtier, a persona rooted in a gestalt that goes beyond the particular form of any momentary rhetorical stance. As Wayne A. Rebhorn has claimed, its essence lies in a perpetual desire to conform to whatever subject or situation is at hand.[19] This driving force demands that one who wears the courtier's mask, like the idealized *letterato* of Bembo's *Prose,* invariably display propriety and measured pace. Castiglione elaborates the notion in Book 2, Chap. 7, through an interlocutor who also figures in the dialogues of the *Prose,* Federico Fregoso: to maintain such conduct the courtier must be circumspect and adaptable, all things to all people. At bottom he

---

16. A general account of the elitism of the Laurentian court is given in Gene A. Brucker, *Renaissance Florence* (New York, 1969), pp. 265–66. For a revisionist view that calls into question the elitism and isolationism traditionally thought to typify Ficino's Florentine circle, see Arthur Field, *The Origins of the Platonic Academy of Florence* (Princeton, 1988), esp. Chaps. 1, 2, and 7. Field's argument however is mainly relevant to conditions of the Florentine context itself, for it rethinks realities of the Laurentian court, rather than the modes by which outsiders typically idealized it.

17. On Bembo's time in Asolo and Urbino, see Logan, *Culture and Society in Venice,* p. 96; Carlo Dionisotti, "Bembo, Pietro," in *Dizionario biografico degli italiani* 8:133–51; and Giancarlo Mazzacurati, "Pietro Bembo," in *Storia della cultura veneta: dal primo quattrocento al concilio di Trenta,* ed. Girolamo Arnaldi and Manlio Pastore Stocchi, vol. 3, pt. 2 (Vicenza, 1980), pp. 1–59.

18. Among recent works that deal with connections between the two see esp. J. R. Woodhouse, *Baldesar Castiglione: A Reassessment of "The Courtier"* (Edinburgh, 1978), esp. pp. 80–82 and passim; Carlo Ossola, *Dal "Cortegiano" al' "Uomo di mondo": storia di un libro e di un modello sociale* (Turin, 1987); Giancarlo Mazzacurati, *Misure del classicismo rinascimentale* (Naples, 1967); Thomas M. Greene, "*Il Cortegiano* and the Choice of a Game," in *Castiglione: The Ideal and the Real in Renaissance Culture,* ed. Robert W. Hanning and David Rosand (New Haven, 1983), esp. pp. 14–15; and Louise George Clubb, "Castiglione's Humanistic Art and Renaissance Drama," in ibid., pp. 191–93, 198–201.

19. See *Courtly Performances: Masking and Festivity in Castiglione's "Book of the Courtier"* (Detroit, 1978), p. 92 and passim.

is a Stoic—or, in the more skeptical interpretations of Rebhorn, Lauro Martines, and others, an avoider of conflicts and harsh realities.[20] "In everything he does our courtier must be cautious, and he must always act and speak with prudence; and he should not only strive to protect his various attributes and qualities but also make sure that the tenor of his life is such that it corresponds with those qualities. . . . in everything he does he should, as the Stoics maintain is the duty and purpose of the wise man, be inspired by and express all the virtues."[21]

All of this stoical decorum adds up to a well-tended, varied *performance,* as the continuation of Federico's explanation makes clear: "Therefore the courtier must know how to avail himself of the virtues, and sometimes set one in contrast or opposition with another *in order to draw more attention to it*" (emphasis mine).[22] The performative quality common to conduct, speech, and literary style, and the flexible social structures it enabled in a city like Venice, will be one of the main themes in my discussion of Venetian verse and music and the salons that nourished them. Style was varied for effect. Federico elaborates the idea in a lengthy analogy between the courtier's mixing of virtues and the painter's chiaroscuro.

> This is what a good painter does when by the use of shadow he distinguishes clearly the light on his reliefs, and similarly by the use of light deepens the shadows of plane surfaces and brings different colors together in such a way that each one is brought out more sharply through the contrast; and the placing of figures in opposition to each other assists the painter in his purpose. In the same way, gentleness is most impressive in a man who is a capable and courageous warrior; and just as his boldness is magnified by his modesty, so his modesty is enhanced and more apparent on account of his boldness.[23]

Yet such contrast *must* be carried off "discreetly" and without obvious "affectation": that is the key to success, since those slight inflections of display will act to entrance the beholder.

Bembo insisted on these qualities for the writer perhaps even more strenuously than Castiglione did for the general courtier. Like Castiglione, Bembo depoliticized

20. See Rebhorn, "The Nostalgic Courtier," Chap. 3 in *Courtly Performances,* and (for related points) Martines, "The Gentleman in Renaissance Italy," pp. 77–93. See also numerous essays in Hanning and Rosand, eds., *Castiglione,* esp. the editors' introduction.

21. Trans. George Bull, Castiglione, *The Book of the Courtier* (Harmondsworth, 1967), p. 114. "[È] necessario che 'l nostro cortegiano in ogni sua operazion sia cauto, e ciò che dice o fa sempre accompagni con prudenzia; e non solamente ponga cura d'aver in sé parti e condizioni eccellenti, ma il tenor della vita sua ordini con tal disposizione, che 'l tutta corrisponda a queste parti . . . di sorte che ogni suo atto risulti e sia composto di tutte le virtù, come dicono i Stoici esser officio di chi è savio" (Baldassarre Castiglione, *Il libro del cortegiano,* ed. Ettore Bonora, 2d ed. [Milan, 1976], p. 111).

22. Trans. Bull, p. 114. "[B]isogna che sappia valersene, e per lo paragone e quasi contrarietà dell'una talor far che l'altra sia più chiaramente conosciuta" (ibid.).

23. Trans. Bull, p. 114. "[I] boni pittori, i quali con l'ombra fanno apparere e mostrano i lumi de' rilevi, e così col lume profundano l'ombre dei piani e compagnano i colori diversi insieme di modo, che per quella diversità l'uno e l'altro meglio si dimostra, e 'l posar delle figure contrario l'una all'altra le aiuta a far quell'officio che è intenzion del pittore. Onde la mansuetudine è molto maravigliosa in un gentilomo il qual sia valente e sforzato nell'arme; e come quella fierezza par maggiore accompagnata dalla modestia, così la modestia accresce e più compar per la fierezza" (ibid.).

Ciceronian rhetorical norms in the process, replacing the dynamic involvement with current affairs that inspired Cicero's oratorical model with cerebral ideals of refined detachment.[24] Indeed, it is this role that Castiglione assigned Bembo as interlocutor in *Il cortegiano* in contriving Bembo's Neoplatonic excursus in the final book, which takes wing just as the work's grounding in social and political reality is all but lost.[25]

Courtly ways were no more excised from the elastic social fabric of Venice than from its literary norms; rather they existed in varying degrees of comfort side by side with indigenous republican ones. The model of the princely establishment even had its analogue in the internal structure of the Venetian government. The doge, although an elected official of the state, had minimal control over policy. He stood in for Venetians as a kind of princely surrogate, divested of real political power but heavily imbued with symbolic force. His principal functions were to guard civic values and to maintain an overarching awareness of public issues. Even the Venetian political historian Gasparo Contarini admitted that the doge's exterior was one of "princely honor, dignitie, and royall appearing shew."[26] This outlook—shared by the Florentine Donato Giannotti—was often taken up and promoted in credulous terms by foreigners, unequipped with any less flattering lens through which to view the figurehead of a powerful state.[27] But it was one created by Venetians themselves, who had vested their doge with both the image of a prince and the power of any garden-variety statesman.

The paradox of the doge remains a telling one. As Edward Muir has written, "in this image one can see the nexus at which many of the tensions in Venetian society

---

24. William J. Bouwsma, *Venice and the Defense of Republican Liberty: Renaissance Values in the Age of the Counter Reformation* (Berkeley and Los Angeles, 1968), discusses the tendency in cinquecento Venice toward standardization and fixity in academic matters, relating its presence in Bembo to his lack of interest in contemporary events of historical importance (pp. 135–40). Thomas M. Greene, *The Light in Troy: Imitation and Discovery in Renaissance Poetry* (New Haven, 1982), similarly links the formal perfection sought by Bembo to a "refusal to respond to contemporary history" (p. 175) and to an effort to avoid the anxieties and political chaos caused by foreign invasions of Italy. Carlo Dionisotti, *Geografia e storia della letteratura italiana* (Turin, 1967), notes in "Chierici e laici" that Bembo's detachment from political consciousness and service represents a striking break from an earlier Venetian tradition of the scholar–public servant (p. 71). On related questions with respect to a slightly earlier period see Vittore Branca, "Ermolao Barbaro and Late *Quattrocento* Venetian Humanism," in Hale, ed., *Renaissance Venice,* pp. 218–43.

Finally, on the Venetian nobility's retreat from the urban realities of commerce, trade, banking, and shipbuilding in the sixteenth century in favor of more idealized existences linked to mainland farming and real estate see Brian Pullan, "The Occupations and Investments of the Venetian Nobility in the Mid- to Late-Sixteenth Century," in ibid., pp. 379–408; and Ugo Tucci, "The Psychology of the Venetian Merchant in the Sixteenth Century," in ibid., pp. 346–78.

25. See Martines, "The Gentleman in Renaissance Italy," p. 93, as well as Ossola, *Dal "Cortegiano" al' "Uomo di mondo,"* pp. 34–37. The inherent conflict between Castiglione's monarchism and Bembo's republicanism is taken up by Woodhouse, *Baldesar Castiglione,* pp. 154–57.

26. From *De magistratibus et republica Venetorum libri quinque* (Venice, 1551), p. 43 (trans. Lewes Lewkenor, *The Commonwealth and Government of Venice* [London, 1599], p. 43); quoted in Muir, *Civic Ritual in Renaissance Venice,* p. 251.

27. On this aspect of Giannotti and other foreigners see Bouwsma, *Venice and the Defense of Republican Liberty,* pp. 160–61.

and politics were revealed and resolved."[28] Tensions of this kind centered on the Venetian attitudes toward sensuality and extravagance that I noted earlier. Herein lay another paradox to catch Venetians in an existential bind: despite the much-restricted ideological place assigned to *luxuria,* the city had more than a healthy share of it in domains outside the strictly communal. This, after all, was the same city that revealed to the artistic world sensuous new realms of color and light and boasted the most beautiful women in Europe. Like its elegant palazzi and gracious waterways, its resistance to invasion, and its invincibility at sea, sensual beauty and luxuriance formed fabled parts of Venetian lore. Many a foreigner commented on the richness and delights to be had in the city, even while remarking on its odd habits of thrift and modesty.

Perhaps most symbolic among its sensual pleasures for the English Coryat and French visitors like Clément Marot and Michel de Montaigne were the great number of courtesans in the city and the unusual abilities cultivated in the upper echelons of the courtesan's trade.[29] "Thou wilt find the Venetian Courtezan," wrote Coryat, "a good Rhetorician and an elegant discourser."[30] By this Coryat had in mind Venice's famed *cortigiane oneste,* its so-called honest courtesans, women of exceptional grace and high rhetorical polish. As well as being skilled conversationalists and writers, many of these courtesans were singers, often apparently improvising and accompanying themselves on instruments such as the lute or spinet—this in an age that sheltered women closely and kept most nonpatrician women illiterate.

The honest courtesan's success in sixteenth-century Venice thus offers a paradigm for how the city, with its pliable and equivocal social structures, could become an extraordinary resource for inhabitants not born into a full measure of its benefits.[31] For her the city's infatuation with courtliness could be appropriated and manipulated to novel ends, to fashion a reputation that inextricably bound the sexual and the intellectual.[32]

---

28. *Civic Ritual in Renaissance Venice,* p. 252, from Chap. 7, "The Paradoxical Prince," the first section of which is headed "The Doge as *Primus Inter Pares* and as *Princeps.*"

29. For the writings of Marot, see his letter to the French duchess of Ferrara, Renée de France, *Epistre envoyée de Venize à Madame la Duchesse de Ferrare par Clement Marot,* in *Les epistres: Edition critique,* ed. C. A. Mayer (London, 1958), pp. 225–31. Montaigne's observations are recorded in his *Journal de voyage en Italie,* in *Oeuvres complètes,* ed. Pléiade ([Paris], 1962), pp. 1183–84. For further on this see Margaret F. Rosenthal, *The Honest Courtesan: Veronica Franco, Citizen and Writer in Sixteenth-Century Venice* (Chicago, 1992), whose ideas helped stimulate the interpretations I put forth in the following pages.

30. *Coryat's Crudities* 1:405.

31. On the importance of the city for enabling women's speech see esp. Ann Rosalind Jones, "City Women and Their Audiences: Louise Labé and Veronica Franco," in *Rewriting the Renaissance: The Discourses of Sexual Difference in Early Modern Europe,* ed. Margaret W. Ferguson, Maureen Quilligan, and Nancy J. Vickers (Chicago, 1986), pp. 299–316; and idem, *The Currency of Eros,* Chap. 5. For an important collection of essays emphasizing the resources offered for the fashioning of identity by the ambiguities and social complexities of early modern city life see Susan Zimmerman and Ronald F. E. Weissman, eds., *Urban Life in the Renaissance* (Newark, Del., 1989).

32. In "Surprising Fame: Renaissance Gender Ideologies and Women's Lyric," Jones proposes what she calls a "pre-poetics," an analysis of "conditions necessary for writing at all" in the "ideological climate of the Renaissance" that is apropos here; in *The Poetics of Gender,* ed. Nancy K. Miller (New York, 1986), pp. 74–95, esp. p. 74.

A few managed to gain fame through the press, plying the arena of public discourse in order to advance their social and economic positions. The most remarkable of these women was Veronica Franco, a *cittadina* and daughter of a procuress who became a major poet in the 1570s and an intimate of the literary salon of Domenico Venier.[33] In her letters and terze rime she made use of considerable literary aplomb to counter malevolent slander. In one noted instance she parried a detractor by boasting an array of linguistic arms.

Prendete pur de l'armi omai l'eletta.
. . . .

La spada, che 'n man vostra rade e fora,
De la lingua volgar veneziana,
S'a voi piace d'usar, piace a me ancora:
E, se volete entrar ne la toscana,
Scegliete voi la seria o la burlesca,
Ché l'una e l'altra è a me facile e piana.
Io ho veduto in lingua selvaghesca
Certa fattura vostra molto bella,
Simile a la maniera pedantesca:
Se voi volete usar o questa o quella.
. . . .

Qual di lor più vi piace, e voi pigliate,
Ché di tutte ad un modo io mi contento,
Avendole perciò tutte imparate.[34]

Take your choice of weapons, then.
. . . .

If you want to use the common Venetian tongue
As the sword that strikes and pierces in your hand,
That suits me equally well;
And if you want to try Tuscan,
Choose a lofty or a lowly style,
For one and the other are clear and easy for me.
I have seen admirable writings of yours
In rustic language,
And others in a learned vein:
If you want to use either one.
. . . .

Choose whichever suits you best,
I am equally contented with them all,
Having learned them all for this purpose.[35]

Franco's bravura served her well in the ambivalent world that cherished the honest courtesan even as it scorned her. As Margaret F. Rosenthal and Ann Rosalind Jones have shown, in speaking out in areas where women had been largely silenced, vaunting her proficiencies in the verbal arts and challenging her defamer in the terms of a male duel, Franco violated a gendered system of rhetorical orthodoxies.[36] Yet in other poems—and herein lies the point—she aligned herself emphatically, if unconventionally, with the rhetoric of the establishment by setting amatory woes alongside patriotic praises of the Serenissima.[37]

Franco was only one of many nonpatricians who ameliorated their marginal social positions by utilizing the city's opportunities for self-promotion and social

33. On Franco (1546–1591) see most importantly Rosenthal, *The Honest Courtesan,* as well as idem, "Veronica Franco's *Terze Rime:* The Venetian Courtesan's Defense," *RQ* 42 (1989): 227–57.

34. *Gaspara Stampa–Veronica Franco: Rime,* ed. Abdelkader Salza (Bari, 1913), no. 16, vv. 109, 112–26 (p. 292).

35. Trans. adapted from Jones, "City Women and Their Audiences," pp. 312–13.

36. See also Sara Marie Adler, "Veronica Franco's Petrarchan *Terze Rime:* Subverting the Master's Plan," *Italica* 65 (1988): 213–33.

37. In no. 12 she asks a lover to replace praise of her with praise of Venice (vv. 10–13): "lodar d'Adria il felice almo ricetto, / che, benché sia terreno, ha forma vera / di cielo in terra a Dio cara e diletto" (Praise the blessed and gracious home of the Adriatic, which, though earthly, has the true form of heaven on earth, cherished and precious to God); trans. Jones, "City Women and Their Audiences," p. 315, who dubs this duality a "contradictory rhetoric."

mobility. Another, outstanding for our purposes, was Willaert's student, the organist, composer, and vernacular author Girolamo Parabosco, a Piacentine who arrived in Venice around 1540.[38] Like Franco, Parabosco manoeuvred himself quickly to the center of the Venetian literary establishment. Like her, too, he came from a bourgeois family. In the humble words he professed to Giovanni Andrea dell'Anguillara:

Huomo al mondo son io di poco merto.	I'm of little merit to the world,
Lombard Cittadin, non nobile Tosco.	A Lombard citizen, not noble Tuscan,
Nudo d'haver, di gran desio coverto.	Bare of possessions, and full of wants.
Mi chiamano le genti Parabosco,	People call me Parabosco,
E la Musica è mia professione,	And music is my profession,
E per lei vita, e libertà conosco.	From which I know life and liberty.
. . . .	. . . .
Son buon compagno, & un dolor	I'm a good chum and only one sorrow
m'accora	grieves me:
Di non poter donar non che un Ducato:	That I can't deed a single duchy,
Ma un Villagio, e una cittate ancora.	Nor even a village, or a city.[40]
Ho sempre un virtuoso amato,	I've always loved a man of virtue
Fosse Spagnuol, Tedesco, ò Taliano,	Were he Spanish, German, or Italian,
Povero, ricco, o in mediocre stato.[39]	Poor, rich, or of middling station.

Not his birth but his virtue makes a man worthy of honor, Parabosco claims, not rank but merit. He himself is no nobleman, not to say *Tuscan*—that is, linguistic aristocratic—but a mere citizen from modest Lombardy. Later in the same *capitolo* he alludes to his eminent position in the city as if only to thank those in Venice more highly placed than he.

La festa haver mi potrete à san Marco,	During a festival you may find me at San Marco,
Che per gratia de miei Signori Illustri,	For thanks to my illustrious signori
Ho ivi di sonar l'organo il carco.[41]	I have the duty there of playing the organ.

Parabosco's was no mean duty. In 1551 he became First Organist of San Marco, one of the most enviable posts of its kind in Europe. With this prestigious title, Parabosco held a trump card among literary colleagues in the city's populous salons,

---

38. Parabosco was born in 1524 and died in Venice in 1557. For his biography see Giuseppe Bianchini, *Girolamo Parabosco: scrittore e organista del secolo XVI,* Miscellanea di Storia Veneta, ser. 2, vol. 6 (Venice, 1899), pp. 207–486; and Francesco Bussi, *Umanità e arte di Gerolamo Parabosco: madrigalista, organista e poligrafò* (Piacenza, 1961). Parabosco's will is preserved in I-Vas, Notarile, Testamenti, notaio Giovanni Battista Monte, b. 706, fol. 230, dated 9 April 1557; a transcription of it appears in Bianchini, pp. 441–42. The will is an ironic reminder of cinquecento disarticulations between the real and the represented: by contrast with Parabosco's satiric projections of libertinism in the *Lettere amorose, Lettere famigliari,* and elsewhere (see Chap. 3 nn. 16 ff.), his will shows a marked conjugal attentiveness to his spouse, Diana. (Bianchini, not surprisingly, is credulous on this score; see, for example, pp. 225–27.)

39. *La seconda parte delle rime* (Venice, 1555), fols. 50–50'.

40. I am unsure of the precise meaning of this verse and the preceding one. Probably *ducato* is a pun ("ducat" as well as "duchy").

41. *La seconda parte delle rime,* fol. 51.

where music was a valued commodity. His position placed him conveniently betwixt and between—between professional musicians and literati, between nobles and commoners—a situation that made good capital in Venetian society. Elsewhere Parabosco pressed the view that real nobility came from inner worth and not from birthright. His letter to Antonio Bargo of 18 November 1549 affected shock at Bargo's attempt to ingratiate him with an unworthy acquaintance, at his wanting him "to believe that it is a good thing to revere men who live dishonorably, so long as they come from honorable families." Until now he had thought Bargo a person who believed (as he did) that "only virtue may make a man noble, and not from being born in this place rather than that other one, nor from this lineage than another, nor from having much rather than little."[42]

Parabosco answered Bargo in the spirit of familiar vernacular invective that had recently been popularized by Pietro Aretino and followers of his like Antonfrancesco Doni. In meting out satiric censure in letters, *capitoli,* and *sonetti risposti,* Parabosco engaged in complicated strategies of challenge and riposte, wielding his interlocutors' rhetoric to his own ends.[43] Like Franco, he draped himself at the same time in the cloak of Venetian patriotism. Defending his comedies against certain nameless critics in a letter to Count Alessandro Lambertino, for instance, he shot off a battery of rejoinders, the last of which protested that "some benevolence" should be shown him in the city of Venice, since with all his "study, diligence, and labor . . . [he] had always sought to show the world with what reverence and love [he] regarded, even adored . . . the gentleness, courtesy, prudence, valor, honesty, faith, and piety of these illustrious Venetian men."[44] By presenting himself simultaneously as moral censor and pious celebrant, couching his ire in the terms of a patriot's defense, Parabosco at once created and authorized his new condition as a Venetian. Some years earlier, writing the literary theorist Bernardino Daniello along similar

42. The complete first part of the letter reads as follows: "M. Antonio amico carissimo, io ho ricevuto la vostra de vinisette del passato, nella qual havete vanamente speso una grandissima fatica, volendomi far credere che sia ben fatto portar riverenza a gli huomini, che dishonoratamente vivono ancora che usciti di honorevole famiglia. se io non credessi che voi lo facesti, perche io cercassi l'amicitia, & benivolenza d'ogniuno: io v'havrei per altro huomo che fin qui non v'ho tenuto. perche fin hora io ho creduto, che voi siate persona che creda, che solamente la virtù faccia l'huomo nobile, & non il nascere piu in questo che quello altro loco, ne piu di questa, che di quell'altra prosapia: ne piu di molto, che di poco havere" (*Il primo libro delle lettere famigliari* [Venice, 1551], fol. 40). Bargo is almost surely the same as Antonio Barges, a Netherlandish maestro di cappella at the Casa Grande of Venice between at least 1550 and 1555 (when he transferred to Treviso) and a close friend of Parabosco's teacher Willaert.

43. For a theoretical account of such strategies from an anthropological perspective see Pierre Bourdieu's *Outline of a Theory of Practice,* trans. Richard Nice (Cambridge, 1977), pt. 1, sect. 1, "From the Mechanics of the Model to the Dialectic of Strategies," pp. 3–9, and for a compelling application of Bourdieu to Elizabethan literature see Maureen Quilligan, "Sidney and His Queen," in *The Historical Renaissance,* ed. Heather Dubrow and Richard Strier (Chicago, 1989), pp. 171–96.

44. "[M]a s'io non credessi parer prosontuoso, direi bene di meritare almeno qualche benivolenza in questa città. Percioche con ogni mio studio, diligenza, & fatica, cosi in questa mia comedia, come in tutte le mie opere, io ho sempre cercato di mostrare al mondo con quanta riverenza, & con quanto amore, io ammiri; anzi adoro (se ciò mi lice fare) la gentilezza, la cortesia, la prudenza, il valore, l'honestà, la fede, & la pietade di questi Illustrissimi Signori Venetiani; ne mancarò per lo avvenire di pregar il Signor Dio che li felici, et renda loro prosperi ogni suo honesto, & santo desiderio: che veramente essi Signori non sono se non pensieri santi, & divini" (*Il primo libro delle lettere famigliari,* fol. 9'); repr. in Bianchini, *Girolamo Parabosco,* pp. 352–53. Letter dated 5 August 1550.

lines, he had softened his claim that the elderly were unsuited to engage in amorous pursuits by pleading loyalty to the Venetian gerontocracy. Again his protestations were voiced in the language of Venetian panegyric as it was handed down in civic mythology—or a quasi-satiric inflation of it. Apart from his position on the issue of love, he insisted, he "always spoke of the aged with infinite reverence, especially in this sanctified and blessed Venice, today sole defense of Italy and true dwelling of faith, justice, and clemency, in which there are an infinite number [of old people], any one of whom with his prudence could easily govern the Empire of the whole world."[45]

With these paradoxical rhetorical stances, writers like Franco and Parabosco could avail themselves of transgressive possibilities inherent in the diverse literary genres newly stimulated by Venetian print, yet still align themselves with the prevailing power structure. They were at once iconoclasts and panderers. In both roles they seized the chance to shape their own public images, as Franco told her adversary so unequivocally.

Doni, the plebeian Florentine son of a scissors maker, represented at its most venal the phenomenon of making capital of the social breach. After an unsatisfying start as a monk, he fled Florence for the life of a nomadic man of letters, arriving in Piacenza in 1543 and in Venice the following year.[46] In a letter to Parabosco published in 1544 he derided the ignorance of certain monied patrons on whom the two were forced to depend. "It's true that sometimes I'm ready to knock my head against the wall when I think that the cure for maintaining ourselves has to come from the rich and the amusement in consoling ourselves from the sages; . . . [W]e have virtue and poverty and they infinite nonsense and a great deal of money. But I hearten myself with having as much patience to die as they have the stupidity to live."[47] Doni only spelled out what Parabosco's *capitolo* to Anguillara had hinted at more furtively, that their wits and wiles would make up for what they lacked in clout and lucre. As if to underscore his irreverent manipulation of printed words and the contradictory strategies that the two of them crafted, Doni's letter then made out as if to return Parabosco's laudatory sonnet with a matching *risposta*.

Like Parabosco's, Doni's skill at social climbing played a role in Venetian madrigalian developments, if one more mercenary than musical. He possessed a rudi-

45. "[I]n generale, io parlo sempre con riverenza d'infiniti; che si sa bene, che per tutto, & massimamente in questa santa, & benedetta Vineggia, hoggidì solo schermo d'Italia, et vero albergo di fede, di giustitia, & di clemenza, ce ne sono infiniti, che potrebbono con la lor prudenza, ogn'un di loro governare, & agevolmente l'Imperio di tutto il mondo" (*I quattro libri delle lettere amorose*, rev. ed. [Venice, 1607], p. 125; see also the *Libro primo delle lettere amorose di M. Girolamo Parabosco* [Venice, 1573], fol. 61′). The letter, undated, comes from the First Book, which was first printed in 1545 as *Lettere amorose*. Cf. Venier's stanza set by Donato, Chap. 4 n. 79 below.

46. For biographical information about Doni, who lived from 1513 until 1574, see Paul F. Grendler, *Critics of the Italian World, 1530–1560: Anton Francesco Doni, Nicolò Franco & Ortensio Lando* (Madison, 1969), pp. 49–65.

47. "Vero è che tal volta io sono per dar capo nel muro quando io considero, che il rimedio del man tenerci ha da venir da ricchi, & il trattenimento del consolar ci da i savi. . . . noi abbiamo virtù, & povertà; & essi infinita asineria, & moltitudine di dinari. Ma io rincoro d'haver cosi patientia à morire come gli hanno gagliofferia à vivere" (*Lettere* [Venice, 1544], fol. ciii′).

mentary education in musical composition and described himself in various letters as an amateur composer.[48] Far more important was his role during the 1540s as a chronicler of Venetian music, regularly inserting references to music and musicians into his familiar letters. In addition to Parabosco, he wrote the organist Iaches de Buus, the Piacentine composer Claudio Veggio, one Paolo Ugone, and a singer called Luigi Paoli.[49] Doni asked the last of these to bring his *compagnia* to his place with their case of viols, a large harpsichord, lutes, flutes, crumhorns, and part books for singing, since they were going to be performing a comedy on the following Thursday.[50] In a letter to Francesco Coccio he jestingly listed musicians who were destined for Paradise—Buus, Willaert, Arcadelt, Francesco da Milano, Costanzo Porta, Giachetto Berchem, and Parabosco.[51] Yet all his attention to music relegated it to the interstices of a project founded in the larger world of Venetian letters.

Doni's eclecticism depended on the city's flexible structures. It leaned away from the elitist, totalizing aesthetic of Bembo toward the grittier, more syncretistic one that the city paradoxically made possible. This is evident in his most famous joining of musical and literary worlds, the *Dialogo della musica,* published in 1544 by Girolamo Scotto shortly after Doni's arrival in Venice, in which he playfully re-created the casual evenings of an academic assembly.[52] However fanciful (and decidedly popularizing in tone), his *Dialogo* nonetheless tried to represent the mechanics of exchange in a musical salon that included *letterati*. As noted by Alfred Einstein and James Haar, the first of the *Dialogo*'s two parts is unmistakably set in provincial Piacenza, where a circle that formed around the poet Lodovico Domenichi took on the title Accademia Ortolana.[53] The participants in Part I are Michele, possibly a composer and here an alto; a soprano named Oste; the Piacentine poet Bartolomeo Gottifredi called "Bargo," who also sings tenor; and Grullone, a professional musician and bass.[54] Within its fictitious dialogue the interlocutors lightly debate current

---

48. For a summary of these see James Haar, "Notes on the *Dialogo della musica* of Antonfrancesco Doni," *Music & Letters* 47 (1966): 198–224, to which we may add the following claim—albeit suspect—from Doni's letter generically addressed "A Poeti, & Musici," in *Tre libri di lettere del Doni e i termini della lingua toscana* (Venice, 1552): "so favellare anche de la Musica" (p. 121); and "io ci ho messo certi Canti ladri, assassinati, stropiati, per farvi dir qualche cosa, & per far conoscere i begli da brutti, & la buona musica dalla cattiva," etc. (pp. 122–23).

49. Those letters appear as follows: to Buus (undated), *Tre libri de lettere,* pp. 183–84; to Veggio, dated 10 April 1544 from Venice, *Lettere,* pp. cx'–cxi; to Ugone, 9 March 1544 from Venice, *Lettere,* pp. cv'–cvi; to Paoli, dated 1552 from Noale, *Tre libri de lettere,* p. 351.

50. "Voi havete à venire Domenica sera da noi con tutta la vostra compagnia, & portate la Cassa con le Viole, lo Stromento grande di penna, i Liuti, Flauti, Storte, & libri per cantare, perche Giovedì si fa la nostra Comedia."

51. *Tre libri di lettere,* p. 209. Only Arcadelt and da Milano had no strong known connection with Venice.

52. Mod. eds. G. Francesco Malipiero and Virginio Fagotto (Vienna, 1964); and Anna Maria Monterosso Vacchelli, *L'opera musicale di Antonfrancesco Doni,* Istituta e monumenta, ser. 2, vol. 1 (Cremona, 1969). Doni was always fascinated by this sort of academic life. He gives an account of current academies in the last pages of his *Seconda libraria* (Venice, 1551).

53. See Haar, "Notes on the *Dialogo della musica,*" pp. 202–5; Einstein, "The *Dialogo della Musica* of Messer Antonfrancesco Doni," *Music & Letters* 15 (1934): 244–53; and idem, *The Italian Madrigal* 1:193–201.

54. For further on the identities of the interlocutors in Part I see Haar, "Notes on the *Dialogo della musica,*" pp. 203–4, and Einstein, *The Italian Madrigal* 1:196.

literary issues and chatter about other literati and musicians. In between they freely interpolate sight-readings of music—mainly madrigals.

At the outset the interlocutors decide on the style of their encounters with characteristic self-consciousness. "So that we don't seem as if we just want to rip off or mimic Boccaccio . . . let's sing and tell stories both at once," says Oste, "because where others just say 'Let's sing it again,' 'That's beautiful,' and make similar chitchat, we'll dwell a little more on discussing poetry, making jokes, telling stories [novelle] and other sweet fantasies [fantasiette] . . . ; and feeding the body that way with a sweet sleep, we'll nourish it with a soft sweetness, or a divine food."[55] Shortly after this they embark on a madrigal of Claudio Veggio's and continue to converse and sing four-part madrigals throughout Part 1.

Once Doni enters the expanded world of Venice in Part 2, new personalities double his resources. Now eight interlocutors are present: Bargo and Michele from Part 1, a woman called Selvaggia, the composers Parabosco and Perissone, Domenichi and Ottavio Landi from Piacenza, and the composer Claudio Veggio, who seems to have been connected with both cities. Pieces handed out from Michele's pouch [carnaiolo] now accommodate up to all eight of those present. Once again the speakers begin with reflections on their relations to one another and remarks on their use of conventions, all the while laughing at their own bows and curtsies.

> SELVAGGIA: Inasmuch as I am among the number of honored women and this music is made out of love for me, I thank you and I am most obliged to Parabosco and everyone.
>
> PARABOSCO: Your Ladyship injures me; for I am your servant.
>
> PERISSONE: Conventional words; are such torrents of theories necessary?
>
> PARABOSCO: Well said. Too much talk in rhetoric.
>
> PERISSONE: I'm just kidding, since you began with servants and such things, which aren't really used by musicians, painters, sculptors, soldiers, and poets.
>
> SELVAGGIA: So that we don't just keep multiplying words, how did you others end yesterday?[56]

---

55. "[P]er non parere che vogliamo rubbare o imitare il Boccaccio, se vi governerete a modo mio canteremo e novelleremo a un tempo: perché dove altri si passa cantando asciuttamente col dire solo 'Diciamolo un'altra volta', 'Quest'è bello', e simili chiachiere, noi ci diffonderemo un poco più nel parlare ragionando di poesia, di burle, di novelle e d'altre dolci fantasiette, come più a sesto ci verrà e a proposito; e così cibando il corpo d'un dolce riposo, pasceremo l'animo ancora d'una soave dolcezza, anzi d'un cibo divino" (Dialogo della musica, p. 8).

56.   S.   Tanto ch'io son nel numero delle donne onorate e che per mio amore si fa questa musica, io vi ringrazio e v'ho tropp'obbligo e con Parabosco e con tutti.

       G.   Vostra Signoria mi fa ingiuria; ch'io le son servitore.

       P.   Parole generali: che bisogna tante scorrentie di teoriche?

       G.   Dì bene: tanto discorrere su le rettoriche.

       P.   Dico appunto baie, come tu hai cominciato di servidore e di certe cose, che fra noi non s'usano alla reale da' musici, da' pittori, scultori, da' soldati e da' poeti.

       S.   Per non moltiplicare in parole, che si terminò ieri da voi altri?

Dialogo della musica, p. 98

At this they move on. Doni continues to aim for the informal realism of a private academy, moving the speakers in and out of their commitment to the discourse and sustaining their self-conscious scrutinies. After the initial gallantries Parabosco announces that their company has been ordered to speak about a beautiful woman by Grullone and Oste. Since neither Grullone nor Oste is there, they sing instead a madrigal about a *donna bella* set by the obscure Noleth. This prompts a trifling speech by Domenichi on what makes a woman beautiful, in the course of which Doni quotes his own epistolary eulogy of the Piacentine beauty Isabetta Guasca—probably the real-life name of the *Dialogo*'s Selvaggia.[57] Domenichi will not let up his lengthy disquisitions and as he prepares yet another, Veggio begins restlessly to hum and finally implores the group to sing Parabosco's setting of Petrarch's *Nessun visse giamai* before letting Domenichi carry on.[58]

In this way Doni presents the salon not only as a dynamic space for arbitrating different styles and tempers but as a vehicle for self-display and self-fashioning. The salon thus functioned like the occasional and intertextual verse of Franco and Parabosco.[59] In a city set up to permit social mobility and obsessed with styling itself according to its wishes, it was natural that by midcentury the growing numbers of private salons should become one of the main marketplaces for the exchange of ideas and artworks. Salons encouraged the sort of juggling for position and exposure common to places of barter. The nobility who formed the salons' main patrons were more receptive to ambitious commoners than they had been before. And by the mid-sixteenth century the means for winning intellectual and artistic recognition within the bustling city had become more diversified and more ample than ever.

Not surprisingly, ambitions proved only more fierce as a result. The ascendency of the private salon following on the heels of Venetian print culture brought quick changes of players, fast renown, rapid dissemination of ideas and artifacts, and above all pressures to excel and adapt quickly to new fashions. The idea of the marketplace, then, is not just metaphorical, for marketplace economies held a material relevance in the city's salons. The salon was not only the concrete locus of patronage, with all that winning patronage entailed; even more crucially, the busy commercial aspect of the city—with its large mercantile patriciate, its steady influx of well-heeled and cultivated visitors, and its thriving presses—increasingly animated

57. *Dialogo della musica,* p. 106. On Guasca see Haar, "Notes on the *Dialogo della musica,*" p. 215, including remarks on Doni's authorship of the piece that follows. Another Piacentine and favorite poet of early madrigalists, Luigi Cassola, addressed her in his *Madrigali* (Venice, 1544), verso of penultimate folio. For the extensive popular literature containing similar encomia of women see Chap. 3 nn. 39, 41–45 below.

58. *Dialogo della musica,* p. 122.

59. For a standard recent argument on early modern Europe's self-fashioning see the so-called New Historicist position delineated in Stephen Greenblatt, *Renaissance Self-Fashioning: From More to Shakespeare* (Chicago, 1980), pp. 1–10 and passim. Prior to Greenblatt's formulation related ideas were developed in text-critical terms by Thomas Greene, "The Flexibility of the Self in Renaissance Literature," in *The Disciplines of Criticism: Essays in Literary Theory, Interpretation, and History,* ed. Peter Demetz, Thomas Greene, and Lowry Nelson, Jr. (New Haven, 1968), pp. 241–64.

toward midcentury the activity taking place in the living rooms of prosperous Venetians.

The heterogeneity and lack of fixity that typified these salons were interwoven threads in a single social fabric. The very immunity of private groups to concrete description, so confounding to the modern historian, lies at the core of their identity. One of their defining characteristics, this loose organization and openness to change was essential to forming competitive groups. Private gatherings in salons, though often described in contemporary literature as *accademie* (a term I use here), were in fact only distant predecessors of more formalized academies that proliferated later in the century.[60] Unlike the latter, they made no by-laws or statutes; neither did they invent titles or keep the sorts of membership lists, minutes, and systematic records that were to become commonplace by the end of the century. Instead, they protected their cultural cachet in the safe seclusion of domestic spaces, where discussion, debate, and performance were private. Rather than demanding fixity from either their activities or adherents, they thrived on the easy accommodation and continual intermingling of new ideas and faces.[61] Through most of the sixteenth century, Venetian academies that stressed vernacular arts were almost exclusively of this type. This is true both of academies that concentrated on literary enterprises in the vernacular—poetry, letters, plays, editions, and treatises on popular theories of love and language[62]—and of those musical academies linked to the circle of Willaert. The gatherings of Venetian noblemen like Marcantonio Trivisano and Antonio Zantani or of transplanted Florentines like Neri Capponi and Ruberto Strozzi are all known only from scattered accounts and allusions.[63]

60. At midcentury such groups mostly went nameless, so that the term *accademia,* like others they used, was not at first part of a proper name. By reducing them all for convenience to the single epithet *academy,* I mean to stress their historical relationship to the later groups, but not to confuse their structures with the formalized ones of those later academies. The generic names applied to academic salons during this time were as changeable as their makeups—*accademia, ridotto, adunanza,* or *cenacolo.* For further explanation of different meanings of the term *accademia* see Gino Benzoni, "Aspetti della cultura urbana nella società veneta del '5–'600: le accademie," *Archivio veneto* 108 (1977): 87–159.

61. From the growing literature on the academies of Venice and the Veneto, especially notable are Benzoni, "Aspetti della cultura urbana nella società veneta"; idem, "Le accademie," in *Storia della cultura veneta: il seicento,* ed. Girolamo Arnaldi and Manlio Pastore Stocchi, vol. 4, pt. 1 (Vicenza, 1983), pp. 131–62; idem, "L'accademia: appunti e spunti per un profilo," *Ateneo veneto* 26 (1988): 37–58. Still informative (if partly outdated), particularly because they incorporate less-fixed academic groups, are the older studies of Michele Battagia, *Delle accademie veneziane: dissertazione storica* (Venice, 1826), and Michele Maylender, *Storia delle accademie d'Italia,* 5 vols. (Bologna, 1926–30). See also Achille Olivieri, "L'intellettuale e le accademie fra '500 e '600: Verona e Venezia," *Archivio veneto,* 5th ser., vol. 130 (1988): 31–56, who explains how academies of the later sixteenth century and beyond came to structure themselves after imaginary collectives in ways that became normative at the time.

62. For general discussions of informal literary academies in sixteenth-century Venice see Logan, *Culture and Society in Venice,* pp. 71ff., and, on the fifteenth century, King, *Venetian Humanism,* pp. 12–18. Outside this pattern are a very few public-minded and philologically oriented academies that grew up earlier in the century; in the early cinquecento this includes the Neacademia of Aldus Manutius, devoted to Greek scholarship, and at midcentury the Accademia Veneziana, also known as the Accademia della Fama, devoted to an encyclopedic agenda of learning and publication. For the Neacademia see Martin Lowry, *The World of Aldus Manutius: Business and Scholarship in Renaissance Venice* (Ithaca, 1979), pp. 195ff., and on the Accademia Veneziana, Chap. 4 nn. 91ff. below.

In the remainder of Part 1, I try to depict the textures of vernacular patronage in Venice by focusing on the private worlds of figures such as these. Chapter 2 begins with the pair of Florentine exiles Capponi and Strozzi, apparently the main private benefactors of Willaert and Rore, respectively, from about the late 1530s until the mid-1540s. As rich aristocrats and singers of domestic music, they represent a kind of private patronage that shunned the popularizing commodifications made by the likes of Parabosco. They stand in sharp opposition to another foreign patron, Gottardo Occagna, who sponsored prints of vernacular music and letters in Venice from about 1545 to 1561. Fictitious printed letters to Occagna from Parabosco that feigned public displays of private diversions suggest he colluded with vernacular artists in mounting the Venetian social ladder. Central to my assessments of both Occagna and the other protagonist of Chapter 3, the patrician Zantani, are the ways in which social images were fashioned through the rhetoric of Petrarchan love lyrics. The juxtaposition of Occagna's and Zantani's cases shows that while those outside the Venetian patriarchy might invert this rhetoric to mobilize their positions, the local aristocracy sought out ennobling texts and images to reinforce their status claims. Zantani probably promoted some of the many encomia of his wife that were made in the rhetoric of Petrarchan praise, and he engineered several printed volumes that could bring him renown, not least an anthology with four of the madrigals from Willaert's (then) still unpublished *Musica nova* corpus.

All of these figures are maddeningly elusive to our backward gaze. It is only in Chapter 4, with the salon of another native patrician, Domenico Venier—a friend of vernacular music whose palace was the literary hub of midcentury Venice—that we come to see the full richness of exchange, the gala of personalities, the competitive forces they set in motion, and the fruitful intersection of art and ideas that the flexible social formation of Venice allowed.

63. Distinctly removed from this mold are several academies on the mainland, most notably the highly organized Accademia Filarmonica of Verona, established at the self-educative initiative of Veronese noblemen—a group that for all its enterprise and interest in fashions on the lagoon lacks the urban nonchalance and elasticity of the Venetians. On academies in the Veneto see Benzoni, "Aspetti della cultura urbana nella società veneta," and Logan, *Culture and Society in Venice,* pp. 72ff.

Chapter 2 · FLORENTINES IN VENICE AND
THE MADRIGAL AT HOME

Throughout much of the 1530s and beyond Venice sheltered a colony of exiled Florentines, the *fuorusciti*. As a group, the *fuorusciti* were highly aristocratic and educated, well versed in music and letters, and eminently equipped to indulge expensive cultural habits.[1] One of them, Neri Capponi, arrived in Venice in 1538 from Lyons. Before long he had established what became the most sophisticated musical academy in Venice, headed by Willaert and graced by the acclaimed soprano Polissena Pecorina. Like other private patrons, Capponi seems to have gathered his academists under his own roof, where they flourished in the early 1540s and almost surely premiered much of Willaert's *Musica nova*. Another Florentine, Ruberto Strozzi, lodged intermittently in the city during the thirties and forties in the course of far-ranging business and political errands that accelerated after his family was banished from Florence in 1534.[2] In the same years Strozzi seems continually to have sought out new madrigals.[3] The Strozzi kept a palace by Venice's Campo San

---

1. The Florentine community had maintained a chapel at the Venetian Chiesa di Santa Maria Gloriosa dei Frari since 1436. The portion of the Frari's archive at I-Vas designated "Scuola dei fiorentini" lacks items for the years 1504 to 1658.

For an informative essay emphasizing the literary aspect of Florentine exiles in Venice see Valerio Vianello, "Tra Firenze e Venezia: il fenomeno del fuoruscitismo," in *Il letterato, l'accademia, il libro: contributi sulla cultura veneta del cinquecento,* Biblioteca Veneta, no. 6 (Padua, 1988), pp. 17–46.

2. Capponi lived from 1504 to 1594 and Strozzi from ca. 1512 to 1566. See further on Capponi's genealogy in n. 11 below.

3. For knowledge about patronage of the madrigal by Florentine exiles in this era, see the crucial findings of Richard J. Agee: "Ruberto Strozzi and the Early Madrigal," *JAMS* 36 (1983): 1–17, and idem, "Filippo Strozzi and the Early Madrigal," ibid., 38 (1985): 227–37. Agee was cautious about concluding definitively that the Neri Capponi of musical fame is the same as the one appearing in many Strozzi letters, but cross-references in the letters combined with Passerini's genealogy cited in n. 11 below confirms that they are one person.

Canciano along the lovely Rio dei Santissimi Apostoli (Plate 7).[4] Even though their presence in Venice was sporadic, various members of the family including Ruberto made stays long enough to establish a base for domestic music making there. In the early to mid-forties, as he tore about Italy and France, Ruberto is known to have bought up madrigals and motets by Cipriano de Rore.[5]

The coincidence of the Florentine presence in Venice with the flourishing of Venetian madrigals was fateful. Florentines made their way into Venice following a long history of political strife in their own city, whose republican edifice by then had collapsed. During the years spent in Florence, these exiles had sustained a long tradition vigorously promoting Italian vocal music. It was only natural that they should have continued it once abroad.

The patronage of both Capponi and Strozzi was aggressively acquisitive, seeking sole ownership of important new settings. But their interest was not mere collection. Each was groomed in gentlemen's musical skills and moved in patrician circles that practiced part singing.[6] Each also studied viol in Venice with the pedagogue Silvestro Ganassi dal Fontego, as Ganassi revealed in dedicating to them in 1542 and 1543 the respective halves of his treatise on viol playing.[7] In both roles—as patrons and as amateur musicians—they met with extravagance the expectations of class and pedigree that they shared with a large network of affluent Florentines abroad, whose cultural heritage placed arts and letters at its center.

In both political and artistic realms the vicissitudes and imaginative powers of Ruberto's father had played a dominant role—a role that is critical for our understanding of the next generation's construction of this heritage and its relationship to Venetian music. Ruberto was the son of Filippo di Filippo Strozzi, the most prominent Florentine banker of the first third of the century and, by many reckonings, for most of his life the richest man in Italy.[8] It was for the Strozzi bank in Lyons that Capponi had served as company manager from 1532 until 1538, when he fled to Venice

---

4. The information comes from a letter from Lione Strozzi, prior of Capua, to Cavalier Covoni, minister of the Strozzi tariffs, addressed to "campo di San Canziano, in ca' Strozzi." The letter appears with documents published in G.-B. Niccolini, *Filippo Strozzi, tragedia* (Florence, 1847), p. 312; see also Agostino Sagredo, "Statuti della Fraternità e Compagnia dei Fiorentini in Venezia dell'anno MDLVI dati in luce per cura e preceduti da un discorso," *Archivio storico italiano,* App. 9 (1853): 447. Sagredo believed that the Strozzi house was "quella ora del Weber dove altre volte era la famosa Biblioteca Svajer" (p. 447), that is, Davide Weber, the famous early-nineteenth-century art collector, and Amedeo Svajer, the bibliophile. This house stands at the Ponte di San Canciano by the so-called Traghetto di Murano and is now numbered 4503 in the *sestiere* of Cannaregio. The ancient Greek reliefs on the exterior, apparently added by Weber, are described by Abbé Moschini, *Itinéraire de la ville de Venise et des îles circonvoisines* (Venice, 1819), pp. 189–91. See further in Giuseppe Tassini, *Alcuni palazzi ed antichi edifichi di Venezia storicamente illustrati con annotazioni* (Venice, 1879), pp. 171–72, which traces the house back to the Morosini family, and idem, *Curiosità veneziane, ovvero origini delle denominazioni stradali di Venezia,* rev. ed. Lino Moretti (Venice, 1988), p. 119.

5. See Agee, "Ruberto Strozzi."

6. See nn. 24–27 below.

7. See his *Regola rubertina* (Venice, 1542), dedicated to Strozzi, and *Lettione seconda pur della prattica di sonare il violone d'arco da tasti* (Venice, 1543), to Capponi. For an English text see the trans. of Hildemarie Peter made from the German ed. of Daphne Silvester and Stephen Silvester (Berlin-Lichterfelde, 1972).

8. Filippo was born in 1488 and died in 1538. For a contemporary view of his wealth see the cinquecento historian Bernardo Segni, *Istorie fiorentine dall'anno MDXXVII al MDLV,* ed. G. Gargani (Florence, 1857), who claimed that "nella ricchezza fu solo, e senza comparazione di qualsivoglia uomo d'Italia" (p. 371).

7 .   Strozzi palace in Venice along the Rio dei Santissimi Apostoli by the so-called
Traghetto di Murano, Ponte di San Canciano. Parish of San Canciano, Cannaregio 4503.
Photo courtesy of Osvaldo Böhm.

in early spring in the face of French demands to release certain of Filippo's funds.[9] Capponi's involvement in Strozzian financial affairs formed part of a protracted union between the two families, which involved a web of marriages around the turn of the century and included the marriage of Ruberto's sister to Luigi Capponi.[10] Neri's father, Gino di Neri, had been wedded to Filippo's sister Caterina. Ruberto and Neri were thus first cousins, and Filippo Strozzi, Neri's uncle.[11] The two families had formed within Florentine society a considerable power base, which had its center in the person of Filippo. By the mid-thirties, however, owing to Strozzi clashes with the new duke, Alessandro de' Medici, Filippo's family and its immediate associates had been cast into a restless and embittered exile. In the course of this, Filippo's banking interests were managed from abroad, mostly by employees from the ranks of the *fuorusciti*. Venice was just one of several cities that received substantial Strozzi business, along with Rome, Naples, Lyons, and Seville.[12]

To clarify the precarious social and political situation in which Filippo, his family, and their Florentine allies found themselves in the 1530s, it is necessary to look briefly back over the long-standing Strozzi relationship with the Medici. In 1508, during Florence's next-to-last republic, the headstrong Filippo became engaged to Clarice de' Medici. At that time her family was banished from the city. The engagement was a brash move on Filippo's part that drew horror and fury from his half-brother Alfonso and members of the extended Strozzi clan, who held at the time at least tentative favor with the Ottimati government.[13] Yet it soon showed his shrewd foresight. With the Medici restoration of 1512 Filippo found himself ideally placed to exploit the financial interests and favor of Clarice's uncle Giovanni, who assumed the papacy as Leo X the following year. In the decades up to 1534 Filippo bankrolled two Medici popes in his role as papal financier, culminating in 1533 with his dowering of a Medici bride for the future king of France, Henry of Orleans, at the staggering sum of 130,000 scudi.[14] In exchange for such favors he received an almost

---

9. See Niccolini, *Filippo Strozzi,* pp. 306–7.

10. See Melissa Meriam Bullard, *Filippo Strozzi and the Medici: Favour and Finance in Sixteenth-Century Florence and Rome* (Cambridge, 1980), pp. 3–4. (Note, however, Agee's cautions concerning some apparent genealogical confusion in her discussion of these marriages, "Ruberto Strozzi," p. 7 n. 27.)

11. This fact, previously unmentioned, helps explain Filippo's willingness to rely on Neri to care for his family finances, particularly by making him executor of his will. The family tree, first noted by James Haar, "Notes on the *Dialogo della musica* of Antonfrancesco Doni," *Music & Letters* 47 (1966): 207 n. 38, is included in the multifascicle work *Le famiglie celebri italiane,* gen. ed. Pompeo Litta (Milan, 1819–1902), which is variously ordered and bound in the different copies that survive. The copy in I-Vas includes 14 vols., with "Capponi di Firenze," ed. Luigi Passerini (1871), in vol. 3, tavola XX. Neri's grandfather is described there as a very rich banker who opened a banking house at Lyons. His mother is given as Caterina Strozzi, who married Gino di Neri Capponi. Our Neri, born 6 March 1504, appears as the oldest of ten children.

12. Filippo speaks of his bank in Venice in various letters and wills; see Niccolini, *Filippo Strozzi,* pp. 315ff., and Sagredo, "Statuti della Fraternità e Compagnia dei Fiorentini," p. 447.

13. On the marriage contract and its aftermath see Bullard, "Marriage Intrigues," Chap. 3 in *Filippo Strozzi and the Medici,* and idem, "Marriage Politics and the Family in Renaissance Florence: The Strozzi-Medici Alliance in 1508," *American Historical Review* 74 (1979): 51–71. For a general account of the hazard perceived by the Ottimati government in Strozzi ambitions see Eric Cochrane, *Florence in the Forgotten Centuries, 1527–1800: A History of Florence and the Florentines in the Age of the Grand Dukes* (Chicago and London, 1973), esp. p. 7.

14. See Bullard, *Filippo Strozzi and the Medici,* pp. 158–62, on the history of this affair.

endless series of venal offices. On a single occasion in 1524, at the institution of the College of the Knights of St. Peter, Giulio de' Medici, then Pope Clement VII, awarded him eleven titles of the office of knight in return for credits totaling 9,130 ducats; he divided them among four of his sons, giving three to Ruberto.[15]

Until Clement VII's death in September 1534 Filippo's political position experienced only one real setback when he abandoned Rome for Florence shortly before the sack in 1527 to take the helm of popular republican leadership. Having failed in that role, he was temporarily forced to pursue interests abroad. But by 1530 he had reforged Medici bonds in Florence and Rome and resumed principal residence in the latter city.

It was only after several years of renewed papal collaboration that Filippo's seemingly unbreakable financial edifice began to crack with the death of the pope—Filippo's primary debtor and Medici supporter. Filippo still boasted a sprawling empire and had much to protect in the continued prestige of the Strozzi family. But any goodwill toward them that remained among Medici at home was dwindling fast. Filippo's wealth and leverage among princes posed an immediate threat to the collateral line of the Medici headed by the dissolute Duke Alessandro, now in firm—and monarchical—command of the *patria* with imperial support. Alessandro grew increasingly suspicious of Filippo and his sons. At last, in December 1534, shortly after Clement's death and after various skirmishes that took the family again out of Florence, Alessandro declared them rebels.[16]

Filippo's story merges at this juncture with that of members of the younger generation who are my main concern here. In August 1536, after a two-year stay in his palazzo at Rome, Filippo finally retired to Venice.[17] His time there was soon cut short, however, by what Benedetto Varchi later described as Lorenzo de' Medici's breathless arrival at San Canciano on 8 January 1537 with news that he had murdered Alessandro.[18] Filippo quickly married off his sons Piero and Ruberto to Lorenzo's sisters. Goaded on by Piero, he also began to organize troops for an assault against the Medici, only to be captured in his first major attempt in the Tuscan hills of Montemurlo on 31 July. The Florentine historian Jacopo Nardi recounted that Filippo's sons retreated the next day toward Venice, tired and defeated and with no alternative but to take stock of their situation and await a better opportunity to strike.[19] By December 1538 Filippo had died in prison, reputedly

15. Ibid., p. 152.
16. Lorenzo Strozzi, *Le vite degli uomini illustri della casa Strozzi,* ed. Pietro Stromboli (Florence, 1892), pp. 173–74.
17. I base this chronology on the first of Neri Capponi's many letters to Filippo written from Lyons. Originally they were addressed to Rome, but beginning on 19 August 1536 they were sent to Venice (I-Fas, CS, Ser. III [95], fol. 23). This initiated a continuous series of letters to Venice until 25 March 1537, when Capponi began writing Filippo at Ferrara (CS, Ser. V [95], fol. 129'). (See Table 1 below.)
18. *Storia fiorentina,* 2 vols. (Florence, 1963), 2:555 (Book 15, Chap. 4). Varchi's account largely agrees with those of Strozzi, *Vite,* pp. 174–75, and Segni, *Istorie fiorentine,* p. 345. Both of the last two include the story that Filippo, once he made up his mind to believe Lorenzo, proclaimed him the Florentine Brutus—just one detail whose repetition suggests a strong narrative filiation among the various versions.
19. *Istorie della città di Firenze,* ed. Agenore Gelli, 2 vols. (Florence, 1858), 2:306.

by his own hand, but most probably at the hands of the Medici.[20] In the years afterward, Ruberto and other anti-Mediceans abroad continued to pursue schemes to retrieve Florence from the Medici until their defeat in the War of Siena in 1552–55 dashed their last real hopes.

I have synthesized events highlighted in Florentine letters and histories in order to emphasize the intrigues and narrowly factional politics that brought elite Florentine patrons into Venice. Far from epitomizing the republicanism idealized in Venice and attached to Filippo in various romanticized representations that appeared after the events of 1537–38, he and his kin differed little in kind from the Medici themselves. In a very real sense, an entrepreneurial merchant-banker on the rare order of Filippo Strozzi—not unlike Jacob Fugger, imperial banker to Charles V—was at once invention and inventor of the princely sponsors who required him to stage their grand schemes. His identity depended on an exchange of mutually productive powers. Born into such a dynasty in the world of early modern power politics, a young man like Ruberto cannot have thought himself much less a prince's son than if his father had been a duke or an emperor, a difference he might have attributed to the winds of fate or to a slight disparity in style or ambitions.

For the Strozzi, empire and culture formed an indivisible alliance. As Pier Paolo Vergerio had put it, not only was "the ability to speak and write with elegance"— and, we might add, to sing—"no slight advantage."[21] Learning and cultural refinement both expressed and bolstered the imperial claims of those born into entitled possession of them. Filippo's passions for high finance and Florentine politics extended almost by necessity to arts and literature, in which he developed considerable abilities. His brother Lorenzo wrote that on all those days that Filippo was free to plan as he liked, his time was divided equally between "the study of letters, private business, and private pleasures and delights."[22] He hired as an intellectual companion and for help with correcting the natural history of Pliny the philologist and composer Bernardo da Pisano.[23] He also composed lyrics of some distinction that were set to music by the likes of Arcadelt, Layolle, and Willaert, and wrote poems for other aristocrats in his circle.[24] Both brothers, according to Lorenzo, were

20. Controversy arose immediately as to how Filippo had really died; see Segni's *Istorie fiorentine,* pp. 370–71. See also Gelli's commentary in Nardi, *Istorie* 2:324 n. 1, and 1:325 n. 1.

21. Quoted in Lauro Martines, *Power and Imagination: City-States in Renaissance Italy* (New York, 1979), p. 194; see also his view of humanistic education and the arts in connection with the ruling classes, passim, esp. Chaps. 11 and 13.

22. "Tutti i giorni della sua vita, che gli fu lecito dispensar per elezione, costumò in tre parti dividere: una alli studi delle lettere, l'altra alle sue private faccende, l'ultima alli suoi privati piaceri e diletti" (Strozzi, *Vite,* p. 200).

23. See Varchi, *Storia fiorentina* 2:274. Filippo was the dedicatee of Pisano's edition of Apuleis, on which see Frank A. D'Accone, "Bernardo Pisano: An Introduction to His Life and Works," *Musica disciplina* 17 (1963): 125–26. D'Accone hesitated to link too securely the identity of this Pisano with that of the musician, but his doubts are certainly cleared up by Varchi's reference to Pisano as an "eccellente musico in que' tempi, che grande e giudizioso letterato" (as noted by Agee, "Filippo Strozzi," p. 229 n. 11).

24. On Layolle's setting of *Gite, sospir dolenti* see Fenlon and Haar, *The Italian Madrigal,* pp. 150, 279, 282. The madrigal was included in the first layer of B-Bc, MS 27.731, which they date to ca. 1535–40. Only a few settings of Filippo's poetry are known today, but given the exclusive patterns of patronage that obtained with Florentine patrons it seems likely that others (ones for which he commissioned settings, for

accustomed to singing part music, not only madrigals but carnival songs and Lamentations, which they performed on feast days publicly and "without shame."[25] Their houses were rich repositories of books and musical instruments, and both Lorenzo and Filippo have been associated with manuscripts central to French and Italian polyphonic repertories of the time.[26] Recent archival unearthings, finally, show Filippo as patron to Bartolomeo degli Organi, a singer named "La Fiore," an instrumentalist called "urbano sonatore," the Roman madrigalist Constanzo Festa, and possibly the Ferrarese composer Maistre Jhan.[27]

The pains Filippo took to reinforce his cultural hegemony naturally included his immediate family. He attended to the humanistic education of his sons by hiring noted tutors and (later) sending his sons to the Studio in Padua. Girolamo Parabosco's description of Ruberto as having "rare judgment in all sciences" may therefore reveal more than the usual hyperbole,[28] for Ruberto's education not only included the Paduan stint but tutoring in Greek letters and law with Varchi.[29]

Ruberto and his brothers sang part music like their father and uncle, as shown by a letter of 19 November 1534 (first noted by Agee) that Ruberto's Lyons-based relative Lionardo Strozzi wrote him in Rome.[30] Lionardo alludes to Ruberto's request

example) simply are not extant. The findings of Agee, "Filippo Strozzi," suggest that literary patrons wrote many more verses for commissioned settings than now survive; see also Thomas W. Bridges, "The Publishing of Arcadelt's First Book of Madrigals," 2 vols. (Ph.D. diss., Harvard University, 1982), p. 29. (Apropos, it might be of interest that while in Lyons Capponi wrote Filippo, then in Venice, to send thanks for a *capitolo* Filippo had composed for him—for singing to music?; 1 December 1536, CS, Ser. III [95], fols. 71′–72′.)

25. "Dilettavasi oltre modo della musica, cantando con modo e ragione; nè si vergognò insieme con Lorenzo suo fratello e altri suoi simili, cantare ne' giorni santi pubblicamente nelle Compagnie di notte, le Lamentationi. Similmente fece per carnevale in maschera per le case le canzoni. Dilettossi anche di comporre nella nostra lingua in prosa e in versi, come per più sue traduzioni e madrigali, che oggi in musica si cantano, puossi conoscere" (Strozzi, *Vite,* p. 202).

26. On Filippo's books and instruments see Frank A. D'Accone, "Transitional Text Forms and Settings in an Early 16th-Century Florentine Manuscript," in *Words and Music—The Scholar's View: A Medley of Problems and Solutions Compiled in Honor of A. Tillman Merritt by Sundry Hands,* ed. Laurence Berman (Cambridge, Mass., 1972), pp. 29–58, and Agee, "Filippo Strozzi," p. 227 n. 2. On Filippo as recipient of the chansonnier in I-Fc, MS Basevi 2442, see Howard Mayer Brown, "Chansons for the Pleasure of a Florentine Patrician: Florence, Biblioteca del Conservatorio di Musica, MS Basevi 2442," in *Aspects of Medieval and Renaissance Music: A Birthday Offering in Honor of Gustave Reese,* ed. Jan LaRue et al. (New York, 1966; repr. New York, 1978), pp. 56–66, and idem, "The Music of the Strozzi Chansonnier (Florence, Biblioteca del Conservatorio di Musica, MS Basevi 2442)," *Acta musicologica* 40 (1968): 115–29, as well as Agee, "Filippo Strozzi," p. 230 n. 12. On Lorenzo Strozzi's extensive connections with the proto-madrigalian manuscript I-Fc, MS Basevi 2440, esp. as poet, see D'Accone, "Transitional Text Forms," pp. 33–35, and idem, "Bernardo Pisano."

27. Filippo created a *mascherata* together with Bartolomeo in 1507 and bought music from him in 1510, as discovered by Frank A. D'Accone, "Alessandro Coppini and Bartolomeo degli Organi: Two Florentine Composers of the Renaissance," *Analecta musicologica* 4 (1967): 52–53. On Filippo's connections with "La Fiore," dating from 1517, see Richard Sherr, "Verdelot in Florence, Coppini in Rome, and the Singer 'La Fiore,'" *JAMS* 37 (1984): 406–8, 410–11. For Filippo's patronage of Festa and "Urbano sonatore" see Agee, "Filippo Strozzi," pp. 229–30 and passim, and for that of a "maestro Janni musico" in 1521 see D'Accone, "Transitional Text Forms," p. 33 n. 16.

28. See Parabosco's dedication of his *Madrigali a cinque voci* (Venice, 1546), quoted in full in n. 65 below.

29. As recounted in the anonymous biography of Varchi, "Vita di Benedetto Varchi," in Benedetto Varchi, *Storia fiorentina,* ed. Gaetano Milanesi, 3 vols. (Florence, 1857), 1:25.

30. Agee, "Ruberto Strozzi," pp. 9–11. For a different translation see Fenlon and Haar, *The Italian Madrigal,* pp. 66–67.

for new music, revealing at the same time that the Lyonnaise circle—of which Ruberto periodically formed a part—sang music at home, "either at your house [i.e., the Strozzi's], or at Niccolò Mannelli's." The current group includes Lionardo himself, Ruberto's brother Vincenzo, the Florentine composer Layolle, as well as Neri Capponi (whom Lionardo familiarly calls "vostro nery Capponi").[31]

Among the most striking aspects of Florentine epistolary exchange are the elitist postures adopted time and again in patrimonial ploys and in the Florentines' observations of outsiders. Florentines pursue what is rare and new, unknown, and decidedly *private*. In the first and best known of their letters, from Ruberto, in Venice, to Varchi of 27 March 1534, Ruberto described his attempt to have an epigram of Varchi's set by Willaert and asked Varchi in return to compose a madrigal in honor of "Madonna Pulissena" (undoubtedly Pecorina). Ruberto's assumption that he would wield influence with the chapelmaster is remarkable in itself. But even more so is the clandestine, cocky way he went about the whole venture. Ruberto presents himself as something of a roué, asking his teacher for a text "with that same boldness that I would use to ask one of my lovers to screw her."[32] He folds his swaggering bravado in love matters into a self-assured cultural elitism. Linking sexual and cultural conquest in a single identity that placed stealth at the strategic node of a sacred bond, Ruberto expressed his hopes through the conjuncture of culture and combat: "I don't want to tell you not to speak to a soul on earth about this [madrigal], because I would do you an injury, as if I lacked faith in you; yet I have more faith in you than the Hungarians have in their swords."[33]

Lionardo's letter of 19 November 1534 evinces the same Florentine attitude toward sharing music. Ruberto's request was specifically meant to procure *new* and unknown music from the Lyonnaise contingent. Lionardo hopes that a canzone that arrived from Florence some eight days earlier will serve; if it's already known in Rome, he'll get some other new pieces for them—not hard for him to do since, as he boasts, a friend in Florence always sends along Arcadelt's latest things. The entire letter turns on this issue of having the latest pieces on hand—and only for restrictive, private use.[34]

31. For general background on music making in sixteenth-century Lyons see Frank Dobbins, *Music in Renaissance Lyons* (Oxford, 1992); pp. 254–56 treat Strozzi patronage.

32. A published repr. of the letter may be found in *Raccolta di prose fiorentine: tomo quinto contenente lettere* (Venice, 1735), *parte terza*, 1:69. For a version based on a copy in I-Fas see Agee, "Ruberto Strozzi," pp. 1–2. I quote from Agee's transcription, which reconciles the printed version with that of a manuscript copy: "Non havendo a chi ricorrere, m'è forza venire a Voi, et certo lo fo con quella baldezza [the printed version has *caldezza*], che se avessi a richiedere una mia innamorata [here, *di chiavarla* is crossed out in the manuscript—the printed version avoids the expression by replacing it with dots]" ("Ruberto Strozzi," p. 2 n. 4).

33. "Non voglio dirvi non ne parliate con homo del mondo, perche io vi ingiurerei, parendovi avessi poca fede in Voi, il che certo non saria, perche ho piu fede in Voi, che li Ungheri nelle spade" (ibid.). Strozzi's outrageousness doesn't stop there; witness the salutation that he juxtaposes immediately afterward: "Fate, lo abbia quanto prima meglio; e senza altro dirvi, raccomandomi a voi *per infinita saecula saeculorum Amen.*"

34. Some years later, on 26 April 1539, a Strozzi employee in Venice may have been emulating the Florentine fervor for novelty by pleading with one Palla Strozzi in Lyons to have a text of his set by Layolle, "*a* 4, but if you would have him do it *a* 5, so much the better"—this just at the time when five-voice pieces were gaining favor over four-voice ones. See Agee, "Filippo Strozzi," pp. 236–37 nn. 37–38.

This was the same tight vise that gripped the new Venetian-styled madrigals of Willaert and Rore. In 1542 Ruberto's employee Pallazzo da Fano angled to have Strozzi send him a new madrigal of Rore's written for Capponi, should he be able to get hold of it.[35] Failing that (his letter reveals), he hopes for "some other lovely thing, but *not one that many people have*—that is, one that might be for a man like messer Nerio. . . . And truly *not a man will have your madrigal that you sent me*, for I know the one to whom I sent it to be of messer Nerio's kind" (emphasis mine).[36] Whoever got the madrigal from da Fano was probably not a Venetian; for the secrecy and exclusivity that marks these transactions are little known in the dealings Venetian patricians had with composers.[37] On the contrary, Venetians largely welcomed printed venues, except at times for their own literary production.

Capponi's tightfistedness was the very quality that so astonished the low-born Antonfrancesco Doni. When his exiled compatriot Francesco Corboli took him to Capponi's salon, Doni was already beginning to fashion a career out of the new livelihood to be earned from the Venetian printing industry and was squirreling away musical works for his forthcoming *Dialogo della musica*. He claimed to be agog on his first encounter with Venetian music making there—not only at the dazzling musical scene but at the total inaccessibility of the music.

> There is a gentlewoman, POLISENA Pecorina (consort of a *cittadino* from my native town), so talented and refined that I cannot find words high enough to praise her. One evening I heard a concert of *violoni* and voices in which she played and sang together with other excellent spirits. The perfect master of that music was Adrian Willaert, whose studious style, never before practiced by musicians, is so tightly knit, so sweet, so right, so miraculously suited to the words that I confess to never having known what harmony was in all my days, save that evening. The devotee of this music and lover of such divine composition is a gentleman, a most excellent spirit, Florentine as well, called Messer Neri Caponi, to whom I was introduced by Messer Francesco Corboli [another Florentine] and thanks to whom I listened, saw, and heard such divine things. This Messer Neri spends hundreds of ducats every year on such talent, and keeps it to himself; not even if it were his own father would he let go one song.[38]

35. The final digit of the letter's date is illegible; for Agee's views of its date see "Ruberto Strozzi," p. 12 n. 39, where he first assigned the date 1541, and idem, "Filippo Strozzi," p. 236 n. 35, where he amended his reading to 1542 based on a subsequent finding. My investigations of Strozzi's whereabouts (as summarized in Table 1 below) indicate that the date must be 1542.

36. Agee, "Ruberto Strozzi," p. 13, letter IIa.

37. Accordingly, composers in Venice, with rare exceptions, were inclined to hand works to the press accompanied by toadying endearments to wealthy dedicatees from whom they hoped for subvention, rather than selling them off piecemeal. On this issue see Jane A. Bernstein, "Financial Arrangements and the Role of Printer and Composer in Sixteenth-Century Italian Music Printing," *Acta musicologica* 62 (1990): 39–56.

38. "Ecci una gentil donna POLISENA Pecorina (consorte d'un cittadino della mia patria) tanto virtuosa & gentile, che non trovo lode sì alte, che la commendino. Io ho udito una sera un concerto di violoni & di voci, dove ella sonava, e cantava in compagnia di altri spiriti eccellenti. il maestro perfetto della qual musica era Adriano Villaert di quella sua diligente invenzione non più usata dai musici, sì unita, sì dolce, sì giusta, sì mirabilmente acconcie le parole, ch'io confessai non avere saputo che cosa sia stata armonia ne' miei giorni, salvo in quella sera. L'infervorato di questa musica, e l'innamorato di tanta divina composizione è un gentil'uomo, uno spirito eccellentissimo pur fiorentino, detto M. Neri Caponi: al quale per mezzo di M. Francesco Corboli uomo Reale fui fatto amico e mercé sua sentii, vidi, et udii

Many have assumed, with good reason, that the music Doni heard at Capponi's house included works printed only fifteen years later in the *Musica nova*.[39] The links between the two repertories are strong. Francesco dalla Viola's dedication of the printed volume maintained that the pieces in the *Musica nova* had been "hidden and buried" so that no one could use them and that consequently "the world came to be deprived" of its contents.[40] The very person who later possessed the collection—presumably after Capponi and before its owner at the time of publication, Prince Alfonso d'Este—was the woman Doni so praised, Polissena Pecorina; it was from her that Alfonso later bought the collection.[41] Doni's claim that Willaert's "diligente inventione" heard at Capponi's had never before been practiced by musicians may even help explain the print's belated designation as "musica nova."[42] Even more than all of this, Doni's letter describes with uncanny closeness the *Musica nova*'s studied, introspective character, its meticulous setting of text, its lofty musical rhetoric ("questa divina compositione," Doni calls the music), and its ability above all to inspire awe—qualities that became touchstones of later descriptions of Willaert's *Musica nova* compositions.[43]

This repertorial link gives a very good idea about one aspect of the musical fare at ca' Capponi—or, more precisely, about its *compositional* substance. Doni offers his Piacentine dedicatee little in the way of concrete information about the

---

tanta divinità. Questo M. Neri dispensa l'anno le centinaia de ducati in tal virtù: e la conserva appresso di sé; né se fosse suo padre darebbe fuori un canto." The letter, dated 7 April, was appended to the tenor part book of Doni's *Dialogo della musica* of 1544, ed. G. Francesco Malipiero and Virginio Fagotto, Collana di musiche veneziane inedite e rare, no. 7 (Vienna, 1964), p. 5.

39. For early views to this effect see, for example, Armen Carapetyan, "The *Musica Nova* of Adriano Willaert: With a Special Reference to the Humanistic Society of 16th-Century Venice" (Ph.D. diss., Harvard University, 1945), pp. 91 and passim, and Edward E. Lowinsky, "A Treatise on Text Underlay by a German Disciple of Francisco de Salinas," in *Festscrift Heinrich Besseler zum sechzigsten Geburtstag* (Leipzig, 1961), pp. 231–51; repr. in his *Music in the Culture of the Renaissance and Other Essays*, ed. Bonnie J. Blackburn, 2 vols. (Chicago, 1989), 2:868–83.

40. In dalla Viola's words, it had been "nascosta & sepolta di modo, che alcuno non se ne potea valere, & il mondo venea à restar privo di cosi bella compositione." The dedication is reprinted in facsimile in Willaert, *Opera omnia*, ed. Walter Gerstenberg and Hermann Zenck, vol. 5 (1957), p. x.

41. On Alfonso's purchasing of the collection from Pecorina in December 1554 see Anthony Newcomb, "Editions of Willaert's *Musica Nova*: New Evidence, New Speculations," *JAMS* 26 (1973): 132–45. The documents surrounding this exchange are now reprinted together with numerous new ones in Richard J. Agee and Jessie Ann Owens, "La stampa della *Musica nova* di Willaert," *Rivista italiana di musicologia* 24 (1989): 219–305. See also David S. Butchart, " 'La Pecorina' at Mantua, *Musica Nova* at Florence," *Early Music* 13 (1985): 358–66.

Doni fashioned for his *Dialogo* a sonnet of his own in homage to Pecorina, *A la bella concordia unica e rara* (p. 318); perhaps he hoped for access to Willaert's much-guarded compositions through her.

42. Einstein's error in translating Doni's "non più usata da i musici" as "no longer followed by musicians" (*The Italian Madrigal* 1:199), still often repeated, would have Capponi spending a fortune on music that was already out of date, rather than on "musica nova." The Italian idiom frequently appears in music prints as an advertising ploy (as in Perissone Cambio's *Madrigali a cinque voci* of 1545, whose title page includes the phrase "non più veduti ne istampati").

43. See, for example, Zarlino's descriptions cited in Chap. 6 below and those of theorists like Vicentino and Stoquerus assembled in Don Harrán, *Word-Tone Relations in Musical Thought: From Antiquity to the Seventeenth Century*, Musicological Studies and Documents, no. 40 (Neuhausen-Stuttgart, 1986), pp. 177–79, 230–32, and passim. In a passage in Chapter 19 of his *Germani de musica verbali* (ca. 1570) Gaspar Stocker claimed that Willaert's music stood at the summit of the new approach to text setting, which all good composers were then following; on this treatise see Lowinsky, "A Treatise on Text Underlay."

performances themselves, except that the concerts included both voices and viols.[44] And Ganassi's dedication in the *Lettione* of the previous year adds nothing else of substance to Doni's description. Together, however, Doni and Ganassi corroborate at least two aspects of the academy's structural makeup: first, that Willaert's role was that of a kind of Promethean maestro, "principio" of what Ganassi called Capponi's "divino e sacro collegio"; and second, that the academy presented itself through the double claims of novelty and exclusivity.

Doni's account also confirms various contemporaneous representations of Pecorina that identify her as a central interpreter of Willaert's music.[45] She may have assumed this role already by the early 1530s. As we saw, Ruberto Strozzi in 1534 requested his teacher Varchi to compose a madrigal text in her honor (most likely *Quando col dolce suono*, later set by Arcadelt, as Agee believes).[46] In the same letter Strozzi remarked that Pecorina sang very well not only to the lute but also from part books.[47] This information virtually clinches the idea that much of the *Musica nova* was composed with her soprano in mind. Indeed Pecorina was so directly identified with the collection that it came to be nicknamed after her.[48] All of this, finally, reinforces the *Musica nova*'s striking position between the dual poles of sacred church and secular home.

Willaert himself set another madrigal lauding Pecorina, the still-anonymous text *Qual dolcezza giamai.*

Qual dolcezza giamai	As much as the sweetness
Di canto di Sirena	Of the Siren's song ever
Involò i sensi e l'alm'a chi l'udiro,	Rapt the senses and the soul of the listener,
Che di quella non sia minor assai	No less than that does the beautiful Pecorina
Che con la voce angelica e divina	Stir the heart with her
Desta nei cor la bella Pecorina.	Angelic and divine voice.
A la dolce armonia si fa serena	At the sweet harmony the air becomes
L'aria, s'acqueta il mar, taccion'i venti,	Serene, the sea calms, the wind turns quiet,
E si rallegra il ciel di gir'in giro.[49]	And the heavens rejoice from sphere to sphere.

(line 5 marked at right)

44. Doni does not say whether Capponi's academists played and sang simultaneously. In treble-dominated pieces we would *expect* that viols often accompanied voices, but Doni leaves us maddeningly uninformed as to whether instruments played some parts alone, without doubling voices—a signal point in madrigals so textually conceived as those in the *Musica nova.*

45. A famous reference is that of Girolamo Fenaruolo, whose *capitolo* urging Willaert not to forsake Venice for Flanders (as he did for a time in 1556) referred to "the good times of Pecorina" (buoni tempi de la Pecorina); printed in Francesco Sansovino, *Sette libri di satire . . . Con un discorso in materia de satira* (Venice, 1573), fol. 193′; repr. in Vander Straeten, ed., *La musique aux Pays-Bas* 6:219.

46. See Agee, "Ruberto Strozzi," pp. 11–12.

47. "Canta sul leuto benissimo, ed in su' libri." Compare this with Ortensio Landi's listing of her among the notable modern musicians in his *Sette libri de cathaloghi a' varie cose appartenenti* (Venice, 1552), p. 512.

48. As Lowinsky pointed out, Stocker cited by way of example a work "referred to by the Italians as *Le pecorine*" ("A Treatise on Text Underlay"). Among other things, the article includes Lowinsky's discovery of a sixteenth-century handwritten notation, "La Pecorina di Ms. Adrian," in a set of part books of the *Musica nova* in Treviso; see ibid., 1:881. See also Newcomb, "Editions of Willaert's *Musica Nova*," pp. 140–41.

49. Verses 7–9 gloss Petrarch's *Hor che 'l ciel,* no. 164, in turn an adaptation of a nightscape in Virgil's *Aeneid;* on both see Thomas M. Greene, *The Light in Troy: Imitation and Discovery in Renaissance Poetry* (New Haven, 1982), pp. 116–17.

I santi angeli intenti	The holy angels, intent,	10
Chinand'in questa part'il vago viso,	Bow their lovely faces earthward,	
S'oblian'ogni piacer del paradiso.	Forgetting every pleasure of Paradise.	
Et ella in tant'honore	And she, so honored,	
Dice con lieto suon "qui regn'Amore."	Says with a happy sound, "Here reigns Love."	

Like Doni's *A la bella concordia* and Varchi's *Quando co 'l dolce suono,*[50] this poem captured Pecorina's renowned vocal élan for an audience probably composed in the main of admirers well-acquainted with her. It glossed Petrarch's praise of Laura from the fourth stanza of the canzone *Chiare freshe et dolci acque,* where flowers falling about her seem to say "qui regna amore" (no. 126, v. 52). Neither this nor any of the celebratory texts or surviving accounts of her support the assumption routinely made by earlier writers that Pecorina was a courtesan.[51] The poem makes no attempt of the sort common in encomia of *cortigiane oneste* to link her vocal charms (or, in other cases, literary aplomb) with physical allurements. In its emphasis on how moving her singing is, lauding her power to transform the natural bodies of earth, sea, and sky, it fashions her image instead as that of a divine enchantress, attracting the beneficent notice of heaven by calling the harmonies of heavenly love to earth. She was thus almost undoubtedly a *gentildonna,* as Doni called her, styled after the musically skilled *donne di palazzo* Castiglione described in Book 3 of *Il cortegiano.*

50. The former was included in Doni's *Dialogo della musica* (mod. ed., p. 318). There is also a setting by Vincenzo Ruffo to a Polissena, *Era lieta Junon*—whether to Pecorina it is less certain.

51. For a typical representation of Pecorina as a courtesan see Einstein, *The Italian Madrigal* 1:175, who assumed that virtually all women active as performers were courtesans. (See also Donna G. Cardamone, ed., *Adrian Willaert and His Circle: Canzone Villanesche alla Napolitana and Villotte* [Madison, 1978], p. ix.) Anthony Newcomb argues a contrary view regarding Pecorina in "Courtesans, Muses, or Musicians? Professional Women Musicians in Sixteenth-Century Italy," in *Women Making Music: The Western Art Tradition, 1150–1950,* ed. Jane Bowers and Judith Tick (Urbana and Chicago, 1986), pp. 105–6. The notion that music making by women was universally regarded in the sixteenth century as leading to licentiousness is put to rest by H. Colin Slim, "An Iconographical Echo of the Unwritten Tradition," *Studi musicali* 17 (1988): 48–49. His central topic, a portrait in the Spada Gallery of Rome by an unidentified north Italian painter, depicts a *gentildonna* with lira and the cantus part of a *strambotto* setting. Similar iconography can be seen in other representations of the time, for example in *Habiti d'huomeni e donne venetiane* (Venice, 1570), an engraving from which is reproduced in Gaspara Stampa, *Rime,* ed. Maria Bellonci and Rodolfo Ceriello, 2d ed. (Milan, 1976), p. [71].

The difficulty of reading evidence to determine whether or not sixteenth-century women were courtesans must be understood to originate in contemporaneous tensions over the appropriation of styles. It was the intended strategy of elevated *cortigiane oneste* to take on the courtly graces of cultivated women—hence the notion of gracious service that underlies the *cortigiano/cortigiana* pairing—and the phenomenon generated a nervous ambiguity that lasted throughout the century. The idea that women who made music were prostitutes was promoted in satiric literature such as Pietro Aretino's *Ragionamenti* (Venice, [1538] 1539); see also Fenaruolo's *capitolo* to Willaert cited in n. 45 above: "Ne si trovano donna cosi strana / Ne tanta casta, che s'egli cantava / Tosto non divenisse una puttana," vv. 122–24 (repr. in Vander Straeten, *La musique aux Pays-Bas* 6:221). Much confusion about how to regard cinquecento women making music seems to stem nowadays from the famous admonition Bembo made in a letter of 1541 to his sixteen-year-old daughter Helena not to play a musical instrument, since doing so is a thing for vain and frivolous women ("il sonare è cosa strana e leggera"); see *Opere in volgare,* ed. Mario Marti (Florence, 1961), pp. 877–78. But Bembo's letter, probably anticipating an eventual public readership, must be interpreted in the context of his concerns about Helena's illegitimacy and his (ultimately successful) efforts to establish her within patrician society: two years after the letter was written he married her off to the Venetian nobleman Pietro Gradenigo (see Chap. 4 n. 20, below).

The configuration of Capponi's academy as I have described it raises questions about the changing place of madrigals in private aristocratic homes. With Willaert installed as director, Pecorina as prima donna, and other top musicians as the corps of singers and instrumentalists (those "altri spiriti eccellenti" who played and sang), all producing what Doni called "concerti," did Capponi, the accomplished part singer and student of Ganassi, still participate in music making as he had in Lyons? Could he have set up his academy to include him as singer or violist?

Probably not, or at least not with as much regularity. The metrical instabilities and contrapuntal independence of Willaert's madrigals would have made them more difficult for amateur singers than the madrigals and chansons of Arcadelt and Layolle sung at Lyons. Most likely secular settings of slightly older vintage complemented the new fare by Willaert and his circle, as happens in Doni's *Dialogo della musica*. There may well have been simple ricercars and instrumental arrangements of vocal music playable by nonprofessionals like Capponi, similar to those Ganassi used to illustrate his manuals. But based on the descriptions of Capponi's academy by Doni and Ganassi and the imitations of Willaert's madrigals made by members of his *cappella* who were both singers and composers, it seems inconceivable that professionals did not play the largest role in performing the music heard at Capponi's house (at least on important evenings attended by outsiders like Doni).[52] In this analysis, the same situation that placed Capponi and his kind at the center of musical patronage pushed them to the margins of music making.

In short, Venice must have worked a sea change on the musical scene in noblemen's homes since Capponi's Lyonnaise days, transshaping their role in the private soirée. Unlike the symmetries described in accounts of earlier meetings, where nobles appear to stand on fairly equal ground, Capponi's new *accademie* observed a definite structural hierarchy (however shadowy and inaccessible they may have been). Meetings now pointed hierarchically to two patriarchal figures, the master of ceremonies and the musical director.

I have belabored this shift and the state of Florentine expatriate patronage generally not because Florentines offered the exclusive or even the primary venues for Venetian madrigals at midcentury (though I believe theirs were crucial ones), but because the conditions of Florentine patronage helped inaugurate a direction of great stylistic and social importance for madrigals generally. Secular music making in the early sixteenth century, as described by Castiglione, was a central occupation of courtly noblemen, one of their masks and avocations. From the time of Filippo's and Lorenzo's involvement in carnival, their singing of Lamentations, polyphonic canzoni, and probably chansons, to their promotion of the new genre of Florentine and Roman madrigals by Festa, Layolle, and Arcadelt, noble patrons shared domestic

---

52. Perissone Cambio would be a central example, an outstanding singer of high parts and an ambitious young composer who first came on the scene about 1544. His *Madrigali a cinque voci,* published in 1545, was the first book to imitate Willaert's settings printed much later in the *Musica nova;* see Chap. 9 below, pp. 341–56.

music as one of their elegant pastimes. It was the patrons themselves who performed, if with the occasional addition of more expert practitioners like Layolle and (we may imagine) Pisano. Whatever went on in Capponi's salon, the newer madrigals were probably no longer the principal province of Capponi and his peers, except in the noblemen's roles as owners, overseers, and auditors. The courtly amateur was gradually becoming the ceremonial host, a position that would become commonplace later in the sixteenth century.

———————

Neri Capponi evidently resided in Venice from at least 1538 until 1544.[53] After that he disappears from view, nowhere to be found in the exiled Strozzi correspondence of the 1540s after June 1543—a correspondence in which he had previously been a central figure.[54] The explanation for this may lie in Capponi's political orientation. Like most other Florentine exiles, Capponi lacked the intense interest in republican revolution that fueled the Strozzi sons. Despite his close financial ties to Filippo Strozzi, who had not only made him manager of the Lyons bank in 1532 but an executor of his will in 1535,[55] nothing in contemporary histories connects him with efforts at Medicean overthrow. Once Filippo had passed away and Cosimo's rule had been securely consolidated, Capponi probably shared the doubts then growing within the exile community about the efficacy of the Strozzi's continued anti-Medicean schemes. Like so many other *fuorusciti,* chances are he slipped back into the shadows of his native city, disappearing from prominence as soon as it was safe enough to do so quietly.[56]

Ruberto Strozzi, on the other hand, continued training his thoughts on revolutionary schemes to play French supporters of the republic against the imperial backers of Cosimo's monarchy. Ruberto's political burden was heavy. By 1537 he was apparently the only one of Filippo's male heirs who had reached his majority still in his father's good graces.[57] Less experienced in arms than his eldest brother, the ruffian Piero,[58] but better suited to diplomacy, Ruberto took on much of the work of forging diplomatic bonds with the French and arranging purchases of arms.

Because of his quixotic, itinerant existence after the family was banished from Florence in 1534, tracking Ruberto's movements is not easy. I offer a provisional attempt for the decade from 1536 to 1546 in Table 1, based primarily on the evidence of locations to which selected letters were addressed. Ruberto's correspondents

53. Niccolini, *Filippo Strozzi,* pp. 306–7.
54. Capponi wrote what seems to be his last extant letter to Ruberto from Venice and mailed it to Ferrara; it dates from 23 June 1543 (I-Fas, CS, ser. V, 1210.10.204).
55. The will, dated 31 December 1537, is reprinted in Niccolini, *Filippo Strozzi,* pp. 323–31; see esp. pp. 327 and 330.
56. Compare the cases of Benedetto Varchi and Vincenzo Martelli mentioned in Cochrane, *Florence in the Forgotten Centuries,* pp. 41–42.
57. See Niccolini, *Filippo Strozzi,* pp. 327–28, where Piero and Vincenzo are cut out (see also p. 307).
58. Ibid., p. cii.

TABLE I

Whereabouts of Ruberto Strozzi, ca. 1536–46, Based on a Selection of Letters

Date of Letter	Sent from RS or to RS	RS's Whereabouts	Source, Remarks
1536			
5 Sept.	From RS	Rome	CS, III (95), 31–31′, to FS in Venice
5 Nov.	From RS	Rome	CS, III (95), 59′–61′, to FS in Venice
4 Dec.	From RS	Rome	CS, III (95), 74′–75′, to FS in Venice
29 Dec.	From RS	Rome	CS, III (95), 85–86, to FS in Venice
1537			
14 Mar.	To RS	Bologna	CS, III (95), 126′–127, from Lionardo Benincasa
3 Apr.	To RS	Rome	CS, III (95), 134′–135, from FS in Venice
7 May	From RS	Rome	CS, III (95), 176–176′, from FS
23 June	From RS	Rome	CS, III (95), 213′–214, FS in Ferrara
13 Aug.	To RS and PS	Venice	Nicc. 257–58, from Cav. Covoni
20 Aug.	To RS	Venice	CS, III (95), 232′, from Card. Salviati at Contrapo; also to his brother the Migliore Covoni
22 Dec.	To RS	imperial court	Nicc. 281, from FS in prison
28 Dec.	To RS	imperial court	Nicc. 286–88, from Lorenzo Ridolfi
1538			
20 Jan.	To RS	Barcelona	CS, III (95), 261′–262, and Nicc. 292–93, from Olivieri Benvenuto
21 Feb.	To RS and LS	Barcelona	Nicc. 297–99, from PS
25 Feb.	To RS and LS	imperial court	Nicc. 300–1, from Benvenuto Olivieri in Rome
17 Apr.	From FS	Lyons	Nicc. 306–7, FS in prison, believes RS is in Lyons; angry at NC for fleeing Lyons ("lasciassi ogni cosa ire in ruine e si fuggisi") when the French demanded funds; fled with his brother Gino and took the road to Venice, leaving Ruberto and Palla "in casa"
10 June	From RS	Nice	CS, III (95), 269′, Nicc. 307–8, to cav. Migliore Covoni in Venice; asks him to send regards to "messer Neri" and show the letter to him and other friends; implies he will soon go to Venice

Date		Place	Reference
27 July	From LS	Venice	Nicc. 312, to Cav. de' Covoni in Venice "in sul campo di San Canziano in ca' Strozzi"; sends regards to RS there
9 Aug.	To RS	Venice	CS, V, 1208.4.162
1539			
26 Apr.	To RS	Venice	CS, V, 1208.4.188
7 Sept.	To RS	Venice	CS, V, 1208.4.195
1540			
9 Apr.	To RS	Venice	CS, V, 1210.10.14
8 June	To RS and PS	Venice	CS, V, 1210.10.21
1541			
15 Feb.	To RS	Venice	CS, V, 1210.10.36, from Bartolomeo Cavalcanti
26 Mar.	To RS	Venice	CS, V, 1210.10.41 and 42
2 Apr.	To RS	Venice	CS, V, 1210.10.46, 50
12 Apr.	To RS	Venice	CS, V, 1210.10.53
24 Apr.	To RS	Venice	CS, V, 1210.10.60, from Luigi del Riccio, Rome
23 Sept.	To RS	Venice	CS, III (97), 1'–2', from PS in Amiens
19 Nov.	To RS	Venice	CS, V, 1210.10.83
11 Dec.	To RS	Venice	CS, V, 1210.10.84, from Lionardo Strozzi
1542			
14 May	To RS	Rome	CS, V, 1210.10.109, from Benedetto Strozzi
25 May	To RS	Venice	CS, III (97), 1–1', from Giovanni Lanfredini, Escleron
29 July	To RS and PS	Venice	CS, V, 1210.10.130, from Card. Trivulzio
26 Aug.	To RS	Venice	CS, V, 1210.10.140, from Luigi del Riccio, Rome
7 Oct.	To RS and PS	Ferrara	CS, V, 1210.10.156, from Card. Trivulzio
9 Oct.	To RS	Ferrara	CS, V, 1210.10.154, from Francesco Corbolo
18 Oct.	To RS	Ferrara	CS, V, 1210.10.160, from NC; see Agee, "Filippo Strozzi," p. 236 n. 35
31 Oct.	To RS	Ferrara	CS, V, 1210.10.169, from Francesco Corbolo
3 Nov. (?)	To RS	Ferrara	CS, V. 1210.10.31, from Pallazzo da Fano in Brescia
6 Nov.	To RS	Ferrara	CS, V, 1210.10.174, from NC
8 Nov.	To RS	Ferrara	CS, V, 1210.10.175, from NC

(continued)

TABLE I (continued)

Date of Letter	Sent from RS or to RS	RS's Whereabouts	Source, Remarks
1543			
27 (?) Apr.	To RS	Ferrara	CS, V, 1210.10.186, from Francesco Corbolo
17 May	To RS	Ferrara	CS, V, 1210.10.192, from Alessandro Bartoli
4 June	To RS	Bologna	CS, V, 1210.10.195
23 June	To RS	Rome	CS, V, 1210.10.204, from NC
26 July	To RS	Rome	CS, V, 1210.10.213, from Lorenzo de' Medici [in Venice]
7 Sept.	To RS	Venice	CS, III (97), 2'–3, from Lorenzo Strozzi in Stene
24 Sept.	To RS	Rome	CS, V, 1210.10.241
1544			
9 Jan.	To RS	Venice	CS, V, 1210.12.?, from PS
10 Jan.	To RS	Rome	CS, V, 1210.12.2
13 (?) Feb. (?)	To RS	Venice	CS, V, 1210.12.76
4 Apr.	From RS	Ferrara	CS, III (97), 5–5', to Luigi del Riccio in Rome
26 Apr.	From RS	Ferrara	CS, III (97), to Luigi del Riccio in Rome (given as being from Venice in CS, III [96], 103')
6 May	To RS	French court	CS, V, 1210.12.45, from Luigi del Riccio
15 May	—	[France]	DG, 106–7, DG in Vicenza tells Lorenzo Ridolfi that RS went to France at order of card. of Ferrara [Ippolito d'Este] (en route to France)
11 July	To RS	Rome	CS, V, 1210.12.54, from Lorenzo de' Medici in Venice
26 July	To RS	Lyons	CS, V, 1210.12.60, from Lanfredini
5 Sept.	—	[Venice]	DG, 111; DG in Vicenza relates that the Strozzi wives are briefly at Venice (and will stay a few days)
20 Oct.	To RS	Ferrara	CS, V, 1210.12.70, LS
28 Oct.	—	[Ferrara]	DG, 113; DG in Vicenza, tells Lorenzo Ridolfi that RS will arrive in Ferrara on Sat. eve.
25 Nov.	To RS	Venice	CS, V, 1210.12.72, from LS at Paris (cf. DG, 114); RS went to Venice for the "ruina del Corbolo"

Date	Direction	Location	Reference
9 Dec.	—	[Venice]	DG, 115; from DG in Vicenza to Lorenzo Ridolfi; "M. Ruberto" will leave soon
23 Dec.	—	[Venice]	DG, 117; from DG in Vicenza to Lorenzo Ridolfi; RS is still in Venice and will leave soon
1545			
5 Jan.	To RS	Rome	CS, V, 1210.12.79
24 Jan.	To RS	Rome	CS, V, 1210.12.90; from Alessandro Lambertini
11 Aug.	From RS	Rome	CS, III (97), 13'–14, to Agnolo Biffoli in Naples
1546			
24 Apr.	—	—	DG, 131; Strozzi wives soon to go to Venice
5 May	From RS	Ferrara	CS, III (96), 117', to Agnolo Biffoli, Naples
24 July	From RS	Venice	CS, III (96), 117', and III (97), 14'–15, to Card. da Rimini

ABBREVIATIONS

CS = Carte strozziane
III (95), 5 = III serie, registro 95, fol. 5
V, 1210.10.5 = V serie, busta 1210, sect. 10, bifolio 5
RS = Ruberto Strozzi
FS = Filippo Strozzi
PS = Piero Strozzi
LS = Fra Leone Strozzi, prior of Capua
NC = Neri Capponi
Cav. = Cavaliere
Card. = Cardinal
Nicc. = G.-B. Niccolini, *Filippo Strozzi, tragedia* (Florence, 1847)
DG = Donato Giannotti, *Lettere italiane (1526–1571)*, ed. Furio Diaz, vol. 2 (Milan, 1974)

Correspondents are noted selectively above.
N.B. Series V is uncatalogued.

were at times as unsure of his whereabouts as we,[59] but in general we can surmise from their letters that Ruberto spent the bulk of his time in Venice from about August or, at latest, October 1538 through at least part of the summer of 1542, where he and his kin were apparently living and being treated "like kings."[60] Titian's famous portrait from 1542 of the little girl feeding a biscuit to her dog, identified as Clarice Strozzi, shows none other than Ruberto's daughter (Plate 8).[61] It is just one token of the family's high style of living there, since portraits of children were rare in the sixteenth century, most of them having been made of royalty.

In these years the Strozzi probably kept a lively household in Venice. Ruberto's teacher Ganassi, in dedicating to him the *Regola rubertina* (glossing his student's name), hinted that the Strozzi salon was one of the most active in the city: "since there is a harmony . . . in giving everyone his due, when thinking to whom I should address this little work, I remembered you, to whom one ought to give more than others since you are more adorned with harmony of the soul, harmony of the body, and vocal and instrumental harmony within your magnificent house, and delight in it more than do others."[62] One of Ruberto's republican compatriots, the historian Donato Giannotti, wrote a letter on 9 December 1544 to Ruberto's brother-in-law Lorenzo Ridolfi that may complement Ganassi's remark.[63] Giannotti explains that Ruberto, in Venice for the previous month, is about to depart for Rome, and then takes up Ridolfi's inquiries about a certain "cantafavola" that Giannotti (then in Vicenza) had composed some time previously. Irked to hear that Ridolfi had got hold of this work, Giannotti

59. Most of the letters I cite are preserved in originals or manuscript copies in the Carte Strozziane at I-Fas. In addition I draw from Niccolini, *Filippo Strozzi,* and Donato Giannotti, *Lettere italiane (1526–1571),* ed. Furio Diaz, vol. 2, (Milan, 1974), for letters that concern Ruberto. Some of my information derives from internal remarks in letters, as noted.

60. Segni, *Istorie fiorentine,* pp. 380–81.

61. Aretino praised the portrait in a letter of 6 July 1542 along with the child's father, that "grave e ottimo gentilhuomo"; *Lettere di M. Pietro Aretino,* 6 vols. (Paris, 1609), 2:288′; mod. ed. *Lettere sull'arte di Pietro Aretino,* commentary by Fidenzio Pertile, ed. Ettore Camesasca, 3 vols. in 4 (Milan, 1957–60), 3/1:217–18, with the portrait given as Plate 30. Patricia H. Labalme thought Aretino might have seen the portrait at Strozzi's house in Venice; see "Personality and Politics in Venice: Pietro Aretino," in *Titian: His World and His Legacy,* ed. David Rosand (New York, 1982), p. 126. On the portrait itself see Harold E. Wethey, *The Paintings of Titian: Complete Edition,* 2 vols. (New York, 1971), vol. 2, *The Portraits,* p. 142, and Plates 106–8 and 110. Titian's painted inscription ANNOR II MDXLII is visible in the upper left-hand corner of the painting. See also Georg Gronau, "Zwei Tizianische Bildnisse der Berliner Galerie: I, Das Bildnis des Ranuccio Farnese; II, Das Bildnis der Tochter des Roberto Strozzi," *Jahrbuch der königlich preuszischen Kunstsammlungen* 27 (1906): 3–12. Wethey, following Gronau, placed Ruberto and his wife in Venice from 1536 until 1542, but this is misleading (cf. Table 1).

62. "[P]erche è armonia . . . il dare ad ogniuno quello, che si conviene, pensando io a chi questa mia operetta si dovesse indrizzare, mè sovvenuta. V.S. allaquale si deve piu che ad altri: quanto essa è piu d'altri ornata de l'armonia de l'anima, de l'armonia del corpo, & de l'armonia vocal & istrumental, con tutta la sua magnifica casa, & piu d'altri se ne diletta" (*Regola rubertina* [Venice, 1542]; facs. ed. BMB, ser. 2, no. 18a [Bologna, 1976]).

63. *Lettere italiane* 2:115–17. Giannotti's correspondence is a rich source of news about the exiled community. See Randolph Starn's edition of some of Giannotti's letters, *Donato Giannotti and His "Epistolae": Biblioteca Universitaria Alessandrina, Rome, M. 107,* Travaux d'humanisme et renaissance, no. 97 (Geneva, 1968), with a good biography and summary of the exiles' machinations in the late thirties and early forties on pp. 45ff. and passim and discussion of Giannotti's patronage by Lorenzino de' Medici on p. 143 n. 7.

8 . Titian, *Portrait of Clarice Strozzi* (daughter of Ruberto Strozzi), 1542. Photo courtesy of the Gemäldegalerie, Staatliche Museen Preussischer Kulturbesitz, Berlin.

protests in typically Florentine fashion that he wanted it to remain "hidden" (*occulta*) and not be recited by friends in Rome where Ridolfi was staying. He wonders if the work was procured from the Strozzi house in Venice. Since Giannotti calls it both a "cantafavola" and "commedia," the work was probably a light one—a pastoral, fable, or fairy tale—and quite possibly to be done with singing.[64]

64. Paolo Fabbri informs me that here the term probably means simply "trifling work," as in Aretino's *Lo ipocrito* (5.24) of 1542, where *cantafavola* appears to be virtually synonymous with "commedia": "LISEO: Signori, poi che colui che ha fatto la comedia, è stato sempre de la fantasia ch'io voglio esser tuttavia, so che gli faccio una grazia rilevata a dirvi che, se la cantafavola vi è piaciuta, l'han caro, e se non vi è piaciuta, carissimo" (private communication). The *Nuovo dizionario della lingua italiana* defines *cantafavola* as a "frivolous fiction."

By the time Parabosco dedicated his *Madrigali a cinque voci* to Ruberto in 1546, Ruberto's ties to Venice had become far more tenuous. Parabosco's is the only surviving musical dedication to Strozzi aside from Ganassi's, yet it shows only a passing acquaintance with him—tellingly, considering Parabosco's usual inclination to flaunt as much familiarity as he could get away with. Here Parabosco instead fashioned a paradoxical opposition of his humble gift with Strozzi's grand station to frame a conceit congratulating his own presumption in risking the dedication.

To the illustrious and generous Signor Ruberto Strozzi

My Lord, knowing music to be as pleasing to you as it is made pleasing to the whole world by your infinite virtues and kindnesses, I did not want to fail to make you a present of these little notes of mine, such as they may be. This, which others would perhaps have desisted from making, has (like everything else) spurred me on and entreated me. . . . Many, my Lord, being ashamed of the humbleness of their gift, or fearing your judgment, would not have done this, but I make you a gift of these little efforts of mine most boldly. I will not be ashamed to present them to you because they are poor, nor will I be afraid because they are not revised. For I am certain that in the greatness of your merits and your judgment, they will be what every large present is. For into the great sea the big rivers disperse just like the little rivulets, and it thus receives one just like the other, benignly and courteously. I do not rest without kissing your hand, infinitely joining my affection to you. Your most devoted servant Girolamo Parabosco.[65]

But the dedication evidently failed to further the ambitions of either party. There is no evidence of Ruberto's involvement with music after this time. Parabosco's book was never reprinted, and after it he all but quit musical composition, never replacing the high-brow Venetian madrigal with anything that could have brought him a wider musical audience.

———————

In sum, the state of affairs concerning Strozzi in the early forties is arresting in two respects: first, his pet object of patronage was the gifted but at first little-known

65. "Allo illustre et generoso Signor Roberto Strozzi Signor mio, sapend'io la Musica esser si grata a V.S. come quella é grata a tutto il Mondo per le infinite sue virtu, & cortesie: non ho voluto manchare di non farle presente di queste mie poche note: quale elleno si siano. & quello, che a cio fare havrebbe forse altrui ritenuto: me quanto ogni altra cosa a spinto, & inviato: che é la grandezza de i meriti di V.S. & il pellegrino giuditio, che ella hâ in tutte le scienze. Molti signor mio vergognandosi per la poverta del presente, o temendo il giuditio di V.S. non havrebbono fatto quello, che facc'io che per questo quanto per darle segno della servitu ch'io le porto, le faccio baldanzosissimamente dono di queste mie poche fatiche. ne mi vergognaro di presentarglile per che elle siano povere, ne temero per che non siano senza emenda: chio mi rendo sicuro, che nella grandezza de i meriti & del giuditio di V.S. esse saranno quello, che saria ogni altro gran presente. che nel grandissimo Mare cosi si disperdono i grandi fiumi, come i picciol rivi, & cosi egli benigno, & cortese riceve l'uno come l'altro. altro non mi resta se non basciar la Mano di V.S. raccordandole la affettion mia verso di lei essere infinita. Devotissimo servo Girolamo Parabosco" (*Madrigali a cinque voci di Girolamo Parabosco discipulo di M. Adriano novamente da lui composti et posti in luce* [Venice, 1546]).

Rore, for whom he remains the main Italian patron known to us before Rore's employment by the dukes of Ferrara (the other being Capponi);[66] and second, Strozzi resided during that period in the same city with which Rore's early madrigal style is identified—even though Rore's own biography remains cryptic. When Pallazzo da Fano's letter was written, surely in November 1542, Rore had apparently been composing in Brescia, where he seems to have been based, and in Venice, where da Fano says the composer traveled and delivered madrigals to Neri Capponi. Wherever Rore's madrigals for Strozzi were composed, therefore, Venice formed a point of convergence for both composer and patron in the early forties, entangled in the larger web of circumstances and interrelations there.

Despite this Venetian nexus we cannot infer with any confidence the actual compositions Rore wrote for Strozzi (by contrast with those Willaert wrote for Capponi). Presumably they consisted mostly of madrigals and perhaps secondarily motets, similar in style to the ones Rore published in 1542 and 1544: the Strozzi correspondence mentions Rore's secular works only with the generic "madrigali." A letter from Capponi in Venice to Strozzi in Ferrara of 18 October 1542 sends Ruberto a sonnet "fecj fare a Cipriano" (done by Cipriano), which accords with the sort of sonnet-filled repertory of Rore's First Book from that same year.[67] And Pallazzo da Fano's letter of the early forties shows interest in a motet that Rore had "gotten into good shape" since returning from Venice, as well as a "madricale . . . che fece a M, nerio" (a madrigal he made for messer Nerio). It hardly seems possible that these were the same works included in Rore's first and second books of madrigals, for why would he have published them?

Ruberto's move from Venice to Ferrara—a court in sympathy with the anti-Medicean French king from whom he hoped for support—took place no later than October 1542. When da Fano's letter was written, in other words, Ruberto had just left Venice. It seems revealing that Rore should have landed in Ferrara just a few years after Strozzi's dealings with the Ferrarese were intensifying, and it is certainly possible that Strozzi could have been influential in securing Rore's foothold there. The impression Rore's musical portfolio made in Ferrara may well mark the beginning of intense Ferrarese interest in Venetian repertory, an interest that was to culminate in Alfonso's acquisition in 1554 and publication in 1559 of the coveted *Musica nova* (see Chap. 3 below). To that extent Ruberto's influence at court concerning Willaert and Rore also marks a stage in the dissemination of Venetian style throughout northern Italy.

There is no reason to think that the Strozzi ever provided a stable presence in Venice's musical life after 1542.[68] Parabosco's hapless dedication inadvertently

---

66. See Capponi's letter of 18 October 1542, cited in Agee, "Filippo Strozzi," p. 236 n. 35.
67. Ibid.
68. A letter of Giannotti's, probably from April 1546, reveals that Ruberto's wife may have moved back to Venice for a time that year. Giannotti tells Ridolfi that Piero's and Ruberto's wives are going to Venice soon, that Piero has resolved to move his wife back to Venice, and that Ruberto may do the same (*Lettere italiane* 2:133).

underscores the waning impact of Florentines on Venetian music. One could hardly have expected that exiles like Filippo, Ruberto, and Capponi, landed in the city's peaceful lap, would have found in it the ultimate resting place—the "Noah's Ark," "Holy City and terrestrial paradise"—that the self-made Aretino did when he drifted into the city in 1527 (never again to leave).[69] The physiognomy of Florentine patronage abroad was essentially one of restless exile. These men were bitterly frustrated, at pains to protect their wealth and patrimony and to assert to the world their continued dominance in culture and politics—the more so since they were by history and inculcation masters of their destinies, princes of the establishment from which they now found themselves disenfranchised with dwindling hope for reversal. The processes of acquiring new music, performing it, admitting one's select audience and coparticipants, trading new works and even information about them all became acts of stealth that defined power and position. The acquisitions themselves were marks of privilege, earned through the same cloak-and-dagger tactics used for trades in arms.[70] To these Florentines, Venice may have been a friendly sanctuary from exile and impossible tensions at home, but also a slightly common place—overly inclusive by comparison with the elect circles in which they were accustomed to move.

69. The characterizations come from additions Aretino made to the revised version of his comedy *La cortigiana* (1st ed. 1525; rev. ed. Venice, 1534) after arriving in Venice; for the panegyric on Venice see *La cortigiana,* act 3, sc. 7, in Pietro Aretino, *Tutte le commedie,* ed. G.B. De Sanctis (Milan, 1968), pp. 168–76.

70. Indeed, the letters to and from Ruberto of 18 October and 3 November 1542 that reveal clandestine procurements of music are dominated by secret plans to procure arms.

Although the manoeuvres of Florentine patronage remain largely hidden, we have seen that the patrons' personalities and social identities do not. By comparison, the identities of non-Florentine patrons of music in Venice, even noble ones, are obscure at best. These figures had nothing of the ultra-high society and finance or international politics to compare with the likes of Strozzi and Capponi. Official historians and heads of state were generally unconcerned with their business and their movements; nor as a rule did hired secretaries or agents keep track of their more sedentary and prosaic lives. By contrast with literary patrons like Domenico Venier, whose constant verbalizing yields a portrait rich in tone if not always in specifics, the doyens of musical patronage kept relatively quiet. Figures interested in music often fell outside the regular patterns of verbal exchange that would have chronicled their lives for future generations. In musical realms it is largely composers themselves and their professional ghost writers, surrogates, or publishers who shed light on musical benefactors, mostly in the conventional form of dedications, sometimes in the less direct and often less intelligible form of dedicatory settings. Only the unprecedented fusion of Venetian literary and musical activities during the 1540s helps expose Venice's non-Florentine musical patrons to our distanced view. In the dialogical bustle that Venetian Petrarchism produced, musical patrons increasingly placed themselves—or were placed by acquaintances—squarely amid the verbal transactions that were the more common preserve of literati. It is this phenomenon that unlocks otherwise sealed doors. To open them I begin with some connections between the business of printing and the business of writing.

In sixteenth-century Venice texts became a major commodity. The local presses that had specialized in meticulous limited editions early in the century were gradually supplanted for the most part by firms that produced a huge number of volumes at great speed. As presses cranked up production, words came to be marketed in a range of forms and sheer quantity that were new to the modern world. Print commerce boomed, moreover, as part of a clamorous urge to engage others in dialogue. A remarkable number of texts issued in the mid-sixteenth century utilized some mode of direct address or concrete reference, or concocted a world of imaginary interlocutors.

By the middle of the century these dual phenomena—the urge to dialogue and the quest for diversity—had brought more authors, more vernaculars, and more literary forms into the hurried arena of published exchange than had ever been there before. Composers and patrons numbered among the many groups who were drawn into increasingly public relationships as a result. For them (as for people of letters), the new public nature of verbal interchange could prove by turns threatening and expedient. On the one hand, it exposed private affairs—or fictitious imitations of them—to social inspection and thus caused tensions over the commodification of what was individual and supposedly personal. On the other hand, it allowed its ablest practitioners to manipulate their social situations, reshape their identities, and, in the most inventive cases, mobilize their own professional rise.

All of this occurred not simply because the quantity of publications had increased but because new mechanisms of literary exchange were encouraged by the vernacular press. These mechanisms took the form of what I will call "dialogic genres." I coin this term principally to interrelate the great variety of writings that fashioned transactions in the form of letters, poetic addresses, and counteraddresses, that fictionalized the interchanges of salons, academies, and schoolrooms, or constructed discourses of address in dedications, dedicatory prefaces, letters, and occasional or encomiastic poems. All of these modes involved speaking to and among others—to patrons, lovers, enemies, and comrades; among teachers and students, scholars and mentors, authors and patrons, courtesans and clients.

In this sense my appeal to the concept of a literary dialogics, however difficult to define, is historically grounded in sixteenth-century Venice, and particularly in the multiplicity of new literary forms linked to an active print commerce. But I also mean for it to resonate with something of the same multivocal plurality with which the Russian literary theorist Mikhail Bakhtin characterized the nineteenth-century novel.[1] Language, for Bakhtin, was continually stratified into social "dialects" by the centrifugal forces of social use. Dispersive and fragmenting, those forces prevented languages from maintaining the sort of uniform character that official doctrines might try to prescribe and perpetuate for them. As part of living acts, language is instead seen to thrive in the face of potential contestations that always reside

---

1. Bakhtin's theories were worked out in a great many texts, most importantly "Discourse in the Novel," written in 1934–35; see *The Dialogic Imagination: Four Essays,* ed. Michael Holquist, trans. Michael Holquist and Caryl Emerson (Austin, 1981), pp. 259–422. Useful introductions to Bakhtin's notion of dialogism and his specialized vocabulary may be found in the Introduction and Glossary of that volume and in Tzvetan Todorov, *Mikhail Bakhtin: The Dialogical Principle,* trans. Wlad Godzich (Minneapolis, 1984).

somewhere between immediate uses and other possible uses. Language always asserts itself against the alien terrain of a listener—or in one of Bakhtin's most famous phrases, it "lies between oneself and another."

For Bakhtin this aspect of language was basic to its status as communication, written or verbal. Yet he argued that not all genres foreground this pervasive condition of language at their stylistic surface. As Bakhtin saw it, while novels were explicitly dialogical, poetry—by claiming to spring from a single authorial voice—pretended to a monological status, albeit one he believed was always ultimately fictitious. We could extend Bakhtin's dichotomy so as to place early modern dialogues, letters, encomia, and dedications on the dialogic side and genres like treatises and theses on the fictively monologic. What I call "dialogic genres" mark out an early modern instance of the general linguistic condition Bakhtin called "dialogism." Indeed, it could be argued that the notion of a pervasive literary dialogics first became relevant at precisely the historical moment when technology—in this case, print technology—acted to multiply and explode the social relations of expression and representation. It is this technologically induced explosion, driving vernacular circulation, that energized in Venice the sort of cultural heteroglossia—that undergrowth of tangled meanings—that Bakhtin described. In early modern Venice, as in the novels Bakhtin discusses, there was a correlated factor at work too: namely, a socially embedded process of imitation that cannot be conceived apart from the multivocal character of Venetian literary production. Imitation functioned as a primary mechanism of vernacular circulation. Through the processes of imitation, tropes and gestures were appropriated and revised, reproduced and perpetuated.[2]

Many of the materials that proliferated through imitation were drawn from Petrarch's *rime,* which came to be treated as a form of fetishized booty.[3] In Chapter 5 I show how Venetian spokesmen for language canonized Petrarch's lyrics as the proposed basis of an official "monological" rhetoric. Yet the city simultaneously remade these lyrics into what W. Theodor Elwert dubbed some time ago a "Petrarchismo vissuto,"[4] a lived Petrarchism that propelled Petrarch's tropes through various cultural reproductions as a virtual form of mimetic capital. Thus at the same time as Petrarch's language affirmed images of Venetian civic identity through its august façade of subjective restraint, his lyrics furnished a cruder source of cultural capital for the city's appropriative strategies of imitation. In these

2. This accords with the "expansive and associative" tendencies of the mid-sixteenth-century lyric described by Carlo Dionisotti, as discussed by Roberto Fedi, *La memoria della poesia: canzonieri, lirici, e libri d'amore nel rinascimento* (Rome, 1990), p. 46. Fedi's thesis regarding the linguistic and generic diffusion caused by the form of the *raccolta,* the lyric anthology, is also relevant (see esp. pp. 43–45).

3. For a stimulating consideration of how print technology bears on the production of Petrarchan commentaries see William J. Kennedy, "Petrarchan Audiences and Print Technology," *Journal of Medieval and Renaissance Studies* 14 (1984): 1–20. Related issues are taken up in Fedi, *La memoria della poesia,* and Roland Greene, *Post-Petrarchism: Origins and Innovations of the Western Lyric Sequence* (Princeton, 1991), Introduction.

4. See Elwert's "Pietro Bembo e la vita letteraria del suo tempo," in *La civiltà veneziana del rinascimento,* Fondazione Giorgio Cini, Centro di Cultura e Civiltà (Florence, 1958), pp. 125–76.

imitative processes dialogic modes figured strongly, even in lyrics: by turning Petrarch's internal, self-reflexive poetics inside out, replacing the absorbed intro-spection of an inward gaze with the reciprocal modes of observation, address, and realistic description, sixteenth-century lyrics often externalized Petrarch's poetics in interactive plays on real-life personalities.

This three-pronged phenomenon—mechanical reproduction, imitation, circula-tion—is distilled in Stephen Greenblatt's expression "mimetic machinery," as recently employed in *Marvelous Possessions* to situate exploration narratives within "social relations of production."[5] Like the voyagers and readers he depicts there, my patrons and composers interacted dialectically in "accumulating and banking" figures and images to "stockpile" them in "cultural storehouses." Musical figures meticulously collected and ordered their tropes in books, archives, galleries, and libraries, whose form and content hold the clues to the mimetic practices they employed. For this reason my immediate concerns with both Petrarchizing and printing do not turn in this chapter on the ideas and tropes Petrarchized per se. Rather, like Natalie Zemon Davis (to whom Greenblatt codedicates his book) and like numerous others following her lead, I look at how such storehouses served, in Davis's phrase, as "carriers of relationships."[6]

It may seem curious to probe these relationships through an ostensibly literary phenomenon, when music is at issue. Yet two cases that I will juxtapose below show how composers as well as their patrons exploited "dialogic" writing (broadly con-ceived) in mutually advantageous ways, profiting if passively at times from verbal interactions that were the typical province of men and women of letters. Not only

---

5. See *Marvelous Possessions: The Wonder of the New World* (Chicago, 1991), pp. 6 and passim. The notion of circulation builds on Greenblatt's earlier *Shakespearean Negotiations: The Circulation of Social Energy in Renaissance England* (Berkeley and Los Angeles, 1988).

6. See "Printing and the People," in *Society and Culture in Early Modern France* (Stanford, 1975), p. 192. The groundwork for an understanding of printing as a facet of social geography in the early mod-ern period was laid in large part by Lucien Febvre and Henri-Jean Martin in 1958 with *L'apparition du livre;* in English *The Coming of the Book: The Impact of Printing, 1450–1800,* trans. David Gerard, ed. Geoffrey Nowell-Smith and David Wootton (London, 1976), esp. Chap. 8, "The Book as a Force for Change." Thereafter came Marshall MacLuhan, *The Gutenberg Galaxy: The Making of Typographic Man* (Toronto, 1962), and the monumental study of Elizabeth L. Eisenstein, *The Printing Press as an Agent of Change: Communications and Cultural Transformations in Early Modern Europe,* 2 vols. (Cambridge, 1979), abridged as idem, *The Printing Revolution in Early Modern Europe* (Cambridge, 1983). MacLuhan's and Eisenstein's studies have been charged with overemphasizing print's break with past oral and man-uscript cultures, in part because of their concentration on intellectual developments in elite, nonephemeral, and relatively mainstream forms of print, by contrast with Febvre and Martin's more sociological approach. Davis's essay represents an early attempt to assess early modern printing in its social relation to nonelite cultures. Her microhistorical approach has been widely favored in recent works dealing with a great variety of printed objects, readers, and modes of circulation. The most vigor-ous voice in current discussions of print culture in the early modern period is Roger Chartier's; see esp. his explanations of the concept of "print culture" in the introduction to *The Culture of Print: Power and Uses of Print in Early Modern Europe,* trans. Lydia G. Cochrane, ed. Roger Chartier (Princeton, 1989), pp. 1–10; and Roger Chartier, *The Cultural Uses of Print in Early Modern France,* trans. Lydia G. Cochrane (Princeton, 1987). Others have followed Chartier's lead in stressing the anxieties generated by print pos-sibilities and the awkward coexistence of print culture with manuscript culture (a theme I take up briefly in Chaps. 4 and 6); see the various essays in *Print and Culture in the Renaissance: Essays on the Advent of Printing in Europe,* ed. Gerald P. Tyson and Sylvia S. Wagonheim (Newark, Del., 1986); and *Printing the Written Word: The Social History of Books, Circa 1450–1520,* ed. Sandra L. Hindman (Ithaca, 1991).

were musicians and musical patrons often part of these dialogic encounters, but the circulation of dialogic varieties of imitation was frequently animated by the unorthodox forms in which they took shape.

In the pages that follow I construct a complementary pair of case studies around two patrons who were long-term residents in Venice. One involves the aspiring immigrant patron Gottardo Occagna. Between 1545 and 1561 Occagna was made dedicatee of at least three books of madrigals and recipient of various letters and literary dedications by Girolamo Parabosco. He died in Venice in 1567, but nothing is known of the last six years of his life. The other involves the Venetian nobleman Antonio Zantani, who died the same year. Zantani sponsored the main musical circle in mid-cinquecento Venice and amassed significant collections in various fields of graphic arts. He was also husband to a beauty exalted in the dialogic and musical literature of the time. By considering the complicities and agendas encoded in writings that accumulated around them, I will try to describe the sensibilities, ideological investments, and social connections with which their patronage of Venetian repertories was aligned.

GOTTARDO OCCAGNA

Let me begin by sketching what I can of Occagna's biography, heretofore unknown. Occagna drew up a will in Venice on 19 February 1548 (see Appendix, A).[7] There he reveals, true to his name, that he is a Spaniard from the little town of Ocaña near Toledo, who has been living for an unspecified length of time in Venice. He calls himself "Gottardo di Ochagna at present resident here in the city of Venice." He names Alfonso de Benites as his father and Suor Maria di San Bernardo, "a nun in the monastery of Seville called Santa Maria di Gratia," to whom he leaves one hundred ducats, as his mother. His brother, to whom he leaves the same sum, he describes as a Dominican monk in the order of the "observanti." Others whom Occagna mentions were also apparently Spanish: an Alberto Restagno de la Niella; his wife, Paula; and a couple named Anzola and Hieronimo Barcharolla.

Occagna's will attests to a certain worldliness and wealth. He refers to the unnamed parts of his estate as being "both here in Venice and in Spain and in every other place." Outside his family his closest connections seem to have been Genoese: his "executor, commissary, and sole heir" Zuanagostino de Marini, in whose house he was staying in the parish of San Moisè; and a "Lorenzo Sansone genovese da Savona fiol de mis*ier* Raymondo mio carissimo." As a maritime, colonializing, and commercial city, Genoa

---

7. Since Occagna's notary used the Venetian calendar, beginning on March 1, the date 19 February 1547 (as it is given) means 1548 in modern usage. So far as I can determine, this is the only document Francesco Bianco notarized for Occagna, nor have my searches of other notaries in the city thus far turned up other documents connected with him (despite the fact that Occagna "cancels and annuls all other testaments previously spoken, written, or ordered" by him).

I am extremely grateful to Giulio Ongaro for his expertise in helping me transcribe and interpret this and other archival documents discussed in Chap. 3. I also wish to thank Julius Kirshner and Ingrid Rowland, especially for help with some of the Latin.

in some ways resembled Venice. It excelled at navigation and cartography, ship-building and various industrial techniques, as well as banking. Once the Genoese shifted in 1528 from serving France to the imperial Charles V of Spain, they also began to manage huge sums and trading ventures for the Spanish crown. Occagna's dual Spanish and Genoese connections thus probably point to mercantile (or possibly diplomatic) activities along a Spanish-Genoese-Venetian axis.

Nothing tells us what the mix of commercial and cultural attractions was that kept Occagna in Venice. Yet it's clear that he integrated himself into aspects of Venetian cultural life in ways other foreign businessmen and diplomats might have envied. One of the recurring concerns of his will, for instance, were the various institutions of charity central to the consciousness of counter-reformational Venetians. Like so many of the city's residents, Occagna had joined a large lay confraternity, the Scuola di Santa Maria della Carità, to which he left twenty ducats so as to have the brothers accompany his body to its burial. He left ten ducats each to the hospitals of the Incurabili and Santissimi Giovanni e Paolo.

Beyond these standard gestures Occagna described himself as fiscal sponsor of a young girl ("putina") Valleria, to whom he had apparently been lending continuous financial assistance ("facto arlevare") for some time through her caretaker, Anzola Barcharolla.[8] For the girl's future marriage or (more likely, as he concedes) her entrance into a convent, he set aside twenty ducats. Such a practice is common enough in wills of the time,[9] but why Occagna should have provided for the child's long-term maintenance is a mystery that suggests a deeper connection—parenthood, either his own or that of a good friend or servant.

While Occagna's will reveals him as well assimilated into Venetian cultural institutions and practices—particularly those involving charity but surely also the larger panoply of rituals connected with church and *scuola*—nothing in it suggests how he was drawn so far into the world of music and letters. Yet we should bear in mind that charitable, religious, and mercantile activities gave ample opportunities for expanding cultural connections from a position outside the establishment—from a position, that is, outside the local patrician class.[10]

8. Apparently the Barcarollas, who lived at San Barnaba, were servants to the French ambassador, though at what rank Occagna does not say.

9. Among personalities discussed in the present study, we encounter it in the wills of Adrian Willaert (see Chap. 1 above, n. 15), Elena Barozza Zantani (as discussed in the present chapter), and Veronica Franco; for the last see Margaret F. Rosenthal, *The Honest Courtesan: Veronica Franco, Citizen and Writer in Sixteenth-Century Venice* (Chicago, 1992), Chap. 2, pp. 65–66, 74–84.

10. Occagna's involvement in the *scuole grandi,* which hired top singer-composers to freelance on special occasions, represents one instance of his cultural networking. (On the hiring of singers at the *scuole grandi* see Jonathan Glixon, "A Musicians' Union in Sixteenth-Century Venice," *JAMS* 36 [1983]: 392–421.) For a fine exegesis of the role assumed in sixteenth-century Venice by local and foreign merchants, including the ways they moralized their positions through codes of honor and virtue and tried to improve their cultural status through the acquisition of musical skills and instruments, see Ugo Tucci, "The Psychology of the Venetian Merchant in the Sixteenth Century," in *Renaissance Venice,* ed. John R. Hale (London, 1973), pp. 346–78, esp. pp. 364–69; see also idem, "Il patrizio veneziano mercante e umanista," in *Venezia centro di mediazione tra oriente e occidente (secoli XV–XVI): aspetti e problemi,* 2 vols., ed. Hans-Georg Beck et al., Fondazione Giorgio Cini (Florence, 1977), 1:335–58.

QVINTVS

MADRIGALI A CINQVE VOCI

PER L'ECCELLENTE MVSICO M. PERISSONE

CAMBIO COMPOSTI A COMPIACIMENTO DE DIVERSI SVOI AMICI,

ET A PREGHI DE I MEDEMI HORA FATTI PORRE A LVCE,

ET PER LO MEDEMO COMPOSITORE CORRETTI ET

REVISTI ET ACCONCI, NON PIV NE VE

DVTI NE STAMPATI.

Quinque Vocum.

VENETIIS M. D. XLV.

Cum gratia & priuilegio.

9 . Perissone Cambio, *Madrigali a cinque voci* (Venice, 1545), title page, quintus part book. Photo courtesy of the Herzog August Bibliothek, Wolfenbüttel, from 2.15.14–18 Musica (4).

Occagna's earliest public link to vernacular arts comes from a composer who is known to have freelanced at the Carità in later years, Perissone Cambio.[11] Perissone dedicated his first print, the *Madrigali a cinque voci,* to Occagna in 1545 (Plates 9 and 10). The print was mutually expedient in aiding the aspirations of both dedicator and dedicatee. In 1545 Perissone had only recently arrived in Venice and was still jobless.[12] Although he had managed to attract some attention as a first-rate singer and promising madrigalist (as attested by Doni's *Dialogo della musica* and other anthologies from 1544), no position within the San Marco establishment could be secured for him until 1548. In order to issue the *Madrigali a cinque voci,* he took his career into his own hands by submitting an application to the Senate for a printing privilege in his name (a practice that was usually carried out by printers). The privilege was granted not for any ordinary settings of madrigals or ballatas but for "madrigali sopra li soneti del Petrarcha."[13] Shortly thereafter the *Madrigali* were issued without a printer's mark as a sort of vanity print.[14]

11. On Perissone's connection with the Carità from 1558, see Glixon, "A Musicians' Union," pp. 401 and 408.

12. See further on Perissone's biography in Chap. 9 nn. 27–30, 38. The best source of biographical information on Perissone is Giulio Maria Ongaro, "The Chapel of St. Mark's at the Time of Adrian Willaert (1527–1562): A Documentary Study" (Ph.D. diss., University of North Carolina at Chapel Hill, 1986).

13. See Chap. 9 n. 38.

14. In the dedication Perissone says that he is having some of his madrigals for five voices printed ("facend'io stampare, alcuni miei Madrigali, à cinque voci").

10. Perissone Cambio, *Madrigali a cinque voci* (Venice, 1545), dedication to Gottardo Occagna. Photo courtesy of the Herzog August Bibliothek, Wolfenbüttel, from 2.15.14–18 Musica (4).

Perissone had clearly found a collaborator in the venture in Occagna. Both on the title page and in the dedication Perissone stressed the fact that encouragement from friends who wanted the music for their own use had been his incentive to print it. As his title page put it, these madrigals had not only been "composed for the pleasure of various friends of his" but were only being "brought to light *at their request*" (emphasis mine). The music Occagna and his friends presumably wanted (and may already have been singing) included the newest and trendiest sort—mostly Petrarch's sonnets set in a motetlike style, though leavened with a few lighter texts done in a more arioso Florentine manner. Only one collection of music had previously been printed in Venice that was at all comparable to this one, namely Rore's First Book from 1542. Perissone's was the first serious attempt to appropriate the style of Willaert and Rore, even quoting from Willaert's unpublished settings of Petrarch. Despite its unassuming origins, then, Perissone's book bore public witness to the new position Occagna had acquired via Petrarchan fashions among the city's cultural elite.

Only a larger dialogic context helps us read the alliances through which Occagna acquired this and other coveted accoutrements of patrimony and patriarchy, a context chiefly provided by various Petrarchizing addresses made to Occagna by Parabosco. Occagna surfaced as literary patron to Parabosco in the same year as Perissone printed his Petrarchan madrigals. Parabosco dedicated to him the first in his series of epistolary handbooks called *Lettere amorose,* zany anthologies of formulaic letters for different amorous situations. These letters extended the familiar letter genre, resurrected for the vernacular by Pietro Aretino only in 1537, into the domain of popular love theory that had been made so fashionable early in the century with Pietro Bembo's *Gli asolani* of 1505.[15] Accordingly, the *Lettere amorose*

15. On Aretino's resuscitation of the familiar letter genre see Amedeo Quondam, *Le "carte messaggiere": retorica e modelli di comunicazione epistolare, per un indice dei libri di lettere del cinquecento* (Rome, 1981), and Anne Jacobson Schutte, "The *Lettere Volgari* and the Crisis of Evangelism in Italy," *RQ* 28 (1975): 639–88.

mixed in a smattering of letters, purportedly to various acquaintances, along with avowedly fictitious and generic ones.

Parabosco specially contrived a dedication that would enfold Occagna in the letters' intimate world. He declined to adopt the obsequious rhetoric conventional in high-styled dedications, advancing in its place the more impertinent tone of eclectic satirists whom Aretino epitomized. Parabosco names three reasons for making this gift: first, knowing Occagna's delight in reading "opere volgari" (he was an afficionado of vernacular letters); second, as a sign of love; and third, because Occagna, who once thought Parabosco an adventurer in love, now knows how far from the truth he had been, as proven by those letters written to assuage his grief. With no further hint, he adds, Occagna will know which were dictated by real passion and which composed fictitiously for the pleasure of friends.[16]

The familiarity Parabosco risked in the 1545 dedication was only a preamble to what was to come in the expanded second edition issued the following year. There he attached an *Aggiunta* in the form of three letters, one to Occagna and two addressed anonymously, plus an extra pseudoletter to Occagna that formed in reality a dedication to the *Aggiunta*.[17] (The typography of this last letter, as printed in the 1549 edition, helps make the letter's dedicatory function clear; see Plate 11).

In the first of the letters Parabosco upped the ante of familiarity in a way that exposes Occagna's complicity in being honored by jocular informality rather than groveling decorum.[18] Parabosco begins by answering Occagna's purported request to explain the workings of the "three [types of] love" (the "tre amori"). In the slow unraveling of allusions that follows, the reader is positioned as privileged onlooker to a private male exchange. Within it, Parabosco tropes the basic Petrarchan tension of an eternally frustrated male infatuated with a chaste, unattainable woman. Yet he quickly and radically alters Petrarchan voice and address. One of the "tre amori" depicts love as a sportman's quest to attain the unattainable, while another celebrates the sweetness of requited love. Unlike Petrarch's poet, who always addresses (ultimately) himself, Parabosco's letters reverse this self-referential strategy to address another lovelorn male. Thus while Parabosco weaves his strands from the private conceits and postures of Petrarch's *rime,* he assumes an ironic—but typically

16. Here is the bulk of the dedication to the *Lettere amorose:* "Al Nobile, et Generoso Sig. Gottardo Occagna. Tre sono le cagioni . . . che mi spingono à farvi dono di queste mie lettere amorose, l'una per conoscer io V. S. dilettarsi & haver sommo piacer di legger l'opere volgari; l'altra per dar segno a quella dell'amore, & della servitù, ch'io le porto, havendomi à ciò astretto le sue infinite virtù; la terza perche conosciate homai, quanto sete lontano del vero, ogni volta che crediate, ch'io sia aventurato nell'amorose imprese, come dite, & di questo ve ne daranno non picciol segno quelle lettere lequali sono scritte, come vederete, piu tosto per disacerbere il dolore, che per speranza di muover pietà ne di altrui cuore. Quelle di tal soggetto la maggior parte della propria passione dettate sono, le altre poi à piacer di diversi miei amici composi. V. S. che è saggio, conoscerà molto bene dall'effetto quelle da queste, però io non le ne darò altro segno." Signed 12 June 1545.

17. I am grateful to Kenneth A. Lohf of Columbia University's Rare Book and Manuscript Library for checking the edition of 1546 and to Jill Rosenshield of Special Collections at Memorial Library of the University of Wisconsin for checking editions printed in 1549 and 1561.

18. For a full transcription of the letter see Appendix, B, Paraboso, *I quattro libri.*

*darui, sia sforzata a sempre lamentarsi, & a sempre
dolersi di cui per ogni ragione la deurebbe addolcire.
rompa homai la mia fedeltà la uostra durezza; & il
mio ardor distruggi,& consumi il freddissimo ghiaccio,
& la crudeltà, di che hauete così cinto il cuore; accio
ch'io canti ad un tempo & la bellezza, & la cortesia
di chi a suo piacer mi puo donar morte, & uita.*

Aggiunta.
Al ualoroso Signor Gottardo Occagna.

IGNOR mio osseruandiß. essendo io
così acceso di mostrare alla S. V. che co
me di lei non uiue al mondo huomo, ne
piu uirtuoso, ne piu gentile; così non è
chi di me piu l'ame,& osserui;non posso macare,che in
ogni occasione,che me ne uenga, io no le scopra l'affet=
tion mia. però hauendo io fatto ristampare le mie lette=
re Amorose,& fattoui una nuoua additione,ho uoluto
farne motto alla S.V.pregandola,che non si sdegni, se
queste poche così saranno adorne del suo nome, come le
molte prime:& io fra tanto studiarò di darle ogni gior
no maggior segno dell'Amor,ch'io le porto. ilquale in
me non lascia albergar pensiero,che non sia di honorar
ui, & riuerirui sempre. Bascio le mani di V. S.

Seruitor Girolamo Parabosco.
IL FINE.

11.   Girolamo Parabosco, *Lettere amorose* (Venice, 1546), "Aggiunta al valoroso Signor Gottardo Occagna," fol. 79ʹ. Photo courtesy of Van Pelt Library, Special Collections, the University of Pennsylvania.

Venetian—position of doubleness, a doubleness in which the subjects' public words annul the implication of intimacy even as they allege it.

Parabosco's letter also inverts parodistically the male-female relation of Petrarch's poetry, as made clear in the second type of love, consisting of a male tactic designed to conquer a particular sort of woman who is won over by the spectacle of a man wallowing in his amorous obsession for her. From their male perspective this is a "sweet love, since loving one of this sort, one . . . doesn't have to suffer through [all] the usual effort." The end is not only attained, but the route to it is eased and quickened. Parabosco claims a man may reach his desired goal by the very *act* of obsessing over it (or, as he says, through the act of "ruminating"), since his coy behavior softens the sympathetic woman. ("How many have there been," he asks, "who have found remedies in cases like this at a point when the wittiest men in the world would not have imagined one in a thousand years?") The amorous huntsman can therefore chalk his catch up to the wits of his own female quarry, who actually exploits his exaggerated grief to justify her tacit but eager complicity in the lovers' game.[19] Parabosco claims to rejoice when friends pull off stunts like these. "[M]y Lord, it doesn't displease me but makes me happy whenever I see a friend of mine giving himself as prey for the loving of such a subject—of which I will say nothing else because I know that *you* know much better than I the sweetness that one draws from *that*" (emphasis mine).[20] The master at this wily love game, Parabosco would then claim, is Occagna himself, the one who arguably backed both print and reprint.[21] This implies a collusion between them not in matters of love but rather in elaborating iconoclastically Petrarch's outer theme of *innamoramento,* of falling in love, to mutually accommodating ends: the double position Parabosco seems to assume in doing so—standing at once between private and public, between inward and outward, and between sober and comic—must be understood as equally Occagna's.

Such subversive inversion is, of course, defined and bound by the thing it subverts, Parabosco's anti-Petrarchism by definition Petrarchan. Several passages from the *Aggiunta* affirm this duality: one of them glosses side by side two of Petrarch's

19. A passage taken from fols. 104–104′ translates: "Oh the great happiness of a lover who is able to see his ultimate goal being fastened, almost in spite of fortune, on his desire through the sublime intellect of his lady. Who could imagine the sweetness that that fortunate man then feels who is at once assured of the love of his beloved and of loving a thing of tremendous value, since the intelligence of the one he loves is no less proven to him than her affection. Beyond that, the man of this second ardor, being of a warm character, can always have more hope of attaining his intended goal than can any other [sort of man]; and no less because of the excuses that such ladies make for his pity than because of their sympathy, each of which they use in similar ways. Those ladies don't have any need to show all that harshness that they are accustomed to enjoy in loving well, because they are so eminent in it or at least much pledged to it. For which reason they are almost always disposed to receive a loving fire."

20. Fol. 104′.

21. Note that the final dedicatory letter to Occagna, included in the *Aggiunte* in the editions of 1546, 1549, and 1558, strongly suggests that Occagna was an actual financial backer (see Plate 10). Although the letter was deleted from Gabriel Giolito's edition of 1561, along with the dedications to Occagna of Books 1 and 3, that of Domenico Farri (another Venetian publisher) dedicated each of its four separately printed books to Occagna in the same year, according to Giuseppe Bianchini, *Girolamo Parabosco: scrittore e organista del secolo XVI,* Miscellanea di Storia Veneta, ser. 2, vol. 6 (Venice, 1899), p. 482.

sonnets—indeed two out of the sixty or so sonnets that were set by Parabosco's teachers and colleagues;[22] while two other passages avow in the most ubiquitous of Petrarch's oxymorons, that of the icy fire, an ardor that destroys and melts the coldest ice.[23]

Parabosco's letters thus suggest several things about the position an upwardly mobile patron like Occagna might assume toward those he patronized: first, that as dedicatee, he was a willing interlocutor in an exchange that made the private public—or pretended to; second, that his tacit participation in literary exchanges formed part of a larger world of vernacular discourse, which embraced music along with various sorts of letters; and third, that a primary discursive mode for all these—and a yardstick from our vantage point—was the collection of tropes provided by Petrarch's lyric sequence. Parabosco (to trope myself) inverts Petrarch's lyric stance in order to stand in it: the unattainable woman becomes attainable, chaste womanhood becomes unchaste, the silent woman (by implication) becomes vocal, and the writer who speaks to himself now speaks out to others. As the internal spiritual struggle of Petrarch's lyrics is externalized in the implicit dialogue of the familiar letter, the most defining aspect of Petrarch's stance is turned inside out. Literary voice and content thus collaborate to lower Petrarch's canonized style to the level of a vulgar popularization.

The very different transformations of Petrarchism that I have noted in Perissone and Parabosco—Perissone's sacred-style Petrarch settings and Parabosco's irreverent verbal plays on Petrarchan poetics—play (broadly speaking) with Venice's tendency at this time to separate styles into high and low. Through its dialogic modes, authors could often slip freely between styles that were otherwise strictly separated. Occagna received two further dedications in the 1540s that exemplify more straightforwardly Venice's tendency at midcentury to stratify styles along such Ciceronian lines. Both match verbal subjects, already matched to linguistic registers, to particular musical idioms.

The first of these came again from Parabosco, but the music was not his. Instead Parabosco dedicated to Occagna a book of *mascherate* by an apparently obscure composer named Lodovico Novello.[24] According to the dedication, Occagna

---

22. See his discussion of the third type of love in the letter given in Appendix, B, *I quattro libri,* which conflates Petrarch's sonnet no. 253, v. 1, with sonnet no. 159, v. 14: "O dolci sguardi, o dolci risi, o dolci parole, che dolci sono ben veramente più che l'ambrosia delli Dei" (fols. 104'–5).

23. These occur at the end of the first letter: "laqual cosa è troppo a far felice un'huomo, ilquale sarebbe degno d'infinita pena, se havendo cotal commodità non rompesse un diamante, o non infiammasse un ghiaccio" (fol. 105); and in this passage from the third: "rompa homai la mia fedeltà la vostra durezza; il mio ardor distrugga, & consumi il freddissimo ghiaccio, & la crudeltà, di che havete cosi cinto il core: accio ch'io canti ad un tempo & la bellezza, & la cortesia di chi a suo piacer mi puo donar morte, & vita" (fol. 108').

24. Title: *Mascherate di Lodovico Novello di piu sorte et varii soggetti appropriati al carnevale novamente da lui composte et con diligentia stampate et corrette libro primo a quattro voci.* The dedication reads: "Al Nobile et gentil Signor Gottardo Occagna / Girolamo Parabosco. Carissimo signor mio, quando io mi ritrovassi privo di quello che da v.s. mi fosse richiesto io me ingegnaria di farmi ladro per contentarvi ne fatica ne timore alcuno o di vergogna o di danno che avenir me ne potesse mi farebbe rimener giamai di cercare ogni via per che fosse adempiuto il desiderio vostro & mio. Essend'io adunque a questi giorni

wanted newly fashioned songs as entertainment for the carnival season and hoped Parabosco could author them. The composer pleaded himself overcommitted, which can hardly have been far from the truth, insisting that he would have stolen them and suffered any shame, damnation, or exertion to procure them had he not chanced miraculously on the four-voice *mascherate* by Novello. Somehow Parabosco was acting as intermediary between Novello and the printer Antonio Gardane, with whom he must have had a working alliance, for he claimed to make the dedication with the "license of one who *has the task of having them printed*" (emphasis mine). These *mascherate* cover "every topic, but all with equal beauty, wit, and ease, and without much gravity, as is fitting," so that "both the melody and words can be understood and enjoyed by everybody." By "every topic" Parabosco means every mask, every get-up—of which there are a great variety: *mascherate* "Da hebree," "Da mori," "Da nimphe," "Da rufiane," "Da scultori," "Da calzolari," "Da vendi saorine," "Da orefici," "Da maestri di ballar," "Da porta littere," "Da fabri," and so on (masks of Jewesses, Moors, nymphs, procuresses, sculptors, shoemakers, mustard vendors, goldsmiths, dance masters, postmen, locksmiths). Occagna's circle must have planned to sing them themselves (just as they sang Perissone's madrigals), for Parabosco closes with advice on how they should go about matching the stanzas to the melodies.

The texts allowed plenty of ribald humor and artisanal double entendre: doctors who nimbly probe the love sores of willing patients; locksmiths who "screw in keys" free of charge.[25] Woven between their lines is a sophisticated tapestry of intertextual references to other lyrics, frottole, dance songs, *napolitane,* epic verse, comedies, and madrigals. Thus the songs could amuse the cognoscenti and invert the official rhetoric they knew all too well, without perplexing the uninitiated.[26]

---

stato richiesto da V.S., di alcune imascherate, & havendo per mille negotii importantissimi come tosto vi sara manifesto l'animo in piu di mille parti diviso io non poteva veramente in modo alcuno servire la S.V. del mio, & mentre mi pensavo ond'io potessi o rubarle o d'haverle in duono fuor d'ogni mio pensiero & senza alcuna mia diligenza quasi per miracolo mi sono venute alle mani queste composte per lo eccellente M. Lodovico Novello per lequali V.S. potra essere apieno sodisfatta d'ogni suo desiderio per che ce ne sono in ogni soggetto ma tutte ugualmente dette con bella & acuta maniera & facile senza molta gravita come si conviene, & cosi il canto come le parole accio che da tutti siano intese & gustate. Io le dedito a V.S. con licenza di chi ha carico de farle stampare. Di queste come V.S. potra vedere tutte le stanze che seguiranno la prima si cantano sopra le noti di essa prima ne qui alcuno potra pigliare errore per che altro canto non ci e che de una sola stanza per ciaschaduna imascherata salvo che di tre, quali sono questi: i gioiellieri, gli fabri, & i Ballarini. di queste tre l'ultima stanza di ogniuna ha un Canto per se & tutte le altre si cantano come la prima, come si comprendera chiarissimamente V.S. le accetta con lieto animo & mi comandi." I add punctuation to a transcription taken from Mary S. Lewis, *Antonio Gardane, Venetian Music Printer, 1538–1569: A Descriptive Bibliography and Historical Study,* vol. 1, *1538–49* (New York, 1988), pp. 527–28, which also includes a list of the print's contents.

It does not seem implausible that "Lodovico Novello" was a pseudonym for Parabosco.

25. The unpublished transcriptions of texts and scores on which I base my discussion of Novello's print are those of Donna Cardamone Jackson. I am very grateful to her for loaning them to me.

26. On the question of how carnival rites served as a "foil" to official rhetoric see Linda L. Carroll, "Carnival Rites as Vehicles of Protest in Renaissance Venice," *The Sixteenth Century Journal* 16 (1985): 487–502. Relevant too is the now widely read study by Mikhail Bakhtin, *Rabelais and His World,* trans. Hélène Iswolsky (Bloomington, 1984).

Many of the masks work Petrarchan figures into their repertory of inside jokes. The mask of the mailmen, for instance, beseeches the "lovely ladies" it addresses to post their love letters with them. But if a killing love death should demand discretion, it offers to send their messages by word of mouth ("a bocca dire")—carnal messages that tell, for instance, "How love makes you die and the spirit and food of a hot impetuous passion, which consumes your afflicted heart, join flesh to flesh and skin to skin."[27] Figures like the "cor afflitto che abbruccia" (afflicted heart that burns) and "amor che fa morire" (love that makes you die) circulated rampantly as common versions of Petrarchan tropes. Thus whoever wrote the texts had no lack of models close at hand. The precise phrase "Amor mi fa morire" was, in fact, well known to Venetian afficionados of vernacular music like Occagna and company, for it troped the incipit of a well-known ballata-madrigal set by Willaert and widely circulated in the 1530s.[28] All the funnier therefore that it should appear here in a raucous, strophic part song. The modest bits of contrapuntal imitation that Novello incorporated into his *mascherata* did nothing to elevate the songs' generally low idiom, their gawky tunes, and sudden metric shifts. On the whole the masks were better suited to outdoor revelries than to genteel drawing rooms, where quiet, ceaseless polyphony was the norm.

This, then, is low style pure and simple, and its proper place is carnival: in short, low style for carnivalesque subjects. At this lower rung of *mascherate* also sat spoken comedy. In 1547, for the third year in a row, Parabosco dedicated a vernacular work to Occagna, this time his comedy *Il viluppo,* citing Occagna's pleasure in reading "simil Poemi."[29] Reading the play aloud—reciting it in a group, that is—may be what Parabosco had in mind, a practice that was widespread among the literate.[30] Here again we find Occagna in the thick of the newly ascendant vernacular arts, engaging in the play of Petrarchism made part of daily life and relishing the diverse styles and levels that the new Ciceronian conceptions of words prescribed.

The high-styled antithesis to masks and comedies came with a work dedicated to Occagna in 1548, attached to an early edition of Rore's Third Book of madrigals printed by Girolamo Scotto (RISM 1548[9]).[31] This dedication assigned Occagna the

27. The passage comes from stanza 3 of the *mascharata* "Da porta lettere": "Se voleti a bocca dire / Qualche cosa et non inscrito / Come amor vi fa morire / Et ch'il spirto vostro e vitto / D'un focoso e gran desire / Che v'abbruggia il cor afflitto / Di congionger dritto adritto / Carne a carne e pelle a pelle."
28. See Chap. 7 above, nn. 18–19.
29. "[E]ssendomi venuto in proposto di stampare questa mia nova Comedia, quale ella si sia, a Vostra Signoria la dono: & perche io so il piacere ch'ella ha di legger simil Poemi." Parabosco used the same address, "Al nobile, & generoso signore Gottardo Occagna."
30. Cf. Donato Giannotti's letter to Lorenzo Ridolfi discussed in Chap. 2 nn. 63–64.
31. The book was printed about the same time as or slightly earlier than an equivalent one by Gardane (RISM 1549[10]). The account books of the Accademia Filarmonica of Verona show that it purchased one of the 1548 eds. (presumably Gardane's) on 19 April 1548; see Giuseppe Turrini, *L'Accademia Filarmonica di Verona dalla fondazione (maggio 1543) al 1600 e il suo patrimonio musicale antico,* Atti e memorie della Accademia di Agricoltura, Scienze e Lettere di Verona, no. 18 (Verona, 1941), p. 37. For bibliographical issues surrounding the print see Alvin H. Johnson, "The 1548 Editions of Cipriano de Rore's Third Book of Madrigals," in *Studies in Musicology in Honor of Otto E. Albrecht,* ed. John Walter Hill (Kassel, 1980), pp. 110–24, and Mary S. Lewis, "Rore's Setting of Petrarch's *Vergine bella:* A History of

slight place he has previously held in historical memory, for the print included Rore's setting of the first six stanzas of Petrarch's final canzone, *Vergine bella*. The brief dedication was signed not by the composer, however, but by the Paduan flutist Paolo Vergelli:

> To the noble and valorous Signor Gottardo Occagna, my most eminent friend and Lord.
>
> My most honored Lord and friend, I know the diligence and effort that you have used recently in order to have those *Vergine,* already composed many months ago by the most excellent musician Mr. Cipriano Rore, your and our most dear friend. Those works having come into my hands, it seemed to me [fitting], both because of the love I bear to you and to satisfy your desire, to have them printed with some other lovely madrigals by the same composer, and some by the divine Adrian Willaert and other disciples of his, so that you might not only be satisfied in your wish, but with it might even bring some praise and merit to the world, which thanks to you will be made rich by this present, truly worthy of being seen and enjoyed by everyone. I kiss your hands. Paolo Vergelli, Paduan musician.[32]

Contrary to Vergelli's claims, Scotto's edition of the *Vergine* cycle suggests that there was no such mutually beneficial collaboration between Occagna and Rore of the kind Occagna had had with Perissone (or Willaert and Rore with the Florentines). If anything, it hints that Occagna's aspirations broke down at such formidable levels. In fact, both bibliographical and musical evidence surrounding the edition make me think the enterprise was surreptitious.[33] First of all, the dedication was not authored by Rore—by then in Ferrara—but by Vergelli, probably as one of Scotto's freelancers. Vergelli noted that Occagna had been trying hard to get hold of the *Vergine* stanzas for some months. He also claimed that both he and Occagna were good friends of Rore's (whom he called "vostro e nostro carissimo amico"). Why then did they let the cycle

Its Composition and Early Transmission," *Journal of Musicology* 4 (1985–86): 365–409. Johnson argues that differences in the title pages of the two editions (there are actually two distinct ones in different part books for Gardane's) leave no doubt that Scotto's was published first; the title pages and dedications are reproduced in Johnson, pp. 111, 114–15, and 121. For the argument that both editions were published by April 1548 see Lewis, p. 381. Gardane's edition bore no dedication until the supplement was issued the following year (see below) and appended to the altus part book, which was dedicated by Perissone Cambio to the poet-cleric Giovanni della Casa.

32. "Al nobile & valoroso Signor Gottardo Occagna compadre & Signor mio osservandissimo. Signor compare honorandissimo. Sapendo io la diligenza, & la fatica che havete usata questi giorni passati per haver quelle vergine, gia molti mesi sono, composte da lo eccellentissimo musico messer Cipriano Rore, vostro et nostro carissimo amico, mi e parso, essendomi le predette compositioni venute alle mani, per lo amor che vi porto, & per satisfare al desiderio vostro, farle stampare con alcuni altri bellissimi madrigali del medemo compositore, & con alcuni del Divinissimo Adriano Villaerth, e de altri suoi discepoli, accio che vostra signoria non solamente sia satisfatta del desiderio suo, ma ne consegua ancora qualche laude & merito appresso il mondo, il quale merce di vostra signoria sara fatto riccho di questo presente, veramente degno di esser veduto, & goduto da ognuno. Et a V.S. baccio le mani. Paolo Vergelli musico padovano." The title page reads: *Di Cipriano Rore et di altri eccellentissimi musici il terzo libro di madrigali a cinque voci novamente da lui composti et non piu messi in luce. Con diligentia stampati. Musica nova & rara come a quelli che la canteranno & udiranno sara palese. Venetiis. Appresso Hieronimo Scotto. MDXLVIII.*

33. Lewis reaches a similar conclusion in "Rore's Setting of Petrarch's *Vergine bella,*" pp. 394–405.

be printed in a form so glaringly incomplete as both poetic and musical structure—especially given that Rore had been instrumental in introducing literary standards to Italian part music that aimed to set poems intact?[34] The six stanzas fell five short of the total eleven, leaving the canzone hanging in midair. Further, in such fragmentary form the music lacked the tonal unity supplied by the last five stanzas once Rore's settings of them were issued in a supplement the following year.[35] Even the supplement was probably only Rore's way of making the best of a bad situation: three years later, a new edition by Gardane included substantial revisions that Rore had made to the whole cycle. If Occagna hoped his identification with the *Vergine* settings would give him the kind of cachet that exiled Florentines got from Willaert's settings, he can only have half succeeded. The upwardly mobile might have envied him, while the real cognoscenti must have sneered at the clumsiness of the effort. Perhaps no one in 1548 could have reaped the benefits of a linkage to Rore's *Vergine* in a legitimate, public arena, but surely not Occagna.

With this evidence in hand we can begin to situate Occagna's position within the kind of ethnography of books I hinted at earlier, one that moves between bibliographical evidence and larger dialogic contexts. It is this hermeneutic move that allows us to consider the extent to which Occagna's link with the *Vergine* cycle put him in cultural company with the city's most select patrons.

What in fact could have been the mechanism that brought about this link, if in fact Occagna had no responsibility for the genesis of the music? Quite simply, he must have offered a subvention to Scotto's printing house. Vergelli probably procured the subvention as part of his moonlighting for Scotto, after having gotten hold of the unfinished music. Occagna for his part cannot have attended much to the niceties of its public debut when presumably he helped finance it. His connection with Rore's *Vergine* thus jibes with ones he made earlier with Parabosco and Perissone. Rather than maintaining his position privately, as nobles tended to do, these addresses and exchanges all helped advance publicly his fledgling reputation in Venetian society.

Occagna's involvements would have been intolerably reckless for the likes of most Venetian aristocrats. In addressing nobles, middle-class authors like Parabosco almost never employed the familiar versions of Petrarchan tropes that Occagna condoned. Even the more dignified tropes of praise that helped define noblemen's patriarchy—and that their patriarchy perpetuated—usually reached them only indirectly. I turn now to Antonio Zantani.[36]

34. Although the trend for complete settings had previously been mainly toward sonnets, it was extended as early as 1544 to longer multistanza poems with cyclic settings of Petrarch's sestine *Alla dolce ombra* (no. 142) by Jachet Berchem, published in Doni's *Dialogo della musica* in 1544, and later to *Giovene donna* (no. 30) by Giovanni Nasco, issued in his *Primo libro a 5* in 1548, the same year that Rore's *Vergine* appeared.

35. The remaining five stanzas can be found as additions to a number of extant copies of the *Terzo libro*, as discussed by Lewis, "Rore's Setting of Petrarch's *Vergine bella*." For further discussion of the music, including the question of tonal unity, see Chap. 10, esp. n. 5.

36. Primary sources give several variant versions of the name, including Zantani, Centani, Centana, and Zentani.

ANTONIO ZANTANI

Zantani gained notoriety in Venetian music history by attempting to print four madrigals from the *Musica nova* in the late 1550s. But his links to Venetian music date from at least 1548 and involve the same Scotto edition in which Rore's *Vergine* cycle was printed. Besides the settings by Rore, this edition included works by Willaert, Perissone, Donato, and others that enhanced its Venetian character.[37] Most of Willaert's contributions were occasional, forming part of the dialogic networks I have attempted to describe here. Among them was a dedicatory setting of Lelio Capilupi's ballata *Ne l'amar e fredd'onde si bagna*,[38] a tribute to a renowned Venetian noblewoman whom Capilupi named with the epithet "la bella Barozza"—Antonio's wife.[39] Its praise of her sets the Petrarchan paradox of the icy fire in a verbal landscape shaped by Venetian geography: her flame, born in the cold Venetian seas, burns so sweetly that the fire from which the poet melts seems frigid beside it.

Ne l'amar e fredd'onde si bagna	In the bitterness and cold in which
L'alta Vinegia, nacque il dolce foco	The great Venice bathes itself was born the sweet fire
Ch'Italia alluma et arde a poco a poco.	That inflames and illumines Italy bit by bit.
Ceda nata nel mar Venere, e Amore	Venus, born of the sea, may yield, and Cupid
Spegna le faci homai, spezzi li strali	May put out the torches and break his arrows;
Chè la bella Barozz'a li mortali	For the lovely Barozza stabs the mortals
Trafigge et arde coi begl'occhi 'l core.	And consumes their hearts with her beautiful eyes.
E di sua fiamma è sì dolce l'ardore,	And there is such a sweet ardor from her flame
Che quell'ond'io per lei mi struggo e coco	That that which makes me melt and burn for her
Parmi ch'al gran desir sia freddo e poco.	Seems frigid and small beside the great desire.

Barozza's full name was Helena Barozza Zantani. In 1548 she already had a reputation as one of Venice's great beauties. She had been painted by Titian and Vasari, venerated by Lorenzino de' Medici, and widely celebrated in verse.[40] These tributes

---

37. A number of these pieces reappear in the manuscript of the Herzog August Bibliothek in Wolfenbüttel, Guelf 293. See Lewis, "Rore's Setting of Petrarch's *Vergine bella*," pp. 407–8, for a list of its contents and concordances.

38. The setting is among those in Wolfenbüttel 293. The poem appears in *Rime del S. Lelio, e fratelli de Capilupi* (Mantua, 1585), p. 31. For my identification of the poet I am indebted to Lorenzo Bianconi and Antonio Vassalli's handwritten catalogue of poetic incipits, which gave me the initial lead on this and a number of other poems.

39. Many sources confirm that Helena was Antonio's wife, including Dragoncino's designation of his stanza "Consorte di M. Antonio" (see n. 42 below); Aretino's paired letters to "Antonio Zentani" and "Elena Barozza" from April and May 1548, respectively (*Lettere di M. Pietro Aretino*, 6 vols. [Paris, 1609], 4:207' and 208'; *Lettere sull'arte di Pietro Aretino*, commentary by Fidenzio Pertile, ed. Ettore Camesasca, 3 vols. in 4 [Milan, 1957–60] 2:215–17); and the wills of Antonio and Helena, as given in Appendix, C and D.

40. Both portraits are described by Pietro Aretino and both are now apparently lost. Vasari's was painted before he left Venice in 1542 (cf. n. 86 below); see Aretino, *Lettere*, 2:304' (no. 420, to Vasari, 29 July 1542, with a sonnet in praise of Barozza) and 4:208' (no. 478, to Helena, May 1548, with reference to both portraits), and *Lettere sull'arte* 1:224 and 2:216–17.

On Lorenzino's unrequited feelings for Helena Barozza, and for the most thorough gathering of information on her, see L[uigi] A[lberto] Ferrai, *Lorenzino de' Medici e la società cortigiana del cinquecento* (Milan, 1891), pp. 343–52, esp. p. 347 n. 2.

placed Helena in the cult of beautiful *gentildonne,* which assigned Petrarch's metaphorical praises to living ladies and generated yet more goods for Venetian printers.[41] Of all these praises, those in lyric forms were most apt to adopt something close to the lightly erotic tone of Capilupi: Giovambattista Dragoncino da Fano's *Lode delle nobildonne vinitiane del secolo moderno* of 1547, for instance, devoted one of its stanzas to the "sweet war" Helena launched in lovers' hearts, ending in praise of her "blonde tresses."[42]

Other encomia conflated her beauty with her moral worth. Confirming the occult resemblance thought to exist between physical and spiritual virtue, they deflected the transgressive possibilities to allure and mislead the unsuspecting to which beauty was also commonly linked. A letter of Aretino's to Giorgio Vasari of 1542 honored Vasari's portrait of Helena for the "grace of the eyes, majesty of the countenance, and highness of the brow," which made its subject seem "more celestial than worldly," such that "no one could gaze at such an image with a lascivious desire."[43] Aretino troped his own letter in an accompanying sonnet, declaring her loveliness of such an honesty and purity as to turn chaste the most desirous thoughts (see n. 43 below). Lodovico Domenichi's *La nobiltà delle donne* similarly joined beauty with virtue by comparing Helena's looks with the Greek Helen of Troy and her honesty with the Roman Lucrezia ("Mad. Helena Barozzi Zantani, laquale in bellezza pareggia la Greca, & nell'honestà la Romana Lucretia . . .").[44] Even the female poet-singer Gaspara Stampa added to her *Rime varie* a sonnet for Barozza, that "woman lovely, honest, and wise" (donna bella, onesta, e saggia).[45]

Like most of the women exalted by this cult, the virtuous Helena was safely sheltered by marriage. This ideally suited her to the Petrarchan role of the remote and unattainable lady, as it was now employed for numerous idolatries of living women.

41. For documentation of the literary activity generated by these cults see Bianchini, *Girolamo Parabosco,* pp. 278–98, and on Helena, pp. 294–96.

42. Fol. [4].

43. Verses 9–11: "Intanto il guardo suo santo e beato / In noi, che umilemente il contempliamo, / Casto rende il pensiero innamorato (*Lettere* 2:304' and *Lettere sull'arte* 1:224).

44. Fol. 261ᵃ in the revised version printed by Giolito in 1551. Domenichi was an interlocutor in Doni's *Dialogo della musica* and a Piacentine comrade of Parabosco's. The theme of Troy echoed again at the end of Parabosco's *I diporti,* as a group of Venice's most prominent literati enthuse over various Venetian women in the popular mode of galant *facezie,* in between recitations of *novelle* and *madrigali.* The Viterban poet Fortunio Spira exclaims, "Che dirò di te . . . madonna Elena Barozzi così bella, così gentile! oh! se al tempo della Grecia tu fossi stata in essere, in questa parte il troiano pastore senza dubbio sarebbe stato inviato dalla Dea Venere, come in luogo dove ella meglio gli havesse potuto la messa attenere!" See Giuseppe Gigli and Fausto Nicolini, eds., *Novellieri minori del cinquecento: G. Parabosco— S. Erizzo* (Bari, 1912), p. 192. (*I diporti* were first published in Venice ca. 1550; see Chap. 4 n. 30 below.) Also directed to Helena may be a letter and three sonnets in Parabosco's *Primo libro delle lettere famigliari* (Venice, 1551) addressed "Alla bellissima, et gentilissima Madonna Helena" and dated 30 April 1550 (fols. 49–50). Parabosco makes intriguing mention there of "il nostro M. A. ilquale compone libri delle bellezze, & delle gratie vostre: con certezza che gli possa mancar piu tosto tempo, che suggetto. io vi faccio riverenza per parte sua, & mia" (our Messer A., who composes books of your beauties and graces, with the certainty that he may be lacking time, rather than a subject. I revere you for his part and mine); fol. 49.

45. *Rime* (Venice, 1554), no. 278; mod. ed. Maria Bellonci and Rodolfo Ceriello, 2d ed. (Milan, 1976), p. 264. On the tributes of Stampa and others to Helena Barozza see Abdelkader Salza, "Madonna Gasparina Stampa, secondo nuove indagini," *Giornale storico della letteratura italiana* 62 (1913): 31.

But it also suggests that the music, writings, and paintings in her honor participated in loose networks of reference and praise that helped situate familial identities within larger civic structures. Indeed, it raises the possibility that some were spousal commissions meant (like Willaert's madrigal) to embellish the domestic household and redound to the family name: Helena's husband, Antonio, could after all count himself among the most avid of aristocratic devotees to secular music at midcentury and a keen patron of the visual arts.

Zantani's vita will set the stage for reexamining relationships between civic identity and patronage at closer range.[46] Antonio was born on 18 September 1509 to Marco Zantani and Tommasina di Fabio Tommasini.[47] His father descended from a line of Venetian nobles, his mother from a family originally from Lucca and admitted to the official ranks of Venetian *cittadini* only in the fourteenth century.[48] In 1532 Antonio gained an early admission to the Great Council,[49] and on 16 April 1537 he and Helena were wed in the church of San Moisè.[50] Their respective wills of 1559 and 1580 identify their residence as being in the congenial neighborhood parish of Santa Margarita (see Appendix, C and D).[51] Inasmuch as Antonio's family clan was very small, they may also have lived at times, or at least gathered, at the beautiful Zantani palace nearby at San Tomà (Plate 12)—quarters that would have suited well the salon over which Zantani presided at midcentury.[52] Most famous of the earlier Zantani was Antonio's

46. For a biography of Zantani see Emmanuele A. Cicogna, *Delle inscrizioni veneziane,* 6 vols. (Venice, 1827), 2:14–17. A briefer and more readily available biography, mainly derived from Cicogna, appears in *Lettere sull'arte* 3/2:528–30. Where not otherwise noted my biographical information comes from Cicogna.

The main contemporaneous biography is that given in the form of a dedication to Zantani by Orazio Toscanella in *I nomi antichi e moderni delle provincie, regioni, città* . . . (Venice, 1567), fols. [2]–[3′]. It is reproduced in Appendix, E.

47. I-Vas, Avogaria di Comun, Nascite, Libro d'oro, Nas. I.285. Marco and Tommasina were married in 1503 (I-Vas, Avogaria di Comun, Matrimoni con notizie dei figli).

48. This information comes from Giuseppe Tassini's manuscript genealogy "Cittadini veneziani," I-Vmc, 33.D.76, 5:37–38, which, however, puts her marriage to Marco in 1505 (cf. n. 47 above). Tommasina drew up her will on 9 August 1566 (I-Vas, Archivio Notarile, Testamenti, notaio Marcantonio Cavanis, b. 196, no. 976), calling herself a resident of the parish of Santa Margherita.

49. See Cicogna, *Inscrizioni veneziane* 2:14. (The date of 1552 given in *Lettere sull'arte* 3/2:528 is wrong.) On the practice of admitting young noblemen to the Great Council before their twenty-fifth birthdays see Stanley Chojnacki, "Kinship Ties and Young Patricians in Fifteenth-Century Venice," *RQ* 38 (1985): 240–70.

50. I-Vas, Avogaria di Comun, Matrimoni con notizie dei figli. A marriage contract survives in the Avogaria di Comun, Matrimoni, Contratti L.4, fol. 381′ (reg. 143/4), but is not currently accessible to the public.

51. Helena's will was kindly shared with me by Rebecca E. Edwards. Cicogna refers to a will of 10 October 1567 that Zantani made just before his death, which is preserved in the Testamenti Gradenigo (*Inscrizioni veneziane* 2:16n.). Presumably it is included in the extensive Gradenigo family papers at I-Vas, which are as yet insufficiently indexed. (I am grateful to Anne MacNeil for inquiring about this.) Michelangelo Muraro cites an ostensible copy of the will at I-Vmc, MS P.D. 2192 V, int. 12, but the document in question is presently missing; *Il "libro secondo" di Francesco e Jacopo dal Ponte* (Bassano and Florence, 1992), p. 382. Cicogna quotes enough of this will, however, to show that Zantani took pains to have his name day celebrated every year thereafter: "Egli fu l'ultimo della casa patrizi Zantani, e col suo testamento ordinò che delle sue entrate fosser ogn'anno de' trentasei nobili dassero in elezione nel Maggior Consiglio."

52. Zantani's clan died out with his death. Nonetheless, Pompeo Molmenti's statement that Antonio lived in the present Casa Goldoni is oversimple; see *La storia di Venezia nella vita privata dalle origini alla caduta della repubblica,* 7th ed., 3 vols. (Bergamo, 1928), 3:360–61. For the information, noted by Dennis Romano, that Venetian patrician families often had residences in several different parishes see Chap. 1 above, n. 1.

12.   Main staircase, Casa Goldoni, formerly Palazzo Centani (Zantani), parish of San Tomà. Photo courtesy of Osvaldo Böhm.

grandfather of the same name, who had reputedly battled the Turks and been brutally killed and dismembered for public display while a governor in Modone.[53] According to one account, it was owing to "the glorious death of his grandfather" that Antonio gained his title of Conte e Cavaliere, bestowed with the accompaniment of an immense privilege by Pope Julius III, who occupied the papacy between 1550 and 1555.[54] Later in life Antonio served as governor of the Ospedale degli Incurabili. One of his memorable acts, as Deputy of Building, was to order in 1566 the erection of a new church modeled on designs of Sansovino.[55] He died before he could see it, in mid-October 1567, and was buried at the church of Corpus Domini.[56]

Music historians remember only two major aspects of Zantani's biography. The first is that he was foiled in trying to publish a collection of four-voice madrigals that included four Petrarch settings from the *Musica nova,* then owned exclusively by the prince of Ferrara. The second is that he patronized musical gatherings at his home—gatherings that involved Perissone, Parabosco, and others in Willaert's circle, as recounted in Orazio Toscanella's dedication to him of his little handbook on world geography, *I nomi antichi, e moderni* (given in full in Appendix, E).

It is well noted that you delight in music, since for so long you paid the company of the Fabretti and the company of the Fruttaruoli, most excellent singers and players, who made the most fine music in your house, and you kept in your pay likewise the incomparable lutenist Giulio dal Pistrino. In the same place convened Girolamo Parabosco, Annibale [Padovano], organist of San Marco, Claudio [Merulo] da Correggio, [also] organist of San Marco, Baldassare Donato, Perissone [Cambio], Francesco Londarit, called "the Greek," and other musicians of immortal fame. One knows very well that you had precious musical works composed and had madrigals printed entitled *Corona di diversi.*[57]

Among the recipients of Zantani's patronage, then, were guilds of instrumentalists and singers, solo lutenists, organists, chapel and chamber singers, and polyphonic composers (primarily of madrigals and *canzoni villanesche*), several of them doubling in various of these roles. Both the Fabretti and the Fruttaruoli were long-established groups. The Fabretti were the official instrumentalists of the doge, performing for many of the outdoor civic festivals, and the Fruttaruoli a confraternity

53. For modern biographies of Antonio's grandfather and father, see Cicogna, *Inscrizioni veneziane* 2:13–14.

54. See Toscanella's dedication to Zantani, *I nomi antichi, e moderni,* fol. [3], with further on Zantani's family, heraldry, etc. The origins of Zantani's knighthood with Julius III would seem to be confirmed by a manuscript book on arms written by Zantani and titled "Antonio Zantani conte e cavaliere del papa Iulio Terzo da Monte," as reported by Cicogna, *Inscrizioni veneziane* 2:16. If Toscanella was right about the immense size of the privilege, this may account for Zantani's apparent increase in patronage in the early to mid-1550s.

55. See Bernard Aikema and Dulcia Meijers, *Nel regno dei poveri: arte e storia dei grandi ospedali veneziani in età moderna, 1474–1797* (Venice, 1989), p. 132, and Muraro, *Il "libro secondo,"* p. 382.

56. The church was secularized in 1810 and later destroyed; see Giuseppe Tassini, *Curiosità veneziane, ovvero origini della denominazioni stradali di Venezia,* 4th ed. (Venice, 1887), pp. 208–10. On Zantani's death date see Cicogna, *Inscrizioni veneziane* 2:16.

57. See Appendix, E, fol. [2']. The passage was first quoted and trans. in Einstein, *The Italian Madrigal* 1:446–47.

that likewise performed outdoor processions.[58] Apparently Zantani paid members of both the Fabretti and Fruttaruoli over a considerable time and, as Toscanella's wording implies, also kept the lutenist dal Pistrino on regular wages, perhaps as part of his domestic staff. Toscanella did not mean to suggest that these musicians all convened ("concorrevano") at once, but he *was* calling up the idea of collective gatherings in the sense of private musical academies.[59]

Zantani's foiled efforts in music printing might be seen as part of a larger attempt to increase his familial patrimony. In approximately 1556–57 he assembled with the aid of another gentleman, Zuan Iacomo Zorzi, the musical anthology that eventually led to his confrontation with agents protecting the interests of the prince of Ferrara. The anthology was to be published with an ornate title page and with the title *La eletta di tutta la musica intitolata corona di diversi novamente stampata: libro primo* (Plate 13).[60] Zorzi contributed a dedication addressed to none other than Zantani himself (Plate 14)—this despite the fact that Zantani was not only the print's backer but in reality its chief owner and producer. Zorzi's dedication praised

---

58. The latter were named for their renowned promenade on the so-called Feast of the Melons, which reenacted an occasion when they had been feted with melons by Doge Steno—an honor that they repeated ritually in every first year of a doge's reign by bearing melons in great flowered chests and small silver basins on a certain day in August and processing with trumpets, drums, and mace bearers from the campo of Santa Maria Formosa through the Merceria and piazza San Marco to the Ducal Palace. For further information see Giuseppe Tassini, *Curiosità veneziane, ovvero origini delle denominazioni stradali di Venezia,* rev. ed. Lino Moretti (Venice, 1988), pp. 266–67: "[L]a confraternita dei Fruttajuoli, eretta fino dal 1423, aveva qui un ospizio composto di 19 camere, ed un oratorio sacro a S. Giosafatte. Quest'arte, unita a quella degli Erbajuoli, aveva un altro oratorio dedicato alla medesimo santo presso la chiesa di S. Maria Formosa. I Fruttajuoli col Erbajuoli erano gli eroi della cosi detta festa dei *Meloni.* Dovendo essi presentare al doge nel mese d'agosto del primo anno del di lui principato un regalo di *meloni* (poponi), solevano nel giorno determinato raccorsi in *Campo di S. Maria Formosa,* e per la *Merceria,* e per la *Piazza di S. Marco,* preceduti dallo stendardo di S. Nicolò e da trombe, tamburri e mazzieri [mace-bearers], recarsi in corpo a palazzo, portando i poponi in grande ceste infiorate, e sopra argentei bacini. Introdotti nella *Sala del Banchetto,* complivano il doge per mezo del loro avvocato, poscia gli facevano offrire da due putti un sonetto ed un mazzolino di fiori, e finalmente fra mezzo le grida di *Viva il Serenissimo!* consegnavano i poponi allo scalco ducale."

59. We can deduce what stretch of time Toscanella's description covered by considering the musicians' biographies. Of the madrigalists mentioned, Parabosco came to Venice around 1540, Perissone at least by 1544, and Donato by 1545, whereas the minor composer and contralto Londariti was hired into the chapel at San Marco only in 1549 (see Chap. 9 below, n. 4 and passim). By 1557 Parabosco had died. Londariti left the chapel around the same time (see Ongaro, "The Chapel of St. Mark's," pp. 187–88, who dates his departure between 6 April 1556 and 10 December 1558), and Perissone had most likely passed away by 1562 (ibid., p. 165 n. 194 and Document 272).

Giulio dal Pistrino is almost undoubtedly the same as Giulio Abondante, who published five books of lute music (three extant) between 1546 and 1587. See Henry Sybrandy, "Abondante, Giulio," in *The New Grove* 1:20, and Luigi F. Tagliavini, "Abondante, Giulio," *Dizionario biografico degli italiani* 1:55–56.

The organists Padovano and Merulo did not enter San Marco until 1552 and 1557, respectively, Merulo having taken Parabosco's place on the latter's death; but Padovano, true to his name, was a Paduan who had long been in the area, and Merulo has been placed in Venice at least as early as 1555. The latest information on these organists has been amassed by Rebecca A. Edwards, "Claudio Merulo: Servant of the State and Musical Entrepreneur in Later Sixteenth-Century Venice" (Ph.D. diss., Princeton University, 1990), to whom I am grateful for sharing various information before her dissertation was filed. On Padovano and his family, see Edwards, p. 94 n. 27. Edwards speculates that since Merulo witnessed a document for Zantani in Venice on 27 November 1555 (p. 214 n. 2) he may have been studying in Venice for some time before 1555, possibly under Parabosco (pp. 269–70). Merulo's close ties with Parabosco can be deduced from the dedication of the latter's *Quattro libri delle lettere amorose* (Venice, 1607) by the editor Thomaso Porcacchi, who called Merulo "ora molto intrinseco del Parabosco che glie l'haveva lasciate [i.e., *le lettere*] in mano avanti la sua morte"; see Edwards, p. 1 n. 1. Edwards also establishes that the printer and bookseller Bolognino Zaltieri, whom Toscanella names as having engaged him to assemble *I nomi antichi, e moderni* ("diede carico à me in particolare di raccorre . . . i Nomi antichi, & moderni," fol. [2]), was one of Merulo's partners; see Chap. 3 and Chap. 4, pp. 217–18.

60. The "corona" was probably a reference to the Zantani family heraldry. See Appendix, E, fol. [3].

13.   *La eletta di tutta la musica intitolata corona di diversi novamente stampata:*
libro primo (Venice, 1569), title page. Photo courtesy of Musikabteilung der Bayerischen
Staatsbibliothek, Munich.

AL L'ILLVSTRE ET
HONORATO SIGNORE
IL SIGNOR ANTONIO ZANTANI
CONTE E CAVALIER MERITISSIMO.

RA TVTTE le cose nobili e che fanno fede qua giu tra noi della marauigliosa grandezza delle cose del cielo: vna è la Musica senza alcun fallo; perciò ch'ella è quasi l'anima delle cose superiori; & l'anima nostra è composta di Musica come vogliano alcuni; la onde non senza cagione ella diletta non solamente gli huomini ma le fere ancora se si die creder a quel che si ragiona d'Orfeo: di questa adunque dilettandomi io sommamente & hauendo raccolto & fatto vna Eletta de cose notabile & honorate in questa materia così stampate come non stampate ho voluto darle al mondo, ma sotto il nome celebre di V. S. Clarissima, percioche douendosi proportionare il dono alla persona a cui se dona io non ho trouato niuno altro mio Signore che sia piu meriteuole a questo presente di V. S. Illustre; conciosia che si noi discorremo le belle qualità dell'animo di V. S. & le honoratissime parte che sono in lei: vedremo vna mirabil Musica non solamente nella proportion del suo corpo ma anco dell'animo; la qual Musica è così dilettuole a coloro che conoscono la S. V. ch'ella è bastante a farueli obligati in eterno come sono io, dall'altro canto: vi si conuiene anco questo presente: percioche per consentimento d'ogniuno V. S. è il padre de Musici: de i letterati de gli Scultori, de gli architetti, de Pittori, Antiquarij; & finalmente d'ogni altra sorte di huomini honorati la onde meritamente vi si debbe, ella adunque con la mano della sua smisurata cortesia aggradisca la mia bona volontà: la quale in questo & in ogni altra cosa è prontissimo a ogni volere di V. S. illustre alla quale humilmente mi raccomando.

D. V. S.

Humilissimo seruitor

Zuan Iacomo di Zorzi.

14 . *La eletta di tutta la musica intitolata corona di diversi novamente stampata: libro primo* (Venice, 1569), dedication from Zuan Iacomo Zorzi to Antonio Zantani. Photo courtesy of Musikabteilung der Bayerischen Staatsbibliothek, Munich.

Zantani as the "'padre' of musicians, literati, sculptors, architects, painters, antiquarians . . . [and] all sorts of honored men."

The anthology (or most of it) was apparently printed by about 1558 but not issued until 1569, ten years after the Ferrarese had brought out the *Musica nova*. It is worth recounting a bit of the well-known story behind the print and its relation to

Willaert's *Musica nova*,[61] because it tells us a lot about Zantani's character and about the new function Petrarchan tropes and styles assumed in helping to define identity in a thickly populated urban world. Zorzi had secured the original privilege for *La eletta* in 1556, but Zantani immediately had it transferred to his own name. Apparently he wanted to avoid the vulgar process of procuring the privilege himself, which it was the usual business of printers to do.[62] On 19 January 1557 Zorzi was granted the privilege for the print along with approval to essay a new printing technique. And both were transferred to Zantani on 29 March 1557.[63]

The anthology was obviously hot property from the start. In addition to Willaert's previously unpublished Petrarch settings, it included new works by Willaert's prominent disciples Donato and Perissone.[64] Unlike the *Musica nova*, *La eletta* was planned from the outset as an appealing four-voice potpourri. The reader for *La eletta*'s Venetian license summarized its literary contents as "diverse types of poems" such as "canzoni, *sonetti*, madrigali, sestine, ballate, and so forth . . . treating youthful topics and amorous emotions."[65]

Ironically, this project brought the Cavaliere more lasting notoriety than any of his other ventures. When Zantani planned the publication he undoubtedly intended the settings from the *Musica nova* to crown it. He probably got hold of them through his connection with Willaert's three protégés, Parabosco, Perissone, and Donato: it was they who, between 1545 and 1553, had published parallel settings imitating those that later became part of Willaert's *Musica nova* collection and who therefore must have had closest access to them.[66] As it turned out, however, Polissena Pecorina had already sold the whole corpus (or something close to the printed version of it) with sole rights to Prince Alfonso d'Este, who meant to have it published by Gardane in an exclusive complete edition. The news that Zantani's

61. For a retelling of the story with illuminating new details and copious documentation see Richard J. Agee and Jessie Ann Owens, "La stampa della *Musica nova* di Willaert," *Rivista italiana di musicologia* 24 (1989): 219–305. The authors were kind enough to share the article with me in typescript before its publication. Since Agee and Owens publish all of the relevant documents thus far known, I cite their article for documents, including ones first unearthed by others.

62. Agee and Owens, "La stampa della *Musica nova*," Document 7, pp. 246–47. The documents directly concerning printing privileges were nearly all first transcribed in Richard J. Agee, "The Privilege and Venetian Music Printing in the Sixteenth Century" (Ph.D. diss., Princeton University, 1982).

63. Ibid., Documents 9 and 10, pp. 248–49 (originally located by Martin Morell), which mention the use of new characters and staves.

64. The settings by Rore, Ferrabosco, Francesco dalla Viola, Heinrich Schaffen, and Ivo had all been published before 1556. The three settings by Donato were not brought out elsewhere until Donato's *Secondo libro a 4* was issued in 1568. Three of Perissone's four were still unique in 1569 (a fourth had come out in Gardane's print *De diversi autori il quarto libro de madrigali a quattro voci a note bianche novamente dato in luce* (Venice, 1554); Vogel/Einstein 1554¹; RISM 1554²⁸). This left only the following settings (in addition to Perissone's) as apparently unique to *La eletta* when it was finally issued: single madrigals by Giachet Berchem and Sperindio and a group of eight settings by Giovan Contino, all clustered toward the end of the volume. In all, its cultural capital had radically dropped.

65. See the reader's report for the license cited in Agee and Owens, "La stampa della *Musica nova*," Document 4, dated 28 November 1556: "ho letto, et ben esaminato alcune rime diverse, poste in canto, et altre volte stampate, come sono Canzoni, Sonetti, Madrigali, Sestine, Ballate, etcetera né in quelle ho ritrovato cosa contra nostra Santa fede né contra l'honore et fama di alcun principe, Et con tutto che trattino materie giovanili, et affetti amorosi, non sono però tali, che non si possino stampare senza pericolo che corrompino gli buoni costumi" (p. 245).

66. See Chap. 9 below.

print was to be issued imminently with Willaert's four-voice madrigals came to the prince's attention only in late 1558, setting off a volley of hostile exchanges between a whole cast of characters, Venetian and Ferrarese: Zantani; the unhappy Ferrarese ambassador in Venice, Girolamo Faleti; Alfonso's secretary at home, Giovanni Battista Pigna; and Alfonso's father, Duke Ercole.[67]

Clearly Zantani had pinned great expectations on his intended *Corona,* in which he had already invested considerable labor and funds by Christmas 1558, when notice of it reached the sponsors of *Musica nova* in Ferrara.[68] In the battle that ensued, Zantani turned hot with anger and humiliation. A famous letter to Faleti from late 1558 sputtered indignantly at the idea that those two "mecanici" Gardane and Zarlino should be allowed to hamper the well-laid plans of a nobleman like himself.

> I would never have thought that you would ever create such displeasure about something by which I am made unhappy or that you would give such trouble as you have to the petition of certain tradesmen like Gardane and Father Gioseffe Zarlino and, without giving me to understand anything, order me now to dispense with the four madrigals taken out of the book of Mr. Adrian . . . (and not even taken out in such numbers as they are [found] in that book); and they have removed your authority ["mezo"] and that of your excellent Duke. To you I am just a servant of yours and moreover to Francesco dalla Viola and those other mercenary people. But you know very well that my father was a *consigliere* and always very favored in his dealings even by the doge and now I on the contrary must accept this offense. I can never believe that the Duke should want to create such vexation not only for me but all my relatives. I tell you now that my privilege is also [at issue] here and in my petition it says that I was making "a selection from all the madrigals both printed and not printed" and this was in 1556. But I turn to you and say that I will be grieved by you interminably that for four madrigals you should use me thus.[69]

67. Pecorina's role and many details of these exchanges were first brought to light by Anthony Newcomb, "Editions of Willaert's *Musica Nova:* New Evidence, New Speculations," *JAMS* 26 (1973): 132–45. Other studies have followed up on this and various other aspects of the *Musica nova*'s printing history, namely David S. Butchart, " 'La Pecorina' at Mantua, *Musica Nova* at Florence," *Early Music* 13 (1985): 358–66, and most recently Agee and Owens, "La Stampa della *Musica Nova.*"

68. Agee and Owens, "La stampa della *Musica nova,*" Document 48, pp. 276–77 (see also n. 71 below).

69. Ibid., Document 45, p. 274: "Io non harei mai pensato che V. S. mi fese mai dispiacer né cosa che per lei mi dolese e dese fastidio che a peticion de certi mecanici come è il Gardana, Pre Isepo Zerlin, senza averme mai fato intender cosa alcuna, farmi far hora comandamento ch'io dispena quatro madrigali tolti fuora del libro di m. Adriano et non più in tanto numero che sono in quel libro et hano tolto il vostro mezo e della eccellentia del signior duca. Io li son ancora mi suo servitor et piu di Francesco Dalla Viola et st'altri mercenarii et sa ben V. S. che sempre che mio padre esta consegier ancio[?] dose si è stato sempre favorevole in le cose sue et che hora mo alincontro per ben io deeba [sic] ricever mal io non posso mai creder che'l signior duca mi voglia usarmi dispiacer non solum a me, ma eciam a tutto il mio parentado. Io ve dicho che'l mio privilegio si è ancian a questo et in la mia suplica dice ch'io ho fato una selta de tutti i madrigali cusì in stampa come non in stampa et questo fo del 1556 ma vi torno adir che [   ] mi dolarò di voi in sempiterno che per quatro madrigali usarme tal termine." The letter is undated, but Agee and Owens note that it was written no later than 6 December 1558. Facs. in *Die Musik in Geschichte und Gegenwart,* vol. 14, cols. 671–72. My translation does not attempt to eliminate the awkwardness of the original.

On the positions held by Antonio's father, who became a *consigliere* to doge Lorenzo Priuli in 1557, see G. B. di Crollalanza, *Dizionario storico-blasonico delle famiglie nobili e notabili italiane estinte e fiorenti,* 3 vols. (Pisa, 1886–90; repr. Bologna, 1965) 3:119.

To Zantani's mind the Ferrarese were launching a direct assault on his kin and his venerable social status. In the wake of the feud Zantani was even contemplating a lawsuit. Owing to the machinations of Pigna he did not follow through on this. Pigna enlisted the efforts of the weary Faleti to urge Zantani away from jeopardizing Prince Alfonso's good graces simply in order to thwart a lowly composer like Francesco dalla Viola, who was only engineering the publication on the prince's behalf.[70] On Christmas Day 1558, after securing Zantani's reluctant cooperation, Faleti wrote a beleaguered report to Duke Ercole, updating him on the current state of affairs. Here we see Zantani's ire in a profoundly Venetian light.[71] The Ferrarese should not imagine that it is in *Faleti*'s power to make the Cavaliere stop sounding his case and stop trying to retain his privilege in order not to lose a "great deal of money that he has spent in printing his work." For "it is the custom of this Republic to let everyone be heard, not to say one of their most principal nobles, for whom so many have by now exerted themselves."[72]

Nonetheless, after all rank had been pulled, it was Ercole and Alfonso who came off victors—courtly princes over city nobles. Zantani apparently agreed reluctantly to delay publication of *La eletta* for a ten-year period. When it was finally issued, with Zorzi's dedication to Zantani, the Cavaliere had been dead for two years.

———————

These musical activities formed part of a dense thicket of patronage activities discernible through both dialogic writings and art-historical chronicles. All told, they reveal Zantani as an avid collectionist, who added music as part of the vernacular arts to other artifacts favored by Venetian antiquarian types, especially medals, antiques, and portraits. All of these were common fare among local patricians, who heaped honor on their families' names by their systematic additions to domestic patrimony. Antonio stands apart from most other patrons in actually performing the labors of some of the artisanal crafts he patronized. In addition to the music-printing technique he invented, he produced his own prints of engraved coins.[73] He practiced the art of engraving himself, as well as painting and, even more surprisingly, the gentler work of embroidery.[74]

Zantani's dual roles as amateur artisan and collector were brought together most intensely in his work with medals. In time he assembled one of the most noted medal collections of his day and by 1548 collaborated with the famous engraver

70. Agee and Owens, "La stampa della *Musica nova*," Document 47, pp. 275–76.

71. Ibid., Document 48, pp. 276–77.

72. "[S]e questi pensano che sia di mio potere il fare che predetto Cavaliere non produca le sue ragioni a diffesa sua et a mantenimento del suo privileggio per non perdere una grossa spesa che ha fatto nel stampar l'opera sua, s'ingannano, essendo costume di questa Republica il dar modo a tutti che siano uditi nelle loro ragioni, ne che a uno de principalissimi suoi gentil'huomeni a favore del quale homai tanti si sono messi" (ibid.).

73. On the former see ibid., Documents 9 and 10, pp. 248–49.

74. See Toscanella, *I nomi antichi, e moderni,* fol. [2′]: "Non è nascoso ancora, che S. S. C. dipinge, ricama, & intaglia sopra ogni credenza bene."

Enea Vico in producing *Le imagini con tutti i riversi trovati et le vite de gli imperatori tratte dalle medaglie et dalle historie de gli antichi. Libro primo,* a book of medals depicting the first twelve Roman emperors together with a large variety of reverses portraying their lives.[75]

Zantani may well have printed *Le imagini* himself, or at least been centrally involved in doing so. Embedded in the elegant title page was the Zantani coat of arms and at the base of the left-hand column Zantani's crest showing a leopard and a scimitar in memory of his grandfather's bravery (Plate 15). On the final recto is Zantani's printer's mark, a device of a leashed dog (Plate 16), decorated with two mottoes that locate the crafts of printing and engraving within standard themes of civic virtue: "Solus honor" and "Malo mori quam transgredi" ("Only honor" and "I would rather die than transgress"). The dog, as it turns out, occupied a special place in Zantani's symbolic system. The only painting Zantani is undisputably known to have commissioned was one done by Jacopo dal Ponte around 1550 of Zantani's two hounds (Plate 17).[76] Moreover, elements of canine iconography found in *Le imagini* reappeared on the title page of *La eletta* (Plate 13), where a leashed dog was positioned at the base of the cartouche with Zantani's mottoes draped around the dog's tree and on the crown at the top. Within this symbolic network the dog represented honor and fidelity. As the first substantial artifact that Zantani bequeathed to posterity, *Le imagini* thus designates an ethical and intellectual space with intriguing symbolic links to the views of patrimonial objects he later expressed concerning *La eletta*. While speaking outwardly to collecting, *Le imagini*'s prefaces and plates moralize ancient history as the vaunted prototype for sixteenth-century forms of patriarchy.

Zantani clearly did not do any of the actual engraving for the volume; rather, he allotted to himself the tasks of writing two prefaces and collecting and organizing the medals' reverses, with representations of the emperors' careers.[77] At the outset of the prefaces Zantani insists that his main labor, that of comprehending the totality of the emperors' lives and deeds in visual portrayals, has been a historical one. The reader's task, he claims, should (like his) be to consider the ancients' actions with the intellect

75. Aretino's praise of this work in a letter dated April 1548 suggests it had been already printed by that month (*Lettere* 4:207'; repr. in *Lettere sull'arte* 2:215–16). The projected second book was never published, and in some copies (like that at Harvard) the words "Libro primo" have been scraped away. On *Le imagini* see also Marino Zorzi, ed., *Collezioni di antichità a Venezia nei secoli della repubblica (dai libri e documenti della Biblioteca Marciana)* (Rome, 1988), pp. 70–71.

76. I am grateful to David Rosand for this information (private communication) and for sending me proofs from Muraro, *Il "libro secondo,"* which documents that the commission was made in 1548 and paid for in 1550 (pp. 70–71). The painting was acquired by the Louvre while this book was in press.

77. This is the division of labor suggested by Vico in his *Discorsi . . . sopra le medaglie de gli antichi divisi in due libri* (Venice, 1558), where he refers to the "medaglie di rame di Augusto, nel libro de' riversi de' primi XII. Cesari da me fatto e gia in luce (di cui è stato autore l'honorato cavalliere m. Anton Zantani)" (p. 84). It is not absolutely certain who published the book, but Zantani is the most likely candidate since his family arms appear on the title page; see Crollalanza, *Dizionario storico-blasonico* 3:119/2, and Eugenio Morando di Custoza, *Libro d'arme di Venezia* (Verona, 1979), *tavola* CCCLXXX, no. 3413. The Latin translation of the work issued in 1553 as *Omnium caesarum verissime imagines ex antiquis numismatis desumptae* replaced Zantani's arms with the lion of Venice and made various other alterations; the entry in the National Union Catalogue attributes the printing of this later volume to Paolo Manuzio, as does Ruth Mortimer, *Harvard College Library, Department of Printing and Graphic Arts: Catalogue of Books and Manuscripts,* pt. 2, *Italian Sixteenth-Century Books,* vol. 2 (Cambridge, Mass., 1974), p. 778.

15.   *Le imagini con tutti i riversi trovati et le vite de gli imperatori tratte dalle medaglie et dalle historie de gli antichi: libro primo* (Venice, 1548), title page. Photo courtesy of the University of Chicago, Special Collections.

16. *Le imagini con tutti i riversi trovati et le vite de gli imperatori tratte dalle medaglie et dalle historie de gli antichi: libro primo* (Venice, 1548), printer's mark. Photo courtesy of the University of Chicago, Special Collections.

as much as to gaze at their portraits with the eyes.[78] This admonishment precipitates an awkward moral lesson. From looking and reading "one sees and appreciates the value of virtue, to what unhappiness wrongdoing leads, of what profit is honest conversation, how easily men's thoughts change, how a virtuous man is really free and an evil one a servant, and finally how no one can escape the providence of God in receiving either penalties or rewards."[79] As the embodiment of the virtues Zantani aimed to depict, the emperors' lives were necessarily idealized to mirror the mythologized self-imagery that made Venice out as a new Rome.[80] This preoccupation with moral ques-

78. "[I]o intendo di dare in luce le imagini de gli imperatori tratte dalle antiche medaglie con tutte quelle maniere di riversi che alle mani pervenute mi sono, come che non picciol fatica in ciò habbi havuta, & aggiugnervi la somma delle vite, & operationi fatte da quegli. . . . Prendete adunque ò lettori questa dimostratione di buona volontate verso voi, & quanto con l'occhio del corpo riguarderete le effigie de gli antichi, tanto con il lume dello intelletto considerate le loro attioni, prendendo que'begli essempi del vivere, che si convengono" (*Le imagini,* p. [4]).
79. "Poca è la fatica di guardare, & di leggere, ma la utilitate, & il frutto è copioso, & grande, perche si vede, & istima quanto può la virtute, à che infelicitade si volga l'errore, di quale giovamento sia l'honesta conversatione, come agevolmente si mutano i pensieri de gli huomini, come uno virtuoso è veramente libero, & uno scelerato servo. & finalmente come niuno fugge la providentia di Dio nel ricevere le pene, ò i premi, ch'egli s'habbia meritato" (ibid., pp. [4]–[5]).
80. Only occasionally did he counterbalance the representations with moral criticism (some of Nero's reverses depict courtesans, plunder, and the like).

17.   Jacopo dal Ponte, *Portrait of Two Hounds* (*Due bracchi*), ca. 1550. Commissioned by Antonio Zantani in 1548, paid for 1550. Private collection.

tions was to return in a little literary composition of his, the "Dubbi morali del cavaliere Centani"—a brief contribution to a popularizing ethics organized into a pedantic series of questions and responses on temperance, abstinence, and honesty.[81]

In the last analysis Zantani begged any exegetical questions that might emerge from these exercises. While he could have "interpreted and made declarations about the reverses," Zantani wrote, he believed such an effort in many ways to be "difficult and vain" and so left this to the judgment of each individual.[82] Even this he turns to moral account, for true judgment is seen as an act of divination, the revelation of a stable reality whose truth is unassailable. After all, "it can easily happen that the contin-

81. Zantani's "Dubbi morali" is found in Book II of the *Quattro libri de dubbi con le solutioni a ciascun dubbio accommodate,* published by Giolito (whose name does not appear on the title page) and ed. by Ortensio Landi (Venice, 1552), pp. 174–76. The volume is discussed by Salvatore Bongi, *Annali di Gabriel Giolito de' Ferrari,* 2 vols. (Rome, 1890–97; repr. Rome, n.d., 1:368–70. On Zantani's composition of "dubbi amorosi" for another volume edited by Landi see Muraro, *Il "libro secondo,"* p. 382 (I have not seen the latter "dubbi").

82. "Io poteva . . . forzarmi nella presente opera de interpretare, & dichiarire i riversci delle medaglie, ma riputando io tale fatica in molte parti essere & difficile, & vana, ho voluto lasciare al giudicio di ciescaduno questa cura, & pensiero" (*Le imagini,* p. [6]).

ual diligence of some students . . . may reveal fitting and true interpretations, [while] many others [are] sooner apt to guess than to judge the truth."[83] "The risk of error is very great," he cautions, "and the fruits dubious and few."[84] His preference was the wordless language of pictures and his pleasure the tasks of taxonomy: organizing the reverses into a visual chronicle, separating copper ones from gold and silver, and the like. Less verbal than many of his fellow patricians, Zantani nonetheless longed for the same moralized polity represented by good olden times and timeless old goods.

The moralizing tone Zantani adopted in *Le imagini* and in the "Dubbi" recalls many writers' emphases on Helena's virtue—a virtue that was mutually produced through encomiastic representations of her and through her own forms of social action. Like many Venetian noblewomen Helena seems not only to have stood for ideals of virtue but to have lived out her personal life in pious acts of charity. Toward the end of her life, on 22 June 1580, she organized such acts in a lengthy and detailed will inscribed by her own hand (Appendix, D). Following Venetian tradition she requested a burial "senza alcun pompa" in the same arch of the church of Corpus Domini where her father-in-law and husband were buried. For the rest she mostly specified distributions of alms: ten-ducat sums to various churches, institutions of charity, and to the prisoners of the Fortezza, altogether totaling one hundred ducats; ten-ducat dowries for three needy girls; all of her woolen and leather fabrics among "our poor relatives"; and the release of all her debtors.[85]

By comparison, Antonio's enactments of virtue took more public and symbolic forms. At the crux of his collecting activities was a family museum that bound civic virtue together with patrimonial fame. In keeping with this, the legacy of Zantani's work with medals not only presents him in the guise of moralist but shows him in the archetypal mold prevalent from the fifteenth century of the Venetian antiquarian engrossed by the ancient world and intent on preserving the past. In some forms, this sort of preservation could take merely fetishistic and sterile forms of

83. "[M]olto bene possa avvenire, che la continova diligenza d'alcuni studiosi, accompagnata dal giudicio, & bello intendimento di varie cose, possa ritrovare acconcie, & vere interpretationi, & molti altri essere atti piu presto ad indovinare, che giudicare la verità" (ibid.).

84. "[I]l rischio di errare è grandissimo, il frutto dubbio, & poco, & molto habbia dello impossibile per l'oscurità delle cose avolte nella longhezza, & nella ingiuria del tempo: percioche le cose dalla memoria nostra lontane sogliono seco recare ignoranza, & l'antichita guasta, & corrompe i segni di quelle" (ibid.).

85. Helena's will resembles those of other patrician women in Venice, whose bequests emphasized private relations with neighbors, servants, and friends, charitable institutions, and bilateral and natal kinship relations over and above the patriline. Among studies that have dealt with this question, see Stanley Chojnacki, "Dowries and Kinsmen in Early Renaissance Venice," *Journal of Interdisciplinary History* 5 (1975): 571–600; Donald E. Queller and Thomas Madden, "Father of the Bride: Fathers, Daughters, and Dowries in Late Medieval and Early Renaissance Venice," *RQ* 46 (1993): 685–711, esp. p. 707; and (most importantly for the sixteenth century) Dennis Romano, "Aspects of Patronage in Fifteenth- and Sixteenth-Century Venice," *RQ* 46 (1993): 712–33, esp. pp. 721–23 on female testators. Romano distinguishes between a "primary system" of patronage, with objects as the *product* (as generated by commissions) and a "secondary system" of patronage with objects as the *sign* (as effected through donations and bequests). Wills, for Romano, formed central instruments for the enactment of secondary forms of patronage, not least because they were relatively public in nature. In Helena's case, they represent a prime documentary source for our knowledge of how such patronage ensured the female patrician's virtue and the salvation of her soul through the care of less fortunate social ranks and thus pulled her acts into a complex circulation of culturally encoded goods and favors between high and low.

collectionism. Yet most Venetian antiquarians did not simply accumulate items piecemeal but made systematic acquisitions of vases, numismata, engraved jewels, and other antique artifacts, organizing them as a means of honoring the ancestral home. This is the end that is consolidated through production of *Le imagini,* as affirmed by the prominent Zantani iconography that decorates its title page.

In the sixteenth century antiquarians increasingly complemented their domestic patrimony with portraiture. Titian's painting of Helena, now apparently lost, could well have been Antonio's commission, forming part of larger patterns of acquisition no longer visible to us.[86] Venetians often purchased Flemish paintings, thus paralleling the acquisitions of Venetian musical patrons.[87] Here we can begin to piece together the cult of Helena, the cultivation of northern polyphony (and painting), and the antique collectionism that in combination marked Antonio's world. All three constituted precious components in the patrimonial order. Objects distant in both time and place formed monuments to the breadth and power of his family estate, in which Helena was central as both image and property. It seems almost inconceivable that an interested party like Zantani, much accustomed to shaping the creative forces around him, did not have a hand in constructing the cult formed around his wife. How different would such constructions have been from a monument to his medal collection like *Le imagini* or a testimonial to his salon like *La eletta?* The allusive networks within which such encomia and commemorations existed—and into which dialogic modes drew their practitioners more generally— were animated by the complex exchanges of goods, favor, speech, and song that created value and fame.[88]

86. Titian's portrait is not dealt with among the lost portraits taken up in the comprehensive catalogue of Titian's works by Harold E. Wethey, who apparently missed Aretino's reference to it; see *The Paintings of Titian: Complete Edition,* 2 vols. (New York, 1971), vol. 2, *The Portraits.* Vasari's portrait did have its genesis in a familial commission, but from Helena's brother Antonio Barozzi. Vasari's notebook records the portrait as follows: "Ricordo come adi 10 di marzo 1542 Messer Andrea Boldu Gentiluomo Venetiano mj allogò dua ritrattj dal mezzo la figura insu[;] uno era Madonna Elena Barozzi et [l'altro era] Messer Angelo suo fratello de qualj ne facemo mercato che fra tuttj dua dovessi avere scudi venti doro cioè scudi 21" (*Il libro delle ricordanze di Giorgio Vasari,* ed. Alessandro del Vita [Rome, 1938], p. 39).

On sixteenth-century collections that mixed antiques and portraits see, for instance, Logan's description, which matches Toscanella's representation of Zantani: "Two possible ancestors of the Renaissance art collection are the collection of family relics and memorials and the antiquarian collection. The first Venetian family museums in the fifteenth century were . . . of the former kind—collections of arms and banners and other family relics—and doubtless in such shrines to the family *lares* and *penates* many sixteenth-century portraits found a natural place. The evidence suggests, however, that the systematic collection of works of art tended to be more closely associated with the collection of antique objects"; see Oliver Logan, *Culture and Society in Venice, 1470–1790: The Renaissance and Its Heritage* (New York, 1972), p. 153.

87. On antiquarianism in Venice and the Veneto see Lanfranco Franzoni, "Antiquari e collezionisti nel cinquecento," in *Storia della cultura veneta,* vol. 3, *Dal primo quattrocento al Concilio di Trento,* pt. 3, ed. Girolamo Arnaldi and Manlio Pastore Stocchi (Vicenza, 1981), pp. 207–66. For a good general discussion of the phenomenon, with analysis of certain Venetian collections described in Marcantonio Michiel's *Anonimo Morelliano,* see Logan, *Culture and Society in Venice,* pp. 152–59. Logan reports that three-quarters of Venetian antiquarians also owned foreign paintings, with Flemish ones predominating. He adds that in general "the number of Flemish works tended to be in proportion to the size of the antique collection" (p. 158), and suggests that some of this may be accounted for by the trade lines through which both were acquired.

88. For a fine anthropological treatment of the politics and forms of commodity exchange in social life see Arjun Appadurai, "Introduction: Commodities and the Politics of Value," in *The Social Life of Things: Commodities in Cultural Perspective,* ed. Arjun Appadurai (Cambridge, 1988), pp. 3–63.

Here we might return to our starting point: the anxieties over the fashioning and winning of fame revealed in the dialogics of print culture by which we mainly come to know the Zantani. These anxieties had been adumbrated two centuries earlier in Petrarch's own verse, which called attention to the poet through his amorous obsession and his paradoxical complaints over the appropriation of his lyrics by the common fold. Central to the Venetians' construction of fame, apropos, was Petrarch's devotion in the *Canzoniere* to the cult of a single woman, a woman now often transformed into real flesh and blood, given voice, and sometimes satirized as sexually available. In all such forms, conventional and inverted, Petrarch's lyrics still provided the Renaissance master trope for figures of praise. As many critics have been quick to point out, moreover, Petrarch's praise of Laura is at root a monument to his own literary creation and the creation of his own self, as symbolized by the poet's laurel (the wreath of poetic achievement) and embodied in the verbal kinship *Laura* and *laurel* are given in his lyrics. This idea subtends the now classic semiotic analysis of Petrarch's poetic strategy proposed by John Freccero.[89] In Freccero's words, Petrarch's laurel is "the emblem of the mirror relationship *Laura-Lauro,* which is to say the poetic lady created by the poet, who in turn creates him as poet laureate."[90] Restated in the balder terms of my analysis, what Petrarch demonstrated to later generations was not only how to praise others but how to make praise of others serve as praise of oneself. This idea is wedded to more recent notions of Petrarch's special role in early modern culture in establishing selfhood not just as an ideological site of subjectivity and autonomy but as a socially embedded site of agency and self-invention—"self-fashioning," as it has come to be called in the coinage of Stephen Greenblatt.[91]

Critics since Freccero have elaborated the importance Petrarch's covert strategies of self-exaltation and self-fashioning assumed for the lyric in subsequent centuries. One of the most provocative commentaries comes from Nancy J. Vickers in her essay "Vital Signs: Petrarch and Popular Culture."[92] Vickers's interest lies in the continuities between Petrarch's tropes and the tropes prevalent in present-day popular lyrics, a continuity she sees made possible by our technological capacity for wide-

---

89. "The Fig Tree and the Laurel: Petrarch's Poetics," *Diacritics* 5 (1975): 34–40.

90. Ibid., p. 37.

91. I refer to Greenblatt's *Renaissance Self-Fashioning: From More to Shakespeare* (Chicago, 1980) but also to more exclusively literary statements on the matter, notably Thomas Greene, "The Flexibility of the Self in Renaissance Literature," in *The Disciplines of Criticism: Essays in Literary Theory, Interpretation, and History,* ed. Peter Demetz, Thomas Greene, and Lowry Nelson, Jr. (New Haven, 1968), pp. 241–64, as well as the general notions of individuality as a salient feature of Renaissance culture, as defined by Jacob Burckhardt in the nineteenth century. On Petrarch's specific role in this process see Arnaud Tripet, *Pétrarque, ou la connaissance de soi* (Geneva, 1967), Giuseppe Mazzotta, "The *Canzoniere* and the Language of the Self," *Studies in Philology* 75 (1978): 271–96, and most recently (and importantly), Albert Russell Ascoli, "Petrarch's Middle Age: Memory, Imagination, History, and the 'Ascent of Mount Ventoux,'" *Stanford Italian Review* 10 (1992): 5–43.

92. *Romanic Review* 79 (1988): 184–95. For Petrarch's ambivalence about his appropriation by the common people see Vickers's analysis on p. 195 of a passage from his *Familiari.* Other studies locating Petrarchism in specific historical time and place that have influenced my recent thinking include those cited in n. 3 above.

spread reproduction of words and sounds. For Vickers, continuities within high lyric verse cannot alone account for the vast temporal and cultural dispersion of Petrarchan texts as material identities. They cannot account for what she calls "the multidirectional exchanges between high, middle, and popular cultures so radically enabled by the reconstitutions of the work of art in the age of mechanical reproduction."[93] Here Vickers speaks of the culture of late-twentieth-century rock music. Yet her observations on how radically dispersed themes are inherited and traded between different social strata resonate with my own. For like her I am interested in how repetitions of Petrarchan tropes served to make famous the objects idolized, as well to create their authors' fame. More specifically, I am interested in how Petrarchan tropes were recast in dialogic forms to fashion fame in a dynamic urban environment. This means an environment receptive to the mobility of a kind of "middle class," of which most professional musicians formed a part, and receptive to the phenomenon of entrepreneurship, in which Venice's many less-established immigrant patrons, as well as musicians, played a role. In the network of compacts formed between patrons and composers we see the dialectic mechanical reproduction formed with Petrarchan music and Petrarchizing words.

APPENDIX: MARCO TRIVISANO

One case that deviates from the norm of the elusive patron as I have characterized it here may be that of Marco Trivisano, to whom Gardane dedicated Willaert's first book of motets for six voices in 1542. According to Gardane's dedication, this Trivisano housed a "most honored *ridotto*" in which "every sort of musical instrument" was kept, where "the most excellent things . . . [were] continuously sung and played" and the most noble persons who delighted in singing and playing habitually retired.[94] More than that, Gardane states that Trivisano himself not only delighted in hearing music but was accomplished in both the theory and practice of it, singing and playing.[95]

The usual presumption holds that this is the same man as the Marcantonio Trevisano (ca. 1475–1554) who served as one of the city's three procurators from 1549 and as doge from 1553 until his death less than a year later. If this is correct, and we may never know for sure, then, owing to his high-ranking position, there are many more writings about him than exist for other musical patrons. Already about sixty-seven years old in 1542, the Trevisano of political fame was remembered for a legendary moral integrity and a personal diffidence that verged on caricaturing the kind of temperament idealized in the official

93. "Vital Signs," p. 185.
94. The passage reads: "io . . . debbo, quanto piu vi posso pregarvi: che con quel bon animo debbiatte, questa cosi . . . rarra coppia di motetti accetare: con il quale à voi, & li dedico, & li sacro & li dono. & etiando fare che essi siano vditi dal Mondo, nel vostro honoratissimo Ridutto a cio eletto: Dove ogni sorte di stromenti Musicali in buona quantita tenete, & ove le piu eccelente cose, che altri cantano, sono continoamente da i piu perfetti Musici cantate, & suonate, & quindi v̀ li piu nobili personaggi, che di canto, di suono si dilettano, molto volentieri si riducono." For a complete reprint of the dedication see Mary S. Lewis, "Antonio Gardane's Connections with the Willaert Circle," in *Music in Medieval and Early Modern Europe: Patronage, Sources and Texts,* ed. Iain Fenlon (Cambridge, 1981), p. 226.
95. "[V]oi siete parimente & nobile & virtuoso, & . . . nella Musica non pure sopramodo vi dilettate: ma di lei ne siete buonissimo professore, ne solamente nella pratica, ma nella Theorica altresi. E si nel Canto, come nel Suono: Impercio che non è stromento Musicale, che con meravigliosa harmonia, & con dolcissima attentione di cui vi ode, non sia da voi ottimamente suonato." Ibid.

state rhetoric I have connected with Willaert's musical style. In his oration for Trevisano's election to the *dogado,* Bernardino Tomitano praised him for serenity, goodness, integrity of mind, innocence of habit, and singular affection for the *patria*.[96] Similarly, an oration composed after his death by Bartolomeo Spathafora devoted four pages to elaborating his qualities of humility, temperance, fortitude, and modesty.[97] And according to Sansovino, Trevisano's mildness and tranquillity of spirit were so great that he would have declined the dogeship but for the duty he felt toward state and kin.[98] One wonders whether Sansovino was trying to rationalize Trevisano's peculiar dogeship, for a controversy arose even during the electoral process over whether Trevisano was too innocent for the task. His subsequent brief rule was distinguished almost entirely by mild Counter-Reformational escalations in civic expressions of piety.[99]

96. *Oratione di M. Bernardino Tomitano, recitata per nome de lo studio de le arti padovano, ne la creatione del serenissimo principe di Vinetia M. Marcantonio Trivisano* (Venice, 1554), fol. 2.

97. *Quattro orationi di M. Bartolomeo Spathafora di Moncata, gentil'huomo venetiano l'una in morte del serenissimo Marc'Antonio Trivisano* . . . (Venice, 1554), pp. 13–33, esp. pp. 23–26. On p. 19 Spathafora wrote, "Egli fu di vita irreprensibile, di prudentia incomparabile, nè solamente giusto, & pietoso, ma liberale, & magnifico in verso la patria."

98. See *Venetia citta nobilissima et singolare descritta in XIII. libri da M. Francesco Sansovino* . . . (Venice, 1581): "Senatore di cosi innocente vita, & singolare per Santità, che si hebbe fatica a fargli accettare il Principato. Perciochè lo huomo ottimo, avezzo a i costumi del tutto lontani dalla mondana grandezza, non sapeva cio che fosse ambitione. Alla fine astretto da i suoi parenti, acconsentì alla volontà loro, contanta humiltà & con tanta modestia, che nulla piu; di maniera che temuto & reverito dall'universale, tenne le cose della giustitia nel suo saldo & inconcusso vigore" (Book 13, fol. 271').

99. For further biographical details see Andrea da Mosto, *I dogi di Venezia nella vita pubblica e privata* (repr., Florence, 1977), pp. 254–59 and 570–71, and Gino Benzoni, ed., *I dogi* (Milan, 1982), pp. 121–22, 145, 188. Trevisano's career up to 1533 may be traced in Marin Sanuto, *I diarii,* ed. Rinaldo Fulin et al., 58 vols. (Venice, 1879–1903).

Chapter 4 · RITUAL LANGUAGE, NEW MUSIC

Encounters in the Academy of Domenico Venier

The previous two chapters have struggled to construct narratives from records of musical patronage that are sketchy at best. My approach has necessarily been bifocal, reading above for concrete particulars and below for deeper cultural meanings, while looking to the dialogics of vernacular exchange to mediate between them. Here I confront a different set of problems in the situation of literary patronage—a patronage at once of and by literati. These figures recorded their ideas and projects in the very media of poems, letters, and dialogues through which I tried to decipher hidden subtexts relevant to musical patronage. They devised the representations of themselves in the same texts in which they pretended to lay themselves bare, manipulating the claims avowed at the outer face of the text. Like the literary critic, the historian must therefore read surface for subsurface, always keeping in view the pressures, pleasures, and performative impulses in which such claims were implicated.

This chapter explores the most prominent literary patron at midcentury, a Venetian patrician named Domenico Venier. Venier lived from 1517 until 1582 and presided for virtually all of his adult life over the most renowned vernacular literary academy in Venice.[1] Consolidated around the mid-forties, the academy became the

---

1. The secondary literature on Venier and his circle is scant. The chief work is Pierantonio Serassi, ed., *Rime di Domenico Veniero senatore viniziano raccolte ora per la prima volta ed illustrate* (Bergamo, 1751), which includes the unique edition of his poetic works as well as a biography. A new edition by Tiziana Agostini Nordio of the Centro Interuniversitario di Studi Veneti, under the general direction of Giorgio Padoan, is currently in preparation. The brief entry on Venier's academy in Michele Maylender, *Storia delle accademie d'Italia*, 5 vols. (Bologna, 1926–30), 5:446, is based on Serassi's work. A few poems are anthologized in Daniele Ponchiroli, ed., *Lirici del cinquecento* (Turin, 1958), pp. 105–12, and Carlo Muscetta and Daniele Ponchiroli, eds., *Poesia del quattrocento e del cinquecento* (Turin, 1959), pp. 1373–77. For a critique of how cinquecento Petrarchists, including Venier, have been anthologized, see Amedeo Quondam, *Petrarchismo mediato: per una critica della forma antologia* (Rome, 1974). On the academy's effects in the second half of the century see some of the literature on Veronica Franco, whom Venier patronized in the 1570s: Riccardo Scrivano, "La poetessa Veronica Franco," in *Cultura e letteratura nel cinquecento* (Rome, 1966), pp. 195–228; Margaret F. Rosenthal, *The Honest Courtesan: Veronica Franco,*

city's crossroads for local and foreign writers and remained so until Venier's death. Nowadays Venier's reputation has dramatically faded, only barely revived by renewed interest in the phenomena of lyric production, dispersion, and collection.[2] Yet in his own day his life was marked by constant accolades that came to assume near-mythic proportions.[3] His fame as an organizer of literary culture continued posthumously—long enough to have been included in the 1640s as interlocutor with Apollo, Aristotle, Plato, Plutarch, Seneca, Guicciardini, and others by an anonymous Florentine satirist lampooning the conversations of the Accademia degli Unisoni.[4]

Let me begin to sketch some formative details of Venier and his circle of patrician friends as they developed in the second quarter of the century. Venier's coterie had been largely schooled together in the 1520s. By the 1530s they had already begun to fashion themselves as virtual heirs apparent to Venice's literary scene. Meanwhile most of them held civic offices and pursued various business interests. In 1546 a worsening case of gout seems to have prevented Venier from continuing to hold offices (as noblemen normally would), and at the same time his academic activities moved into high gear.[5] His palazzo at Santa Maria Formosa quickly became the

<hr />

Citizen and Writer in Sixteenth-Century Venice (Chicago, 1992), pp. 89–94, 154–55, 179–80, and passim; and Alvise Zorzi, *Cortigiana veneziana: Veronica Franco e i suoi poeti* (Milan, 1986), pp. 59–90. Discussions of Venier's own poetry are taken up in Dámaso Alonso and Carlos Bousoño, *Seis calas en la expresión literaria española (prosa, poesía, teatro),* 4th ed. (Madrid, 1970), pp. 51 and 92–94; Edoardo Taddeo, *Il manierismo letterario e i lirici veneziani del tardo cinquecento* (Rome, 1974), pp. 39–70; and Francesco Erspamer, "Petrarchismo e manierismo nella lirica del secondo cinquecento," in *Storia della cultura veneta: il seicento,* vol. 4, pt. 1, ed. Girolamo Arnaldi and Manlio Pastore Stocchi (Vicenza, 1983), pp. 192–97.

2. See, for example, Roberto Fedi, *La memoria della poesia: canzonieri, lirici, e libri d'amore nel rinascimento* (Rome, 1990), esp. pp. 43–46.

3. The large number of sixteenth-century references mentioned below represents merely a fraction of what exists. Despite this, Venier's academic activities have not been well documented elsewhere—hence the rather heavy documentation that follows.

4. This comes from a manuscript of satires entitled "Sentimenti giocosi havuti in Parnaso per L'Accademia degli Unisoni," I-Vmc, Misc. P.D. 308C/IX. Other manuscript copies of these satires are listed by Ellen Rosand, "Barbara Strozzi, *virtuosissima cantatrice:* The Composer's Voice," *JAMS* 31 (1978): 250 n. 31.

5. According to the electoral records of the Great Council, Venier was voted in as a senator on 26 October 1544 for a sixteen-month term that ended on 15 March 1546, after which he apparently did not serve for many years; I-Vas, Segretario alle voci, Elezioni del Maggior Consiglio, registro 2 (1541–52), fols. 40'–41. Zorzi summarizes the various offices held by Venier in *Cortigiana veneziana,* pp. 83–84 (without citing documents that provide the information but giving an overview of pertinent archives). The results of my archival searches have thus far agreed with Zorzi's information. On senatorial ranks see Robert Finlay, *Politics in Renaissance Venice* (London, 1980), pp. 59–81, and the glossary, p. xvi, and Oliver Logan, *Society and Culture in Venice, 1470–1790: The Renaissance and Its Heritage* (New York, 1972), p. 25.

The secondary literature alluding to Venier's academy shows some discrepancy concerning the academy's date of origin. Serassi's claim of 1549 is based on the far-fetched reasoning that Michele Tramezzino's dedication to Venier of 1548 (see n. 29 below) omits to mention the illness that ostensibly prompted Venier to drop out of political life and focus full time on cultural activities. Serassi's date is repeated in Pompeo Molmenti, *La storia di Venezia nella vita privata dalle origini alla caduta della repubblica,* 7th ed., 3 vols. (Bergamo, 1928), 2:374. Already in May 1548, however, Pietro Aretino referred to "l'Accademia del buon Domenico Veniero, che in dispetto della sorte, che il persegue con gli accidenti delle infermità, ha fatto della ornata sua stanza un tempio, non che un ginnasio" (the Academy of the good Domenico Venier, who in spite of fate, which persecutes him with the misfortune of illness, has made of his ornate salon a temple, not a mere schoolroom); letter to Domenico Cappello, *Lettere,* 6 vols. (Paris, 1609), 4:274, quoted in Girolamo Tiraboschi, *Storia della letteratura italiana,* vol. 7, pt. 3 (Milan, 1824), p. 1684. And as early as 1544, Bembo referred to Venier's "dilicata complessione" (see n. 19 below).

meeting place for writers of every stripe: patrician diplomats and civil servants, cultivated merchants, editors, poets, classicists, theorists, and playwrights.[6] Some of them were professional, others amateur, and (most strikingly) many had no clearly defined social-professional position of any sort.

Many references in the prolific occasional literature of the time make note of the various personalities involved. Among the closest to Venier were the patrician poet Girolamo Molino, whose posthumous biographer counted Venier's salon the most influential in Molino's experience,[7] and the *letterato* Federigo Badoer—an exact contemporary, though intermittently much occupied with diplomatic missions prior to his founding of the Accademia Veneziana in 1558.[8] Others included the Paduan scholar Sperone Speroni; a host of vernacular poets like Fortunio Spira, Anton Giacomo Corso, Giovanni Battista Amalteo, and Giacomo Zane, and others whose lyrics appeared in the copious poetic anthologies of midcentury; and polygraphs like Girolamo Parabosco and Lodovico Dolce.[9] Parabosco named many of these in a much-cited *capitolo* to Count Alessandro Lambertino, along with the satirist Aretino, who had at least a tangential relationship to the group.[10]

<hr />

6. Francesco Flamini, *Storia letteraria d'Italia: il cinquecento* (Milan, 1901), identified the location of Venier's palazzo as the Venier house at Santa Maria Formosa (p. 180)—i.e., that of Sebastiano Venier who was made famous by his victories against the Turks at Lepanto in 1571—an assertion echoed elsewhere in secondary literature. Venier's tax report, I-Vas, Dieci savi alle Decime (166–67), b. 130, fol. 653 (located by David Butchart and graciously shared with me), confirms the general location, but the genealogies give no reason to think that the house was the same.

7. In naming Molino's many friends and colleagues in Venice, Giovan Mario Verdizzotti wrote that "of all these honored conversations he frequented none more often than that of Domenico Venier . . . whose house is a continuous salon of talented people, both noblemen of the city and all sorts of other men in the literary profession and others rare and excellent" (di tutte queste honorate conversationi niuna egli più frequentava, che quella del M. Domenico Veniero . . . la casa del quale è un continuo ridutto di persone virtuose così di nobili della città, come di qual si voglia altra sorte d'huomini per professione di lettere, & d'altro rari, & eccellenti); Molino, *Rime* (Venice, 1573), p. [7]. Sansovino listed him among the other great Venetian writers of the time ("M. Gieronimo Molino è noto a ciascuno, però non ve ne parlo"), as he did Venier—both through the droll mouth of "Venetiano"; *Delle cose notabili che sono in Venetia. Libri due, ne quali ampiamente, e con ogni verità si contengono* (Venice, 1565), fol. 33′. Molino lived from 1500 until 1569.

8. Badoer (1518–1593) was precisely contemporary with Venier. A satiric *capitolo,* in praise of Badoer by Girolamo Fenaruolo to Venier, recounts how Fenaruolo, while walking through the Merceria, hears the news that Badoer has been made *Avogadore;* Francesco Sansovino, *Sette libri di satire . . . Con un discorso in materia de satira* (Venice, 1573), fols. 196–200′.

9. Most of the writers listed by "Venetiano" as being in Venice can be linked to Venier: in addition to "Bargarigo" [*sic,* i.e., Niccolò Barbarigo] and Molino it includes Gian Donato da le Renghe, Pietro Giustiano (historian), Paolo Ramusio, Paolo Manutio, Giorgio e Piero Gradenighi (Gradenigo), Luca Ieronimo Contarini, Di Monsi, Daniel Barbaro, Agostino da Canale (philosopher), Bernardo Navaiero (Navagero), "prestantissimo Senatore," Iacomo Thiepolo, Agostin Valiero, Lodovico Dolce, Sebastiano Erizzo" (fols. 33′–34). "Et se voi volete Huomeni forestieri," he continues, "ci habbiamo M. Fortunio Spira, gran conoscitor de tutte le lingue, M. Carlo Sigonio che legge in luogo d'Egnatio che fu raro a suoi dì, Bernardo Tasso; Hieronimo Faleto orator di Ferrara, Sperone Speroni habita la maggior parte del tempo in quest' segue. Il vescovo di Chioggia non se ne sa partire. Girolamo Ruscelli, dopo molto girar per Italia, finalmente s'è fermato in questa arca" (*Delle cose notabili,* fol. 34). We will encounter many of these figures below.

10. Aretino's acquaintance with Domenico and other members of the Venier family goes back to the 1530s; see Aretino's letters to Lorenzo Venier of 24 September 1537 (Aretino, *Lettere* 1:163), to Gianiacopo Lionardi of 6 December 1537 (*Lettere* 1:233′–34), and to Domenico of 18 November 1537 encouraging his literary talents (*Lettere* 1:190–190′).

Andarò spesso spesso a ca' Venieri,	I'll go ever so often to the Veniers' house
Ove io non vado mai ch'io non impari	Where I've never gone for four whole years
Di mille cose per quatr'anni intieri;	Without learning about a thousand things.
Per ch'ivi sempre son spiriti chiari,	For eminent spirits are always there
Et ivi fassi un ragionar divino	And folk reason divinely there
Fra quella compagnia d'huomini rari.	Among that company of rare men.
Chi è il Badoar sapete, e chi il Molino,	Who Badoer is you know, and who Molino is,
Chi il padron della stanza, e l'Amaltèo,	Who the father of the stanza, and Amalteo,
Il Corso, lo Sperone, e l'Aretino.	Corso, Sperone, and Aretino.
Ciascun nelle scienze è un Campanèo,	Each one in the sciences is a Capaneus,
Grande vo' dire, et son fra lor sì uguali,	Great, I mean, and so equal are they
Che s'Anfion è l'un, l'altro è un Orfeo.[11]	That if one is an Amphion, the other is an Orpheus.

Parabosco composed the *capitolo* as a bit of salesmanship, hoping to induce Lambertino to visit the city, and he bills the salon as one of the town's featured spots.[12] Some of the writers he mentions are practitioners of high lyric style, like Molino and Amalteo; others, like Aretino, dealt in satire and invective; and still others—Speroni for one—in philosophy. The mix seems representative, since everything points to a scene that was generously eclectic.

Some measure of this eclecticism clearly extended to include music. Although the academy's agenda was essentially literary, Parabosco's presence in its regular ranks is telling. He was one of several stars from the San Marco musical establishment who had connections with Venier's group, which also included various solo singers—probably of less professional cast—who declaimed poetry to their own accompaniments. Not surprisingly, some of the literary members had strong musical interests too—interests that can be documented through sources outside Venier's immediate group.

As the major center for informal literary exchange in mid-cinquecento Venice and one that embraced musicians, Venier's academy articulates concerns relevant to the

---

11. *La seconda parte delle rime* (Venice, 1555), fols. 61–61ʹ.

12. Parabosco was involved with Venier from at least 1549 when Aretino mentioned to Parabosco in a letter from October of that year that it was Venier who had introduced them ("avermi insegnato a conoscervi"); *Lettere sull'arte di Pietro Aretino*, commentary by Fidenzio Pertile, ed. Ettore Camesasca, 3 vols. in 4 (Milan, 1957–60), 2:308. In July 1550 Parabosco wrote Venier a letter of praise and affection from Padua, which suggests by its wording that the two had had a more extensive correspondence: "ho ricevuto una di V.S. a li ventisette del passato" (I received one of your [letters] on the 27th of the past [month]); *Il primo libro delle lettere famigliari* (Venice, 1551), fols. 4–4ʹ. In 1551, finally, Parabosco published a letter to one Pandolpho da Salerno characterizing the group around Venier as a definite body: "Io sto qui in Vinegia continuando la prattica del Magnifico M. Domenico Veniero, & del Magnifico Molino, & del resto della Accademia: i quali sono tutti quei spiriti pelegrini, & elevati che voi sapete" (I remain here in Venice continuing the activities of the magnificent Messer Domenico Venier, and the magnificent Molino, and the rest of the Academy, all of whom are those rare and lofty spirits whom you know); (*Lettere famigliari*, fol. 14ʹ). The letter could well have been written earlier than 1551. It is undated, but most other letters in the collection bear dates between the years 1548 and 1550. Parabosco's reference to the "spiriti pelegrini" is ambiguous. For evidence surrounding this mysterious appellation, associated with an academy of Doni's, see Maylender, *Storia delle accademie* 4:244–48. Maylender voices doubts about whether it ever existed (4:248), as does James Haar, "Notes on the *Dialogo della musica* of Antonfrancesco Doni," *Music & Letters* 47 (1966): 202.

intensely literary orientation of Venetian music. Yet the academy has found its way into surprisingly few musical studies of the cinquecento, and then only in passing.[13] The elusive state of evidence about the group's musical activities no doubt accounts for some of this neglect, for nothing of a direct nature survives. Nonetheless, the history of Venier's circle is rich, and an attempt to reconstruct its values and practices yields valuable insight into the processes by which literary ideas were absorbed by makers of music.

THE LEGACY OF PIETRO BEMBO, RATIFIED AND RECAST

Venier and his peers grew up under the spell of Pietro Bembo. Until receiving his cardinalate in 1539 Bembo lived in semiretirement at his villa in Padua, so that only a few privileged literati, including some members of Venier's circle, could have managed much contact with him before he departed for Rome. Venier was only twenty when Aretino named him in a fanciful, irreverent account of a dream about a Bembist Parnassus. As Aretino nears the garden he finds Domenico and his brother Lorenzo among a group of callow youth seated at Bembo's feet. In the idyllic excerpt below Bembo is reading aloud his *Istorie veneziane* to a rapt and adoring audience.

> I take myself to the main garden and as I draw near it I see several youths: Lorenzo Venier and Domenico, Girolamo Lioni, Francesco Badoer and Federigo, who signal me with fingers to their lips to come quietly. Among them was the courteous Francesco Querino. As they do so the breath of lilies, hyacinths, and roses fills my nostrils; then, approaching my friends, I see on a throne of myrtle the divine Bembo. His face was shining with a light such as never before seen; sitting on high with a diadem of glory upon his head, he had about him a crown of sacred spirits. There was Giovio, Trifone, Molza, Nicolò Tiepolo, Girolamo Querino, Alemanno, Tasso, Sperone, Fortunio, Guidiccione, Varchi, Vittore Fausto, Pier Francesco Contarini, Trissino, Capello, Molino, Fracastoro, Bevazzano, Bernardo Navaier, Dolce, Fausto da Longiano, and Maffio.[14]

---

13. Such references begin in the mid-nineteenth century with Francesco Caffi, *Storia della musica sacra nella già cappella ducale di San Marco dal 1318 al 1797*, 2 vols. (Venice, 1854), 1:112–13, 121, and 2:49–50, 129. His suggestions were pursued by Armen Carapetyan, "The *Musica Nova* of Adriano Willaert: With a Reference to the Humanistic Society of 16th-Century Venice" (Ph.D. diss., Harvard University, 1945), pp. 74–75, and Einstein, *The Italian Madrigal* 1:446, and were taken up by (for example) Francesco Bussi, *Umanità e arte di Gerolamo Parabosco: madrigalista, organista, e poligrafo* (Piacenza, 1961), pp. 36–37, and Dean T. Mace, "Pietro Bembo and the Literary Origins of the Italian Madrigal," *The Musical Quarterly* 55 (1969): 73. None of these contains more than a few sentences.

It should be mentioned that Serassi assumed more musical activity and patronage in connection with Venier's salon than evidence collected thus far will support—namely, that "nè capitava in Venezia Musico o Cantatrice di conto, che il Veniero non li volesse udir più d'una volta; e se accadeva ch'essi fossero veramente eccellenti, non solo li premiava secondo il merito loro, ma li celebrava ancora co' suoi bellissimi versi" (*Rime di Domenico Veniero*, pp. xiv–xv). Serassi's view surely contributed to the assumption prevalent in music histories that Venier's was equally a literary and a musical academy.

14. "Mi lascio menare a l'uscio del giardin principale, e ne lo appressarmici, veggo alcuni giovani: Lorenzo Veniero e Domenico, Girolamo Lioni, Francesco Badovaro e Federico, che col dito in bocca mi fér cenno ch'io venga piano: fra i quali era il gentil Francesco Querino. Intanto il fiato dei gigli, de' iacinti e de le rose mi empieno il naso di conforto; onde io, acostandomi agli amici, veggo sopra un trono di mirti il divin Bembo. Splendeva la faccia sua con luce non più veduta; egli sedendo in cima col

Aretino's spoof played on the kind of doting admiration he must have observed in Venice. At midcentury Bembo's beliefs in linguistic purity and the imitation of models and his rhetorical principles for writing prose and poetry still formed the near-exclusive stylistic guides for mainstream vernacular writers, especially in the Venetian literary establishment that Venier came to represent. In Chapter 5, I show how volumes of writings on vernacular style produced by Venetian literary theorists of the generation that succeeded Bembo reproduced and gradually transformed his views. For the moment I wish only to point up some contexts in which Bembo's theories were propounded within the academy and the range of mechanisms by which they were transmitted.

Lodovico Dolce, possibly the most dogged Bembist at midcentury and one of Venier's closest adherents, provides a link between Bembist ideology and Venier's literary practice. Dolce was an indigent polymath who earned a meager livelihood off the Venetian presses. In 1550, three years after Bembo's death, he published his *Osservationi della volgar lingua* as a kind of zealous reaffirmation of official vernacular ideology. Many of its catchiest passages obediently echo the judgments and jargon of Bembo's *Prose della volgar lingua*. Dolce reinforces his "Venetocentric" view by naming as the best lyric stylists five comrades, including Domenico Venier and at least three other Venetian poets tied to his circle—Molino, Bernardo Cappello, and Pietro Gradenigo.[15] Other writings, seen in juxtaposition with Dolce's, imply that after Bembo left the Veneto, Venier filled the patriarchal void he left behind.[16] The cosmopolitan Girolamo Muzio cast Venier as a kind of literary *padron* in his verse treatise *Arte poetica*. Dedicated to Venier in 1551, it exploited the folk rhetoric of didactic *capitoli*.

Ricorrerò ai maestri de la lingua,	I'll apply myself to the masters of language,
Al buon Trifon Gabriello, al sacro Bembo.	To the good Triphon Gabriele, to the sacred Bembo.
Andrò in Toscana al Varchi, al Tolomei,	I'll go to Tuscany to Varchi, to Tolomei,
E correrò a Vinegia al buon Veniero.[17]	And I'll race to Venice to the good Venier.

diadema de la gloria in capo, aveva intorno una corona di spirti sacri. V'era il Iovio, il Trifone, il Molza, Nicolò Tiepolo, Girolamo Querino, l'Alemanno, il Tasso, lo Sperone, il Fortunio, il Guidiccione, il Varchi, Vittor Fausto, il Contarin Pier Francesco, il Trissino, il Capello, il Molino, il Fracastoro, il Bevazzano, il Navaier Bernardo, il Dolce, il Fausto da Longiano, il Maffio" (quoted from *Lettere sull'arte* 1:97–98). The letter is dated from Venice, 6 December 1537. The figures not fully identified are Paolo Giovio, Triphon Gabriele, Francesco Maria Molza, Luigi Alemanno, Bernardo Tasso, Sperone Speroni, Giovanni Francesco Fortunio, Giovanni Guidiccione, Benedetto Varchi, Giangiorgio Trissino, Bernardo Capello, Girolamo Molino, Girolamo Fracastoro, Marco Bevazzano, Bernardo Navagero, Lodovico Dolce, and Maffio Venier.

15. Dolce argues that to write the best Tuscan one need not be Tuscan, as proved by Bembo and others in Venice, "who, writing often in this language, produce fruits worthy of immortality, such as [Bernardo] Capello, Domenico Venier, M. Bernardo Zane, Girolamo Molino, Pietro Gradenigo, and many others" (che in essa lingua, spesso scrivendo, producono frutti degni d'immortalità; si come il Capello, M. Domenico Veniero, M. Bernardo Zane, M. Girolamo Molino, M. Piero Gradenigo Gentilhuomini Vinitiani, e molti altri); *Osservationi nella volgar lingua* (Venice, 1550), fol. 9. Compare the protestations of Girolamo Muzio, Chap. 5, n. 32 below.

16. The view appears repeatedly in sixteenth-century accounts, as well as in modern ones; see, for instance, Flamini, *Storia letteraria*, p. 180, who calls Venier "l'erede e successore del Bembo."

17. *Arte poetica*, fol. 94.

The political prominence of Venier's noble family and his early education at San Marco with the renowned teacher of humanities, Giovanni Battista Egnazio, made him well suited to the role he came to assume.[18] In their correspondence of 1544, Bembo praised the young Venier for "a lovely, pure, and well-woven style" (un bello, casto, e ben tessuto stile), the same qualities championed in the *Prose*.[19] Indeed, the strands of their relationship were not only literary but included the larger familial web of Venetian patrician society: the manuscript letters of Pietro Gradenigo, Bembo's son-in-law and Venier's literary cohort, reveal that in the mid-forties Venier actually became godfather to two of Bembo's grandsons.[20]

Venier's most explicit advocacy of Bembist canons came in the commemorative sonnets he composed after Bembo's death in 1547 and published in 1550 in the third volume of the famed series of anthologies known as the *Rime diverse,* or *Rime di diversi*.[21] Venier adapted the norms of Bembist style to the purposes of a fervid encomium. By stressing in Bembo the traditional virtues of Venice, he fixed his predecessor's fame in the lasting domain of Venetian civic mythology. An especially typical embodiment of this comes in the sonnet *Pianse non ha gran tempo il Bembo,*[22] a double tribute to Bembo and another patriarchal contemporary (and close colleague of Bembo's), the Venetian poet-scholar Triphon Gabriele, who died in 1549.[23]

Pianse non ha gran tempo il Bembo, ch'era,	Not just as much as the sun circles the Adriatic shore,
Scevra l'alma dal corpo al ciel salito,	But as much as it turns from morning to evening,
D'Adria non pur, quanto circonda il lito,	[Had Venice] wept not long ago for Bembo, who had risen
Ma quanto gira il Sol da mane a sera.	To Heaven, his soul severed from his body.

4

18. See the reference to Venier's schooling by Lodovico Dolce cited in *Rime di Domenico Veniero,* p. iv. On Egnazio see James Bruce Ross, "Venetian Schools and Teachers, Fourteenth to Early Sixteenth Century: A Survey and a Study of Giovanni Battista Egnazio," *RQ* 29 (1976): 521–60.

19. "Ho tuttavia con grande piacer mio in essa vostra lettera veduto un bello & casto & ben tessuto stile: ilquale m'ha in dubbio recato, quali più lode meritino, o le rime vostre o le prose" (*Delle lettere di M. Pietro Bembo . . . di nuovo riveduto et corretto da Francesco Sansovino,* 2 vols. [Venice, 1560], 2: *libro* 10, fol. 131). The letter is dated 31 July 1544, from Rome.

20. Their father, Pietro Gradenigo, one of the poets singled out for mention by Dolce (see n. 15 above), was a nobleman and husband to Bembo's illegitimate daughter Helena. The information comes from a series of letters in manuscript, "Lettere inedite di Pietro Gradenigo Patrizio Veneto Scritte a diversi," I-Vnm, MSS It. Cl. X, 23 (6526), fols. 9 and 13. A letter on fol. 9 of 15 April (no year but probably from 1544 based on the surrounding letters) speaks of the birth of their son Alvise: "ho elletto per compari Domenico Veniero, e Federigo Badoero miei antichi, et cari amici, et compagni, et S*ign*ori devotissimi di V*ost*ra S*igno*ra R*everendissi*ma oltre ad alcuni altri gentilhuomini" (I have chosen as godfathers Domenico Venier and Federigo Badoer, my old and dear friends and comrades, and most loyal sirs of your Republic, in addition to some other gentlemen). Elsewhere Pietro writes to his father-in-law: "Marti prossimo passato battezzammo il mio bambino, et li ponemmo nome Paolo. . . . I compari che l'hanno tenuta al battesimo sono stati questi, lo ecc*elle*nte ms. Giacomo Bonfio . . . , Mons*ignor* Franco, il S*ign*or Girardo Rambaldo, ms. Federigo Bado*er,* ms. D*ome*nico Veniero, ms. Ant*onio* Moresini, et ms. Marc' Ant*onio* Contarini. Gentilhuomini tutti di gran valore, et miei cari amici et compagni" (Last Tuesday we baptized my baby boy, and named him Paolo. . . . The godfathers who held him at the baptism were the excellent Messer Giacomo Bonfio . . . , Monsignor Franco, Signor Girardo Rambaldo, Messer Federigo Badoer, Messer Domenico Venier, Messer Antonio Moresini, and Messer Marc' Antonio Contarini, all gentlemen of great worth and my dear friends and comrades); fol. 13.

21. *Libro terzo delle rime di diversi nobilissimi et eccellentissimi autori nuovamente raccolte* (Venice, 1550).

22. Folio 197'.

23. Gabriele was a principal interlocutor of Daniello's *La poetica,* on which see Chap. 5 below. In 1512 Bembo sent to him the first two books of his *Prose della volgar lingua* in manuscript; see Mario Marti's preface to his edition *Opere in volgare* (Florence, 1961), pp. 265–68, and for a reprint of the letter Bembo

Piange te parimente, hor ch'a la vera	Now that to the true Fatherland, dying,
Patria morendo e tu TRIFON se gito,	You too have gone, Triphon, all of Venice
Venezia tutta, e quanto abbraccia il sito	Weeps for you equally, as much as it yet embraces
Qua giuso ancor della mondana sfera.	The site of the worldly sphere here below.[24] 8

D'egual senno ambo duo, d'egual bontate	Of equal wisdom both, of equal goodness
Foste, a communi studi ambo duo volti,	Were you, both turned to common studies
D'una patria, d'un sangue, e d'una etate;	From one homeland, one blood, and one age. 11

Nodo par d'amistade insieme avolti	An equal knot of friendship wound round both
Tenne sempre i cor vostri alme ben nate,	Always held your hearts, well-born souls;
Ed hor ancho v'ha 'l cielo ambo raccolti.	And now even Heaven has gathered you both. 14

Here Venier placed the memory of his two mentors in the discourse of Venetian myth by stressing in them qualities attached to traditional conceptions of the state—goodness and wisdom—as well as their derivation from a common race. Though Venier distinguishes between Heaven, the "vera patria," and Venice, the "mondana sfera," his affections seem to lie chiefly with the latter. From the opening image of the sun circling the Adriatic shore (the "lito") he links in a linguistically rich evocation both Venetian geography and the notion of the homeland to the patriotic rhetoric of the Serenissima.[25] The poem's emphasis on the moral content of Venetian mythology ("d'egual bontade") demonstrates that Venier's depiction of Bembo and Gabriele as model figures was not meant to be just literary and scholarly but ethical as well, charged with a moral imperative.

In other poems on Bembo's death Venier made clear the nature of this imperative, as seen in a sonnet that asks Dolce too to mourn Bembo.

DOLCE, possente a raddolcir il pianto,	Dolce, powerful enough to sweeten the mourning
Ch'è per alta cagion pur troppo amaro,	That from a great cause is all too bitter,
Piangendo il Bembo à tutto 'l mondo caro,	Weeping for Bembo, dear to the whole world,
Poi che sua morte ha tutto 'l mondo pianto,	Now that the whole world has wept for his death: 4

Perche seco habbia il duol di gioia alquanto,	Since grief contains some joy,
Anzi vada il gioir col duolo a paro,	Or rather joy goes paired with grief,
Segui 'l tuo stile, e non ti sia dischiaro	Follow your style, and let it not displease you
Di lagrimarlo in sì soave canto.	To lament him in such a sweet song. 8

wrote accompanying the manuscript, pp. 713–15. A manuscript in I-Vmc entitled "Accademie in Venezia" (MS Gradenigo 181) lists Gabriele's circle in Padua under "Adunanze virtuose" (fol. 148'). A few remarks on Gabriele's circle may be found in Paul Lawrence Rose, "The *Accademia Venetiana:* Science and Culture in Renaissance Venice," *Studi veneziani* 11 (1969): 200.

24. For vv. 1–2 Nino Pirrotta kindly offers the alternative "Not just what is surrounded by the Adriatic shore [i.e., Venice], but all the land circled by the sun from morning to evening" as clarification of the distinction Venier later draws between Venice and the "worldly sphere" (private communication).

25. Bembo used a related lexicon and imagery in his own sonnet, "Questo del nostro lito antica sponda, / Che te, Venezia, copre e difende" (*Opere in volgare,* ed. Marti, no. 93, pp. 300–301).

Questo farà, che 'l suon de tuoi lamenti	This will make the people hear ever more
Gioia non men che duolo altrui recando	Eagerly the sound of your laments,
Sempre piu disiose udran le genti.	Bearing joy to others no less than grief: 11
Tal che ferendo in un l'alme e sanando,	So that at once wounding and healing the souls,
Fama eterna il tuo stil ne l'altrui menti,	Your style, like Achilles' lance,
Come l'hosta d'Achille, andrà lasciando.[26]	Will leave eternal fame in people's minds. 14

Throughout the poem Venier pursued the Petrarchan opposition of *gioir* and *duolo* to develop the poem's thematic strategy, while punning his recipient's name: to make his sadness felt most keenly Dolce should lament Bembo's death in sweet tones. His conceit tempers the sense of both terms, joy and grief, with distinctly Petrarchan reserve, each straining to uphold and assert its meaning in the face of its antonym.

At its surface, then, the injunction for Petrarchan paradox is simply a thematic one. But its stylistic basis finds an explanation in Ciceronian codifications of vernacular style that prevent words from registering too firmly on a single semantic or stylistic plane. By reducing the expression of sorrow through its opposite and exhorting Dolce to a sweet style even for the dark subject of death, Venier thus also claimed for his contemporaries the same canon of moderation earlier urged by Bembo. The road he treads is dutifully narrowed by Bembist precepts. And his insistence in the sestet that a lament is best heard mixed with contrasting sentiments invokes Bembo's advocation of Ciceronian variation and restraining decorum as the vehicles of rhetorical persuasion.

Such reserved expression also recalls the Venetian patriciate's artfully orchestrated self-image and its tendency to insist on well-monitored emotions in the civic sphere. Decorum, in this sense of reserve, formed the literary counterpart of *virtù*, purity, wisdom, and good judgment. As we have seen, these qualities, basic to Venetian communal identity, were epitomized for Venetians by Petrarch's lyric style. The academic and self-conscious brand of Petrarchism that proliferated in Venier's milieu, in catering to the needs of a highly disciplined state, thus served to reinforce the self-identity that was so emphatically articulated in the political and social rhetoric of the republic.

Yet, paradoxically, the ideological force that suppressed the poet's voice joined blithely with a candid quest for individual public acclaim. And so, ironically, Venier sugars the end of his sonnet with assurances that "Fama eterna il tuo stil ne l'altrui menti . . . andrà lasciando." The Bembist path to literary perfection might be unyieldingly self-effacing, but the promised compensation for taking it was poetic immortality.

---

26. *Libro terzo delle rime di diversi*, fol. 211, in the Newberry Library copy [recte: fol. 195].

Venier was well accustomed to the position of civic literary advisor he assumed in these sonnets. Although he wielded as much power as any vernacular author in Venice, he seems to have eschewed print by and large, publishing little and participating mainly in a manuscript culture that circulated verse by hand, post, perhaps even word of mouth.[27] Publicly he served primarily as a mentor to the many fledglings of the bourgeoisie, aristocratic dropouts, and patrician dilettantes who flocked to his door. Despite the power and esteem he accumulated, Venier resembled other noble literati in producing no *canzoniere* or other literary opus while he lived. His role instead was that of arbiter of Venetian poetic tastes. Like the printed anthologies to which he sometimes added his prestigious name, his salon and his acquaintance were stepping stones to public status for numerous literary aspirants of backgrounds less privileged than his, striving for acknowledgment or remuneration and a firm place within the active literary discourse of the day.[28] In this capacity Venier appeared as dedicatee of a number of volumes issued from the prolific Venetian presses, and much of the poetry that he and his comrades produced responded indirectly to the new public nature of words.[29] Generated out of the larger fabric of Venetian society, this poetry often transformed the contemplative, soloistic poetics of Petrarchan-Bembist lyric models into the more externalized and explicitly dialogic forms that I identified in Chapter 3 — sonnet exchanges, dedica-

27. On this phenomenon see Armando Balduino, "Petrarchismo veneto e tradizione manoscritta," in *Petrarca, Venezia e il Veneto,* ed. Giorgio Padoan, Civiltà veneziana, Saggi 21 (Florence, 1976), pp. 243–70.

28. Venier's sporadic contributions to the printed literature may be compared with those of several other Venetian poets, highly placed in the social and literary worlds, whose writings circulated in manuscript. Molino, also of noble birth, must have been known primarily in manuscript, since his *Rime* were printed only posthumously. The same is true of Giacomo Zane, who died in 1560 and whose *Rime* were issued in 1562; see Taddeo, *Il manierismo letterario,* p. 101 n. 1. I am inclined to think that there was a tendency among the uppermost crust to emulate aristocratic Florentine manuscript culture (in addition to the Tuscan language) by avoiding a wholesale participation in the culture of printed words as being beneath their station. Poets, including Molino, Celio Magno, Giuliano Goselini, and others, frequently entered into the world of print via musical sources, and only later poetic ones; see Lorenzo Bianconi and Antonio Vassalli, "Circolazione letteraria e circolazione musicale del madrigale: il caso G. B. Strozzi," in *Il madrigale tra cinque e seicento,* ed. Paolo Fabbri (Bologna, 1988), pp. 125–26.

29. Among volumes dedicated to Venier are the *Lettere volgari di diversi nobilissimi huomini, et eccellentissimi ingegni scritte in diverse materie* (Venice, 1542), with a dedication by the publisher and editor Paolo Manutio; an edition of Ficino's *Tre vite* entitled *Marsilio Ficino fiorentino filosofo eccellentissimo de le tre vite* (Venice, 1548), translated into the vernacular by Giovanni Tarcagnota (pseudonymously called Lucio Fauno in a preface to the readers) and dedicated by the publisher Michele Tramezzino; the *Rime diverse del Mutio Iustino Politano* (Girolamo Muzio), including the *Arte poetica* (Venice, 1551), dedicated by the author; and the *Rime di Mons. Girolamo Fenaruolo* (Venice, 1574), dedicated by Fenaruolo's posthumous biographer Marc'Antonio Silvio. Venier also figured among the inflated number of dedicatees (loosely so-called) scattered throughout Antonfrancesco Doni's *Libraria* (Venice, 1550), fol. 16'; on the various editions of the work, two of which date from 1550, see C. Ricottini Marsili-Libelli, *Anton Francesco Doni, scrittore e stampatore* (Florence, 1960), nos. 21, 22, and 70. In addition, many of the poems in the *Libro terzo delle rime di diversi* stem from the Venier circle and include a great many encomiastic praises of both Bembo and Venier — for example, Dolce's *Venier, che dal mortal terreno chiostro,* fol. 184, Giorgio Gradenico's (Gradenigo) *Venier, che l'alma a le crudel percosse,* fol. 98', and Pietro Aretino's *VENIERO gratia di quel certo ingegno,* fol. 183'. The *Libro terzo* was the first of the *Rime di diversi* series to represent large numbers of poets connected with Venier, including Dolce, Giovanni Battista Susio, Giovanni Battista Amalteo, Parabosco, Giorgio Gradenigo, Fortunio Spira, Bernardo Tasso, Giacomo Zane, Bernardo Cappello, Anton Giacomo Corso, and Venier himself (although a number had already been included in the *Rime di diversi nobili huomini et eccellenti poeti nella lingua thoscana. Libro secondo* [Venice, 1547] — Corso, Cappello, Susio, Parabosco, and Dolce).

tory poems, stanzas in praise of women, patriotic encomia, and so forth. It thus became fundamentally a poetics of correspondence and exchange, but also of competition, which often took the form of ingenious and ultrarefined verbal games.

One of the works that best reveals the evolving direction of Venier's academy at midcentury is Parabosco's *I diporti*. First printed (without date) by 1550, *I diporti* is a colorful, Boccaccesque series of novellas in the form of conversations between various men of letters.[30] The interlocutors are mostly linked with Venier's group: Parabosco himself, Molino, Venier, Badoer, Speroni, Aretino, the scholar Daniele Barbaro, Benedetto Corner (Venier's interlocutor in a dialect *canzoniere* discussed below), the editor and poet Ercole Bentivoglio, Count Alessandro Lambertino (recipient of Parabosco's *capitolo* cited earlier), the philosopher and classicist Lorenzo Contarini, and the poets Giambattista Susio, Fortunio Spira, and Anton Giacomo Corso, among others.[31]

During a lengthy digression toward the end of the stories the participants enumerate the requisite qualities of different lyric genres—madrigal, *strambotto, capitolo,* sestina, pastoral canzone, and sonnet.[32] Madrigals must be "sharp with a well-seasoned, charming invention" (acuti e d'invenzione salsa e leggiadra) and must derive their grace from a lively spirit.[33] They must be beautifully woven, adorned with graceful verses and words and, like the *strambotto,* have a lovely wit (arguzia) and inventiveness. To exemplify these qualities Sperone recites one of Parabosco's madrigals, applauding its manipulation of a pretty life-death conceit. Corso then recites a witty *capitolo* (again Parabosco's), full of anaphora, prompting Badoer to effuse on its "begli effetti amorosi."[34] The sestina, Contarini insists, allows the exposition of beautiful things and is a very lovely poem (poema molto vago).[35]

---

30. I cite from the mod. ed. in *Novellieri minori del cinquecento: G. Parabosco—S. Erizzo,* ed. Giuseppe Gigli and Fausto Nicolini (Bari, 1912), pp. 1–199, hereafter *I diporti*. On the date of the first edition see Bussi, *Umanità e arte,* p. 77 n. 1. As Giuseppe Bianchini reported, Parabosco mentioned the existence of *I diporti* in a letter (also undated), which in turn probably stems from 1550; *Girolamo Parabosco: scrittore e organista del secolo XVI,* Miscellanea di Storia Veneta, ser. 2, vol. 6 (Venice, 1899), p. 394. On this basis Bianchini suggested 1550 as the date of the first edition. Ad[olphe] van Bever and Ed[mond] Sansot-Orland, *Oeuvres galantes des conteurs italiens,* 2d ser., 4th ed. (Paris, 1907), pushed the compositional date to a slightly earlier time (pp. 219–20), but without real evidence. The hope Doni expressed in the *Libraria* (Venice, 1550) that Parabosco would soon issue "un volume di novelle" (p. 23) would seem to secure the date of 1550, since Doni's book was published in that year.

31. The mix of Venetians and non-Venetians overlaps a good deal with other descriptions of Venier's circle, like the one in Parabosco's *capitolo* cited in n. 11 above. Characteristically, a number of figures (as Parabosco states in the *ragionamento* to the *Prima giornata)* are non-Venetians but all spent time in Venice: Bentivoglio and Lambertino from Bologna, Susio from Mirandola, Spira from Viterbo, Corso from Ancona, and Speroni from Padua (*I diporti,* p. 10). Speroni was also a main interlocutor in Bernardino Tomitano's *Ragionamenti della lingua toscana* (see Chap. 5, pp. 129–30 below). The towering Aretino, quite fascinatingly, though counted by Parabosco among the non-Venetians, is the only one given no native origin. For further identifications of these and other interlocutors in *I diporti* see Bianchini, *Girolamo Parabosco,* pp. 395–98. On Baldassare Donato's encomiastic setting of a sonnet on Contarini's death see Chap. 9 n. 76.

In the decade after *I diporti* M. Valerio Marcellino published a series of conversations called *Il diamerone* that were explicitly set among the Venier circle (Venice, 1564); see Chap. 5 below, n. 139.

32. *I diporti,* pp. 177–91.

33. Ibid., p. 177.

34. Ibid., pp. 179–80.

35. Ibid., pp. 182–83.

In each genre, then, grace and beauty are paramount. But no less important in their estimation are invention, wit, and technical virtuosity. When they come to the labyrinthine sestina, this stance takes the form of a little apologia, as Corso and Contarini argue that the genre is no less suited than the canzone to expressions of beauty and no more difficult to compose.[36] After more madrigals of Parabosco are recited—and amply praised by as harsh a judge as Aretino—the whole company assembles to assess the formidable sonnet.

Toward the end of their exchange they cite several sonnets of Venier, whose virtuosic verbal artifice won him widespread fame in the sixteenth century. Whereas the madrigals described earlier aimed at a tightly knit and clever rhetorical formulation, these sonnets employ technical artifice in a somewhat different role. To construct the following, for example, Venier systematically reworked corresponding triads of words—no fewer than four of them in the first quatrain alone.

Non punse, arse o legò, stral, fiamma, o laccio	The arrow, flame, or snare of Love never
D'Amor lasso piu saldo, e freddo, e sciolto	Stung, burned, or bound, alas, a heart more
Cor, mai del mio ferito, acceso,	Steady, cold, and loosed than mine, wounded, kindled,
e 'nvolto,	and tied
Gia tanti dì ne l'amoroso impaccio.	Already so many days in an amorous tangle. 4
Perc'haver me 'l sentia di marmo e ghiaccio,	Because I felt marble and ice within me,
Libero in tutto i' non temeva stolto	Free in everything, I foolishly did not fear
Piaga, incendio, o ritegno, e pur m'ha colto	Wound, fire, or restraint, and yet
L'arco, il foco, e la rete, in ch'io	The bow, the fire, and the net in which I lie have
mi giaccio.	caught me. 8
E trafitto, infiammato, avinto in modo	And pierced, and inflamed, and captured in such a way
Son, ch'altro cor non apre, avampa, o cinge	Am I that no dart, torch, or chain opens, blazes, or clasps
Dardo, face, o catena hoggi più forte.	Any other heart today more strongly. 11
Ne fia credo chi 'l colpo, il caldo,	Nor, I believe, may it be that the blow, and the heat, and
e 'l nodo,	the knot
Che 'l cor mi passa, mi consuma, e stringe,	That enter, break, and squeeze my heart
Sani, spenga, o disciolga altri, che	Could be healed, extinguished, or unloosed by any other
morte.[37]	but death. 14

Parabosco's interlocutors submit a panegyric on Venier after the mention of this puzzlelike poem and its sister sonnet, *Qual più saldo, gelato e sciolto core.* Both poems were well enough known to the interlocutors to forego reading them aloud. *Non*

36. Ibid., p. 182.
37. In addition to its mention in *I diporti,* p. 190, and its inclusion in the *Libro terzo delle rime di diversi,* fol. 198, the sonnet appeared in numerous subsequent printed anthologies and a large number of manuscripts. For a partial listing of these see Balduino, "Petrarchismo veneto e tradizione manoscritta," pp. 258–59. I give an early version of the sonnet as it appeared in the *Libro terzo delle rime di diversi,* to which I have added some modern diacritics.

punse, arse o legò, Spira avows, is one of the "rarissimi e bellissimi fra i sonetti mara-vigliosi di Venier."

Non punse, arse o legò initiated a subtle shift in the stylistic premises that Venier's circle had maintained for years. Its formal type, dubbed by the modern critics Dámaso Alonso and Carlos Bousoño the "correlative sonnet,"[38] seems to have been Venier's invention, created by extending to their utmost Petrarchan tenden-cies toward wit and *ingegno* that appear in earlier cinquecento poetry in far less extreme guises. The essential strategy of the correlative sonnet lies in its initial presentation of several disparate elements ("punse" / "arse" / "legò") that are continually linked in subsequent verses with corresponding noun, verb, or adjec-tive groups ("stral" / "fiamma"/ "laccio"; "saldo" / "freddo" / "sciolto," and so forth). Although the high-level syntactic structure is highly syntagmatic, the immediate syntax of the poetic line tends to lack coordination and subordination of elements except that of a crisscrossed, paratactic sort.

Very possibly *Non punse, arse o legò* and *Qual più saldo* had even been written some time before 1550, as Spira seems to imply in describing them as the models imitated by another sonnet and the source of Venier's wide renown as a "raro e nobile spirto."[39] They thus represent an early and radical extension of the Petrarchan penchant for witty wordplay, one that was carried out in less systematized forms in Petrarch's own sonnets and imitated in less extreme ways by others in the sixteenth century—Luigi Tansillo, Annibale Caro, Benedetto Varchi, and Gaspara Stampa.[40]

38. For their analysis of this sonnet see Alonso and Bousoño, *Seis calas,* p. 56. See also Taddeo, *Il manierismo letterario,* pp. 57–58, and Erspamer, "Petrarchismo e manierismo," pp. 190–91, who names the basic rhetorical figure with the Latin *rapportatio.* The sixteenth-century Daniello characterized the phe-nomenon as "corrispondenze e contraposizioni" in his discussion of Petrarch's sonnet no. 133, *Amor m'ha posto come segno al strale; La poetica* (Venice, 1536), p. 79 (see n. 40 below and Chap. 5 below on Daniello). For an analysis of the sonnet's correlations see Dámaso Alonso, "La poesia del Petrarca e il petrarchismo (mondo estetico della pluralità)," *Studi petrarcheschi* 7 (1961): 100–4.

39. *I diporti,* p. 190. The two sonnets appear on the same page in the *Libro terzo delle rime di diversi.* One candidate for the imitations Spira refers to is Parabosco's sonnet *Sì dolce è la cagion d'ogni mio amaro;* its first tercet reads: "Non fia però ch'io non ringratia ogn'hora / La fiamma, il dardo, la cathena, e Amore / Che si m'arde per voi, stringe, & impiaga" (Parabosco, *Il primo libro delle lettere famigliari,* fol. 50).

40. Consider, for example, the more leisurely correlations in Petrarch's sonnet no. 133, "Amor, m'ha posto come *segno* al *strale,* / Come al *sol neve,* come *cera* al *foco,* / Et come *nebbia* al *vento,*" in which two and a half lines (vv. 1–3) are needed to correlate four pairs of elements a single time. The second quatrain brings back their substantive forms ("colpo," "sole," "foco," "vento") just once, and the first tercet corre-lates only the first three pairs of elements ("saette," "sole," "foco" / "mi punge," "m'abbaglia," "mi di-strugge"). The last tercet concludes the whole by turning its final rhetorical point around a reorientation of the last element: the "dolce spirto" of the beloved that becomes the breeze ("l'aura") before which the poet's life flees. Petrarch's four-pronged correlations thus number a total of four for the whole sonnet, as compared with twelve for Venier's three-pronged correlations in *Non punse, arse o legò.*

For an example in Bembo, see sonnet no. 85, *Amor, mia voglia e 'l vostro altero sguardo* (*Opere in vol-gare,* ed. Marti, p. 497), which structurally resembles Petrarch's *Amor, Fortuna e la mia mente* (no. 124). Alonso and Bousoño, *Seis calas,* pp. 85–106, discuss two-, three-, and four-pronged correlations in son-nets by Petrarch, Ariosto, Luigi Tansillo, Vincenzo Martelli, Benedetto Varchi, Gaspara Stampa, Camillo Besalio, Pietro Gradenigo, Annibale Caro, Maffio Venier, Luigi Groto, and Giambattista Marino. A good example, though not as rigorously organized as this one, exists in Stampa's no. 26, which may be significant in view of her association with Venier; see Fiora A. Bassanese, *Gaspara Stampa* (Boston, 1982), pp. 9–12, 18, 37–38, and nn. 66–75 below. The first quatrain of the poem reads: "Arsi, piansi, cantai; piango, ardo, canto; / Piangerò, arderò, canterò sempre / Fin che Morte o Fortuna o tempo stempre / A l'ingegno, occhi e cor, stil, foco o pianto" (*Rime,* ed. Maria Bellonci and Rodolfo Ceriello, 2d ed. [Milan, 1976], p. 97). Like Petrarch, Stampa reorders the triad in its different reincarnations.

Though the correlative sonnet represents only one subgenre in the poetry of Venier, it nonetheless presents a vivid example of the growing tendency in the Venetian lyric to invest the sanctioned Ciceronian properties of grace and moderation with greater technical complexity.[41]

POLYPHONY AND POETRY, HIGH AND LOW

The infatuation with *ingegno* that inspired Venier's correlative sonnets must have found congenial exemplars in the madrigalian practice recently ascendent in Venice. Both correlative sonnets and polyphonic madrigals depended on an audience immediately at hand, ready to be engaged and impressed and to reflect on its currency in the world of vernacular arts. And both were rooted in a kind of intellectual *luxuria* that was necessary to champion what might otherwise have seemed intolerably arcane creations.

The reshaping of Venetian madrigals in knotty church polyphony parallels the academic, self-conscious impulse toward intellectual sophistication that lay beneath Bembo's thinking about vernacular style and that reached extremes in correlative verse. Such impulses were the very sort encouraged by the competitive lather of Venetian academic life and the commercialization of art with which it intersected. Yet they contradict the prevailing norms of decorum that control both Venetian sonnets and sonnet settings to produce a basic tension in Venice's high vernacular arts: like Venier's most intricate poems, the madrigals produced by Willaert and his circle seem to want to emerge unruffled from the competitive fray as both the most urbane and the gravest emblems of aristocratic culture—to win eminence in the domain of virtuosity without jeopardizing the aristocratic values to which they are beholden.

Ultimately the extremes of complexity in both Willaertian madrigals and Venier-styled verse threatened to upset the Bembist balance between calculated artifice and natural grace. Both labor in a ponderous rhetoric whose guiding hand is an overriding consciousness of noble *gravitas,* without embracing the elegance—the *sprezzatura*—that was de rigueur in Florentine music and letters or in those of courts like

---

41. Other famous examples of Venier's correlative verse include *M'arde, impiaga, ritien, squarcia, urta, e preme (Rime di diversi . . . Libro quinto* [Venice, 1552], p. 299) and *Maladetto sia 'l dardo, il foco, e 'l laccio* (ibid., p. 300).

The source tradition may indicate that Venier revised such sonnets with a view to perfecting technical aspects of them. In the radically revised version of *Non punse, arse o legò* that was issued in vol. 5 of the *Rime di diversi,* p. 297, for example, he changed vv. 5 and 6 from: "Perc'haver me 'l sentia di marmo, e ghiaccio / Libero in tutto i non temeva stolto" to: "Saldo et gelato più, che marmo, et ghiaccio, / Libero & franco i non temevo stolto," adding an extra two sets of correlations and allowing every verse in the sonnet to participate in the correlative pattern. Multiple variant readings from various manuscripts are given in Balduino, "Petrarchismo veneto" (p. 259), who also lists sixteenth-century prints that include this sonnet (p. 258 n. 26). Balduino cites other sorts of revisions that show Venier's increasing concern for technical perfection, for example the two versions of the sonnet *Mentre de le sue chiome in giro sparse* (pp. 254–58). Venier apparently rewrote the initial quatrain in a later version, changing the first verse, from "*in giro* sparse" to "*a l'aura* sparse" and thus introducing a pun and play of sounds between the ends of vv. 1 and 4 ("Vedea sotto il bel cerchio aurato starse")—that is, "a l'aura sparse" / "aurato starse."

Mantua and Ferrara. On the contrary, the new Venetian products were strangely mannered by comparison with those produced elsewhere in northern Italy and in ways perhaps unimaginable without Venice's combative pressure to adapt afresh new techniques and styles. Beneath its virtuosic displays Venice managed to maintain as a Procrustean bed ideals of the *ordene antiquo* that were deeply rooted in Venetian consciousness.

Although no direct reports tell of Venetian madrigals performed in the Venier household (or in most others, for that matter), fictive re-creations like Doni's make it clear that madrigals found their main abode in drawing rooms. Clearly the primary occupation of the Venier house was vernacular literature, with musical performances playing a decidedly secondary role. Yet much evidence suggests that music nonetheless occupied a regular niche in the academy's agenda. Several central figures linked with Venier's household sustained strong connections with the culture of written polyphony: in addition to Parabosco the literati Girolamo Fenaruolo and Girolamo Molino, to whom I will turn shortly. Two other star pupils of Willaert's were known to its members: Perissone Cambio and Baldassare Donato. Perissone formed the subject of a double sonnet exchange between Venier and Fenaruolo following his death, probably in the early 1560s.[42] And the promising Donato was given the task no later than 1550 of setting three of Venier's stanzas for large civic celebrations—this at a time when Venier's academy was still in its youthful stage and Donato himself no more than about twenty.[43] Even Willaert appears in what may be suggestive proximity to Venier, namely the postscript to Parabosco's *capitolo* characterizing Venier's salon to Lambertino of 1555.[44] Perhaps Willaert—aging, heavily burdened, and slowed by ill health—would not have spent much time there late in life, but there is no doubt that he kept in touch with many of its intimates.

———————

Serious polyphonic madrigals stand at the forefront of developments in Venetian secular music. But like Venier's correlative sonnets for Venetian literati and vernac-

42. See Chap. 9 nn. 65–66 below, and for the sonnets the Appendix to Chap. 9.

43. See Giulio Maria Ongaro, "The Chapel of St. Mark's at the Time of Adrian Willaert (1527–1562): A Documentary Study" (Ph.D. diss., University of North Carolina at Chapel Hill, 1986), p. 125.

Yet another polyphonist, Gasparo Fiorino of Rossano, was directly acquainted with Venier, although probably in a later decade. Fiorino flourished from about 1571–74 in Ferrara and apparently had social connections with Rome as well (see Iain Fenlon, "Fiorino, Gasparo," in *The New Grove* 6:601–2). Fiorino was recipient of a dedicatory sonnet by Venier, which was attached to his *Libro secondo canzonelle a tre e a quatro voci*, fol. [2], a collection "in lode et gloria d'alcune signore et gentildonne genovesi," published in 1574. Fenlon speculated that Fiorino had been a singer at St. Mark's in the middle of the century. Although the documentary work of Ongaro, "The Chapel of St. Mark's," now makes this very doubtful, the sonnet addressed to him by Venier does confirm that he was a singer (*Rime di Domenico Venier,* no. 98).

44. Parabosco, *La seconda parte delle rime,* fol. 63'–64. Earlier scholars treated the juxtaposition of their names as evidence that Willaert frequented Venier's house, even though the poem makes no such explicit claim; see Gaetano Cesari, "Le origini del madrigale cinquecentesco," *Rivista musicale italiana* 19 (1912): 395–96, and Carapetyan, "The *Musica Nova* of Adriano Willaert," p. 74.

ular poetry more broadly, they represented only one of several genres available to musicians. Bembo's call for discrete stylistic levels echoed as profoundly in vernacular music as it did in literature. And while Venetian composers now generally reserved their most serious secular efforts for madrigal books, the same composers also began, in 1544, to publish in separate volumes stylized genres of light music—*canzoni villanesche alla napolitana* and *villotte*.[45] Many of the dialect songs were obscene and invariably had something comic, rustic, or earthy about them. The *canzoni villanesche* that emanated from Venice reworked Neapolitan polyphonists' three-voice settings of popular Neapolitan songs by expanding the models from three voices to four and shifting the original popular tune from its prominent place in the soprano to a more hidden location in the tenor. They often Tuscanized the poems' dialect and reduced the number of stanzas. These transformations made the whole genre into something less soloistic and more madrigalistic—that is, more a matter of shared choral singing according to the elevated northern ideal of equal-voiced polyphony. They also invested the settings with self-conscious artifice—lowly tunes uplifted by northern wit, as it were—in ways that could appeal to Venetian intellects. Many prints of Venetian *canzoni villanesche* met with immense success—numerous reprints and many arrangements for solo lute.

Dialect songs likely formed part of the academy's fare, just as madrigals did. One collection of *villotte* was produced in 1550 by Willaert's close Netherlandish friend Antonio Barges and dedicated by Barges to Venier's cohort Fenaruolo.[46]

To the Magnificent and Reverend Monsignor Mr. Girolamo Fenaruolo, my lord:

Being the custom of almost everyone who wants to print some little thing of his to erect a defense against a certain sort of person who, either out of a bad nature or not to appear ignorant, censures the efforts of everyone, good and bad alike, I too on that account would have to address these flowers of mine (rather than fruits) to someone who by his profession had toiled and acquired more in music than in any other science. But all the same I will not do so. For in this case it's enough for me that I've forced myself as much as I could not to deviate from the teaching of the only inventor of true and good music, the most excellent Adrian, who was not only my most diligent teacher but the very best father to me. I therefore dedicate these little efforts of mine to you—you who are a friend and who, besides belles lettres and

45. The primary work on lighter genres is that of Donna G. Cardamone, *The "Canzone villanesca alla napolitana" and Related Forms, 1537–1570,* 2 vols. (Ann Arbor, 1981), esp. Chaps. 5 and 6. On pp. 164ff. Cardamone discusses misgivings of northerners about the moral influence of part-songs in dialect, but their Counter-Reformational statements seem to have appeared only after the mid-fifties. Willaert first published a collection of *napolitane* (as they were sometimes called) with the printer Girolamo Scotto in 1544, but only a single gathering of the tenor part book survives (see Cardamone 2:35–36). In 1545 Antonio Gardane brought out a version of the same book, *Canzone villanesche alla napolitana di M. Adriano Wigliaret a quatro voci . . . novamente stampate* (RISM 1545²⁰), and one by Perissone, *Canzone villanesche alla napolitana a quatro voci di Perissone novamente poste in luce.* . . . Donato published a book of *napolitane* in 1550 (cited in n. 78 below).

46. Full title: *Di Antonino Barges maestro di cappella alla Casa grande di Venetia il primo libro de villotte a quatro voci con un'altra canzon della galina novamente composte & date in luce* (Venice, 1550). Barges was maestro at the Casa Grande until 1563. He witnessed Willaert's will of 8 December 1562 shortly before the latter's death; see Vander Straeten, *La Musique aux Pays-Bas* 6:246.

gracious habits, are so adorned with that sweet virtue, and who gladly hear my works. Not that they were made with the goal that they might be printed, but rather composed at various times at the wishes of my different friends (although now perforce being sent out, so as to appear a grateful friend with little praise rather than an ungrateful musician with much). I also send you a few sweet compositions by the Magnificent Cavalier S. Andrea Patricio da Cherso, which I believe you'll like a lot. This, my sir, is how much I now give you evidence of the love I bear to you, and I do so ardently, being certain that you know clearly (and much better than many others) how true that thought is; for he who does what he can do does therefore what he ought. Not that anyone should therefore blame me for not sending them to the very worthy and gentle M. Stefano Taberio, since in sending them to you not only do I make a richer gift to M. Stefano, who loves you so much, but also to the gentle M. Marco Silvio, both of whom, living in you as you live in them, love and honor the one who loves and honors. I kiss your hand, my lord, and I wish for that dignity that your good qualities merit, begging you to be kind enough to sing these little *canzonette* of mine now and then with your Silvio and with those gentlemen, among the pleasantries and delights of the most merry Conegliano; and love me since I love and honor you. Antonino Barges.[47]

Barges's *villotte*—some of which are really *villanesche alla napolitana,* others Venetian dialect arrangements—were among the more northern, complex examples of light music. They justify his claim to be following closely his "ottimo patre," Willaert, and his linking of *villotte* with the seemingly high literary circle of Fenaruolo.

Barges pointedly avoided praising Fenaruolo's own musical skills, emphasizing instead his devotion to musicians and citing the genesis of the print's *villotte* among amateur appreciators like Fenaruolo and friends. Clearly he did expect that they could render their own performances of the songs, for he asked Fenaruolo to sing them "now and then" together with his other literary cohorts. Barges's expectation

---

47. "Al Magnifico & Reverendo Monsignore M. Girolamo Fenarolo Signor suo. Essendo costume quasi d'ogn'uno che voglia mandare alcuna sua fatica in luce, proccaciarsi diffesa contra una certa sorte di persone, che o per lor trista natura, o per mostrar di non esser ignoranti biasimano cosi le buone come le triste fatiche d'ogn'uno. anch'io percio doverei indrizzar questi miei piu tosto fiori che frutti, ad alcuno che per sua professione piu havesse sudato & aquistato nella musica che in altra scientia. ma non lo farò altrimenti, perche in questo mi basta ch'io mi son forzato per quanto ho potuto, di non deviare dalla dissiplina de l'unico inventore della vera & buona musica l'Eccellentissimo Adriano il quale non solamente m'é stato diligente maestro, ma ottimo patre, Io dunque â voi che oltre le bellissime litere, & i gratiosi costumi, sete ancho ornato di questa dolcissima virtu mi sete amico, & udite voluntieri le mie compositioni dedico queste mie picciole fatiche, non gia fatte a fine ch'andassero alle stampe, ma in diverse volte a voglia di diversi amici miei composte quatunque adesso, (piu tosto per parer grato amico con poca lode, che ingrato musico con molta) sia forzato mandarle fuori. Mandovi ancora alcune poche ma soavi compositioni del Magnifico Cavalliero il S. Andrea Patricio da Cherso, le quali credo che molto vi piaceranno. Questo é signor mio quanto hora vi posso dare in testimonio dell'amore ch'io vi porto, & lo faccio arditamente essendo certo che voi (& assai meglio di molt'altri) conoscete chiaramente quanto sia vera quella sententia, che quello che fa quanto puote, conseguentemente fa quanto deve. Ne sia percio alcuno che mi biasimi, non le mandandole a V.S. non solamente ne faccio piu ricco dono a M. Stefano che tanto v'ama, ma insieme al gentilissimo M. Marco silvio, i quali vivendo in voi, si come voi in loro vivete, amano, & honorano, chi v'ama, & honora. Vi bascio la mano signor mio, & vi desidero quella dignita che meritano tante vostre buone qualita, pregandovi che mi siate tal'hor cortese di cantar queste mie canzonette con il vostro silvio, & con quei gentil'huomini, tra le amenita & le delitie del giocondissimo Conegliano: & amatemi per ch'io v'amo & honoro. Antonino Barges."

that his recipient would sing the pieces recalls those of Perissone and Parabosco in dedicating prints to Gottardo Occagna (see Chap. 3, pp. 53–60). Like Perissone, Barges claims not to have composed these works for print but for the pleasure of literary friends—Silvio, Stefano Taberio, and Fenaruolo. In any case, they were not so hard to negotiate as Perissone's five-voice madrigals, which required a firmer grasp of singing written counterpoint from part books.

Fenaruolo knew other musicians too, including Willaert, to whom he addressed a satiric *capitolo* in 1556, and Perissone, whose death he mourned with Venier, the dedicatee of Fenaruolo's posthumous *canzoniere.*[48] Venier's academy seems a likely setting for the sort of light music dedicated to Fenaruolo, since it was one of his main venues. *Napolitane* may even have been heard there in equal measure with serious madrigals, as was true at the Accademia Filarmonica of Verona from the time of its founding in 1543.[49]

With their earthy tones and often obscene Neapolitan or Venetian texts, these songs correspond musically to bawdy dialect verse composed by Venier himself and others in his circle, verse that formed the subject of a letter from Aretino to Venier in November 1549.

> Just as the coarseness of rustic food often incites the appetite to gluttony, Signor Domenico—more than the great delicacy of high-class dishes ever moved to the pleasure of eating in such a way—so too at times the trivial aspects of subjects in the end sharpen the intellect with a certain eager readiness, which as fate would have it never showed itself with any epic material. So that in composing in the Venetian language, style, and manner in order to divert the intellect, I especially praise the sonnets, *capitoli,* and *strambotti* that I have seen, read, and understood by you, by others, and by me.[50]

48. Remo Giazotto has published eight sonnets concerning numerous members of Willaert's circle and assigned their authorship to Fenaruolo; see *Harmonici concenti in aere veneto* (Rome, 1954). Inexplicably, no other reference to the book said to have contained the sonnets can be found, including by the staff at the Biblioteca Nazionale Centrale in Rome (private communication). I have searched over forty libraries in Italy and many others elsewhere in Europe and in North America.

49. See Giuseppe Turrini, *L'Accademia Filarmonica di Verona dalla fondazione (maggio 1543) al 1600 e il suo patrimonio musicale antico,* Atti e memorie della Accademia di Agricoltura, Scienze e Lettere di Verona, no. 18 (Verona, 1941), p. 184, Appendix A, passim; and the newer publication, idem, *Catalogo delle opere musicali: città di Verona, Biblioteca della Società Accademia Filarmonica di Verona,* BMB, ser. 1, no. 18 (Bologna, 1983). See also Cardamone, *The "Canzone villanesca alla napolitana"* 1:175–78.

50. "Sì come bene ispesso; la grossezza de i villani cibi, ò Magnifico S. Domenico; incitano l'appetito a una avidità di gola, che altra delicatura di signorili vivande, non mai la mossero al piacere del mangiare in tal' modo; così alle volte il triviale de i suggetti infimi aguzzano lo ingegno, con certa ansia di prontitudine, che in sorte d'alcuna Heroiche materia non dimostròssi mai tale. Sì che nel comporre per recrear' lo intelletto in lingua, in stile, & in foggia Venetiana, laudo sommamente, i Sonetti, i Capitoli, & gli Strambotti, che ho visti, letti & intesi da voi; da altri, & da me" (*Lettere* 5:218'). (Aretino's trio of triads in the last sentence—lingua / stile / foggia; sonetti / capitoli / strambotti; visto / letti / intesi—undoubtedly plays on Venier's correlative technique.) Girolamo Ruscelli also mentioned Venier's *capitoli* satirizing pedantry (now apparently lost), in *Del modo de comporre in versi, nella lingua italiana* (Venice, 1559): "Molto vagamente pur' in quest'anni stessi hanno il mio Signor Domenico Veniero, et altri nobilissimi ingegni introdotto di scrivere in versi Sciolti, & di Terze rime, alcuni soggetti piacevolissimi, & principalmente volendo contrafar la pedanteria. . . . & non so se questa, nè altra lingua habbia sorte di componimento così piacevole. De' quali io ò in questo stesso volume, ò (se pur questo venisse soverchiamente grande) in qualche altro spero di farne dar fuori alcuni, che sieno per pienamente dilettare ogni bello spirito" (Even in these very years my Signor Domenico Venier and other most noble

Until recently nothing else has been known of this aspect of Domenico's literary activity (unlike that of his brother Lorenzo and nephew Maffio, both famous dialect poets). But a codex at the British Library, MS Add. 12.197, preserves a full-length autobiographical *canzoniere* in dialect composed as an exchange between Domenico Venier and another nobleman named Benedetto Corner.[51] The collection turns on the two men's relations with a woman named Helena Artusi, whom both claim to have "chiavà" (screwed). The opening sonnet "del Venier a i Lettori" describes the authors of the poems: "One has the name Domenico, the other Benedetto; one comes from ca' Corner, the other from ca' Venier, and is sick in bed" (Un ha nome Domenego, e Benetto / L'altro; questo si se da ca Corner; / L'altro è da ca Venier, ch'è gramo in letto; vv. 9–11).[52]

The collection is organized as a risqué *canzoniere,* a low dialect countertype to Petrarch's *Rime sparse.* Some of the poetic forms stand outside, in some cases beneath, the Petrarchan *canzoniere,* including *capitoli,* sonnets "con ritornelli," *madregali, madrigaletti,* and *barzellette;* others—canzoni and sonnets "senza ritornelli"—are standard Petrarchan types.[53] Many are in dialogue, mainly with Helena, and a few mention various contemporaries—a "Cabriel Moresini" and the mid-sixteenth-century poet "Domenego Michiel," for example.[54] In order to expand the conceit into a larger social-literary exchange, they also pin Helena's name as alleged author to fictitious rejoinders to their own defamatory verse.

It may seem paradoxical that Venier, like the madrigalists, should have simultaneously practiced two such opposed stylistic levels with equal zeal. But it was not so

talents have very charmingly introduced writing in blank verse and terze rime on some very light subjects, principally wanting to make a burlesque on pedantry . . . and I don't know if this, or any other language may have a sort of composition so pleasing. Some of these I, either in this same volume, or [should it yet become excessively long] in some other one, hope to issue, so that they may delight utterly every beautiful spirit); p. lxxviii.

51. Perhaps this Corner is the one Aretino called "il Cornaro patron mio" in the same letter excerpted in n. 50 above.

52. The manuscript, which I chanced upon at the British Library, had never been discussed in any secondary sources until I shared it with Tiziana Agostini Nordio. She examined my film of the manuscript, corroborated my suspicion of its authenticity, and pointed me to the Aretino excerpt cited above. She has since published a descriptive account of the manuscript, "Poesie dialettali di Domenico Venier," *Quaderni veneti* 14 (1991): 33–56, listing the identifications of Briquet numbers that I made based on my watermark tracings and supplying some information on Helena Artusi (pp. 37–38). I might modify the last of these with the information that Artusi's death was lamented in a sonnet set by Giovanni Nasco and printed in his Second Book for five voices in 1557, "Hor che la frale e mortal gonna è chiusa" (see Einstein, *The Italian Madrigal* 1:460), providing a probable terminus post quem of 1556/57 for the codex. Some of the poems ascribed to Maffio Venier (Domenico's nephew) in I-Vnm, MSS It. cl. IX, 173 (6282), probably belong to Domenico, as indicated by their references to his physical condition; see Antonio Pilot, "Un peccataccio di Domenico Venier," *Fanfulla della domenica* 30 (1906; repr. Rome, 1906). (Though evidently unaware of the British Library MS, Pilot points out, pp. 6–8, that the Marciana codex exchanges dialect verse with a Corner, refers to a Helena, and to Venier's illness.)

For a discussion of dialect verse generally among the Veniers see Rosenthal, *The Honest Courtesan,* pp. 17–19, 37–38, 51–57, 186–89, and passim; and Bodo L. O. Richter, "Petrarchism and Anti-Petrarchism among the Veniers," *Forum italicum* 3 (1969): 20–42.

53. All of these are detailed in the prefatory *sonetto caudato* on fols. 1'–2.

54. Michiel is surely not the Domenico Micheli of Bolognese musical fame, but a poet anthologized at midcentury. The latter has sixteen poems published under the name "Domenico Michele" in the *Libro terzo* and *Libro quarto* (1550 and 1551) of the *Rime di diversi* series—in all fifteen sonnets and one *capitolo.* One of the sonnets in the *Libro terzo* is dedicated to Venier.

in the world of Renaissance styles and conventions, epitomized by the Venetians' pragmatic acceptance of such contradictory modes and their arduous attempts to explain and order them by appeal to Cicero. As early as 1541 a composer called Varoter—apparently a Venetian nobleman fallen on hard times—dedicated his four-voice *villotte* to no less a patron than Duke Ercole of Ferrara with the apologia that "just as a man whose ears are filled with grave and delicate harmonies, satiated as at a royal banquet, feels a desire for coarse and simple fare, so I have prepared some in the form of rustic flowers and fruits."[55]

It is hardly surprising that a prominent patrician and former senator would have kept such activities close to the vest. Venier was a figurehead in a different sense from Willaert. The civic ideals that the chapelmaster was expected to reflect in his official capacity were ones that Venier was obliged to embody as their very font. While Venier and his noble friends might act in paradoxes among one another, these were not for everyone to see. Unlike professional, salaried musicians, they sent works to the press not as the servants of consumer audiences but as representatives of their class. And what they did *not* send the press—whether high or low—was as much a register of class differences as what they did. The pervasive presence of a variety of stylistic registers through all social classes should therefore not be taken as erasures of class differences at the base of social structure. On the contrary, the modes in which styles, and the tropes and dialects attached to them, circulated on the whole maintained, rather than surrendered, the claims of class.

IMPROVISED SONG

In addition to vernacular polyphony, high and low, the academy's music included unwritten song, the sung (and probably at least partly improvisatory) recitations of poetry that formed a continuous part of the indigenous Italian culture so eloquently described by Nino Pirrotta.[56] Castiglione's *Cortegiano* provides evidence that both solo song and written part-song were favored by aristocratic amateurs, and Willaert's transcriptions of Verdelot's madrigals for lute and voice could well have been done by Polissena Pecorina or less virtuosic counterparts.[57] Accordingly,

55. Varoter continues: "I have made so bold to sing Your Excellency's virtues in new melodies and to send them with other canzoni of mine to Your Excellency" (si come quella, che havendo il petto e le sue orecchie piene di gravi e delicate armonie, satia con altrimenti che di regie vivande, voglia descender a grossi e naturali cibi: Liquali io di fiori e frutti rusticani gli ho preparati . . . ho havuto ardimento cantar per modi novi le vostre virtuti, e quelle insieme con altre mie Canzoni mandare alla E. V.). The author's real name was Alvise Castellino. The passage is quoted and translated in Einstein, *The Italian Madrigal* 1:379.

56. See various essays in *Music and Culture in Italy from the Middle Ages to the Baroque: A Collection of Essays* (Cambridge, Mass., 1984), especially "The Oral and Written Traditions of Music," pp. 72–79, and "*Ricercare* and Variations on *O rosa bella*," pp. 145–58. See also James Haar's essay "*Improvvisatori* and Their Relationship to Sixteenth-Century Music," in *Essays on Italian Poetry and Music in the Renaissance, 1350–1600* (Berkeley and Los Angeles, 1986), pp. 76–99, and William F. Prizer's "The Frottola and the Unwritten Tradition," *Studi musicali* 15 (1986): 3–37.

57. On types of music making in Castiglione's milieu see Baldassarre Castiglione, *Il libro del cortegiano*, ed. Ettore Bonora, 2d ed. (Milan, 1976), Book 2, Chap. 13, and James Haar "The Courtier as Musician: Castiglione's View of the Science and Art of Music," in *Castiglione: The Ideal and the Real in Renaissance Culture,* ed. Robert W. Hanning and David Rosand (New Haven, 1983), pp. 171–76.

references to solo singing recur often in the Venier literature—always in conjunction with women, who, until later in the century, had no other apparent place within the academy's ranks.[58]

Several female singers who come to us through encomiastic literature had connections with Venier. In later years a series of letters by the renowned courtesan-poet Veronica Franco, printed in her *Lettere familiari* of 1580, establish Venier as her mentor, and two of them contain suggestive references to music making at home. The ninth one, addressed anonymously like nearly all her letters, invites friends to visit for an occasion in which she will make music at home (an "occasione in ch'io faccio la musica"). She asks to borrow a "stromento da penna," either a kind of harpsichord—probably the more portable spinet—or possibly a lute or guitar.[59] Another (no. 45) tells a friend that on the following day there will be "musica per tempo" at her house and that before the start of this "suono musicale" she hopes to take delight in his "dolcissima armonia de' soavi ragionamenti."[60] Since music was not at the top of Franco's accomplishments, these letters may have provided little more than formulas for epistolary exchange that could be adapted for use by others. Yet her allusions nonetheless point to situations in which music served as social adornment. At issue is not whether Franco herself could really sing and play, or do so well enough for Venier's salon, but rather how her claims match the more generalized expectations of courtly ladies and well-graced *cortigiane oneste*.[61]

Other women praised by Venier were accomplished singers who provided their own accompaniments. To one of them he wrote:

Con varie voci or questa, or quella corda	With various words, now this, now that string
Tocca da bella man sul cavo legno	Does the lovely hand touch on the hollow wood,
Mirabilmente il canto si al suon accorda.	Miraculously tuning her song to its sound.

(no. 68, vv. 9–11)

Willaert's transcriptions of Verdelot appeared in *Intavolatura de li madrigali di Verdelotto de cantare et sonare nel lauto, 1536,* Renaissance Music Prints, vol. 3, ed. Bernard Thomas (London, 1980), facs. ed. Archivum Musicum, Collana di testi rari, no. 36 (Florence, 1980). See Haar's comments on the latter in "Notes on the *Dialogo della musica*," p. 206, and evidence in Doni, *Dialogo della musica,* p. 315.

58. Apropos, a passage from Parabosco's *Lettere amorose* to a woman turns on the conceit that his love and hers issue from a concordant harmony: each of them might play and sing in separate rooms in perfect harmony, their thought in perfect agreement, so perfectly are they tuned to the same (Neoplatonic) music. The air they play is none other than the treble-bass formula called "Ruggiero" after the tradition of reciting stanzas from Ariosto's *Orlando furioso* in solo song; she is compared to Bradamante, he to Ruggiero (*I quattro libri delle lettere amorose,* ed. Thomaso Porcacchi [Venice, 1561], fols. 107–8).

59. The term "stromento da [or 'di'] penna" generally means simply plucked keyboard instrument, as, for example, in the description of the Florentine *intermedi* of 1518, in Lorenzo Strozzi, *Le vite degli uomini illustri della casa Strozzi,* ed. Pietro Stromboli (Florence, 1892), p. xiii; reported in Howard Mayer Brown, *Sixteenth-Century Instrumentation: The Music for the Florentine Intermedi,* Musicological Studies and Documents, no. 30 ([Rome], 1973), p. 87. Nino Pirrotta kindly informs me that since *penna* refers to a plectrum it may also be used synonymously for any instrument played with one—hence guitars and lutes, as well as plucked keyboards (private communication).

60. I thank Margaret F. Rosenthal for bringing these letters to my attention. See Veronica Franco, *Lettere dall'unica edizione del MDLXXX,* ed. Benedetto Croce (Naples, 1949), pp. 19–20.

61. On such questions see Rita Casagrande di Villaviera, *Le cortigiane veneziane del cinquecento* (Milan, 1968); Georgina Masson, *Courtesans of the Italian Renaissance* (New York, 1975); and Anthony

The singer vaunted here is Franceschina Bellamano, as confirmed by the sonnet's contemporary editor Dionigi Atanagi.[62] As early as 1545 the music theorist Pietro Aaron's *Lucidario in musica* listed Bellamano among Italy's renowned "Donne a liuto et a libro."[63] In Ortensio Landi's *Sette libri de cathaloghi* of 1552 she ranked with Polissena Pecorina and the elusive Polissena Frigera as one of three most noted female musicians of the modern era.[64] Like Venier's sonnet, the *Sette libri* emphasized her instrumental skill by punning her name as "bella mano."

Several other solo singers appear in encomiastic literature linked to Venier. In one sonnet Venier joined the chorus of praises sung posthumously to the precocious singer-lutenist Irene di Spilimbergo, mythologized after her untimely death by members of his circle (Molino, Fenaruolo, Dolce, Amalteo, Muzio, Pietro Gradenigo, and Bernardo Tasso). In another he praised the singer and gambist Virginia Vagnoli, wife of Alessandro Striggio.[65] But the most lauded solo singer usually associated with the first decade of Venier's academy was the famed poet Gaspara Stampa. Although she was probably not a regular at their meetings, her close ties with intimates of the academy—especially Parabosco and Molino—and the sonnet she addressed to Venier make her presence there very likely.[66] Stampa's

---

Newcomb, "Courtesans, Muses, or Musicians? Professional Women Musicians in Sixteenth-Century Italy," in *Women Making Music: The Western Art Tradition, 1150–1950*, ed. Jane Bowers and Judith Tick (Urbana and Chicago, 1986), pp. 90–115.

62. See *Rime di Domenico Veniero*, p. xv; the sonnet, *Ne 'l bianco augel, che 'n grembo a Leda giacque*, is no. 68 in Serassi's edition, p. 37. It appears in the anthology *De le rime di diversi nobili poeti toscani, raccolte da M. Dionigi Atanagi, libro secondo, con una nuova tavola del medesimo . . .* (Venice, 1565), fol. 11, where Atanagi's annotated *tavola* reads, "Ad una virtuosa donna, che cantava, & sonava eccellentemente di liuto, detta Franceschina Bellamano: al qual cognome allude nel primo Terzetto" (fol. K/2 4). See also Bussi, *Umanità e arte*, p. 36.

63. Fol. 32. See also the references to Bellamano in Einstein, *The Italian Madrigal* 1:447 and 2:843. Einstein considered her—without evidence—to have been a courtesan, as he did virtually all female musicians; see Chap. 2 n. 51 above for a reassessment of the problematics involved.

64. The full title of the former is *Sette libri de cathaloghi a' varie cose appartenenti, non solo antiche, ma anche moderne: opera utile molto alla historia, et da cui prender si po materia di favellare d'ogni proposto che si occorra* (Venice, 1552); she is listed as "Franceschina bella mano" on p. 512. I am indebted to Howard Mayer Brown for the reference and for the use of his copy of the book. Parabosco addressed a letter to Polissena Frigera (Frizzera) in his second book of *Lettere amorose*; see *Libro secondo delle lettere amorose di M. Girolamo Parabosco* (Venice, 1573), fol. 11'.

65. For the verses to Spilimbergo see *Rime di diversi nobilissimi, et eccellentissimi autori, in morte della Signora Irene delle Signore di Spilimbergo. Alle quali si sono aggiunti versi Latini di diversi egregij Poeti, in morte della medesima Signora*, ed. Dionigi Atanagi (Venice, 1561), with Venier's poem on p. 33. Like Venier's sonnet to Franceschina Bellamano, this one plays with the words *bella man*. This might seem to suggest that the former could also have been intended for Irene or another female singer-lutenist other than *Franceschina* Bellamano, but Atanagi's authority as editor of both volumes (cf. n. 62 above) makes this unlikely. On the volume dedicated to Irene see Marcellino, *Il diamerone*, p. 5; Elvira Favretti, "Una raccolta di rime del cinquecento," *Giornale storico della letteratura italiana* 158 (1981): 543–72; and Anne Jacobson Schutte, "Irene di Spilimbergo: The Image of a Creative Woman in Late Renaissance Italy," *RQ* 44 (1991): 42–61. For a reprint of the table of contents see idem, "Commemorators of Irene di Spilimbergo," *RQ* 45 (1992): 524–36.

The information about Vagnoli was kindly related to me by David Butchart. It appears in a sonnet of Venier's (not included in Serassi's ed.) cited by Alfredo Saviotti, "Un'artista del cinquecento: Virginia Vagnoli," *Bulletino senese di storia patria* 26 (1919): 116–18.

66. The sonnet to Venier is no. 252 in her *Rime varie*; mod. ed., *Rime*, ed. Bellonci and Ceriello, p. 247. On the question of Stampa's involvement in ca' Venier see Abdelkader Salza, "Madonna Gasparina Stampa, secondo nuove indagini," *Giornale storico della letteratura italiana* 62 (1913): 1–101, who delivers a negative opinion while adducing much evidence that can be interpreted to the contrary (pp. 22–23).

singing was continually exalted with the topos of weeping stones; Parabosco's letter in his *Lettere amorose* of 1545 is only one of many such references: "What shall I say of that angelic voice, which sometimes strikes the air with its divine accents, making such a sweet harmony that it not only seems to everyone who is worthy of hearing it as if a Siren's . . . but infuses spirit and life into the coldest stones and makes them weep with sweetness?"[67]

We know little of how these soloists' unpreserved music sounded. I imagine Stampa singing fairly stock melodic formulas for poetic recitation not unlike the ones printed in Petrucci's Fourth Book of Frottolas of 1505 as "modi" or "aeri," which matched different melodies to different poetic forms—sonnets, *capitoli,* and so forth.[68] Such melodies were entirely apt for the poet-reciter, for whom display of original verse was the main point. They could be invented or borrowed, and reapplied stanza after stanza with creative variations and ornamentation, the patterns reshaped according to the poem's thematic development and the performer's inspiration.

The process is simple enough to try by applying Petrucci's melodies to Stampa's own verse. What emerges from such an exercise is how very singable her lyrics are—not only in the musicality of their scansion and sound groups, but in their thematizing of the very process of reciting in song.[69] Frequently Stampa's verse begins by summoning a friend, lover, or muse with a vocative rhetorical device in a way that might invite some kind of musical intonation. In the opening of Stampa's *capitolo* no. 256 we hear an apostrophic call to a muse that suggests this kind of intonation, replete with allusions to singing, melodic qualities, and the emotions they engender.[70]

Musa mia, che sì pronta e sì cortese	My muse, you who were so quick and so kind
A pianger fosti meco ed a cantare	To weep with me and to sing
Le mie gioie d'amor tutte, e l'offese	Of all my joys of love, and the hurts
In tempre oltra l'usato aspre ed amare	In modes beyond the usual harsh and bitter ones,[71]
Movi meco dolente e sbigottita	You move with me dolefully and dismayed,
Con le sorelle a pianger e a gridare . . .	With your sisters weeping and crying out . . .

67. "Che dirò io di quella angelica voce, che qualhora percuota l'aria de' suoi divini accenti, fa tale sì dolce harmonia, che non pura a guisa di Sirena fa d'ognuno, che degno d'ascoltarla . . . ma infonde spirto e vita nelle più fredde pietre, facendole per soverchia dolcezza lacrimare?" (*Libro primo delle lettere amorose di M. Girolamo Parabosco* [Venice, 1573], fol. 21′). Molino also referred to Stampa as a siren ("Nova Sirena"); see Salza, "Madonna Gasparina Stampa," p. 26, and for Ortensio Landi's praise of her musical prowess, pp. 17–18.

68. This book (RISM 1505⁵) contains untexted melodic formulas for a "Modo de cantar sonetti" (fol. 14) and an "Aer de versi latini" (fol. 36), as well as a texted "Aer de capituli," *Un solicito amor* (fol. 55′), for which different texts in *capitolo* form can be supplied. It is reprinted in Ottaviano Petrucci, *Frottole, Buch I und IV: Nach dem Erstlingsdrucken von 1504 und 1505 (?),* ed. Rudolf Schwartz, Publikationen älterer Musik, vol. 8 (Leipzig, 1935; repr. Hildesheim, 1967).

69. The latter forms the subject of a study by Janet L. Smarr, "Gaspara Stampa's Poetry for Performance," *Journal of the Rocky Mountain Medieval and Renaissance Association* 12 (1991): 61–84.

70. See also sonnet 173, *Cantate meco, Progne e Filomena,* and Ann Rosalind Jones's analysis of it as "an exchange of sympathy and song," *The Currency of Eros: Women's Love Lyric in Europe, 1540–1620* (Indianapolis, 1990), pp. 138–39.

71. I should emphasize that my use of "modes" for *tempre* here does not mean to imply the full panoply of technical traits linked with sixteenth-century modal theory. I intend instead the more general

In recitation for terze rime such as these the three poetic lines of the *capitolo*'s stanzas would each be matched with a single musical phrase and the overall poetic prosody of each strophe thus shaped by a larger tripartite architectural scheme. Tunes for reciting such stanzas typically have a simple progressive shape that defines the keynote at the start, migrates above it, and then sinks to a clear return. The anonymous setting of Jacopo Sannazaro's *capitolo Se mai per maraveglia alzando 'l viso,* as arranged by Franciscus Bossinensis for lute and voice and printed by Petrucci in *Tenori e contrabassi intabulati col soprano in canto figurato . . . Libro secundo* in 1511, suits Stampa's *capitolo* especially well (see Ex. 1, where the music is given with Sannazaro's text replaced by Stampa's).[72] The arrangement offers up a preludial series of freely iterated, improvisatory chordal arpeggios that preface the recitative-like opening of the tune. This in turn leads into a more melodious excursion at the tune's center.[73] In Ex. 1 I have underlaid the first stanza of Stampa's *capitolo* to which she could have applied grace notes, cadential decorations, rhythmic alterations, and other forms of improvisation here and in subsequent stanzas.

Of course, Stampa could also have used newer formulas, or made them up herself. A remarkable discovery by Lynn Hooker concerning Stampa's only two canzoni, nos. 68 and 299, lends supports to the latter alternative.[74] Hooker points out that the two share precisely the same versification scheme and, moreover, that the first of them, *Chiaro e famoso mare,* bases its content, narrative, and verse structure on Petrarch's *Chiare fresche et dolci acque.* We know that canzoni were among the least fixed of repetitive forms and therefore the least susceptible to repetitive melodic formulas; they could use stock melodic archetypes traditionally linked with *settenari* and *endecasillabi,* respectively, but the method of pairing, separating, concatenating, and varying the melodies has to have been keyed (at minimum) to the particular formal scheme of each individual canzone. The unusual formal identity of the canzoni in this trio (including Stampa's two and Petrarch's *Chiare fresche*) might alone be grounds to suspect that Stampa performed all three with the same melodic

sense of melodies or melodic gestures using characteristic intervallic relationships, especially as they might have been conceived within a broad cultural consciousness as evoking affects.

72. Knud Jeppesen, *La Frottola,* 3 vols. (Copenhagen, 1968), 1:118, lists the piece as "Laude?" My attribution of the poem to Sannazaro is based on Iacobo Sannazaro, *Opere volgari,* ed. Alfredo Mauro (Bari, 1961), pp. 210–11, where it is given with the rubric "Lamentazione sopra il corpo del Redentor del mondo a' mortali."

73. This example seems to me to suit Stampa's poem for use as a *capitolo* formula better than the generic "aer de capituli" published by Petrucci in RISM 1505⁵, since the latter is more lyrical than recitational and rather foursquare in its metric-melodic contours. (See fol. v' of Petrucci's Book Four, ed. Kroyer, p. 99.) Kevin Mason shows how unusual the idiomatic, improvisatory style of Bossinensis's ed. of *Se mai per maraviglia* is among early- to midcentury lute books; see "Per cantare e sonare: Lute Song Arrangements of Italian Vocal Polyphony at the End of the Renaissance," in *Playing Lute, Guitar, and Vihuela: Historical Practice and Modern Interpretation,* ed. Victor Coelho (Cambridge, forthcoming). See also Howard Mayer Brown, "Bossinensis, Willaert and Verdelot: Pitch and the Conventions of Transcribing Music for Lute and Voice in the Early Sixteenth Century," *Revue de musicologie* 75 (1989): 25–46, who argues that Bossinensis initiates a tradition for publishing lute books that largely demonstrate how to arrange "apparently vocal polyphony" for solo performance (rather than how to play lute accompaniments in the idiomatic, improvisatory style).

74. Hooker's study was produced in my seminar on Petrarchism at the University of Chicago. In its current form it bears the title "Gaspara Stampa: Venetian, Petrarchist, and *Virtuosa*" (seminar paper, Winter 1992).

E x . 1 .   Anon. *capitolo* setting, *Se mai per maraveglia alzando 'l viso*, with a *capitolo* text by Gaspara Stampa substituted for Sannazaro's *capitolo*; in *Tenori e contrabassi intabulati col sopran in canto figurato per cantar e sonar col lauto: libro secundo. Francisci Bossinensis* (Venice, 1511), fols. v^v-vi.

formulas and that the formulas were either her own or adapted by her to suit the special requirements of the three canzoni's shared formal structures. Hooker virtually clinches the argument that this was so by relating the nexus of canzoni to Orazio Brunetti's letter to Stampa in which he begs re-entry into her salon with the plea that he has missed her marvelous singing and especially her rendition of Petrarch's *Chiare fresche*.

Whether the melodies were Stampa's inventions or adaptations from preexistent formulas, her practice would almost certainly have matched melodic phrases to poetic lines, rather than to syntactic structures (which in any case do not always correspond to line lengths). This approach is far from high-styled Venetian madrigalian practice. It comes closer to madrigalian styles linked in their text-music relationships, harmonic patterns, and free treble-dominated declamatory rhythms to the world of *improvvisatori,* the most striking manifestations of which are the *madrigali ariosi.*[75] The music's role in both solo singing and polyphonic imitations thereof—but especially in singing *by* the poet her- or himself—was to provide the verse with a musical dress. This did not mean that the goal of moving the listener through the efficacious joining of words and voice was any less strong for song than polyphony; indeed the reverse could have been true. It means instead that song did not aim for a sovereign aesthetic equal to the poetry in the same way elaborate polyphonic settings did.

——————

In 1547 the madrigalist Perissone Cambio dedicated to Stampa his *Primo libro di madrigali a quatro voci,* praising her musical talent, her "sweet harmonies," and recalling her epithet of "divine siren."[76] Perissone's dedication confirms the connection we might infer from Parabosco's letter to her cited earlier—a connection, that is, between Stampa, the *cantatrice,* and Venetian polyphonists. Yet the volume's contents show even more importantly that their distinct performing traditions—written polyphony and recited song—at times merged. Perissone's four-voice madrigals set two distinct kinds of verse: weighty Petrarchan sonnets and lighter *ottave,* madrigals, and ballatas, most of which were short. Frequently homophonic, these four-voice settings traded in great melodic charm. They strike a course midway between the tradition of melodious song practiced by Stampa and the thick, motetlike style found in the new five- and six-voice Venetian madrigals. Perissone, in other words, brought to many of his four-voice madrigals that

75. *Madrigali ariosi* were issued by the Roman publisher Antonio Barrè in three different editions, first printed in 1555, 1558, and 1562, respectively. See James Haar, "The *Madrigale Arioso:* A Mid-Century Development in the Cinquecento Madrigal," *Studi musicali* 12 (1983): 203–19, and (with particular attention to the relations of harmony, melodic phrasing, and verse lines) Howard Mayer Brown, "Verso una definizione dell'armonia nel sedicesimo secolo: sui *madrigali ariosi* di Antonio Barrè," *Rivista italiana di musicologia* 25 (1990): 18–60.

76. The dedication and translation are given in Chap. 9, p. 373. A facsimile of the dedication also appears in my edition of the book, Sixteenth-Century Madrigal, vol. 3 (New York, 1989), p. xvi.

indefinable, memorable, and tuneful quality that Pirrotta linked to the Italians' notion of "aria"[77]—a quality particularly striking in them since they were published after Perissone issued his first book of five-voice madrigals in a style close to the *Musica nova*.

The more tuneful approach of Perissone's *Madrigali a quatro voci* resembles Donato's four-voice settings of Venier's three patriotic stanzas for the dual celebration of Ascension Day and the Marriage of Venice to the Sea.[78] I offer the text of one of them below.

Gloriosa, felic'alma, Vineggia,	Glorious, happy soul, Venice,		
Di giustitia, d'amor, di pace albergo,	Shelter of justice, of love, of peace,		
Che quant'altre città più al mondo pregia	You who, first in honor, leave behind		
Come prima d'honor ti lassi a tergo.	All other cities praised in the world:	4	
Ben puoi tu sola dir città d'egregia;	Well may you alone be called city of renown;		
Stando nell'acqu'in fin al ciel io mergo,	I immerse myself up to Heaven in water,		
Poichè mi serb'anchor l'eterna cura,	Since the eternal cure still serves me,		
Vergine, già mill'anni intatt'e pura.[79]	Virgin, a thousand years intact and pure.	8	

Donato's setting (Ex. 2) avoids the blurred outlines of the new Willaertian madrigal—a style in which the young composer was by then already proficient.[80] Instead it celebrates the poem's association of the Virgin with the Marian virtues of Venice by means of lucid textures and well-defined successions of textual units. The simple F-mollis tonality concentrates its cadences exclusively on F and C and continually emphasizes the unassuming modal degrees of F, C, and A to create pleasing melodic outlines. Its graceful arioso melodies are enhanced by a fairly harmonic bass line, both treble and bass thus recalling characteristics of songlike genres. In this way the words project clearly to suit what was probably an outdoor performance on the occasion for which it was written, with instruments doubling vocal parts. But it may also have been heard with reduced forces in chamber performances at salons like Venier's. In such a venue

---

77. See Pirrotta's "Willaert and the *Canzone villanesca*," in *Music and Culture in Italy*, p. 195, and Nino Pirrotta and Elena Povoledo, *Music and Theatre from Poliziano to Monteverdi*, trans. Karen Eales (Cambridge, 1982), pp. 247ff.

78. They appeared in *Baldissara Donato musico e cantor in santo Marco, le napolitane, et alcuni madrigali a quatro voci da lui novamente composte, corrette, & misse in luce* (Venice, 1550). See Ellen Rosand, "Music in the Myth of Venice," *RQ* 30 (1977): 527–30, with particular attention to the modernized reinterpretations of Venetian civic mythology in Venier's poems.

79. *Rime di Domenico Veniero*, p. 40. (Here and elsewhere, I give the orthographical variants as they appear in the musical source.) Parabosco seemingly glossed the first line of the poem as the last line of his own *Stanze in lode de l'inclita città di Vinegia*, first published in his *Rime* (Venice, 1547), fols. 19–21′: "di virtù tante Iddio t'adorna, et fregia, / felice gloriosa alma Vinegia" (15.7–8). Perhaps Venier's stanzas already existed by that time. For a modern edition of Parabosco's *Stanze* see Bianchini, *Gerolamo Parabosco*, pp. 461–64.

80. When only about eighteen years old Donato had already published a highly proficient madrigal in the Willaertian style, a setting of Petrarch's sonnet *S'una fed'amorosa, s'un cor non finto* (see Chap. 9 n. 70 below). It was included in Cipriano de Rore's *Terzo libro di madrigali a cinque voci* of 1548 (RISM 1548⁹); for a mod. ed. see my "Venice and the Madrigal in the Mid-Sixteenth Century," 2 vols. (Ph.D. diss., University of Pennsylvania, 1987), 2:656–67.

Ex. 2. Donato, *Gloriosa, felic'alma, Vineggia* (Domenico Venier), incl.; *Le napolitane, et alcuni madrigali a 4* (Venice, 1550), p. 20.

Ex. 2 *(continued)*

18

Co - me pri - ma d'ho-nor ti las - - si a ter - go, ti las -

Co - me pri - ma d'ho-nor ti las - si a ter - - - go, ti las-si a ter - go, ti

- gia   Co - me pri - ma d'ho-nor ti

mon-do pre - - gia Co - me pri - ma d'ho-nor ti las-si a ter - go.

24

si a ter - - go.   Ben   puoi tu so - - la dir

las - si a ter - go.   Ben puoi tu so-la dir,   (ben puoi tu so-la dir)___

las - si a ter - go. Ben puoi tu so-la dir, ben   puoi tu so - - la dir

Ben   puoi tu so-la dir,   (ben puoi tu so - - la dir)___

30

ci - tà   d'e-gre - gia; Stan - do nel-l'a - qu'in fin al ciel io mer -

___ ci-tà d'e-gre - gia;   Stan - do nel-l'a - qu'in fin al ciel io mer -

ci - tà   d'e-gre - gia; Stan - do nel-l'a - - - qu'in fin___ al ciel io

___ ci-tà d'e-gre - gia; Stan - do nel-l'a - - qu'in fin   al ciel io mer -

(continued)

111

its text could articulate the academy's alliance with the same civic values that sound less directly in the copious Bembist lyrics its members produced.

Since musical activity in Venier's salon functioned as a pastime rather than a central activity, and since the academy kept no formal records of its meetings, concrete evidence of links between musicians and men of letters is scarce. Parabosco, as a key figure in both the musical establishment at San Marco and the literary circle of Venier, forms the primary liaison between musicians and writers. Among literati the most intriguing link may be found in the figure of Molino, Venier's aristocratic poet friend and acquaintance of Parabosco (who sent him two books of his *Lettere amorose*).[81] Molino's stature in Venetian society was considerable, despite family battles that cost him an extended period of poverty and travails (on which more in Chap. 6).[82] A bust sculpted by Alessandro Vittoria for the tiny Cappella Molin in Santa Maria del Giglio—where a great number of reliquaries owned by the family are still preserved—portrays Molino as the embodiment of gerontocratic wisdom (Plate 18).

In 1573 his posthumous biographer, Giovan Mario Verdizzotti, wrote that of all the arts Molino had delighted in understanding music most of all.[83] The remark is supported by earlier evidence. Several composers based in Venice and the Veneto—Jean Gero, Francesco Portinaro, and Antonio Molino (no relation)—set Molino's seemingly little-accessible verse to music before its publication in 1573, four years after the poet's death.[84] As early as 2 April 1535 Molino seems to have tried to obtain a frottola, *Se la mia morte brami,* by one of the genre's greatest exponents, Bartolomeo Tromboncino. The work had been requested of Tromboncino (then in Vicenza) by the Venetian theorist Giovanni del Lago, who apparently was in such a hurry to procure it that Tromboncino had no time to rewrite the original lute-accompanied version in a more madrigalesque vocal arrangement with the addition of an alto part, as had apparently been asked of him.

> You ask me for the draft of *Se la mia morte brami,* and I send it to you most happily, advising you that I have written it only for singing to the lute, that is, without alto. For this reason, for whoever should want to sing it [a cappella], the [missing] alto would produce a serious wrong. Had you not had so little time, I would have

81. Cited in Bianchini, *Girolamo Parabosco,* pp. 420–21 n. 2.

82. See Chap. 6 nn. 11–14 below. The most extensive modern work on Molino is that of Elisa Greggio, "Girolamo da Molino," 2 pts., *Ateneo veneto,* ser. 18, vol. 2 (Venice, 1894), pp. 188–202 and 255–323.

83. "[D]i Musica . . . egli sommamente intendendosene dilettava" (Molino, *Rime,* p. [6]).

84. The settings are *Amore, quanta dolcezza* in Gero's *Book 2 a 3,* 2d ed. (Venice, 1556), of which the first ed. is lost; and *Come vago augellin ch'a poco a poco* in Portinaro's *Book 1 a 4* (1563), the latter also set in Antonio Molino's *I dilettevoli madrigali a quatro voci* (1568). The publication of Molino's posthumous *canzoniere* in 1573 led to many further settings, including three by Andrea Gabrieli, one by Luca Marenzio, five by Massaino, three by Pordenon, and twenty-four by Philippe de Monte, none of them listed in *Il nuovo Vogel.*

18.   Alessandro Vittorino, *Bust of Girolamo Molino,* Cappella Molìn, Chiesa di Santa Maria del Giglio, Venice. Photo courtesy of Osvaldo Böhm.

arranged it for singing in four parts, with no one part obstructing any of the others, and on my return to Venice, which will be at the beginning of May, if such an occasion arises, I shall fashion one of the sort mentioned above in order to make you understand that I have been and always shall be at your service. But please do me this favor: remember me to the magnificent and kindly Messer Girolamo Molino, that lover of artists ["virtuosi"], whom God by his grace should grant hundreds and hundreds of years of life.[85]

85. "V.S. mi richiede la minuta de :Se la mia morte brami: et così molto voluntier ve la mando, ad vertendovi ch'io non la feci se non da cantar nel lauto cioè senza contr'alto. Per che chi cantar la volesse il contr'alto da lei seria offeso. Ma se presta [*sic*] non haveste havuto, gli n'harei fatta una che se canta ria a 4 senza impedir lun laltro et alla ritornata mia a Venetia che sera a principio de maggio se accadera gli nefaro una al modo supra dicto facendovi interder [*sic*] ch'io fui et sempre sero minor vostro facendomi pero questo piacere racomandarmi al magnifico et gentilissimo gentilhomo amator de i virtuosi ms Hyeronimo molino che Dio cent'e cent'anni in sua gratia lo conservi." In musical contexts the term

Tromboncino's allusion to the rushed nature of the request that prevented him from producing the four-voice version and his warm regards to Molino suggest that the work was wanted for a specific occasion and probably by Molino, rather than del Lago. The work is lost, but we may assume that it was either a traditional frottola or rather akin to one. As a genre, of course, the frottola was related to the tradition of solo singing practiced by Molino's good friend Gaspara Stampa.

Molino himself may have performed solo song, as Stampa seems to hint in a sonnet dedicated to him with the words "Qui convien sol la tua cetra, e 'l tuo canto, / Chiaro Signor" (Here only your lyre is fitting, and your song, / eminent sir).[86] In Petrarchan poetry the idea of singing, and singing to the lyre, is of course a metaphorical adaptation of classical convention to mean simply poetizing, without intent to evoke real singing and playing. But Stampa's poems make unusual and pointed separations between the acts of "scrivere" and "cantare" that suggest she meant real singing here.[87]

Other contemporaries specifically point up Molino's knowledge of theoretical and practical aspects of music. Six years after Tromboncino's letter was written, in 1541, Giovanni del Lago dedicated his extensive collection of musical correspondence to Molino, whom he declared held "the first degree in the art of music" (nell arte di Musica tiene il primo grado). Further, he claimed, "Your Lordship . . . merits . . . the dedication of the present epistles, in which are contained various questions about music. . . . And certainly one sees that few today are found (like you) learned . . . in such a science, but yet adorned with kindness and good morals."[88] Del Lago's correspondence, as will be seen in Chapter 6, was theoretically oriented in church polyphony. One of its most striking aspects is its recognition of connections between music and language that parallel those embodied in the new Venetian madrigal style. Del Lago insisted that vernacular poetry be complemented with suitable musical effects and verbal syntax with musical phrasing. In

---

virtuosi generally referred to musicians, so here Molino is probably being called specifically a "lover of musicians." Quoted from I-Rvat, MS Vat. lat. 5318, fol. 188; Einstein, *The Italian Madrigal* 1:48, gives a translation along with a somewhat different version of the text, as does Jeppesen, *La frottola* 1:150–1. The entire manuscript of Vat. lat. 5318 has been transcribed and published along with glosses of each letter in English by Bonnie J. Blackburn, Edward E. Lowinsky, and Clement A. Miller, eds., *A Correspondence of Renaissance Musicians* (Oxford, 1991), with Tromboncino's letter on p. 869. I am indebted to Bonnie Blackburn for reminding me of the latter and sharing substantial portions of the *Correspondence* with me prior to its publication.

86. No. 261, vv. 12–13, from her *Rime varie*.

87. Franco, who may also have done solo singing, does so too; see, for example, *capitolo* no. 2, v. 169, in *Gaspara Stampa—Veronica Franco: Rime,* ed. Abdelkader Salza (Bari, 1913), p. 241. I suspect that this is a feature of poetry conceived for an immediate audience—a distinctive aspect of a musician's verse, as both Stampa's and (to a lesser extent) Franco's was. This is a point made by Smarr, "Gaspara Stampa's Poetry for Performance." One should also note Venier's sonnet to Molino (*Rime di Domenico Venier,* no. 48, p. 26), which refers to the "suon delle tue note" (v. 6)—again, possibly with literal intent.

88. "Vostra segnoria . . . merita . . . la dedicazione delle presenti epistole, nellequali si contengono diversi dubbij di Musica. . . . Et certo si vede che pochi al di d'hoggi si trovano (come voi) dottata . . . di tale scienza, ma ancora di gentilezza, et costumi ornata." This is the same collection of correspondence that contains Tromboncino's letter cited in n. 85 above—MS Vat. lat. 5318 (fol. [1′]).

discussing these relationships he developed musically the Ciceronian ideals of propriety and *varietas*.[89] His dedication to Molino therefore presents a fascinating bridge between patronage in Venier's circle and developments in Venetian music. Yet taken in sum these sources show Molino's musical patronage embracing two different traditions, each quite distinct. one, the arioso tradition of improvisors and frottolists; the other, the learned tradition of church polyphonists. Molino's connection with both practices reinforces the impression that Venetian literati prized each of them.

Indeed, informal salons like Venier's, with their easy mixing of diverse personal and artistic styles, were ideally constituted to accommodate different traditions. They were well equipped to nurture the kind of interaction of musical and literary cultures necessary to achieve a profitable exchange and, at times, a fusion of disparate traditions. As we have seen, this was accomplished in a variety of ways: in the appropriation of literary ideals by composers, so evident in the new Venetian madrigal; in the bifurcation of secular genres according to Italian and dialect, high and low; and in the continued commingling of the ideals of song with those of imitative counterpoint, seen both in Perissone's four-voice book of polyphonic madrigals and in Donato's settings of Venier's stanzas.

AFTERWORD

By the late 1550s, certain urban groups began crystallizing into more definite structures. Titled, formalized academies such as were to become the norm late in the century now made their first appearance.[90] The most celebrated of these was the brainchild of Venier's lifelong friend Federigo Badoer, who in 1557 began forming a highly public academy called the Accademia Veneziana, or Accademia della Fama.[91] This extravagant organization was a large, ambitious, and fatally costly undertaking designed formally along the lines of the Aldine Neacademia to serve the public needs of scholarship in science, arts, and letters.[92] Its parallel in Florence was the Medici-supported Accademia Fiorentina. The Accademia Veneziana ultimately consisted of an administrative staff with four notaries and a secretariat, headed by a

---

89. I summarize these points in "The Composer as Exegete: Interpretations of Petrarchan Syntax in the Venetian Madrigal," *Studi musicali* 18 (1989): 203–38, esp. pp. 219–23.

90. The only real formal ancestor to this phenomenon in Venice was the Aldine Neacademia, which thrived from 1496 to ca. 1515 and had its official constitution in Greek. See Martin Lowry, *The World of Aldus Manutius: Business and Scholarship in Renaissance Venice* (Ithaca, 1979), pp. 195ff.

91. The most important modern studies of the Accademia Veneziana are those of Rose, "The Accademia Venetiana," pp. 191–242; Pietro Pagan, "Sulla Accademia 'Venetiana' o della 'Fama,' " *Atti dell'Istituto Veneto di Scienze, Lettere ed Arti* 132 (1973–74): 359–92 (with corrections to some of the documents transcribed in Rose); and Lina Bolzoni, "L'Accademia Veneziana: splendore e decadenza di una utopia enciclopedica," in *Università, accademie e società scientifiche in Italia e in Germania dal cinquecento al settecento*, ed. Laetitia Boehm and Ezio Raimondi, Annali dell'Istituto Storico Italo-Germanico, no. 9 (Bologna, 1981), pp. 117–67. A brief entry appears in Maylender, *Storia delle accademie* 5:436–43.

92. Another notable precursor, though much more modest in scope, is the Accademia degli Uniti founded in 1551, which did have official *capitoli;* see Antonio Pilot, "Gli ordini dell'Accademia Veneziana degli Uniti 1551," *Ateneo veneto* 35 (1912): 193–207.

chancellor, Bernardo Tasso, to whom it paid a handsome salary equivalent to Willaert's as chapelmaster of San Marco—two hundred ducats. Its separate departments, the Consiglio Iconomico, Consiglio Politico, Consiglio delle Scientie, and Oratorio, were intended collectively to embrace the whole of the Renaissance encyclopedia and thereby ensure the moral and scientific education of the state. As announced in a series of three published constitutions, various *suppliche,* and letters, it aimed to cover the full range of disciplines, since all pertained "to the public and private interests."[93] Official members were eventually enrolled in scores of categories—even Zarlino was listed under the rubric of "musico."[94]

The academy was defunct after less than four years. The phenomenon of its abrupt rise and fall marks an anxiety deeply embedded within the opposed alternatives of private and public, which forms a major theme in midcentury Venice. Particularly revealing are the intersections between Badoer's ambitiously titled Accademia Veneziana and the decidedly nameless *accademie* at ca' Venier.

Both Venier and Molino helped out with the planning and execution of the Accademia Veneziana in its formative phase. In September 1557 Venier joined the signers of a letter to Camillo Vezzato inviting him to participate in Badoer's academy—"a company" they claimed already to have "bound together," though in actual fact it was still in its founding stages.[95] Molino, for his part, wrote to Bernardo Tasso on behalf of the Accademia Veneziana on 22 January 1558 singing its praises.[96]

> In recent days a noble company of learned and flourishing talents has joined together under the title Accademia Veneziana, having the intention of profiting literati and the world by putting into their hands books of philosophy and other disciplines. And not only in order to purge these of infinite errors and mistakes, which in truth they do contain, much to the grief of scholars, but to compile them with many useful annotations, discourses, and scholarly notes and, translated from various languages, bring them to light with the most beautiful printing and paper ever seen. Beyond this they intend to send forth new works, both by them and by others, never before printed; and indeed (from what I have understood) they have a great number of them prepared. This undertaking appears vast and very difficult; however, knowing the excellence and energy of those who have taken it upon themselves makes me believe that it will undoubtedly go forward fortuitously. Indeed they have rented the most elegant shop with the most lovely view in our whole Merceria, which they soon intend to open.[97]

93. The words are Badoer's, from a *supplica* of 12 July 1560 to the Procuratori asking to shift the academy from his house to the rooms of the Biblioteca Sansovino at San Marco, newly finished by Titian; see Rose, "The *Accademia Venetiana,*" p. 229. See also the letter of Badoer's from 1559 quoted in Rose, p. 193.
94. Maylender, *Storia delle accademie* 5:442.
95. Pagan, "Sulla Accademia 'Venetiana,'" p. 361 n. 7.
96. *Delle lettere di M. Bernardo Tasso,* 3 vols. in 2 (Padua, 1733–51), 2:358–61.
97. "[A'] giorni passati s'è congregata insieme una nobile compagnia, sotto titolo di Accademia Veneziana, di alcuni dotti, e fioriti ingegni, avendo intenzione di giovare a letterati, e al mondo, col metter le mani così nei libri di Filosofia, come di altre facultà: e non solo purgar quelli degli infiniti errori, e incorrezioni che nel vero portano seco attorno, con molto danno degli studiosi, ma farli insieme con molte utili annotazioni, e discorsi e scolj, e tradotti appresso in diverse lingue, uscire in luce nella più

All of this was simply a prelude to a request that Tasso place his newly written *Amadigi* in their hands. Molino adds that most of these "Signori Accademici" are his friends; it is they who entreated him to make this request, together with "various of their protectors, among whom are Federigo Badoaro and Domenico Veniero."[98]

While Molino knows something about the various plans he mentions, he hardly seems to count himself as one of the official academists. Much of what he relates sounds secondhand, as if he had been prepped by them to try to acquire the prestigious work for publication and went through with the task only as a favor.[99] Venier's role, the letter suggests, might have been parallel to Badoer's at this early stage. But other documents lead me to believe that it could not have extended much beyond that of an initial financial backer.

Indeed Molino's distanced tone seems to presage the future relationship between Venier's private circle and the grand scheme conceived by Badoer. Neither Venier nor Molino can be found in documents emanating from the academy after these initial ones. The original business charter of 14 November 1557 did not include them, and neither of them signed the by-laws of the Accademia Veneziana in 1559.[100] Contrary to what is stated in virtually all of the literature on Venier's circle, moreover, nothing suggests that Venier's group merged with the Accademia Veneziana only to return to its separate, private, and informal state after the Accademia Veneziana's demise.[101]

The small—and finally nonexistent—place Venier and Molino occupy in the documents can be no accident; on the contrary their absence is remarkable. To read the documents otherwise misconstrues the spirit that informed Venier's enterprise, for although Badoer started from a combination of civic and literary ideals that were partially epitomized by Venier's academy at that time, he institutionalized them in

bella stampa, e carta che si sia ancor veduta. Oltra di ciò intendono dar fuori Opre nuove, e non più stampate, sì per loro, come per altre composte; e già (per quel ch'io ho inteso) essi ne hanno gran numero apparecchiato. La qual' impresa, ancor che paja grande, e difficile molto; tuttavia il conoscere il valore di quei che l'hanno sopra di se tolta, e il buon polso loro, mi fa credere che ella anderà innanzi con felice corso senza dubbio. E già hanno tolta ad affitto la più bella bottega, e nella più bella vista che sia in tutta la nostra Mercería, intendono tosto aprila" (ibid., 2:359–60).

98. "[T]anto più volentieri vi do questo ricordo, quanto questi Signori Accademici; che sono per lo più miei amici . . . me ne hanno fatto instanza" (ibid., 2:360); and later, "io ne sono stato pregato da questi Signori miei amici, e da diversi loro protettori, tra' quali è'l Clarissimo M. Federigo Badoaro, e M. Domenico Veniero; in nome de' quali io la prego insieme di questo favore" (ibid., 2:361).

99. For further on the letter's references to *Amadigi* see Bolzoni, "L'Accademia Veneziana," pp. 124 and 128–29.

100. See Documents 1 and 2 given in Rose, "The *Accademia Venetiana*," pp. 216–24, and other Documents given in his Appendix.

101. The idea is implied by Serassi, *Rime di Domenico Venier,* p. xvii. Zorzi's recent *Cortigiana veneziana* states outright that the gatherings at ca' Venier transferred directly to the house of Badoer (p. 81), as if to suggest that Venier's salon simply emptied out during this time. Both Tiraboschi, *Storia della letteratura italiana* 7/1:253 and 7/3:1684, and Bolzoni, "L'Accademia Veneziana," pp. 119–20, tie the birth of the Accademia Veneziana closely to Venier's inner circle, albeit without claiming such a direct causal relationship. As far as I can determine, the freshest reading of Venier's relationship to the Accademia Veneziana based on known documents is that of Pagan, "Sulla Accademia 'Venetiana,' " esp. pp. 359–66.

ways antithetical to the mood of casual artistic exchange at ca' Venier.[102] The ambitious agenda formulated in the Accademia Veneziana included a new philological emphasis that had had little place in the informal salon. Translations into the vernacular proposed in the summa of the Accademia Veneziana included an expanded corpus of authors in line with the academy's encyclopedic leanings.[103]

This is not to say that Badoer's venture bore no fruit after financial corruption brought on its ruin. When the Accademia Veneziana foundered in 1561 Venier's salon seems to have absorbed some of its stranded *letterati* along with something of their more Aristotelian and eclectic literary perspectives.[104] Venier's gradual turn in the sixties and seventies to philological inquiry into Provençal and Latin forms, metrical experiments with non-Bembist verse forms like the *capitolo* and the poetic genres of satire, pastoral, and elegy were undoubtedly related to the new directions they explored.[105] And its philological focus seems to have led in time to acceptance of a wider range of literary models than strict Bembist views had allowed.[106] But Venier's academic tastes were better accommodated in the atmosphere of the informal *accademia,* thriving in the slippery space between private elitism and public fame that drawing rooms could provide.

102. Cf. Iain Fenlon and James Haar's characterization of the way the Accademia Fiorentina evolved under Medici support around 1540 as a means of systematizing and centralizing Florentine intellectual life in ways that were pedantic and countercreative; *The Italian Madrigal in the Early Sixteenth Century: Sources and Interpretation* (Cambridge, 1988), p. 85.

103. See further in Bolzoni, "L'Accademia Veneziana," pp. 128–38, who characterizes Badoer's academy as a "syncretistic plurality" (p. 133).

104. New adherents set adrift by Badoer's failed academy include Girolamo Fenaruolo, Marc'Antonio Silvio, and Celio Magno.

105. On this later period see Rosenthal, *The Honest Courtesan,* pp. 177–78. Taddeo, *Il manierismo letterario,* also hints at this development but without much in the way of a chronological perspective (p. 56). In later years Venier pursued his interest in archaic metrics and linguistics through correspondence with Ludovico Castelvetro and Giovanni Maria Barbieri and prepared an edition, never completed or published, of the verse of the troubadour poets Peire d'Alvergne and Peire Rogier; see Santorre Debenedetti, *Gli studi provenzali in Italia nel cinquecento* (Turin, 1911), pp. 67–68, 159–60, and 228. He also made a translation of the *Odes* of Horace.

106. Badoer's academists, notably Bernardo Tasso in his *Ragionamento della poesia,* exalted Bembo's *Prose della volgar lingua* for generating the rebirth of a poetic Italian language but did not embrace his mandate that Petrarch and Boccaccio be its sole models.

Part 2 · RHETORICAL
UNDERPINNINGS

Chapter 5 · CURRENTS IN VENETIAN LITERARY AND LINGUISTIC THEORY

The Consolidation of Poetry and Rhetoric

We have already seen in Venetian salons that certain interests tended to overwhelm all others. When Venier entreated Dolce to eulogize Bembo's death with a wistful sweetness, his concern was with the poetic tone that Dolce should adopt; the object of tribute barely hovered in the periphery of his vision, except as an implied poetic muse. Similarly, looming largest in Doni's report to Annibale Marchese Malvicino on the brilliant music at Capponi's house—inseparable from the substance of the music itself—was the polished delivery of Pecorina and company. What most commanded the attention of both Venier and Doni, in other words, was not inner content but outward effects. Both were fixated on style.

Venetians were hardly unique in making style central to aesthetic interests. Writers across fourteenth- and fifteenth-century Italy, responding to medieval writing as dry and inelegant, had gradually displaced absolute content in favor of style in innumerable varied and covert ways. By the early sixteenth century discussions not only of language and literature but of painting, architecture, sculpture, manners, and music were thickly overgrown with problems of style.[1] This is not to say that sixteenth-century observers were innocent of semantic dimensions in art or human action; rather that they were more likely to explain meaning (or avoid doing so) through recourse to the ways things, ideas, and persons presented themselves in the world.

From the disciplinary standpoint, this meant explicating old works and inventing new ones within the framework of rhetoric, where concerns about locution and

---

1. For an extension of rhetorical analysis to visual arts see Michael Baxandall, *Giotto and the Orators: Humanist Observers of Painting in the Renaissance and the Discovery of Pictorial Composition* (Oxford, 1971). On the centrality of style to musical thinking in this period see James Haar, "Self-Consciousness about Style, Form, and Genre in 16th-Century Music," *Studi musicali* 3 (1974): 219–31.

gesture dominated both exegesis and compositional process. Venice differed from the rest of the peninsula only in its extraordinarily single-minded, obedient attention to rhetorical modes that placed style at the very center of critical and creative thinking. Conceived this way, rhetoric could not confine itself to writing in any pure, timeless form, but necessarily involved transactions between author and audience. The enormous "dialogical" literature I have dealt with in Part I stands witness to this phenomenon, drawing for its multifaceted modes—of argument, commentary, criticism, praise, poetics, and history—from the arena of oratory.

Thinkers in Venice and its dominions, and especially Pietro Bembo, led Italy in codifying language through rhetoric. Bembo was ideally positioned to secure a loyal following by the time his dialogue on the vernacular, *Prose della volgar lingua,* was published in 1525.[2] Early in the century he had already established himself in the upper crust of philological academia through ties with Aldus Manutius's press and had won favor with vernacular readers with his Neoplatonic dialogue on love, *Gli asolani.* After the *Prose* was drafted in 1512–16, manuscript copies circulated widely in literary circles, and Bembo had come to be regarded as a de facto dean of Italian letters.[3]

At its surface the *Prose* simply attempts to gain Italian equal status with Latin and provide it with a set of practical guidelines for use. In its actual working out, however, Bembo's fixation on style, and especially on the style of Petrarch's lyrics, led him to codify a fairly comprehensive system of Italian poetics. To this end his second book recast Cicero's dialogues on oratory, adding to them precepts from Horace's rhetorically inspired verse epistle, *Ars poetica:* Bembo fused Cicero's advocacy of oratorical diffidence and variation and his advice on suiting style to particular audiences with Horace's conception of poetry as a kind of staged performance, carefully gauged to manipulate the reader according to the author's fancy. Through this consolidation, Bembo aimed for nothing less than a new vernacular program— a project he carried off with singular success. More than anyone else, Bembo was instrumental in fixing the fledgling art of poetry, only recently hatched from its medieval state as an adjunct of grammar and rhetoric, within the more generalized framework of oratory. It was also he who devised a comprehensive theoretical accompaniment to the increasingly social role literary language was coming to play in public and private spheres. Far from sequestering language in any abstract philosophizing, Bembo instead based his guidelines on the rhythms, timbres, and cadences of immediate sounding speech to produce a practical apparatus for reading and writing the vernacular that was well tuned to verbal sound. The result was highly prescriptive but also pragmatic—a program addressing real readers, listeners, and interlocutors.

---

2. On Bembo's life and work see esp. W. Theodor Elwert, "Pietro Bembo e la vita letteraria del suo tempo," in *La civiltà veneziana del rinascimento,* Fondazione Giorgio Cini, Centro di Cultura e Civiltà (Florence, 1958), pp. 125–26, and the literature cited in Chap. 1 n. 16 above.

3. On the date of the *Prose* and the manuscript tradition that preceded its publication see the introduction to Mario Marti's ed., *Prose della volgar lingua* (Padua, 1967), pp. vii–ix. Citations below refer to Marti's ed., which is based on the definitive third edition of the *Prose* from 1549.

The sonorous aspects of Bembo's *Prose* have attracted much attention from musicologists,[4] who have tried hard in recent decades to show how composers translated Bembo's ideas into notes. Musicologists have, above all, asked how Bembo's views on sound and prosody—vowels and consonants, syllable lengths, line lengths, rhyme schemes, accents, and verse types—combined to generate passages and entire works of varying expressive weights, from light and pleasing to grave and harsh. This has seemed a rich line of inquiry, for as Dean Mace stressed some years ago, Bembo's conceptions of words did not assign them fixed meanings but regarded them within various and changing sound contexts in ways that compare strikingly with Venetians' musical settings. But the same scholars have been less inclined to consider how Bembo's arguments relate to Venetian expressive practices more broadly. My argument repositions our past emphasis on Bembist sound to place it within what I identify as the *Prose*'s overarching rhetorical principle of decorum. Important in two different, but related, ways, decorum signaled a commitment to preserve moderation but also to achieve separate stylistic levels matched to subject matter. We have already encountered this duality in earlier chapters—in Tomitano's portrait of the Venetian gentleman and Venier's counsel to Dolce to temper grief with joy.

Surprisingly, the symbiotic interrelations of decorum's dual meanings are as yet barely hinted at in the growing secondary literature on cinquecento vernacular theory. In the present chapter I extend my study of these interrelations beyond Bembo into a larger field of grammarians, rhetoricians, poetic theorists, and popular *trattatisti* to reveal something of the process by which such untidy stylistic collapses were inscribed and reinscribed in a larger textual-critical tradition—one I identify as distinctly Venetian. I show that in the face of multiplicitous linguistic usages Venetians' repeated conflations of moderation and propriety helped assert an official, unitary language by systematizing rules for language use. Venice was engaged in two contradictory modes—asserting an atemporal language to project the official rhetoric of moderation and propriety while simultaneously generating numerous time-bound linguistic styles that often undermined the "official" one.

---

4. See, most importantly, Dean T. Mace, "Pietro Bembo and the Literary Origins of the Italian Madrigal," *The Musical Quarterly* 55 (1969): 65–86. Although Mace argued the relevance of Bembo's thinking to the genesis of the madrigal in Florence and Rome, he illustrated his essay with two examples from Willaert's *Musica nova* and one by Wert. Notable for situating Bembo in various musico-historiographic contexts are Gary Tomlinson, "Rinuccini, Peri, Monteverdi, and the Humanist Heritage of Opera" (Ph.D. diss., University of California at Berkeley, 1979), pp. 37–55, which develops the Ficinian context of Bembo's theories; Howard Mayer Brown, "Words and Music: Willaert, the Chanson and the Madrigal about 1540," in *Florence and Venice, Comparisons and Relations: Acts of Two Conferences at Villa I Tatti in 1976–1977*, vol. 2, *Il Cinquecento*, ed. Christine Smith with Salvatore I. Camporeale (Florence, 1980), pp. 217–66, relating Bembo's ideas to Willaert's madrigals; and Claude V. Palisca, *Humanism in Italian Renaissance Musical Thought* (New Haven, 1985), pp. 355–68, which extends Bembo's ideas to an analysis of the opening of Willaert's madrigal *Aspro core et selvaggio et cruda voglia*. Earlier than any of these are Nino Pirrotta's remarks following Walter H. Rubsamen's paper "From Frottola to Madrigal: The Changing Pattern of Italian Secular Vocal Music," in *Chanson & Madrigal, 1480–1530: Studies in Comparison and Contrast*, Isham Memorial Library, 13–14 September 1961, ed. James Haar (Cambridge, Mass., 1964), pp. 76–77.

This chapter concentrates on analyzing the former as it was articulated in written doctrines, keeping the latter in peripheral view in anticipation of issues that will arise in Chapters 7–10.

BEMBISM ON THE *TERRAFERMA* AND IN THE LAGOON

In the second quarter of the sixteenth century, after Bembo's *Prose* was published, theoretical writers in Venice and the Veneto formed two broad sociogeographic groups. The first consists of teachers and scholars situated in Padua, the second, of popularizing polygraphs based mainly in Venice; in the former group I consider Bernardino Daniello, Sperone Speroni, and Bernardino Tomitano, and in the latter, Francesco Sansovino, Lodovico Dolce, and Girolamo Muzio.[5] The regional split is significant. Theorizers in each city played substantially different roles, with Paduans oriented in the didactic worlds of the schools, universities, and formalized academies, and Venetians often working as editors, translators, and freelancers for local presses. While Venetians were accommodating a more commercial public, eager to have the mushrooming quantities of vernacular wisdom made readily digestible, Paduans served up many of the same issues in somewhat headier concoctions. Despite these differences, Paduans and Venetians did a good deal of intermixing. It will be useful to sketch their profiles and some of their major contributions.

According to Alessandro Zilioli's manuscript biography, Daniello had come from his native Lucca to Padua, where he taught letters to boys.[6] While there he composed orations and Italian poetry, translated classical texts (notably the *Georgics* of Virgil), and assembled commentaries on Dante and Petrarch.[7] His *Poetica,*

---

5. I should note, however, that the first Italian poetics printed in the region following Bembo's *Prose* was *La poetica* (Books 1–4: Vicenza, 1529) by the Vicenzan nobleman Giangiorgio Trissino. Trissino employed a wide reading of both Greek and Latin classics, but his treatise is mainly a handbook on versification. Based in large part on Dante's *De vulgari eloquentia* and Antonio da Tempo's *De rithimis vulgaribus,* Trissino's poetics emerged in seeming isolation from those of other theorists of the Veneto who were active at the time. The first edition, including Books 1–4, promised two more; they did not appear until 1562, although they seem to have been written by at least 1549, possibly some years earlier. All six books are included in Bernard Weinberg, ed., *Trattati di poetica e retorica del cinquecento,* 4 vols. (Bari, 1970–74), 1:21–158 and 2:5–90 (hereafter *Trattati*); see also the facsimile of Books 1–4 in the series Poetiken des Cinquecento, vol. 4, ed. Bernhard Fabian (Munich, 1969). Trissino's fifth and sixth books of *La poetica* are significant mainly as paraphrases of Aristotle's *Poetics,* whose importance had already begun to be widely appreciated by the time they were published, as discussed below. See Weinberg's discussion of Books 5 and 6 in *A History of Literary Criticism in the Italian Renaissance,* 2 vols. (Chicago, 1961), 2:719–21, and in *Trattati* 1:590–91 and 2:653–54. For a summary of Trissino's importance in this period see Baxter Hathaway, *Marvels and Commonplaces: Renaissance Literary Criticism* (New York, 1968), pp. 10–13.

6. "Istoria delle vite de' poeti italiani, di Alessandro Zilioli veneziano," I-Vnm, MSS It. cl. X, No. 1 (6394), p. 140. Zilioli was a literary scholar who died in 1650. See also the biographical information on Daniello by M. R. De Gramatica, "Daniello, Bernardino," in *Dizionario biografico degli italiani,* 32:608–10, which fixes his date of birth in the late 1400s and the date of his move to Padua ca. 1525. He died in 1565.

7. Of special interest is his ed. and commentary of Petrarch, *Sonetti, canzoni, e triomphi di Messer Francesco Petrarca con la spositione di Bernardino Daniello da Lucca* (Venice, 1541); see Luigi Baldacci, *Il petrarchismo italiano nel cinquecento,* rev. ed. (Padua, 1974), pp. 66–68.

printed in 1536, is notable as one of the earliest vernacular poetics and the first firmly rooted in the Ciceronian tradition.[8] Adopting the fashionable dialogue form, it portrays a group of Venetians as visitors to an academic Arcadia in the Veneto with Daniello as schoolmaster.[9] The scene takes place in the bucolic Bressano on the Brenta in May 1533. There Daniello meets his mentor, Triphon Gabriele—also based in Padua at the time—along with Gabriele's two nephews, Andrea and Iacopo. As the group convenes, Daniello espies a shyly hidden copy of Horace's *Ars poetica* in Andrea's hand and embarks on a series of impromptu lessons on poetry. Thereafter the dialogue unfolds as a didactic-moral rereading of Cicero, taking Bembo's *Prose* as its point of departure and hardening it into pedagogic dogma.[10]

Daniello was a minor scholar-didact, if a skilled linguist, commentator, and theoretician. His prestige paled beside that of Sperone Speroni, who counts as the dominant literary figure on the *terraferma* in the generation following Bembo.[11] During the early 1520s Speroni studied with the Aristotelian philosopher Pietro Pomponazzi and by the 1530s had become a major light at Padua. In the year 1540 he helped found and shape the Paduan Accademia degli Infiammati.[12]

---

8. Fabian, ed., *Poetiken des cinquecento,* vol. 2 (Munich, 1968); repr. in *Trattati* 1:227–318, which includes the original pagination referred to here. For a useful summary see Ralph C. Williams, "The Originality of Daniello," *Romanic Review* 15 (1924): 121–22.

9. On the adoption of Cicero's model of the dialogue by quattrocento humanists see David Marsh, *The Quattrocento Dialogue: Classical Tradition and Humanist Innovation* (Cambridge, Mass., 1980). Virginia Cox, *The Renaissance Dialogue: Literary Dialogue in Its Social and Political Contexts, Castiglione to Galileo* (Cambridge, 1993), approaches sixteenth-century dialogue from the broad perspective of the cultural economy of communicative exchange. For the later sixteenth century see also Walter J. Ong, *Ramus, Method, and the Decay of Dialogue: From the Art of Discourse to the Art of Reason* (Cambridge, Mass., 1958), and Jon R. Snyder, *Writing the Scene of Speaking: Theories of Dialogue in the Late Italian Renaissance* (Stanford, 1989).

10. Early on in the work, Daniello recounts another conversation heard in Padua, a Platonic defense of poetry involving at least two more Venetians, the poet Giovanni Brevio and the senator and *letterato* Domenico Moresini. In connection with vernacular arts, it is noteworthy that two of Brevio's ballate were set to music by Rore prior to their publication in poetic eds.; see Chap. 8 n. 10 (and on Parabosco's and Perissone's settings, Chap. 9, esp. n. 17). A prelate at the Roman court after 1542, Brevio reputedly had friendships with Bembo, Pietro Aretino, Giovanni della Casa, and other luminaries. The identification of Moresini comes from Verdizzotti's biography of Molino in *Rime di M. Girolamo Molino* (Venice, 1573), p. [6]. Moresini is also mentioned in Tomitano's letter to Longo (see the Preface, n. 2 above) as the "magnifico Mess. Domenico Moresini" (p. 386).

On *La poetica*'s Platonic defense of poetry see Weinberg, *A History of Literary Criticism* 2:721–22, and for an overall prospectus of its content, 2:721–24. See also De Gramatica's article on Daniello in the *Dizionario biografico degli italiani,* which provides a précis of the *Poetica* and a list of Daniello's Venetian contacts (including Aretino, Federigo Badoer, and Iacopo Bonfadio) based on his correspondence. Despite these references the extent of Daniello's interaction with Venice remains unclear (see Weinberg, *Trattati* 1:611). For an attempt to clarify Daniello's relationship with Gabriele see Ezio Raimondi, "Bernardo Daniello, lettore di poesia," in *Rinascimento inquieto* (Palermo, 1965), pp. 23–69. Daniello was also connected with Parabosco, as revealed in Parabosco's letter to him (first published in 1545) in the first book of the *Quattro libri delle lettere amorose,* ed. Thomaso Porcacchi (Venice, 1561), fols. 95′–98′.

11. Speroni lived from 1500 until 1588. For his life see Mario Pozzi, ed., *Trattatisti del cinquecento,* vol. 1, *Bembo, Speroni e Gelli* (Milan and Naples, 1978), pp. 471–509 (and the Nota ai testi, pp. 1178–94, with references to earlier biographies).

12. On Speroni's role in the Infiammati see Florindo [V.] Cerreta, *Alessandro Piccolomini: letterato e filosofo senese del cinquecento* (Siena, 1960), pp. 23–31 (who fixes Speroni's leadership from November 1541 to March 1542); Francesco Bruni, "Sperone Speroni e l'Accademia degli Infiammati," *Filologia e letteratura* 13 (1967): 24–71; and Valerio Vianello, *Il letterato, l'accademia, il libro: contributi sulla cultura veneta del cinquecento,* Biblioteca Veneta, no. 6 (Padua, 1988), Chaps. 3–5, the last of which also deals with Tomitano.

Speroni's *Dialogo delle lingue,* set in 1530 and composed soon afterward, offered the most probing philosophical response to linguistic issues raised by Bembo.[13] On the surface it constituted an attempt to arbitrate debates about the choice of a vernacular language and extract a truce from the embattled lines drawn around them. The main sides in the conflicts were represented by Lazaro Buonamici as a hardnosed antivernacular classicist, an anonymous courtier who favors spoken vernaculars, and Bembo as champion of old Tuscan. But the deeper problematic for Speroni stood outside the choice of language. In fact, language hardly constitutes the real site of polemic at all (as Francesco Bruni has noted), for although Lazaro and Bembo take different sides in the discussions, each displays a fundamental methodological faith in Ciceronian rhetorical ideals.[14] The true conceptual divide emerges in a larger conflict introduced surreptitiously through an interpolation in the latter half of the dialogue, where a new interlocutor recounts a discussion between Pomponazzi (called Peretto) and the humanist scholar Giovanni Lascari. Revealingly, this interlocutor, bearing the quiet epithet "Scolare," boasts himself ignorant of all languages. Introduced not as an expert but as a "disinterested" yet perceptive witness, he narrates a scene of conciliation in which the philosopher and his humanist opponent make two new claims that will now be used to mediate the terms of the initial linguistic dispute: the first is for the pragmatic value of all languages for cognitive and scientific purposes; the second for the ultimate inferiority of any language to philosophy.

Speroni's little *Dialogo* thus lays out a dialectical tension between rhetoric and philosophy that inevitably arose within the Paduan university elite, where Aristotelianism was the coin of the realm.[15] In that respect it may seem a departure from the resolutely rhetorical and Bembist themes I have set out to trace in this chapter, as in part it is. But when the conversation comes back to the principal interlocutors the last word goes to Bembo, who reiterates his pro-Tuscan position with the admonition that "if you . . . want to compose canzoni or *novelle* in our way— that is, in a language different from Tuscan and without imitating Petrarch or

13. See Piero Floriani, "Grammatici e teorici della letteratura volgare," in *Storia della cultura veneta: dal primo quattrocento al concilio di Trenta,* vol. 3/2, ed., Girolamo Arnaldi and Manlio Pastore Stocchi (Vicenza, 1980), pp. 175–77; Raffaele Simone, "Sperone Speroni et l'idée de diachronie dans la linguistique de la Renaissance italienne," in *History of Linguistic Thought and Contemporary Linguistics,* ed. Herman Parret (New York, 1976), pp. 302–16; Bruni, "Sperone Speroni," pp. 31ff.; Riccardo Scrivano, "Cultura e letteratura in Sperone Speroni," in *Cultura e letteratura nel cinquecento* (Rome, 1966), pp. 121–26; and Snyder, Chap. 3 in *Writing the Scene of Speaking,* pp. 87ff. (on Speroni's dialogues). For briefer mentions see G. A. Padley, *Grammatical Theory in Western Europe, 1500–1700: Trends in Vernacular Grammar II* (Cambridge, 1988), pp. 63–64, and Robert A. Hall, Jr., *The Italian "Questione della lingua": An Interpretative Essay,* University of North Carolina Studies in the Romance Languages and Literature, no. 4 (Chapel Hill, 1942), p. 17.

I cite from the edition of Pierre Villey [-Desmeserets], *Les sources italiennes de la "Deffense et illustration de la langue françoise" de Joachim du Bellay,* Bibliothèque littéraire de la renaissance, ser. 1, vol. 9 (Paris, 1969), pp. 111–46. Another ed. may be found in Speroni's *Opere,* 5 vols. (Venice, 1740), 1:166–201, and in *Trattatisti del cinquecento* 1:585–635.

14. "Sperone Speroni," p. 32.

15. For a broad assessment of this theme see Jerrold Seigel, *Rhetoric and Philosophy in Renaissance Humanism: The Union of Eloquence and Wisdom, Petrarch to Valla* (Princeton, 1968).

Boccaccio—perhaps you will be a good courtier but never a poet or orator."[16] This, he adds (reminiscent of Venier's advice to Dolce), may bring you temporary fame but not everlasting glory. Speroni thus accepts the vitality of Bembo's Tuscan for new literary production at the same time as he takes pains to circumscribe it within a limited intellectual domain.

Speroni's *Dialogo* helps explain some of the motifs and conflicts that arise in other Paduan texts, notably the *Ragionamenti della lingua toscana* of Bernardino Tomitano, dubbed by Baxter Hathaway Speroni's "Boswell."[17] Tomitano, to recall my Preface, was a Paduan lecturer in the Aristotelian discipline of logic, as well as a *medico*. He published his *Ragionamenti* in 1545, republishing them with further additions from the rhetorics of Aristotle and Cicero the following year.[18] The dialogues were set during the year 1542 in the house of Speroni, "prencipe & governo" of the Accademici Infiammati. At the outset Speroni is heard proudly announcing their lofty goal: "The occasion for assembling this noble and generous company of men having become known and arrived at by us for no other end than to add some light and beauty and dignity to this language, which we call Tuscan, and not to make a popular fraternity or Babel, I wish we were of no other opinion than to have people read Petrarch and Boccaccio."[19] Speroni's opener provides a key to the sociointellectual context of the work. Its interlocutors appear as a kind of academic brotherhood, members of a tightly structured fraternity of the sort that was still anathema in Venice. Their mission is twofold: first, to advance trecento Tuscan as the exclusive literary vernacular against the claims of any current spoken tongue; and second, to propose as its sole models the same two authors Bembo singled out for verse and prose, Petrarch and Boccaccio. Tomitano's text thus reconfirms retrospectively that even the more philosophically oriented Speroni accepted Bembo's case insofar as it applied to modern literature. Indeed the *Ragionamenti* bluntly rebutted those like Baldassare Castiglione and Giangiorgio Trissino who advocated an eclectic composite of modern languages, the so-called *lingua cortigiana,* exalting instead Bembo's revival of Tuscan by assimilating it to Cicero's cultivation of Latin.[20]

---

16. "[S]e voglia vi verrà mai di comporre o canzoni o novelle al modo nostro, cioè in lingua che sia diversa dalla thoscana, et senza imitare il Petrarca o il Boccaccio, peravventura voi sarete buon cortigiano, ma poeta o oratore non mai" (p. 146).

17. Tomitano lived in Padua ca. 1517–76. For Hathaway's compelling account of Tomitano's indebtedness to Speroni, especially in the area of poetic imagination, see *The Age of Criticism: The Late Renaissance in Italy* (Ithaca, 1962), pp. 310–15. On their relationship see also Bruni, "Sperone Speroni," pp. 24–31.

18. Both were printed in Venice. I cite from the later edition, *Ragionamenti della lingua toscana di M. Bernardin Tomitano. I precetti della rhetorica secondo l'artificio d'Aristotile & Cicerone nel fine del secondo libro nuovamente aggionti* (Venice, 1546).

19. "Essendo a noi trapelata, & pervenuta l'occasione di adunare questa nobile & generosa compagnia d'huomini non per altro fine, che per accrescere alcun lume & vaghezze & dignita a questa lingua, che noi Toscana addomandiamo, & non per farne una popolaresca frataglia ò sinagoga; vorrei che non fussimo d'altra opinione che di far leggere altro che il Petrarca, & il Boccaccio" (ibid., p. 18).

20. In Book 3 Tomitano compares Cicero's synthesis of the best in Roman literature to Plato's synthesis of Greek philosophers, likening both to Aesculapius's restoration of the members of Hippolytus's lacerated body and assigning the same synthetic role in Tuscan literature to Bembo. He concludes: "Tra Toscani pochissimi vi sono stati, & per dire meglio un solo; il BEMBO dico, hora la Dio merce Cardinale

All of this may make Tomitano appear more orthodox than Speroni's views in the *Dialogo delle lingue* would have led us to expect. Yet other passages in the *Ragionamenti* confirm Tomitano's entanglement in Speroni's philosophical biases. Tomitano's prologue asserts, for example, that "sapere et conoscere"—that is, the cognition of *things*—is what separates men from beasts, not (as the rhetoricians typically claimed) the faculty of speech.[21] *Res,* in other words, sits higher in Tomitano's philosophical conception than *verbum,* or, as he put it: "Things make a man wise, and words make him appear so. The voice makes us similar to beasts, while thoughts, separating us from them, make us resemble God."[22]

Tomitano's allegiances, like Speroni's, were thus mixed, exalting Tuscan (and Petrarch) for *verbum,* but demoting language per se in the larger philosophical scheme of *res.* Owing to this tension, and to a strong dose of Aristotelian encyclopedism, the *Ragionamenti* fail to develop along hard and fast Bembist lines. The last two of its three books consist of a prolix treatment of style and rhetoric, applying to Italian all the major rhetorical ideas of Cicero and Aristotle and drawing at various times on virtually every major classical writer on language. Despite obeisances to Bembo, the philosophical interests that Tomitano and Speroni cultivated make them more independent than their counterparts in Venice. (We will see that this is also true of Daniello.)

Once again, different preoccupations correspond to differences of audience. Unlike the Paduans, whose audience would look to them for scholarly, or at least schoolmasterly, erudition, Sansovino, Dolce, and Muzio had to attract an urban market of relatively unsophisticated readers through seductive packaging of rhetorical ideas. Each of them did so with varying degrees of selectivity and different formulas, but recognizing that in the economy of vernacular knowledge that circulated in Venice, greater density meant fewer readers.

Sansovino typified this peculiarly Venetian breed of author. Of Florentine descent, he was born in Rome in 1521 but following the Sack of 1527 moved with his sculptor father, Jacopo, to Venice, where he died in 1586. Although Sansovino had studied law at Padua, Florence, and Bologna from 1536, his attraction to vernacular letters drew him back to his adoptive home in 1542. He spent his days in Venice cranking out poetry, fiction, translations, editions, bizarre catalogues, chronicles, genealogies, and popular histories (what Paul Grendler has called "scissors-and-

---

illustrissimo & signor mio: la cui diligenza si come in tutte le forme del dire è stata non men cara che rara" (Among writers in Tuscan there were very few, and to put it better, only one: Bembo, I declare, now, thanks to God, most illustrious Cardinal and my master, whose assiduousness in all forms of discourse was no less esteemed than rare); p. 269.

21. *Ragionamenti,* pp. 3–4. The usual rhetoricians' view may be seen at the beginning of Bembo's *Prose,* p. 5.

22. "[L]e cose fanno l'huomo saggio, et le parole il fan parer. La voce con le bestie ci rende communi et simigliant, il pensiero da quelli separandoci, con Iddio ci rassimiglia" (*Ragionamenti,* pp. 40–41). For a searching evaluation of Tomitano's attitudes about the conflict between *res* and *verbum,* its relation to Speroni's thought, and other aspects of Tomitano's *Ragionamenti,* see Vianello, "Tra velleità di riforma e compressi con la tradizione per un'identità di competenza," Chap. 6 in *Il letterato, l'accademia, il libro,* pp. 107–37, and "Nella prospettiva di una nuova mediazione: l'esigenza della 'letterarietà,'" Chap. 7, pp. 139–72.

paste compilations")[23] and from 1560 managed to make sizable profits by starting his own press. His *Arte oratoria* of 1546 is one of the earliest rhetorics of its kind, summarizing and simplifying Ciceronian oratory for application to the archaic Tuscan championed by Bembo.[24] Much of the *Arte oratoria* addresses questions pertaining specifically to oratory, such as argumentation and ethics. But Sansovino approaches the issue of persuasion largely through the vernacular poets, in keeping with other contemporaneous rhetorics, and shows the same concern for sound typical of the new poetic theorists.

Sansovino's links to vernacular publishing thus resemble Dolce's, as I characterized them briefly in Chapter 4. By 1550, when Dolce published his popular gloss on Bembo's *Prose,* the similarly titled *Osservationi nella volgar lingua,* Bembo's work was already a generation old. Developments between 1525 and 1550 had changed conditions for the reception of linguistic and literary theory even among less-educated readers. In 1535 Dolce had added a vernacular translation of Horace's *Ars poetica* to the growing Horatian literature—one of the vast number of translations he produced before his death in 1568.[25] A year later Alessandro de' Pazzi put Aristotle's *Poetics* into general circulation by publishing it in a respectable Latin translation.

Meanwhile critical reaction to Bembo's views was gaining a good deal of weight. By the late decades of the century his program for the Italian language (if not his poetics as a whole) was to win the day. Still to be reckoned with at midcentury, however, were the feisty Florentines, members of the Accademia Fiorentina like Giovambattista Gelli, Vincenzo Borghini, and Pierfrancesco Giambullari, who rejected Bembo's narrow literary boundaries in favor of spoken Florentine (as Machiavelli had done before them).[26] On top of that Venice itself was sheltering a more biting variety of polygraph than the likes of Sansovino and Dolce—writers like Doni and Niccolò Franco, who had been satirizing Bembist models in print since 1539.[27]

---

23. For a summary of Sansovino's life with attention to his role as a popular historian see Paul F. Grendler, "Francesco Sansovino and Italian Popular History, 1560–1600," *Studies in the Renaissance* 16 (1969): 139–80; see also idem, *Critics of the Italian World, 1530–1560: Anton Francesco Doni, Nicolò Franco & Ortensio Lando* (Madison, 1969), pp. 65–69. Further information on Sansovino's life and an annotated catalogue of his works may be found in Emmanuele A. Cicogna, *Delle inscrizioni veneziane,* 6 vols. (Venice, 1834), 4:31–91.

24. The full title of the volume was given as *L'arte oratoria secondo i modi della lingua volgare, di Francesco Sansovino divisa in tre libri. Ne quali si ragiona tutto quello ch'all'artificio appartiene, cosi del poeta come dell'oratore, con l'autorità de i nostri scrittori* (Venice, 1546) and the internal books as *Dell'arte oratoria nella lingua toscana di F. Sansovino. Libro primo [-al terzo].* Reprints were issued in 1569 and 1575 and a variant version called "In materia dell'arte libri tre ne quali si contien l'ordine delle cose che si ricercano all'Oratore" was included in an anthology of orations that Sansovino published called *Diversi orationi volgarmente scritte da gli huomini illustri de tempi nostri* (Venice, 1561). The *Arte oratoria* may have been intended as the prospectus for an immense work of twenty-three books on the topic, never completed, as the first paragraph of Sansovino's little manual *La retorica* of 1543 suggests (see Weinberg, *Trattati* 1:453 and 631).

25. *La poetica d'Horatio* (Venice, 1535), dedicated to Pietro Aretino. See Weinberg, *A History of Literary Criticism* 1:101–2.

26. See Padley, *Grammatical Theory,* pp. 27–35 and passim, and R. G. Faithfull, "On the Concept of 'Living Language' in Cinquecento Italian Philology," *Modern Language Review* 48 (1953): 278–92.

27. Among the earliest such writings are Franco's *Petrarchista* (Venice, 1539), *Le pistole vulgari* (Venice, 1539), and *La Philena* (Mantua, 1547). Doni published his *Inferni* in Venice in 1553. See Grendler, *Critics of the Italian World,* passim.

By 1550, therefore, an audience was ready-made for Dolce's handbook. Cobbled together with its simply argued defense of Bembo were remarks distilled from the *Prose* itself, glosses from Gianfrancesco Fortunio's *Regole grammaticali* of 1516, paraphrases of Donatus's Latin grammar, and (in Book 4) a superficially Aristotelian poetics, all presented with a plainness and simplicity that transformed Bembo's subtle precepts into a sort of folk wisdom. Bembo of course had died just three years before, and in Dolce's heroic account his stature was that of a modern Cicero. "There are some who don't like Bembo's works," he admitted. "To them one can answer in the way Quintilian once answered those overly severe men of his century who didn't like Cicero's works: let each one know without a doubt that he must take great profit from Bembo's lessons in poetry and prose."[28]

Where Dolce converted Bembo's *Prose* into a canon for the common man, Muzio exploited the epistle form to bolster his precepts through familiarizing didactic address to a second-person "lettor." Generically the *Arte poetica* emulated the verse epistle of Horace, which provided both the formal model and poetic principles through which Bembo's linguistic biases were filtered.[29] But compared with the droll servility with which Dolce's compilation paid homage to the Bembist tradition, Muzio's endorsement in the verse treatise *Arte poetica* of 1551 was more equivocal. As a Paduan and cosmopolitan courtier who served numerous princes on the peninsula, often carrying out delicate diplomatic missions,[30] Muzio virulently opposed the arrogation of linguistic authority that he attributed to the Florentines. His position could at times appear comically contradictory, advocating trecento Tuscan (or what he preferred to call "Italian") in some works, while passionately resenting Tuscan elitism in others.[31] Yet Muzio's defense of non-Tuscans' right to theorize Tuscan literature nevertheless helps explain the Veneto's curious dominance in the revival and codification of a language that was both foreign to it as well as archaic. In a letter to the Florentine literati Gabriello Cesano and Bartolomeo Cavalcanti he bristled:

> [P]erhaps you will laugh that I, a non-Tuscan, want to discourse about Tuscan writers. But laugh on, as I too often laugh at those Tuscan writers who, believing

---

28. "[S]ono alcuni, aiquali l'opere del Bembo non piacciono. A costoro si puo rispondere nella guisa, che gia rispose Quintiliano a que glihuomini troppo severi del suo secolo, aiquali non piacevano l'opre di Cicerone: conosca indubitatamente ciascuno di dover dalla lettione cosi de' versi, come delle prose del Bembo ritrar grandissimo profitto" (*Osservationi nella volgar lingua* [Venice, 1550], fols. 9–9'). Dolce later annotated Cicero's works in *Opere morali di Marco Tullio Cicerone: cioè tre libri de gli uffici, due dialoghi, l'uno dell'amicitia, l'altro della vecchiezza, sei paradossi secondo l'openione de gli storici*, trans. Francesco Vendramin (Venice, 1563).

29. Modern ed. in *Trattati* 2:163–209.

30. Muzio, known as Giustinopolitano, lived at Ferrara, Pesaro, and Urbino among other places and spent his last years in Rome and Tuscany. He wrote manuals for courtiers, including *Il duello* (Venice, 1550) on duelling and *Il gentiluomo* (Venice, 1571). Among various discussions of Muzio, see the *Dizionario enciclopedico della letteratura italiana* 4:97–99; Benedetto Croce, *Poeti e scrittori del pieno e del tardo rinascimento*, 2d ed., 3 vols. (Bari, 1958), 1:198–210; and Padley, *Grammatical Theory*, pp. 40–41.

31. Muzio voiced his strongest resentment in the late *Varchina* (Venice, 1573), a retort to Benedetto Varchi's *L'Hercolano*, which had been published in 1570 (see n. 33 below). Some of Muzio's other late writings on language survive in *Battaglie . . . per la diffesa dell'italica lingua . . .* (Venice, 1582), in which he took Trissino's part against pro-Tuscans like Varchi and Claudio Tolomei.

only themselves suited to write in this language, know less of it than the non-Tuscans. . . . To me it seems that in Tuscany what may come to pass is what used to happen in those countries where the most precious wines were produced: the foreign merchants, buying the best ones, carried them off, leaving the less good ones to the peasants.[32]

Muzio's anxieties were not groundless. As late as 1564, when Varchi drafted his *L'Hercolano*, his interlocutor Count Cesare Hercolano was made to say, "It seems to me a strange thing that a foreigner, however learned and talented, should give the rules and teach the way of good writing and graceful composition in the language of others, and I have heard someone say that . . . [Bembo] was bitterly reproved as both presumptuous and arrogant by I don't know how many of your Florentines."[33]

Yet as strangers to the dialect of the *trecentisti*, Venetians needed to make systematic, self-conscious guidelines in order to achieve stylistic and grammatical regularity. Their readiness to adapt themselves to an alien mode sets them apart from those champions of the courtly spoken dialect like Castiglione, whose *Cortegiano* warned against any kind of linguistic affectation.[34] Bembo's aspirations to courtly grace, purity, classicism, and restraint did not preclude archaisms that seemed intolerably ostentatious to Castiglione-styled courtiers.[35] Indeed, this tendency, perhaps more than any other, is paradigmatic for the Venetians' reception and transformation of a foreign musical idiom to their own classicizing ends.

POETRY AS CICERONIAN ORATORY

In the sixteenth century no art was more assimilated to oratory than poetry,[36] and nowhere more than in Venice, where oratorical standards served as the foremost means of poetic prescription, creation, and evaluation. Many have linked the special persistence with which Venice pursued oratorical paradigms to the strangely liminal

---

32. "[V]oi forse vi riderete, che io non Thoscano voglia de gli scrittori Toscani ragionare. Ma ridete pure; che anche io bene spesso rido di que' Thoscani, i quali soli credendosi essere atti a scrivere in questa lingua, ne sanno meno che i non Thoscani. . . . À me pare che nella Thoscana sia avvenuto quello, che suole avvenire in que' paesi, dove nascono i vini piu pretiosi: che i mercatanti forestieri i migliori comperando quelli se ne potano, lasciando à paesani i men buoni" (*Lettere* [Venice, 1551], fol. 99).

33. "Egli mi pare strana cosa, che un forestiero, quantunque dotto, e virtuoso habbia à dar le regole, e insegnare il modo del bene scrivere, e leggiadramente comporre nella lingua Altrui, e ho sentito dire à qualcuno, che egli ne fu da non sò quanti de' vostri Fiorentini agramente, e come presontuoso, e come arrogante ripreso." This comes from *L'Hercolano dialogo di Messer Benedetto Varchi, nelqual si ragiona generalmente delle lingue, & in particolare della Toscana, e della fiorentina . . .* (Venice, 1570), p. 19. On Varchi's position with respect to larger issues in the *questione della lingua* debate see Padley, *Grammatical Theory*, pp. 37–40, and Thérèse Labande-Jeanroy, *La question de la langue en Italie* (Strasbourg and Paris, 1925), p. 169.

34. See Ettore Bonora, ed., 2d ed. (Milan, 1976), Book 1, Chaps. 28–39, where the view is put forth by Count Giuliano de' Medici.

35. Some who extended his ideas even systematized these archaisms; see for instance Sansovino, *L'Arte oratoria*, fols. 55'–56.

36. Weinberg's essay in *Trattati* 1:541–61 and the monograph of Ezio Raimondi, *Poesia come retorica* (Florence, 1980), are instructive on the general question of connections between poetry and oratory (though the latter deals primarily with the later cinquecento).

state in which the city was caught after the shock of the League of Cambrai and before the rising pressures of Inquisition trials, political uncertainty, and the plague of the 1570s forced an awakening of social and political consciousness later in the century. During the second to fifth decades Venetians seemed to ignore much of the political reality that surrounded them, or reshaped it into their own imagined versions. In this state of "Venice Preserved," to borrow William J. Bouwsma's rubric, they clung to an idealized world, defined and authorized by words, that served as a hedge against frightening recognitions of current realities.[37] The Venetian histories of Gasparo Contarini and Pietro Bembo and the interviews of Triphon Gabriele recorded in Giannotti's *Libro della repubblica de' vinitiani* attest (as Bouwsma has shown) to ways that Venetians viewed even affairs of the present and recent past through the scrim of civic myth. Literary creation, linguistic theorizing, and history writing all sought out idealized realities not unlike those Tomitano distilled in his letter to Francesco Longo.[38]

It is not hard to see the kinds of dilemmas this worldview posed for the *Prose* and works like it. If Bembo's standards exemplified a more general Venetian posture of insulated detachment, what expressive range was allowed to writers aspiring to meet them?[39] In particular, if writers adapted Ciceronian rhetoric with hardly a trace of its vigorous social side, what attitudes could they hold toward the problems of literary *subjects*? Since Cicero's teachings urged orators to match style to subject matter, these questions profoundly affected the compositional process from start to finish.

Hidden away in the manuscript letters of Pietro Gradenigo at the Biblioteca Nazionale Marciana is a small corpus of informal poetic criticism that helps clarify the ways in which Venetians confronted such questions, replacing thematic concerns with the problems of rhetoric.[40] Gradenigo was Bembo's son-in-law and a member of Domenico Venier's innermost circle. He was thus centrally located among Venice's literary elite and, as was the case with his aristocratic peers Venier and Girolamo Molino, his poems were not published in a *canzoniere* during his lifetime but scattered through midcentury anthologies. Similarly his poetic criticism (such as it is) is preserved only in an epistolary manuscript.

Among the most intriguing items in this corpus are letters exchanged with an otherwise unknown woman named Signora Lucia Albana Avogadria of Brescia. In one of his responses to her Gradenigo offered a critique of a sonnet of hers.[41] We have only the last two lines (13–14) of the poem she sent him, which he quotes.

---

37. See *Venice and the Defense of Republican Liberty: Renaissance Values in the Age of the Counter Reformation* (Berkeley and Los Angeles, 1968), Chap. 3, esp. pp. 135–39 on Bembo, and Preface, nn. 8–10 above.

38. Preface, nn. 2–7 above.

39. See Thomas M. Greene on the Ciceronian search for "synchronic purity" in this period and its relation to an atemporal vision of art and language; *The Light in Troy: Imitation and Discovery in Renaissance Poetry* (New Haven, 1982), p. 175. (See also Chap. 1 n. 24 above.)

40. I-Vnm, MSS It. cl. X, 23 (6526); see Chap. 4 n. 20 above.

41. Ibid., fol. 74', from a letter dated 7 October 1560 from the Villa Bozza.

| Teco havendo portare altiere e sole | With you having to bear proud and alone |
| Spoglie dal tempo, Mondo, e Morte rea. | The spoils of time, the world, and evil death. |

From this fragment we can only guess that Avogadria's poem tried to paint a portrait of bereavement in grand, sweeping tones. Her theme left Gradenigo silent. His attentions focused instead on the rhythmic disposition of the lines, for which he suggests a revision.

| Teco spoglie portando altere: e sole | With you bearing spoils proud and alone, |
| il Mondo, e 'l Tempo vinto, e Morte rea. | The world and time overcome, and evil death. |

or:

| Vinto il Mondo e 'l Tempo, et Morte rea. | Overcome the world and time and evil death. |

These changes, he claims, will alter "only a little the arrangement of the words."[42] By collapsing the phrase "havendo portare" of v. 13 to simply "portando" and introducing the past participle "vinto" in v. 14, Gradenigo replaced the clear, symmetrical syntax of the original versification with weightier, proselike diction to strengthen the rhetorical momentum in the approach to the final verse. To justify these changes he adduced the wisdom of Petrarch and Bembo, who "used the form very often, . . . along with all the good writers and . . . the Latins as well."[43] He suggested one further change, to alter the words "la vede" to "la scorge" in the fourth verse, "in order to vary the locution" (per variar la locutione). In closing, Gradenigo praised the sonnet for "being in all ways lovely, charming, and beautiful, having beautiful invention, lovely disposition, and charming locution."[44]

With that triple accolade Gradenigo gives away his game. In keeping with his other concerns, these were the three components of Cicero's compositional process on which every modern Ciceronian dwelt.[45] Invariably, they were preceded in theoretical discussions by a distinction made between *materia* and *forma*—essentially things (subjects) and words. And it was the latter that occupied Gradenigo.

Bembo's *Prose* sheds light on what is at stake here. Book 2 begins with the initial Ciceronian distinction between *materia* and *forma* but quickly introduces an additional division of *forma* into *elezione* and *disposizione*—the procedures of choosing

42. "[S]arano però quei suoi istessi versi, mutata, se non un poco la collocatione delle parole" (ibid.).

43. "[A]ssoluto modo usata frequentissimo dal Petrarca, dal Bembo, e da tutti i buoni Scrittori; et da i Latini anchora" (ibid.).

44. "[A] tutte le vie vago, leggiadro, e bello, havendo bella inventione; vaga dispositione, et leggiadra locutione" (ibid.).

45. Note, for instance, Muzio: "Drizzate gli occhi con la mente intenta / Ai chiari esempii che d'ingegno e d'arte / V'ha sì ben coloriti il secol prisco. / Gli scrittori d'Atene e quei di Roma / Daranno al vostro dir materia e forma" (*Arte poetica*, fols. 68'–69, vv. 50–55). See also Daniello, *Poetica*, pp. 69–70. The distinction entirely underlies Giulio Camillo Delminio's *Trattato delle materie che possono venir sotto lo stile dell'eloquente,* [ca. 1540]; modern ed. in *Trattati* 1:319–56.

and arranging words. It then subdivides *disposizione* into the processes of *ordine*, *giacitura,* and *correzione* (ordering, arranging, and revising words) and finally spends the rest of the book on a detailed consideration of elocution. In other words, the purportedly generative element in Cicero's threefold compositional process, invention—the production of, or settling on, the material itself—barely appears in Bembo's system, an absence that repeats itself tellingly in Gradenigo's criticism and in aspects of Bembo's discussion that we will encounter elsewhere.[46]

Other poetics produced in and around Venice also ran the risk of being eviscerated thematically by their heavy dependence on oratory.[47] In Daniello's *Poetica* rhetorical traditions not only furnish compositional procedures for poetry writing but give poetry its form. According to Daniello, a poem should consist of a prologue, an argument, and a conclusion, designed respectively to draw the reader into the topic, to instruct, and to move. The last is fundamental—the orator's art of persuasion—for as Bembo wrote following Cicero, "to define and describe well and completely the nature [of persuasion] it would be necessary to recount all that has been written of the art of oratory, which is . . . a great deal, since that whole art teaches us nothing else and strives for no end but to persuade."[48]

This perspective owed its conception to Horace as well as to Cicero, since Horace's *Ars poetica* largely translated Ciceronian rhetoric into poetic principles.[49] First printed in Italy around 1470, the *Ars poetica* became widely known in Cristoforo Landino's annotated Florentine edition published in 1482. Landino's annotations established the pattern for a hermeneutics that mixed more and more of the rhetorical tradition (as well as bits of Plato and Aristotle) into the *Ars poetica*.

---

46. Bembo explicitly discussed *elezione* under the category of the "modo col quale si scrive" (the way in which one writes), i.e., *forma*—by Bembo's admission the only one of the two major Ciceronian terms with which he concerns himself (*Prose,* p. 54). As Tomlinson points out, Bembo's word *elezione* corresponds schematically to Cicero's *inventio,* but "*inventio* embraces for Cicero broad decisions about subject matter which are not broached by Bembo" ("Rinuccini, Peri, Monteverdi," p. 44 n. 99). See also Weinberg on Daniello, who claims that "in Daniello's system nothing is invented," that instead "art consists in the judicious handling of fairly fixed materials" (*A History of Literary Criticism* 2:723, and my critique of Weinberg, nn. 91–92 below).

47. It is just as true that rhetorically styled grammars like Niccolò Liburnio's *Tre fontane* of 1526, handbooks like Sansovino's *Arte oratoria* and *La retorica,* and even the more Aristotelian *Della eloquenza* of the Venetian Daniele Barbaro (drafted in 1535) draw most or all of their illustrations from poetry, especially Petrarch's. Barbaro's work was published in Venice in 1557 with a dedication by Girolamo Ruscelli to the Accademici Costanti (of which the Paduan composer Francesco Portinaro was a member). Ruscelli dated the work from Padua around 1535, but it shows evidence that later writings were subsequently incorporated too (see Weinberg's notes, *Trattati* 2:673–80, and his mod. ed., ibid., 2:335–451). On Liburnio's *Tre fontane* see Carlo Dionisotti's illuminating "Niccolò Liburnio e la letteratura cortigiana," *Lettere italiane* 14 (1962): 33–58.

48. "[A] dissegnarvi e a dimostrarvi bene e compiutamente, quale e chente ella è, bisognerebbe tutte quelle cose raccogliere che dell'arte dell'orare si scrivono, che sono . . . moltissime, per ciò che tutta quella arte altro non c'insegna, e altro fine non s'adoperà, che a persuadere" (*Prose,* pp. 85–86). Compare Daniello's paraphrase of Horace: "Ne basta solamente che il Poema sia grave, sia vago, sia di ciascun colore, & arte ornato del dire: s'egli non havera poi seco la Persuasione, nella quale tutta la virtù et grandezza del Poeta è riposta" (Nor is it sufficient that the poem be grave, lovely, adorned with color and art of speech if it does not also encompass in itself persuasion, in which the whole power and greatness of the poet dwells); *Poetica,* p. 40.

49. Note, for example, vv. 38–45 and 104–18 on decorum; vv. 24–31 and 48–53 on moderation; and vv. 323–46 and passim on eloquence.

Cicero's ideas on decorum and variety, as well as the *inventio-dispositio-elocutio* process, all found their way there until Ciceronian and Horatian ideas became nearly indistinguishable by the mid-sixteenth century.[50] The particular set of stylistic axioms codified by Horace were especially fruitful for the Italian poetics that emanated from northern Italians like Trissino, Daniello, and Muzio.[51]

From Horace, in addition, came the premise that poetry should both instruct and delight, a notion that became universal with humanistic consolidations of wisdom and eloquence. Even in a lighthearted work like Parabosco's *Diporti,* one of the interlocutors, Federico Badoer, exhorts the others to this principle before the *novelle* begin.[52] To draw again from Tomitano's richly argued letter to Longo, "utility without pleasure is cold, just as pleasure without profit is vain." For Tomitano the components of this Horatian bond were indivisible—so commonplace by midcentury that he credits it simply to the "antichi"—requiring that "the praise of one" depend on "the perfection and sweetness" of the other. Implicitly, Tomitano ties the notion to the dynamics of aural performance: one who tries to write in many languages without a taste for noble arts and without possession of the kind of knowledge that brings him closer to God is like one whose fingers play a lute with perfect technique and tuning but without any knowledge of its art; and conversely, one who has knowledge without the eloquence to make it perceptible to others resembles an excellent organist who plays the pipes, touching the keys with great skill, but without being heard.[53] Tomitano returns from these analogies to the conclusion that equal measures of profit and pleasure are as essential to all the "scienze" as they are to the playing of instruments. With typically philosophical bent he claims to favor "nourishing the mind with laudable arts rather than delighting the ears with the words of a false Siren." But his ultimate compromise would have sat well with any Horatian: "I would still rather combine a medium level of knowledge with a middling eloquence than have a full measure of either separately, since everything that is understood with the mind must at last be explained and expressed with the voice."[54]

50. On this process see Weinberg, *A History of Literary Criticism* 1: Chaps. 14 and 15.

51. For individual discussions of Horatian concepts in their writings see Weinberg, *A History of Literary Criticism* 2: Chap. 14, 719–24, 729–31; see also 1: Chaps. 3 and 4.

52. "[A] me parebbe, se così a voi fosse il piacere, che tra noi divisassimo qualche ragionamento utile e piacevole, il quale avesse lungo spazio a rimaner fra noi; onde ciascuno parli di qual soggetto più gli pare a proposto che si ragioni, ché poscia tutti insieme eleggeremo quello che più a tutti parrà che ci arrechi utilità e diletto" (Parabosco, *I diporti* [Venice, ca. 1550], p. 15).

53. "Certo a me pare colui, che si dà tutto dì ad imparare molte lingue, scrivendo in quelle di molte composizioni senza gusto delle arti nobili, e senza la illustre possessione di quella cognizione che tanto ci rende vicini alla perfezione di Dio, ch'egli sia simile ad uno, che con le dita tocchi un liuto perfettissimo e bene accordato senza aver alcuna cognizione dell'arte, con la quale si suona quell'istrumento. E pel contrario chi tiene la cognizione senza saperla con eloquenzia spiegare e far sentire, stimirei a niun'altra cosa esser più simile, che ad un eccellente sonatore di organo, il quale, levate le canne, tocasse nondimeno i tasti con grand'arte senza esser sentito. Dove appare che molto più ci contentarebbe udire un mediocre sonatore, il quale con mediocre arte tocasse uno di quegl'istrumenti ch'io dissi; imperocchè l'uno non giova, e l'altro non diletta, siccome fa in qualche particella il temperamento del terzo" (Tomitano, in *Operette,* ed. Jacopo Morelli, vol. 3 (Venice, 1820), p. 391).

54. "[E]leggerò piuttosto di pascer l'animo con l'arti lodevoli che dilettare l'orecchie con voci d'una fallace Sirena. Stimerò ancora che sia da antiporre una mediocre cognizione con mezzana eloquenza al colmo dell'una e dell'altra separatamente. Adunque tutto quello, che nell'animo con la cognizione s'intende, si deve ottimamente con la voce spiegare, *ed esprimere*" (ibid., p. 393).

All of this reinforces a picture of the writer as a performer, one that sent some theorists scurrying for existential clarity. What role, they wondered, would the poet play? Tomitano's *Ragionamenti* struggled at length to carve out a separate niche for poets by proposing that "the first distinction born between the orator and the poet is that one seeks to persuade and the other to imitate, from which proceeds the rule and norm of speech, inasmuch as the orator uses words loosed from the ties of feet and free from the obligation of syllables and rhyme while the poet is constrained by both laws."[55] Here Tomitano distinguishes poets for their role as imitators and for the rhythmic aspect of their art. A later amplification on the question reduced differences between poets and orators to just one: while the orator avoids the use of fables and embraces instead laws, customs, examples, and histories, the poet makes the false appear true.[56]

Tomitano was broaching the delicate subject of the poet's relation to truth that had been newly animated by the rediscovery of Aristotelian poetics. Aristotle's own formulation had revolved around a comparison of the poet to the historian, which saw the former as representing universal truths, what people would *probably or necessarily do,* and the latter as relating absolute truths, what people *had done.*[57] The historian performed the less noble function. Otherwise both were rhetoricians of a sort, as Daniello had argued nine years earlier.[58] If poets and historians differed little, it was because Venetian rhetoricians conflated both their disciplines with the rhetorical arts, with equal emphasis on styles of expression and their effects on listeners.

DECORUM, IMITATION, AND THE CANONIZATION OF PETRARCH

In tying all this to the question of decorum, it makes sense to start where *cinquecentisti* did, with Cicero, by recalling two tenets that he asked his orator to heed in order to claim the listener's attention and goodwill. He illustrated the first of these, decorum, with the declaration that "perfumes compounded with an extremely

---

55. "La prima differenza che tra l'oratore nasce, et il poeta è che l'uno ricerca il persuadere, et l'altro l'imitare, à cui succede la regola, & norma di parlare, in quanto che l'oratore usa parole sciolte da legami de i piedi, & libere dall'obligo delle sillabe & delle rime, & il poeta è astretto all'una & l'altra legge" (*Ragionamenti*, p. 273).

56. "L'oratore fugge l'uso delle favole, & in vece di quelle abbraccia le leggi, i costumi, gli esempi & l'historie; la dove che il poeta dando co 'l penello della persuasione colore alle menzogne, ci fa parere il falso verosimile" (ibid., p. 281).

57. Aristotle drew the distinction in *Poetics* 9.4. On the close links between rhetoric, poetry, history, and other arts of discourse see Weinberg, *A History of Literary Criticism* 1: Chap. 1.

58. Daniello's lengthy comparison between poets and historians confined differences between the two to Aristotelian criteria of truth, but otherwise portrayed both as rhetoricians. "Sono così dell'uno, come dell'altro proprie l'Amplificationi, le Digressioni, le Varietà. Ambo studiano in muover gliaffetti, il decoro di ciascuna cosa in ciascuna cosa, et materia servando. Ambo insegnano, dilettano, & giovano parimente. Ambo le cose ne dipongono; & quasi davanti a gliocchi le ci pongono" (Proper to both are amplifications, digressions, and variety. Both study how to move the affections, each of them having decorum and serving the subject matter. Both teach, delight, instruct equally. Both depict things and virtually place them before our eyes); *Poetica*, p. 42.

sweet and penetrating scent do not give us pleasure for so long as those that are moderately fragrant."[59] Along with many other examples, this one aimed to show that a good thing too much indulged in would ultimately lose its allure. The second tenet follows naturally from the first: in order to ensure that the listener not become overly satiated with a particular effect, the orator must always seek variety in his rhetoric. For as Crassus warns in *De oratore,* "a style . . . that lacks relief or check or variety cannot continue to give pleasure for long, however brilliantly colored the poem or speech may be."[60] Both poets and musicians, Cicero claimed, appreciate the necessity of modulating their works through variation.[61] Related to these two tenets was the notion of the three stylistic levels, plain, middle, and high (or vigorous), which allow the orator to "decide what is needed at any point" and "be able to speak in any way the case requires."[62]

These are the intersecting principles I have pointed to in connection with decorum—in both senses of moderation and of matching styles to subjects—and variety. Modern-day critics easily miss the interdependencies between them precisely because they were taken for granted and intermingled by cinquecento thinkers. Dolce exemplifies this in an amusing explanation of how to match styles to subjects, as he haughtily admonishes poets to maintain propriety by preserving each of the three levels. By varying slightly and thus alleviating a too-strict adherence to any one level, a shrewd poet could succeed in striking a decorous stylistic balance.

> The wise poet must try with all his might while writing about humble material not to debase himself too much and go crawling around like a child on all fours—which can easily happen, every virtue having within its bounds vice—and likewise, when writing in the middle style not to enter the high, or writing in the high style not to spill over into bombast, as so many do.[63]

Dolce warns the poet to pursue all stylistic levels with restraint in order to avoid extremes.[64] Lurking behind this Ciceronian advice is the now familiar idea that an admixture of devices belonging to different styles should be called on to help

---

59. *De oratore* 3.25.99. On Cicero's probable borrowing of the term *decorum* from Aristotle's *Rhetoric* see Marvin T. Herrick, "Decorum," Chap. 5 in *The Fusion of Horatian and Aristotelian Literary Criticism, 1531–1555,* Illinois Studies in Language and Literature, vol. 32, no. 1 (Urbana, Ill., 1946).

60. *De oratore* 3.25.100.

61. Ibid. 3.26.102: "Neque id actores prius viderunt quam ipsi poetae, quam denique illi etiam qui fecerunt modos, a quibus utrisque summittur aliquid, deinde augetur, extenutur, inflatur, variatur, distinguitur."

62. *Orator* 21.70.

63. "[D]ee l'accorto Poeta a tutta sua forza procurar, che mentre egli scrive di materia humile, non s'abbassi tanto, che a guisa di fanciullo, vada carpone per terra; ilche puo avvenir facilmente, havendo ogni virtù per confino il vitio. è così volendo darsi allo stil mezano, non trappassi all'alto; o applicandosi all'alto, non passi alla gonfiezza; vitio, dove di leggero sono trabboccati, e trabboccano molti" (*Osservationi,* fol. 94).

64. Cf. *De oratore* 3.25.100 and *Ars poetica* 24–31. Bembo had set this precedent in vernacular literature by cautioning that the "extremes of virtue" are wont to resemble the "beginnings of vice" (La vicinità e la somiglianza che aver sogliono i principi del vizio con le stremi della virtù); *Prose,* p. 85.

temper each one, with one main level predominating. In compositional terms this is what early modern writers generally had in mind by "variety" and why they dwelt at the local levels of words and phonemes in trying to guide aspiring writers toward stylistic success. In talking about *elezione, disposizione,* and *ordine* Bembo had alluded to just this process of simultaneously keeping styles separate while intermixing them to avoid extremes.

> One must then choose the words; if speaking of lofty material, grave, high, resonant, clear, and brilliant ones; if of low and vulgar material, light, flat, humble, popular, quiet ones; if of material in between these two, then likewise middle and temperate words which incline as little toward one or the other of these two poles as possible. It is necessary, nonetheless, in these rules, to observe moderation and avoid above all satiety.[65]

In other words, since the devices proper to any given style must not be pursued too far, the secret to good writing is to emphasize one stylistic level while judiciously borrowing words and devices from others.

As growing attention to genre made it necessary to decide how propriety should be applied to epic and dramatic poetry, commentators following Bembo extended his ideas to include characters. Daniello warned that one needed not only to see that "the parts of the material treated have propriety among them but that those assigned to persons also be most suitable, proper, and fitting; and beyond those, that the speech given to them be of a smoothness, mildness, gravity, happiness, grief, and in sum, full of all the affects according to the quality, dignity, habits, office, and age of each one."[66] This, Daniello explained, was what the Latins called "decoro" and the moderns "convenevolezza" (fittingness).

Later theorists articulated more clearly the relations between the concept of stylistic levels and new Aristotelian notions of genre. In working out such ideas, they tried to determine which characteristics were essential to different genres, especially whether they were inherently low, middle, or high, and what sorts of circumstances allowed departures from the norms. Among the earliest to publish works attending specifically to questions of genre were Girolamo Ruscelli and Francesco Sansovino. Ruscelli's *Del modo de comporre in versi nella lingua italiana,* published in Venice in 1559, offered separate chapters describing each of the different lyric types: stanze, terze rime, madrigals, ballate, canzoni, and sonnets.[67] One year later Sansovino's

65. "Da scegliere adunque sono le voci, se di materia grande si ragiona, gravi, alte, sonanti, apparenti, luminose; se di bassa e volgare, lievi, piane, dimesse, popolari, chete; se di mezzana tra queste due, medesimamente con voci mezzane e temperate, e le quali meno all' uno e all' altro pieghino di questi due termini, che si può. E di mestiero nondimeno in queste medesime regole servar modo, e schifare sopra tutto sazietà" (*Prose,* p. 55).

66. "[L]e parti delle materie che si prendono a trattare, habbiano fra loro convenientia, ma che quelle ancora che alle persone si mandano, convenientissime, proprie, & accommode siano; et oltre a ciò, che il parlar che si dà loro sia di soavità, di mansuetudine, di gravità, d'allegrezza, di dolore, e finalmente pieno degli affetti tutti, secondo però la qualità, la degnità, l'abito, l'ufficio e l'età di ciascuna" (*Poetica,* pp. 35–36).

67. This direction was widely taken up later in the century in endeavors like Cesare Crispolti's "Lezione del sonetto," presented to the Accademia Insensata of Perugia about 1592. See the ed. and com-

little *Discorso sopra la materia della satira* drew stylistic boundaries for a genre that was fundamentally defined by the nexus between literary topic and tone.[68]

Deep at the heart of all these commentaries on stylistic levels and propriety lay a horror that *gonfiezza* (bombast) and *asprezza* (harshness) might invade the official literary language—qualities even less readily accommodated in the simplifying poetics of popularizers like Dolce than in Bembo's poetics. The insurgence of Petrarchan satirists at the presses during the 1540s made members of the Bembist establishment increasingly nervous—so much so that Dolce could chastize Giulio Camillo (Delminio) for *gonfiezza* with a verse as innocent as "Quando l'alta salute de le genti" and even censure Petrarch for the swollen vowels of "Giunto Alessandro a la famosa tomba."[69]

Although few theorists fired off criticisms with as little provocation as Dolce, the impulse to expel any gesture that seemed immodest, unpretty, raw, or harsh, or could in any way be accused of excess, was widespread. In the last analysis it accounts for the tendency among Venetian theorists to make aesthetic dogma out of edicts that in Cicero had stemmed more from practical exigencies. Bembists supplanted the pragmatics of oratory with unbudging expressive biases that ossified the demands imposed on Castiglione's courtier to uphold codes of modesty, elegance, and charm.

These biases led Bembo to his now famous condemnation of Dante, whose writing he claimed allowed unacceptable breaches of decorum.[70] Reproving linguistic transgressions in the *Inferno,* Bembo insisted that Dante would have been better off avoiding horrifying subjects than resorting to the gruesome language he sometimes used to describe them.

> And if it still sometimes happens that that which we intend to write about cannot be explained with proper words, but rather it is necessary to bring in vile or harsh or spiteful ones—which I scarcely believe can happen, there being so many ways and modes of speaking, and so much variety, and the human tongue being suited to taking diverse forms and diverse likenesses, and almost colors—but if it nonetheless

mentary in *Trattati* 4:193–206 and 420–21. On the relation of this phenomenon to Aristotelian criticism as it applies to the last two decades of the century see Weinberg, *A History of Literary Criticism* 2: Chap. 13, "The Tradition of Aristotle's Poetics V: Theory of the Genres." For a critique of Weinberg's explanation how genre theory came to emerge in the mid-sixteenth century and an attempt to account for it through attention to contemporary poetic practice (and not just the new understanding of Aristotle's *Poetics*) see Daniel Javitch, "Self-Justifying Norms in the Genre Theories of Italian Renaissance Poets," *Philological Quarterly* 67 (1988): 195–217.

68. In *Sette libri di satire . . . Con un discorso in materia della satira,* first published in 1560 (Venice, 1573), fols. [5]–[7], esp. fols. [6']–[7]; mod. ed. of the "discorso" in *Trattati* 2:513–18.

69. *Osservationi,* fol. 94'.

70. For other sixteenth-century attitudes toward Dante, especially late in the century, see Michele Barbi, *Della fortuna di Dante nel secolo XVI* (Pisa, 1890); Weinberg, *A History of Literary Criticism* 2: Chaps. 16 and 17; Giancarlo Mazzacurati, *Misure del classicismo rinascimentale* (Naples, 1967), pp. 221–62; and most recently Deborah Parker, *Commentary and Ideology: Dante in the Renaissance* (Durham, 1993). This polemic, and particularly the opposed sides that literati in Florence and Venice took in the debate, forms a backdrop to my "Rore's 'selva selvaggia:' The *Primo libro* of 1542," *JAMS* 42 (1989): 547–603; see esp. pp. 547–50 and 589–91.

happens, I declare that whatever part cannot be expressed properly should be left silent rather than marring the rest of the writing by expressing it, especially where necessity does not press or force the writer—from which necessity poets, above all others, are far removed.[71]

With this Bembo set the stage for a poetics tyrannically ruled by the demands of a puristic *elocutio*. By going so far as to eliminate particular subjects, he imposed a highly restrictive view of the oratorical poet as a kind of virtuosic manipulator of words, rather than thoughts—a poet with virtually no philosophy.

Bembo's view was later more gently reasoned in Tomitano's *Ragionamenti*, which reflected that, though Petrarch was indeed the better poet, Dante was the better philosopher.[72] The problem as Tomitano formulated it was that Dante so greatly excelled in invention and understood so well the various states of the soul and the issues of theology and philosophy that "he forgot many times to be a poet."[73] Petrarch, by contrast, had much in his heart with which to grace language but only hinted at a concrete knowledge of the natural world. When one interlocutor questions whether, since philosophy is a necessary gift of a poet, the better philosopher is not the better poet, Tomitano counters (through the mouth of Speroni), "I do not concede that Dante, although he may be a better philosopher, is a more serious poet than Petrarch. For Petrarch understood as much of philosophy *as is necessary to bring spirit and fullness to his rhymes,* so that in beautiful elocution, from which a poet takes his name, . . . he was better than Dante. From which one must conclude that he was a better poet than Dante" (emphasis mine).[74]

Tomitano's compromise notwithstanding, Bembo's indictment of Dante became axiomatic in Venetian academies. By 1551 Muzio was singing the Petrarchan line in catechistic verse: "a pure and graceful writer was Petrarch / above all others . . . / audacious to excess was Alighieri."[75] Not surprisingly, it was Dolce who took up the gauntlet, discounting Dante's poetic judgment—and just at the time when members of the Accademia Fiorentina were launching a public defense of Dante's poetic reputation.[76]

71. "E se pure aviene alcuna volta, che quello che noi di scrivere ci proponiamo, isprimere non si possa con acconce voci, ma bisogni recarvi le vili o le dure o le dispettose, il che appena mi si lascia credere che avenir possa, tante vie e tanti modi ci sono da ragionare e tanto variabile e acconcia a pigliar diverse forme e diversi sembianti e quasi colori è la umana favella; ma se pure ciò aviene, dico che da tacere è quel tanto, che sporre non si può acconciamente, più tosto che, sponendolo, macchiarne l'altra scrittura; massimamente dove la necessità non istringa e non isforzi lo scrittore, dalla qual necessità i poeti, sopra gli altri, sono lontani" (*Prose*, pp. 55–56).
72. "Il Petrarca [è] maggior poeta di Dante, si come Dante miglior philosopho di M. Francesco" (*Ragionamenti*, p. 286).
73. "[S]i dimenticò più volte d'esser poeta" (ibid., p. 285).
74. "Non vi si concede, che Dante quantunque sia maggior philosopho: venga ad esser piu grave poeta del Petrarca. Percio che il Petrarca quel tanto di philosophia intese, che a recar spirito & fermezza alle sue rime bastava: la dove che poi nella bella elocutione, della quale si denomina il Poeta, . . . fu di Dante migliore. Onde conchiuder si dee egli esser stato di Dante miglior poeta" (ibid., p. 287).
75. "Fu 'l Petrarca scrittor puro e leggiadro / Sopra ad ogn' altro . . . / Di soverchio fu audace l'Aldighieri" [*sic*] (*Dell'arte poetica*, vv. 183–84 and 187).
76. On the issue of style Dolce claimed that "l'autorità di Dante . . . non vale. percioche egli cosi nella elettion della lingua, come anco d'intorno alle bellezze Poetiche, non hebbe quel buono & perfetto

In a general way the pro-Petrarchan position depended on imitation theory, which once again took inspiration from classical rhetoricians.[77] The Veneto led sixteenth-century Italy in trying to standardize vernacular practices of imitation.[78] As early as 1513 Niccolò Liburnio discussed imitation in the third of his dialogues *Le selvette*. But neither Liburnio, here or in his later *Tre fontane* of 1526,[79] nor Gianfrancesco Fortunio, in his *Regole grammaticali della volgar lingua* of 1516, tried to exalt a *single* exclusive model. Unlike Bembo, who reduced the number of acceptable models to two (Petrarch for poetry and Boccaccio for prose),[80] Liburnio and Fortunio sanctioned the whole trecento triumverate. They agreed with Bembo only in rejecting contemporary authors as models—authors whose practices were less susceptible to totalizing description and reproduction by their contemporaries. In this sense all three were taking part in a trend toward linguistic standardization that both promoted and was inspired by projects of editing and publication.

Bembo's ostensible claim was for two models, but in fact he relied almost solely on Petrarch for prosody, diction, themes, genres, and lexicon. Bembo's single-model position raised theoretical hackles early in his career, setting him apart from more flexible, empirically minded courtiers whom he otherwise often resembled. It was in part this difference that stood behind the famous dispute on imitation between Bembo and Gianfrancesco Pico della Mirandola, as preserved in a Latin epistolary exchange from the second decade of the sixteenth century.[81]

Pico insisted that the author of original texts had to sort through a wide range of models, selectively commandeering what suited his own nature and guarding against the appropriation of anachronistic, ill-fitting aspects of others' works. Each person was endowed with an individualized mental simulacrum of beauty, which could be violated only at one's peril.[82] In countering Pico's argument, Bembo claimed to have sought in vain for this simulacrum, for some Neoplatonic mirror of

---

giudicio, che si vede havere havuto il Petrarca: come bene e dottamente è mostrato dal Bembo nelle sue prose" (The authority of Dante . . . does not count. Because in the choice of language, as in the matter of poetic beauty, he did not have that good and perfect judgment that one sees Petrarch to have had, as has been shown well and learnedly by Bembo in his *Prose*); *Osservationi*, fol. 7ʳ.

77. For further on theories of imitation, rhetoric, and their relation to Petrarchism see Greene, "Sixteenth-Century Quarrels: Classicism and the Scandal of History," Chap. 9 in *The Light in Troy;* Hathaway, "Poetry as Imitation," Part One in *The Age of Criticism;* and for related musical issues, Howard Mayer Brown, "Emulation, Competition, and Homage: Imitation and Theories of Imitation in the Renaissance," *JAMS* 35 (1982): 1–48.

78. For general treatments of the topic see Greene, *The Light in Troy,* and G. W. Pigman III, "Versions of Imitation in the Renaissance," *RQ* 33 (1980): 1–32, and the copious literature cited there.

79. See Padley, *Grammatical Theory,* pp. 54–57 and 65–67, and Floriani, "Grammatici e teorici," pp. 164–65.

80. For further on this point see Floriani, "Grammatici e teorici," pp. 141–43.

81. For analyses of the dispute see Baldacci, *Il petrarchismo italiano,* pp. 11–27; Greene, *The Light in Troy,* pp. 171–76; and the introduction to Giorgio Santangelo, *Le epistole "De imitatione" di Giovanfrancesco Pico della Mirandola e di Pietro Bembo* (Florence, 1954).

82. See the edition of Santangelo, pp. 27–28: "[Natura] Ideam igitur ut aliarum virtutum, ita et recte loquendi subministrat, eiusque pulchritudinis affingit animo simulachrum; ad quod respicientes identidem et aliena iudicemus et nostra" (Nature supplies us with a pattern for speaking well, as for the other virtues, and creates in our mind a similacrum of this beauty with reference to which we habitually judge both what is not ours and what is); trans. from Greene, *The Light in Troy,* p. 172.

perfection, in his own youthful mind.[83] Having failed, he turned to the models of Cicero for prose and Virgil for verse. At first he tried merely to mimic them, but said he could later *emulate* them—a higher and ostensibly more creative act. Lesser models, according to Bembo, would have been useless in implanting this consummate paradigm in the mind of the aspiring poet.[84] And what did he try to imitate? Only style. "The activity of imitating is nothing other than translating the likeness of some other's style into one's own writing."[85] As Bembo describes him, the imitator offers no heuristic resistance, no challenge to the model, but surrenders himself as a passive medium, a clear pool of water ready to take the dye.

Bembo's recommendation that a writer copy another authoritative author, widely accepted by the second quarter of the sixteenth century, resulted in an academized rigor that exceeded even his own prescriptions. As taken up by critics like Delminio—and inveighed against by Aretino—the notion of imitation was flattened into a deadly sort of thieving.[86] To be sure, Daniello sought to enrich the idea with Aristotle's theory of mimesis, a more imaginative notion of poetry as an imitation of the actions of men and thus of nature itself.[87] Others, like Tomitano, sounded the same call, but their contexts were tacitly Horatian. Tomitano exemplified this in describing the poet as an "imitator of human actions *who arouses admiration in the listener*" (emphasis mine).[88] In adhering to Horatian concerns for sonorous effects— and of necessity its rhetorical adjunct of imitation-as-emulation—Tomitano typified the midcentury fusion of Horace and Aristotle that Marvin T. Herrick has characterized.[89]

Even as late as 1560, Bernardino Parthenio's dialogue *Della imitatione poetica* avoided dealing centrally with Aristotelian imitation.[90] Parthenio was a former stu-

83. On the idea of the mirror in Renaissance literary imitation see M. H. Abrams, *The Mirror and the Lamp: Romantic Theory and the Critical Tradition* (Oxford, 1953), esp. pp. 30–42.

84. On the problematic question of imitating lesser models see JoAnn Della Neva, "Reflecting Lesser Lights: The Imitation of Minor Writers in the Renaissance," *RQ* 42 (1989): 449–79.

85. "Nihil est enim aliud totum hoc, quo de agimus, imitari; nisi alieni stili similitudinem transferre in tua scripta" (Santangelo, *Le epistole,* p. 45).

86. On this aspect of Delminio see Greene, *The Light in Troy,* p. 177. In a letter to Dolce of 25 June 1537 Aretino compared such "thieves" to those who "trample herbs to gather condiments" (gli ortolani sgridano quegli: che calpestano l'herbicine da far' la salsa, e non coloro; che bellamente le colgano); *Lettere,* 6 vols. (Paris, 1609), 1:122.

87. See E. N. Tigerstedt, "Observations on the Reception of the Aristotelian *Poetics* in the Latin West," *Studies in the Renaissance* 15 (1968): 7–24, for a discussion of this aspect of the Renaissance tradition of Aristotle's *Poetics.* On Aristotelian verisimilitude see Hathaway, *Marvels and Commonplaces,* pp. 9–19 and Part 2. For a clarification of issues relevant to music late in the century see Gary Tomlinson, "Madrigal, Monody, and Monteverdi's *via naturale alla immitatione,*" *JAMS* 34 (1981): 60–108.

88. Tomitano, *Ragionamenti,* p. 226; see Weinberg, *A History of Literary Criticism* 1:384.

89. Herrick's *The Fusion of Horatian and Aristotelian Criticism* remains the best treatment of the subject.

90. On the two types of imitation Parthenio says there is "Una, la qual consiste nell'esprimere eccellentemente le nature & i costumi di quelle persone, che ci proponiamo d'imitare. . . . Ma di queste sorti di imitation lasciando la cura ad Aristotele, solamente tratteremo dell'altra, laquale consiste nelle parole & ne modi di dire" (There is "one, which consists in expressing excellently the natures and habits of those persons whom we propose to imitate. And this is the end goal of poetry, which is meant to express human actions. . . . But leaving the care of this sort of imitation to Aristotle, we treat only the other type, which consists in words and modes of discourse"); Bernardino Parthenio, *Della imitatione poetica* (Venice, 1560), pp. 93–94.

dent of Giovanni Battista Egnazio (the teacher of Venier and his circle), and his interlocutors included literati from the region: Gabriele, Paolo Manuzio, and Trissino. Unlike theorists late in the century for whom Aristotle's poetics of mimesis became the primary theoretical matrix, Parthenio gave only cursory attention to the imitation of nature, and this mainly as a byway to the main issues of sound and meter.

The foremost modern historian of these texts, Bernard Weinberg, was dismayed by what he perceived as the sullied fusions of ancient sources devised at midcentury and the indifference of midcentury theorists toward the integrity of canonical ancient texts.[91] This put him at odds with the basic working methods of writers like Tomitano and Parthenio, who habitually compiled their arguments by drawing loosely from ancient texts. For Weinberg that spelled damning impurity, philological sloth and ignorance, and lack of resources—icing without cake. More than this, Weinberg viewed the replacement of Ciceronian imitation of models by Aristotelian imitation of nature as a teleological victory of the late sixteenth century that midcentury authors, with their constant backsliding into rhetoric, had failed to pull off. Rhetoric, as he viewed it, simply lacked substance.

Yet in turning everything to rhetorical account, treatises like Parthenio's were not so barren as Weinberg made out. The rhetorical vision that led Venetians to read in universally Ciceronian-Horatian terms also prompted them to innovative meditations on rhythmic and musical properties of verse.[92] In searching for listener appeal, Venetians hoped to convey meaning *through* sound and awaken readers to interactions *between* sound and meaning. These interactions were the musical basis of their attraction to Petrarch's verse and their theoretical basis for conflating it with Ciceronian oratory. By careful attention to sound, theorists invigorated the decorum/variation conjuncture thought to form common ground between Petrarchan poetics and Ciceronian rhetoric, explaining how meanings were manipulated through variations of sonorous effects.

VARIAZIONE AS MUSICAL DIALECTIC

Variazione is the process by which Bembist thinking finds its implementation in real compositional practice. In analyzing how the principle operated, Bembo and others presented readers with the means to create their own Petrarchan styles, their own simulacra of ideal models. For students of lyric and madrigal, these discussions offer remarkably detailed hints for understanding the sanctioned processes of generating new texts—or, in the case of music, new text settings.

Variazione as a precept proceeds from the stylistic levels delineated in ancient theory. Cicero's *Orator* rejected the plain, severe style of the Attic logicians (chiefly Brutus and Calvus) by boasting brilliant results for his three oratorical styles. In the

---

91. See Weinberg, *A History of Literary Criticism* 1:145–47 and 280–81.
92. Indeed, Weinberg discusses this contribution of Parthenio in *A History of Literary Criticism* 1:281.

plain style the orator would adhere to common words and modest metaphors; his speech would be subdued in ornament, with few figures of speech, and "sprinkled with the salt of pleasantry."[93] The orator of the middle style would minimize vigor and maximize charm; though all figures of speech and ornaments could lie at his disposal, his language had above all to be "brilliant and florid, highly colored and polished."[94] The orator of the grand style was "magnificent, opulent, stately, and ornate."[95] But it was the diversity that the orator brought to each of these that gave the new brand of oratory its great appeal, as Cicero claimed in explaining the effects of his early attempts: "The ears of the city . . . we found hungry for this *varied style of oratory,* displayed equally in all styles, and we were the first, however poor we may have been and however little we may have accomplished, to turn them to an amazing interest in this style of oratory" (emphasis mine).[96]

A lucid reading of Bembo's *Prose* depends on understanding how far its seemingly disparate themes relate similarly to variation. Early in Book 2, Bembo explains the three styles and recasts *variazione* as a dialectical principle intended to guide all composition and criticism. "One could consider how much a composition does or does not merit praise, . . ." he claimed, "by means of . . . two aspects . . . that make all writing beautiful, *gravità* and *piacevolezza*" (gravity and pleasingness).[97] *Gravità* contains honesty, dignity, majesty, magnificence, and grandeur ("l'onestà, la dignità, la maestà, la magnificenza, la grandezza"), while *piacevolezza* encompasses grace, smoothness, loveliness, sweetness, playfulness, and games ("la grazia, la soavità, la vaghezza, la dolcezza, gli scherzi, i giuochi").[98]

The schemata by which *gravità* and *piacevolezza* intersect with high, middle, and low styles are deliberately imprecise—and nowadays widely misunderstood. Theoretically, each stylistic level is discrete and dependent on subject matter, while *gravità* and *piacevolezza* in turn function as extreme dialectical poles within any one of them. In explaining how various authors have actually used *gravità* and *piacevolezza,* however, Bembo implicitly links *gravità* to the high style and *piacevolezza* to the middle or low. Some authors, he says, have dwelt excessively on one or the other—Dante on a style too often unrelieved in its *gravità,* Cino da Pistoia on one too *piacevole.* Only Petrarch had moderated the two with a perfect feel for variety, attaining "each of these qualities marvelously, to such a degree that one cannot choose in which of the two he was the greater master."[99] Ideally every author

93. *Orator* 24.81–26.90.
94. Ibid. 26.91–28.96.
95. Ibid. 28.97.
96. Ibid. 30.106. Cicero elaborates the performative aspects of this style not only in terms of varied language but of modulation of the voice, physical gestures, and facial expressions (ibid. 17.55–18.60).
97. "Dico che egli si potrebbe considerare, quanto alcuna composizione meriti loda o non meriti . . . per . . . due parti . . . che fanno bella ogni scrittura, la gravità e la piacevolezza" (p. 63). These resemble the "mild and pleasing" and "emotional and vehement" styles in Cicero's *De oratore* 2.42.179–53.215, as Tomlinson observes, "Rinuccini, Peri, Monteverdi," p. 47 n. 104.
98. Bembo, *Prose,* p. 63.
99. Ibid.

would achieve the same equilibrium, choosing from the three styles "at times grave words tempered with light ones and temperate ones with light ones, and vice versa—the latter with some of the former, the former with some of the latter, neither more nor less."[100]

Slipping freely between the three styles and between *gravità* and *piacevolezza*, Bembo confounds the reader in search of a systematic theory. His treatment conflates two outwardly different systems—the one vertical and rigidly hierarchical, the other lateral and inherently dialectical. Yet in so doing he made tangible the real purpose of introducing *gravità* and *piacevolezza* in the first place: only through them is the constant intermixing and tempering process that Bembo believed necessary to the proper working of separate levels set in motion. The dual system enabled him to grant the concept of stylistic levels a certain dynamism, as long as each level maintained a baseline of decorum. In later adaptations of Bembo's model, paired, intersecting systems became a normative means to support the principle of variation, even for eclectics like Tomitano.[101]

Even though Bembo linked *gravità* and *piacevolezza* clearly to *variazione,* he reiterated the latter theoretically in enumerating three qualities that "fill out and comprise" the former pair: namely, "il suono, il numero, la variatione"[102]—a schematic duplication that suggests at once how much variation counted in Bembo's system and how very loose that system was. It will be useful to examine *suono* and *numero* more closely, since the rest of Book 2 is mainly devoted to an explanation of them.

Suono in Bembo's definition is "that concord of sounds and that harmony that is generated in prose by the arrangement of the words and in verse also by the arrangement of the rhymes."[103] Bembo built explanations of *suono*'s musical effects on a tradition that goes back to ancient times with Cicero,[104] and in the Renaissance to grammars like Fortunio's *Regole grammaticali*. Yet Fortunio had regarded sound mainly within the restricted sphere of orthographical and morphological questions.[105] For Fortunio gemination, for instance, was permissible in prose but not in poetry; without it the latter could "flow more sweetly" since "gemination of

---

100. "[V]ariando alle volte e le voci gravi con alcuna temperata, e le temperate con alcuna leggera, e così allo 'ncontro queste con alcuna di quelle, e quelle con alcuna dell'altre né più né meno" (ibid., p. 55).

101. See, for instance, the *Ragionamenti,* pp. 466–67: "Il poeta dovere co 'l giudicio dell'orecchie mescolare insieme le voci rotonde, con l'humili, l'humili con le sonore, le sonore con le languide, & queste con le gravi. onde la grandezza dell'una temperata con la humilità dell'altre venga à fare una mescolatura perfetta, & un condimento soave" (The poet must, with the judgement of the ear, mix together full-toned words with humble ones, humble with sonorous, sonorous with languid, and languid with grave; so that the loftiness of one tempered with the humbleness of another comes to make a perfect mixture and sweet seasoning). Further comments on *variazione* occur on p. 474.

102. "[E] le cose, poi, che empiono e compiono queste due parti, son tre, il suono, il numero, la variazione" (*Prose,* p. 63).

103. "[Q]uel concento e quel armonia, che nelle prose dal componimento si genera delle voci; nel verso oltre a ciò del componimento eziando delle rime" (ibid.).

104. For Cicero's use of these terms see *Orator,* 48 to the end.

105. Carlo Dionisotti contextualizes the orthographical questions raised by Fortunio in "Marcantonio Sabellico e Giovan Francesco Fortunio," Chap. 2 in *Gli umanisti e il volgare fra quattro e cinquecento* (Florence, 1968), pp. 23ff.

consonants is not without some harshness" and was thus to be avoided, "especially in amorous verse."[106] This is as far as Fortunio would go in connecting sound with meaning. Quite new in Bembo, by contrast, is the extension of sound's importance from simply a bearer of sensory traits to an actual signifier.[107]

Suono operated for Bembo through two main vehicles: the phonetic (letters) and the metric (rhymes). Letters make their effects both separately and in various combinations, with different criteria applied to vowels and consonants. Gary Tomlinson has shown how Bembo's hierarchical ranking of vowels according to the amount of air expelled to pronounce them followed the Ficinian theories with which Bembo had grown up, and which he had already popularized in *Gli asolani*.[108] The letter "A makes the best sound because it sends forth the most air, since this air is expelled with more open lips and more towards Heaven."[109] The other vowels descend from *A* in the order *E, O, I, U,* all of them making "a better sound when the syllable is long than when it is short."[110] The rules, however, are complex and contingent, dependent on context. Open *O*'s, for instance, resound more than closed ones and hence sit higher in the hierarchy, accented *E*'s sit higher than unaccented ones, and so forth.

Bembo also graded consonants for affect and in some cases for "spirito." The *L* is "soft and agreeable and the sweetest of all the letters in its family." The *R* has the opposite quality, "harsh," although of a "generous breath." Located somewhere between the two are the *M* and the *N*, the sound of which Bembo mysteriously describes as "almost crescent- and horn-shaped" within words—apparently a metaphor for their nasal, prolonged quality.[111] The sound of the *F* is "somewhat dense and resonant" but "quicker" than that of the *G. C* is equally dense and resonant but more "halting than the others." *B* and *D*, on the other hand, are "pure, graceful, and fluent," and *P* and *T* are even more so. *Q* has a "poor and dead" sound, but adds "resonance and flesh" to the letter by which it stands as kind of servant, that is, the *U*.[112]

---

106. In verse "più dolcemente corrano: perche la geminatione delle consonanti non è senza alcuna durezza; & specialmente nell'amorose rime è da doversi schifare" (fols. 39–39′); quoted from the rev. ed. published by Manutius in 1545.

107. The generalization also holds for Cicero, for whom "good" *sonus* meant euphony and smoothness in speech and *numerus* meant prosody structured in balanced metrical arrangements—both designed to win over the audience. In Cicero's usage the terms lack the quantitative, semantic, and dialectical dimensions that their equivalents have for Bembo.

108. See "Rinuccini, Peri, Monteverdi," pp. 17–55, esp. p. 48.

109. "Di queste tutte miglior suono rende la A; con ciò sia cosa che ella più di spirito manda fuori, per ciò che con più aperte labbra nel manda e più al cielo ne va esso spirito" (*Prose*, p. 100).

110. Ibid.

111. For Bembo's figurative usage of "lunato e cornuto" see the *Nuovo dizionario della lingua italiana*. The two terms had wider planetary associations that may relate to Bembo's Neoplatonic cosmologies.

112. The complete passage on consonants reads: "Molle e dilicata e piacevolissima è la L, e di tutte le sue compagne lettere dolcissima. Allo 'ncontro la R aspera, ma di generoso spirito. Di mezzano poi tra queste due la M e la N, il suono delle quali si sente quasi lunato e cornuto nelle parole. Alquanto spesso e pieno suono appresso rende la F. Spesso medesimamente e pieno, ma più pronto il G. Di quella medesima e spessezza e prontezza è il C, ma più impedito di quest'altri. Puri e snelli e ispediti poi sono il B e il D. Snellissimi e purissimi il P e il T, e insieme ispeditissimi. Di povero e morto suono, sopra gli altri tutti,

On another structural level—that of multiple lines of poetry—a poem's relative weight results from the distance between rhyme words. More distant rhymes have a graver quality, closer ones are more pleasing.[113] By this reckoning sestine, lacking rhymes within stanzas, are the gravest of all. In all other verse forms, rhymes must not be farther apart than three to five lines, so as "to serve the propriety of time."[114] Unlike the fixed sestina and the nearly fixed sonnet and ballata, *suono* imparts considerable variety to canzoni and madrigals because their rhyme schemes and verse lengths can differ so much.[115]

Bembo explains *numero* in similarly hierarchic terms: "Number is none other than the time given to syllables, either long or short, created by virtue of the letters which make up the syllables or by reason of the accents which are given to the words, and sometimes by both."[116] Quantity in Italian is determined by accent, with tonic accents being long and syllables preceding them short. The arrangement of accents at the ends of verses also affects verses' *numero*. Antepenultimate accents give lightness ("leggerezza"), while final accents make verses heavy ("peso")— hence *versi sdruccioli* create *piacevolezza* and *versi tronchi* create *gravità*. Furthermore, words whose syllables abound in vowels and consonants lend verses a certain *gravità;* those that have few create *piacevolezza*.[117] To exemplify the grave style, Bembo cited the second verse from the opening sonnet of Petrarch's *Canzoniere, Voi ch'ascoltate in rime sparse il suono,* for its diphthongs and consonantal clusters: "Di quei sospiri, ond'io nudriva il core," and at a far greater extreme the famous "Fior', frond', erb', ombr', antr', ond', aure soavi."[118]

The principal job of the poet, in short, is to create well-proportioned, felicitous mixtures of sonorous and articulative elements. In a charming analogy Daniello compares this process with the work of a mason.

---

ultimamente è il Q; e in tanto più ancora maggiormente, che egli, senza la U che 'l sostenga, non può aver luogo. La H, per ciò che non è lettera, per sé medesima niente può; ma giugne solamente pienezza e quasi polpa alla lettera, a cui ella in guisa di servente sta accanto" (*Prose,* p. 66). Bembo discusses the problems of *S* and *Z* on pp. 65–66, mainly in historical-linguistic terms.

113. "[P]iù grave suono rendono quelle rime che sono tra sè più lontane; più piacevole quell'altre che più vicine sono" (ibid., p. 68).

114. "[A] servare ora questa convenevolezza di tempo" (ibid. p. 70).

115. "[L]e canzoni, che molti versi rotti hanno, ora più vago e grazioso, ora più dolce e più soave suono rendono, che quelle che n'hanno pochi" (ibid.). As examples of light canzoni with a proliferation of seven-syllable lines Bembo cited Petrarch's *Chiare, fresche e dolci acque,* no. 126, and *Se 'l pensier che mi strugge,* no. 125 (ibid., p. 71). Along these lines Dolce noted that even sonnets could have more or less "grandezza," depending on whether the tercets used three different rhymed endings (e.g., cde dce) or two (e.g., cdd dcc) (*Osservationi,* fol. 99). In the latter case the more frequent rhymes make the sonnet less high and grave.

116. "Numero altro non è che il tempo che alle sillabe si dà, o lungo o brieve, ora per opera delle lettere che fanno le sillabe, ora per cagione degli accenti che si danno alle parole, e tale volta e per l'un conto e per l'altro" (*Prose,* p. 73).

117. "Gravità dona alle voci, quando elle di vocali e di consonanti, a ciò fare acconce, sono ripiene; e talora piacevolezza, quando e di consonanti e di vocali o sono ignude e povere molto, o di quelle di loro, che alla piacevolezza servono, abbastanza coperte e vestite" (*Gravità* is imparted to words when they are full of vowels and consonants that are conducive to it, and at times *piacevolezza* [is imparted] when they are stripped and destitute of vowels and consonants, or are sufficiently clothed and dressed with those that produce *piacevolezza*); ibid., p. 74.

118. Ibid., pp. 80–81. The line is v. 5 from no. 303, *Amor che meco al buon tempo ti stavi.*

I declare that number is none other than a disparate parity [or, balance of disparates] and harmony that results from speech. And therefore, I would commend you, lads, were you not to disdain to imitate in your writings the master stonemasons who, before setting themselves to the task of building . . . choose those stones or tiles which seem to them most suited to the composition of the wall. . . . And then, having chosen them, begin to adapt and compose them with one another—now a large with a small, now a narrow with a wide; now a whole with a broken; sometimes one lengthwise, another one crosswise, placing one one way, another another way, until the wall reaches that height which it must in order to be beautiful and well proportioned.[119]

Like Bembo, Daniello expected the poet to create suitable poetic mixtures, more sonorous words with less sonorous, "high and grave" with "low and light," and final accents with penultimate accents.[120] Nouns and verbs were to be used in different positions, with different vowels, persons, numbers, and in different guises. Even the positions of caesurae—like the landings placed every ten or fifteen steps apart to allow one to catch one's breath on the staircases of great palaces—should be variously interspersed depending on the accentual positions of the particular words found in the vicinity of the caesurae. With *comune* words (penultimate accented), caesurae will fall after the third, fifth, or seventh syllables; with *mute* (final accented) after the fourth or sixth; with *sdrucciolose* (antepenultimate accented) after the sixth or the eighth.[121]

All of this wisdom leads to a single broad axiom: that just as we praise youth for maturity and the aged for youthful delicacy, so we should greatly extol verse that resembles prose and prose that reflects the *numero* of verse.[122] Bembo had not made the equation between poetry and prose so precise. In doing so Daniello captured a great tangle of Bembist criticism in a single net, suggesting much about the proselike shape madrigals were to assume at the hands of Venetian composers.

By the 1540s theorists were expanding Bembo's observations on sound and number to account for ever more specialized cases, some of which will become relevant

119. "[D]ico, il numero non esser altro che una dispari parità & harmonia, che risulta del parlare. Et per tanto vi loderei io figliuoli, che voi non vi deveste sdegnare d'imitare nelle vostre scritture i maestri di murare, i quali prima ch'a fabricar si ponghino . . . eleggono quelle pietre o que matoni, che loro pare che piu si confacciano alla composition del muro. . . . Et poi ch'essi scielte l'hanno, incominciano ad adattarle & comporle insieme l'una con l'altra, hora una grande, con una picciola, hora una sottile, con una grossa; hora una intera con una spezzata; quando questa per lungo, quando attraverso quell'altra & quale in una, & qual in altra guisa ponendo, insino a tanto che il muro a quella altezza che dee bello & uguale ne cresce" (*Poetica,* pp. 118–19).
120. "[V]engasi . . . alla compositione di esse voci, ponendone quando una piu sonora, con una meno; & mescolandone hora un'alta & grave; con una bassa & leggieri; & le tronche con l'intere" (ibid., p. 119; cf. also p. 121).
121. Ibid., pp. 123–24.
122. "Oltre a tutto cio cosi come noi sogliamo spesse fiate molto commendar quel fanciullo, ch'alcuna maniera & costume di canuta etade in se ritiene: Et allo'ncontro quel vecchio nel quale alcuna cosa si scorga di giovenile delicatezza. Cosi etiando è da grandemente commendar quel verso che tiene della prosa: Et conseguentemente quella prosa che numero si veda havere di verso" (ibid., p. 126).

to my interpretations in later chapters. Tomitano for one noted that words having the consonants *R, S,* and *T* and the vowel *O* create greater *numero,* or, as he gives us to understand, greater *gravità*—words like "soggiorno, rapido, antro, ardori, acerbo," and so forth.[123] *Collisioni* also make lines more numerous, as in

Deh porgi mano all'affannato ingegno,

or the "full, melodious, grave, and magnificent"

Rodan' Hibero, Rhen, Sen' Albi' Her' Ebro.[124]

Sometimes a poet has to avoid ending with a sound with which the next word begins, since this creates too much noise. Thus it is better to say

Quand'io son tutto volto in quella parte

than to have the two words with *T*'s side by side, as in

Quand'io son volto tutto,

which generates a strange, bad sound.[125] At other times a poet will purposely draw a verse out so that it doesn't gather too much speed, as in

Aspro core, & selvaggio, & cruda voglia,

which is more hesitant than

Aspro, selvaggio cor' & cruda voglia.[126]

Occasionally a writer wants to "split the ears with noise" and at other times to create a "numero tranquillo," as at the beginning of an oration in order to "make listeners attentive." Tomitano exemplifies "tranquil number" with the start of Petrarch's canzone *Nel dolce tempo de la prima etade.*[127] At other times one should slip along with haste, which happens in a verse having two "voci sdrucciolose."

L'odorifero e lucido Oriente.[128]

---

123. *Ragionamenti,* p. 469. Tomitano cited as poems that exemplify this Petrarch's sonnets *Rotta è l'alta colonna, e 'l verde lauro* (no. 269) and *Ite rime dolenti al chiuso sasso* (no. 333).

124. Ibid., p. 470. As Daniello explains, the poet may (in some cases) adjust the orthography and (in most cases) drop vowel endings of words so as to make them *mute, comune,* or *sdrucciolose,* and thus more or less grave, as happens here (*Poetica,* p. 122).

125. *Ragionamenti,* p. 471.

126. "Tiene alcuna volta il poeta il verso à bada co 'l sostenerlo in maniera, che non venga à precipitarsi per la troppa velocità, 'Aspro core, & selvaggio, & cruda voglia', che piu riposata divenne, che il dire 'Aspro, selvaggio cor'& cruda voglia', Il qual verso tanto divenne volgare, quanto quell'altro fu degno de gli orecchi di M. Francesco" (ibid., pp. 471–72).

127. Ibid., p. 472.

128. Ibid., pp. 472–73. The line is v. 2 from no. 337.

Petrarch never composed a whole verse out of these *sdrucciolose* words, Tomitano cautions—as here where he tempered "odorifero" and "lucido" with a word of "numero grave," "Oriente."[129] An excess of *voci sdrucciolose* could cause "languidezza" (poetic languor), so serene effects had to be achieved in alternative ways. Tomitano's perfect example of this is the famous opening quatrain from Petrarch's sonnet no. 164, *Hor che 'l ciel et la terra e 'l vento tace*. He described the evocative gloss on Theocritus's calm sea and silent night that opens the poem as lacking "noise." Even though inherently the material was prone to "languidezza,"[130] it embodied a "perfect tranquillity" through its ideal balance of *gravità* and *piacevolezza*.

The question of languor brings Tomitano to structural and affective questions involving caesurae. Although caesurae commonly occur at either the fourth or sixth syllable in an *endecasillabo*, the first of these is "the more magnificent and grave" and thus (implicitly) superior.[131] A caesura on the fifth syllable should be disdained as too languid.[132]

Additional structural repetitions, finally, may add to a verse's beauty. Alliteration generally creates greater number. Words not participating in the alliteration may be interpolated between those that are, and the effect is quite graceful when one alliterated word finishes a line and another starts the next.[133] This prose-like device calls to mind Daniello's claim that resemblance to prose is an asset to verse. Further, words that divide other words from one another, such as "et, hor, ne, si come," make a verse beautiful, as in the line "Et temo Et spero Et ardo Et sono un ghiaccio."[134]

Even Sansovino's *Arte oratoria* added to the wisdom on sound and number, although Sansovino was more concerned with rhetoric and less with poetry than Daniello or Tomitano had been. He affirms that the guidelines designating which words are naturally grave, pompous, base, and so forth—based largely on sound— had their origins in oratory. Despite the fact that it treats oratory, the *Arte oratoria* (like other rhetorics) exemplifies these guidelines with poetry. Sansovino concludes that old Tuscan words may add a certain *gravità* to one's style exactly *because* of their antiquity and their foreignness. Some words, such as "troba, heroe, anno, frôba," carry with them a natural grandeur that is pompous ("gonfie") by nature, while others, like "sante, veste, cinto, via fuoco," call up a base quality because of their languid sound.[135]

Like Daniello, Sansovino shows how words that are "mute," "comune," and "sdrucciolose" can be used by the orator to make greater or lesser *harmonia*.[136] Even

---

129. Ibid., p. 478. In fact Petrarch never ended lines with *parole sdrucciole*.
130. Ibid., p. 473.
131. Cf. Ruscelli, *Del modo de comporre*, on accents; he assigns the principal accents in *endecasillabi* to the fourth, sixth, or eighth positions, in addition to the tenth (p. xlix).
132. *Ragionamenti*, pp. 474–76.
133. Ibid., pp. 486–87.
134. Ibid., p. 489.
135. *L'arte oratoria*, fol. 56.
136. Ibid., fol. 56ʹ.

more important, he explains the division of sentences and the formation of cadences. A cadence is "none other than a harmonious and sweet finishing of the period, more conclusive and easier in verse than in prose. This is because in verse one must not leave the listener in any doubt or in any way less than fully satisfied from a lack of number or a paucity of sound ["harmonia"]. And this sound depends on a well-proportioned joining of words, one with another."[137]

In the decade after 1550 Venetian rhetorics and poetics maintained a lively interest in Bembo's aesthetics, and this at a time when Willaert's students were still setting scores of Petrarchan sonnets. Parthenio's *Della imitatione poetica,* though not pitched to a vernacular readership, borrowed much of what Bembo had to say about sound, since (it explained) "words are chosen according to variety."[138] Marco Valerio Marcellino's first "Discorso" in *Il diamerone* invoked Bembo's authority in citing Petrarch and Boccaccio as vernacular models. Couched as an old-styled apologia, it defended the Tuscan vernacular for its especially melodious character.[139] The most ambitious of the midcentury writings was Ruscelli's *Del modo de comporre in versi nella lingua italiana* (signed in 1558 although not published until 1559), which applied Bembist norms to a wide range of lyric genres. A Viterban polygraph based in Rome before his move to Venice in 1548, Ruscelli was among the best known and respected of vernacular theorists in the city.[140] His *Del modo de comporre* tried to

137. "[La] cadenza . . . altro non è che harmonico e dolce finimento del periodo, tanto piu nella prosa difficile, quanto nel verso è piu terminato e piu facile; perche in quello conchiudendo attamente non si dee lasciar l'ascoltatore dubbio e non a pien sodisfatto, o per il mancamento del numero, o per la poca harmonia che vi si ode; laqual harmonia risulta dalle commessure delle parole, l'una all'altra proportionalmente congiunte" (ibid., fol. 57′).

138. "Le parole secondo la varieta s'eleggerano" (p. 241). Thus, for example, *A* and *O* are the fullest, hence weightiest, vowel sounds; clusters of consonants make for *gravità*, sparseness of consonants makes for *piacevolezza* (see esp. p. 80 and in Book 4, pp. 191–93 and 199–201).

139. The work was dated 10 April 1561 and published three years later. The *discorsi* published in *Il damerone* (Venice, 1564) were set in ca' Venier (cf. Chap. 4 above, nn. 31 and 65). For Bembist allusions see fols. [c], [c ii]–[c ii′]. On the melodious quality of the vernacular, note the following: "le nostre voci volgari, sono quasi tutte composte d'una cosi ordinata mescolanza di vocali, & di consonanti, che acquistano un dolce cominciamento, un regolato mezzo, & un soavissimo fine. Per la qual cosa, se queste parole sono con giudicio da dotta, & leggiadra mano composte, & con una politezza gentile congiunte, & serrate insieme: il loro congiungimento, non puo divenir nè duro, nè aspro, nè molle, nè languido: ma fa riuscire l'oratione dolce, soave, composta, unita, & tutta uguale: in maniera, che ogni nostro concetto puo esser da noi partorito vivo, et quasi vestito di carne & d'ossa; quando egli ci comparisce avanti vestito di cosi ricca, & cosi ben tessute veste" (Our vernacular words are almost all made up of an ordered mixture of vowels and consonants, which acquire a sweet beginning, a regulated middle, and a most smooth end. For which reason, if these words are composed by a learned and graceful hand and joined and bound with a courtly polish, then their conjoining can become neither hard nor harsh, nor soft nor languid, but rather the speech will succeed in being sweet, smooth, poised, unified, and completely consistent in such a way that our every concept can be endowed with life and virtually clothed in flesh and bones, since it appears before us dressed in such a rich and well-woven vestment); ibid., fols. [b v]–[b v′]. Following this, Marcellino gives examples of all the different sounds that Italian can make—long and short syllables in different combinations, different vowels, accents, and so forth—concluding that "da questo si puo comprendere . . . che la nostra favella ha perfettamente tutta questa numerosa armonia; che in essa i nostri moderni . . . hanno cominciato à scrivere" (from this one can comprehend . . . that our tongue contains perfectly all this numerous harmony with which our moderns have begun to write); fols. [b vi]–[b vi′].

140. Parabosco was among those acquainted with him, as indicated in a letter to Anton Giacomo Corso discussing Corso's sonnet in Bembist terms: "Io hebbi dal dottissimo, & gentilissimo Ruscello, una di V.S. con la risposta al sonetto ch'io le mandai. io l'ho molto bene essaminato, & considerato; perche egli è degno di molta consideratione, & hollo giudicato degno d'infinita lode; ne voglio in questo caso cedere, di giuditio a nessuno, & non gli defraudere in parte nessuna il nome della sua bellezza, gra-

show how to write in all the standard lyric forms, as well as in *versi tronchi* and *versi sdruccioli*. The thoroughness with which he embarked on this task, with chapters devoted to each form, remains his most useful contribution and, for students of contemporaneous madrigals, his attention to the sonnet is especially helpful.[141]

Ruscelli mainly occupied himself with the sonnet's prosodic possibilities, principally enjambment. For, as he stated, "the breaking of the verse and then finishing the construction of the thought is the principal [source of] grandeur in style."[142] Because of this, a sonnet devoid of enjambments, like *Piangete donne, et con voi pianga Amore* (no. 92), embodied simplicity, or the humble style. Petrarch's *Mentre che 'l cor dagli amorosi vermi* (no. 304), broken as it is by continual enjambments, embodied the high style.[143] As a rule, however, enjambments were not to be made one after another in either sonnets or *capitoli,* since this "could generate a vexing continuousness of style. But above all one eschews [enjambments] in the first verses of quatrains [and] tercets."[144]

All these elaborations of *variazione* along Bembo's dialectical lines suggest we rethink Weinberg's dismissal of midcentury arts of poetry. The years 1525–60 produced some preliminary challenges to Bembo's views on models, imitation, and the choice of language; but more than that they produced a wealth of embellishments on the sonorous functions of vernacular poetry. The rhetorical concerns for harmony, number, sound, and structure all stood at the center of poetic criticism, since language and especially poetry had come to be conceived as vehicles for performance more than cognition and contemplation. Indeed there is a striking resemblance between the focus of cinquecento theorists and of modern ones (most notably Gianfranco Contini, as reflected in a famous essay of 1951), who have been

---

vità, leggiadria, & facilità" (I received from the most learned and kind Ruscelli one of yours with the *risposta* to the sonnet that I sent him. I have examined and considered it well, for it is worthy of much consideration, and I have judged it worthy of infinite praise. In this case I do not want to cede judgment to anyone, and deprive it in any way of the labels of beauty, gravity, loveliness, and facility); *Il primo libro delle lettere famigliari* . . . (Venice, 1551), p. 6.

141. A chapter on the sonnet may also be found in Dolce's *Osservationi,* fols. 96′–100′, but Dolce's treatment is more perfunctory than Ruscelli's.

142. "Lo spezzar . . . in verso, e quivi venir à finir la costruttione della sentenza, è la principal grandezza dello Stile"; *Del modo de comporre,* p. 113.

143. "Et queste spezzature, che non lascino andar à finir le costruttioni, e le sentenze tutte piane nel fin de' versi, son quelle, che, come ho detto, hanno le principal parte nella gravità dello stile" (ibid., p. 115). Torquato Tasso's *Lezione recitata nell'Accademia Ferrarese sopra il sonetto "Questa vita mortal" ecc. di monsignor della Casa,* written ca. 1565–72, praised della Casa's *O sonno, o della queta, umida ombrosa Notte* precisely for its frequent enjambments. On the question of enjambment in this work see Edoardo Taddeo, *Il manierismo letterario e i lirici veneziani del tardo cinquecento* (Rome, 1974), pp. 233–37; and Tomlinson, "Rinuccini, Peri, Monteverdi," pp. 55–57. Tasso had met Ruscelli in Venice during a journey of 1559–60, after which he made Ruscelli an interlocutor in his *Minturno.*

144. "[Q]uesto spezzar di versi si faccia spesso, ove commodamente può farsi, ma che non però si faccia sempre, cioè, in tutti i versi d'un Sonetto, ò d'un Capitolo, che, come dissi, potrebbe generar fastidio la continuata somiglianza dello stile. Ma che sopra tutto si fugga di non farlo ne' primi versi de' Quatternarii, nè de' Terzetti, che allora . . . parebbe importantissimo vitio, & con molta cura fuggito da tutti i Scrittori per ogni tempo" (*Del modo de comporre,* p. 117). (Note, however, that this is not true of *Mentre che 'l cor* nor of della Casa's *O sonno.*)

Aside from Ruscelli and Tasso, considerations of enjambment are rare in the sixteenth century. See also Weinberg's discussion of Vincenzo Toralto's *La Veronica, o del sonetto* (Genoa, 1589), in *A History of Literary Criticism* 1:228, and Crispolti's Lezione on "Mentre che 'l cor," mod. ed., *Trattati* 4:193–206.

gradually more receptive to recognizing the priority of rhythmic over semantic properties in Petrarch's poetics, or at least their interdependencies.[145]

Much of the motivation behind Venetians' literary theorizing during the first half of the sixteenth century stemmed of course from their anxiety to elevate the vernacular. The new local culture linked with the press was shaped increasingly by Italian and less and less by Latin. Steps had to be taken to secure acceptance of the vernacular, improve it as a vehicle of communication, and give it a certain cachet. This way learned writers, once in print, could be made accessible to a less-learned reading public, and aspiring writers of humble origins could, conversely, be groomed for higher realms of literary discourse.[146] The welcoming attitude toward foreignness and archaism that Venetians assumed in codifying trecento Tuscan sprang from a desire to add luster to their adopted tongue. Such arcana were anathema to proponents of the *lingua cortigiana* who prized unruffled elegance. But in Venice a writer like Parthenio could claim (with Sansovino and others) that strange and little-used words gave living language a heightened *gravitas*.[147] Even though Parthenio was writing about imitation and drew examples from Latin and Tuscan, he shared with collectors and patrons like Antonio Zantani widespread attitudes that sought elite status by appropriating the cultural objects and instruments of distant times and places.

More than any other Italian city, Venice domesticated a foreign idiom for vernacular music, using a full-blown northern polyphony that was fundamentally sacred, austere, hieratic, and complex with which to set high-styled Tuscan texts. The linguistic equal of this polyphony was Petrarchan syntactic complexity, which endowed the new vernacular with its needed cultural capital.[148] The cachet attached to complex syntax goes a long way toward explaining the new status of the sonnet among midcentury poets, who often published almost nothing else in the copious anthologies issued around 1550 from the Venetian presses.[149] Many of these sonnets were conventional by literary standards, yet settings of them by Willaert and Rore adapted their linguistic possibilities to music in novel ways that transformed the symbolic relations of sacred and secular. Before considering this phenomenon more closely, we will attempt to mediate between theories of words and settings of words by considering how they were reconciled by Venetian music theorists.

---

145. See Gianfranco Contini, "Preliminari sulla lingua del Petrarca," in *Varianti e altra linguistica: una raccolta di saggi (1938–1968)* (Turin, 1970), pp. 169–92. For related views see Umberto Bosco, "Il linguaggio lirico del Petrarca tra Dante e il Bembo," *Studi petrarcheschi* 7 (1961): 121–32; Giulio Herczeg, "La struttura delle antitesi nel *Canzoniere* petrarchesco," *Studi petrarcheschi* 7 (1961): 195–208; idem, "La struttura della frase nei versi del Petrarca," *Studi petrarcheschi* 8 (1976): 169–96; Fredi Chiapelli, *Studi sul linguaggio del Petrarca: la canzone delle visioni* (Florence, 1971); and Robert M. Durling, ed., *Petrarch's Lyric Poems: The "Rime sparse" and Other Lyrics* (Cambridge, Mass., 1976), pp. 11–18.

146. On the relationships between the press, the standardization of the vernaculars, and their links to national identities see Lucien Febvre and Henri-Jean Martin, "Printing and Language," Chap. 8, pt. 4 in *The Coming of the Book: The Impact of Printing, 1450–1800*, trans. David Gerard, ed. Geoffrey Nowell Smith and David Wooten (1958; London, 1976), pp. 319–32.

147. "Le parole nuove, et inusitate aggiungono gravità, et maraviglia come anchora ricordò Aristotele" (*Della imitatione poetica*, p. 192).

148. On this point see Floriani, "Grammatici e teorici," p. 165.

149. I refer here especially to those in the *Rime di diversi* series; see Chap. 4 above, n. 21 and passim.

Chapter 6 · CURRENTS IN VENETIAN MUSIC THEORY
The Consolidation of Music and Rhetoric

As a preface to his remarks on *numero,* Bernardino Tomitano wrote in the *Ragionamenti della lingua toscana* that words made in time delight us because they are rhythmic ("numerose") and fill the soul with endearing intervals and musical proportions.[1] Tomitano went on to explain the ramifications of *numero* in both poetry and music. Strings, reeds, and human voices all produce number and harmony through high and low pitches that delight the ears. These in turn generate many other musical parts ("voci") by which the intervals and their proportions can combine to satisfy the listener and bring forth a more perfect sound.[2] To signify the harmonious sounding of unlike tones Tomitano depicted "[t]his loving discord or discordant lovingness" as "a most sweet procuress who, with the enticements of her sweetnesses, lures the soul into that happiness with the state of loving an unknown ['un non so che'], whom we know not well."[3] The conceit of the sweet procuress is an allegory of beauty, who charms the soul into a contentment with loving. The love thus inspired in the listener resembles the one described by Renaissance Neoplatonists, that is, a love for God as yet vaguely and dimly realized. It corresponds more precisely—if only by suggestion—to the Neoplatonic construct of earthly beauty as a seductive manifestation of the ideal proportions of the divine and of beautiful music as an aid to souls in traversing the series of emanations that lead them back to their divine origins.[4]

1. "Le parole, che noi diciamo, fatte a tempo cotanto ci dilettano, non per altro, che perche sono numerose, & empiono l'anima nostra di amichevoli intervalli & musiche proportioni" (Tomitano, *Ragionamenti della lingua toscana* [Venice, 1546], p. 460). As in Chap. 5, I cite from the second edition.
2. Ibid., p. 461.
3. "Questa amichevole scordanza, ò discorde amicitia, è una ruffiana dolcissima, laquale con le lusinghe delle sue dolcezze tira l'anima in quel contento ad amare un non so che, che noi non bene sappiamo" (ibid.).
4. In the next breath Tomitano acknowledges Pythagoras and Plato as his sources (ibid.). The idea relates, of course, to the notion of *discordia concors,* which recurs throughout medieval and Renaissance

These proportions, Tomitano went on to explain, represent only one type of *numero,* however. There is another type in the measure of sound produced by human voices. This is a gauge not of pitch but of how words are properly timed and weighed to delight the soul of the listener or reader. In stressing the aural aspect of a spiritual ontology Tomitano was taking up Bembo's lead in *Gli asolani,* which had followed Ficino in attributing supernatural powers to sung words. As described by Lavinello in Bembo's dialogue, love displayed itself as the dual desires for beauty of the body and beauty of the soul, the one attained through sight, the other through sound.[5]

In one crucial respect Tomitano's discussion differs from those in either *Gli asolani* or in Bembo's *Prose,* namely in connecting directly sonorous aspects of verse with their translations into musical settings. One of the main reasons Tomitano exhorts poets to pay close aural attention to the verses they write is that well-timed verse makes music sweeter: "Musicians will sing beautiful and well-measured verses more sweetly and they will delight us more than when singing rough and badly composed ones."[6] This prefatory axiom grounds and justifies Tomitano's unusually detailed account of poetic sound and number as I have summarized it in the previous chapter.

Like Tomitano and other writers on language, theorists of music in midcentury Venice were trying harder and harder to forge the link between language and sound. The first notable attempt comes from the priest Giovanni del Lago, who showed a striking recognition of rhetoric's growing importance to musical developments. This is something of a surprise, for del Lago's contributions to music theory were otherwise largely unoriginal. They lay mainly in his assembling a vast collection of correspondence to which his own offerings are the least ingenious part. In fact del Lago's mind was not only derivative but almost totally speculative, since he lacked experience in composition. The real practical and theoretical consolidation of words and notes did not come until the monumental *Istitutioni harmoniche* of Gioseffo Zarlino, published in its first edition in 1558, which showed Zarlino as a keen observer of contemporaneous polyphonic practice. Between these two sources, with del Lago's preliminary attentions to language and Zarlino's massive speculative theories and analytical assessments of contemporary compositional practices, I attempt to reconstruct

---

theory, but finds a particularly avid reformulation at the hands of Florentine Neoplatonists. On this idea see Claude V. Palisca, *Humanism in Italian Renaissance Musical Thought* (New Haven, 1985), pp. 17–21 and Chap. 8, "Harmonies and Disharmonies of the Spheres."

5. "È adunque il buono amore disiderio di bellezza tale, quale tu vedi, e d'animo parimente e di corpo, et allei, sì come a suo vero obbietto, batte e stende le sue ali per andare. Al qual volo egli due finestre ha: l'una, che a quella dell'animo lo manda, e questa è l'udire; l'altra, che a quella del corpo lo porta, e questa è il vedere. Perciò che sì come per le forme, che agli occhi si manifestano, quanta è la bellezza del corpo conosciamo, così con le voci, che gli orecchi ricevono, quanta quella dell'animo sia comprendiamo" (Pietro Bembo, *Prose della volgar lingua, Gli asolani, Rime,* ed. Carlo Dionisotti [Turin, 1966], p. 468). On Ficino's philosophies of magical songs see Gary Tomlinson, *Music in Renaissance Magic: Toward a Historiography of Others* (Chicago, 1993), Chap. 4, and for a summary of Bembo's adaptations of Ficino's theories idem, "Rinuccini, Peri, Monteverdi, and the Humanist Heritage of Opera" (Ph.D. diss., University of California at Berkeley, 1979), pp. 37–43.

6. "[P]iu dolcemente canteranno i musici i belli & misurati versi, & piu ci diletteranno, che cantando i rozzi & mal composti" (*Ragionamenti,* p. 462).

an emergent consciousness of rhetorical issues in music among Venetian musicians and trace their growing confidence about how to apply them.

THE NASCENT CICERONIANISM
OF GIOVANNI DEL LAGO

Del Lago was born sometime in the late fifteenth century during the heyday of courtly song.[7] His teacher, as he related in a letter of 15 September 1533, was the Paduan frottolist Giovanni Battista Zesso. By 1520 del Lago had become a priest at the tiny parish church of Santa Sofia in the Venetian *sestiere* of Cannaregio and had begun what was to become a copious correspondence with other music theorists. As Bonnie J. Blackburn has discerned, the addresses of various of these letters show that del Lago lodged in a series of unassuming neighborhood quarters, one near the dump by Santa Sofia, another by the barbershop there, and another presumably near the church of Santa Eufemia on the Giudecca.[8] In the course of his professional life del Lago also received mail at three different churches (Santa Sofia, Santa Eufemia, and San Martino delle Contrade in Castello), though his only lifelong association remained the tiny Santa Sofia. Even there, del Lago had to climb laboriously through the church hierarchy, where (as Blackburn has noted) he was promoted from subdeacon to deacon in 1527 and from deacon to titular priest in 1542, but never reached the highest post of curate by the time he died on 8 March 1544.

Del Lago's correspondence is preserved today in the Biblioteca Apostolica Vaticana, MS Vat. lat. 5318.[9] This manuscript consists of three distinct layers. One contains primarily correspondence del Lago received from Pietro Aaron, Giovanni Spataro, Bartolomeo Tromboncino, and various minor musicians;[10] another, letters from Spataro and other theorists to Aaron (these make up layers two and three). Only one layer (the first) collects del Lago's own letters and in a most intriguing form: with one exception the items there have been transcribed by a scribe in a fair copy with the clear intention of readying them for publication. Appended to the many letters contained therein is a dedication preceded by a full title page.

7. I am grateful to Bonnie J. Blackburn for sharing with me much information and many insights about del Lago over a number of years. The biographical notices that follow are largely indebted to her. For del Lago's collected correspondence see Bonnie J. Blackburn, Edward E. Lowinsky, and Clement A. Miller, eds., *A Correspondence of Renaissance Musicians* (Oxford, 1991) (hereafter *Correspondence*).

8. For a precise and chronological identification of these see Blackburn et al., *Correspondence,* Chap. 6. Much of this information is the result of Blackburn's successful foray through the church archives, which had been given up by earlier scholars.

9. Prior to the *Correspondence* the most important inventories of this manuscript were those of Raffaele Casimiri, "Il codice Vatic. 5318: carteggio musicale autografo tra teorici e musici del sec. XVI dall'anno 1517 al 1543," *Note d'Archivio per la Storia Musicale* 16 (1939): 109–31, with an annotated chronological listing of its contents and an index of persons, and especially Knud Jeppesen, "Eine musiktheoretische Korrespondenz des früheren Cinquecento," *Acta musicologica* 12 (1940): 3–39, which provides information on other copies of these letters and sources of the manuscript.

10. These include Joannes Legius, Paulo de Laurino, Pietro de Justinis, Don Laurenzio Gazio, Nicolaus Olivetus, Francesco di Pizoni, Fra Seraphim, Francesco Lupino, Hieronymo Maripietro, and Bernardino da Pavia. See the *Correspondence,* pp. 979–1020.

Epistole composte in lingua volgare nellequali si contiene la resulutione d'e molti reconditi dubbij della Musica: osscuramente trattati da antichi Musici, et no*n* rettame*n*te intesi da Moderni a comune utilita di tutti li studiosi di tale liberale arte novamente in luce ma*n*date dal molto di cio studioso Messer Gioanne del Lago ~~dia-cono~~ prete nella chiesa di Santa Sophia di Vinegia. Et scritte al Ma*gnific*o Messer Girolamo Molino patricio Venetiano. (fol. [1])

Epistles composed in the vernacular language in which are contained the resolution of many recondite questions on music, obscurely treated by the ancient musicians and not fully understood by the moderns, for the common use of all the students of such liberal art, newly brought to light by the most learned Messer Giovanni del Lago ~~deacon~~ priest in the church of Santa Sofia of Venice. And written to the magnificent Messer Girolamo Molino, Venetian patrician.

Del Lago fashioned his title in the rhetoric of printed volumes, deploying phrases like "novamente mandate in luce" and "non più vedute" that first editions typically used to attract buyers. Other components of the title tried to pitch the contents to a wide readership, noting its use of the vernacular and the simplified explanations of complex theoretical problems that interested "studiosi" would find in it. Perhaps most notably, del Lago assembled his various explications into one of the "dialogic" forms that had just recently emerged in the era of high-volume printing, the episto-lary anthology—a genre that had had its debut in print only with Pietro Aretino's *Primo libro delle lettere* of 1537.[11]

We have already encountered the dedicatee of these literary-styled "Epistole," Girolamo Molino, among the literary patriarchs who gathered at ca' Venier in the company of Domenico Venier, Federico Badoer, Lodovico Dolce, Girolamo Muzio, Girolamo Parabosco, and scores of other literati. Contemporary theorists such as Dolce and Bernardino Daniello listed Molino as one of the city's cardinal poets, but del Lago's dedication chronicles for the first time the nature of Molino's curiosity and skill in music.[12]

To the magnificent Mr. Girolamo Molino, Venetian patrician, most honored patron.

It is a natural instinct, magnificent sir, to desire that which one knows to be similar to oneself. Being yourself then full of virtue and celebrated among others for that, you merit not only the dedication of the present epistles in which are contained vari-

11. On the genre as a whole, including a catalogue of epistolary collections by men and women of letters, see Amedeo Quondam, *Le "carte messaggiere": retorica e modelli di comunicazione epistolare, per un indice dei libri di lettere del cinquecento* (Rome, 1981). See also Margaret F. Rosenthal, *The Honest Courtesan: Veronica Franco, Citizen and Writer in Sixteenth-Century Venice* (Chicago, 1992), Chap. 3; various essays in *Writing the Female Voice: Essays on Epistolary Literature*, ed. Elizabeth C. Goldsmith (Boston, 1989); and on seventeenth-century France Elizabeth C. Goldsmith, *Exclusive Conversations: The Art of Interaction in Seventeenth-Century France* (Philadelphia, 1988).

12. For the literary references see Chap. 4 nn. 15 and 31 and the Afterword to Chap. 4. On Molino's musical side, see Chap. 4 nn. 81–88, esp. the letter of April 1535 from Tromboncino to del Lago, cited in Chap. 4 n. 85, which sends regards to Molino.

ous questions about music, but you are to be esteemed for every other honor. And certainly one sees that few today are found (like you) gifted not only in such a science but also adorned with kindness and good morals. Therefore not finding to whom one could better submit such questions to be judged, and you being one who holds the first degree in the art of music among your other virtues, and also to show you some sign of the love and benevolence that I bear to you for infinite obligations, I make you a present. Even if it is a small gift to you (to whom much more worthy ones are due), nonetheless owing to your benign kindness it will please you to accept this little gift and it will indeed be welcome coming from one of your most faithful servants.[13]

As further confirmation of Molino's understanding of music, del Lago addressed to him a lengthy treatiselike letter, undated, giving assorted technical definitions of intervals and musical genera.[14]

It may be that Molino's patronage did not materialize into the subvention del Lago needed to publish the "Epistole"; as Blackburn notes, much of Molino's life was passed in a state of financial embarrassment owing to a family dispute over money, which he spent years fighting in court.[15] Or it may have become clear to del Lago that Molino, who kept his own works from public view, would be better honored by a gift in manuscript.

Precisely when del Lago first assembled the "Epistole" that make up layer one is not entirely clear. The fair copy was presumably made sometime between May 1535, the date of the latest letter in the "Epistole," and June 1538, that of the first letter in the following series. It seems likely that del Lago was inspired to assemble an epistolary volume only after Aretino's letters had their riveting effect on Venetian readers—that is, between 1537 and early 1538. In 1540 del Lago incorporated parts of the "Epistole"'s contents into what was to be his only published work, the treatise *Breve*

13. "Al Mag*ni*fico Messer Girolamo Molino patricio venetiano patrone Honorandissimo. É instinto naturale Mag*ni*fico Sig*nore,* desiderare quello, che a sé proprio si conosce simile. [Es]sendo adu*n*que vostra segnoria di virtu piena, et tra gli altri p*er*cio celebrata, merita nonsolamente la dedicatione delle presenti epistole, nellequali si contengono diversi dubbij di Musica, ma esser essaltata ad'ogni altro honore. Et certo si vede che pochi, al di d'hoggi si trovano (come voi) dottata no*n* solamente di tale scienza, ma anchora di gentilezza, et costumi ornato. Onde per no*n* trovare à chi meglio si possino tali dubbij rimettere ad esser giudicati, et per esser voi quello, il quale nell'arte di Musica tiene il primo grado fra le altre virtute, et anchora per mostrare alcuno segno de l'amore, et benivolentia ch'io vi porto per infinite obligationi, ve ne fo uno presente, il quale anchora che sia picciol dono a' vos*tra* Signoria (alla quale maggior più degni si conviriano) no*n*dimeno per vostra benigna cortesia vi piacerà, [di a]ccetare questo picciolo dono et sara poi grato venendo da uno suo fedelissimo servitore" (fol. [1']).

14. The letter appears without date on fols. 110'–115'.

15. For reference to this see Molino's posthumous biographer Giovan Mario Verdizzotti, in Girolamo Molino, *Rime* (Venice, 1573), who wrote that he was "per lo spatio di trenta & piu anni di continuo con fiera crudeltà fin al punto estremo della sua vita a gran torto travagliato, & lacerato con molti litigii, & insidie dalla malignità & perfidia di chi gli era piu congiunto di sangue" (p. [8]). Relevant archival documents are noted in Elisa Greggio, "Girolamo da Molino," *Ateneo veneto,* ser. 18, vol. 2, pt. 1 (1894): 194–95, and a lengthy "Difesa di se stesso al Consiglio di Dieci" survives at I-Vmc, Cod. Cic. 1099, fols. 70–92. Molino's letter to Bernardo Tasso of January 1558, partially quoted at the end of Chap. 4 above, n. 97, begins by describing the legal resolution of the battle (*Delle lettere di M. Bernardo Tasso,* 3 vols. [Padua, 1733–51], 2:358–59).

introduttione di musica misurata.[16] Afterward he continued to make additions and revisions to the manuscript letters, as indicated by the textual relationship of many marginal additions to them to portions of the treatise.[17] In fact, Blackburn's biographical sleuthing allows us to take del Lago's change of title from "diacono" to "prete" on the manuscript's title page as verification that he was still going about revisions in 1542 when he got his last promotion.

Originality and philological rigor fell low on del Lago's list of priorities and bore almost no relevance to the kind of publication planned for the "comune utilità di tutti li studiosi di [musica]" that he hoped to launch. Much of what found its way into the "Epistole" was cobbled together from letters del Lago had arrayed before him, some of which were actually addressed to him and others of which he had simply gotten hold. He took this miscellanea and added cribbings from any number of classical and modern sources, freely patching together each letter to form his final version. All of his writings are highly derivative as a result, as the patient philological work of Blackburn et al. now makes clearer than ever.

Despite this, the "Epistole"'s opening letter, addressed to an obscure Servite monk named Fra Seraphin and first discussed in modern times by Knud Jeppesen in 1940, commands interest as one of the earliest efforts to lay out the linguistic and grammatical principles necessary to a composer of music. Styled as a little tract, the letter occupies a sizable nine folios (fols. 2–10) complete with marginal rubrics marking the various topics. The letter is not the work of the scribe who copied the rest of the "Epistole," but an autograph. Del Lago evidently added it to the front of the corpus after the creation of layer one and affixed the date 26 August 1541, thus postdating the publication of the *Breve introduttione* as well as his initial assembling of the "Epistole."

Like many other letters in the "Epistole"—and in epistolary collections generally—the date is at least partly fictitious, since much of the letter had already been written much earlier. Several textual and physical factors help clarify the history of the letter's compilation. Only the initial section on the modes responds to queries by Fra Seraphin, who replied in turn on 30 April 1538.[18] In 1540 it became one of two major sections that del Lago incorporated into his *Breve introduttione,* the other ostensibly dealing with composing music in parts.[19] In the treatise the second of

16. Full title: *Breve introduttione di musica misurata, composta per il venerabile Pre Giovanni del Lago Venetiano: scritta al Magnifico Lorenzo Moresino patricio Venetiano patron suo honorendissimo* (Venice, 1540); facs. ed. BMB, ser. 2, no. 17 (Bologna, 1969). Connections between the two are investigated in Don Harrán, "The Theorist Giovanni del Lago: A New View of the Man and His Writings," *Musica disciplina* 27 (1973): 107–51.

17. See Martha Feldman, "Venice and the Madrigal in the Mid-Sixteenth Century," 2 vols. (Ph.D. diss., University of Pennsylvania, 1987), 1:80–81.

18. MS Vat. lat. 5318, fol. 74.

19. See Harrán, "The Theorist Giovanni del Lago," pp. 121–29. The two sections appear on pp. [29]–[30] and [39]–[43] of the treatise.

these was called "Modo, & osservatione di comporre qualunche concento," but it had more to do with text setting and grammar than counterpoint.

The letter also contains two lengthy interpolations that were not part of the *Breve introduttione,* in addition to the minor reworkings of numerous treatise-derived sections that occur throughout. The first interpolation (on fol. 5) presents definitions of "accento, discritione, pronuntiatione, [e] modulatione." The next (on fols. 7–8') offers a grammatical summary of syllables, syllable length, the qualities of letters, and so on. Both interpolations were compiled separately from the main body of the letter: written on paper of a smaller size, the verso of the first interpolation (fol. 5') has been left entirely blank, while the end of the second interpolation is mostly blank (fol. 8), and both lack the marginal rubrics that run throughout the large-format portions of the letter. Most likely del Lago first authored all the parts in large format, probably before 1540, included them in his *Breve introduttione,* and subsequently inserted new sections when preparing the letter version, which he then dated 1541.[20] This hypothesis is supported by the numerous insertions of smaller passages that were added to the side and bottom margins of the original folios— glosses to the main text that qualified or enlarged on the topics at hand—all of which the printed treatise lacks.

What was the point of such a seemingly inchoate text? No easy answer suggests itself, but some clues are hidden in its clumsy structure. Immediately after his exposition of the modes, del Lago shifted without warning into an explanation of composing music for a text. "As to the observation on composing a harmony, it should be noted that every time you wish to compose a madrigal, or sonnet, or *barzelletta,* or other canzone, it is first necessary, searching diligently with the mind, to find a melody suited to the words . . . that is, one that suits the material."[21] This is a simple recasting of the traditional rhetorical maxim of propriety, the fitting of style to subject so often taken up by contemporaneous literary theorists. It was one voiced by medieval musicians from Guido d'Arezzo and Jacques de Liège to Franchinus Gaffurius and Martin Agricola in more recent decades.[22] Del Lago formulated it in conventional Ciceronian language by calling for an "aëre *conveniente*" able to match ("convenire") the "materia."[23] Unlike earlier theorists, he made no mention of Latin texts but conceived propriety in specific connection with vernacular forms. In fact

---

20. Harrán, working from a copy of Vat. lat. 5318 in I-Bc, MS B. 107, 1–3, was unaware of these physical differences in the original and, therefore, of the fact that each must have been compiled at a separate time.

21. "Quanto alla osservatione di comporre un concento primieramente è da notare, ogni volta che vorrete comporre un madrigale, o sonetto o barzeletta, o, altra canzone, prima bisogna con la mente diligentemente cercando ritrovare uno aere conveniente alle parole . . . cioè che convenga alla materia" (fol. 3; = *Breve introduttione,* p. [39]).

22. See the references to these and other theorists' statements in Don Harrán, *Word-Tone Relations in Musical Thought: From Antiquity to the Seventeenth Century,* Musicological Studies and Documents, no. 40 (Neuhausen-Stuttgart, 1986), Appendix, Nos. 15–42, pp. 364–73. Many of these theorists advocate propriety in connection with modal ethos; we will see that del Lago did the same.

23. Zarlino also consistently used forms of the verb *convenire.* This idea is discussed in the context of Aristotelian imitation by Walther Dürr, "Zum Verhältnis von Wort und Ton im Rhythmus des Cinquecento-Madrigals," *Archiv für Musikwissenschaft* 15 (1958): 89–90 and passim.

del Lago took over the preoccupation of his literary counterparts with the proper accommodation of Italian (and, by extension, secular vocal genres). By *madrigale* he means the sixteenth-century poetic form and adds the *sonetto,* the *barzelletta*—that lower-brow and shorter version of the ballata common in frottola settings—and other canzoni (that is, lyric poems in general). Like contemporaneous madrigalists, del Lago viewed these Italian forms as discrete and essentially poetic categories—by implication representing different poetic *levels*—to which appropriate musical styles would be matched.[24]

Outwardly del Lago's sudden transition from modal issues at the beginning of his letter to grammatical ones seems disjointed, but the juxtaposition may have had more to it than meets the eye. Once the reader knows the modes, he or she is then taught to make the (modal) melodies of each part fit the kinds of texts that will be set. The next passage clarifies the logic of this pedagogy. Proceeding from the explanation of the modes to the Ciceronian dictum on secular text setting cited above, del Lago returns immediately to the matter of modal properties. "Whenever learned composers have to compose a song, they are wont first to consider diligently within themselves to what end and to what purpose they create and compose it, that is, what affects of the soul they ought to move with their composition, or in what tone [or mode] they ought to compose it."[25] Not only are mode and secular music linked, but the two of them specifically with modal ethos. These linkages point suggestively toward developments in Venetian secular music of the time, which was just then starting to pay special attention to mode through modal orderings of madrigal prints.[26] The textual history behind del Lago's advice to "learned composers" sheds still more light on this question. As Claude V. Palisca discovered, del Lago lifted the passage just cited from Mattheo Nardo, probably a Florentine resident in Venice and an acquaintance of Aaron;[27] and Nardo, as it happens, was a student of Giovanni Battista Egnazio, the same humanist who taught Venier and others in Venier's circle.[28] Following the transmission of knowledge forward, a line descends in the early sixteenth century from Egnazio's schoolroom, with Nardo,

24. On the phenomenon of identifying Italian musical genres by poetic forms in this period see the classic essay of Don Harrán, "Verse Types in the Early Madrigal," *JAMS* 22 (1969): 27–53.

25. "Quante volte, che i dotti compositori hanno da comporre una cantilena, sogliono prima diligentemente fra se stessi considerare a che fine, et a che proposito quella potissimamente instituiscono, o componghino. Cioè quali affetti d'animo conquella cantilena movere debbino, cioè di qual tuono si debba comporre" (fol. 3).

26. In the next years several prominent books would be ordered by mode: the *Madrigali a cinque voci* of Cipriano de Rore published in 1542, the *Madrigali a cinque voci* of Perissone Cambio published in 1545, and Perissone's *Primo libro dei madrigali a quatro voci* of 1547 (see Chaps. 8 and 9 below and Tables 6, 10, and 12). Harold S. Powers, "Tonal Types and Modal Categories in Renaissance Polyphony," *JAMS* 34 (1981): 428–70, speculates that there may have been a connection particular to *secular* music between modal ordering of prints and the general desire for what he calls "pathic and ethic effects" (p. 446).

27. See *Humanism in Italian Renaissance Musical Thought,* p. 342, where Nardo's statement (preserved in I-Rvat, MS Vat. lat. 5385) appears in columns parallel to del Lago's.

28. Palisca, arguing that Nardo's text probably preceded that of del Lago, tentatively dates it between 1522 and 1536 when Nardo's friend, Pietro Aaron, was involved (along with Egnazio) in the Aldine intellectual circle in Venice. According to his funeral oration, Egnazio was learned in music (see Palisca, ibid., p. 344 n. 30), though it seems unlikely that his learning surpassed the general knowledge that was imparted in any standard account of the seven liberal arts.

Venier, and his circle, and divides laterally to Aaron and del Lago by the late 1530s—a tantalizing crossing of musical and literary genealogies.

From this point onward, del Lago's letter sticks closely to matters of text setting, grammar, and rhetoric, all the while borrowing freely and abundantly to expand material from the *Breve introduttione*. In a continuation of themes bearing on modal ethos, del Lago next appears to paraphrase (unacknowledged) a passage from Sebald Heyden's *De arte canendi* (Nuremberg, 1540) to explain why composers ought to consider the affects of various modes.[29] "Some [modes] are happy, others pleasant, others grave and sedate, others mournful and lamenting, still others wrathful and others impetuous. And so too the melodies of the songs—one moving in one way, one in another—are variously distinguished by musicians."[30] Here del Lago sets out more clearly the Greek theory of modal ethos, which had already emerged in medieval writings on chant and was reconstituted for various discussions of Renaissance polyphony. Neither Heyden nor del Lago had a special hand in reviving the direction, of course: Gaffurius and Aaron had already made the traditional medieval juxtaposition between suiting words to music and moving the passions of the soul through various modal affects.[31] Once again, the only unique aspect of del Lago's discussion is his pointed effort to relate modal ethos to secular music.

In a somewhat later passage, del Lago extended the underlying principle of propriety, insofar as it pertains to affect, to the succession of intervals in a polyphonic composition. "Force yourself to make your harmony such that it may be happy, soft, full, sweet, resonant, grave, and fluid when sung, that is, composed of consonants in common usage, as are thirds, fourths, fifths, sixths, and octaves."[32] Even though the framework for his discussion here is propriety, del Lago tacitly assumed that *proprietas* was symbiotically hinged to its classical and modern twin in literary sources, *varietas*. Being no composer himself, he made no effort to turn the idea into a workable compositional principle but simply tossed it into the shuffle of general admonishments. Nevertheless, his naming of contrasting, even opposed, qualities ("allegro," "grave"), conceived at the level of individual intervallic progressions, indicates that local attention to variety and a belief in adapting properly the available compositional materials were beginning to spill over from literary into musical theory. Like his literary counterparts—and we will see the same to be overwhelmingly

29. Ed. and trans. Clement A. Miller, Musicological Studies and Documents, no. 26, AIM ([Rome]; 1972), Book II, Chap. 8. The relationship between the two passages is pointed out by Blackburn et al., *Correspondence,* p. 877 n. 4.

30. "[P]erche altri sono allegri, altri plausibili, altri gravi, et sedati, alcuni mesti, et gemibondi, di nuovo iracondi, altri impetuosi, così anchora le melodie de canti, perche chi in un modo, et chi in un'altro commuovono, variamente sono distinte da Musici" (fols. 3–3'; = *Breve introduttione,* p. [39]).

31. Citations are given in Harrán, "The Theorist Giovanni del Lago," p. 115 nn. 32–33; see also a similar statement by Martin Agricola from his *Rudimenta musices* (Wittenberg, 1539), fol. D ij. Palisca provides a useful table contrasting the attributions of affect to various modes made by Aaron, Nardo, and Gaffurius in *Humanism in Italian Renaissance Musical Thought,* p. 345, with a comparison of the role of modal ethos in each of their writings on pp. 345–47.

32. "Sforzatevi di far il concento vostro che sia allegro, suave, pieno d'harmonia, dolce, resonante, grave, et [a]gevole nel cantare, cioè di consonantie usitate, come sono terze, quarte, quinte, seste, et ottave" (MS Vat. lat. 5318, fol. 4'; = *Breve introduttione,* p. [40]).

true of Zarlino—del Lago pointedly confined the principle to pleasant, consonant intervals. Dissonant ones he discouraged as "mali agevoli a pronuntiar[e]," awkward to declaim.[33]

From comments relating to mode and affect, del Lago slipped into a lesson on musical and verbal cadences. However limited in understanding the subtleties of compositional procedures, he nevertheless tried here to recognize the syntactic importance of cadences, an effort in which he implied his contemporaries were often negligent.

> Cadences are truly necessary and not optional, as some thoughtlessly say, especially in songs composed on words; and this is so as to distinguish between the parts of the text, that is, to make the distinctions of comma, colon, and period, so that the meaning of the complete text may be understood, both in verse and in prose—because the cadence in music is like the full stop in grammar.[34]

The distinctions of comma, colon, and period that del Lago advocated were age-old,[35] but a certain disparity of opinion over whether, or how much, contrapuntists needed to respect them had arisen once, after Josquin's time, the linear aspect of music became complicated by the vertical dimension and overlapping mechanisms of continuous, equal-voiced (or what is sometimes called "simultaneous") polyphony. In 1533 the Brescian theorist Giovanni Lanfranco had declared in his *Scintille di musica* that divisions of words in plainchant were made according to their meaning, whereas in polyphony such divisions were made according to the arrangement of the counterpoint and the need for rests. Only as an afterthought did Lanfranco add that even polyphonists should show some concern for verbal meaning.[36] Del Lago tried to counter such views with his insistence that cadences gauged to grammar and sense were "necessary and not optional," especially in texted music

---

33. MS Vat. lat. 5318, fol. 4ʳ.

34. "Le cadentie veramente sono necessarie et non arbitrarie, come alcuni inconsideratamente dicono, massimamente nel canto composto sopra le parole, et questo per distinguer le parti della oratione, cioè far la distintione del comma, et colo, et del periodo, accio che sia intesa la sententia delle parti della oratione perfetta, si nel verso, come nella prosa. perche la cadentia in musica è come il punto nella Gramatica" (MS Vat. lat. 5318, fol. 4; = *Breve introduttione*, p. [40]).

35. For medieval and Renaissance sources voicing similar ideas see the various statements on syntax compiled in Harrán, *Word-Tone Relations in Musical Thought*, Appendix, Nos. 89–115, pp. 388–97. See also Palisca's brief discussion of the relationship between articulation in grammar and in music as discussed by Guido d'Arezzo and John Cotton, in *Humanism in Italian Renaissance Musical Thought*, pp. 338–39. Ritva Jonsson and Leo Treitler, "Medieval Music and Language: A Reconsideration of the Relationship," in *Music and Language*, Studies in the History of Music, vol. 1 (New York, 1983), pp. 1–23, clarify the importance of medieval theory in upholding such basic correspondences between grammar and music.

36. "Or e da sapere, che le distintioni delle parole si fanno nel canto Misurato: ma non come nel Fermo: perche in questo la distintione si fa secondo la sentenza delle parole: & in quello secondo che porta l'ordine del contrapunto, & la necessità delle Pause, benche il Compositore de avertire di far la cadenza, overo distintione generale secondo la sentenza, & distintione delle parole" (Now it should be known that divisions of words are made in mensural music, but not as in plainchant, because in the latter the division is made according to the meaning of the words and in the former according to the arrangement of the counterpoint and the necessity for rests, although the composer should pay heed to making cadences or general divisions according to the meaning and division of the words); *Scintille di musica* (Brescia, 1533), p. 68; facs. ed. BMB, ser. 2, no. 15 (Bologna, 1970).

where words had to be made intelligible. He adduced the idea while discussing polyphony and applied it equally to settings of poetry and of prose: "Be careful then to make cadences where the parts of the text (or one of its portions) finish and not always in an identical place—because the proper place for cadences is where the thought within a group of words finishes, since it is fitting to extend and conclude together [i.e., simultaneously] the articulations of the words and notes."[37] In other words, it is the composer's duty to see that his musical composition corresponds to the grammatical structure of the texts he sets; composers should heed *syntax* over *prosody* in setting verse since syntactic settings are rhetorically clearer. His reason ("la sententia . . . delle parole"), only alluded to here, was made explicit in an earlier passage which upheld the necessity "that the meaning of the words sung be understood."[38] Del Lago's view represents a turn away from the practice of composers like his teacher Zesso and toward the proselike readings of the most recent Venetian madrigalists.

Despite del Lago's apparent lack of sophistication with polyphonic composition, not all the subtleties of a syntactically based polyphony were lost on him. Witness, for example, his discussion of "feigned cadences," roughly comparable to what Zarlino would later call "evaded cadences." "Sometimes feigning the cadence and then, at the end of it, arriving at a consonance not near to that one is commendable." This, he adds, "is intended for the soprano or another part, but the tenor in that case always makes the cadence, or division, so that the sense of the words may be understood."[39] The mechanics of del Lago's contrapuntal strategy—that when one of the cadential voices avoids the final consonance it should not be the tenor (or perhaps bass) voice—are straightforward enough. More striking is the underlying objective of clear text expression that led him to propose the idea in the first place.

---

37. "Siate adunque diligente di far le cadentie, dove la parte dell'oratione, overo il membro finisce, et non sempre in un medesimo luoco, perche il luoco proprio delle cadentie è dove finisce la sententia del contesto delle parole, perche gliè cosa conveniente tendere, et parimente insieme finire la distintione, et delle parole, et delle notule" (MS Vat. lat. 5318, fol. 4; = *Breve introduttione,* p. [40]). As noted by Blackburn et al. in the *Correspondence* (pp. 878–79 nn. 6–7), this passage resembles one in Stefano Vanneo's *Recanetum de musica aurea* (Rome, 1533): "Cadentiarum denique numerus, maior quam deceat, non fiat, mira enim debet esse paucitas, nec in eodem semper loco. . . . Legitimus autem peculiarisque Cadentiarum locus est, ubi verborum contextus desinit sententia, nec immerito, decet enim et verborum et notularum distinctionem pariter tendere, unaque desinere" (fol. 93′; fasc, ed. BMB, ser. 2, no. 16 [Bologna, 1969]). Harrán cites the two passages in close proximity in *Word-Tone Relations in Musical Thought,* pp. 391–92.
38. "Che sia intesa la sententia delle parole cantate" (ibid., fol. 3′). Palisca (*Humanism in Italian Renaissance Musical Thought,* p. 341) reads the passage on fol. 4 differently, relating the phrase "non sempre in un medesmo luoco" (see n. 36 above) to Johannes Tinctoris's seventh rule of counterpoint in the *Liber de arte contrapuncti* stating that two cadences should not be made on the same *note.* But I would argue that the continuation of del Lago's passage, "perche il luoco proprio delle cadentie è dove finisce la sententia del contesto delle parole," suggests instead that del Lago is thinking of the place in the *text* where cadences ought to occur, not the pitches in the melody. (See also Harrán, "The Theorist Giovanni del Lago," p. 117.)
39. "Alcuna volta finger di far cadentia, et poi nella conclusione di essa cadentia pigliare una consonantia non propinqua ad essa cadentia per accommodarsi è cosa laudabile, et questo se intende con il soprano, o altra parte, ma bisogna che sempre il tenore in questo caso, faccia egli la cadentia, o ver distintione, accio che sia intesa la sententia delle parole cantate" (MS Vat. lat. 5318, fol. 3′; = *Breve introduttione,* p. [39]). Harrán's rendering of the passage in "The Theorist Giovanni del Lago," p. 111 n. 19, based on the Bologna copy of the manuscript, is misleading.

Del Lago's grammatical digest continues with a lengthy discussion of accent under the marginal caption "Che cosa è Gramatica?" Here he tried to cover the meaning, derivation, and function of accent, the three types in Latin and Italian, respectively, and the locations of accents in Italian verse.[40] In the way typical of ancient grammars, he formulated much of his pedagogy as admonishments to avoid errors ("barbarismi" he calls them in traditional grammatical jargon).[41] In all of this del Lago was eager to demonstrate his erudition through an eclectic rehearsal of different sources; yet in amassing them to raise his prestige, he often clouded his meanings for the same readers he was trying to impress. An ironic and maddening instance of this occurs in his caveat against the "barbarismi" of setting long syllables with short notes and vice versa. "Take care not to commit barbarisms in composing notes to words; that is, do not place long accents on short syllables or short accents on long syllables, which is against the rules of grammar, without which no one can be a good musician. Grammar teaches how to declaim and write correctly."[42] Del Lago adduces the authority of the Latin grammarian Isidore of Seville to defend the rule, stating that accent has "quantità temporale."[43] Are we to infer from this that del Lago was thinking of quantitative accent and that his sources were anachronistic for the purposes of his case? Probably so, but he is characteristically vague about the precise context at hand. We will see that he subsequently attempts a discrete treatment of vernacular accent that unwittingly confuses quantitative with qualitative accent.

This notwithstanding, del Lago's most inventive contribution to music theory comes in connection with accent and text underlay as they relate to vernacular verse. The three types of final accents, he explains, include antepenultimate, which makes the sound "sdruccioloso"; ultimate, which makes it "grave"; and penultimate, which makes it "temperato."[44] This occurs in one of the few passages in which del

40. MS Vat. lat. 5318, fols. 4′–6′; = *Breve introduttione,* pp. [40]–[42].
41. See, for example: "siate cauto di non far barbarismi nel comporre le notule sopra le parole" (fol. 4′, and the related statement at the end of fol. 6′); and later, "schivatevi adunque dal barbarismo il quale . . . è enuntiatione di parole corrota la letera, over il suono." On the fixation of ancient and Renaissance grammarians on avoiding errors see Keith W. Percival, "Grammar and Rhetoric in the Renaissance," in *Renaissance Eloquence: Studies in the Theory and Practice of Renaissance Rhetoric,* ed. James J. Murphy (Berkeley and Los Angeles, 1983), pp. 324–25. For an essay that traces reactions against barbarism in sixteenth-century musical criticism see Don Harrán, "Elegance as a Concept in Sixteenth-Century Music Criticism," *RQ* 41 (1988): esp. 420ff.
42. "Siate cauto di non far barbarismi nel comporre le notule sopra le parole, cioè non ponete lo accento lungo sopra le sillabe brevi, o ver l'accento breve sopra le sillabe lunghe, quia est contra regulam artis grammaticcs, senza la quale niuno po esser buono Musico, la quale insegna pronuntiare et scrivere drittamente" (MS Vat. lat. 5318, fol. 4′; = *Breve introduttione,* p. [40]). On this aspect of the letter see Dürr, "Zum Verhältnis von Wort und Ton," pp. 91ff.
43. As noted by Blackburn et al., it comes from the *Etymologariae,* 1.32.1 (*Correspondence,* p. 880 n. 11); originally cited by Harrán, "The Theorist Giovanni del Lago," p. 118 n. 42.
44. "Quanto à gli accenti nel verso volgare, sono tre modi: primo, quando cade nella sillaba antepenultima, quale rende il suono sdruccioloso; quando cade poi sopra l'ultima sillaba, rende il suono grave; et quando cade sopra la penultima, rende il suono temperato" (As to accents in vernacular verse, there are three types: first, when one falls on the antepenultimate syllable, which makes the sound slippery; then when it falls on the final syllable, making the sound grave; and when it falls on the next to last, making the sound temperate); MS Vat. lat. 5318, fol. 6′; = *Breve introduttione,* p. [41]).

Lago broaches the question of affective function, and it clearly derives from current literary theory as found in Bembo's *Prose della volgar lingua* and in Daniello's *La poetica*.[45] Next he notes, after Bembo, that a line of vernacular poetry—by which he actually meant an eleven-syllable line—cannot have accents except in three syllabic positions, the fourth, sixth, or tenth:[46] lines with their accents arranged otherwise risk not being verse at all.[47] This much is clear enough, but in an unhappy conflation of his meager Latin learning with Bembo's vernacular theory, del Lago goes on to claim that "one does not place accents except on long syllables."

Ostensibly, del Lago here is still simply describing the nature of the *endecasillabo* in poetic terms. Yet Bembo himself had said something quite different—first, that *numero* has to do with the amount of time given to syllables, and second, that this is a function both of the letters that make up syllables and of the accents they receive. For Bembo vernacular accent existed a priori, and he went out of his way to make the point that the vernacular language differs from classical languages in this respect. "Speaking of accents, I do not wish to say what the Greeks do about them, more suited to their language than to ours. But I do say just this: that in each word in our language *that syllable is always long on which the accents fall and all those [syllables] that precede them [are] short* (emphasis mine)."[48] If del Lago really meant to tell musicians where they should place *musical* accents, he might have said either that musical accents must fall on accented syllables, since length in *real* terms could only

45. Cf. the *Prose*, where Bembo says that accents should be arranged so as to fall in one of three syllabic positions: "uno di tre luoghi suole avere nelle voci, e questi sono l'ultima sillaba o la penultima o quella che sta alla penultima innanzi, con ciò sia cosa che più che tre sillabe non istanno sott'uno accento comunemente, quando si pone sopra le sillabe, che alle penultime sono precedenti, ella porge alle voci leggerezza; per ciò che . . . lievi sempre sono le due sillabe, a cui ella è dinanzi, onde la voce di necessità ne diviene sdrucciolosa. Quando cade nell'ultima sillaba, ella acquista loro peso allo 'ncontro; per ciò che giunto che all'accento è il suono, egli quivi si ferma, e come se caduto vi fosse, non se ne rileva altramente"; p. 74 in the ed. of Mario Marti (Padua, 1967). See also Bernardino Daniello, *La poetica* (Venice, 1536), on the three accentual types with respect to individual words: "le voci tutte o sono sdrucciolose, o comuni, o mute: (Sdrucciole quelle sono che hanno sempre nella loro innanzi penultima l'accento: Comuni quelle, che nella penultima: Mute quelle che l'hanno nell'ultima)" (p. 121); mod. ed. in Bernard Weinberg, ed., *Trattati di poetica e retorica del cinquecento*, 4 vols. (Bari, 1970–74), 1:308.
46. Cf. Bembo: "a formare il verso necessariamente si richiegga che nella quarta o nella sesta o nella decima sillaba sieno sempre gli accenti" (*Prose*, p. 78). This idea may be compared with the exposition of accents within verse by Giovan Giorgio Trissino, *La poetica*, pts. 1–4 (Vicenza, 1529), fols. xix'–xx', which relates these accentual positions to the positions of caesurae (repr. in *Trattati* 1:62–64). See also the remarks of Daniello dealt with in Chap. 5 above, n. 121, and of Girolamo Mei on accent, summarized in Palisca, *Humanism in Italian Renaissance Musical Thought*, pp. 348–55, as well as the more general comments on accent in idem, *Girolamo Mei (1519–1594): Letters on Ancient and Modern Music to Vincenzo Galilei and Giovanni Bardi*, Musicological Studies and Documents, no. 3, AIM ([Rome], 1960; 2d ed. 1977), 117.
47. Bembo continues: "ogni volta che qualunque s'è l'una di queste due positure non gli ha, quello non è più verso, comunque poi si stiano le altre sillabe" (*Prose*, p. 78).
48. See Bembo (partially quoted in Chap. 5 n. 116, above): "Numero altro non è che il tempo che alle sillabe si dà, o lungo o brieve, ora per opera delle lettere che fanno le sillabe, ora per cagione degli accenti che si danno alle parole, e tale volta e per l'un conto e per l'altro. E prima ragionando degli accenti, dire di loro non voglio quelle cotante cose che ne dicono i Greci, più alla loro lingua richieste che alla nostra. Ma dico solamente questo, che nel nostro volgare in ciascuna voce è lunga sempre quella sillaba, a cui essi stanno sopra, e brievi tutte quelle, alle quali essi precedono" (Number is none other than the time that is given to syllables, either long or short, now because of the letters that make up the syllables, now by reason of the accents that one gives to words, and sometimes on both accounts. And, first speaking of accents . . . [here begins the passage translated in my main text]), ibid., p. 73.

have been at issue in setting Latin texts; or (better) that in setting the vernacular they should reconcile the demands of quantity—heuristically determined by vowel and consonantal weight, consonantal clusters, and the like—with those of stress.[49]

Del Lago's tendency to stray from compositional praxis was both his bane and his boon. His injunctions on "measuring" accent roved far from any practical realities of Italian verse settings; yet, taken in sum, his attentions to vernacular prosody and its rhetorical links to text setting did at least recognize some of the ways in which accent served to articulate musical rhetoric. As we saw, he thought it necessary to acknowledge the three final accentual positions in Italian verse. And in addition, he dealt in a later passage with caesurae as defined by internal accentual positions—an issue treated by several literary theorists of the time. To this end del Lago concluded his discussion of prosody by contriving a principle, unique to his writings, to govern the setting of three Italian verse types, *settenario, ottonario,* and *endecasillabo.*

> Note finally this rule: that in vernacular verses of seven syllables the penultimate always receives [the accent], and in all those of eight, the third and penultimate, and in all those of eleven, the sixth and penultimate, and sometimes the fourth, but rarely both. But when it should happen to rest on the fourth, do not hold the sixth but rather the fourth and the penultimate. And this is done because of the verse and in order to avoid and escape the barbarism that can occur in composing notes to words.[50]

The final folios of del Lago's letter (fols. 7–10) cover a wide array of linguistic and metrical topics common to virtually all works on the *questione della lingua* and on rhetoric and poetics in the early sixteenth century. In its final form, this last section begins with the longest of the letter's interpolations, that on syllables and letters.[51] Syllables are defined by their "tenore" (accent), "spirito" (mood), "tempo" (unit of time), and "numero" (number, that is, of letters). Del Lago attributes affect only to "spirito," which may be either "aspero" (harsh) or "lene" (delicate, or sweet). Nothing is said about how syllables are made so by poets or composers, or even why composers might try to discern their affect; presumably the materials in this section were submitted as general wisdom for musicians' edification.

---

49. This is much like what Thomas Campion tried to do in Elizabethan England; see my "In Defense of Campion: A New Look at His Ayres and Observations," *Journal of Musicology* 5 (1987): 226–56.

50. "Notate ultimamente questa regola, che in tutti i versi volgari di sette sillabe, sempre la penultima si tiene, et in tutti quegli di otto, la terza, et la penultima, et in tutti quegli de undeci, la sesta et la penultima, et qualche volta la quarta, ma rare volte accade. Ma quando accadesse tenere la quarta, non terrete la sesta, ma la quarta et la penultima. Et questo si fa per la ragione del verso, et per schivare et fuggire il barbarismo che po accadere, componendo le notule sopra le parole" (MS Vat. lat. 5318, fol. 6'). Bembo makes a similar statement with respect to vernacular metrics in the *Prose,* pp. 77–78. See also Palisca on Mei cited in n. 46 above.

51. See the translation in Harrán, "The Theorist Giovanni del Lago," pp. 123–24. As shown by Blackburn et al., the sources of this passage include Priscian, Bede, Sulpicius, and Diomedes (*Correspondence,* pp. 882–83).

Next del Lago returned to the structure of Latin verse, advising that the composer "have a knowledge of meter or verse, that is, know what a foot is and how many syllables it can have, which are long, which are short, and which are common; and know how to scan a verse and where one makes caesurae and elisions between vowels; and similarly, know where the comma, and the colon, and the period fall, both in verse and in prose."[52] He wanted to make all of these tools basic to the composer's trade and threw in the caveat that the composer must be familiar with linguistic meter and rhythm, underscoring the point (as usual) with a string of borrowed definitions.[53] Of greatest interest here again is his reiteration that such knowledge applies equally to poetry and prose.

With his usual detachment from real practice, del Lago made little serviceable use of his formidable inventories. Rather inanely he made himself out as a kind of apostle, come to proselytize the unconverted to a higher consciousness of language. His preaching probably fell on few ears, for those who would convert were engaged in more profound reconciliations of musical and linguistic phenomena than del Lago was able to reckon with. He played a role that was not proactive but reactive—not a molder of his time, but a measure of it, a gauge of the new interdependencies between language and music that were already being formed within Venetian academies and private homes. If del Lago now seems to have been incapable of formulating a coherent musical poetics, we must remind ourselves that this was never his importance among theorists or composers of his day.

Nevertheless, in the late 1530s the practical recognition of these interdependencies still lay largely outside the discourses of music theory. Aaron had adumbrated some of the issues, as revealed in Spataro's 1531 letter answering Aaron's criticisms of text setting in Spataro's *Virgo prudentissimo*.[54] Spataro's retort argues the conservatist party line for a kind of *Absolutmusik*, accusing Aaron of wanting to "take the free will from music and make it subject to grammatical accents," and chiding him for his pickiness, since neither of them was a grammarian.[55] At that point Aaron had been in Venice for about nine years, during which time he had periodically served

---

52. "E necessario chel compositore habbia cognitione del metro, o, verso cioè saper che cosa è piede, et quante sillabe può havere, et quali sono lunghe, et quali sono brevi et quali sono comune. Et saper scandere il verso et dove si fa la cesura, et la collisione. Et similmente saper dove cade lo coma, et lo colo, nel periodo, si nel verso, come nella prosa" (MS Vat. lat. 5318, fol. 9; = *Breve introduttione*, p. [42]).

53. Much of this is taken from Gaffurius, *Practica musicae*, who provided translations (not of his own making) of the Greeks Aristoxenus and Nichomachus (cf. MS Vat. lat. 5318, fol. 10'; = *Breve introduttione*, p. [43]). For further details see Blackburn et al., *Correspondence*, no. 93 nn. 39–40.

54. MS Vat. lat. 5318, fols. 228–29'; *Correspondence*, no. 36, pp. 445–55.

55. Spataro wrote, "voleti tore el libero suo arbitrio al musico et farlo subiecto a li accenti grammatici" and later, "Io non scio dove proceda che hora in le compositione de li altri andati con tanti respecti grammatici, ma credo chi bene cercasse per le vostre compositione se trovaria che non haveti havuto tanti respecti, perché la gramatica non è vostra nè mia professione."

as a courier for Willaert, fetching and delivering pieces of music.[56] In addition to his views on text setting, Aaron's writings seem to anticipate other strains in Venetian thinking that are only fully played out in Zarlino. In his *Lucidario* he justified his use of Italian—in reality the only language he was equipped to handle—by submitting praises of the *tre corone* of the trecento and a defense of Italian music and musicians.[57] Situated thus in the *questione della lingua,* Aaron's discussion followed directions generally set by Venetians. But he was also the first to present, in Book 2 of his *Toscanello in musica,*[58] a comprehensive view of simultaneous composition and triadic chords, redolent of Venetian ideals of sonority and harmony; and he showed a decided absorption with the modal questions that were to become a preoccupation of Venetian writings and musical collections soon after his *Trattato della natura et cognitione di tutti gli tuoni di canto figurato* appeared in 1525.[59] In recalling these incipient signs of a Venetian mindset in Aaron's writings, we should remember too that Aaron published with Venetian presses. Like Zarlino he was trying to resolve practical compositional problems for a fairly broad group of Italian readers that only the vernacular press could reach. Undoubtedly, del Lago hoped for the same, and through a much more voluminous, innovative form than he ever saw to fruition.

CICERONIANISM MATURED IN *LE ISTITUTIONI HARMONICHE* OF GIOSEFFO ZARLINO

For the observer some four and a half centuries hence, Gioseffo Zarlino explains the compositional practice of Willaert and ratifies its humanistic basis more thoroughly than any other musician of the sixteenth century. Zarlino defined his mission in his first and most ambitious publication, the massive *Istitutioni harmoniche* of 1558. His title glossed Quintilian's encyclopedic rhetorical treatise *Istitutio oratoria,* which had similarly served to codify the practice of Quintilian's master and model, Cicero. The

---

56. The evidence about his connections with Willaert comes from the letters of Spataro. See Peter Bergquist, "The Theoretical Writings of Pietro Aaron" (Ph.D. diss., Columbia University, 1964), pp. 45 and passim; on Aaron's years in Venice from 1522 to 1535, see pp. 35–49.

57. For the justification of the Italian language see the preface "a lettori" to his *Lucidario in musica* (Venice, 1545); fasc. ed. BMB, ser. 2, no. 12 (Bologna, 1969). Aaron's list of Italian musicians, in Book IV, Chap. 1, fols. 31′–32, including "Cantori a libro," "Cantori al liuto," and "Donne a liuto et a libro," shows above all how little Italian musicians of the first decades of the century had entered the polyphonic mainstream (Costanzo Festa, Marc'Antonio Cavazzoni, Bartolomeo Tromboncino, and Marchetto Cara are the only well-known contrapuntists mentioned). The Italians' fame was instead as singers and improvisors.

58. Title of the 2d ed. (Venice, 1529); the first ed. was called *Thoscanello de la musica* (Venice, 1523).

59. Aaron wanted to regularize modes by emphasizing "regular" cadences over "irregular" ones. See the discussion in Bernhard Meier, *The Modes of Classical Vocal Polyphony Described according to the Sources,* trans. Ellen S. Beebe, rev. ed. (New York, 1988), Pt. 1, Chap. 4, pp. 105–6; orig. *Die Tonarten der klassischen Vokalpolyphonie* (Utrecht, 1974). He also connected mode to secular music, if indirectly, by specifically claiming that tenors could determine mode in *any* kind of composition, even those sorts unrelated to psalmody like the *madrigale* (*Trattato della natura et cognitione di tutti gli tuoni di canto figurato* [Venice, 1525]; facs. ed. BMB, ser. 2, no. 9 [Bologna, 1970], Chap. 2).

Mode figures as well in the supplement added to the 1529 edition of *Toscanello.* Essential on Aaron's concept of mode is the article by Harold S. Powers, "Is Mode Real? Pietro Aron, the Octenary System, and Polyphony," *Basler Jahrbuch für historische Musikpraxis* 16 (1992): 9–52 (which relates Aaron's *Trattato* to the Venetian context on p. 20).

title page, conspicuously learned with its Greek motto, recorded his concern for musical issues pertaining to poets, historians, and philosophers (Plate 19):

> The harmonic institutions of Mr. Gioseffo Zarlino of Chioggia in which, beyond materials pertaining to music, one finds explained many passages by poets, historians, and philosophers, as may be clearly seen in reading them.

Zarlino's choice of disciplines affirms his broader orientation toward the fivefold curriculum of the *studia humanitatis,* including poetry, history, and moral philosophy in addition to grammar and rhetoric, which were necessary to the first three. He emphasized both the practical and the philosophical—writing and thinking— and it is surely no coincidence that, like Tomitano, he opted to impart his teachings through the "reasoned" genre of treatise rather than the discursive one of dialogue. Zarlino's admission to the ranks of the short-lived Accademia Veneziana about the same time the *Istitutioni* were issued undoubtedly showed its founders' perception of him as a figure of wide learning, not only in music but in logic, philosophy, and ancient philology.

Despite these philosophical and encyclopedic leanings, Zarlino invoked in the proem to the *Istitutioni* the traditional humanistic tenet that man's superiority rests in speech: as speech was perfected and made beautiful over time, music was gradually added to it. In this way, through praises chanted to the gods, men could redeem their souls, move their wills, and reduce their appetites in order to lead a more tranquil and virtuous life. Zarlino's claim for music's power lying in its ability to persuade men to a better life with beautifully ornamented speech corresponds to that traditionally advanced by humanistic teachers.[60] As the study and practice of music eventually brought it to a separate disciplinary status from language, Zarlino continued, it fell on hard times, losing its former "veneranda gravità."[61] In modern times, however, music had found a redeemer: "The great God . . . has bestowed the grace of making Adriano Willaert born in our time, truly one of the rarest intellects who has ever practiced music, who . . . has begun to elevate our times, leading music back to that honor and dignity that it formerly had."[62] The agenda of the *Istitutioni* was thus to demonstrate how and why Willaert's method of composing had restored music to its ancient status.

In settling so fixedly on one composer Zarlino tacitly embraced Bembo's singlemodel theory of imitation as argued in *De imitatione,* which had largely held sway

---

60. For a fundamental essay arguing the view that a belief in eloquence and the power of persuasion was the most distinctive aspect of humanistic thought see Hanna H. Gray, "Renaissance Humanism: The Pursuit of Eloquence," *Journal of the History of Ideas* 24 (1963): 497–514; repr. in *Renaissance Essays from the Journal of the History of Ideas,* ed. Paul Oskar Kristeller and Philip P. Weiner (New York, 1968), pp. 199–216.

61. *Istitutioni harmoniche,* p. 1.

62. "L'ottimo Iddio . . . ne ha conceduto gratia di far nascere a nostri tempi Adriano Vuillaert, veramente uno de più rari intelletti, che habbia la Musica prattica giamai essercitato: il quale . . . ha cominciato a levergli, & a ridurla verso quell'honore & dignità che già ella era" (ibid., pp. 1–2).

LE ISTITVTIONI
HARMONICHE

DI M. GIOSEFFO ZARLINO DA CHIOGGIA;

Nelle quali; oltra le materie appartenenti

ALLA MVSICA;

Si trouano dichiarati molti luoghi

di Poeti, d'Hiſtorici, & di Filoſofi;

Si come nel leggerle ſi potrà chiaramente vedere.

¶ Θεῦ διδόντος, οὐδὲν ἰσχύει φθόνος.
Καὶ μὴ διδόντος, οὐδὲν ἰσχύει πόνος.

Con Priuilegio dell'Illuſtriſſ. Signoria di Venetia,
per anni X.

IN VENETIA   M D LVIII.

19.   *Le istitutioni harmoniche* (Venice, 1558), title page. Photo courtesy of the
University of Chicago, Special Collections.

in Ciceronian circles over the multiple-model theory of Pico. It is no surprise that Zarlino based his teaching on a modern-day master and not on one two centuries past, as champions of the *lingua toscana* had done, for even more than verbal languages, musical idioms were inextricably bound up with available technologies of composition.[63] Happily for Zarlino, his aged paragon had already been elevated to Parnassus in his own lifetime.[64]

Zarlino's Ciceronianism reached beyond the questions of technical or idiomatic imitation, however, into the deeper aesthetic crevices of his theoretical constructs. As for Bembo, beauty for Zarlino required elegance, purity, and restraint, all of which superseded other expressive demands. For this reason Zarlino issued several stern lectures to singers, cautioning them to perform only "with moderated voices, adjusted to the other singers." By singing in any other way, he warned, they would only create more "noise than harmony," and harmony could only be found by "tempering many things in such a way that no one [thing] exceeds the other."[65] For Zarlino these principles were universal. He assured singers that composers would try to outfit them with easily singable parts, organized by "beautiful, graceful, elegant movements," so that those who hear them might be "delighted rather than offended."[66] At this point in the *Istitutioni* he had already canonized beauty and grace in enumerating the six basic requirements of good composition: the second requirement dictated that music "be composed principally of consonances and only incidentally of a number of dissonances," and the third, that the voices "proceed properly, that is, through true and legitimate intervals born of the sonorous numbers, so that we acquire through them the use of good harmonies."[67]

The theme of avoiding offense resounds all through the *Istitutioni*. Some of Zarlino's famous observations on text setting seem superficially to free him from this Ciceronian straitjacket. A well-known passage (to which I will return), for instance, enjoins composers to match each word with the right musical sentiment

---

63. On this issue see Howard Mayer Brown, "Emulation, Competition, and Homage: Imitation and Theories of Imitation in the Renaissance," *JAMS* 35 (1982): 1–48.

64. The data presented by Creighton Gilbert, "When Did a Man in the Renaissance Grow Old?" *Studies in the Renaissance* 14 (1967): 7–32, indicate that by 1558, when Willaert was at least sixty-five, he would have been considered quite aged. For a summary of ways Willaert was mythologized during and after his lifetime see Einstein, *The Italian Madrigal* 1:321–24.

65. "Ma debbe cantare con voce moderata, & proportionarla con quelle de gli altri cantori, di maniera che non superi, & non lassi udire le voci de gli altri; La onde più presto si ode strepito, che harmonia: conciosia che l'Harmonia non nasce da altro, che dalla temperatura di molte cose poste insieme in tal maniera, che l'una non superi l'altra" (*Istitutioni harmoniche*, p. 204). Zarlino also admonished in this chapter against excessive physical gestures by singers (ibid.), as Cicero had done for orators (*Orator* 17.55–18.60), with an emphasis on the impact on audience. See Hermann Zenck, "Zarlinos *Istitutioni harmoniche* als Quelle zur Musikanschauung der italienischen Renaissance, *Zeitschrift für Musikwissenschaft* 12 (1929–30): 577.

66. "Cercarà . . . il Compositore di fare, che le parti della sua cantilena si possino cantar bene, & agevolmente; & che procedino con belli, leggiadri, & eleganti Movimenti; accioche gli auditori prendino diletto di tal modulationi, & non siano da veruna parte offesi" (*Istitutioni harmoniche,* p. 204).

67. "La Seconda è, che sia composta principalmente di consonanze, dipoi habbia in sè per accidente molte dissonanze, collocate in essa con debiti modi. . . . La terza è, che le parti della cantilena procedino bene, cioè che le modulationi procedino per veri, & legittimi intervalli, che nascono da i numeri sonori; accioche per il mezo loro acquistiamo l'uso delle buone harmonie" (ibid., p. 172).

and to allow enough dissonance "so that when [the text] denotes harshness, hardness, cruelty, bitterness, and other similar things, the harmony may be similar to it, namely rather hard and harsh." Yet even here Zarlino continued with the caveat "but not to the degree that it would offend."[68] The expressive boundaries that had impelled Bembo some decades earlier to repudiate the "harsh, vile, and spiteful words" he perceived in Dante's *Inferno* were still firmly drawn.[69]

The same views led Zarlino to reject vehemently the claims of the chromaticists voiced in Nicola Vicentino's *L'antica musica ridotta alla moderna prattica* (Rome, 1555). In Part III, Chapter 80, Zarlino took passionate exception to the chromaticists' readiness to admit all the various intervals for what they professed were the oratorical ends of moving the affections. This was "most improper, for it is one thing to speak 'familiarly' and another to speak in song."[70] Nondiatonic steps, he argued, destroy modal identity—a pressing concern for contrapuntists who built their systems on the firm ground of diatonic modality.[71] In response to those who had warmed to chromatic theory he blustered, "I have never heard an orator . . . use in his speech such strange, garbled intervals as they use, and if they did I can't see how they could sway the mind of the judge and persuade him to their will, as is their goal; rather the contrary."[72] Perhaps this was Zarlino's sticking point with Rore, whose style on the whole would seem to have supported his precepts well; in any case, it is surprising that he cited—and perfunctorily at that—a mere three of Rore's works in the whole *Istitutioni*.

Like literary Ciceronians, for whom Bembo hovered censoriously in the background, Zarlino constantly advocated "variation" as insurance against excess. This principle grounds Part III, Chapter 29, which entreats musicians "to vary constantly the sounds, consonances, movements, and intervals," and thus "through diversity . . . attain a good and perfect harmony."[73] Zarlino's purpose in conveying these ideas is especially clear in Part III, Chapter 41, on the need to avoid parallel unisons

68. "Debbe avertire di accompagnare . . . ogni parola, che dove ella dinoti asprezza, durezza, crudeltà, amaritudine, & altre cose simili, l'harmonia sia simile a lei, cioè alquanto dura, & aspra; di maniera però che non offendi" (ibid., p. 339).

69. Cf. Chap. 5 below, nn. 70–71, and for the views of Tomitano, Girolamo Muzio, and Lodovico Dolce, nn. 72–76.

70. "E grande inconveniente: imperoche altro è parlare famigliarmente; & altro è parlare modulando, o cantando" (*Istitutioni harmoniche*, p. 291).

71. In addition to Zarlino's theoretical remarks see Mary S. Lewis on Zarlino's designation of the modes in the tenor part books of his 1549 book of motets, "Zarlino's Theories of Text Underlay as Illustrated in His Motet Book of 1549," *Music Library Association Notes* 42 (1985–86): 239–67. Zarlino's adherence to modal diatonicism should not be confused with his attitude towards modal ethos. For good reason Palisca has seen Zarlino's belief in modal ethos as half-hearted (*On the Modes: Part Four of "Le Istitutioni Harmoniche," 1558,* trans. Vered Cohen and ed. with an introduction by Claude V. Palisca [New Haven, 1983], p. xv).

72. "Ne mai hò udito Oratore (poi che dicono, che bisogna imitar gli Oratori, acciache la Musica muova gli affetti) che usi nel suo parlare quelli cosi strani, & sgarbati intervalli, che usano costoro: perciache quando li usasse, non so vedere, in qual maniera potesse piegar l'animo del Giudice, & persuaderlo a fare il loro volere; si come è il suo fine; se non per il contrario" (*Istitutioni harmoniche,* p. 291). Cf. the passages from Cicero cited in Chap. 5 nn. 59–62, above.

73. "[C]ercare di variar sempre li Suoni, le Consonanze, li Movimenti, & gli Intervalli; & per tal modo, dalla varietà di queste cose, verremo a fare una buona, & perfetta harmonia" (ibid., p. 177).

and octaves. Poetry, grammar, and rhetoric, he began, have all taken their cue from music, which teaches about good order and the hazards of repetition. To exemplify this in language one may consider a verse like "O fortunatam natam me consule Romam," where the reiteration of the syllables "natam," combined with the like-sounding final syllable "-mam," "give the listener little pleasure."[74] Repetition precludes beauty. "It is not permissible to use these strange modes of speech [i.e., repetition] either in prose or in poetry, except as used artificially or for special effects. The musician most particularly must eliminate from his works every unpleasant sound and whatever might offend the hearing. . . . He must regulate [his compositions] in such a way that one hears in them only good things."[75] Beauty, then, can only be grasped through the merging of elegance with diversity—that is, of decorum with variation.

ZARLINO'S PEDAGOGY OF THE *SOGGETTO* AND *IMITATIONE*

Several of Zarlino's most insightful formulations stemmed from a desire to explain the localized contrapuntal heterogeneity that pervaded the Willaertian style of his day in terms of rhetorical *varietas*. Two major and interrelated instances of this play themselves out in his innovative discussions of the *soggetto* and of *imitatione*, procedures that form the aesthetic nucleus of the new style.

At its initial appearance as the first of the six requirements for good composition enumerated in Part III, Chapter 26, the *soggetto* corresponds simply to the rhetorical idea of *materia*. It is analogous to the "story or fable" of an epic poem. The *soggetto* in music, as in literature, may be either borrowed or invented anew. Zarlino followed Horace in advising that the *soggetto* should also "serve and please the listener," forming the very basis "on which the composition is founded . . . , [and] adorning it with various movements and various harmonies."[76] Up to this point the notion of the *soggetto* seems almost metaphorical, but when Zarlino resumes his characterization of it at the end of the chapter it becomes more concrete. A *soggetto* that comes from another composition may be a plainchant serving as tenor or as cantus firmus in another part, or it may be taken from *canto figurato*, that is, from a

74. "[Il] Grammatico, il Rhetore, & il Poeta hanno dalla Musica questa cognitione, che la continovatione di un suono, cioè il replicare molte volte una Sillaba, o una littera istessa in una clausula di una Oratione, genera . . . Cativo parlare, o Cativa consonanza; come si ode in quel verso, *O fortunatam natam me consule Romam;* per il raddoppiamento della sillaba *Natam,* & per la terminatione del verso nella sillaba *Mam,* che porgono all'udito poco piacere" (ibid., p. 194).
75. "[Repetitione] non è lecito, ne in Prosa, ne in Verso (salvo se non fusse posto cotal cosa arteficiosamente, per mostrar qualche effetto) porre questi modi strani di parlare; maggiormente il Musico debbe bandire dalle sue compositioni ogni tristo suono, & qualunque altra cosa possa offendere l'udito. . . . ma debbe regolare in tal maniera li suoi concenti, che in loro si odi ogni cosa di buono" (ibid.).
76. Ibid., pp. 171–72.

polyphonic work. It may be placed in more than one voice and may take any number of forms, including canon.[77]

Once Zarlino begins to explain how counterpoint relates to a *soggetto* that is *not*
borrowed, however, things become rather stickier. If there is no *soggetto* to start
with, then "whatever part is first put into action or starts the composition—whatever it may be or however it may begin, low, high, or middle—that will always be
the *soggetto*."[78] The composer will adapt the other parts in canon (*fuga*), as answers
(*consequenze*), or however he likes, "matching the harmonies to the words according
to their content (*materia*)."[79] So far so good. But which part is to be understood as
the *soggetto* in the very free method of "simultaneous" composition prevalent in
Zarlino's orbit? His answer, decidedly indeterminate, begins now to touch the heart
of the elusively varied style he aimed to describe.

> When the composer draws the *soggetto* from the parts of the composition—that is,
> when he obtains one part from another and gets the *soggetto* that way, composing all
> the parts of the work together . . .—then that portion that is obtained from the other
> parts, on which he then composes the parts of the composition, will be called the
> *soggetto*. Musicians call this method "composing by fantasy"; one could also call it
> counterpointing [*contrapuntizare*], or making counterpoint, as one likes.[80]

Here the tangibility of the *soggetto* threatens to vanish once again. Zarlino only
clarifies the passage in Chapter 28 by stating outright, in a reversal of his earlier
assertion, that the *soggetto* is *not* necessarily the first voice to sound, "but the one
that observes and maintains the mode and [the one] to which the other voices are
adapted, whatever their distance from the subject."[81] In the same place he refers the
reader to his own seven-voice setting of the "Ave Maria" salutation from the Lord's
Prayer (Ex. 3). (Zarlino included no quotations of the repertory that he cited, so it
seems he expected students either to know it or, if not, to learn it.) According to his

77. "[P]uò essere un Tenore, overo altra parte di qualunque cantilena di Canto fermo, overo di
Canto figurato; overo potranno esser due, o più parti, che l'una seguiti l'altra in Fuga, o Consequenza,
overo a qualunque altro modo: essendo che li varij modi di tali Soggetti sono infiniti" (ibid., p. 172).

78. "[Q]uando non haverà ritrovato prima il Soggetto; quella parte, che sarà primieramente messa
in atto; over quella con la quale il Compositore darà principio alla sua cantilena, sia qual si voglia, &
incomincia a qual modo più li piace; o sia grave, overo acuta, o mezana; sempre sarà il Soggetto" (ibid.).

79. "[A]ccommodando le harmonie alle parole, secondo che ricerca la materia contenuta in esse"
(ibid.).

80. "[Q]uando il Compositore andrà cavando il Soggetto dalle parti della cantilena, cioè quando
caverà una parte dall'altra, & andrà cavando il Soggetto per tal maniera, & facendo insieme la compositione . . . ; quella particella, che lui caverà fuori delle altre, sopra laquale dipoi componerà le parti della
sua compositione, si chiamerà sempre il Soggetto. Et tal modo di comporre li Prattici dimandano
Comporre di fantasia: ancorache si possa etiandio nominare Contrapuntizare, o Far contraponto, come
si vuole" (ibid.).

81. "Ma si debbe avertire, che io chiamo quella la parte del Soggetto, sopra la quale sono accommodate le altre parti in consequenza, & è la principale, & la guida di tutte le altre. Io non dico quella, che
prima d'ogn'altra incomincia cantare; ma quella dico, che osserva, & mantiene il Modo sopra laquale
sono accommodate le altre distanti l'una dall'altra per qual si voglia intervallo" (ibid., p. 175).

Ex. 3. Zarlino, *Pater noster* (secunda pars): *Ave Maria*, mm. 1–7; *Musici moduli liber primus* (Venice, 1549), p. 33.

explanation, the *soggetto* in this excerpt is not the first but the second of the three voices to "sing in fugue"—presumably not the quintus but the altus. This verifies (as he has already argued) that it is possible to have opening voices that do not carry the *soggetto*, voices that may in some cases be "discordant" with one another. That is to say, such voices may utilize nonessential steps of the mode, although, he warns, it will bother the singers if the composer does this too much. (In this instance, the opening voice departs from the essential *soggetto* halfway through the second measure, but it adheres to scale degrees that unambiguously define the mode.)

Chapter 43 pushes this discussion further into the complexities of real practice by trying to teach how to write diminished counterpoint either on a diminished subject derived from a polyphonic work or on one newly composed. Zarlino now summarizes the situation very simply: the subject can in fact be "either the first part to be written or the *first to be imagined by the composer*" (emphasis mine).[82] His account of free counterpoint on given *soggetti* has awaited this chapter and the following one, Chapter 44, which deals essentially with rhythmic possibilities. Chapter 43 is quite terse. It begs the question of how such counterpoint actually works, claiming that "one cannot give particular rules, since the individual cases are infinite." Instead Zarlino refers the reader to two two-part examples, the second of which demonstrates the technique of *contrapuntizare* on an original subject (Ex. 4).[83] This musical example clarifies what Zarlino's text does not tell us explicitly, namely that *soggetti* heard over the course of an extended composition are multiple, as we would expect. There are three distinct *soggetti* in the passage, as marked, each of them part of overlapping contrapuntal expositions. Each exposition has a separate motivic identity and ends with a cadence. A given exposition may contain repeated statements of the *soggetto,* as in the lower voice of the second one, mm. 13–16. Or, in typical motet style, transformed versions of the *soggetto* may supplant the original one; witness the motive first sounded in the upper voice at the upbeat to m. 17.

In such a simple two-voice passage, one voice will often imitate the other's opening motive exactly, or almost exactly. Since each is equally melodious, at least at the start, the guide (or initiating) voice can be thought to present the essential form of the *soggetto,* unless it explores "discordant," nonessential areas of the mode. An interesting exception to this exists in the third *soggetto.* There the lower voice leads off in m. 21 with a version that is rhythmically slightly diminished compared with the one subsequently sounded in the upper voice at m. 22. Retrospectively the lower-voice version sounds like a varied form of the upper voice of mm. 22ff., especially once the lower voice brings the *soggetto* back in its seemingly more essential form at the upbeat to m. 28.

Much of the difficulty we now have in determining what is "supposed" to be the *soggetto* in a given passage stems from the fact that Zarlino described the *soggetto* as a precompositional construct for use by composers. He named and explained it as a real procedural part of the precompositional toolkit for use at the most preliminary stages of the creative act, thus elusive to the observer after the fact. Once set down in finished form, compositions in an idiom like Willaert's, with their continual shifting of materials, naturally tend to confound our attempts to "discover" the "essential" materials that went into crafting them early in the compositional process. Zarlino reiterates that the voice(s) bearing the *soggetto* will use essential degrees of

---

82. "Soggetto io chiamo quella parte, che si ponen avanti le altre parti nella compositione; overamente quella parte, che il Compositore si hà primieramente imaginato di fare" (ibid., p. 200).

83. The examples offered here from *Le istitutioni harmoniche* are transcribed without reduction of note values so as to aid in following Zarlino's discussions.

the given mode, but the question remains what sort of rhythmic profile each voice assumes—whether a so-called primary form or altered—and the answer to this can be less obvious.

Chapter 44 offers some rhythmic guidelines. By and large they bear little clear relation to questions involving the *soggetto* but illustrate instead other aspects of his thinking relevant to variation principles. In a discussion of the duration of rests between entries of parts, for instance, Zarlino explains that in an exposition the second voice may enter off the tactus when minims are involved—even at the minim immediately following the entrance of the first voice. Such a device he calls a "sospiro" (sigh); an example is shown in Ex. 5, not taken from the *Istitutioni* but from Willaert's setting of *O Invidia* from the *Musica nova*.

Had Zarlino's definition of the *soggetto* aimed to describe an idiom with less motivic flexibility than Willaert's, it undoubtedly would have been easier to explain. Owing to this flexibility, the *soggetto* can best be understood when viewed in conjunction with Zarlino's novel reflections on *imitatione*.[84] In traditional discussions of imitation, theorists had enumerated a precise series of technical procedures connected with *fuga*. Yet *fuga* denoted techniques that were inherently fixed and restrictive.[85] Zarlino intended with *imitatione* to include freer techniques through which the composer could explore a variety of motivic possibilities.[86] The difference between the two, as revealed in Part III, Chapters 51 and 52, respectively, was that fugue involved strict reflection of the intervals in a *dux* (in his lexicon, the "guide"), whereas imitation did not. Either could be made in parallel or contrary motion. But imitation, as Zarlino defined it, did not "show *in its course* intervals in the consequent voices identical to those formed in the guide."[87] The consequent voices in imitation would "proceed only with the same *steps*" as the guide, but not necessarily with "regard for the precise *intervals*" (emphases mine).[88]

Zarlino claimed that both fugue and imitation could be made in continuous form, called *legata,* or in passages that are broken off from one another, called *sciolta*. In reality, although both types of fugue can readily be found in contemporaneous Venetian repertory, *imitatione legata* is a rarity.[89] As James Haar has noted, the kind of procedure that is characteristic of Willaert's freely varied contrapuntal technique is the kind that Zarlino called *imitatione sciolta*.

To make this kind of "loosed" imitation, Zarlino says, "one may extract the consequent from the guide partly through imitation [i.e., *sciolta*] and partly through consequence [presumably, exact imitation], partly in similar and partly in contrary motion."[90] In Chapter 51 he had explained specifically that in imitation (again,

---

84. On this question see the fundamental study of James Haar, "Zarlino's Definition of Fugue and Imitation," *JAMS* 24 (1971): 226–54.

85. See ibid., pp. 231–34, on the comments of theorists who preceded Zarlino.

86. For a discussion relating these distinctions to mannerist tendencies see Maria Rika Maniates, *Mannerism in Italian Music and Culture, 1530–1630* (Chapel Hill, 1979), pp. 196–97.

87. "Imitatione . . . non camina per quelli istessi intervalli nelle parti consequenti, che si ritrovano nella Guida" (*Istitutioni harmoniche,* p. 217).

88. "[I]l consequente imitando li movimenti della Guida, procede solamente per quelli istessi gradi, senza havere altra consideratione de gli intervalli" (ibid.).

89. Zarlino gives a rather theoretical example of it, *Istitutioni harmoniche,* p. 218 (transcribed in *The Art of Counterpoint: Part Three of "Le istitutioni harmoniche," 1558,* trans. Guy A. Marco and Claude V. Palisca [New York, 1976], as Ex. 94, p. 137), which in fact is a strict canon at the third. The relationship of *comes* and *dux* is inexact because imitation is at an imperfect interval.

90. "Si debbe dipoi avertire, che nelle Sciolte si può cavare il Consequente dalla Guida, parte per imitatione, & parte in consequenza. Cosi parte in movimenti simili, & parte in movimenti contrarij;

sciolta) the rhythmic and melodic figures of the two parts, like their intervallic relationships, are only similar, not identical.[91] Indeed, as Zarlino's extended two-voice example shows (Ex. 6), they are often quite different in melodic direction, diminutions, interval size, and cadential rhythms. As he had done with the *soggetto*, Zarlino claims it would take "too long, even if one wanted, to explain every minute particular" of how these freed-up imitations work, but much of it we can deduce from the passage itself. The upper-voice consequent at m. 3 alters the opening *soggetto* by syncopating the entry and inverting the melody. In m. 10 the imitation begins in contrary motion with dissimilar intervals and immediately switches by m. 11 to similar motion; in the continuation some intervals differ from those of the guide voice by as much as a perfect fifth (in m. 11 compare the aa–e drop in the guide with the e–E drop in the consequent). In the final imitation, starting at mm. 17–18, only the rhythmic shape is common to both voices and the upper voice dissolves into a series of semiminims in mm. 19–20 that are not found in the guide. Typically, Zarlino concentrates the imitative process at the beginning of each exposition and makes the approach to the cadence more episodic (as in the second half of mm. 19 to the end). The basic rhythmic and (especially) metric design of the guide generally turns out to be mimicked most exactly in the consequents. (We will see in the Venetian

---

dilche sarebbe troppo lungo, se'l si volesse dar notitie particolare di ogni cosa minima" (*Istitutioni harmoniche*, p. 218).

91. See, for example, "Et in cotesto modo di comporre, il Compositore non è obligato di osservare la equalità delle figure, & di porre le Pause simili, ne osservare altri simili accidenti; ma può far quello, che più li piace; si come, che una parte proceda per Minime, & l'altra proceda per altre figure, cioè per Semibrevi; & similmente per Minime & Semiminime insieme mescolate; come si osserva di fare nelli Contrapunti fatti sopra'l Canto fermo" (ibid., p. 213).

E x . 6 .   Zarlino, *Le istitutioni harmoniche* (Venice, 1558), p. 217.

repertory of Willaert and his followers that motivic expositions often start not with precise pitches imitated but with all the parts imitating a particular textual rhythm.)

Zarlino's reluctance to systematize his explication of free imitation carries a crucial message, since the expressivity of the repertory he aimed to explain depends on a level of motivic and contrapuntal variation that eludes formulaic prescription. It may be telling, as Haar suggests, that the only theorist prior to Zarlino who made a point of confining the word *fugue* to strict intervallic imitation was Pietro Aaron, who spent many years at Venice.[92] Without actually using the word imitation, Aaron cautioned in his *Lucidario* of 1545 against calling inexact imitative writing "fugue."[93] "Among us [i.e., Venetians?]," he claimed, "there has often been talk of the heedlessness and wrong opinion of those who believe themselves to be writing in their music what musicians call fugue."[94] As an example of nonfugal writing, Aaron gave a brief passage that corresponds to what Zarlino later named "imitatione sciolta."[95]

92. "Zarlino's Definition of Fugue and Imitation," pp. 232–34.
93. *Lucidario,* Book 2, fol. ix.
94. "Gia dannoi molte volte fu havuto consideratione alla poca avertenza, & vana oppenione di alcuni, i quali si credono creare nelle loro compositioni quello, che dal musico è chiamato Fuga" (ibid.).
95. Haar also points out that this sort of imitative thinking is conceived within a diatonic modal framework and does not warrant chromatic alterations through *ficta* to create precise imitations of motives ("Zarlino's Definition of Fugue and Imitation," pp. 248–53). In doing so Haar counters the opinion of Edward E. Lowinsky, ever the chromatic maximalist, who had advocated preserving solmizations through the addition of *ficta* in transpositions of motives one or two fifths downward in Willaert's ricercars; see Lowinsky's foreword to H. Colin Slim, ed., *Musica nova accommodata per cantar et sonar . . . ,* Monuments of Renaissance Music, vol. 1 (Chicago, 1964), p. ix.

In confronting both the *soggetto* and the question of imitation, then, Zarlino was attempting to make sense of a highly mutable system of motivic construction. In both domains he analyzed the application of an old contrapuntal pedagogy to new compositional principles. Like contemporaneous paradigms of *variazione* articulated by Ciceronian literati, the processes he was examining involved ongoing, local transformations. Ciceronians writing on rhetoric and poetics similarly imagined variation in terms of contrasting, paired qualities, as epitomized by Bembo's *gravità* and *piacevolezza*. Theories of words and notes resemble one another at this conceptual level, within which style functions as a dialectical system of contrasts.

Zarlino's proclivity toward dualistic thinking may be inferred from the way he linked affects with intervals in Part IV, Chapter 32, "In what way harmonies may suit the words set." There Zarlino obliquely associated imperfect minor intervals with qualities Bembo connected with *piacevolezza* and major intervals with *gravità*. Yet in delineating harmonic effects appropriate to different kinds of words Zarlino initially set up his own dichotomy as one of harshness versus sorrow. As we saw earlier, he advised that the composer "be careful to accompany each word in such a way that when the word denotes harshness, hardness, cruelty, bitterness, and other things of this sort the harmony will be similar to these qualities, namely somewhat hard and harsh." By contrast, "when any of the words expresses complaint, sorrow, grief, sighs, tears, and other such things, the harmony should be full of sadness."[96] The schematics of Bembo's and Zarlino's affective dichotomies might be compared as follows:

Bembo *gravità*	Zarlino *[harshness]*		Bembo *piacevolezza*	Zarlino *[sorrow]*
onestà	asprezza		grazia	pianto
dignità	durezza		soavità	dolore
magnificenza	crudeltà		vaghezza	cordoglio
maestà	amaritudine		dolcezza	sospiri
grandezza			scherzi	lagrime
			giuochi	

While seeming to differ substantially from Bembo's, Zarlino's descriptions of the intervals that contribute to each of these two types reveal that the reason minor intervals are associated with sorrowful affects is that they create the qualities of *dolcezza* and *soavità*—qualities Bembo had ascribed to *piacevolezza*. In expressing grief

96. "Debbe avertire di accompagnare in tal maniera ogni parola, che dove ella dinoti asprezza, durezza, crudeltà, amaritudine, & altre cose simili, l'Harmonia sia simile a lei, cioè alquanto dura, & aspra. . . . Simigliantemente quando alcuna delle parole dimostrarà pianto, dolore, cordoglio, sospiri, lagrime, & altre cose simili, che l'harmonia sia piena di mestitia" (*Istitutioni harmoniche*, p. 339).

and sorrow, Zarlino advised composers to use linear movements of minor seconds, minor thirds, and "similar intervals" and minor sixths or minor thirteenths above the lowest note of the composition, "these being by nature sweet and soft."[97] In other words, he identified melodic minor seconds and thirds and harmonic minor sixths and thirteenths with sorrowful expressions, tears, plaints, and the like.[98] But in calling them "dolci, et soavi" he suggested a kind of wistfully lyrical complaint, rather than a dramatic lament.[99] His qualities of "asprezza, durezza, crudeltà, [and] amaritudine," conducive to virile expressions of anger, pomp, scorn, excitement, and even bombast presumably by means of melodic major seconds, major thirds, harmonic major sixths, and so forth, have seemingly little to do with this melancholy affect.[100] Bombast was precisely the quality literary theorists often dreaded in Ciceronian gravity (recall that Lodovico Dolce even decried it in Petrarch's "Giunto Alessandro alla famosa tomba").[101]

In Zarlino's musical conception, then, the antipole to *gravità* seems to have been partially redefined for musical purposes. Zarlino clearly linked accidental flat signs with affects of sweet sorrow and not with any chromatic dissonance that we might more readily have connected with expressive harshness. While Bembo's *piacevolezza* may embrace the sweetly sorrowful qualities Zarlino is thinking of, it also embodies quite different notions of playfulness ("gli scherzi" and "i giuochi") and enchanting beauty ("la vaghezza").

In addition to conceiving *variazione* as a means to expressive contrast, Zarlino also tied it to a general aspiration toward natural musical symmetry and proportion—one of the ways that it related to the notion of decorum. In this his explanations call to mind Daniello's simile of the mason who builds a well-proportioned wall from a varied assortment of stones.[102] "Variety," Zarlino wrote, "gives our emotions great

97. "Quando vorrà esprimere li secondi effetti, allora usarà . . . li movimenti, che procedeno per il Semituono: & per quelli del Semiditono, & gli altri simili; usando spesso le Seste, overo le Terzedecime minori sopra la chorda più grave della cantilena, che sono per natura dolci, et soavi" (ibid., p. 339).

98. Even though Zarlino omitted to mention *melodic* minor sixths (and thirteenths) in the *Istitutioni,* Venetian composers, as we will see, clearly associated them too with expressions of sweet sorrow. Words like *dolcezza* and *soave* are nearly always set with flatted inflections, imperfect minor leaps, and the like.

99. Note, for example, the minor seconds on "dolcezza" in the well-known exordium of Willaert's setting of *Cantai, hor piango,* as in the cantus of m. 11 (*Opera omnia,* vol. 13, *Musica nova, 1559: Madrigalia,* ed. Hermann Zenck and Walter Gerstenberg [{Rome}, 1966], pp. 73–79 and Ex. 45a below).

100. In practice we know that what Zarlino called "harshness" could also be interpreted by dissonant suspensions, and that the suspensions used to interpret gentler forms of melancholy tended to be less dissonant.

101. *Osservationi nella volgar lingua* (Venice, 1550), fol. 94'; see Chap. 5 n. 69 above.

102. See Chap. 5 above, n. 119. Parabosco troped the same idea in comparing physical and musical beauty: "Non si puo dire, che fa la bellezza le vogliono solamente le parti belle: ma convien dire, che la bisogna una proportion uguale, & una concordanza de' membri, & che questo sia vero comprendetelo in questo che gli occhi neri da ogn'uno sono giudicati i piu belli; nientedimeno in qualche viso compariscono assai meglio gli occhi persi, & in altri gli occhi bianchi, & che talmente della lor bellezza rendono testimonianza, che gli huomini sono sforzati di dire, che tutta la vaghezza di quel viso consista solo nel color di quegli occhi, & è vero, che cosi come il buon Musico meschiando le consonanze perfette con le imperfette, & con le dissonanze, rende più vaga, & più soave la melodia, che non farebbe facendole tutte perfette: cosi ancho alle volte gli occhi, una bocca, un naso renderà nel volto, over si troverà, posto si grato, & si dolce vedere, che farà stupire chiunque lo vederà" (One cannot say that beauty requires only lovely parts: but one can say that it needs an equal proportion and a concord of the parts. That this is

pleasure. Therefore every composer should follow such beautiful order, for he will be thought good insofar as his procedures resemble nature."[103] In the idealized world of Neoplatonic harmonies, nature manifests ideal proportions; it "hates things without proportion and delights in those that have propriety between them."[104] Reasoning countermanded the legitimacy of any music not founded on good proportion and symmetry. Since Zarlino assumed in all beings a primal sympathy for natural proportions, man's senses would necessarily yearn for likeness to nature, and music provided one means to approach it.

ZARLINO ON SYNTAX AND CADENCE

Zarlino wrote in the wake of a tradition that had long assumed a similarity between verbal and musical structures. Among medieval commentators the notion that music reflected grammatical relationships through its cadences was a commonplace. Virtually all commentators related the grammatical hierarchy of comma, colon, and period to musical phrasing. Fifteenth- and early-sixteenth-century theorists of polyphony, however, had gone some way toward severing this connection for the sake of counterpoint (as we saw in Lanfranco's *Scintille* and in Spataro's retort to Aaron). In his writing about cadences in polyphonic music, Aaron therefore had to make a point of advocating (albeit tentatively) that composers resume the old grammatical alliances, arguing in his *Trattato* that without the proper cadences a texted composition simply could not be well understood: "The cadence is a sign by which composers make an indirect ending ["mediato fine"] according to the sense of the words."[105]

Extending the recent tradition of rhetorically minded polyphonic theorists (including del Lago), Zarlino insisted repeatedly that the cadence in *polyphony* needed to correspond to meaningful divisions of words. In the *Istitutioni,* admonishments appear prominently in Part III, Chapter 53, on cadences, where only after emphasizing several times the need to coordinate musical with verbal cadences Zarlino admits that cadences in polyphony sometimes do "emerge from a certain con-

---

true you understand by the fact that black eyes are judged the most beautiful by everyone, but nonetheless in some faces dark eyes look much better and in others light eyes, and they render such account of their beauty that men are compelled to say that all the loveliness of that face consists only in the color of those eyes. And it's true that as the good musician mixing perfect consonances with imperfect and with dissonances makes the melody more lovely and smooth than he would if he made them all perfect, so will eyes, a mouth, or a nose at times seem in a face—that is, one will find something so pleasing and sweet that it will amaze anyone who sees it); *Lettere amorose* (Venice, 1607), pp. 103–4; see also the *Libro primo delle lettere amorose di M. Girolamo Parabosco* (Venice, 1573), fol. 51.

103. "Varietà molto piacere porge alli nostri sentimenti. Debbe adunque ogni Compositore imitare un tale, & tanto bello ordine: percioche sarà riputato tanto migliore, quanto le sue operationi si assimigliaranno a quelle della Natura" (*Istitutioni harmoniche,* p. 177).

104. "La natura odia le cose senza proportione, & senza misura; & si diletta di quelle, che hanno tra loro convenienza" (ibid., p. 185).

105. "Cadenza non è altro che un certo segno del quale gli Compositori per alcun senso delle parole fanno un mediato fine" (*Trattato,* Chap. 8 [unpaginated]).

trapuntal design initiated by the composer."[106] Lanfranco had described this circumstance as the norm; for Zarlino it was something to be conceded "out of necessity."[107] No other theorist of the Renaissance showed as clearly as Zarlino how to reflect textual syntax and (though to a lesser extent) meaning in music. This is not inscribed so much in his rules of text underlay—many of which, as Don Harrán has shown, are derived from Lanfranco[108]—but in the totality of his teachings on cadences, rests, text repetition, and underlay.

In Part III, Chapter 50 ("Delle pause"), Zarlino theorized questions of rests (like so many others) through the principle of variety. Rests enabled composers to vary the numbers of voices singing at any given point in a work in order to make compositions "lovely and delightful." Just as important, rests functioned like cadences in demarcating text. They were "not to be placed except at the ends of *clausule* or *punti* in the text . . . and at the end of every *periodo*." Composers were to make sure that rests allowed the parts of the text and the meanings of the words to be fully heard and understood, so that they would have a "true function" and not just be random: "In no case should they be placed . . . in midclause, for anyone who would do so would show himself to be a veritable sheep, an oaf, and an ignoramus."[109] In Part IV, Chapter 32, on accommodating harmonies to words, Zarlino added that composers should neither make a cadence *nor* use a rest larger than a minim in any place where the meaning of the words is incomplete.[110]

The attention Zarlino gave to meaningful divisions of the text included textual repetitions, which he otherwise rarely discussed. The portion of text repeated, he

106. "[S]i debbe avertire, che le Cadenze nelli Canti fermi si fanno in una parte sola: ma nelli figurati si aggiungono altre parti. Et in quelli si pongono finita la sentenza delle parole; in questi poi non solamente si fanno, quando si ode la Clausula perfetta nella oratione; ma alle volte si usano per necessità, et per seguire un certo ordine nel Contrapunto, principiato da Compositore" (*Istitutioni harmoniche*, p. 221).

107. Gaspar Stoquerus expressed the relationship of words and cadences similarly, at least by implication, in *De musica verbali* of ca. 1570, also based on Willaert's practice. Stoquerus made the traditional equation of music and speech and exalted those composers who were actually capable of realizing it: "therefore *for the more learned and careful musicians,* a phrase is the same as for the grammarians" (emphasis mine) (Quare doctis quidem et diligentioribus musicis sententia eadem est cum grammaticis; Chap. 20, fol. 30ʳ; See *De musica verbali, libri duo: Two Books on Verbal Music,* ed. and trans. Albert C. Rotola, S.J., Greek and Latin Music Theory [Lincoln, Neb., and London, 1988], pp. 204–5).

108. See "New Light on the Question of Text Underlay prior to Zarlino," *Acta musicologica* 45 (1973): 24–56.

109. "[N]on porre tali Pause, se non nel fine delle Clausule, o punti della Oratione, sopra la quale è composta la cantilena, & simigliantemente nel fine di ogni Periodo. Il che fa dibisogna, che li Compositori etiandio avertiscano; accioche li Membri della oratione siano divisi, & la sentenza delle parole si oda, & intenda interamente: percioche facendo in cotal modo, allora si potrà dire, che le Pause siano state poste nelle parti della cantilena con qualche proposito, & non a caso. Ne si debbeno porre per alcun modo, avanti che sia finita la sentenza, cioè nel mezo della Clausula: conciosia che colui, che le ponesse a cotal modo, dimostrarebbe veramente essere una pecora, un goffo, & uno ignorante" (*Istitutioni harmoniche*, p. 212).

110. "Si debbe . . . avertire, di non separare alcuna parte della Oratione l'una dall'altra parte con Pause, come fanno alcuni poco intelligenti, fino a tanto, che non sia finita la sua Clausula, overo alcuna sua parte; di maniera che 'l sentimento delle parole sia perfetto; & di non far la Cadenza; massimamente l'una delle principali; o di non porre le Pause maggiori di quelle della minima, se non è finito il Periodo, o la sentenza perfetta della Oratione" (ibid., p. 340).

insisted, should make sense as a unit. One should therefore avoid single-word and (needless to say) single-syllable repetition, as explained in the eighth of his rules of text underlay, Part IV, Chapter 33: "[I]n mensural music such repetitions are tolerated; I am certainly not talking about one syllable or one word, but of some part of the text whose idea is complete."[111] Textual repetitions, when they did occur, were to be kept to a minimum and reserved for words bearing "serious thoughts worthy of consideration."[112]

The same view of symbiotic syntactic and semantic functions that governed Zarlino's recommendations on text repetition and cadence led him to insist on faithful musical accentuations of words. Following theorists from Guido to Gaffurius and beyond, he held that long syllables should be matched to long notes and short ones to short notes,[113] placing this at the head of his famous decalogue, or ten rules of text setting. Yet in doing so he was not just nodding obediently toward old grammatically based traditions of music theory.[114] Neither, as Don Harrán has argued, did he mean for the rule to apply only to Latin quantitative verse, as the preponderance of Italian madrigals among his examples attests.[115] Instead, his attitude corresponded to that of Vicentino's *L'antica musica ridotta alla moderna prattica,* published three years earlier, which lamented that too many composers were inclined to go their own compositional way without considering the nature of words, their accents, and syllable length, *whether in the vernacular or in Latin.*[116]

More than Vicentino, though, Zarlino conceived the coordination of syllable and musical length in the specific context of Venetian repertory, as suggested in the wording of rule 1: "The first rule then will be always to place on a long or short syllable a corresponding note, in such a way that no barbarism is heard. For in mensural music every note that is separate and not tied (excepting the semiminim and all notes smaller than the semiminim) carries its own syllable."[117] Here, first of all,

111. "[N]el [canto] figurato tali repliche si comportano; non dico gia di una sillaba, ne di una parola: ma di alcuna parte della oratione, quando il sentimento è perfetto" (ibid., p. 341). This conforms to what Stoquerus later said, allowing for repeats of sentences, but not individual words. See Harrán, *Word-Tone Relations in Musical Thought,* p. 460, nos. 380–81.

112. "[I]l replicare tante fiate una cosa (secondo 'l mio giuditio) non stia troppo bene; se non fusse fatto, per isprimere maggiormente le parole, che hanno in se qualche grave sentenza, & fusse degna di consideratione" (*Istitutioni harmoniche,* p. 341).

113. See Harrán, *In Search of Harmony: Hebrew and Humanistic Elements in Sixteenth-Century Musical Thought,* Musicological Studies and Documents, no. 42 (Neuhausen-Stuttgart, 1988), pp. 92ff.; and idem, *Word-Tone Relations in Musical Thought,* pp. 10–15 and 375–87.

114. See Franchinus Gaffurius, *Practica musicae* (Milan, 1496), 2.1, fol. 21′, who cites the Latin grammarians on the point, ed. and trans. Clement A. Miller, Musicological Studies and Documents, no. 20, AIM ([Rome], 1968), pp. 69–72; facs. ed. BMB, ser. 2, no. 6 (Bologna, 1972).

115. *In Search of Harmony,* pp. 92–97.

116. "Molti Compositori che nelle loro compositioni attendono à far un certo procedere di compositione à suo modo, senza considerare la natura delle parole, ne i loro accenti, ne quali sillabe siano lunghe ne brevi, cosi nella lingua volgare come nella latina" (*L'antica musica,* Book 4, Chapter 29, fol. P i′); facs. ed. Edward E. Lowinsky, Documenta musicologica, ser. 1, Druckschriften-Faksimiles, no. 17 (Kassel, 1959).

117. "La Prima Regola adunque sarà, di porre sempre sotto la sillaba longa, o breve una figura conveniente, di maniera, che non si odi alcuno barbarismo: percioche nel Canto figurato ogni figura quadrata si accommoda la sua sillaba" (*Istitutioni harmoniche,* p. 341).

Zarlino explicitly exhorts composers to *syllabic* text setting, which was normative in midcentury Venetian polyphony. As rule 4 specifies, however, only in rare circumstances—justified expressively—could the declamation occur on semiminims and smaller notes; the actual rhythmic structures of the style are such that most of the syllabic declamation occurs on semibreves and minims.[118] In adding in rule 1 that each note should carry one syllable as long as the note does not fall within a ligature and is not *smaller than a minim,* Zarlino presupposed the composite minim rhythm that pulsates at the declamatory surface of Venetian repertory when the voices are configured in their typical staggered relationships. The longs and shorts that he, along with his predecessors, relied on as a traditional means of description hardly pointed to strict quantitative poetics, with two values corresponding to a spoken syllable length. Rather, a system of two surface durations of a 2:1 ratio now reflected local practice, which confined itself almost solely to the declamatory values of semibreve and minim, organizing the syllables in a free arrangement of fluctuating tonic and agogic stresses.[119]

———

All of this is considerably simpler than the questions surrounding cadence. Along with rests, cadences formed one of the two main devices articulating verbal syntax. Zarlino surpassed any previous polyphonic theorist in trying to account for the multiplicity, variety, and subtlety of cadential events that were possible in an irregular contrapuntal texture. In such a context the tenor-superius framework on which cadences had traditionally hinged was all but gone or, at minimum, was seriously threatened. The main melodic materials—the *soggetti*—could not necessarily be found in any particular voice or imitated in any particular form, nor would they necessarily even be imitated at all. Even the way text was divided did not warrant a separate category of articulation, as Zarlino made clear in his definition of cadence at the outset of Part III, Chapter 53, "On the Cadence, what it is, its species, and its use." "The cadence," he explained, "is a certain act that the voices of a composition make in singing together, which denotes either a general repose in the harmony or the perfection of the sense of the words on which the composition is based. Or we could say that it is a termination of a part of the whole harmony at the middle or end, or an articulation of the main portions of the text."[120] A text-determined environment of

---

118. Rule 4 reads: "La Quarta, che rare volte si costuma di porre la sillaba sopra alcuna Semiminima; ne sopra quelle figure, che sono minori di lei; ne alla figura, che la segue immediatamente" (ibid.). In rule 6, Zarlino adds that when one syllable is placed under a semiminim another may be placed under the following note: "La Sesta, quando si porrà la sillaba sopra la Semiminima, si potrà anco porre un'altra sillaba sopra la figura seguente" (ibid.).

119. See the respective Latin- and Italian-texted musical examples from the *Musica nova* in Harrán, *In Search of Harmony,* pp. 96–97.

120. "La Cadenza adunque è un certo atto, che fanno le parti della cantilena cantando insieme, la qual dinota, o quiete generale dell'harmonia, o la perfettione del senso delle parole, sopra le quali la cantilena è composta. Overamente potemo dire, che ella sia una certa terminatione di una parte di tutto 'l concento, & quasi mezana, o vogliamo dire finale terminatione, o distintione del contesto della Oratione" (*Istitutioni harmoniche,* p. 221).

the kind Zarlino describes here made it difficult to distinguish the purely musical components of cadences. Zarlino opted to define cadential events as comparable syntactically (at least in theory), whether they brought to an end harmony or text (or both). Thus, certain passages might be deemed cadences that were not articulative in contrapuntal terms. In principle, cadences could even include events involving neither the suspended dissonances nor the imperfect-to-perfect intervallic movements that we normally associate with classic Renaissance polyphony.

Nevertheless, cadences that consist of contrapuntally discernible structures do have clearly defined musical features.[121] According to Zarlino's description, they routinely consist of two voices moving through three successive dyads, with at least one of the simultaneities progressing in contrary motion. Zarlino first says that cadences arrive on unisons or octaves, then admits that they may also arrive on other intervals, such as fifths or thirds (and even additional ones). Cadences on octaves and unisons are perfect (i.e., with a major sixth to octave progression for the last two of the three dyads, or a minor third to a unison), while those on other intervals are imperfect since they are not strictly speaking cadences ("non assolutamente cadenze"). Later on Zarlino adds that an imperfect cadence is a "cadenza impropiamente" (improper cadence).[122] Either type, perfect or imperfect, may be simple—that is, unornamented, homophonic, and fully consonant; or diminished—that is, varied rhythmically and including dissonant suspensions.

Once Zarlino begins to discuss specific cases he implicitly calibrates cadences from strong to weak, though decidedly not in any rigid, categorical, or (often) explicit way. For Zarlino perfect cadences carried the most weight. They were to be used when ending all the parts in a work or when punctuating complete sentences.[123] Zarlino's stance on them was unequivocal, but in his detailed contrapuntal descriptions he made other (sometimes ambiguous) refinements regarding weight. Imperfect cadences, by contrast with perfect ones, were to be used for "intermediate divisions of the harmony or for places where the words have not completely reached the end of their thought." Whether ending on thirds, fifths, or sixths, imperfect cadences always had to move into their last sonority from a third and with the upper voice ascending stepwise.[124] As with his descriptions of the *soggetto* and *imitatione,* Zarlino saw that many instances in current practice transcended his guidelines, making it impossible to illustrate every case: cadence types

121. For what follows I am indebted to Meier, *The Modes of Classical Vocal Polyphony,* Part I, Chap. 4; Siegfried Hermelink, "Über Zarlinos Kadenzbegriff," in *Scritti in onore di Luigi Ronga* (Milan, 1973), pp. 253–73; Karol Berger, *Musica ficta: Theories of Accidental Inflection in Vocal Polyphony from Marchetto da Padova to Gioseffo Zarlino* (Cambridge, 1987), pp. 122–39; and Michele Fromson, "The Cadence in Zarlino's *Le istitutioni harmoniche*," Chap. 1 in "Imitation and Innovation in the North Italian Motet, 1560–1605" (Ph.D. diss., University of Pennsylvania, 1988). Fromson provides a close reading of Zarlino's Part III, Chapters 53 and 54 and parts of 61, with astute analyses of his musical examples.

122. *Istitutioni harmoniche,* p. 224.

123. "[S]e le Cadenze furono ritrovate, si per la perfettione delle parti di tutto il concento; come anco, accioche per il suo mezo si havesse a finire la sentenza perfetta delle parole" (ibid., p. 225).

124. Ibid., p. 224.

are "almost infinite," he claimed, "for the contrapuntist . . . seeks new ones, constantly searching for new procedures."[125]

In order to suggest some of the possible exceptions, Zarlino embedded in a passage of continuous polyphony a group of examples that he later, in the 1573 edition of the *Istitutioni,* dubbed "extravagant cadences." In this passage (Ex. 7), we find a welter of melodic syncopations that descend and return by step, but no orthodox cadential progressions. Six of these syncopations occur in the lower voice (mm. 1–2, 2–3, 4–5, 6–7, 9–10, 11–12) and just one in the upper voice (the last one, mm. 13–14). The nonsyncopated voice in some cases makes an unconventional descent by leap to the cadential pitch (m. 3, g to c; mm. 4–5, g to c; m. 10, e to c; and m. 12, c to a); in other instances it stays put from the penultimate to the final sonority, instead of changing pitch at the point of cadence, as usually happens (e.g., the c over mm. 1–2; the c in m. 7). Furthermore, a number of the syncopations do not form dissonances with the counterpoint (as in mm. 1, 7, 10, and 13). What Zarlino seems to be drawing attention to here is the cadential impulse inherent in these syncopated melodic figures; he seems to be grappling with the Willaertian blur between such syncopated figures and the expectations of cadence that they set up in the listener.

Since the contrapuntal events in Ex. 7 lack orthodox cadences, their implied hierarchic strength will be low. In principle, they should carry less weight on our deduced scale than those described in Chapter 54 under "fuggir la cadenza," or "evading the cadence." Zarlino describes the latter as involving a "certain event in which the parts, pointing toward the desire to make a perfect ending according to one of the procedures shown above, turn elsewhere."[126] In other words, unlike the variety of figures grouped under extravagant cadences, evaded cadences should theoretically have all the necessary conditions of true cadences, *up until the final sonority.*

---

125. "Sarebbe cosa molta tediosa, se io volesse dare uno essempio particolare di ogni Cadenza propia, & non propia; conciosia che sono quasi infinite; onde è dibisogna, che'l Contrapuntista s'ingegni di ritrovare sempre di nuove, investigando di continuovo nuove maniere" (ibid.).

126. " '[L]Fuggir la Cadenza sia . . . un certo atto, il qual fanno le parti, accennando di voler fare una terminatione perfetta, secondo l'uno de i modi mostrati di sopra, & si rivolgono altrove" (ibid., p. 226).

But in real use the designation "fuggir la cadenza" turns out to be a catchall for any kind of cadence that appears to start out normally and ends up going astray. This includes imperfect cadences ending on thirds, fifths, or sixths in connection with which Zarlino first introduces the term at the end of Chapter 53. Evaded cadences are useful, Zarlino tells us, "when the composer has a lovely passage on his hands which would suit a cadence perfectly, but the words have not come to an end." Then it would "not be honest" to insert one, so the composer instead evades it.[127] To show techniques for evading the cadence, apart from the imperfect cadences already demonstrated, Zarlino again adduces a lengthy continuous passage, thirty-five breves in all (about half of which is given in Ex. 8).

The passage begins with a canon at the fifth, spaced at the semibreve. The guide in m. 2 sets up a typical syncopated cadential figure but fails to return by ascent to the pitch of preparation. Owing to the close spacing of the canon, the consequent initiates an identical syncopated figure in the middle of m. 2, so that the two end up overlapping in mm. 2–3. Had the upper voice returned to the f at the beginning of m. 3, the cadence would still have been unorthodox, since the lower voice would

127. "[Q]uando si vorrà fare alcuna distintione mezana dell'harmonia, & delle parole insieme, le quali non habbiano finita perfettamente la loro sentenza; potremo usar quelle Cadenze, che finiscono per Terza, per Quinta, per Sesta, o per altre simili consonanze: perche il finire a cotesto modo, non è fine di Cadenza perfetta: ma si chiama fuggir la Cadenza; si come hora la chiamano i Musici. Et fu buono il ritrovare, che le Cadenze finissero anco in tal maniera; conciosia che alle volte accasca al Compositore, che venendoli alle mani un bel passaggio, nel quale si accommodarebbe ottimamente la Cadenza, & non havendo fatto fine al Periodo nelle parole; non essendo honesto, che habbiano a finire in essa; cerca di fuggirla, non solamente al modo mostrato: ma nella maniera ch'io mostrerò nel seguente capitolo" (ibid., p. 225).

then have anticipated its own cadential pitch. By moving instead to d, it forms a suspended 2–3 dissonance with the consequent. Zarlino fails to sustain the d long enough for it to sound against the lower voice's resolution to b, leaping instead to g in m. 3 on the second part of the implied cadence's second sonority. The lower-voice consequent then undergoes the same lack of resolution as had the guide, b moving to a in m. 3. To double the injury done to the expected cadence at the third beat of that measure, the upper voice leaps again, now down to f and finally (in m. 4) to c.

More obvious deflections away from cadences affect the syncopated voice later in the passage. In m. 6, it leaps up from e to g. In m. 11 what had seemed to be a perfectly prepared Phrygian cadence to aa/a finds the diminished voice dropping suddenly a fifth to c to form an evaded cadence on a minor third. And in m. 19, the Phrygian cadence set up so conventionally is undercut by the sudden disappearance of the upper voice at the moment of final cadence.

To summarize, although Zarlino's discussion does not fix hierarchical relationships of cadence and text in an absolute or exhaustive way, certain hierarchical relationships emerge implicitly from his remarks. Perfect cadences, which mark off complete sentences or thoughts, rank highest.[128] They sit above imperfect cadences, which mark off incomplete sections of text. Evaded cadences seem to carry syntactic weight in proportion to the extent to which they set up cadential expectations. Thus if all the conditions of cadence are present but one (such as the actual cadential pitch in one of the voices), then the evaded cadence may rank fairly high. Those that go astray in more ways, and hence imply cadences less strongly, are weaker syntactically. The so-called extravagant cadences, having little resemblance to conventional cadences apart from the syncopated melodic figure, would seem to be weakest of all.[129]

Taken together, Zarlino's remarks on cadences, rests, textual repetition, and text underlay constitute a novel effort to conceptualize the new relation between text and music in the highly irregular and variegated polyphony of Willaert's circle. Zarlino fused his broad learning and acculturation in literary circles with his exceptional musical perspicacity and practical experience to codify Willaert's vocal polyphony within the terms of current rhetorical issues. These combined gave him a unique place in mediating between the new preoccupations of Venetian literary culture and the long-standing technical traditions of polyphonists bred in the church.

128. It might seem to us that perfect cadences would be strongest when their lowest voice leaps up a fourth or down a fifth, yet Zarlino asks that such leaps be confined mainly to the bass in multivoice polyphony. This is because he views cadences essentially as two-voice contrapuntal progressions.

129. We might have hoped Zarlino's ranking of appropriate cadential degrees would complement the foregoing, but he was not very effective in this respect. His chapters on individual modes (Part IV, 18–29) subsume each under a rationalist arithmetic system that unrealistically favors root, third, and fifth. This directly contradicts contemporary practice (as pointed out by Palisca, *On the Modes,* pp. xiii–xvi; Meier, *The Modes of Classical Vocal Polyphony,* pp. 105–7; and Carl Dahlhaus, *Untersuchungen über die Entstehung der harmonischen Tonalität* [Kassel, 1968], p. 198). Aaron gives a better idea of how modal counterpoint was actually being written (*Trattato,* Chaps. 9–12), even though his discussion is largely based on chant.

Part 3 · PETRARCHISM AND THE REPERTORY OF VENETIAN MADRIGALS

Adrian Willaert did not burst onto the Venetian scene as Rore was to do some years later. By the time he took up the position of chapelmaster at San Marco in 1527 he had already been a key figure at the Ferrarese court for over a decade, having joined the large musical establishment of the worldly, flamboyant Cardinal Ippolito I d'Este, brother of Duke Alfonso I, in 1515 or 1516.[1] When Ippolito died in September 1520 Willaert had shifted to the duke's service, where he had remained as a chapel singer until 1525, and had spent the years until 1527 serving another Este, Alfonso's son Cardinal Ippolito II.[2] Nor had Ferrara formed the limit of Willaert's contact with Italy and points east. In 1517, when Ippolito I left Ferrara to carry out duties as bishop of Eger in Hungary, Willaert had accompanied him, returning to Ferrara only in August 1519, and at some point during the pontificate of Leo X (1513–21) he had also visited Rome.[3]

1. The first discovery that Willaert was a singer in the court chapel at Ferrara under Duke Alfonso I came from René Lenaerts, who placed him there from 1522 until 1525; see "Voor de biographie van Adriaen Willaert," in *Hommage à Charles van den Borren: Mélanges,* ed. Suzanne Clercx and Albert vander Linden (Antwerp, 1945), pp. 205–15. Lewis Lockwood has shown that Willaert joined the Ferrarese establishment of Cardinal Ippolito I d'Este as early as July 1515 and certainly by 1516; see "Josquin at Ferrara: New Documents and Letters," in *Josquin des Prez: Proceedings of the International Josquin Festival-Conference, New York, 21–25 June 1971,* ed. Edward E. Lowinsky and Bonnie J. Blackburn (London, 1976), pp. 118–21. For a fuller account of Willaert's years with Ippolito I, including discussion of the relevant documents, Willaert's time in Hungary, the patronage of Ippolito I, and an inventory of some works from the period, see idem, "Adrian Willaert and Cardinal Ippolito I d'Este: New Light on Willaert's Early Career in Italy, 1515–21," *Early Music History* 5 (1985): 85–112. Lockwood suggests that Willaert's services were probably obtained by Ippolito through contacts with the French Royal Chapel, of which his teacher Jean Mouton was a member (see esp. pp. 87–88). The only book-length biographical study of Willaert is that of Ignace Bossuyt, *Adriaan Willaert (ca. 1490–1562): Leven en werk, stil en genres* (Louvain, 1985).

2. Lenaerts, "Voor de biographie," pp. 209–13.

3. Information about Willaert's visit to Rome comes from an anecdote told by Gioseffo Zarlino, *Le istitutioni harmoniche* (Venice, 1558), p. 346. All of these residencies and travels took place after several youthful years spent in Paris, first studying law, then music as a pupil of Jean Mouton. See Zarlino's *Dimostrationi harmoniche* (Venice, 1571), pp. 11 and 221; facs. ed. Ridgewood, N.J., 1966.

By 1527, then, Willaert had already been cultivating his skills in Italian soil for well over a decade. During that time many of his works had found their way into important Roman manuscripts (the Medici Codex and Cappella Sistina 16) and manuscripts of north Italian provenance (Bologna Q 19, known as the Rusconi Codex), while additional works had been printed by Antico and others.[4] Among them were masses, motets, and chansons—genres that still formed the mainstays of the pan-European polyphonic tradition in the 1520s and the proving grounds for any composer aspiring to international acclaim.

By contrast, none of Willaert's works presently datable to his Ferrarese years set Italian texts.[5] Indeed, whether Willaert set any Italian much before his first five madrigals appeared in 1534 remains an open question, since little is known of the madrigal's early history at Ferrara. Yet as Iain Fenlon and James Haar have shown, the madrigal of the 1520s was decidedly a Florentine and secondarily a Roman phenomenon.[6] Ferrara—along with Mantua and other northern courts—had instead been a center of the frottola, a genre that waned in the 1520s and was not clearly replaced in the north by madrigals until the following decade.[7] Although Ferrara did sustain musical ties with Rome, there was no clearly perceptible Florentine-Ferrarese axis of the sort that would establish a link to the decade's principal exponent of madrigals, Philippe Verdelot.

The scant knowledge relating to Maistre Jhan and Alfonso dalla Viola, the two other composers active in Ferrara during the 1520s who eventually produced madrigals, tends to confirm the impression that madrigal writing was just beginning to

---

4. On the Medici Codex (I-Fl, MS Acquisti e doni 66), a presentation manuscript containing fifty-three motets, see Edward E. Lowinsky, ed., *The Medici Codex of 1518: A Choirbook of Motets Dedicated to Lorenzo de' Medici, Duke of Urbino*, 3 vols., Monuments of Renaissance Music, vols. 3–5 (Chicago, 1968), vol. 3, and the review of it by Leeman L. Perkins in *The Musical Quarterly* 55 (1969): 255–69. On Cappella Sistina 16, a papal manuscript from the later years of Leo X's reign (i.e., probably between about 1515 and 1521) containing seven motets and one mass (the *Missa Mente tota tibi supplicamus* a 6) by Willaert, see Josephus M. Llorens, *Cappellae Sixtinae codices, musicis notis instructi sive manu scripti sive praelo excussi*, Studi e testi, no. 202 (Vatican City, 1960), pp. 29–31. The motet manuscript in I-Bc, Q19, is also taken up in Perkins's review cited above, pp. 265–67, where it is claimed as a manuscript of northern Italian provenance contemporaneous with the Medici Codex; see also David Crawford, "A Review of Costanza Festa's Biography," *JAMS* 28 (1975): 208, who dates the manuscript to ca. 1518 and suggests Bologna as its provenance. A number of Willaert's motets also mention members of the Milanese Sforza family. Important as well are the manuscripts in I-Pc, MS A 17, and I-Rv, MS S¹ 35–40 (olim Inc. 107bis, S. Borromeo E. II.55–60), the latter known as the "Vallicelliana manuscript"; see Lowinsky, "A Newly Discovered Sixteenth-Century Motet Manuscript at the Biblioteca Vallicelliana in Rome," *JAMS* 3 (1950): 173–232; rev. version in *Music in the Culture of the Renaissance and Other Essays*, ed. Bonnie J. Blackburn, 2 vols. (Chicago, 1989), 2:433–82. An important early printed source for Willaert is the printer Andrea Antico's anthology *Motetti novi e chanzoni franciose* (Venice, 1520). The anonymous print *Libro primo de la fortuna* (including Willaert's famous chromatic experiment *Quid non ebreitas*), of which a single altus part book survives at I-Bc with the shelf no. MS R 141, probably derives from somewhat later. Recently Iain Fenlon and James Haar have dated it to ca. 1526; see *The Italian Madrigal*, pp. 218–20, as well as their discussion of the apparently related *Messa motteti Canzonni Libro primo*, pp. 210–11.

5. Even these French and Italian settings owe much to Italian influences, however. For a persuasive assessment of the Italian impact on Willaert's later chansons, see Lawrence F. Bernstein's ed. of Antico's multifaceted collection of 1536 (with many chansons by Willaert), *La couronne et fleur des chansons a troys*, 2 pts., Masters and Monuments of the Renaissance, vol. 3 (New York, 1984), Chap. 5.

6. *The Italian Madrigal*, pp. 7–9 and passim.

7. Ibid., pp. 9–10, 74–75, and 320.

get under way in Ferrara during Willaert's time there. Of their Italian settings nothing is assignable to the 1520s save a single work in the Florentine manuscript known as the Newberry part books from about 1527–29—anonymous in that source but attributed in a later one to Maistre Jhan.[8] Another of Maistre Jhan's madrigals was subsequently published in the *Libro primo de la serena* of 1530 (RISM 1530[2]).[9] Dalla Viola's madrigals do not survive in early manuscript sources at all, and his first madrigal book was published only in 1539.[10] Though his madrigals show fluent acquaintance with Verdelot's Florentine style of the 1520s and clearly served as private fare for the Ferrarese court for some time before their publication, nothing indicates that dalla Viola composed any of them as early as the mid-twenties. Furthermore, Willaert's madrigals, once printing of them began, appeared not as the sudden release of a reservoir but as a steady trickle—five in 1534, followed by one in 1538, five more in 1540, and so forth.

The implications of these bibliographical artifacts are simple and profound: the genesis of Willaert's entire corpus of madrigals was quite likely Venetian. Willaert's earliest settings from 1534 owe much to the still-dominant Florentine tradition, but over the following decade they quickly began to replace Florentine traits with nascent Venetian ones. By the 1540s Willaert and other Venetian madrigalists had either displaced Florentine style almost entirely or reserved it for setting poetic madrigals, ballata-madrigals, and other lighter Italian verse forms. Their new products accommodated northern polyphonic techniques to Bembist literary ideals, layering part upon part with scrupulous attention to the affective values of sound, the strength and articulation of syntactic components, and the weighty canons of decorum.

This novel style had its most radical and influential embodiment in the Petrarchan sonnet settings of Willaert's *Musica nova*. During the mid-forties and fifties the *Musica nova* style, still known only through an aural and manuscript culture, was disseminated by Willaert's students in madrigals that modified its syntactic and expressive rigors for the purposes of print, making it more palatable for public consumption. Even though Willaert's own settings of Petrarch's sonnets were

---

8. US-Cn, Case MS-VM 1578. M91, fols. 82–83; the altus part book is in Sutton Coldfield, Oscott College, Old Library MS Case B, No. 4.

9. The two, respectively, are *Deh quanto e dolc'amor* and *Hor vedete madonna*. The former was attributed to Maistre Jhan only in his *Primo libro*, published posthumously in 1541. Its presence in the Newberry manuscript, otherwise almost wholly devoted to Verdelot, is peculiar (see H. Colin Slim, ed., *A Gift of Madrigals and Motets*, 2 vols. [Chicago, 1972], 1:88–89). *Hor vedete madonna*, conversely, reappeared *without* attribution in Arcadelt's *Libro secondo a 4* (1539; repr. 1541). On Maistre Jhan's biography see Lewis Lockwood, "Jean Mouton and Jean Michel: French Music and Musicians in Italy, 1505–1520," *JAMS* 32 (1979): 230.

10. Alfonso's *Primo libro a 4* was issued by Bulghat of Ferrara. For further on this book and the question of early Ferrarese madrigal writing see Leonardo Julio Waisman, "The Ferrarese Madrigal in the Mid-Sixteenth Century," 4 vols. (Ph.D. diss., The University of Chicago, 1988), Chaps. 1 and 3. Waisman is inconclusive about whether any of Alfonso's madrigals were written in the 1520s and dubious that any of Willaert's were (p. 40). Madrigals *were* performed at Ferrarese banquets given in 1529. Among composers for the banquets was dalla Viola, but he is not mentioned in the famous cook's account as a composer of madrigals per se; see Howard Mayer Brown, "A Cook's Tour of Ferrara in 1529," *Rivista italiana di musicologia* 10 (1975): 216–41.

withheld from publication during this time, a smattering of madrigals he wrote setting less complex verse appeared in a variety of printed anthologies. This twofold division represents a recurring pattern in Venetian madrigalian history: expressive weight was aligned with private settings and less imposing styles with public ones— a pattern that grounds my presentation in the remainder of the present chapter and one to which I will point more than once in those that follow.

PUBLIC STYLES AND PRINTED ANTHOLOGIES

The *Musica nova* preserved the only madrigal corpus Willaert published in his lifetime. His other madrigals, thirty in all over almost as many years, survive almost exclusively in anthologies and in prints devoted to other composers.[11] As shown in Table 2, the bulk of these (four-fifths) came out between 1534 and 1549. Many went on being reprinted periodically, but only six new ones cropped up in prints issued between 1554 and 1563.

Through the year 1541 Willaert's madrigals appeared only in collections otherwise mainly devoted to Philippe Verdelot—Verdelot's second books for four and five voices of 1534 and 1538, respectively, his only six-voice book of 1541, and a number of reprint editions (starting with RISM 1540[20] and 1540[18]).[12] It was not until 1542 that Willaert's madrigals first appeared in non-Verdelot editions. The printer Girolamo Scotto's collection of his own madrigals, *Madrigali a quatro voci . . . con alcuni a la misura breve, et altri a voce pari,* included Willaert's two settings of canzone stanzas by Petrarch, *Qual più diversa e nova cosa* and *Quante volte diss'io.* And the first of Gardane's *Madrigali . . . a misura di breve* series included a single sonnet setting by Willaert. Both of these editions advertised themselves in connection with the fashionable new black-note madrigals.

In subsequent years, nine more new madrigals came out in five-voice editions of Rore: three in Rore's eclectic second book of 1544, five in Scotto's edition of Rore's third book of 1548, and in 1557, finally, one in his fourth book. These and the settings published in Verdelot prints account for all but five of the thirty anthologized

---

11. The sole exception is Scotto's posthumous print of 1563, the *Madrigali a quatro voci,* a sentimental commemorative collection that unites the more accessibly scored four-voice madrigals with examples of Willaert's *canzoni villanesche.* The print has a number of what appear to be clear misattributions, but much of it consists simply of reprinted madrigals. It contains only a single unicum (discussed below).

12. Much has been made of these joint appearances as an indication that the two composers may have been connected in some way, especially given Willaert's role in arranging madrigals of Verdelot for lute and voice, *Intavolatura de li madrigali di Verdelotto da cantare et sonare nel lauto, intavolati per Messer Adriano, novamente stampata . . .* (Venice, 1536). For Verdelot's possible influence on Willaert see Lowinsky, "The Vallicelliana Manuscript," p. 194, and Einstein, *The Italian Madrigal* 1:326; see also Wolfgang Osthoff, *Theatergesang und darstellende Musik in der italienischen Renaissance,* 2 vols. (Tutzing, 1969), 1:286 and 305, for an argument contradicting the latter's view that Willaert's style emerged from Verdelot. But Verdelot's biography after 1528–29 remains as mysterious as ever, and he could well have perished during the plague that hit Florence then. The best biography of Verdelot is that in Slim, *A Gift of Madrigals and Motets* 1:41–65; see also idem, "Verdelot, Philippe," in *The New Grove* 19:631–35. In lieu of more concrete information, the possibility remains a good one that the editions of Verdelot were in some sense commemorative and that Willaert's place in them was that of a first among various equals, brought together to embellish the works of an old master.

Table 2
Willaert's Madrigals in Anthologies and Single-Author Prints*

First publ. RISM/ Abbreviated Title	Incipit	No. Pts.	Signature/ Cleffing/ Final	Mens.	Poetic Form	Remarks
1536[7] Verd 2 a 4	Amor mi fa morire	4	b/g2/d	¢	ballata-madrigal	Poet: Dragonetto Bonifazio
	Signora dolce	4	b/c1/g	¢	madrigal	
	Quando gionse per gli occhi	4	b/c1/f	¢	madrigal	
	Madonna, il bel desire	4	b/g2/g	¢	ballata-madrigal	
	Grat'e benigna donna	4	b/c1/f	¢	madrigal	
1538[21] Verd 2 a 5	Tant'alto sei, signore	5	b/c1/F	¢	canzone-madrigal	occasional, for [Card.] Hieronimo [Aleander], datable April–May 1538 (H. Meier, *Opera omnia* 14:x)
1540[20] Verd 1 & 2 a 4	Già mi godea felice	4	-/g2/c	c	madrigal	Setting in Festa *1 a 4* (1538)
	Qual anima ignorante	4	b/c1/A	¢	whole sonnet	5v setting by Willaert in Rore *2 a 5*
	Così vincete in terra	4	b/c2/F	¢	madrigal	anon. setting in I - Bc, Q21
1540[18] Le dotte a 5	Qual dolcezza giamai— A la dolce harmonia	5	-/c1/G	¢	madrigal	occasional, for [Polissena] Pecorina
	Quanto più m'arde— Non è ghiaccio	5	-/c1/G	¢	ballata	Festa setting in Arcadelt *3 a 4* (1539)
1541[16] La più divina a 6	Rompi de l'empio cor	6	-/c1/E	¢	madrigal	Poet: Filippo Strozzi (comp. Aug. 1537– Dec. 1538)
1542[17] Misura di breve 1 a 4	Chi volesse saper	4	-/c1/g	o	whole sonnet	
1542[19] Scotto 1 a 4	Qual più diversa e nova cosa	4	-/g2/d	c	canzone stanza	Poet: Petrarch, no. 135, stanza 1
	Quante volte diss'io	4	b/c2/F	c	canzone stanza	Poet: Petrarch, no. 126, stanza 5
1544[17] Rore 2 a 5	Sciocco fu 'l tuo desire	5	b/c1/F	¢	ballata-madrigal	invective poem in a female voice ("Chiara")
	Qual anima ignorante	5	b/c2/A	¢	whole sonnet	on attribution see Einstein, *The Italian Madrigal* 1:329
	Qual vista sarà mai	5	b/c2/A	¢	madrigal	

(continued)

TABLE 2 *(continued)*

First publ. RISM/ Abbreviated Title	Incipit	No. Pts.	Signature/ Cleffing/ Final	Mens.	Poetic Form	Remarks
1548[9] *Rore 3 a 5*	Amor, da che tu vuoi— Gentil coppia eccellente	5	b/g2/A	¢	madrigal	set by Perissone *1 a 4* (1547) and *2 a 5* (1550); on possible addressees see H. Meier, *Opera omnia* 14:x–xi
	Dove sei tu, mio caro— Chi mi ti tols'oimè?	5	b/c2/A	¢	whole sonnet	set in two pts.; on the death of a young man
	Mentre al bel letto— In te Marte	5	-/g2/d	¢	whole sonnet	occasional, for Pierluigi Farnese's assumption of the dukeship of Parma (Sept.–Oct. 1545) (H. Meier, *Opera omnia* 14:x)
	Se la gratia divina	5	b/c2/G	¢	ballata-madrigal	
	Ne le amar'e fredd'onde— Ceda nata nel mar Venere	5	b/g2/c	c	ballata	Poet: Lelio Capilupi; occasional, for [Helena] Barozza [Zantani]
1549[34] *Fantasie . . . a 3*	Se 'l veder voi m'ancide	3	b/c2/a	¢	ballata-madrigal	
1554[28]	Quando i begli occhi	4	-/c1/G	¢	whole sonnet	
1557[23] *Rore 4 a 5*	Ingrata è la mia donna— Ingrat'hai lasso l'amo	5	b/c1/F	¢	whole sonnet	set in two pts.
1559[19]	Madonna, s'io v'amai	5	b/c1/d	¢	madrigal	
1562[5]	Son già molt'anni— Son giont'al fin	5	-/c1/G	¢	madrigal	
1563 *Willaert Madr a 4*	Con doglia e pietà	4	b/c2/A	¢	madrigal	altus missing
1563[7]	Pianget'egri mortali	5	b/c2/A	¢	pseudo–terza rima	poem glosses Sannazaro's spiritual *capitolo Se mai per maraveglia* (*Opere*, pp. 210–11)

*This accounting omits secular Latin works (i.e., the *Aeneid* settings) and lighter works, as well as the two madrigals attributed to Leonardus Barré in RISM 1540[20], *Oimè il bel viso* and *Lagrime meste*.

Note that where no poet is given, the text remains anonymous.
Table uses short-title references. For full citations see the Bibliography.

settings Willaert made of Italian literary verse that survive (omitting his secular Latin settings and lighter dialect settings); the remaining five were issued singly in sundry editions of 1549, 1554, 1559, 1562, and 1563.

This publication pattern corresponds to Willaert's general rate of productivity over his lifetime, which showed a steady decline from about the mid-1540s. A famous anecdote in Zarlino's *Sopplimenti musicali* of 1588 reveals through the mouth of Parabosco that even Willaert's pupils came to think of him as an immaculate but slow worker.[13] Giulio Ongaro has corroborated this through a remarkable report he located, which relates that in 1547 the Procuratori of San Marco gave Willaert's young pupil Baldassare Donato the task of "keeping Willaert occupied in composing" (tenir solicitato esso maistro Adriano a tal composition).[14] Willaert's slowness in composing may have been exacerbated by increasingly poor health, for by 1549 a series of wills and codicils begin to describe him as ill and confined to bed.[15] In combination with such evidence, the anthologized madrigals provide a means to chronicle the evolving (and diminishing) pattern of Willaert's compositional production.

All of this suggests the existence of a counternarrative to the heroic tale of monumental production on which Willaert's posthumous reputation has always rested—an undercurrent of creative hesitation and generic fragmentation beneath the *Musica nova*'s exterior of extraordinary invention, conceptual unity, and generic consolidation. Aside from biographical data, the evidence of Willaert's anthologized madrigals provides many insights into the broader cultural economies of Venetian madrigal production. Unlike those of the *Musica nova,* the anthologized madrigals contain a great thematic diversity and formal variety. Poetic madrigals and hybrid forms of ballata-madrigal and canzone-madrigal predominate early on, but after 1540 they appear in equal numbers with sonnets, canzone stanzas, ballatas, and even a variant of terza rima. The settings range between nearly *Musica nova*–like gravity in a few to numerous others that are light, with passages of homorhythm, triple time, and the like. The majority use standard cut time, but a few use black notes. Some are in one part, others have some sort of formal division into two. Many, like *Mentre al bel letto,* written to celebrate the creation of Parma's dukedom in 1545, were obviously occasional. Others were encomiastic—the tributes to Polissena Pecorina, *Qual dolcezza giamai,* and Elena Barozza Zantani, *Ne le amar'e*

13. The *Sopplimenti musicali* were published in Venice. The story relates Parabosco's conversation with a self-important, little-known "maestro," who claims he can write a mass in an evening like one he has just heard by Willaert—one that Willaert had allegedly worked on for two months. Parabosco trumps him by replying, "I believe you and I am surprised that you did not write ten of the sort in that time," then goes on to explain Willaert's method of composing: "Adriano quando compone metto ogni suo studio et ogni sua industria, e pensa e studia molto bene quello che abbia da fare avanti che dia fine, et mandi alla luce una sua compositione; il perche, non per altro che per questo, è riputato il primo de' nostri tempi" (Adriano when he composes puts all his learning and all his industry and thinks and studies very well what he must do before he considers a piece finished and sends his composition out into the world; for no other reason than that is he reputed to be the best in our time); p. 326.
14. See "The Chapel of St. Mark's at the Time of Adrian Willaert (1527–1562): A Documentary Study" (Ph.D. diss., University of North Carolina at Chapel Hill, 1986), pp. 88–90 and Document 170.
15. See those reproduced in Vander Straeten, *La musique aux Pays-Bas* 6:227–46.

fredd'onde, discussed in earlier chapters.[16] They may have been used for particular events or simply satisfied the more general wishes of interested fans and patrons.

These particulars begin to elaborate the striking bifurcation within Venetian repertory that must have governed the creation and dissemination of the many different madrigal types to which I pointed above. On one side stood the monolithic repertory of the *Musica nova,* representing so implacably a musical embodiment of the classic, "authentic" Petrarchism prized by the literary elite. On the other stood the heterogeneous repertory of anthologized works that were mostly more immediate in their appeal, with no obvious claims for a transcendent musical poetics. Unlike the "hidden" state in which the *Musica nova* was cultivated and preserved in manuscript, many of Willaert's madrigals for printed anthologies probably entered the commercial marketplace without much delay. By contrast with those of the *Musica nova,* they display Willaert at his most accessible.

In the genre's earliest Florentine and Roman forms, of course, accessibility—if not *public* accessibility—was part of madrigal's temper, and it was within this frame of reference that Willaert started out. His first group of four-voice madrigals, published in Verdelot's *Secondo libro* in 1534 and reprinted in 1536 and 1537, adapted the chansonesque style identified with Verdelot and Jacques Arcadelt. Each of these madrigals arranges its poetic lines as a series of elegant, charming melodies. Sometimes the lower voices assume autonomous roles, expressively or contrapuntally (particularly in imitative passages), but most of the time musical prominence is ceded to the cantus. All five of Willaert's madrigals from the 1534 group set either the new cinquecento form of poetic madrigal or the most common hybrid variety derived from the ballata.[17]

The early madrigalists' preference for ballatalike structures forms a useful point of musical departure, for it reveals their continuing attachment to the balanced formal return offered by song forms. Rounded ballata-madrigals yielded rounded musical madrigals. In setting Dragonetto Bonifazio's ballata-madrigal *Amor mi fa morire* (see Ex. 9), Willaert capitalized on the text's vestigial resemblance to the repetitive, sectionalized structure of the ballata: the poem has a brief *ripresa* (vv. 1–2), an irregular passage of *mutazioni* (vv. 3–9—normally two *piedi* equaling two verbal periods, but here three), and a quasi-*volta* (vv. 10–12) that elides midway into a *ripresa.*[18] As shown below in my schematization of melodies carried (characteristically) by the cantus, Willaert mirrors—even outstrips—the text's elision into the *ripresa,* postponing it musically beyond the poetic return—that is, until the end of v. 11 (cf. mm. 3–5 with mm. 59–60).

16. See above Chap. 2 n. 49, and Chap. 3 nn. 38–39.
17. On these hybrid forms see Don Harrán, "Verse Types in the Early Madrigal," *JAMS* 22 (1969): 27–53.
18. On this poem see ibid., p. 32 n. 20. The rhyme of v. 10 matches that of v. 9, as the beginning of a *volta* should do. On the poet Bonifazio (Bonifacio) see Erasmo Percopo, "Dragonetto Bonifacio, marchese d'Orio: rimatore napoletano del sec. XVI," *Giornale storico della letteratura italiana* 10 (1887): 197–233, with *Amor mi fa morire* on p. 219.

EX. 9.   Willaert, *Amor mi fa morire* (Dragonetto Bonifazio), incl.; in Verdelot, *Secondo libro a 4* (Venice, 1536) (RISM 1536[7]), no. 1.

(continued)

(continued)

Ex. 9 *(continued)*

Rhyme scheme	Phrases (cantus)[19]		
a	A1	Amor mi fa morire	Love makes me die
a	A2; A3	E pur il vo seguire.	And still I wish to follow it.
B	B1	Non è gran duol il mio tenac'e forte	Is my strong, tenacious knowledge
B	B2	Conoscer ch'io vo dietro alla mia morte?	That I am going back to my death no great grief?
b	C	Sotto ch'acerba sorte	Under what bitter fate 5
C	D1	Nacqui nel mondo, che morir mi sento,	Was I born into the world, that I feel myself dying
C	D2	E d'abbracciar mi piace 'l mio tormento.	And yet I am happy to embrace my torment.
C	E	Deh, voi ch'udite 'l mio grave lamento,	Ah, you who hear my grave lament,
D	D1'	Dite, per Dio, se 'l dir non v'è molesto:	Say, by God, if the words do not trouble you:
d	B2' (end)	Non è miracol questo,	Is this not a miracle 10
a	F	Ch'Amor mi fa morire	That love makes me die
a	A2'; A3; A4	E pur il vo seguire?	And still I wish to follow it?

Willaert's setting adheres to the phraseology of French and Italian song styles that binds each poetic line to a single musical phrase. His rendition favors a reading based on versification, so much so that even the enjambment of lines 5 and 6 produces two distinct musical phrases.[20] Yet it still practices a northern art of imitation.

At a higher level the setting divides the twelve poetic lines into structural groups formed around five verbal periods:

ripresa	*mutazioni?*			*volta/ripresa*
vv. 1–2	vv. 3–4	vv. 5–7	vv. 8–9 →	vv. 10–12
A phrases	B phrases	C → D phrases	E; D (reused)	loop back w/B; F → A (reused)

Each of these poetic divisions in turn finds support in an interwoven system of melodies and cadences (see Table 3), still wholly based in the traditional tenor-

---

19. Note that the prime sign (') below indicates varied repeat of a phrase.

20. Although sixteenth-century madrigals were often performed with instruments taking at least some of the parts or doubling voices, my critical discussions in Chapters 7–10 treat all voices as if they were sung. Since all of the madrigals I discuss in Part 3 were conceived in such a way that all parts would provide viable poetic readings when performed by voices, this seems reasonable analytically but it should not be taken to dismiss or minimize the historical existence of other kinds of performances.

Readers wishing fuller access to the madrigals under discussion should consult modern editions of them, as listed below. My identifications of poets come from *Il nuovo Vogel* except where otherwise noted. I have added poetic sources wherever possible. I am grateful to Lorenzo Bianconi and Antonio Vassalli for use of their handwritten catalogue of sixteenth-century poetic incipits and to Michael Keller, Anthony Newcomb, and Shuli Roth for use of the computer database of cinquecento poetry at the University of California at Berkeley.

Table 3

TABLE 3
Cadence Plan of Willaert's *Amor mi fa morire*

Bar	Poetic Line	Cadential Pitches/ Voices	Bass or Lowest Pitch	Cadence Type/ Remarks
4	1	cc♯/e (C/T)	a	half
7	2	f/F (A/B)	F	perfect
10	2	aa/a (C/T)	D	Phrygian
17	3	f/F (T/B)	F	perfect
18	3	f/F (T/B)	F	perfect/Landini
23	4	d/d (C/A)	D	perfect
27	5	dd/d (C/T)	b-flat	
29	6	c/E (T/B)	E	evaded
31	6	c/F (T/B)	F	evaded
33	6	cc/F (C/B)	F	
34	6	cc/c (C/B)	c	evaded
35	6	f/F (T/B)	F	evaded
39	7	g/G (A/B)	G	perfect
40	7	g/G (C/T)	E-flat	perfect
42	7	g/G (C/T)	G	perfect
47	8	ee/g (C/T)	C	half
49	9	cc/c (C/B)	c	evaded
51	9	cc/c (C/T)	c	perfect
54	10	f/F (T/B)	F	perfect
57	11	d/D (A/B)	D	perfect
60	11	-/d ([C]/T)	D	evaded
62	12	f/F (A/B)	F	
65	12	aa/a (C/T)	F	Phrygian
66	12	c/C (A/B)	C	perfect/Landini
68	12	dd/d (C/T)	D	perfect
70	12	—	D	plagal

superius framework.[21] The madrigal proceeds from a d-mollis tonality strongly polarized with A. Its first important cadence, between the cantus on aa and tenor on a over D in the bass (m. 10), rounds off the opening two *settenari*. As the poetic refrain that will close the piece, these lines need to be firmly anchored, and Willaert does so by treating line 1 as an antecedent, brought to a half cadence (m. 4), and line 2 as a consequent. By letting line 2 cadence fleetingly on f/F (altus-bassus, m. 7) and then, more strongly, on the D-major chord (m. 10), Willaert's setting makes the whole into a tiny, but balanced, bar form aimed toward the final. F retains its status as a secondary

21. The designation of pitches in Table 3 and elsewhere follows Renaissance practice, with each octave conceived as proceeding upward from pitch G and c designating our "middle c." When speaking of pitch class generally, without reference to particular register, I simply use upper-case letters.

cadential degree and D as a primary degree as the quasi-*mutazioni* first cadence in a decorative suspension to f/F at mm. 17–18 and then in a hollow open-fifth at m. 23. The last resounds with D in no fewer than three voices (cantus, altus, bassus), while the tenor lingers on the a it had sung in the penultimate cadential sonority. It might seem surprising that this otherwise traditional tenor should retire contrapuntally at a moment of such clear structural definition. But doing so enables it to leap dramatically to center stage, its unexpected high f-sharp attack at m. 24 beaconing the tonal reorientation to come with the "bitter fate" of the third period.

F-sharp is an outsider in the D/A tonal world of the *ripresa*. The diminished-fourth cross relation it forms with the alto's bb-flat—and that bb-flat's augmented-fourth cross relation with the cantus's ee (m. 25)—subverts the tonal calm that had prevailed in the *ripresa*. Ultimately the tonality is riveted to a new axis of pitches, F and C, which dominate the medial third and fourth poetic periods, approached through a detour past G at line 7 (m. 42).[22] The shift amounts to a change of modal orientation from Hypoaeolian to Hypolydian that first emerges in a series of evaded cadences at midverse, with falling fourths, ff to c, in the cantus (mm. 31, 33, etc.). Eventually the cadences take up more clear-cut positions at verse endings (mm. 35, 47, 51), reinforcing the shift of modality. Only after D is summoned back with phrase B2 and the start of the last period, "Non è miracol questo," does the madrigal meld seamlessly into a return of the opening.

In *Amor mi fa morire,* then, Willaert put northern contrapuntal skills to novel expressive use. Pitch emphases, voice leading, and modal relationships all quietly shape prosodic structures at the two levels of verses and periods. The madrigal's new coloristic expressivity—the cross relation between ee-flat and e at the very opening (m. 3) and cross relations highlighting the "bitter fate" in mm. 24–25 noted earlier—introduces a refined dramatic tension into the handling of the verse structure. Some of the madrigal's rhetorical gestures, like the abrupt pause and textural shift to near-homorhythm at the exclamatory "Deh, voi ch'udite 'l mio grave lamento" in the midst of otherwise staggered declamation, are boldly new. Its imaginative transitions between verses call to mind the formal subtlety often heard in Arcadelt's madrigals of the 1530s, most famously *Il bianco e dolce cigno* from the *Primo libro* of 1539. And yet with all this, musical accents are allied to words in melodies free enough to allow a virtually infallible diction.

Despite these novelties, Willaert's *Amor mi fa morire* is closer to Verdelot's style than to anything Willaert composed in later years. The music remains syllabic with many short phrases, cadences (including many Landini cadences) at the end of nearly every verse, minimal text repetition, frequent four-square metric patterns,

---

22. This sort of medial modal contrast parallels that undertaken in contemporary chansons, as Howard Mayer Brown pointed out with respect to Willaert and Verdelot; see "Words and Music: Willaert, the Chanson, and the Madrigal about 1540," in *Florence and Venice, Comparisons and Relations: Acts of Two Conferences at Villa I Tatti in 1976–1977,* vol. 2, *Il cinquecento,* ed. Christine Smith with Salvatore I. Camporeale (Florence, 1980), pp. 217–66. Comparable events in chansons are generally managed within a much more controllable verbal space—four or five lines of equal length and rhythmic character.

enlivened chordal textures built mainly around tenor and cantus, and a rounded formal structure. The musical treatment of vv. 1–2 as a single bipartite unit—the latter part essentially a variation of the former with a "half cadence" separating the two (m. 4)—recalls the handling of seven-syllable couplets typical in the repertories of both frottola and early madrigal. These qualities serve as a reminder that Willaert largely preserved the formalistic approach that Howard Mayer Brown identified in likening one of his chansons to a madrigal of Verdelot's.[23]

What is more, the novelties I have noted in *Amor mi fa morire* move it farther from Verdelot's style than any of the other madrigals in the 1534 collection do. A typically Verdelot-styled setting of a ballata-madrigal is Willaert's *Madonna, il bel desire,* whose melodic repetitions are far more schematic:[24]

Verses/Rhyme scheme	Musical phrases
1 a	A
2 B	B
3 a	C1
4 a	C2
5 B	B′
6 c	A′
7 C	B
8 D	D
9 D	D
10 a	A″
11 A	B; B

Like many early-sixteenth-century song settings, *Madonna, il bel desire* assembles jigsaw fashion four distinct melodic strains. Each of these strains plays a discrete rhythmic-harmonic role: phrase A that of an initiating gesture for *settenari;* phrase B a more elaborated melody for *endecasillabi,* tracing a falling-ff-to-final-g curve; phrase C a short open-ended melody for paired *settenari,* supported frottola-like by

23. Ibid.

24. The madrigal has a mixed attribution history. In RISM 1534[16], 1536[7], and 1537[10], it is assigned to Willaert. In 1540[20], Scotto's combined edition of Verdelot's first and second books for four voices, it appears to be attributed to Verdelot, as Gardane apparently believed in assigning it to Verdelot in 1541[18]. As Stanley Boorman has argued, however, this is probably only a result of the fact that the madrigal begins in the middle of a recto with Verdelot's name in the header and with a madrigal of Verdelot's immediately preceding *Madonna, il bel desire.* In 1540[20] Willaert's name does not appear until the header of the verso on which *Madonna* is completed. See Boorman, "Some Non-Conflicting Attributions, and Some Newly Anonymous Compositions, from the Early Sixteenth Century," *Early Music History* 6 (1986): 125–27 and 157.

For scores of *Madonna* and other madrigals by Willaert not published in the *Musica nova* see Willaert, *Opera omnia,* Corpus mensurabilis musicae, no. 3, AIM, vol. 14, ed. Helga Meier (Neuhausen-Stuttgart, 1977).

Willaert, *Signora dolce, io te vorrei parlare,* cantus, mm. 1–11; in Verdelot, *Secondo libro a 4* (Venice, 1536) (RISM 1536[7]), no. 2.

a homorhythmic minim chain with a weak-beat ending; and phrase D a medial *endecasillabo* melody arching from bb-flat up to dd and down to d below.

There is even more archaism, albeit of an eclectic sort, in other madrigals from 1534. *Quando gionse per gli occhi al cor, madonna* recalls the old Florentine ballate of Heinrich Isaac, Alessandro Coppini, and Bartolomeo degli Organi: strong metrical rhythms and syncopations, triple-meter shifts, and passages of homorhythm (mm. 31ff.). And the quasi-medieval floating lines and fragile melismas of *Signora dolce, io te vorrei parlare,* a chivalric offer of secret servitude to a "sweet lady," harken back to the chansons of the fifteenth-century *rhétoriqueurs.*[25] (See the opening bars of the cantus in Ex. 10.)

By 1540 Willaert's anthologized madrigals, even the ones for four voices, had already grown distant from Verdelot's balanced songlike conception. The difference is striking in *Già mi godea felice ogni mio bene,*[26] one of Willaert's contributions to Scotto's reprint edition *Di Verdelotto tutti li madrigali del primo, et secondo libro a quatro voci* (1540[20]). This piece sets a little eight-line madrigal, disposed in the near-symmetrical scheme ABbA CddC.

Già mi godea felice ogni mio bene,	Once I gladly enjoyed all my good fortune,
Hor, sì longo al mio ben, tal doglio sento,	Now, so far from my loved one, I feel such grief
Che più crudel tormento	That I have never had a more cruel torment,
Non hebbi hormai, nè sì gravose pene.	Nor such a grave pain as now.
Felic'era 'l mio amor, felic'ero io;	Happy was my love, happy was I;
Hor, benchè sia 'l mio core	Now, though my heart is
Sì lontan dal suo amore,	So far from its love,
Fie volendo felice l'amor mio.	Let my love be happy if it wishes.[27]

The poem is a study in simple symmetries, yet Willaert's setting counteracts nearly all of them: the anaphora, repetitions of rhymes, and evenly deployed paradoxes. Its melodies wind out motet-style in a formidable 99 breves (not much shy of the 120

25. This funny little text does not even scan as proper seven- and eleven-syllable lyric verse.
26. Willaert may have gotten the text from Constanzo Festa's setting in the latter's *Primo libro* of 1538. No poetic source is known.
27. I am grateful to Elissa Weaver for help in translating several poems in this chapter, including this one.

or so typical of his sonnet settings), with little regard for the length or overall rhythmic character of each verse. The declamatory pacing varies widely, from the opening, dominated by breve and semibreve declamation, to subsequent passages declaimed continuously in minims (Ex. 11). Added to all this are several extended melismas, all of these thwarting any clear perception of the poem's versification.

Nevertheless, Willaert did not ignore the poem's larger verbal structures altogether. On the contrary, he magnified the rhetorical-rhythmic closes, culminating the ends of each half with multiple textual repetitions that stretch line 4 over 23 breves and line 8 over 16 1/2. Other tactics gather momentum toward these final cadences too: the cantus makes a prolonged ascent to gg shortly before the close of the first half and florid, sequenced melismas before the very end. As he did in setting *Amor mi fa morire,* Willaert brought into relief the internal apex of the poem by carrying line 4 to the madrigal's farthest point of modal remove—in this case an evaded, overlapped cadence on f/D—and then turned almost immediately back to the original tonality of C durus.[28]

Ironically, Willaert spun out these simple verses with more pliant, elongated melodies than he had ever used before, forsaking the prosodic rhythms that had previously been fundamental to Italian lyric song. *Già mi godea* and other madrigals of 1540 also mark the beginning of Willaert's experimentation with subtle manipulations of timbre, generated by variously blending and reblending different vocal groups. Certainly none of his earlier expositions looks anything like the one in Ex. 11, which weaves a highly individuated cantus and altus into a spare duo for eight long measures before finally repeating v. 1 *a quattro.* The madrigal's subsequent dispositions of text continue to project varied groupings that intersect and overlap one upon another, as at line 6 (mm. 71–79), where three high voices replace three low ones. The technique is strikingly new in a four-voice texture and profoundly unsettling to the traditional cantus-tenor edifice on which the madrigal's earlier song textures—even less conventional ones like *Amor mi fa morire* (Ex. 9)— had been built.

Scotto's four-voice reprint of Verdelot presented two more of Willaert's madrigals. One set a lengthy madrigal text, *Così vincete in terra,*[29] a fourteen-line encomium of a woman, in a style much like that of the 1534 collection. But the other introduced Willaert's first published sonnet setting, *Qual anima ignorante over più saggia* (set *in toto,* as all his essays in the sonnet were to be). *Qual anima ignorante* is a Petrarchan lament loosely modeled after Petrarch's *In qual parte del ciel* (no. 159), complete with repetitive rhetorical constructions and pervasive antitheses. Its only debt to repetitive song forms is an internal refrain, lines 3–4 returning as lines 7–8.

---

28. After the close of v. 4 nearly all the cadences land on C (e.g., m. 75, m. 80, m. 91), with the exception of mm. 66–67.

29. An anonymous setting of the same text survives in I-Bc, MS Q21, which dates from ca. 1526; see Fenlon and Haar, *The Italian Madrigal,* pp. 137–39.

Ex. 11.   Willaert, *Già mi godea felice ogni mio bene,* mm. 1–17; in *Di Verdelotto tutti li madrigali del primo, et secondo libro a 4* (Venice, 1540) (RISM 1540[20]), p. 47.

Qual anima ignorante over più saggia	What soul ignorant or more wise,
Qual huom mortal, qual dio, qual donn'o diva,	What mortal man, what god, what woman or goddess
Che non sappia 'l mio mal onde deriva,	That might not know from whence my woe derives
E del mio grand'ardor pietà non haggia.	And might not pity my great ardor? 4
Qual selv'è sì riposta o sì selvaggia	What woods so hidden or so savage,
Qual lauro in aria cresce o qual oliva,	What laurel rising in the air or what olive tree
Che non sappia 'l mio mal onde deriva,	That may not know from whence my woe derives
E del mio grand'ardor pietà non haggia.	And may not pity my great ardor? 8
Qual part'hoggi del mondo, che non sia	What part of the world today that is not
Delle lagrime pien'e di lamento,	Full of tears and of laments,
Delle voci, sospir'e doglia mia.	Of voices, sighs, and my griefs? 11
Non giace cosa hormai sotto la via	Not a thing now lies beneath the path
Del ciel che non conosca 'l mio tormento,	Of heaven that does not know my torment
Se non sola colei, ch'io sol vorria.	But her alone whom I alone desire. 14

Willaert's setting of *Qual anima ignorante* continued the trajectory of other madrigals from 1540, though the basic conception differs from that of sonnet settings in the *Musica nova*. Willaert made no *seconda parte* for the sestet or any double-bar division at all and matched the poetic refrain with the same music. In these respects the setting follows conventional norms for setting the lighter forms of the ballata and madrigal. Yet some of the elastic pacing and varied vocal scoring of *Già mi godea* finds its way into *Qual anima ignorante,* especially in the last tercet, where the previously languorous rhythms unexpectedly pick up. Here too Willaert loosed the restraints of a prosodic approach by fully recognizing the poetic enjambment with a continuous musical phrase (mm. 110–11).

All three of the poets in 1540[20] have continued to elude identification. The point is suggestive, for it relates to Willaert's general disengagement in anthologized madrigals from verse authorized by classical tradition or having pretensions to the highest literary pedigree. If the poets' voices remain so consistently unrecoverable in our day, they were probably muted in Willaert's too. More than theirs, it was probably Willaert's voice that resonated "authorially" among buyers and auditors in salons and print shops. This does not mean that poems were typically chosen through Willaert's agency or authority: the mechanisms through which he acquired texts remain mysterious and the impetuses for his settling on one or another were probably as fragmentary and diverse as their printing venues.

Both of Willaert's two five-voice madrigals featured in Scotto's anthology *Le dotte, et eccellente compositioni de i madrigali a cinque voci* (RISM 1540[18]) may have arisen at the behest of particular patrons or for special occasions.[30] One of these is

30. As Fenlon and Haar point out, the composers listed in this print appear in "what looks like a descending order of importance" (ibid., p. 313): Willaert, "suo discipulo" Leonardo (Leonardus) Barré, Verdelot, Arcadelt, Festa, Corteccia, Berchem, and so on (the order thereafter becomes slightly less

the famous homage to Polissena Pecorina, *Qual dolcezza giamai* (the text of which appears in Chap. 2, pp. 34–35). *Qual dolcezza giamai* is the only madrigal from these years that essays an explicitly celebratory style, with appealing melodies that have little place in Willaert's Petrarch settings. The graceful, catchy *soggetto* in Ex. 12, announced by the tenor under a shimmery alto countersubject and imitated at m. 5 by the cantus, has no analogues among expositions in the *Musica nova*. Einstein viewed this kind of five-part writing as technically new; "the choral response, the vocal coloring (one might call it 'vocal glazing'). Just as a painter covers over but does not conceal a shining ground color with another one, delicate and transparent, so Willaert superimposes upon a prominent voice, the bearer of the *espressivo,* another purely radiant one."[31] Einstein did not link this to the celebratory nature of the text. But he did note the new dramatic potential inherent in such textural flexibility and particularly the rhetorical and timbral possibilities in treating the five-part madrigal as two four-part textures (as happens at the beginning of the *seconda parte*). (The only text for which Verdelot uses such a technique in the same print is an actual dialogue.) In making the words easily perceptible, Willaert also kept the declamatory meter uniform, even when the parts give out different rhythms and melodies on the same words. His short, simple formulas for acclamations like "Desta nei cor" usually repeat the same motive (as shown in Ex. 13) but also vary it with the more athletic motion of the bassus (Ex. 13b) or the rising movement of the altus (Ex. 13c). Willaert pitched settings like these to a lighter—hence lower—stylistic level than his settings for the *Musica nova* (even switching to a near-homorhythmic triple time at "Et si rallegra in ciel di gir'in giro").

Though *Qual dolcezza giamai* progresses through an accumulation of enjambments (vv. 1–3, 5–6, 7–8, 10–11, 13–14), Willaert's setting still largely ties its phrases and contrapuntal articulations to the poem's versification.[32] Superficially the parts appear to function autonomously, but Willaert stitches them to a series of cadences that coordinate the parts at moments of prosodic definition (note the four upper voices at m. 13, Ex. 12).[33] The combination of relatively short melodious strains and frequent multivoice cadencing keeps the words clear and the texture delightfully transparent.

Both *Qual dolcezza giamai* and the other setting in *Le dotte,* the ballata *Quanto più m'arde e più s'accende il foco,* may owe their existence to local sources of patronage.

---

straightforward)—an arrangement only a little different from that given on the title page of the cantus part book. The undated print RISM [1538]²⁰ (*Il nuovo Vogel,* no. 2883) is undoubtedly a later reprint of 1540¹⁸, as established by Mary S. Lewis, "Antonio Gardane and His Publications of Sacred Music, 1538–55" (Ph.D. diss., Brandeis University, 1979), p. 629, and Fenlon and Haar, *The Italian Madrigal,* p. 313.

31. *The Italian Madrigal* 1:327–28.

32. The only exception is that of the strong enjambment that opens the second part, "A la dolce armonia si fa serena / L'aria, s'acqueta il mar, taccion'i venti" (At the sweet harmony the air becomes / serene, the sea calms, the wind turns quiet), for which Willaert provided a separate exposition for "A la dolce armonia," and then made what follows continuous.

33. Some of these cadences involve as many as all five voices, for example, mm. 79, 84, and the general pause preceding the triple-time passage, m. 63. For the full setting see Willaert, *Opera omnia* 14:65–70.

EX. 12. Willaert, *Qual dolcezza giamai*, mm. 1–13; in *Le dotte, et eccellente compositioni de i madrigali a 5* (Venice, 1540) (RISM 1540¹⁸), p. 1.

EX. 13. Willaert, *Qual dolcezza giamai:* a, m. 33; b, mm. 32–33; and c, mm. 36–37; in *Le dotte, et eccellente compositioni de i madrigali a 5* (Venice, 1540) (RISM 1540¹⁸), p. 1.

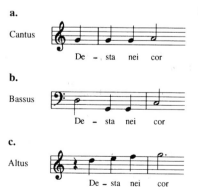

Quanto più m'arde had recently been published (like *Già mi godea*) in a setting by Constanzo Festa,[34] and in light of Festa's previous settings of both texts one cannot discount the possibility of a Strozzi connection. Both *Quanto più m'arde* and *Già mi godea* remain without poetic identifications. But an important poet-patron of Festa's (and one not represented in surviving literary sources) had significant Venetian connections, namely *Filippo* Strozzi. One of Willaert's anthologized madrigals, the six-voice *Rompi dell'empio core il duro scoglio,* published the year after *Le dotte* in Verdelot's six-voice print *La più divina musica* (1541[16]), set Strozzi's invective on his incarceration by the Medici. By 1541 Filippo had been dead for about three years (as noted in Chapter 2), but his trusted nephew Neri Capponi and sons Piero and Ruberto maintained a Strozzi presence in Venice. Since Festa benefited from Filippo's patronage and set his poems to music,[35] it is tempting to consider whether Willaert may have reset texts set by Festa because they were Strozzi's.

Such a scenario seems plausible in view of Willaert's having composed music for both texts. And *Quanto più m'arde* shares with an attributed Strozzi poem set by Willaert about 1542, *Rompi dell'empio cor il duro scoglio,* a darker, more dramatic expression than found in any of Willaert's previous settings. Einstein singled out Willaert's *Quanto più m'arde* for the violent rhetoric it used to assail the poem's mass of Petrarchan oppositions: death is sweet, pain a jest; ice does not freeze, or fire burn, grief grieve, or death kill; thus does the poet beg Love to freeze, inflame, and kill him.[36]

In lieu of such additive development, *Rompi dell'empio cor* weaves a bitter address to a "cruel lady" into the theme of Filippo's imprisonment.

Rompi dell'empio cor il duro scoglio	Break the hard reef of your evil heart,
Depon gli sdegn'e l'ire	Put down your ire and your disdain,
Hormai, donna crudel, depon l'orgoglio,	Now, cruel lady, swallow your pride;
Nè ti rincresc'udire,	Don't be unhappy to hear
Com'io, giont'al morire,	How I, having arrived at death, 5
Non più di te d'amor del ciel mi doglio.	No longer grieve for you, for love of Heaven;
Ma sol qual cign'in trist'accenti chieggio,	But only like a swan in sad tones ask
Che se m'odiast'in vita	That if you hated me in life,
Non mi niegh'un sospir alla partita.	You not deny me a sigh at my departure.
Ah, dove folle son, come	Ah, where am I going mad, why do
vaneggio?	I rave on? 10
Qui non m'od'o risponde	Here no one hears or answers me
Altri che de Mugnon le riv'e l'onde.	But the shores and waves of Mugnone.

34. Festa's setting was printed in Arcadelt's *Terzo libro a 4* (Venice, 1539). There is also a setting of the poem in Scotto's *Primo libro a 4* of 1542.

35. See Richard J. Agee, "Filippo Strozzi and the Early Madrigal," *JAMS* 38 (1985): 227–37.

36. *The Italian Madrigal* 1:329, where the text is not mentioned by incipit.

Given the continued presence in Venice of the Strozzi sons, especially Ruberto, Willaert's setting may have served as a eulogy, with its deep tessituras and large scoring (it is his only anthologized setting for six voices).[37]

In 1542 Willaert published his second sonnet setting, *Chi volesse saper che cos'è umore*, again in one complete part. The setting was included in Scotto's *Madrigali a quatro voce con alcuni alla misura breve* as one of the black-note madrigals, though it bore the unusual time signature O (*tempus perfectum, prolatio imperfecta*). In the same year Willaert also published what are now his first firmly datable settings of Petrarch, *Qual più diversa e nova cosa* and *Quante volte diss'io* (*Canzoniere*, nos. 135 and 126). Remarkably, canzone stanzas are Willaert's only known Petrarch settings outside of the *Musica nova*.

Then in 1544 came the three settings in *Di Cipriano il secondo libro de madregali a cinque voci insieme alcuni di M. Adriano et altri autori a misura comune novamente posti in luce a cinque voci* (RISM 1544[17]), nominally Rore's second book albeit with only eight of his madrigals. Willaert's settings assume an almost equal symbolic position in the collection next to Rore's,[38] with both composers arranged as symmetrical frames for the rest: the print begins with a madrigal each by Rore and then Willaert and ends with the reverse—perhaps a bow to age. Otherwise it resembles other books issued by Venetian printers in the 1540s that presented works by local Willaertians like Perissone, Jachet Berchem, Leonardus Barré, and Parabosco.[39] More will be said about the print in Chapters 8 and 9. For the moment it is important to note how many rhetorically conceived settings clustered in it all at once, signaling the gradual displacement of Florentine madrigalian style in the face of a growing consolidation and diffusion of Venetian practices.

Notwithstanding this, Willaert's anthologized madrigals continued setting texts outside the literary canon of Petrarch, Bembo, Sannazaro, and Ariosto. All the verse in

37. Possibly Willaert resorted to mode 3 for the same reason. His use of Hypophrygian for one of the only two sonnets from the "in morte" portion of Petrarch's *Canzoniere* included in the *Musica nova* (*Mentre che 'l cor dagli amorosi vermi*) makes me think he may have.

For identification of *Rompi dell'empio core* and its sources see Eugenia Levi, ed., *Lirica italiana nel cinquecento e nel seicento fino all'Arcadia* ... (Florence, 1909), pp. 307, 419, and 445.

38. It should be noted that Einstein doubted the authenticity of the second, a resetting of *Qual anima ignorante*, on the grounds of its voice leading and what he took to be removal of the attribution to Willaert in later editions of Rore's *Secondo libro* (*The Italian Madrigal* 1:329). To be sure it is difficult to explain the presence of a passage with parallel fifths between tenor and bassus, like that from the upbeat of m. 53 to m. 55. Yet the madrigal is also attributed to Willaert in various reprint editions (see *Il nuovo Vogel* 2:1487–88).

39. See Table 8. Similar prints include the 1546 reprint of Verdelot's six-voice volume *La piu divina, et piu bella musica*, originally issued by Gardane in 1541 and later reprinted by him as *Madrigali di Verdelot et de altri autori a sei voci novamente con alcuni madrigali novi ristampati & corretti a sei voci* (RISM 1546[19]) with madrigals by Noletto (Nolet or Noleth, known from Doni's *Dialogo della musica*), Jachet Berchem, Parabosco, and Perissone, among others; and Rore's third book, *Di Cipriano Rore et di altri eccellentissimi musici il terzo libro di madrigali a cinque voci,* as published by Scotto in 1548 (1548[9]) with madrigals by Rore, Perissone, Donato, Willaert, Gabriele Martinengo, and Zarlino. Venetian composers are also scattered throughout Scotto's Verdelot reprint *Le dotte, et eccellente compositioni de i madrigali a cinque voci da diversi perfettissimi musici fatte. Novamente raccolte, & con ogni diligentia stampate* (RISM 1540[18]), reprinted in 1541 and 1549, which includes works of Verdelot, Willaert, Barré, Constanzo Festa, Arcadelt, Corteccia, Berchem, Yvo, and Nolet.

the 1544 group remains anonymous and some of it ventures strategies of voice and address foreign to conventional lyrics of the early cinquecento. The unorthodox *Sciocco fu 'l tuo desire*—a lengthy ballata-madrigal couched in the invective of a woman called "Chiara" who rails against the folly and ills of a noble lover—turns on its head the notion that Venetian polyphonists adhered to strictly Bembist literary norms.

Sciocco fu 'l tuo desire	Foolish was your desire
Veramente pensando ch'a miei danni	In truly imagining that at my expense
Teco n'entrassi a gli amorosi affanni.	I should enter into amorous troubles with you.
Mi maraviglio, quando	I wonder that
Non anchor chiaro sei del foll'errore,	You are not yet certain of the foolish error, 5
E come desiando	And how you lost days and hours
L'amor mio ne perdest'i giorni e l'hore.	In craving my love.
Donna cortes'e humana	A courteous, humane woman
Con vil amante certo mal s'accorda.	With a vile lover surely is badly matched.
Non mi conosci, o cieca mente insana	You do not know me, o blind twisted mind 10
Di bastardo, nè vo' che per me leggi	Of a bastard, nor do I want you to read me
El suon di privileggi	The sound of your
Tuoi ch'ogni orecchia assorda.	Titles, which deafen every ear.
Hor tienti al mio consiglio:	Now take my advice:
Pon giù, se puoi, l'insania e cangia	Set aside, if you can, your madness and change
l'ire,	your wrath, 15
Ch'assembr'al vespertil e non al giglio.	Which resembles bats, not lilies.
Chiara son io, qual fui, nè mi scompiglio	I am Chiara, as I was, nor do I
A fart'il vero udire:	Trouble myself to make you hear the truth:
Se di te mai pensai, poss'io morire.	If I ever thought about you, I might die.

The poem's harsh, chiseled diction replaces Petrarch's lyric meditations with the direct discourse not just of a real-life lover but a female one, no less, and frames her speech in vituperative secular protestations linked with class. Chiara's low-styled cannonade on her lover's high-born vice foregrounds the matter of social rank as it inverts it. She delivers her tirade in a familiarizing second-person singular, crescendoing from *passato remoto* to present tense (v. 8) and finally to a rebuke aimed, at last, not (Petrarchistically) at herself but at him. Even the familiar turn to dying for the final rhetorical point does not propose a *Petrarchan* love-death—a love that ambivalently relishes love pangs as welcome death—but rather hints formally at Petrarch's paradox to reject it. The poem resembles Veronica Franco's invective retorts to challenges to her class and virtue from later in the century (cf. Chap. 1, n. 35). Yet madrigalian settings of texts spoken either in a woman's voice or even in a voice overtly aligned with class were rare throughout the sixteenth century, making this one striking despite the relatively neutral treatment Willaert gave it. Rather than embodying the text's invective realism in musical events, Willaert realized it by continuing to experiment with different three- and four-voice choral responses, especially at the most heated and direct parts of Chiara's tirade—the declamation of

v. 12, "El suon di privileggi," whipping by in minims and fast registral shifts of dialogue, or again for the imperative of v. 14, "Hor tienti al mio consiglio."

It is instructive to recall that the madrigals in Rore's *Secondo libro* were published in the same year Doni described Neri Capponi hoarding Willaert's music, music undoubtedly kept from print for a long time afterward (see Chap. 2 above, nn 38–39). This coincidence underscores the impression that social polarities were crucial in segregating public madrigals from private ones, and that the madrigals of the *Secondo libro* were textual and stylistic exemplars of the former ilk, while those kept by Capponi were marked by *Musica nova*–like reserve. More than that, the stylistic, thematic, bibliographical, and biographical evidence clustering on each side of this polarity suggests that social contexts actually worked to exaggerate differences between them.

From this point on Willaert essentially reworked approaches he had developed by the early to mid-forties. The five madrigals published in Rore's Third Book set occasional texts, with only one or two exceptions, but did not experiment with new approaches.[40] Nothing in subsequent publications surprises much either, except perhaps a spiritual madrigal published posthumously in 1563—a modified terza rima that turns out to be a gloss of Jacopo Sannazaro's *capitolo Se mai per meraviglia alzando il viso* (note the adaptation of Sannazaro's second, third, sixth, and part of the fourth stanzas indicated below).

Poem Set by Willaert (with rhyme scheme)	Stanze from Sannazaro's Poem
a Piangete' egri mortali,	3 Piangete il grave universal dolore
B Piangete l'aspra morte del Signore,	Piangete l'aspra morte e 'l crudo affanno
B Se spirto di pietà vi punge il core.	Se spirto di pietà vi punge il core.
C Volgete gli occhi in qua c'hoggi dimostra	2 Volgete gli occhi in qua, che ve presente
D Non quella forma, oimè, non quel colore	Non quella forma (ahimè), non quel dolore
C Che finge forse i sensi in mente vostra.	Che contemplaron gli occhi de la mente.
e Vedete 'l volto esangue	6 Ecco che hor vi dimostra il volto exangue
F Le chiome lacerate, il capo basso,	Le chiome lacerate: el capo basso
E Qual rosa che calcata in terra langue.	Come rosa dismessa in terra langue.
G O mirabil pietà, o dolce pegno,	
e O sacrosanto sangue,	
G Si largamente sparso al duro legno;	4/v.2 Pende come vedete al duro legno.

40. See Table 2. *Amor, da che tu vuoi* exemplifies texts that are not specifically occasional, but use the playfully direct voice prevalent in anthologized madrigals: "Amor, da che tu vuoi pur ch'io m'arischi / In udir e vedere / Sirene e Basilischi? / Fammi gratia, signore, / S'egli avvien che mi strugga lo splendore / Di due occhi sireni, e ch'io sia preda / D'un ragionar accorto, / Che chi n'ha colpa creda / Che per udir e per veder sia morto. / Gentil coppia eccellente, / Chi vi mira et ascolta / Solamente una volta / E non mor di piacere, / Può gir arditamente / Ad udir e vedere / Le Sirene d'amor e i Basilischi" (Why do you still want me to endanger myself / By hearing and seeing / Sirens and basilisks? / Do me a favor, Lord, / If it happens that the splendor / Of two serene eyes melts me, and that I am prey / To a crafty reasoning; / For one who is guilty of this believes / That by hearing and seeing he may die. / Gentle excellent couple, / He who gazes at you and listens / Just once / And doesn't die of pleasure / Can turn ardently to listen and see / The sirens of love and the basilisks).

h   O rara, o nuova legge,
J   Humiliarsi a morte acerba e dura
H   Quel che 'l ciel e la terra e 'l mar corregge.

J   Piangi mond'orbo, piangi egra natura:
H   Morto è 'l pastor per liberar lo gregge,
J   Come agnel mansueto alla tonsura.

The similarities between Willaert's and Sannazaro's texts, and especially the publication in 1511 by Franciscus Bossinensis of Sannazaro's text in an anonymous frottola setting, presents a potentially fascinating link between Willaert's written polyphony and the *capitolo* in terza rima so closely identified with oral tradition. Recall that the anonymous setting in Bossinensis's lute book gave every indication of having its genesis in improvised song, indeed song of an epic recitational sort (see Chap. 4 nn. 72–73). As Willaert's only effort at setting terza rima, we might expect to find some semblance of oral genesis in *Piangete' egri mortali,* but Willaert's madrigal lacks all the traces of oral prehistory that mark the Bossinensis arrangement. The vestigial affinities with oral traditions found in written Italian polyphony from the 1520s and 1530s, even in Willaert's own madrigals of 1534 and his lute intabulations of Verdelot's madrigals from 1536, found no place here.

———

The collective diversity evinced by the madrigals that Willaert anthologized from the 1530s to 1550s resembles the physiognomy of vernacular literary production during the same period. The earlier end of this span coincides with the beginnings of a phenomenon that parallels our modern-day "journalism," a period when professional polygraphs like Lodovico Domenichi, Lodovico Dolce, Ortensio Landi, Antonfrancesco Doni, and Niccolò Franco began to adapt a wide variety of subjects for popular consumption, often framing them in what I earlier called "dialogic" modes. In 1537 Aretino's *Primo libro delle lettere* inaugurated the familiar vernacular letter; in 1539 the first anti-Petrarchan parody, Niccolò Franco's *Il Petrarchista, dialogo . . . nel quale si scuoprono nuovi secreti sopra il Petrarca,* appeared; in 1543 Landi's satirical popularization of the classical genre of paradox *Paradossi cioè, sententie fuori del comun parare;* and (not least) in 1544 Doni's quasi-comic dialogue evoking the meetings of a musical academy, *Dialogo della musica.* The playful poetics found in many of Willaert's anthologized texts, the occasional, even biographical side of others, and the appealing musical persona of the settings share the public consciousness of those eclectic literary publications. Both kinds of literary and musical production were designed for the largest possible audience, an audience that thrived on the direct speech and referentiality of realistically situated verse and on the diminutive forms, ludic inversions, and general accessibility to be had in simple plays on Petrarchan courtly love.

Many of the poems set in Willaert's anthologized corpus must have been written by professional polygraphs styling themselves after the prototypes of Franco and Doni, or else by courtier-academists like Spira, Muzio, or Dolce. These new eclectics abounded in the commercializing culture of sixteenth-century Venice, transforming Petrarchan tropes and reworking Petrarch's lyric meditations into the speeches of real-life lovers. The amorous pleas of *Quanto più m'arde* and pointed diatribes of *Rompi dell'empio cor* or *Sciocco fu 'l tuo desire* exemplify the immediacy such verse offered over standard Petrarchan lyrics, even over the shorter canzone stanzas by Petrarch that Willaert anthologized. Still, those canzoni stanzas, alleviated by an admixture of *settenari* and structurally similar to cinquecento poetic madrigals, offered some relief from the weightiness of Petrarch's ponderous sonnets. Of the anthologized madrigals only seven are sonnet settings and of these Willaert only divided two into two parts. None of the sonnets' authors is known; indeed, only three poets apart from Petrarch can as yet be named for any of Willaert's anthologized settings.

Standing wholly apart from these is the remarkable collection that apparently went so little seen for nearly two decades until it was finally printed with the title *Musica nova*. Nothing distinguishes the two repertories more than the absence of even a single sonnet by Petrarch among the miscellanea as compared with twenty-four settings of Petrarch's sonnets in the *Musica nova,* all of which Willaert divided into two parts after the manner of the contemporary motet.

The *Musica nova* owed its unique complexion to a symbiosis of musical and literary interests that transcends our usual notions of conscientious text setting. Inspired by the wave of Ciceronianism in current literary theory, the madrigals in the collection presented themselves as self-conscious exemplars of a high, serious style. They formed an explicitly secular counterpart to *Musica nova*'s motets (which they followed physically in the print) by their division into two parts, their austerity, the inclusion of four-, five-, six-, and seven-voice settings (like the motets), and the searching nature of their poems. The juxtaposition of Petrarch's sonnets with many motet texts drawn from the Old Testament and dealing with issues of sin and penitence further reinforced the madrigals' parity with the motets.[41]

If the tonal makeup of the four- and seven-voice pieces is any indication, Willaert may have had a direct hand in the structural paralleling of sacred and secular, for motets and madrigals share a partial identity and order that can be seen by comparing Tables 4a and 4b. These tables list what Harold S. Powers has called the "tonal types" employed for the works in each genre, including signatures (or "systems"), cleffings, and finals.[42] Those of the four-voice motets are identical to the four-voice madrigals, with only a minor exception in the inner-voice cleffings of the fourth

41. See Willaert, *Opera omnia* 5:iv.
42. See "Tonal Types and Modal Categories in Renaissance Polyphony," *JAMS* 34 (1981): 428–70.

No.	Title	System	Ambitus	Final
1	Domine, quid multiplicati sunt	b	c3c4c4F4	GG
2	Dilexi, quoniam exaudiet	—	c1c2c3c4	C
3	Confitebor tibi Domine	—	c3c4c4F4	GG
4	Recordare Domine	—	c4F4F3F5	EE
5	O admirabile commercium	—	c2c3c4c4F4	D
6	Miserere nostri Deus omnium	b	c3c4c4F3F4	FF
7	Sub tuum praesidium confugimus	b	c3c4c4F3F4	GG
8	Beati pauperes spiritu	—	c1c3c4c4F4	GG
9	Sustinuimus pacem	—	c2c3c4c4F4	GG
10	Omnia quae fecisti	b	c2c2c3c3F3	A
11	Veni Sancte Spiritus	b	g2c1c2c3c3F3	G
12	Avertatur obsecro	b	c1c3c3c4c4F4	GG
13	Alma Redemptoris Mater	b	g2c1c2c3c3F3	F
14	Peccata mea	b	g2c2c2c3c4F3	A
15	Salve sancta Paren	b	c1c2c3c4c4F4	GG
16	Audite insulae	—	c1c3c3c4c4F4	GG
17	Aspice Domine	bb	c4c4F3F4F4F5	C
18	Pater, peccavi	—	g2c1c2c3c3c4	G
19	Victimae paschali laudes	b	g2g2c2c3c3F3	G
20	Mittit ad Virginem	b	c2c3c3c4c5F4	FF
21	Haec est domus Domini	—	c1c2c3c4c4F4	E
22	Huc me sidereo	b	g2c2c2c3c4F3	a
23	Praeter rerum seriem	b	c1c2c3c3c3c4F4	GG
24	Inviolata, integra	b	c1c1c2c3c4c4F4	FF
25	Benedicta es coelorum Regina	—	c1c1c3c3c4c4F4	GG
26	Verbum supernum	—	c1c2c3c4c4c4F4	GG
27	Te Deum Patrem ingenitum	b	g2g2c1c2c3c3F3	A

pair, while the seven-voice works (including the last four of the five seven-voice motets) are identical except for the signatures in the penultimate pair. Notwithstanding these differences, it is hard to see how such a sequentially ordered pattern of triadic correlations (i.e., system-cleffing-final) could have arisen by coincidence.[43] They raise at least two possibilities: first, that the correspondences between what are mostly unusual tonal types occurred because the paired madrigals

43. For the same reason, it seems unlikely that it was the printer Gardane who fashioned the correspondences postcompositionally, rather than Willaert. Gardane might ultimately have seen to it that "tonal types" in each genre appeared in identical order, but what is remarkable is that four pairs of virtually identical types should have existed at all. Moreover, as I note, the particular combinations of tonal constituents were unusual among Willaert's works. The possibility that Willaert shaped this patterning is all the more intriguing in view of the fact that his motet books were ordered in less extensive ways,

No.	Title	System	Ambitus	Final
1	Io amai sempre	b	c3c4c4F4	GG
2	Amor, Fortuna	—	c1c2c3c4	C
3	Quest'anima gentil	—	c3c4c4F4	GG
4	Lasso, ch'i ardo	—	c4c5F4F5	EE
5	O invidia	b	c3c4c4F3F4	D
6	Più volte già	—	c3c3c4c4F4	G
7	Quando fra l'altre donne	b	c2c3c4F3F4	FF
8	L'aura mia sacra	b	c3c4c4F3F4	FF
9	Mentre che 'l cor	b	c2c2c3c3F3	A
10	Onde tolse Amor	—	c1c3c4c4F4	GG
11	Giunto m'ha Amor	b	g2c2c3c4F3	G
12	I begli occhi	b	c1c3c4c4F4	GG
13	Io mi rivolgo	—	c2c3c3c4F4	EE
14	Aspro core	—	c2c3c3c4c4F4	GG
15	Passa la nave	b	g2c2c2c3c3F3	G
16	I piansi, hor canto	—	g2c1c2c3c3c4	G
17	Cantai: hor piango	—	c1c3c3c4c4F4	E
18	In qual parte del ciel	—	c2c3c3c4F4F5	EE
19	I vidi in terra	b	c1c3c3c4F3F4	FF
20	Ove ch'i posi gli occhi	—	g2c2c2c3c3c4	D
21	Pien d'un vago pensier	b	g2c1c2c3c3F3	F
22	"Quando nascesti, Amor?"	b	c1c2c3c3c4c4F4	FF
23	"Liete e pensose"	—	c1c1c3c3c4c4F4	GG
24	"Che fai, alma?"	b	c1c2c3c3c4F3F4	GG
25	"Occhi piangete"	b	g2c1c2c3c3c4F3	A

and motets were to be performed by identical forces in a single venue when they first came into being; and second, that Willaert may even have originally considered planning the madrigal and motet sections as tonal-timbral mirrors of one another. Even though evidence to establish the second of these is lacking, it is useful to recognize that by extending other parallelisms in the collection, such an arrangement would have substantially strengthened the collection's implicit Bembist assertion

grouped primarily by signatures. This was a habit of Gardane's, on which see Lewis, "Antonio Gardane and His Publications of Sacred Music," pp. 184–91.

As Tables 4a and 4b show, there is a wide array of so-called tonal types in the collection as a whole, including the five- and six-voice works. It almost seems as if one of its goals was to provide as much variety of tonal and performative possibilities as the print's dimensions would permit. Among the madrigals no type appears more than twice (as happens six times; eleven tonal types make only one appearance). The motets include eighteen tonal types in all (as compared with nineteen for the madrigals), with just one occurring as many as four times (♮-c1-G), two three times (♭-c1-G and ♭-g2-A) and two twice (♭-c3-G and ♭-g2-G).

that the two categories, sacred and secular, Latin and vernacular, could stand on an equal footing.

Willaert heightened the madrigalistic genre not primarily in these four- and seven-voice works, however; the four-voice works represent the least complex essays in the new style, and the seven-voice works are dialogues that typically pit three- and four-voice groups against one another in large-scale, often homophonic alternations. Instead, the collection is dominated by the madrigals for five and six voices, which incarnated the style at its most sober and introspective and posed the most challenging alternative to preexisting madrigalian norms. Verdelot's five- and six-voice predecessors had shown no signs of pushing the genre toward such a thoroughly polyphonic state. If anything, Willaert's resembled more the continuous, thick polyphony of Gombert's motets, the banderole of post-Josquin international polyphony.

Yet Willaert's idiom differed from both Verdelot's and Gombert's in taking its cue to a far greater extent than either of them did from the words. His settings consistently articulated syntactic structures with musical structure and rhetorical nuances with musical gestures and textures. In accomplishing this in the general "dialect" of the motet, Willaert's *Musica nova* madrigals participated in the larger project of elevating the vernacular. Now the singing of Italian lyrics could claim a universal significance parallel to the motet's.

This goes far toward explaining what made the sonnet Willaert's ideal vehicle. Sonnets carried rhetorical weight without overwhelming size and naturally invited bipartite division. As a formal genre and one of the most fixed of lyric forms, the sonnet had served as the traditional lyric vehicle for expressing archetypal states of emotion.[44] Literary theorists like Bembo, Ruscelli, and Tasso repeatedly noted that an inevitable corollary of the sonnet's distantly spaced rhymes and long lines (its *suono* and *numero*) was an intrinsic *gravità*. Within such obdurate matrices as these, poets could impose temporal order on a wide-ranging conceptual space.

Venetian composers found numerous possibilities for musical interpretation of the many temporal-formal schemes that sonnets offered. In the following pages I explore this idea in connection with Petrarch's *Pien d'un vago pensier che me desvia*. Among sonnets set by Willaert, *Pien d'un vago pensier* typifies one of the genre's essential strategies, that of locating a spiritual journey within fixed boundaries and demarcating its progress at a series of structurally articulated stages.[45]

44. See Christoph Kleinhenz, "The Art of the Sonnet," in *Francis Petrarch, Six Centuries Later: A Symposium,* ed. Aldo Scaglione, North Carolina Studies in the Romance Languages and Literature, Symposia, no. 3 (Chapel Hill and Chicago, 1975), esp. p. 190.

45. For discussions related to this kind of temporal structuring see Fredi Chiappelli, "An Analysis of Structuration in Petrarch's Poetry," in *Francis Petrarch, Six Centuries Later,* ed. Scaglione, pp. 105–16; and (more specifically on temporal order in the sonnet) Kleinhenz, "The Art of the Sonnet," ibid., pp. 177–91.

The lyric development I describe is completely undone in Bernardino Tomitano's inversion and rewriting of the sonnet's parts—vv. 1–8 as 8–1 and 9–14 as 14–9—in a poem included in *Rime de' piu illustri poeti italiani scelte dall'abbate Antonini. Parte prima,* ed. Annibale Antonini (Paris, 1731), fol. O v', no. 166.

Pien d'un vago pensier che me desvia	Full of a yearning thought that makes me stray away
Da tutti gli altri, e fammi al mondo ir solo,	From all others and go alone in the world,
Ad hor ad hor a me stesso m'involo,	From time to time I steal myself away from myself,
Pur lei cercando che fuggir devria;	Still seeking her whom I should flee; 4
E veggiola passar sì dolce e ria	And I see her pass so sweet and cruel
Che l'alma trema per levarsi a volo,	That my soul trembles to rise in flight,
Tal d'armati sospir conduce stuolo	Such a crowd of armed sighs she leads,
Questa bella d'Amor nemica e mia.	This lovely enemy of Love and me. 8
Ben, s'io non erro, di pietate un raggio	Surely, if I err not, I do discern a ray
Scorgo fra 'l nubiloso altero ciglio,	Of pity on her cloudy, proud brow,
Che 'n parte rasserena il cor doglioso:	Which partly clears my grieving heart: 11
Allhor raccolgo l'alma, e poi ch'i aggio	Then I collect my soul and when I have
Di scovrirle il mio mal preso consiglio,	Decided to discover to her my ill-taken counsel,
Tanto le hò a dir che 'ncominciar non oso.	I have so much to say to her that I dare not start.[46] 14

Petrarch begins with fantasy, his most fluid medium of movement. The kinetic force that governs this movement is the "vago pensier," the elusive thought that never finds satisfaction in its own self-expression. Steadily the poet moves through a series of unbounded spatial zones. Pulled in turn from the world, from himself, and toward Laura, his soul threatens to take flight, only to be regained unfulfilled. In the end he circles back to his starting point—love unexpressed. Lack of fulfillment and the continual, billowing movement it generates are thus the beginning and end of the poem and the driving impulse throughout.

Successively Petrarch aligns this series of plastic states with the sonnet's compositional structure, matching the migrations of the poet's soul with its four main sections. The first couplet removes him from the world at large to a state of solitude, while the next one rounds off the quatrain with the poet's flight from himself and quest for the beloved. The second quatrain flirts with a potential but frustrated flight of the spirit—a fantasy within the fantasy as he imagines his beloved. In the first tercet the poet hesitantly takes heart from the lady's pity, her half-lucid brow half-clearing his heavy heart. Encouraged, he braces himself to regain his soul ("raccolgo l'alma") in the last tercet—though, predictably, to no avail. These migrations are strung together with enough semantic instability and syntactic fluidity to yield a nearly continual sense of motion. Petrarch's real theme is a spiritual ebbing and flowing, a swaying of the mind. Such psychic movement is the underlying theme of the *Canzoniere,* a series of internal fluxes that never fully comes to rest and continually refers back to itself. Since the motion is constant, however, it is also static, forever circling with no intended destination but its own self-created world.

46. Here and below I have taken the liberty of adapting and arranging in verse lines Robert M. Durling's translations of Petrarch's sonnets, *Petrarch's Lyric Poems: The "Rime sparse" and Other Lyrics* (Cambridge, Mass., 1976). His translations have been invaluable to my work.

Willaert's sacred idiom, with its long-breathed lines constantly overlapping in subtly varied guises and its continual changes of textures and timbres, must have found close company in Petrarch's poetics. Through a continuous, unstable polyphonic web, it realized the meandering syntax Petrarch often utilized to embody his themes of spiritual uncertainty, evoking in musical abstractions effects parallel to Petrarch's verbal ones. (For the complete score see Ex. 14.) Indeed, Willaert set *Pien d'un vago pensier* without a single notable cadential break except for the one that divides the two parts. The few cadences that occur are so thickly buried in artful counterpoint that they pose little threat to the madrigal's general continuity. Tension is created through constant gesturing toward resolution and turning away, gesturing that recalls Zarlino's descriptions of evaded and extravagant cadences.

Willaert created this kind of polyphony by manipulating the blandest of melodic materials. His melodies largely move in conjunct paths and most of the motives are so mildly profiled as to be almost indistinct from one another. The imitations are generally loose because motivic variation frees up each voice for an independent recitation of the words. Frequently Willaert's melodies move along in chains of minims or alternate unremarkably between minims and semibreves. His *soggetti* tend to reinforce such regularities, falling out in binary repeated-note groups (as in the opening measures). With few exceptions, the composite declamatory unit holds resolutely to the minim. Most important, this relentlessly even declamation is predicated on a syllabic delivery of the words, with melismas placed few and far between.

Like plainchant, Willaert's declamation and parsing of verse make it seem almost like spoken text, with a resulting emphasis on asymmetrical linear and grammatical constructions. (Notice the localized syntactic articulation given the text at the beginning of the *seconda parte*.) Through these various musical techniques, *Pien d'un vago pensier* (like other madrigals in the *Musica nova*) emerges as a subdued musical counterpart of the decorum advocated by Venetian literati and statesmen.

At the same time, the madrigal develops its own musical version of the Bembists' corollary of *variazione* through its use of constantly shifting materials and forms. The principle of *variazione* manifests itself most clearly in the changing motivic shapes and accents assigned to different segments of the text. Willaert's preoccupation with diction meant that all the different versions declaimed (*soggetti* and their variations) had to contain equally accurate patterns of accentuation but not the same rhythmic profile, and the actual pitch content of different statements often seems almost immaterial. Thus, although the same *syllables* may be stressed in each statement of a textual fragment, the *means* of accentuation generally differ. Measures 93–103, for example, encompass disparate, overlapping versions of v. 11 in altus, cantus, and quintus. Willaert renders the third syllable of "rasserena"—the sixth of the *endecasillabo* and the line's chief poetic accent—in three different ways, each equally suited to the poem's prosody: the altus places -*re*- on the tactus in a lengthy dotted semibreve (m. 95); the cantus syncopates it on a semibreve (m. 96);

EX. 14. Willaert, *Pien d'un vago pensier che me desvia* (Petrarch, no. 169), incl.; *Musica nova* (Venice, 1559), no. 21.

(continued)

Ex. 14 *(continued)*

(continued)

Ex. 14 *(continued)*

(continued)

(continued)

(continued)

and the quintus returns it to the tactus with a ubiquitous double-minim figure (m. 97). Both altus and cantus apply agogic accent—prolongation—while the quintus relies wholly on the always unambiguous tonic accent. (A comparable kind of variety obtains with the secondary accent, *par-* of "parte" near the beginning of the line.) The combined effect of this technique is a lack of any unified polyphonic assertion of meter. In its place a constantly shifting metric polyphony coalesces—faint in its overall level of stress, but pulsating with gentle, inexorable uniformity in the background.

Only on rare occasions, when striking sounds or rhythms appear in the verse, did Willaert project text with a *single* rhythmic gesture. By contrast with the foregoing, for instance, witness in Ex. 15 the relatively consistent way he set "e rompr'ogn'aspro scoglio" (v. 6 from the five-voice *Giunto m'ha Amor fra belle e crude braccia*), with its coarse mouthfuls of *r*'s, double and triple consonantal clusters, and sonorous *a*'s and *o*'s.[47]

This avoidance of clear motivic and metric definition has a parallel in Willaert's cultivation of variegated textures. As successive combinations of freely overlapping voices roam alternately toward homophonic or imitative poles, the various parts constantly rearrange themselves in new configurations. And since every evolving configuration brings with it a new combination of voices, Willaert's vocal color takes on the look of an ever-turning kaleidoscope.[48]

47. See also the setting of "Romper le pietre," mm. 98ff. from *Mentre che 'l cor.*
48. Jonathan Marcus Miller extends my work on Willaert and Rore to argue that both composers constructed their textures in such a way as to bring out clusters of sound, which were in turn designed to help project textual meaning; see "Word-Sound and Musical Texture in the Mid-Sixteenth-Century Venetian Madrigal" (Ph.D. diss., University of North Carolina at Chapel Hill, 1991).

E x . 15 .　Willaert, *Giunto m'ha Amor fra belle e crude braccia* (Petrarch, no. 171), mm. 52–59; *Musica nova* (Venice, 1559), no. 11.

These kaleidoscopic effects do not diminish Willaert's ability to shape Petrarch's conceptual patterning in music, as the structural summary of *Pien d'un vago pensier* in Table 5 makes plain. The schemata of Table 5 necessarily give only a crude picture of the real articulative events in the piece, since the cadences, while intelligible contrapuntally as two-voice formations, are almost always obscured and enervated by the surrounding polyphonic activity of the other voices. Note, for example, that the first cadence, to the perfect octave c/C in tenor and bassus in m. 16, is thoroughly overlapped by multiple, varied assertions of the motive on "e fammi al mondo ir solo" throughout the upper registers. However clear-cut such a two-voice cadence may be, the overall impression conveyed is one of continuity. In a texture like this one, fine gradations in articulation can be projected through the relative strength of preparation and resolution. But such preparation and resolution are rarely unequivocal except at

TABLE 5
Musico-Poetic Structure in Willaert's
Pien d'un vago pensier che me desvia

Bar	Poetic Line Ended	Grammatical Unit	Cadential Pitches/ Voices	Bass or Lowest Voice	Cadence Type/ Remarks
16	2	dependent clause	c/C (T/B)	C	perfect (with T continuing to a)
23	3	1st main clause (start)	ee/c (C/T)	c	half, improperly resolved
30	4	1st main clause	ff/a (C/T)	F	evaded (to m 13th)
32	4	1st main clause	cc/C (VI/B)	C	bass drops P 5th
34	4	1st main clause	f/b-flat (V/T)	b-flat	P 5th
36	4	1st main clause	ff/dd (C/VI)	b-flat	m 3rd
46	5	2d main clause (start)	a (A)	F	
63	8	double period (vv. 1–8) completed	cc/c (C/T)	c	perfect (with T continuing)
68	8	double period (vv. 1–8) completed	g/C (A/B)	C	P 5th
71	8	double period (vv. 1–8) completed	cc/c (VI/V)	c	perfect
73	8	double period (vv. 1–8) completed	—	C	plagal
87	10	if-then main clause	cc/c (C/A)	C	perfect
95	10	if-then main clause	g/c (VI/B)	c	P 5th
(99)	11	if-then main clause	cc/g (C/VI)	C	strong textual cadence only
(102)	11	if-then main clause	a/c (V/T)	F	strong textual cadence only
(103)	11	if-then main clause	d/B-flat (A/B)	B-flat	strong textual cadence only
105	12a	final point	ff/b-flat (C/V)	B-flat	P 5th
108	12a	final point	f/F (T/B)	F	perfect
128	14	final point	f/F (VI/V)	F	perfect

the end of the *prima* or *seconda parte* or at exceptional rhetorical moments and, in any case, are always complicated by other factors—especially texture.

The next cadential gesture at the end of v. 3 (mm. 22–23) presents a different situation, related to the ubiquitous technique that Zarlino dubbed "fuggir la cadenza." The cadence is conspicuously prepared but its resolution is foiled as it moves from an intended penultimate sonority on a C-major triad to one on c-minor. The cadential cantus falls silent at its expected moment of arrival on ff at m. 24 (one of Zarlino's standard "evasion" techniques), replaced by a jarring cross relation, ee/e-flat, with the quintus.

Despite this constant undercutting, Willaert's complex cadential formations do not hinder the goal of supporting Petrarch's linguistic and thematic articulations.

Quite the contrary; they aid it by complementing Petrarch's verbal hierarchy with a musical one, at least within the subtle band of utterance Willaert's idiom allows. Willaert's *Musica nova* settings generally vary the degree to which cadences are made strong or weak through a judicious deployment of perfect and imperfect cadences, extravagant cadences, different sorts of evasions, and rests. In *Pien d'un vago pensier* Willaert varied articulative weight, modifying the number of cadential gestures successively deployed by shifting voice pairs for a given portion of text. Mild but calculated cadential repetition is key to such a strategy. By means of sheer repetition, Willaert strengthened the conclusions of each of the independent clauses that end the two quatrains (mm. 30, 32, 34, and 36; mm. 63, 68, 71, and 73)—even though the gestures taken singly are not especially strong—and in accordance with Zarlino's dictum that textual repetitions be limited to significant parts of a text. Cadences are also positioned carefully in different tessituras according to grammatical weight. Thus while the lower voices bury their cadence under continuous upper-voice melody when ending a mere dependent clause at m. 16, three of the four cadences that end the main clause of the first quatrain are exposed in the uppermost register (mm. 30–36).

Verse 12 shows how shrewdly Willaert coordinates these articulations with the main structural divisions of the sonnet. At this juncture, two striking cadences demarcate the poet's progress following the rhetorically crucial "Allor raccolgo l'alma." Though standing in formal isolation, prosodically unhinged, these words signal the poem's spiritual turning point. Willaert's setting highlights them with an independent melody and a turn to somewhat broadened rhythmic gestures. As the declamation slows, the semibreves allow the resonant *a*'s, *o*'s, and the double consonants to breathe, creating assonance in accented and unaccented syllables alike and a deceleration that marks at once the text's grammatical structure and its "grave" rhetorical character.[49]

The value of Willaert's reading is both immediate and contextual, since it sets up the musico-dramatic pacing of the remainder of the sonnet. The long phrases subsequently assigned to "e poi ch'i aggio / Di scovrirle il mio mal preso consiglio" (vv. 12–13) in order to span the enjambment contrast with the relatively short ones that have just been heard. Further, by returning to a predominant minim motion, the music resumes its insistent pace and starts to marshall the more bustling texture with which Willaert generally approached sectional endings. Willaert sustains both qualities through the final verse and heightens their rhetorical effects with a flood of closely spaced entrances for "Tanto le ho à dir," a new voice entering nearly every semibreve from mm. 116 to 123.

Willaert's organization of cadences supports these subtle interactions of meaning and prosody as much as it does grammatical weight. To consider how this operates,

49. Willaert generally used this technique to distinguish the articulations between quatrains and tercets. See, for instance, the transitions from vv. 4–5 in *L'aura mia sacra* (m. 49) and *Giunto m'ha Amor* (mm. 39–40); and from vv. 11–12 in *L'aura mia sacra* (mm. 92–93) and *Cantai, hor piango* (mm. 96–97); Willaert, *Opera omnia*, vol. 13.

let us assume (with Zarlino) that a background modal conception underlies the madrigal's overall pitch plan. Zarlino assigned *Pien d'un vago pensier* to mode 11,[50] transposed Ionian authentic as conceived within Glareanus's twelve-mode numbering system, or mode 5 (authentic Lydian) in the traditional eight-mode system. Cantus, tenor, and quintus are all in authentic ranges, sextus, altus, and bassus in plagal. Willaert's setting concentrates cadences on the primary cadential degrees of the mode, the final F and confinal c. As shown in Table 5, the dependent clause of vv. 1–2 moves to the confinal, while three of the cadences ending the main clause in v. 4 (mm. 30, 34, and 36) form cadences on the final (albeit enfeebled by lower voices moving to the secondary degrees a, b-flat, and dd, respectively). In this mode all theorists of modal polyphony ranked the medial a just below the final and confinal in terms of cadential weight, and most named E, D, G, and b-flat as secondary degrees, permissible for internal cadences.[51] The remainder of the *prima parte* constructs a neat bit of tonal architecture, with a supporting the main clause that begins the second quatrain (m. 46) and a series of cadences emphasizing the final's antipole of C in the approach and conclusion of the octave. Not until the clause "Allor raccolgo l'alma" returns in v. 12 does Willaert cadence again on the final, and there he does so twice—once on the fifth ff/b-flat (m. 105), next on a perfect octave, f/F (m. 108).

Yet the point should be made again that none of these cadences comes close to halting or delaying the ongoing polyphonic motion. As a result of this continuity, everything takes place within a general gestalt of sameness, a contrapuntal feature of all *Musica nova* madrigals but a particular tonal characteristic of those in F-mollis. As if dabbing on empty canvases Willaert brightened them only with the lightest coloristic touches, in bursts like firefly shimmer, to conjure up vivid local moments.

Pitch color thus manages—and is managed by means of—two basic strategies: one involves choosing pitches gauged to help bring out hierarchic interrelationships of poetic syntax; the other involves accommodating the exigencies of these syntactic concerns to the subdued demeanor of the whole collection. At the local level of coloristic events Willaert pits relative stability against instability toward expressive ends, just as he does at the more architectonic level of cadential design. Just before restoring the final F in v. 12, for example, he presses B-flats and E-flats plaintively on the "cor doglioso" of the relative clause in v. 11. This turn to the flat side easily catches the ear, despite its mildness, because Willaert uses it only rarely. (Another set of E-flat inflections [mm. 19 and 24] follows the self-exodus narrated in v. 3, "Ad hor ad hor a me stesso m'involo.")

Flatted inflections often participate in larger processes of stabilization and destabilization that are regulated by Willaert's frequent use of circles of fifths. The preva-

---

50. *Istitutioni harmoniche,* p. 333.
51. For a summary of theorists' writings on this matter, see Bernhard Meier, *The Modes of Classical Vocal Polyphony Described according to the Sources,* trans. Ellen S. Beebe, rev. ed. (New York, 1988), pp. 101–22 (and for discussion of the cadence plan of a work by Wert in the same mode, pp. 158ff.).

lence of circle-of-fifth progressions offsets the potential that the melodies and coun-terpoint might be enervated by a certain aimlessness. In the passage just discussed, Willaert explores the flat side within fifth progressions in a way that reinforces poetic motion toward the syntactic/rhetorical goal: the E-flat triad of m. 18 moves backward through a circle of fifths all the way to one on a-minor (m. 21); and a briefer circle of fifths from a B-flat-major triad to one on d-minor (mm. 23–25) over-arches the false resolution of the C-major sonority to c-minor.[52] This regulation of the flat side through the strong harmonic directedness of fifth progressions allows Willaert to convey the text in a way that appeals directly to the senses, instead of simply matching the poet's flight in a purely formal or iconic way.

Some of these circles of fifths do not project verbal meaning directly but simply help propel the counterpoint toward an imminent syntactic goal. In mm. 120–22, for instance, Willaert intensifies the repetitions of "tanto le ho a dir" by means of a fifth progression from a d-minor triad to one on B-flat. This is only the longest of several sequences of fifths that help strengthen the drive toward the final cadence (cf. mm. 114–16 and 125–26). In tonally static madrigals like this one, which oscillate along an F-C axis with little real movement toward an alternate tonal target, the sense of harmonic direction provides a vital source of kinetic energy.[53]

Willaert's coloristic techniques play another role in subtly resolving local syntac-tic ambiguities. To understand the interaction of tonal color and syntax at this local level, one needs to consider how Willaert copes with Petrarch's complex verbal con-structions. Invariably, *Musica nova* settings parse words as prose rather than as verse, ostensibly linking proselike readings with dignity and gravity in the same way literary theorists like Daniello and Tomitano did in advocating proselike syntax for poets writing high lyric verse.[54] In these madrigals the juncture between words and music had thus fully shifted from the poetic line to the syntactic unit. As noted ear-lier, this meant that the enjambments favored by literati for sonnets ran rampant in Venetians' musical phrasings,[55] causing the textual units to fall out in unpoetic and highly asymmetrical arrangements.

Even this rule of thumb could not produce all the necessary solutions about how to parse a given text, however, since not all verbal constructions unequivocally sug-gested a single prose reading. Indeed, *Pien d'un vago pensier* includes one of the most ambiguous, Latinate lines Petrarch ever wrote, v. 8: "Questa bella d'Amor

---

52. Cf. also the circle of fifths from the end of m. 96 to m. 98.

53. Gary Tomlinson has noted this phenomenon as part of the pastoral topos employed by Wert, Marenzio, and Monteverdi, in *Monteverdi and the End of the Renaissance* (Berkeley and Los Angeles, 1987); see also Chap. 8 below, nn. 24 and 25.

54. See Chap. 5 above, nn. 122 and 133.

55. In addition to the comments on enjambment cited in Chap. 5 above, nn. 142–44, see also Torquato Tasso's praise of Giovanni della Casa's use of the technique in his "Lezione sopra *Questa mor-tal vita*," discussed in Gary Tomlinson, "Rinuccini, Peri, Monteverdi, and the Humanist Heritage of Opera" (Ph.D. diss., University of California at Berkeley, 1979), pp. 55–57.

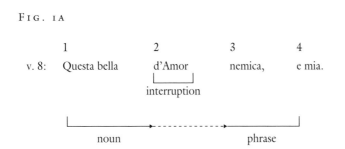

nemica, e mia."[56] Structurally, this is a line that evokes the mercurial quality of Petrarch's elusive lady. It rends the Petrarchan oxymoron on the beloved, the "bella nemica," with the intrusive "d'Amor" to form four disconnected grammatical units, as shown in Fig. 1a. Here the four constituents stand in a kind of chiastic relationship to one another, each of them one position removed from its proper neighbor. But the elements can also be considered in another way, as suggested in Fig. 1b. In this reading "questa bella" forms a complete and independent substantive, if a disarmingly casual one in Petrarchan discourse for reference to Laura. "Nemica" then counts as a second noun phrase troping "questa bella," and "d'Amor" a prepositional phrase defining simply "nemica." The possessive "mia," free-floating outside the main frame of the line, might be thought to define either "bella" or "nemica," or both, depending on how the reader perceives the line; its indeterminacy proceeds from the vagueness of the substantive, without which "mia" has no point of reference. Since Petrarchan commentators of Willaert's time seem consistently to have read the line as in Fig. 1a (as we will see Willaert appears to have done also), it seems fair to take this as our point of departure.[57]

The severed noun phrase of line 8 surprises, since even Petrarch's mannered norms did not usually allow for it. But the ambiguities thus created are a vital part of the line's rhetorical effect and its meaning. "Amor" is not only the intruder in the syntactic process but the culprit in the fractious vision of the poem as a whole. As hinted above, the witty dissociation of "e mia," combined with the line's lack of an unambiguous substantive, robs it of a clear grammatical affiliation and hence mean-

56. For a fuller discussion of Willaert's syntactic strategies see my "Composer as Exegete: Interpretations of Petrarchan Syntax in the Venetian Madrigal," *Studi musicali* 18 (1989): 203–38, of which pp. 212–16 have been adapted for what follows. A broader appraisal of medieval and Renaissance concepts of syntax may be found in W. Keith Percival, "Deep and Surface Structure Concepts in Renaissance and Medieval Syntactic Theory," in *History of Linguistic Thought and Contemporary Linguistics,* ed. Herman Parret (Berlin and New York, 1976), pp. 238–53.

57. Sixteenth-century commentators tended to restore the oxymoron with the paraphrase "Questa bella nemica d'Amor, e mia," with no comma after "bella" that would designate it a noun. See, for example, *Sonetti, canzoni, e triomphi di Messer Francesco Petrarca con la spositione di Bernardino Daniello da Lucca* (Venice, 1541), fol. 113; and *Le rime del Petrarca brevemente sposte per Lodovico Castelvetro . . .* (Basel, 1582), p. 312.

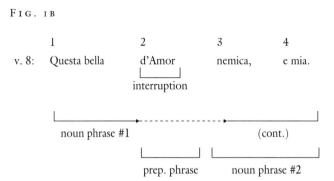

ing (*my* lovely one? *my* lovely enemy? *mine* and Love's?). The disorientation of "mia" comments on the slippery nature of the thing possessed; yet its dangling isolation, a structural means of semantic emphasis, accentuates at the same time the quality of possession.

Given Willaert's concern for linguistic coherence the line presented declamatory problems and perhaps inevitably invited multiple, fragmentary readings.[58] By offering a number of different fragments of the line Willaert was able to comment both on the nature of the fragmentation and on the grammatical interrelationships of the verse. Much of it he parsed in such a way as to unify the noun phrase "questa bella nemica": two outer voices initially present "questa bella" alone with a separate, lingering melodic figure, but immediately afterward all six declaim the verse in integral phrases up to the word "nemica." This bit of text, the one most frequently stated, fuses in a single melodic gesture the subject "nemica" with its qualifying adjective "bella." We might say that Willaert admitted the ambiguity and then resolved it: "Questa bella . . . ," "Questa bella *d'Amor nemica.*"

In the tenor, by contrast, beginning in m. 62, Willaert linked the other disjointed verbal elements indicated in Fig. 1a by deploying a different textual fragment: "d'Amor nemica, e mia." This is the only time in this lengthy exposition when "e mia" joins directly any other portion of the verse, and the reason for it seems clear. Without the suspended adjectives "questa bella," no consolidation of the noun phrase (as obtained by ending with the word "nemica") is required. The phrase "d'Amor nemica, e mia" instead serves to unify words that function in essence as two prepositional phrases: "d'Amor" and "e mia" (that is, "d'Amor, e di me"). Now, for the only time in the whole passage, "e mia" is sung twice in a row (tenor, mm. 65–67)—repeated, that is, *without* first returning to an earlier part of the verse. Through this repetition and other isolated statements, Willaert took advantage of the line's grammatical self-sufficiency up to the word "nemica" to heighten the broken pathos that "e mia" inflicts on the octave's ending.

58. For another example of varied parsing in Willaert's settings (of which there are many) see my comments on his *Cantai, hor piango, e non men di dolcezza,* vv. 1–2, in Chap. 9 nn. 41ff., below.

Just as telling as the many textual fragments that Willaert used here are those he avoided. Most important, the whole verse is never set to an unbroken melodic phrase. We should not underestimate the significance of this in a lengthy passage that provides so many diverse statements. Willaert seems to have considered presentation of the verse in a single phrase unintelligible, or insufficiently interpretive. Also, the words of the prepositional phrase "d'Amor" are invariably joined to the succeeding subject "nemica," as if one were a necessary rhetorical consequent of the other. Willaert's consistent linking of these words reduces the confusion created in the verse by the interjected "d'Amor" while preserving its descriptive role (this of-Love enemy).

To return, finally, to the question of tonal color, Willaert exploits the contrast of stable and unstable pitches to help underscore syntactic articulations. The dispassionate pitches F and C function as recurrent, if fleeting, points of repose for the words *nemica* and *mia,* words that conclude the severed syntactic units to which each belongs. The effect is striking at the two perfect cadences on C of mm. 63 and 71 and at the cadence on the perfect fifth g/C at m. 68. But it can also be perceived at numerous melodic markers. If we follow the *soggetto* in the cantus from m. 53 through the cadence in m. 63 and continue tracing the text repetitions in the cantus through to m. 73, we find an almost dogged insistence on ff and cc as points of departure (mm. 60, 63, and 70), arrival (mm. 60, 63, 69), and melodic accentuation (m. 57, 59, 65, and 66). When the *soggetto* appears in the altus in m. 64, its melodic line is anchored between F and c at mm. 68 and 71, respectively.

The way these pitches function tonally echoes the madrigal's placid opening exposition, especially in mm. 1–17, where F and C dominate the tonal space, undulating back and forth but essentially locked in tonal stasis. They form a striking contrast to the delicate E-flat inflections in the setting of v. 8, which instead suggest incompleteness and uncertainty. Willaert uses these accidentals to shade the text locally: they occur only on the syntactically open and ambiguous words "bella" and "d'Amor"—a pair of E-flats on the first syllable of "bella" in m. 56 and one on the first syllable of "d'Amor" in m. 62. In this way, both here and elsewhere in the madrigal, flatted inflections form restless counterpoises to more tranquil surrounding areas.

In singling out *Pien d'un vago pensier* for discussion I have tried to represent Willaert's private style at its most undemonstrative—which is to say its most typical. Where he might have opted for gripping contrasts or dramatic expressivity, Willaert instead kept to a subdued poetic reading. The paucity of all but the weakest articulation, the ubiquitous motivic variation, shifting textures, and kaleidoscopic shifts of vocal color yield a sense of continual, quiet unfolding that Willaert's discursive declamation does little to disturb. The constantly varied materials that produce such a dense contrapuntal web served, I have argued, to project the attitude of decorum advocated by Venetian literati. Beyond this, the sacred rhetoric Willaert adapted encoded the quality of reverence—a reverence that points outwardly toward the unattainable woman, but covertly to a rarified discourse of self-contemplation and lyric creation.

It was thus precisely through this highly localized process of incessant, subtle variation, rather than a patchwork of contrasts, that Willaert's late madrigals were able to meet contemporary rhetorical ideals of decorum and variation. This localized instantiation of rhetorical principles is consistent with the particular way in which Bembo codified them. Recall that his dialectic of *variazione* took shape through the opposing qualities of *gravità* and *piacevolezza,* whose interactions he (and his followers) mostly illustrated in shadings of local events. At the level of the poetic line this meant contrasts of accents, phonemes and letters, elisions, and syllable lengths; and at the next higher level those of line lengths, rhymes, and rhyme schemes. As a rule Willaert departed from making delicate chiaroscuro effects through timbre, meter, and pitch only when his text embodied clear-cut oppositions that cried out for bald contrasts. One such instance, much-cited in modern literature, is the exposition of his six-voice *Aspro core e selvaggio e cruda voglia* (no. 265), whose opening two verses are particularly susceptible to dialectical opposition.[59]

Aspro core e selvaggio e cruda voglia	A harsh, savage heart and cruel desire
In dolce, humile, angelica figura	In a sweet, humble, angelic form

Willaert echoed the verses' natural declamatory rhythms by contrasting the choppy dissonance of the poet's charges in v. 1 with the graceful *sdrucciolo* accent of his encomiastic "angelica" in v. 2 (Ex. 16). The declamation of the first is martial, based on the tactus; much of the second gently syncopated. As Claude V. Palisca has pointed out, a wealth of linear and contrapuntal progressions also articulate qualities of *gravità* and *piacevolezza.* Major sixths moving to perfect fifths and parallel major thirds—both described by Vincenzo Galilei as justifiable transgressions of counterpoint rules for the sake of imitating the text—dominate the harmonic movement in the first verse, but disappear in the flatted environment of the second.[60] Verse 1

59. See the discussions by Dean T. Mace, "Pietro Bembo and the Literary Origins of the Italian Madrigal," *The Musical Quarterly* 55 (1969): 78–80, Claude V. Palisca, *Humanism in Italian Renaissance Musical Thought* (New Haven, 1986), pp. 357–67, and Armen Carapetyan, "The *Musica Nova* of Adriano Willaert: With a Special Reference to the Humanistic Society of 16th-Century Venice" (Ph.D. diss., Harvard University, 1945), pp. 188 and 255–57.

60. The rule violated is one making imperfect consonances go to the closest perfect ones. Palisca notes that Galilei drew attention to the device in his *Fronimo dialogo, nel quale si contengono le vere, et necessarie regole del intavolare la musica nel liuto* (Venice, 1568), p. 13: "Patisce secondariamente eccettione ne l'imitatione delle parole, come bene lo manifestò fra gl'altri eccellenti musici in piu luoghi il famoso Adriano, & particolarmente nel principio di quella sua dotta Canzone, che gia compose à sei voci, qual comincia. Aspro core, & et seluaggio & cruda voglia, dove passa piu volte (per esprimere con gratia tal concetto,) non Solo dalla Sesta maggiore alla Quinta ma da una Terza maggior à l'altra col mouimento congiunto, & piacendoui serverò à vn'altra volta il mostrarui maggiormente l'eccelentia di questo condimento della musica" ([This may be broken] in imitating the words, as the famous Adrian did (among other composers) in the beginning of that learned music he composed for six voices on the sonnet of Petrarch which begins *Aspro core, e selvaggio, & cruda voglia.* There several times, in order to express the subject with grace, he passes not only from a major sixth to a fifth, but from a major third to another by conjunct movement. I shall save for another time to demonstrate the excellence of this musical seasoning); quoted in *Humanism in Italian Renaissance Musical Thought,* pp. 357 and 362 n. 60.

E x . 16. Willaert, *Aspro core e selvaggio e cruda voglia* (Petrarch, no. 265), mm. 1–22; *Musica nova* (Venice, 1559), no. 14.

(continued)

moves largely by melodic major seconds and major thirds and v. 2 by minor seconds and thirds and minor sixths, thus complementing the first verse's consonantal clusters and the liquids of the second (and recalling Zarlino's injunctions in Part IV, Chapter 32). Palisca also notes the tendency of the bass to move up by fifth and down by fourth for v. 1 and vice versa (down by fifth and up by fourth) for v. 2, tendencies Galilei associated with happiness, excitation, virility, and naturalness on the one hand and sad and subdued effects on the other.[61]

Willaert's interest in such dichotomies may seem clear in this instance, but it is rare that his *Musica nova* settings conform so straightforwardly to Bembist principles. Only three other cases, all again mainly notable for their *exordia,* are as striking in this respect as *Aspro core.* These include the pair of six-voice settings, *I piansi, hor canto, che 'l celeste lume* and *Cantai, hor piango, et non men di dolcezza,*[62] and the seven-voice *Liete e pensose, accompagnate e sole.*[63] Both of the first two begin with vivid antitheses that Willaert matched with madrigalisms: florid upturned melismas for singing and doleful sustained notes for weeping. In *I piansi* the image of weeping also invites a chain of suspensions (a virtual requirement at midcentury), here realized in varied entries of a stepwise descending motive alternating on arsis and thesis. (Quite unusually Willaert delayed the entrance of "hor canto" all the way until m. 9 and with it the establishment of the minim surface rhythm, which normally prevails after the first measure or two.)

The third setting that plays obviously with this sort of musical dialectic again embodies dualities codified by Bembo, especially in its octave.

"Liete e pensose, accompagnate e sole,	"Happy and sad, in company and alone,
Donne che ragionando ite per via:	Ladies who go talking by the way,
Ov'è la vita, ove la morte mia?	Where is my life, my death?
Perché non è con voi com'ella sòle?"	Why is she not with you as she is wont to be?" 4
"Liete siam per memoria di quel sole,	"Happy are we in thinking of that sun;
Dogliose per sua dolce compagnia	We are sad because we lack her company,
La qual ne toglie invidia et gelosia	Which envious jealousy takes from us,
Che d'altrui ben quasi suo mal si dole."	Grieving at another's good as if at its own harm." 8

61. See Vincenzo Galilei, *Dialogo della musica antica, et della moderna* (Florence, 1581), p. 76.

62. As in Petrarch's *Canzoniere,* the *Musica nova* places them side by side (though in reverse order). Discussions of this pair in the secondary literature can be found in Einstein, *The Italian Madrigal* 1:335–37; Willaert, *Opera omnia* 13:iv and v; Carapetyan, "The *Musica nova* of Adriano Willaert," pp. 164, 188, and 259–60; and Howard Mayer Brown, *Music in the Renaissance* (Englewood Cliffs, N.J., 1976), pp. 200–202. On *Cantai, hor piango* see also Bernhard Meier, "Rhetorical Aspects of Renaissance Modes," *Journal of the Royal Musical Association* 115 (1990): 183–84.

63. *Opera omnia* 13:108–14. *Liete e pensose* is one of the two madrigals (along with *Aspro core*) singled out by Mace for discussion ("The Literary Origins of the Italian Madrigal," pp. 80–83). Among the many other discussions of the madrigal are: Erich Hertzmann, *Adrian Willaert in der weltlichen Vokalmusik seiner Zeit: Ein Beitrag zur Entwicklungsgeschichte der niederländisch-französischen und italienischen Liedformen in der ersten Hälfte des 16. Jahrhunderts* (Leipzig, 1931), p. 53; Carapetyan, "The *Musica nova* of Adriano Willaert," pp. 118, 148, 185–86; Einstein, *The Italian Madrigal* 1:339; Willaert, *Opera omnia* 13:v; Helga Meier, "Zur Chronologie der *Musica Nova* Adriaen Willaerts," *Analecta musicologica* 12 (1973): 78; B. Meier, *The Modes,* pp. 126–28, 415; and David Alan Nutter, "The Italian Polyphonic Dialogue of the Sixteenth Century" (Ph.D. diss., University of Nottingham, 1978), 1:55.

These were lines ripe for the madrigalist's picking. Throughout the octave positive sentiments are keyed to the bright vowels *e* and *i* ("liete" and "vita," as well as the more neutral *a*, as in "accompagnate") and gloomier ones to the dark vowel *o* ("pensose," "sole," "morte," "dogliose"). Some of the contrasting terms are set in parallel structures that help tag rhythmically both meaning and sound: in v. 1 "liete" and "accompagnate" pair up as the first and corresponding terms in each syntactic entity and "pensose" and "sole" as the second—the second half of the verse thus echoing the first.

By articulating the syntactic inflections with rests and providing certain bright-voweled words with rising melodies and dark-voweled words with descending ones, Willaert intensified such parallelisms, as seen in Ex. 17. The four-voice group assigned to the first quatrain is divided into four sections, essentially one for each adjective. Willaert distinguished each through the contrast of major and minor intervals, both vertical and linear, in the uppermost voice: the major chords G and C and a melodic major second fall on "liete" and the minor chords a and d and a prominently accented melodic minor second, f to e, on "e pensose." Thereafter the "morte"/"vita" antithesis of v. 3 is expressed through similar means and further set off by parallel melodic motives in the altus—three repeated d's turning upward on "vita," downward on "morte."

Verse 5 summarizes the diverse syntactic and sentimental elements of the initial quatrain. By transferring to its outer limits both the words flanking v. 1—"liete" and "sole"—Petrarch clarified their semantic relationship. The ladies' metaphoric recollection of Laura as that "sole," still resonating with its initial adjectival meaning, reminds the informed reader that she represents inseparably both happiness and loneliness. The new context of "liete" and "sole" in v. 5 thus enriches the words' meaning and consolidates them syntactically. As "Liete e pensose, accompagnate e sole" is recast as: "Liete siam per memoria di quel sole," that same "sole" which first conveyed desolation becomes, after the triple pun, a metaphor for the beloved who "sole" (both "alone" and "like the sun") in her radiance can produce happiness. Willaert's setting of v. 5 reflects this consolidation of symbol, syntax, and sense by delivering it in a single phrase, uninterrupted save short rests by cantus and sextus. It also reinterprets the final a-minor chord of v. 1's "sole" (m. 8) as A-major for that of v. 5 (m. 41). Moreover, the sextus and tenor, in mimicking the opening melodic material of septimus and altus, strengthen the correspondence between this verse and the first, helping to reinforce its special role in the octave.

I have touched on these four madrigals not only because all four trade in what are for Willaert uncommonly extroverted exordia, but because they have been the works most often cited from the *Musica nova*. In an important sense, they have formed the basis of widespread conceptions about Willaert's style. Their exemplary status in the musicological literature has lent support to certain representations of

EX. 17.   Willaert, *Liete e pensose, accompagnate e sole* (Petrarch, no. 222), mm. 1–42; *Musica nova* (Venice, 1559), no. 23.

(continued)

E X . 1 7 *(continued)*

256

Willaert's new style as expressively vivid and given to musical symbolism, a representation first made by Gustave Reese. In asserting this, Reese isolated in the encyclopedic preserves of *Music in the Renaissance* only one tiny passage from the collection, a brief melisma on "cantando" from the otherwise archly spare *Mentre che 'l cor.*[64] His account of *Musica nova* style antedated the cross-disciplinary thinking that has since linked Willaert's madrigals to Bembo's ideas; it fell in better with teleological portrayals of madrigalian developments that sought to show the genre's increasing skill at mimesis over the course of the century. Like other such portrayals, a baldly mimetic approach seemed to offer the only tangible evidence of music's growing bond with words. It is not surprising that Reese had little else to say about the collection, since the reified textual-motivic links he wished to exemplify had in reality no prominent place in it.

Subsequent accounts have refined thinking about this repertory, yet something of the literalist impulse that guided Reese seems to underlie the expectations that have determined not only *how* we interpret but *what* we interpret—which examples have been chosen for close readings. Implicitly, at least, this literalism seems also to have shaped conceptions about the sorts of factors that must have governed Willaert's own readings, especially about how he realized Bembo's ideas: hence the censure, especially of Willaert's stark melody and undifferentiated pacing, that so often alloys praise of Willaert's late music, and the worrying over its lack of contrast.[65] Yet if, as I have insisted, strong juxtapositions were anathema to a Bembist idea of style, then Willaert's expressive reticence should cause neither surprise nor disappointment. I would view his subtly varied *soggetti,* plain rhythm, modest melody, and continuous musical fabric instead as carefully marshalled participants in his *musica nova,* a secular music intended to have no precedent or equal in weight and restraint. Willaert's personal conception—shared by his patrons, performers, and listeners—of the *Musica nova* as a monument to a newly conceived secular genre of the highest order seems clear from any number of features, both internal and external, that I have discussed: its compendious nature including four-, five-, six-, and seven-voice works, its mixing of madrigals with motets, its almost exclusive setting of Petrarch's poems, and its setting of complete sonnets.

Even those works by Willaert farthest from the *Musica nova,* his *canzoni villanesche,* seem to confirm the idea that his serious madrigals emerged from a

---

64. Rev. ed. (New York, 1959), p. 324.
65. See Edward E. Lowinsky, who suggests that humanistic demands for perfect declamation were the culprit hindering Willaert's ability to write good melodies: "Willaert's music has no easy appeal. Despite its masterly construction and notwithstanding its virtues of conciseness and elegance, its richness in harmonic color, its unexcelled adaption of the text, its variety of rhythmic and metric structure, it has a certain heaviness, hard to define, rooted perhaps in the absence of a true melodic inspiration. Yet the much freer flight of melody in his four-part *ricercari* suggests that the exigencies of a humanistically impeccable text setting in all the voices of a polyphonic complex of four, five, six, and more parts worked as a serious impediment to the free unfolding of melody" (*Medici Codex* 1:80). Similar reservations are voiced in Brown, "Words and Music," p. 228, and Carapetyan, "The *Musica Nova* of Adriano Willaert," pp. 115 and 147.

Bembist, hence Ciceronian, conception of stylistic propriety.[66] His conscious sense of purpose is evident from the way he codified the lighter style and segregated it (with help from Venetian printers) in separate publications. Indeed, the wholesale bifurcation of secular music into discrete genres, high and low, in Venetian musical production of the 1540s provides one of the clearest signs that Willaert's decorous fashioning of the madrigal was no failure of inspiration but one of the most concerted acts of Ciceronianism to emerge from early modern Venice.[67]

66. The point is mentioned in Brown ("Words and Music," p. 229), who suggests that diverse genres in the music of Willaert and his students reflected Bembo's classical advocation of different stylistic levels. See also James Haar, who discusses the concern for genre in the period of Bembo's influence in *Essays on Italian Poetry and Music in the Renaissance, 1350–1600* (Berkeley and Los Angeles, 1986), pp. 117–18; and idem, "Self-Consciousness about Style, Form, and Genre in 16th-Century Music," *Studi musicali* 3 (1974): 219–31; and Nino Pirrotta, "Willaert and the *Canzone Villanesca*," in *Music and Culture in Italy from the Middle Ages to the Baroque: A Collection of Essays* (Cambridge, Mass., 1984); p. 179.

67. The argument laid out in Michèle Fromson's "Themes of Exile in Willaert's *Musica nova,*" *JAMS* 47 (1994): 442–87, first came to my attention as this book was in press. Fromson's study contributes to our understanding of the religious background of Florentine republicans but reduces the multivalent cultural geography in which the *Musica nova* evolved to a single Florentine solution, reading the print's motet and Petrarchan sonnet texts as having registered solely in Florentine terms. I perceive a Florentine accent in Rore's first book but much less of one in Willaert's *Musica nova,* and I would question whether the romantic narrative of "heroic struggle" and "suicide" (pp. 465–66) that Fromson imposes on Florentine exiles (cf. p. 29 above) can be readily made to fit Neri Capponi, who is in fact the only known Florentine patron of the print. The crucial evidentiary basis of Fromson's thesis is the claim that Willaert's motets and madrigals evoked the Florentines' situation by quoting chants linked to loss and exile, but it is useful to remember here that Willaert's whole modal-melodic language was chant-based and that his melodic style in any case avoided distinctive motives.

Books One and Two for Five Voices

Willaert's madrigals, like his orderly place in Venice's cultural institutions, form a study in temperance and regularities. Smooth rhythmic pace, orderly projection of syntax, controlled polyphony, and subdued motivic gestures all merged in the style Willaert cultivated for the *Musica nova*. The consolidation of musical and personal identities with civic image that Willaert embodied as Venice's chief representative of musical decorum stemmed from mutual accommodations between composer and state. Indeed, as we saw in the Preface, the Procuratori who had hired Willaert expressly commended him as a deliberate, cautious man—a reputation admirers elaborated in his role as patriarchal head of the Venetian musical establishment.

Against the patterns of order and moderation that repeat themselves with such uniformity throughout Willaert's biographical and musical legacy, Rore cuts a decidedly more eccentric figure. This is something of a puzzle, since it was Willaert and Rore together whose madrigals of the 1540s formed the pillars of a single musico-literary project. Even a cursory comparison of the madrigals in Willaert's *Musica nova* with those in Rore's *Primo libro a 5* of 1542 reveals correspondences between them that support this association. Both collections are based on Petrarchan sonnets set motetlike in two parts in a broad, contemplative vein. Both embed Petrarch's convoluted language in a dense mass of freely imitative polyphony, shaping it in motives that subtly change from voice to voice. And most important, both attend scrupulously to rhetorical qualities of text—sound, accent, verbal figure, and syntax.

At the same time, Rore showed remarkable independence at age twenty-six when his first book emerged seemingly out of nowhere—independence in both musical style and manner of presentation. In 1542 his works had apparently never been printed before, even in anthologies. Despite this, his *Primo libro* included, rather unusually, only his own works. Both that book and his *Secondo libro* of 1544 lacked the dedications to patrons who typically helped support composers and underwrite their prints. Neither book contains any of the same Petrarchan lyrics found in the *Musica nova,* although at least some of Willaert's settings of them must have existed by those years. Moreover, the *Primo libro* transmits some of the most tortured lyrics in Petrarch's *Canzoniere,* together with several remarkably dramatic modern texts. Whatever external impulses may have urged these poetic choices on him, Rore stands apart in this respect. Not until his *Terzo libro a 5* of 1548 did he print a setting of a sonnet also set by Willaert, *Quando fra l'altre donne ad hora ad hora* (no. 7 in the *Musica nova*). Yet any deeper affinities to which such a coincidence might hint pale beside the technical and stylistic departures of the *Terzo libro* as a whole. With this book came radical innovations in madrigalistic conception, including the transformation of the Venetian madrigal's penchant for the monumental into the form of an immense madrigal cycle, the famed setting of Petrarch's *Vergine bella.*[1]

Some inkling of these innovations might be inferred from Rore's earlier books. Already in the early 1540s Rore's language was considerably more extroverted than Willaert's. The bold motivic strokes, erratic declamatory pacing, florid melismas, and disjunct melody that appear regularly in Rore's madrigals barely exist in Willaert's, and neither does the graceful cantilena to which they form a foil.[2] Furthermore, Rore accommodated an expanded range of rhythmic values by using black notation for all but two of his madrigals in the *Primo libro,* a notational style Willaert adopted only a few times in his career.[3] The widened expressivity allowed by black notation made for more expansive madrigals: Willaert's sonnet settings, with their steady declamation, average about 120 measures, whereas Rore's stretch to as many as 164 and routinely over 150.[4] Finally, whereas Willaert invariably broke sonnets into two parts after the octave, Rore divided a number (unconventionally)

1. Rore's was not the first madrigal cycle to be written but the most ambitious to date. Berchem's six-part setting of Petrarch's sestina *Alla dolc'ombra,* ranging from three to six voices, is more typical. It appeared in Doni's *Dialogo della musica* in 1544.

According to Vergelli's dedication to Gottardo Occagna, Rore's *Vergine* cycle was known in Venice for at least some months before its publication ("già molti mesi fa"), presumably by April of that year (see Chap. 3 above, n. 32, and the purchase entry in the records of the Accademia Filarmonica di Verona cited by Giuseppe Turrini, *L'Accademia Filarmonica di Verona dalla fondazione (maggio 1543) al 1600 e il suo patrimonio musicale antico,* Atti e memorie della Accademia di Agricoltura, Scienze e Lettere di Verona, no. 18 (Verona, 1941), p. 22.

2. See James Haar's observations on Rore's melodic grace and individuality and his distinctive exordia, in *Essays on Italian Poetry and Music in the Renaissance, 1350–1600* (Berkeley and Los Angeles, 1986), p. 120.

For full scores of madrigals discussed in this chapter see Cipriani Rore, *Opera omnia,* ed. Bernhard Meier, Corpus mensurabilis musicae, no. 14, AIM, vol. 2 ([Rome], 1963).

3. The exceptions are nos. 19 and 20. On this issue see Don Harrán, "Rore and the *Madrigale Cromatico,*" *Music Review* 34 (1973): 66–81, and James Haar, "The *Note Nere* Madrigal," *JAMS* 18 (1965): 22–41. Willaert's black-note madrigals include three in the *Musica nova,* nos. 11, 12, and 13, and four published in anthologies (see Table 2).

4. The longest is *Il mal mi preme e non spavento un hora* (164 mm.) in Book One. Close behind it are *Quanto più m'avincino al giorno estremo* (162 mm.), *La vita fugge e non s'arresta un'hora* (155 mm.), and *Perseguendomi amor al luogo usato* (152 mm.), all also from Book One. The sonnet settings in Book Two are somewhat shorter on average, in the range of 130 measures. (I am speaking, of course, of modern transcription, with either the breve in white notation or the semibreve in black notation equivalent to a transcribed measure.)

after the first quatrain, in line with rhetorical suggestions in their texts; for others he made no division at all.[5]

We can scarcely begin to weigh these differences without adding into the balance the mysteries of Rore's biography before he arrived at his earliest known post, in Ferrara, at latest in April or May 1546.[6] The only patrons who can be linked definitively to him in his pre-Ferrarese years in Italy are Ruberto Strozzi and Neri Capponi. As I showed in Chapter 2, Strozzi spent most of his time between about July 1538 until the late summer of 1542 in Venice. To recapitulate the most salient data on Venice's Florentine colony, the dedication to Strozzi by his viol teacher Silvestro Ganassi dal Fontego strongly suggests that musical gatherings took place at the Strozzi's Venetian house at San Canciano, probably with Ganassi participating. Capponi, who bought music from Rore as well, was evidently settled in Venice from late 1538 through at least 1544. In the early 1540s, Rore made one documented trip to Venice—and probably many more—when he visited Capponi's salon, delivered madrigals to him, and apparently made revisions (possibly with Willaert's advice).[7] From what we know, Rore probably lived mainly in Brescia, rather than Venice, before moving to Ferrara. But throughout the early 1540s his stock must have been high among cognoscenti and publishers in Venice and Ferrara (where Strozzi would surely have championed him with the duke): all the evidence suggests Rore stood at the center of those guarded Florentine exchanges that saw the new Italo-Netherlandish idiom as a prized commodity.

These circumstances form the backdrop to Rore's first two books. In a different way each book raises questions about Rore's relationship to Venice: Book One to the genesis of Venetian style, to newer Venetian developments like modal ordering and black notation that appeared in the most modish prints, and to Willaert; Book Two to the eclecticism and occasional side of Venetian print culture, to the genre of anthologistic prints it produced, and to the directions taken up by less celebrated contemporaries. The remarkable changes appearing in Rore's Third Book lead ultimately out of the muted rhetoric practiced by Venetian madrigalists and into the more demonstrative style of Rore's late madrigals and madrigals by his students Giaches de Wert and Luzzasco Luzzaschi working in northern Italian courts. I will return to these directions in Chapter 10, after assessing the response Willaert's immediate students at San Marco made to the stylistic equipoise—this narrow play of alternatives—that was formed between Willaert's *Musica nova* and Rore's first two books.

---

5. Sonnets that divide after the quatrain include nos. 9, 15, and 16 in Book One and nos. 16, 20, and 24 in Book Three. Sonnets set with no division include no. 6 in Book One and no. 21 in Book Three. Willaert sometimes did the same, as in *Qual anima ignorante,* published in Rore's Book Two, but never in setting Petrarch's sonnets.

6. See Jessie Ann Owens, "The Milan Partbooks: Evidence of Cipriano de Rore's Compositional Process," *JAMS* 37 (1984): 270–98. Further citations for what follows can be found in Chap. 2 above, nn. 3 and 35.

7. This was shortly after Strozzi left Venice. See Richard J. Agee, "Ruberto Strozzi and the Early Madrigal," *JAMS* 36 (1983): 12–13, and Chap. 2 above, n. 35 and Table 1.

MADRIGALI A CINQUE VOCI (1542): PETRARCHAN WOODS IN THE SHADOW OF DANTE

The twenty poems of Rore's First Book form a corpus of intriguing thematic tendencies. Several overlapping textual motifs recur often enough to raise the possibility that a loosely related thematics influenced the way the book was shaped, even if it carried no overarching lyric program. Central to these thematics is what I have elsewhere described as a dissident strain of Danteism manifest in extremes of *materia* and *forma*—harsh subjects delivered in rough-hewn language—that most contemporary critics must have sensed as dangerously uncontained.[8] To be sure, the book's outward alliance with the puristic variety of Petrarchism found in Venice, which was just then being adapted to musical repertory, belies this "Dantean" strain: twelve of the book's twenty settings are of Petrarch. Nonetheless, the combination of dramatic Petrarchan sonnets and starkly graphic modern ones betrays leanings quite alien to the orthodox Petrarchism of Bembo and his adherents.

To its audience in 1542 what must have seemed most remarkable about the collection were the sixteen sonnets, grouped contiguously as nos. 2–17, that make up the main body of the print, as shown in Table 6.[9] No previous book of music had collected so many sonnet settings in one place or rendered them with such intensity. Situated at the peripheries of the print are four lighter poems in less weighty forms—one at the start and three at the end. An informed observer might have noticed symmetries in the placement of these outer numbers too. At the book's extreme ends are its only two ballate, both by the Venetian poet Giovanni Brevio, whose reputation in the city included his minor role in Bernardino Daniello's *La poetica* published six years earlier.[10] Just inside them sit, toward the front, Petrarch's sonnet *Hor che 'l ciel e la terra e 'l vento tace* (no. 2) and, at the back, an anonymous cinquecento madrigal *Hor che l'aria e la terra* (no. 19) that glosses some of the former's famous themes and lexicon. Rore's *Hor che l'aria* reinforces the parallel by dividing the madrigal's eleven lines (quite unusually) into two halves along the lines of his sonnet setting.

These structural features of the book's layout are compatible with its systematic (and more widely recognized) organization by mode.[11] The *Primo libro* is the first book known to have been successively ordered by mode according to the traditional numbering 1 to 8 (see Table 6). The plan extends only through no. 17,

---

8. See my "Rore's 'selva selvaggia': The *Primo libro* of 1542," *JAMS* 42 (1989): 547–603.

9. The many later editions of the book altered this arrangement substantially through additions, deletions, and reorderings. For listings of these see *Il nuovo Vogel* 2:1479–85 (nos. 2389–2400) and for Gardane's edition of 1544, Mary S. Lewis, *Antonio Gardane, Venetian Music Printer, 1538–1569: A Descriptive Bibliography and Historical Study,* vol. 1, *1538–49* (New York, 1988), pp. 429–35 (no. 57).

10. See Chap. 5 above, n. 10. The poems appear in Giovanni Brevio, *Rime e prose volgari di M. Giovanni Brevio* (Venice, 1545), fols. B V and C III'.

11. On modal organization in Rore's madrigals see Bernhard Meier, *The Modes of Classical Vocal Polyphony Described according to the Sources,* trans. Ellen S. Beebe, rev. ed. (New York, 1988), and Jessie Ann Owens, "Mode in the Madrigals of Cipriano de Rore," in *Essays in Italian Music in the Cinquecento,* Altro Polo, ed. Richard Charteris (Sydney, 1990), pp. 1–15.

TABLE 6
Cipriano de Rore, *Madrigali a 5* (1542)

Incipit; Poetic Form; Poet and Poetic Source*	System	Cleffing	Final	Mode
1. Cantai mentre ch'i arsi del mio foco	b	g2	**G**	1
14-line ballata: ABBA CDEDCEEFFA				
Giovanni Brevio, *Rime e prose volgari,* fol. B V				
2. Hor che 'l ciel e la terra e 'l vento tace	b	g2	D	
ii. Così sol d'una chiara fonte viva	b	g2	**G**	1
sonnet				
Petrarch, no. 164				
3. Poggiand'al ciel coll'ali del desio	b	g2	D	
ii. Tal si trova dinanzi al lume vostro	b	g2	**G**	1
sonnet				
Anon.				
4. Quand'io son tutto volto in quella parte	b	c1	A	
ii. Così davanti ai colpi della morte	b	c1	**GG**	2
sonnet				
Petrarch, no. 18				
5. Solea lontana in sonno consolarme	b	c1	D	
ii. Non ti soven di quell'ultima sera	b	c1	**GG**	2
sonnet				
Petrarch, no. 250				
6. Altiero sasso lo cui gioco spira	—	c1	**E**	3
sonnet (complete)				
Francesco Maria Molza, in *Libro terzo delle rime di diversi,*				
fol. 4; *I fiori delle rime,* fol. 221				
7. Strane ruppi, aspri monti, alte tremanti	—	c1	GG	
ii. A guisa d'hom da soverchia pena	—	c1	**E**	3
sonnet				
Luigi Tansillo (or Luigi Alemanni); on sources see Feldman,				
"Rore's *selva selvaggia,*" pp. 565–66				
8. La vita fugge e non s'arresta un'hora	—	c1	A	
ii. Tornami avanti s'alcun dolce mai	—	c1	**E**	3
sonnet				
Petrarch, no. 272				
9. Tu piangi e quella per chi fai tal pianto	—	c2	A	
ii. Lei tutta intenta al lume divo e santo	—	c2	**EE**	4
sonnet				
Antonio Tebaldeo, *Rime di M. Antonio Tibaldeo,* fol. [g v']				
10. Il mal mi preme e mi spaventa il peggio	b	g2	C	
ii. Ben ch'i non sia di quel grand'honor degno	b	g2	**F**	5
sonnet				
Petrarch, no. 244				

TABLE 6 *(continued)*

Incipit; Poetic Form; Poet and Poetic Source*	System	Cleffing	Final	Mode
11. Per mezz'i boschi inhospiti e selvaggi	b	g2	C	
ii. Parmi d'udirla udendo i rami e l'ore	b	g2	**F**	5
sonnet				
Petrarch, no. 176				
12. Quanto piu m'avicino al giorno estremo	b	c1	C	
ii. Perchè con lui cadrà quella speranza	b	c1	**FF**	6
sonnet				
Petrarch, no. 32				
13. Perseguendomi amor al luogo usato	b	c1	FF	
ii. Io dicea fra mio cor perchè paventi	b	c1	**FF**	6
sonnet				
Petrarch, no. 110				
14. Chi vol veder quantunque po natura	—	g2	D	
ii. Vedrà s'arriva a tempo ogni virtute	—	g2	**G**	7
sonnet				
Petrarch, no. 248				
15. Quel sempre acerbo et honorato giorno	—	g2	G	
ii. L'atto d'ogni gentil pietate adorno	—	g2	**G**	7
sonnet				
Petrarch, no. 157				
16. Far potess'io vendetta di colei	—	c1	GG	
ii. Così gli afflitti e stanchi pensier miei	—	c1	**GG**	8
sonnet				
Petrarch, no. 256				
17. Amor, che vedi ogni pensiero aperto	—	c1	D	
ii. Ben veggio di lontano il dolce lume	—	c1	**GG**	8
sonnet				
Petrarch, no. 163				
18. Ben si conviene a voi	b	g2	**D**	1
9-line madr: aABccbBCC				
Anon.				
19. Hor che l'aria e la terra	b	c1	A	
ii. Sol nel mio pett'ogn'hor lasso si serra	b	c1	**GG**	2
11-line madr: aBccB AdDaEE				
Anon.				
20. Da quei bei lumi ond'io sempre sospiro	—	c1	**E**	3
13-line ballata: ABBA CDECDEdFF				
Giovanni Brevio, *Rime e prose volgari*, fol. C III'				

*Table uses short-title references. For full citations see the Bibliography.

however, the same place that marks the end of the bank of sonnets.[12] What was given modal order, in other words, was essentially the sonnet.[13] And what was new about the print was therefore not just modal ordering, but the nexus of modes and sonnets.[14]

All in all, then, Rore's book was a novel essay in sonnet setting. Despite the many occasional sonnets written in the mid-sixteenth century, sonnets remained a primary vehicle for remote, archetypal forms of expression (as we saw in Chap. 7). Accordingly, the book avoids occasional verse almost completely,[15] emphasizing instead two interrelated themes: death—both feared and augured—and the untamed wilderness. The recurrence of these themes casts a veil of despair over the whole book, a feeling epitomized by the burst of vengeance that opens Petrarch's *Far potess'io vendetta di colei* (*Canzoniere,* no. 256).

Far potess'io vendetta di colei	Could I but take vengeance on her
Che guardando et parlando mi distrugge	Who gazing and speaking destroys me
E, per più doglia, poi s'ascond'e fugge,	And then, to increase my pain, hides herself and flees,
Celando gli occhi a me sì dolce e rei!	Taking from me her eyes so sweet and cruel!

Far potess'io vendetta explores a soundscape that challenges the limits of what Bembo later described as "materia grande" and the vocabulary he called "gravi, alte, e sonanti."[16] Consonantal clusters and abundant *a*'s and *o*'s slow the poem's rhythmic pace, especially in v. 2 ("Che guardando e parlando mi distrugge"), and fill its

12. Does this mean that nos. 18–20 must have been a "foreign body incorporated only after the original had been submitted for printing," as Bernhard Meier assumed (Rore, *Opera omnia* 2:iii)? Apropos, we might consider that had the two madrigal texts (nos. 18 and 19) been interpolated among settings in modes 1 and 2 and Brevio's second ballata (no. 20) among settings in mode 3, the book's solid bank of sonnets would have been interrupted. Why the first Brevio ballata (no. 1) should not have been relegated to the back of the book as well apparently had to do with the bookmakers' notion that madrigal prints should not open with a sonnet but with something lighter. To judge from the makeup of subsequent collections published by Willaert's students, the *Primo libro* set a precedent for avoiding weighty sonnets at the starts of books in which they otherwise dominated. All of the following sonnet-filled prints open with cinquecento madrigals: Perissone Cambio, *Madrigali a cinque voci* (1545), with twelve sonnets out of sixteen settings; idem, *Il secondo libro de madregali a cinque voci* (1550), with fifteen sonnets out of twenty-three; Girolamo Parabosco, *Madrigali a cinque voci* (1546), with eight out of twenty; and Baldassare Donato, *Il primo libro d'i madregali a cinque & a sei voci* (1553), with thirteen out of twenty-six.

13. It may be relevant here that the one ballata that departs from the pattern, no. 1, consists of fourteen lines of *endecasillabi*.

14. This is not at all the same as saying that the meanings of the individual sonnets were keyed to modal affect, a different matter that I will take up briefly below. It does seem likely, however, that there is a connection between modal ordering and a highly literary vernacular. For a suggestion that composers sought "pathic and ethic effects" of modes particularly in secular (hence almost always vernacular) music, see Chap. 6 above, n. 26.

15. Even *Altiero sasso* (no. 6), described by Einstein as a "threnody on the death of a Roman" (*The Italian Madrigal* 1:393), is couched in a generalized poetics, with no direct hint of its subject's identity. The only other quasi-occasional text in the book is no. 18, a chivalric madrigal for an anonymous "Rosa": "Ben si conviene a voi / Così bel nome, alma mia rosa poi / Che con quella beltà che 'l monda honora, / Vincete i più bei fiori / E i più soavi odori" (Well does such a lovely name suit you, my life-giving Rosa, since with that beauty that the world honors, you surpass the loveliest flowers and the sweetest aromas).

16. *Prose della volgar lingua*, ed. Mario Marti (Padua, 1967), p. 55.

rhymes with what Bembo had called a "meravigliosa gravità."[17] This "grave" diction culminates in the clamorous rhymes of the sestet ("caccia" / "sciolta" / "minaccia", "volta" / "abbraccia" / "s'ascolta") and the bitter rebuke of its final point, where Petrarch embeds the *o*'s in a slew of hissing *s*'s: "Non rompe il sonno suo s'ella l'ascolta" ([My lamenting soul] does not break her sleep, if she is [even] listening).

Even though *Far potess'io vendetta* does not explicitly portend loss, it comes from a sonnet cluster that brings the entire *Canzoniere* to a nadir of despair with Laura's death in no. 264, and the beginning of the sonnets "in morte." This sonnet cluster, beginning with no. 250, positions the poet's fantasy on the edge of reality by slipping repeatedly into scenes of tormented sleep. Rore also set the very first of the group, *Solea lontana in sonno consolarme* (Accustomed from afar to console me in sleep), in which Laura announces in a nocturnal vision her imminent death ("Non sperar di vedermi in terra mai" [Do not hope to see me on earth ever again]). Several other poems in Rore's book deal centrally with death—*Poggiand'al ciel coll'ali del desio* (no. 3), an anonymous gloss on the motif of Icarus who flies so high from love that his wings are melted by the sun, *Altiero sasso lo cui gioco spira* by Francesco Maria Molza (no. 6), a eulogy on a Roman (see n. 15 above), and Petrarch's *La vita fugge e non s'arresta un'hora* (no. 8) and *Chi vol veder quantunque po natura* (no. 14)—and most of the other poems in the book touch on death at least tangentially.

The related topos of the savage wilderness staged at the center of Rore's book had its most gripping prototype in Dante's *Divina commedia,* particularly (as I have argued elsewhere) as the "selva oscura" with which Dante begins his prologue scene.[18] In the *Commedia,* of course, the dark woods represents a space of primitivity and spiritual blindness. Its power to terrorize the soul motivates the beginning of a conversion that will take the poet on a harrowing odyssey through Hell and into those linguistic regions that were forbidden by the codifiers of Tuscan who later prevailed in Venice.

The three sonnets that pursue the topos in Rore's *Primo libro* (nos. 6, 7, and 11) aspire to varying degrees of Dantean intensity. The most moderate, Petrarch's *Per mezz'i boschi inhospiti e selvaggi* (no. 11), mediates between Dantean and Petrarchan extremes. Its evocative nature scene is painted as a familiar symbol of spiritual loss, but also of comfort—a symbol caught, in typically Petrarchan fashion, in a web of uncertainties.

Per mezz'i bosch'inhospiti e selvaggi	Through the midst of the inhospitable savage woods,
Onde vanno a gran rischi'homini et arme,	Where even armed men go at great risk,
Vo secur'io, che non po spaventarme	I go without fear, nor can anything terrify me
Altri che 'l sol, c'ha d'Amor vivo i raggi;	Except the sun that has rays from living Love.

4

17. Ibid., p. 81.
18. Feldman, "Rore's 'selva selvaggia,' " from which some of what follows is drawn. For antecedents to Dante's exploration, particularly those of Virgil, see *The Divine Comedy,* ed. and trans. Charles S. Singleton, 3 vols. (Princeton, 1970), vol. 1, pt. 2, pp. 4–5; and John Freccero, "The Prologue Scene," Chap. 1 in *Dante: The Poetics of Conversion,* ed. Rachel Jacoff (Cambridge, Mass., 1986).

E vo cantando (o pensier miei non saggi!)	And I go singing (oh my unwise thoughts!)
Lei che 'l ciel non poria lontana farme,	About her whom the heavens could not put far from me,
Ch'i' l'ho ne gli occhi, e veder seco parme	For she is before my eyes and with her I seem to see
Donn'e donzelle, e sono abeti e faggi.	Ladies and damsels, and they are but firs and beeches. 8
Parmi d'udirla, udendo i rami e l'ore	I seem to hear her when I hear the branches and breeze
E le frondi, e gli augei lagnarsi, e l'acque	And the leaves, and birds lamenting, and the waters
Mormorando fuggir per l'herba verde.	Murmuring, fleeing across the green grass. 11
Raro un silentio, un solitario horrore	Rarely has the silence, the solitary horror
D'ombrosa selva mai tanto mi piacque,	Of a shady wood pleased me so much;
Se non che dal mio Sol troppo si perde.	Except that I lose too much of my Sun. 14

Unlike the dread that shadows Dante's journey, here the lover willingly seeks uninhabited places since nothing can harm him but the sun—metaphor, that is, for Laura and for the enlightened, hence civilized, life. In this pagan forest love is ubiquitous and comforting, yet also ambiguously elusive, as we learn in v. 4 and again in the last tercet. There the shaded woods of Dante's *Commedia* reappear, but since they offer solace (protection from the sun) their meanings are enervated by Petrarchan ambivalence. They point at once to the presence and absence of the beloved. By contrast with the sonnets of Rore's southern contemporaries that I will take up shortly—sonnets that delve deeply into the penumbral wilderness Dante had explored—Petrarch's sonnet leans at once in and out, tempering and softening its linguistic signs in a way that appealed to Venetian literati.[19]

As a text that reconciles these verbal-thematic extremes, *Per mezz'i boschi* offers a valuable way to consider the range of discursive possibilities that Rore's readings made use of. His setting is far more animated than those of Willaert, defined by clear contrasts and lively gestures (see the complete setting in Ex. 18). This squares well with the Rore of the late fifties whom Claudio Monteverdi later called the father of the *seconda prattica*—those experiments in extravagant harmonic and voice-leading effects in the service of text expression that he compared with the more constrained *prima prattica* employed by composers from Josquin to Willaert. Yet in the early forties Rore's language evinced virtually none of the harmonic experiments or overt text painting that were to invite that label. How his earliest settings managed to construe text so vividly is a question that must be searched out in other domains—in the way his rhetoric simultaneously shapes verbal syntax and meaning.

19. Meier misrepresents the sonnet by reducing it to an expression of Petrarch's fearlessness in imagining Laura—this by way of explaining Rore's use here of fifth mode, traditionally conceived as cheerful (*The Modes,* p. 394). Petrarch's contradictory relationship to sun and light, and thus to Laura, is a theme that runs throughout the *Canzoniere* (e.g., nos. 18 and 22). Indeed the originary fiction of the *Canzoniere* describes the day he first sighted Laura as "il giorno ch'al sol si scolararo / per la pietà del suo fattore i rai"—that is, the anniversary of Christ's Crucifixion (no. 3, vv. 1–2). Far from being avoided by madrigalists, such contradictions were sought out.

Rore, *Per mezz'i bosch'inhospiti e selvaggi* (Petrarch, no. 176), incl.; *Madrigali a 5* (Venice, 1542), no. 11.

(continued)

(continued)

(continued)

Seconda parte

(continued)

(continued)

We can begin to uncover this rhetoric by looking at Rore's treatment of the sonnet's formal articulations, as provisionally described in Table 7. Although the ambiguities of Rore's counterpoint render such descriptions problematic,[20] Table 7 nonetheless shows that his setting foregrounds the sonnet's verse structure by using suspension cadences repeatedly at the ends of all but one of the sonnet's main sections (cf. vv. 4, 8, and 14). The only section that lacks such a cadence is the first tercet, with a single cadence to end v. 11 at m. 105, but here Rore reinforces the articulation through other means (as I discuss below). Furthermore, suspension cadences sound at the ends of virtually every clause (the only exceptions are the very last cadences that close each of the two parts).

This structural overview allows us to see profound differences between Rore and Willaert. Rather than trading in suspension cadences and sharp motivic differentiations, Willaert tended to work with speechlike recitation, often marking textual cadences through the simple use of rests.[21] Willaert's madrigals must have offered trenchant models for how to define formal details of text with subtle rhythmic and harmonic nuances and delicate textural shifts; but Rore sought out more explicit rhetorical definition.[22] While Willaert's madrigals usually deploy few contrapuntally conceived cadences, *Per mezz'i boschi* typifies Rore's tendency toward a highly articulated reading.

This profusion of contrapuntal cadences was just one way Rore's articulation differed from Willaert's, however, and perhaps not even the most obvious one. For Rore, semantic content held equal sway with linguistic form. More than Willaert's, his music indulged in vivid text painting and sharp verbal contrasts, bold motivic shapes and striking expositions. One result of these tendencies was a less regular rhythmic surface. Thus, where Willaert's declamation distributes durations fairly evenly over words in the course of a sonnet, Rore's moves between this Willaertian "speech time" and what we might usefully distinguish as "expressive time," time played out in alternately lingering or quickening affective gestures and pictorial effects. In short, Rore forewent some of Willaert's rigorous adherence to the

20. As with Willaert's *Pien d'un vago pensier* (see Table 5), Rore's setting is not wholly congenial to this kind of simplified description. Both the contrapuntal ambiguities and the subtle and diverse means by which articulations are made defy efforts to summarize the forms of many cadences or even to identify all their locations. Rore parses the text not just through contrapuntal devices but through textural shifts, changes in declamatory speed, text repetition, and a host of other means. Table 7 lists all of the cadences involving suspended dissonances, as well as others that I deem especially significant, but for the reasons given above I do not aspire to a universal or wholly systematic approach in tabulating cadences.

21. The total lack of suspension cadences in the *prima parte* and inclusion of only two in the *seconda parte* of Willaert's *Mentre che 'l cor* find no equivalent in Rore's books. Meier's tabulations of cadences for several madrigals from the *Musica nova* might seem to suggest otherwise, but his examples happen to be drawn from the most cadence-laden works in the book. See the sections on *Giunto m'ha Amor* and *Quando fra l'altre donne* in *The Modes,* pp. 144–45 and 159 (I do not count the seven-voice dialogues that Meier discusses on pp. 126–27 and 145 because they operate according to different principles of articulation).

22. For a study aimed at demonstrating Rore's mastery in reflecting textual structure through bass patterns, tonal structure, and cadential repetitions see Jessie Ann Owens, "Music and Meaning in Cipriano de Rore's Setting of *Donec gratus eram tibi,*" in *Music and Language,* Studies in the History of Music, vol. 1 (New York, 1983), pp. 95–117, on his setting of an ode by Horace.

Table 7
Musico-Poetic Structure in Rore's
Per mezz'i bosch'inhospiti e selvaggi

Bar	Poetic Line Ended	Cadential Pitches/ Voices	Bass or Lowest Voice	Cadence Type/ Remarks
9	1	f- (V-)	B-flat	evaded
17	2	f/F (V/B)	F	perfect
25	3	cc/c (C/V)	c	perfect
30	4	f- (V-)	b-flat	evaded
32	4	c/F (B/T)	F	evaded (P 5th)
35	4	ff/f (C/A)	D	perfect
53	6	aa/a (A/V); f (T)	a-F	Phrygian, then evaded to close text on f-c (A+T/Q)
55	7a	ff/f (C/A)	D	perfect
57	7a	dd/b-flat (C/A)	b-flat	Phrygian evaded to M 3rd
66	8a	c- (T-)	a	evaded
67	8b	cc/F (C/B)	F	P 5th
70	8b	f/Bb (A/B)	B-flat	P 5th
72	8b	c- (V-)	a	m 3rd
73	8b	cc/c (C/A)	F	disjunct progression to perfect cadence
75	8b	—	C	plagal
81	9a	d- (A-)	d	evaded
94	10b	cc/c (C/T)	C	perfect
105	11	f/F (T/B)	F	perfect
107	12a	c/C (V/B)	C	perfect
113	13a	f- (T-)	b-flat	evaded
115	13b	cc/c (C/T)	E	perfect (cf. mm. 93–94)
119	13a	c/c (T/B)	c	unison approached by leap
122	13a	ff- (C-)	F	evaded
126	14a/14	c/C (T/B)	C	octave approached by leap
130	14+14a	f/f (V-T)	F	perfect
138	14+14a	aa/a (A/B)	a	Phrygian
145	14+14a	f/f (V-T)	F	perfect (cf. mm. 129–30)
154	14	—	F	plagal

tempos, accents, and cadences of a spoken reading in favor of a more semantic interpretation.

Per mezz'i boschi carefully balances such formal and expressive considerations in the transitions between major structural divisions. When the first quatrain draws to a close, for example, a series of brilliant melismas gestures the word "raggi" repeatedly toward cadence (quintus, mm. 28–30; bassus, mm. 30–32; cantus, mm. 33–35). Crowning the quatrain with their whimsical swirling motions launched across sevenths and propelled in thirds and fourths, these melismas bring about the quatrain's tonal-grammatical resolution to the final, F. At the same time, by calling attention with their sudden absence to the poet's singing in v. 5 ("E vo cantando") and the beginning of the new poetic thought, they also exaggerate retrospectively the loss of motion in m. 35. To employ stasis for the sake of contrast at such a moment is a touch ironic, of course, since Rore can exploit it only by slighting the prevailing convention that prescribed florid melody for allusions to singing. But in pitting such a spare passage against the previous spate of melismas—condemning the poet's reckless song to a spell of semantic impoverishment—Rore found an efficacious formal-cum-expressive solution to the structural transition.

"E vo cantando" forms only the first part of a clause whose direct object "Lei" is displaced in enjambment to line 6 through an extraordinary interruption. It is worth pursuing these verses a little further to notice the ingenious syntactic solution given to Petrarch's exclamatory "(o pensier miei non saggi!)"; for Rore offset it with rests, as if to mark it as a parenthetical mental flash, and also reintroduced a declamatory rhythm at the semibreve (mm. 37–38) not heard since the opening. The new pacing marks the poet's "unwise thoughts" as intrusive and other, an effect heightened by the flat-footed binary figures that declaim "E vo cantando." Only when the phrase elides into v. 6 to complete the interruption—"E vo cantando . . . Lei"—is the stasis of v. 5 lifted; trace the quintus from m. 37 to 41, for instance, and note the continuous and rising phrase that accompanies "saggi!) Lei" at each appearance.[23] The quintus, leading off as surrogate bass, immediately introduces a proliferation of voice crossings with the tenor that obscure and destabilize the sense of a bass line (mm. 37–39 and 44–45). Shortly afterward, the altus's flatted inflections herald a raft of minor triads, which otherwise scarcely appear in the madrigal (note the c, g, and a of mm. 39–41). None of the polyphony to this point has been tied off with a cadence. Indeed, for the first time in the madrigal, two whole verses go by before a suspended cadence sounds at the end of v. 6 (m. 53)—both the first Phrygian cadence and the first on the medial degree aa/a (altus and quintus), albeit immediately extended.

To summarize, vv. 4–6 gloss Petrarch's text in a way that moves between two different rhetorical goals: syntactic clarification and semantic expression. Whereas Willaert made interpretation of localized grammar an overriding concern—indeed often the sole means of enhancing the sense of the words—Rore's music wrested meaning directly from text. So doing, it balanced the competing demands of linguistic form and meaning.

---

23. As Willaert did with the interruption in v. 8 of *Pien d'un vago pensier* (see Chap. 7 above, nn. 56–58), Rore clarified the words' syntactic autonomy by setting them off musically from the first part of the clause they interrupt, "E vo cantando." He also, like Willaert, linked the delayed completion of the main clause, "Lei," to the disruptive interjection: hence "(o pensier miei non saggi!) Lei" became a single syntactic unit.

Such balance proves expressively vital for the wonderfully pictorial first tercet, a catalogue of natural phenomena that Rore depicted in vivid musical images. Each item—branches, breeze, leaves, and birds—forms collectively part of a sonorous contrapuntal thicket used to animate Petrarch's scenery. To mimic the sound of the breeze whipping light rain over a field, for instance ("e l'acque / Mormorando fuggir per l'herba verde"), Rore set voices fluttering from part to part (mm. 93–105) and underpinned the effect with a rocking bassus at mm. 94–97 and 99–102. Such rich iconic tapestries were unusual at the time, even in Rore's own madrigals. In the future, rapid declamation combined with repeating note pairs such as Rore applied to "fuggir per l'herba verde" were to become a prominent musical topos for depictions of pastoral landscapes. They surface in black-note madrigals of the 1540s, of which those in Rore's *Primo libro* are early, if atypical, examples, and they continue to appear in madrigals of the *seconda prattica*. Rore's *Terzo libro* of 1548 is the first to make extensive use of such pictorial passages, which finally became part of an established tradition in the pastoral settings of Andrea Gabrieli, Wert, Marenzio, and Monteverdi.[24]

Even the bravura multiple counterpoint Wert fashioned for *Vezzosi augelli*, a stanza from Tasso's *Gerusalemme liberata* published in his *Ottavo libro a 5* of 1586 (Ex. 19), finds its prototype in *Per mezz'i boschi*. Wert's madrigal pits a melodious trio of "singing birds" for Tasso's first two verses against monotonal chanting for the murmuring breeze of v. 3. Not dissimilarly, Rore assigned separate motives to "l'acque / Mormorando" and "Fuggir per l'herba verde." To do so he had forcibly to disengage the verbal parts, for their syntax alone does not call for them to be parsed as such. The separations he artificially forced on them provide the basis for what we might call prospectively a Wertian counterpoint, which takes shape in the overlappings of mm. 95–97 and 100–102. They form a striking precedent for the sort of simultaneous counterpoint Monteverdi was to cultivate so extensively beginning in his *Secondo libro a 5* of 1590.[25]

Rore projected another efficacious rhetorical-grammatical shift by articulating the division of the tercets with the perfect cadence on f/F in m. 105. The reasons for this are evident, as Rore starts the brief "Raro un silentio" in near homorhythm and quickly ends with yet another perfect cadence in m. 107 (these being the only two to bring as many as four voices to a simultaneous close). The textural tranquillity thus achieved and enhanced by an all-vocal rest in turn sets up the poem's key phrase, "un solitario horrore / D'ombrosa selva mai tanto mi piacque." At this point the texture unravels just slightly until, reaching their second statement, the voices begin to hurtle toward an enormous coda.

Rore placed unprecedented weight on the last verse. Melismas now proliferate as each voice echoes the final verse six, seven, or more times, working out at last the

24. See Gary Tomlinson, *Monteverdi and the End of the Renaissance* (Berkeley and Los Angeles, 1987), pp. 49–50, and Chap. 7 above, n. 53.

25. Tomlinson, ibid., relates Wert's *Vezzosi augelli* to Monteverdi's setting of Tasso's lyric poem *Ecco mormorar l'onde,* another paratactic nature scene, which was published in Monteverdi's *Secondo libro.*

EX. 19. Giaches de Wert, *Vezzosi augelli infra le verdi fronde* (Torquato Tasso), mm. 1–9; in *Ottavo libro a 5* (Venice, 1586), p. 11.

(continued)

E X . 1 9 *(continued)*

abundant polyphonic energy collected in the previous hundred-plus measures. Through all this the bass leaps back and forth between the two tonal axes, F and C, as if purging the tonal terrain of all the alien inflections that had invaded earlier. This is a fitting climax to a work that set new standards of vigor for polyphonic madrigals.

Both of the other sonnets that explore the topos of the woods were the work of poets contemporary with Rore, and both are darker than Petrarch's *Per mezz'i boschi*. The first (no. 6) is Molza's *Altiero sasso*.

Altiero sasso lo cui gioco spira	Proud stone whose ridge breathes
Gli antichi honor del gran popul di Marte,	The ancient honor of the great populace of Mars;
Fiume che fendi questa e quella parte,	River that breaks this way and that,
Hor quieto e piano, hor pien di sdegno et ira,	Now quiet and still, now full of rage and fury; 4
Piaggie che 'l mondo ancor ama e sospira,	Slopes that all the world still loves and desires,
Consecrate da tante e da tai carte,	Consecrated by so many and such writings;
Memorie eterne e voi reliquie sparte	Eternal memories and you, Spartan relics,
Ch'ogni bon'alma con pietà rimira:	On which every good soul gazes with devotion: 8
Parmi d'udir fuggendo a voi d'intorno	I seem to hear flying all about you,
Sospirar l'onde e i rami e i fiori	Sighing, the waves, and branches, and flowers,
e l'ora	and the breeze
Lagnarsi, e per dolor romper i sassi;	Lament, and the stones break from grief, 11
Che già del pianto s'avicina el giorno	Since already the day of tears draws near
Che 'l bel viso ch'Italia tutta honora,	When the beautiful face that all of Italy honors,
Cinti d'horror al suo partir vi lassi.	Wrapped in horror at his departure, will leave you. 14

Altiero sasso apostrophizes deserted formations in the Roman out-of-doors—a stony mountain face, raging river, slopes, and Spartan relics. The poem sustains a level of Dantean gloom throughout the octave, then shifts to a lighter Petrarchan vein, conjuring up in waves, branches, flowers, and breeze the memory of the beloved. This first tercet is, of course, a gloss on the analogous one in *Per mezz'i boschi*. But here day breaks to provide a mere foil for the final tercet. The sonnet resumes its lamenting tone at v. 12, now draping the octave's rocky landscape in a Dantean "horror" to convey the air of deathly departure at the sonnet's end.

Rore set *Altiero sasso* in ♮-CI-E, or mode 3, the same tonality he called on for an even more desolate version of the topos in *Strane ruppi* (no. 7), which immediately follows.

Strane ruppi, aspri monti, alte tremanti	Strange cliffs, harsh mountains, high quivering
Ruine, e sassi al ciel nudi e scoperti,	Ruins, and stones naked and exposed to Heaven,
Ove a gran pena pon salir tant'erti	Where with great effort such steep clouds
Nuvoli, in questo fosco aer fumanti,	Of smoke rise in this gloomy, fuming air, 4
Superb'horror, tacite selve, e tanti	Proud horror, silent woods, and so many
Negr'antr'herbosi, in rotte pietre aperti,	Black grass-grown caves in broken-open stones,
Abbandonati, sterili deserti,	Abandoned, barren deserts
Ov'han paur'andar le belve erranti:	Where even wandering wild beasts go in fear: 8
A guisa d'hom che da soverchia pena	As a man who, with a sad heart, torn with
Il cor trist'ange, fuor di senn'uscito,	Excessive pain, out of his mind,
Se 'n va piangendo, ove la furia il mena,	Goes crying wherever his madness leads him, 11
Vo piangend'io tra voi, e se partito	I go weeping among you: and if Heaven does not
Non cangia il ciel, con voce assai più piena	take my side, with a much fuller voice
Sarò di là tra le mest'ombre udito.	Will I be heard from there among the sad shades. 14

Though attributions of its authorship are mixed, *Strane ruppi* appears to be the work of the Neapolitan Luigi Tansillo, who was noted for his extraordinarily raw diction.[26] Its trembling rocks, clouds of smoke, and lifeless woodland depict the spoils of a volcanic eruption. In evoking them with such graphic language, Tansillo departs radically from the Petrarchan mainstream, as well as from the idyllic Arcadian world of his Neapolitan predecessor Sannazaro.[27] Here the poetic persona is set in a stark and terrifying place that transforms the usual pastoral scenes of Petrarchan verse: unlike their docile woods and groves, these spaces are rugged and

---

26. I expand on questions of authorship in "Rore's 'selva selvaggia,'" pp. 565–66. On Neapolitan Petrarchism see Aldo Vallone, "Di alcuni aspetti del petrarchismo napoletano (con inediti di Scipione Ammirato)," *Studi petrarcheschi* 7 (1961):355–75, and Giulio Ferroni and Amedeo Quondam, *La locuzione artificiosa: teoria ed esperienza della lirica a Napoli nell'età del manierismo* (Rome, 1973).

27. On settings of Tansillo in the sixteenth century see my "Rore's 'selva selvaggia,'" p. 566 n. 30.

uninhabitable. All the poet's emotions are projected through this violent landscape, whose images express a total loss of civilization and, by extension, the loss of reason that defines a cultivated being. At the verbal level madness is dramatized most acutely in the octave, with its fragmentary vocatives distancing it from the equivocal syntactic convolutions of Petrarch's verse.

Elsewhere I have proposed that Tansillo drew from Dante's *Commedia* for specific words and meanings and more generally from the cacophonous sounds of the *Inferno*.[28] The "tremanti ruine" of *Strane ruppi* recall the rumblings of Purgatory Dante feels in Hell, to which he is doomed but for the grace of Heaven.[29] In the *Inferno* he learns through a series of cryptic allusions that the tremors signify a soul's completion of penance in Purgatory.[30] In *Purgatory* 20, the pilgrim and his guide hear violent quaking accompanied by cries of "Gloria in excelsis Deo" given out by shades ("ombre") who afterwards return to a state of eternal weeping.[31] This final point (as I have argued) confirms the specific inspiration of Tansillo's sonnet in the *Commedia* and provides a Dantean key to the whole poem, with its final allusion to the underground shades. More than this, it reveals a precise musical association with the quaking that must have made the poem appealing for musical setting, despite—or even because of—its lyric eccentricities.

The extravagant Neapolitanism of *Strane ruppi* finds a unique place among Venetian collections, a place that is unthinkable in Willaert's oeuvre. But it forms part of a distinctly southern stream running through Rore's *Primo libro,* also fed by poets like the Roman Molza and (so it seems) the anonymous author of the Neapolitan-styled Icarus sonnet *Poggiand'al ciel*.[32] Sitting at the extreme end of Rore's early expressivity in a style that borders on expressionism, Rore's

28. I am indebted to Linda Armao, who first brought the thematic connection to my attention.

29. According to Christian tradition, the rumblings commemorate Christ's Crucifixion and his harrowing of Hell. In Matt. 27:51, for example, the earth shudders after the Crucifixion: "And behold the veil of the temple was rent in twain from the top to the bottom, and the earth did quake, and the rocks rent." See also Mark 15:38: "And the veil of the temple was rent in twain from the top to the bottom."

30. For the specific references and lexical connections see Feldman, "Rore's 'selva selvaggia,' " pp. 567–68.

31. *Purg.* 20.124–44: "Poi cominciò da tutte parti un grido / tal, che 'l maestro inverso me si feo, / dicendo: 'Non dubbiar, mentr' io ti guido. / *'Gloria in excelsis'* tutti *'Deo'* / dicean, per quel ch'io da' vicin compresi, / onde intender lo grido si poteo. / No'istavamo immobili e sospesi / come i pastor che prima udir quel canto, / fin che 'l tremar cessò ed el compiési. / Poi ripigliammo nostro cammin santo, / guardando l'ombre che giacean per terra, / tornate già in su l'usato pianto" (Then began such a cry on all sides that my master drew toward me saying, "Do not fear while I guide you." *"Gloria in excelsis, Deo,"* all were saying, by what I understood from those nearby, where the cry could be heard. We stood motionless and in suspense, like the shepherds who first heard that song, until the quaking ceased and it was ended. Then we took up our holy way again, looking at the shades that lay on the ground, already returned to their wonted plaint).

32. Vallone, "Di alcuni aspetti del petrarchismo napoletano," stresses southern poets' use of comparison and simile, their wielding of naturalistic imagery to heighten contrasts between the poet's interiority and the physical world, and manipulations of naturalistic invocations to balance rhetorical artifice—all qualities found in these poems. Vallone cites Tansillo's employment of the winged-flight motive in comparative form on p. 367. For Ernest Hatch Wilkens's description of the Icarus motif as an emblem of "soaring inspiration," see *A History of Italian Literature,* ed. Thomas Bergin, rev. ed. (Cambridge, Mass., 1974), p. 245.

settings of Southern imagery stimulated unexpected antecedents to his late madrigalian style.

Expressionistic qualities are most striking in the opening quatrain, where Rore ignored the norms of classical vocal counterpoint that assigned one main *soggetto* to each word group by threading a descending tetrachord through four distinct verbal phrases in the way of a virtual leitmotif. (See Ex. 20, where the four are numbered in the cantus and other instances bracketed.) With their staggered exordial entrances, these tetrachords translate musically the jagged cliffs of v. 1. They find their most gripping exposition in the opening measures—texturally spare, broad in rhythm, jostled by ubiquitous suspensions, and hardened in parallel major thirds

Ex. 20. Rore, *Strane ruppi, aspri monti, alte tremanti* (prob. Luigi Tansillo), mm. 1–28; *Madrigali a 5,* no. 7.

(continued)

E x . 2 0 *(continued)*

(the quintus and bassus of mm. 2–3).[33] Obsessively repeated, they give special force to the melodic whole tones that Zarlino later mentioned in connection with "asprezza, durezza, crudeltà, [ed] amaritudine" (harshness, hardness, cruelty, [and] bitterness).[34]

From this stark beginning Rore drew the tetrachords into increasingly turmoiled counterpoint. With the appearance of "harsh mountains" and "trembling ruins" in m. 5 come more dissonances, declamatory ruptures, and shifts of texture. By m. 7 the suspension chains, now in diminution, generate faster harmonic shifts and remarkable dissonances. The bassus's suspended a of m. 8 becomes the middle member of a tone cluster whose outer notes (tenor g and quintus b) arrive by leap; its note of resolution, g, sounds with it not only simultaneously but in unison. As if to underscore the dissonance, the bassus rumbles through a subterranean run on "Ruine" to bring the noun phrase to an end.

In all of this, Rore made the most of the poem's noisy vowels and consonants by chiseling each of its paratactic parts into a separate musical phrase. The chain of broken syntactic bits thus receives an asymmetric musical parsing that Daniello (for one) had linked to proselike *gravità* in verse.[35] Deliberately measured, Rore's setting stuffed the poem's bloated diction—its *a*'s and *o*'s, *r*'s, *s*'s, *t*'s, and consonantal clusters,[36] with jarring discords compounding its instabilities of theme and phraseology.

The gritty style that emerged has much to do with Rore's individuality as a contrapuntist. Within the bounds of post-Josquinian, continuous polyphony, the music's surface is unusually restless. No sooner are words cranked up to a clattering, speechlike tempo than the surface turns lushly melismatic.

These two declamatory styles—recitational and melismatic—always stand in a kind of counterpose, one quickly mutating into the other. Rore individualized them contrapuntally by linking each of them to different types of chordal events and different kinds of voice leading. Crisp syllabic declamation—even and metrically stable—is usually accompanied by passages that are tonally less stable. Thus Rore often unleashed a succession of quick, erratic chordal shifts while holding the declamation steadily at the quarter note (here semiminim), as happens at the allusion to caves and stones of v. 6 (see Ex. 21, especially mm. 49–50).[37] Conversely, when the declamation unfolds in luxuriant melismas, harmonic changes become slower and

---

33. Recall here that conjunct motion by major thirds, as well as from major sixths to perfect fifths, were later explicitly linked to gravity and harshness by Vincenzo Galilei in his *Fronimo dialogo, nel quale si contengono le vere, et necessarie regole del intavolare la musica nel liuto* (Venice, 1568), p. 13 (quoted in Claude V. Palisca, *Humanism in Italian Renaissance Musical Thought* [New Haven, 1985], p. 357 n. 60); see also Chap. 7 n. 60 above. Zarlino proscribed parallel major thirds in *Le istitutioni harmoniche* (Venice, 1558) because of the cross relations they cause (Part III, Chap. 29, p. 177).

34. *Istitutioni harmoniche,* p. 339.

35. See above, Chap. 5 n. 124.

36. All of these were variously remarked by contemporary literary theorists for their fullness, gravity, and dissonance. On *a*'s and *o*'s see the views of Bembo, Tomitano, and Parthenio cited in Chap. 5 nn. 109, 110, 123, 138–39; on the consonants *r, s,* and *t,* see Bembo cited Chap. 5 nn. 111–12 and Tomitano, nn. 123–25, among others. See also nn. 117–18 on vowel- and consonant-filled syllables.

37. Still more so are the erratic shifts at "questo fosco aer fumanti" from v. 4, esp. m. 33; see the complete setting in Rore, *Opera omnia* 2:29–34.

less adventuresome: witness the poet's "fury" in v. 11 (Ex. 22), where melismas weave their way through a mild progression of fifths, C-G-C-F-C-G (mm. 100–105). Despite the wide registral spans and wild contours in some of these melismatic passages (e.g., quintus, mm. 106–7), however, Rore's voice leading minimizes the destabilizing effects of voice crossing. In this respect, such melismatic passages contrast with the many instances of chordal declamation, where voice crossing often abounds (in Ex. 20, note mm. 13–16).

This process of broadening out from syllabic textures to more florid ones that resolve instabilities of tonality and voice leading takes place repeatedly in the madrigal. It seems unlikely that Rore developed the technique by simply extending expressive possibilities he learned from Willaert, for Willaert made such pronounced

Rore, *Strane ruppi, aspri monti, alte tremanti* (prob. Luigi Tansillo), mm. 100–108; *Madrigali a 5* (Venice, 1542), no. 7.

juxtapositions only at the most exceptional passages, like his setting of the paradox that opens *Cantai, hor piango* (see Ex. 45a). More typical is the diffident rhetoric of *Pien d'un vago pensier* (Ex. 14).

Almost invariably Rore's settings make use of Willaertian rhetoric but only for expressive contrast and rarely in so reticent a state as Willaert's own. Even a passage that explicitly recalls Willaert's plain idiom such as "Abbandonati, sterili deserti" (Ex. 23) is too idiosyncratic for Willaert in its contrapuntal construction. Here the passage earlier seen in Ex. 21 (mm. 47–54) devolves into an unsettled motivic counterpoint once all the voices have formed a perfect cadence on G. Pulled apart grammatically, the separate nouns and adjectives create ephemeral effects of a kind generally unknown in midcentury Venetian madrigals—contrapuntal disintegrations

EX. 23. Rore, *Strane ruppi, aspri monti, alte tremanti* (prob. Luigi Tansillo), mm. 54–62; *Madrigali a 5* (Venice, 1542), no. 7.

that we might call, after Anthony Newcomb's descriptions of the cadences in late Ferrarese madrigals, "evaporated."[38] In mm. 55–57 the fifth motion that animates the bassus provides a little momentum and direction to help the music retain its bearings, but by mm. 57–61 a sense of disorientation begins to set in again. The lowest-sounding note constantly migrates from part to part, switching back and forth from tenor to bassus as the texture is intermittently abandoned by one voice and then another. Finally these stark motives seem to go nowhere and end in the empty major third at m. 61. Both the textural disorder and spare, sharply etched motives foreshadow Rore's later experiments of the 1550s, as well as the Luzzaschian and Monteverdian madrigals of the 1590s. The eloquent minor-sixth leap in the altus of

38. *The Madrigal at Ferrara, 1579–1597*, 2 vols. (Princeton, 1980), 1:120 n. 6.

mm. 54–55 even brings to mind the kind of barren pathos evoked in the famous opening of Monteverdi's *Vattene pur crudel*.[39]

Strane ruppi shows other extremes foreign to Willaert beyond those exemplified here. Occasionally they crop up quite unexpectedly, as in the madrigal's voluptuous, sequence-filled *fioriture*—one in the cantus on "erranti" (mm. 72–76), for example, and another for the final "ombre udito" (mm. 141–42). Other melismas are surprisingly angular, like the triadic tenor at m. 27 and the quintus at mm. 22–24, seen in Ex. 20.

What is remarkable, then, is not the boldness of any one such gesture viewed in isolation, but the general saturation of them. When the book first appeared, the public was unused to such intense expression applied to vernacular poetry; nor would it have been used to hearing such dramatic poetry sung to music. In fact, neither *Strane ruppi* nor *Altiero sasso* was ever set again, despite the popularity of Rore's book, and the same can be said of a number of other poems Rore published in it.[40] *Per mezz'i boschi* was not reset until later decades, by the Nicosian Pietro Vinci and the Mantuan Wert. Only late in the century did its topos become a favorite in the form of Petrarch's *Solo e pensoso, i più deserti campi,* where it found memorable expositions at the hands of Wert and Marenzio in the 1580s and 1590s. In 1542 that topos was—and would remain for many decades—a rarity.

———————

There is a lighter side to the *Primo libro,* however, one that is mostly evident in its settings of madrigals and ballate. Of these, the former evince more realism than the book's other poems, though all four settings differ poetically from even the book's most restrained sonnets. The least facile—and most influential—of them was the opening madrigal, *Cantai mentre ch'i arsi del mio foco,* which will figure in the next chapter in connection with resettings by madrigalists even younger than Rore, the San Marco musicians Perissone and Parabosco. For the other poems Rore turned to a more cantabile idiom, a more modest elocution, and a style that is altogether less weighty and highly wrought.

The contrast of light and weighty styles reveals itself in the exordia Rore wrote for the madrigal *Hor che l'aria e la terra* and the sonnet to which it is loosely related, *Hor che 'l ciel e la terra e 'l vento tace* (Exx. 24 and 25). The two share the same basic declamatory rhythms through the first eight syllables. But in the usual high Venetian manner *Hor che 'l ciel* pits a syncopated entrance of the quintus against unsyncopated entrances in the other voices and a moment later varies the *soggetto* in the altus with a new dotted rhythm (mm. 3–4). These irregularities instantly complicate the metric edifice. By contrast, the exordial rhythms of *Hor che l'aria* are

———————

39. See Claudio Monteverdi, *Tutte le opere,* ed. G. Francesco Malipiero, 17 vols. (Asolo, 1926–42; Venice, 1966), vol. 3 (1926), p. 48. Rore achieves a similar effect for the exposition of *Altiero sasso.*

40. These include no. 3, *Poggiand'il ciel,* no. 9, *Tu piangi,* no. 10, *Perseguendomi amor,* and no. 15, *Quel sempre acerbo,* as well as both of the madrigals (nos. 18 and 19).

virtually uniform through all five entrances and only vary with the reentry of the tenor in mm. 3–4. Similarly, while the opening measures of *Hor che 'l ciel* are drenched in semitones—D-E♭, G-F♯, B♮-C—*Hor che l'aria* is completely diatonic.

The vigorous rhetoric Rore fashioned for a poem like *Hor che 'l ciel* was unsuited to most madrigals, ballate, and small canzone stanzas. Perhaps the most unequivocal expressive departure of *Hor che 'l ciel* from the milder *Hor che l'aria* comes at the ravishing contrasts of vv. 5–6, where Petrarch jolts the sonnet from the serenity of the first quatrain to introduce a sudden shift to first-person parataxis. By contrast with the tranquil scene painting of vv. 1–4, the verbs of v. 5 move along in an unsettled, if weary, *dissolutio*. Suddenly, as the parataxis breaks, the verse tumbles in enjambment toward the oxymoron of v. 6.

EX. 25. Rore, *Hor che 'l ciel e la terra e 'l vento tace* (Petrarch, no. 164), mm. 1–12; *Madrigali a 5* (Venice, 1542), no. 2.

Hor che 'l ciel e la terra e 'l vento tace	Now that the heavens and the earth and the wind are silent,
E le fere e gli augelli il sonno affrena,	And sleep reins in the beasts and the birds,
Notte 'l carro stellato in giro mena	Night drives her starry chariot around
E nel suo letto il mar senz'onda giace	And in its bed the sea lies without a wave.
Veggio, penso, ardo, piango, e chi mi sface	I am awake, I think, I burn, I weep; and she who destroys me
Sempre m'è inanzi per mia dolce pena;	Is always before me, to my sweet pain;

Rore's setting orchestrates the resultant interplay of syntax and rhetoric in vv. 5–6 while maximizing the expressive possibilities broached by the instabilities of the exordium (Ex. 26). It sets off the syntactic disjunction of the verbs in v. 5 by

EX. 26. Rore, *Hor che 'l ciel e la terra e 'l vento tace* (Petrarch, no. 164), mm. 37–56; *Madrigali a 5* (Venice, 1542), no. 2.

suddenly slowing the declamatory speed. Each verb is declaimed in a plaintive two-note gesture (often a simple minor second) and isolated by rests. Measures 37–44 move through an unpredictable harmonic course, irregular rhythms, and a texture wholly variable in density and weave. Ultimately, this passage forms a foil to the music starting at mm. 44–45 by distinguishing the shift to third person at the end of v. 5 ("E chi mi sface / Sempre m'è innanzi") with a return to the standard declamatory rate and counterpoint. First set off by rests, the clause is realized in a rhythmic parallel that energizes the enjambment and embodies it iconically through various rising and falling melodies, at the same time as it accentuates the words' expressive asymmetries.

Rore's *Primo libro*—and especially the play of these two text settings—nonetheless attests to the continued vitality of lighter poetic forms in Venetian printed repertories, not least because it represents the first printed madrigal book of such weight. Some of the lighter settings published alongside sonnets undoubtedly carried a whiff of nostalgia for the prettier, more chansonesque idioms of Verdelot and Arcadelt. Others offered more neutral versions of the new Venetian style, possibly more congenial to the amateurs who had purchase on printed books. Rore's Second Book, a printer's compilation drawn from a variety of styles and authors, furnished numerous examples of these earlier idioms, along with retrospective settings and new-styled Venetian sonnet settings.

SECONDO LIBRO A 5 (1544): ANTHOLOGY IN THE GUISE OF SINGLE-AUTHOR PRINT

The distinctive makeup of Rore's second book sharpens the contrast between Petrarchan sonnet settings and settings of lighter and (in part) more realistic verse seen in his first. Of its scant eight madrigals by Rore, four set sonnets of Petrarch, two set occasional sonnets, one an occasional cinquecento madrigal, and one a little ballata-madrigal (see Table 8). All four of the Petrarch settings are placed consecutively (as nos. 15 to 18), the others, all by unidentified poets, ranged throughout the print (nos. 1, 3, 14, and 26). We will see that, as in Book One, this rough bifurcation of sonnets and nonsonnets throws into relief a general stylistic one.

With less than a third of its twenty-seven settings by Rore, however, we can hardly take at face value the title under which Gardane marketed the book: *Di Cipriano il secondo libro de madregali a cinque voci insieme alcuni di M. Adriano et altri autori a misura comune novamente posti in luce a cinque voci.*[41] Rore's contributions form only a few points on a map that plots a significant corner of the northern madrigalian dialect. Among the other madrigals in the volume, the most prestigious and prominently placed are Willaert's. The *Secondo libro* was the first publication to print Willaert's and Rore's madrigals in quasi-symmetrical proximities: Willaert's first setting, no. 2, was wedged between Rore's first two and his final one, no. 27, just after Rore's last (as if giving Willaert the last word). No. 2, the lengthy ballata-madrigal *Sciocco fu il tuo desire* (see Chap. 7, pp. 221–22), was followed by a sonnet setting of Rore's; and no. 27, the ten-line madrigal *Qual vista sarà mai,* came after Rore's little ballata-madrigal *Deh, se ti strins'amore.* Thus two "pairs" framed the book at front and back, with madrigals roughly equivalent in weight and size by each composer making up each pair. It is not surprising that the centerpiece of the book, Rore's four settings of Petrarch's sonnets, is unmatched by Willaert's contributions, since Willaert published none of his Petrarch sonnet settings until 1559.

Of the other contributors, the Roman-based Fleming Hubert Naich follows Rore in number with seven madrigals (nos. 4, 10–12, 19, and 24–25). His settings probably served as fillers, however. They are among the least engaged in the Venetian style that otherwise stamps the print—the least concerned with textual rhetoric or polyphonic breadth—and but for one setting of a Petrarch sonnet (no. 24), bizarrely truncated after seven verses, they are almost wholly disengaged from the high-styled literary verse prevalent among Venetians.[42]

The single madrigals by Arcadelt and Ferrabosco (nos. 20 and 21), both of whom had ties not to Venice but to Rome, also stand outside the book's Venetian charac-

---

41. In addition, eight of the madrigals in the book had appeared (undoubtedly before Gardane's edition) in Scotto's reprint of Rore's First Book of the same year, of which six of the madrigals were Rore's. See *Il nuovo Vogel* no. 2391 (2:1480–81) and no. 2401 (2:1485–86)—Scotto's reprint of Book One and Gardane's edition of Book Two, respectively—and see the comments of Lewis, *Antonio Gardane,* p. 436, and the forthcoming catalogue of Scotto's printing house by Jane A. Bernstein.

42. Another sonnet of Naich is apparently occasional, addressed to the "sacrato impero" and set in one part (no. 12). Four other settings are of madrigals (nos. 10, 11, 19, and 25) and another a short canzone (no. 4), all anonymous. For a good biography of Naich and summary of his madrigalian style see Don Harrán's foreword to his edition of *The Anthologies of Black-Note Madrigals,* Corpus mensurabilis musicae, no. 73, AIM, 5 vols. (Neuhausen-Stuttgart, 1978), 1:xxix, and idem, "Hubert Naich, Musicien, Académicien," *Fontes artes musicae* 28 (1981): 177–94. It should be noted that all of Naich's madrigals had been published around 1540 by the Roman printer Antonio Blado in Naich's *Exercitium seraficum* (Rome, [ca. 1540]).

T A B L E 8

Cipriano de Rore, *Secondo libro a 5* (1544), ed. Gardane

[RISM 1544[17]]

Incipit; Composer; Poetic Form; Poet and Poetic Source	System	Cleffing	Final
1. **Cantiamo lieti il fortunato giorno**	b	c1	C
ii. **La terra di novelle et vaghi fiori**	b	c1	F
sonnet			
Anon.			
2. Sciocco fu 'l tuo desire	b	c1	FF
ii. Donna cortese'e humana	b	c1	FF
Adriano [Willaert]			
19-line ballata-madr: aBBcDcDeFEGgfhAHHaA			
Anon.			
3. **Sfrondate, o sacre dive**	b	g2	G
10-line madr: aBCcDEbEFF			
Anon.			
4. Gentil, almo paese	b	g2	G
Hubert Naich			
canzone stanza: abCabC ddCD			
Anon.			
5. Che cosa al mondo far potea natura	b	c1	A
ii. Fu del fattor mirabil magistero	b	c1	GG
Pierresson [Perissone Cambio]			
sonnet			
Anon.			
6. Lasso, che desiando	b	c1	A
Iachet Berchem			
canzone stanza			
Petrarch, no. 73, stanza 6			
7. L'occhio, la man, la bocca, il collo, il petto	b	c1	A
Unattributed			
9-line ballata-madr: ABB CDDC BB			
Anon.			
8. Vaghe faville, angeliche beatrici	b	c1	GG
Leon Barré			
canzone stanza, *sirima* only			
Petrarch, no. 72, stanza 3			
9. Qual anima ignorante over piu saggia	b	c2	A
Willaert			
sonnet (complete)			
Anon.			
10. I soventi martiri	—	c1	A
Hubert Naich			
11-line madr: aBbAAcDdEFF			
Anon.			

(continued)

TABLE 8 *(continued)*

Incipit; Composer; Poetic Form; Poet and Poetic Source	System	Cleffing	Final
11. Mirate altrove vita mia che offende Hubert Naich 9-line madr Anon.	—	c1	**A**
12. L'alta gloria d'amor gli alti trophei Hubert Naich sonnet (complete) Anon.	—	c1	**A**
13. Anima bella, da quel nodo sciolta Hieronimo Parabosco octave Petrarch [and Parabosco?] lines 1–4 = Petrarch, no. 305	—	c1	**A**
14. **Scielgan l'alme sorelle in li orti suoi** ii. **Ardir, senno, virtù, bellezza e fede** sonnet Anon.	— —	c1 c1	**GG** . **E**
15. **O dolci sguardi, o parolette accorte** ii. **Et se talhor da begli occhi soavi** sonnet Petrarch, no. 253	— —	c1 c1	A **EE**
16. **I' mi vivea di mia sorte contento** ii. **O natura pietosa et fera madre** sonnet Petrarch, no. 231	— —	c4 c4	A **EE**
17. **Padre del ciel, dopo i perduti giorni** ii. **Hor volge, signor mio, l'undecimo** sonnet Petrarch, no. 62	b b	g2 g2	D **G**
18. **Fu forse un tempo dolce cosa amore** ii. **Ogni mio ben crudel morte m'ha tolto** sonnet Petrarch, no. 344	b b	g2 g2	D **A**
19. Poscia che 'l tempo in vano adopra Hubert Naich 12-line madr: aBBcDDCeFfgG Anon.	b	g2	**G**
20. S'infinita bellezza [Jacques] Archadelt 7-line madr: ABCDBdd Anon.	b	g2	**G**
21. Più d'alto pin ch'in mezzo un orto sia ii. Ma se del mio tormento non ti cale [Domenico] Ferabosco sonnet Anon.	b b	g2 g2	G G

TABLE 8 *(continued)*

Incipit; Composer; Poetic Form; Poet and Poetic Source	System	Cleffing	Final
22. Lasso, qual fia giamai Unattributed 15-line madr: aBBCDCeFEGgHhII Anon.	b	c1	**G**
23. Aprimi, Amor, le labbia, esci soavi di lor Unattributed 6-line madr: ABcCdd Anon.	b	g2	**G**
24. Dolce ire, dolci sdegni, et dolci paci Hubert Naich sonnet, vv. 1–7 only Petrarch, no. 205	—	g2	**D**
25. Dolce pensier, che spesso mi rimembri Hubert Naich 9-line madr: ABCdECCEF Anon.	—	g2	**D**
26. **Deh, se ti strins'amore** 9-line ballata-madr: aBB cDcDEE Anon.	—	c1	**E**
27. Qual vista sarà mai, occhi miei lassi Adriano [Willaert] 10-line madr: AbbaCdcDeE Anon.	b	c2	**A**

N.B. Settings by Rore are given in boldface, as are finals; confinals are given in regular type.

ter,[43] but each of the other contributors was in some way aligned with Venice stylistically and, in most cases, biographically. Clearest among these were Willaert's students Perissone Cambio and Girolamo Parabosco. Perissone's bipartite setting of a spiritual sonnet (no. 5) and Parabosco's setting of an octave adapted from Petrarch (no. 13) are both unmistakably Venetian works that will be taken up in Chapter 9. For both composers, the *Secondo libro* was the venue of their first secular vocal publications, along with Doni's *Dialogo della musica* of the same year.

Less obvious but sound enough claims to Venetian provenance fall to two final contributors, Jacquet Berchem and Leonardus Barré. The prolific Berchem spent time in Venice during the 1540s and may well have been sponsored by an ostensible

43. Harrán, ed., *Anthologies of Black-Note Madrigals* 1:xxix.

Ex. 27.   Giachet Berchem, *Lasso, che desiando* (Petrarch, no. 73, stanza 6): a, mm. 18–24; b, tenor, mm. 8–11; c, cantus, mm. 24–28; *Di Cipriano il secondo libro de madregali a 5* (Venice, 1544) (RISM 1544[17]), no. 6.

patron of Willaert's, Marcantonio Trevisano.[44] Yet his contribution of a Petrarchan canzone stanza, *Lasso, che desiando* (no. 8), shares little of the syntactic and accentual precision or rhetorical logic of Willaert's settings, and the same is true of the Petrarchan settings, six in all, in his first book of 1546.[45] *Lasso, che desiando* does make modest efforts at Willaertian rhetoric, but it also contains instances of awkward text setting of a sort that virtually never mar the settings of Willaert's immediate circle. (Note, for example, in Ex. 27: a) the unvaried misaccentuation of "solamente" and the quintus's broken "sola-, solamente" [mm. 18–20]; b) the tenor's clumsy declamation of the cadential "non puot'in alcun modo"; and c) likewise, the misaccented cadence on "Ch'Amor circund'alla mia lingua.")

The work of the lesser-known Barré shows surprisingly deeper sympathies with Venetian practices than Berchem's. Barré had already debuted as a member of the

---

44. See Appendix to Chap. 3, as well as Dale Emerson Hall, "The Italian Secular Works of Jacquet Berchem" (Ph.D. diss., The Ohio State University, 1973), esp. pp. 21–22 and passim; and George Nugent, "The Jacquet Motets and Their Authors" (Ph.D. diss., Princeton University, 1973).

45. Mod. ed. Jessie Ann Owens, The Italian Madrigal, vol. 1 (New York, 1993). The ambiguities of text underlay in Berchem's book almost never appear in those of Willaert's students at San Marco.

Leonardus Barré, *Vaghe faville, angeliche beatrici* (Petrarch, no. 72, vv. 37–45),
mm. 1–6; *Di Cipriano il secondo libro de madregali a 5* (Venice, 1544) (RISM 1544[17]), no. 8.

(then fledgling) Venetian school in the five-voice anthology *Le dotte, et eccellente compositioni de i madrigali a cinque voci da diversi perfettissimi musici fatte,* printed by Scotto in 1540 (RISM 1540[18]).[46] Though he was a papal singer, the print's title page dubbed him a "discipulo" of Willaert's. The claim is not sustained by other biographical findings, but the style of his *Vaghe faville, angeliche beatrici* (no. 8), a setting of the *sirima* from the third stanza of Petrarch's canzone no. 72, makes it entirely plausible. Barré set the text in a motet texture, with meticulous accentuation and declamation and all the choice gauging of musical to verbal cadence emphasized by Willaert and Zarlino. As seen in Ex. 28, the first three voices of the exposition immediately preempt the possibility of a dominating tactus by staggering their entrances at the minim with the device that Zarlino called a "sospiro."[47] Subsequent entries are equally irregular, metrically and melodically, and delicately inflected with e-flats in a way that prefigures the nuanced Venetian-styled reading of subsequent passages.

A few observations, then. First, the *Secondo libro,* like Doni's *Dialogo della musica,* already evinces the diffusion of Venetian style beyond the chapel members and Rore to a larger circle. In this respect, the book offers a useful way to see the two composers now regarded as the style's most illustrious practitioners in relation to

46. See Fenlon and Haar, *The Italian Madrigal,* pp. 313–16.
47. See *Le istitutioni harmoniche,* Part III, Chap. 44, and Chap. 6 above, Ex. 5. The exposition's *soggetto* likewise collaborates in shaping Barré's introverted style: carried by the cantus and tenor as the third and fifth voices to enter, it conforms to the kind of exposition cautiously approved by Zarlino in which non-*soggetto* voices enter first, adapting themselves to a "real" *soggetto* that materializes only later. See *Le istitutioni harmoniche,* Part III, Chap. 28, and Chap. 6 above, n. 81.

surrounding lesser lights.[48] Second, to date none of the poets who authored verses in the *Secondo libro* has been identified save Petrarch (and provisionally the Petrarchan adaptation, no. 13). Given increasingly useful (if still limited) apparatuses for searching cinquecento poetic sources, this profusion of anonymous poetry looks less and less coincidental. Even in its own time the book probably divided roughly into anonymous poetry, on the one hand—synonymous with poetry never meant for collection or preservation outside of music—and Petrarch's poetry, on the other. Perhaps only one other print of Venetian provenance displays a division as strict, namely Perissone's *Primo libro a 4* of 1547, which figures in my discussion in Chapter 9. Third, the rough division of poetry into two large branches—lighter anonymous and weightier Petrarchan—has broader ramifications. Petrarch's poems form the basis of a higher, more remote expression, while the anonymous ones run the gamut: some are set in styles close to those of the Petrarch settings, others are much lighter in tone. (The same sort of bifurcation marks Willaert's entire corpus, of course—a bifurcation duplicated in its patterns of preservation.) By juxtaposing Petrarchan settings with settings of anonymous verse, composers set a probing and timeless aesthetic against the simpler, more mundane countertypes produced by transient Petrarchan imitators.

The latter have their most characteristic embodiment in settings of occasional verse, whose worldly aspect manifests itself in three of Rore's four non-Petrarch settings, all of them celebratory: two wedding sonnets (nos. 1 and 14) and an encomium of one Isabella of Cremona (no. 3). Verse like this was much at home in the madrigalian anthology, since both celebratory settings and printed anthologies bore the social signs of commodification. Whether vended by composers or printers, both were publicly produced for capital consumption with an ear to easy appeal.

The opening madrigal of the *Secondo libro,* a sonnet for a Gonzaga wedding, speaks precisely out into this public space. The text opens in the first-person plural, familiar from songs for carnival and theater, calling up the image of costumed singers staging their song for assembled wedding guests.

Cantiamo lieti il fortunato giorno	Let us sing joyously about the happy day
Che strins'a un nodo sacr'almo e tenace	That bound in a sacred, life-giving, constant knot
Coppia si degna e con ardente face	Such a worthy couple, and adorned this
Il fe divino amor leggiadro adorno.	Divine, happy love with an ardent light. 4
Cantiamo lieti, che già d'ogn'intorno	Let us sing joyously, for heaven is already rejoicing
S'allegr'il cielo, l'aria e 'l vento tace,	All about, the air and the wind are silent,

48. An inverse pattern of dissemination can be seen in the 1546 reprint of Verdelot's six-voice madrigals, *Madrigali di Verdelot et de altri autori a sei voci novamente con alcuni madrigali novi ristampati et corretti* (originally titled *La piu divina . . . musica* in 1541), printed, like the original ed., by Gardane. Its inclusion of works by Willaert, Parabosco, Perissone, Berchem, and Nollet (all of them represented in Doni's *Dialogo della musica*), along with those of Verdelot, Festa, Arcadelt, Maistre Jhan, and others, justifies Fenlon and Haar's description of the reprint as having "a more Venetian cast" than the original ed. (*The Italian Madrigal,* pp. 317–18).

E 'l bel sereno appare, e già si sface	And the weather appears serene, and already
A tutti gli animanti un bel soggiorno.	A beautiful site is arrayed before all the lively ones. 8
La terra di novelli e vaghi fiori	The earth paints itself with new and lovely flowers
Ovunque si dipinge e copre il manto	And covers the mantle,
Di la felice et aurea età presaga:	Foreshadowing the happy and golden age: 11
Verà che sol il mondo acqueti e honori	It will come to pass that the sun may appease and honor the world
Da l'alto seme glorioso santo	Through the great, glorious, saintly seed
D'il fiero Marte e l'unica Gonzaga.	Of the proud Mars and the unique Gonzaga.[49] 14

Rore's setting revels in sparkly melodies, with episodes of patter declamation, speechlike rhythms, and (intermittently) extended periods reminiscent of song. In the cantus's first fifteen measures a continuous strain arches from f to cc and back, with graceful diminutions cadencing on the final in the approach to the "Coppia si degna." In keeping with this melodious character, the setting's large-scale structure is more sectionalized than those Rore designed for Petrarch's sonnets. Highlighting the refrainlike anaphora of the first two quatrains, verses 4 and 6 both cadence with the full complement of five voices and on the final, which dominates the setting, followed by the unpretentious modal degrees a (mm. 30, 67, and 89) and c (mm. 61 and 84). Rore executes all this with crisp dispatch—a mere 114 measures for fourteen *endecasillabi,* whereas his settings of Petrarch's sonnets generally average between 130 and 160 measures. His other wedding sonnet, *Scielgan l'alme sorelle,* is equally short and similar in style, with buoyant rhythms, brisk declamation, and several multivoice cadences. In a way almost unknown in Rore's Petrarch settings (and more in keeping with later pastoral styles), many of its melismas are wholly unsyncopated (see the one drawn from the cantus in Ex. 29).

Even though the ethos of *Scielgan l'alme sorelle* is far lighter than that of Willaert's Petrarchan sonnet settings, the work exploited certain *Musica nova*–like techniques to evoke local rhetorical events without recourse to contrapuntal cadences. Most remarkable in this respect is the way in which Rore gives definition to the catalogue of virtues that opens the sestet (and the *seconda parte;* see Ex. 30). The passage did not escape Einstein's attention, and for good reason.[50] Yet his claim that "in 1540 only Rore could write a section as 'articulated'" as this one does not hold up in the face of an analogous passage from Petrarch's *I vidi in terra angelici costumi* set by Willaert; like Rore's exordium, Willaert's also opens the sestet and *seconda parte* (Ex. 31). In composing "Ardir, senno, virtù, bellezza e fede," the anonymous poet of

---

49. The poem, for a spring wedding between a female member of the Gonzaga family and (possibly) a member of a Roman family, is difficult to translate because the grammatical relationships in vv. 3–4 and v. 12 are unclear. I am grateful to Stefano Castelvecchi for his help with it.

For Rore's setting see Rore, *Opera omnia* 2:108–12.

50. See *The Italian Madrigal* 1:401.

EX. 29. Rore, *Scielgan l'alme sorelle in li orti suoi,* cantus, mm. 72–76; *Di Cipriano il secondo libro de madregali a 5* (Venice, 1544) (RISM 1544[17]), no. 14.

EX. 30. Rore, *Scielgan l'alme sorelle in li orti suoi,* mm. 62–67; *Di Cipriano il secondo libro de madregali a 5* (Venice, 1544) (RISM 1544[17]), no. 14.

Scielgan l'alme sorelle surely glossed the rhythms, words, and word sounds of "Amor, senno, valor, pietate e doglia" from Petrarch's *I vidi in terra.* But did Rore's setting gloss Willaert's? This question raises issues of both chronological and musical relationships between the two. A definitive resolution of chronology is not possible, though it is likely that Willaert's setting came first. Einstein's view that in general the Second Book represents the earliest stylistic layer in Rore's oeuvre, that the pieces in it were leftovers from the First Book, and that *Scielgan l'alme sorelle* dates from 1540 (a claim unsupported by circumstantial evidence) was undergirded by his teleological view of the repertory.[51] It conflicts with the model I propose for Venetian madrigals in which different styles endured concurrently in connection with different kinds of poetry, for different kinds of occasions, and for dissemination in different kinds of sources. Probably the works printed in 1544 were mostly newer

51. "Rore's eight compositions for this book . . . seem to me to represent a mere gleaning, all of which antedates the first book of 1542. This follows not only from their notation but also from their character, which is less sharply defined. One of them, *Deh, se ti strins'amore,* is a youthful work, still wholly in the style of Verdelot; others are occasional pieces whose early date will perhaps be determined someday by inferences from the texts" (ibid.).

than those of 1542—at least in part—and more suited (as I have suggested) to inclusion in an anthologistic potpourri.

Questions of musical relationships are less difficult, for the two employ a fragmentary motivic counterpoint that is much alike. Despite differing pitch systems—♭-cI-F for Willaert's, ♮-cI-E for Rore's—each madrigal also begins its *seconda parte* with a circle of fifths starting on a triad based on A. Willaert's passage moves from an A-major chord, carrying over the raised third from the harmony that ended the *prima parte,* through a fully major circle of fifths to a triad on E-flat, both favorite devices of his. By contrast, Rore's *seconda parte* begins on an a-minor triad proper to the mode, though the next sonority is D major (and in the identical spot to Willaert's) and the circle continues until m. 64. Even if Rore did not parrot Willaert here, the passage nonetheless suggests that he attended more closely to Willaert's music than it usually appears.

At least one other passage in the Second Book raises similar questions, a line from the madrigal *Sfrondate, o sacre dive,* v. 8, "Sgombrino l'altre voglie aspr'e selvaggie." This line echoes the incipit of Petrarch's sonnet no. 265, *Aspro core e selvaggio e cruda voglia,* just as Rore's setting echoes the striking exordium of Willaert's *Musica nova* setting of it. As noted in Chapter 7, Claude Palisca (among others) has remarked on the harsh parallel major thirds and major-sixth-to-perfect-fifth progressions of Willaert's exposition, as well as its copious deployment of melodic major seconds and thirds (see Ex. 16).[52] As seen in Ex. 32, Rore's setting makes comparable parallel motion at the words "aspr'e selvagge" and deploys linear major seconds copiously between the respective syllable pairs "a - spr'e" and "sel - vag-," with their descending tetrachords. (Minor seconds, by contrast, more often *connect* the two words to each other.) Given the intensity and exposed position of the parallel-third motion, later proscribed by Zarlino,[53] Willaert's passage bears signs of having served as the model.

Even so, correspondences like these suggest only a very partial obeisance toward Willaert on Rore's part, in addition to confirming Rore's participation in Willaert's practice through their mutual preoccupations with dense five-voice polyphony, Petrarch's sonnets, bipartite settings, and the like. Other aspects of Rore's madrigals—even general ones like choices of sonnets, ordering of sonnets by mode, extensive use of black notation, expansive proportions, and florid melismas—have little or no precedent in Willaert.

Again the musical clues to this relationship rest mainly on the *Primo libro,* for the *Secondo libro* is not really a single-author monument, as its title would have it—not a book *by* Rore at all, but one made to honor and profit from him. For us the *Secondo libro* helps situate Rore's early practice by clarifying his relationship to some of his contemporaries and affirming his recently gained status as Willaert's equal. In

52. See n. 33 above and Zarlino, *Le istitutioni harmoniche,* Part IV, Chap. 32.
53. See nn. 33 and 52 above. Vincenzo Galilei first drew attention to Willaert's breaking of the rule in *Aspro core* in order to justify it as an instance of imitation; see also Chap. 7 above, n. 60.

Rore, *Sfrondate, o sacre dive*, mm. 57–61; *Di Cipriano il secondo libro de madregali a 5* (Venice, 1544) (RISM 1544[17]), no. 3.

this regard we should recall that Rore was the only composer in the *Secondo libro* by whom there were settings of Petrarch's sonnets at all, save the seven odd lines set by Naich. The only other complete settings of sonnets (both anonymous) are those of Willaert and his pupil Perissone, the latter of whom managed, through an ambitious act of entrepreneurship, to become the first acolyte to issue a book dominated by sonnet settings after Willaert's and Rore's leads.

Taken together, Willaert and Rore make an odd pair of figureheads: the one eminently visible to historical view, the other cloaked in mystery; the one moored in a single symbolic space, the other seemingly aloof from the enveloping constraints of place. The aesthetic hegemony that Rore was able to elude was rabidly Ciceronian and anti-Dantean. Even with such minimal information on Rore's ties and whereabouts as we now have, much can be understood by perceiving that his allegiances to Venice, with the many taboos and biases it demanded, must have been far more tenuous than Willaert's. To say so constitutes a substantial revision of long-standing assumptions initiated in the mid-nineteenth century by Francesco Caffi, who claimed that Rore had been a singer in the Chapel of San Marco.[54] Caffi evidently played off two notions that remain much discussed in more recent literature: one was a tradition dating back to the mid-sixteenth century for referring to Rore as Willaert's disciple, which emerged only in 1548 with the dedication of Scotto's edition of Rore's Third Book to Gottardo Occagna;[55] the other was the problematic

---

54. See Francesco Caffi, *Storia della musica sacra nella già cappella ducale di San Marco in Venezia (dal 1318 al 1797): riedizione annotata con aggiornamenti bibliografi (al 1984)*, ed. Elvidio Surian, rev. ed. (Florence, 1987); Surian corrects Caffi on p. 94 n. 2.

55. See Chap. 3 n. 32, above. In 1549 Scotto again described works by "Adriano Vuigliart, et Cipriano de Rore suo discepolo" on the title page of the print *Fantasie, et recerchari a tre voci* (RISM

assumption that whoever was chapelmaster must have had priority in fashioning the new style. The possibility that Caffi's assertions might someday prove right has now been effectively nullified by Giulio Ongaro's detailed documentary study of the chapel in Willaert's time,[56] but Caffi's opinion forms only the first in a line that has long viewed Rore unproblematically as Willaert's student.[57]

All the same, if Rore was as unfettered in the early forties as he seems—freelancing for worldly, nomadic Florentines and the like—we should recall that the allegiances to which Willaert was bound were multiple as well. Even the staunch, seemingly monolithic Venetianism Willaert served was fused with Tuscan tastes—not only through the elitism imposed on him by Capponi but by the Tuscan linguistic norms that Venetians promoted. In the ensuing chapter we will see some of the madrigalistic choices this alliance drew from students who appropriated and disseminated Venetian musical norms in the 1540s and 1550s.

1549[34]). The works in question include five madrigals, centrally placed and printed in alternation by composer (three by Rore and two by Willaert), in addition to seven ricercars by Willaert. A still more equal association between the two was implied two years later by Antonio Gardane's inclusion of two three-voice settings of "Regina caeli, laetare," one each by Willaert and Rore, in a related print (RISM 1551[16], containing seven of the ricercars by Willaert that were printed in 1549[34]). These two settings used the same cantus firmus and were printed on facing pages.

56. "The Chapel of St. Mark's at the Time of Adrian Willaert (1527–1562): A Documentary Study" (Ph.D. diss., University of North Carolina at Chapel Hill, 1986).

57. See Einstein, *The Italian Madrigal* 1:384, and Meier, ed., Rore, *Opera omnia* 2:ii.

By the mid- to late forties Willaert was producing music more and more slowly. He printed his last sizable cache of madrigals (five) in Scotto's edition of Rore's Third Book of 1548, and this after a dry spell of four years. During the same time the pursuit of madrigals by vernacular connoisseurs in Venice like Antonio Zantani, Gottardo Occagna, and Domenico Venier was rising with the increased production of what I have called dialogic volumes around midcentury. With "the good times of la Pecorina" nearly gone, these connoisseurs could have little chance to fill their shelves and parlor rooms with new music by the aging chapelmaster. And Rore—chapelmaster in his own right at Ferrara by the spring of 1546—must have been all but inaccessible.

Willaert's young corps of students at San Marco was eager to fill the void. Girolamo Parabosco had been studying with Willaert since about 1540.[1] Perissone Cambio made his way to the city by 1544 and had joined the chapel by 1548. His tutelage under Willaert probably started earlier, since he was already skilled at Willaertian composition by 1544–45. Baldassare Donato arrived perhaps only slightly later than Perissone (to judge from the raise in the nominal salary he received as a *zago*, a boy singer in training, early in 1546).[2] As we saw in Chapter 7,

1. H. Colin Slim notes that Parabosco may have studied with Willaert as early as the late 1530s, for in 1540 two of his ricercars appeared along with Willaert's in the instrumental print called *Musica nova*; see *Musica nova accommodata per cantar e sonar sopra organi; et altri strumenti, composta per diversi eccellentissimi musici. In Venetia, MDXL,* ed. H. Colin Slim, foreword by Edward E. Lowinsky, Monuments of Renaissance Music, vol. 1 (Chicago, 1964), pp. xxix and passim. According to Zarlino's *Sopplimenti musicali* (Venice, 1588; facs. ed. Ridgewood, N.J., 1966), Parabosco was present in Venice by at least 1541 (p. 326).
2. See Mary S. Lewis (who learned it from Jonathan Glixon), "Rore's Setting of Petrarch's *Vergine bella:* A History of Its Composition and Early Transmission," *Journal of Musicology* 4 (1985–86): 371 n. 13, and Ongaro, "The Chapel of St. Mark's at the Time of Adrian Willaert (1527–1562): A Documentary Study" (Ph.D. diss., University of North Carolina at Chapel Hill, 1986), p. 125 and Document 164.

Donato was enough in his teacher's graces by 1547 to have been given the tasks by the Procuratori of acting as Willaert's scribe and keeping him "occupied in composing."[3] And Francesco Londariti (called "il Greco"), who attended Zantani's gatherings along with the other three, joined the chapel in June 1549.[4]

For musicians at the chapel, training in counterpoint formed an essential part of a general musical education. Counterpoint taught singers how to adapt part music according to the norms of *musica ficta,* how to make the correct consonances and progressions, and how to improvise over a cantus firmus—a practice alluded to by the Venetian dialect author Andrea Calmo in a letter to Willaert.[5] A knowledge of counterpoint (as Margaret Bent has argued) was thus virtually as necessary for singing as for composing. For chapel members, Willaert's counterpoint lessons were part of the weekly agenda, and singers who ignored them (like one Zorzi Carpenello) risked censure from the upper echelons of the church.[6] It did not follow that all performers of part music were also composers, yet one of the most significant coincidences in the social, aesthetic, and economic conjunctures by which vernacular music emerged in Venice was that Willaert's three main disciples excelled in both roles. All but Londariti published solo madrigal books at the same time as they won considerable fame as performers.[7] These composer-performers were among the most successful entrepreneurs in the private worlds of Venetian music making, even though none of them seems to have formed the elitist pacts with patrons that Willaert and Rore did. On the contrary, what distinguished the new generation were careers marked by struggle, entrepreneurship, and mobility. Unlike Willaert's and Rore's prints of Petrarchan sonnet settings, theirs were interlaced with numerous lighter-weight settings of madrigals, canzone stanzas, ballate, and ottave rime, and all of them were underwritten by dedicatees. By recasting elite styles in sunnier guises, they disseminated them in forms that could better appeal to commercial consumers.

3. Donato was also to notify the bureaucracy of any new works that Willaert had composed (see Chap. 7 above, n. 14).

4. Ongaro, "The Chapel of St. Mark's," pp. 128–29 and Document 180.

5. "La vostra componidura amice dulcissime è destilà a sete lambichi, e purgà in nuove acque, e affinà a quatro fuoghi, propio alla condicion de l'Aurum potabilem; mo vegnimo sun questa difficultae, che puochi la sà resolver, tanto la xe difficile, e contrapontizar all'improviso del canto fermo, altro cha dir vilote, ni zorziane, ni barzelete" (Your compositions are distilled in seven stills, purged in fresh water, and sharpened over four fires, just like *aurum potabilem*. But let's turn now to this difficult business, so hard that few can manage it, of improvising a counterpoint over a cantus firmus: how much harder than improvising villotte, *zorziane,* or *barzellette*); *Delle lettere di M. Andrea Calmo libro terzo. Nel quale si contiene varij, & ingeniosi discorsi filosofici, in lingua Veneta composti,* 4 vols. (Venice, 1572), vol. 3, fol. 30.

6. See Ongaro's report of an interrogation of Willaert by one of the Procurators, Giovanni da Lezze, made on 8 August 1538, "The Chapel of St. Mark's," pp. 105–9 and Document 343. For an argument that studying counterpoint in the chapel ranks was an advanced, rather than elementary, training for adult singers, see the interpretation offered on pp. 109–11. For Bent's views on the necessity of counterpoint both for correct composing and singing see "*Resfacta* and *Cantare Super Librum*," *JAMS* 36 (1983): 371–91, esp. p. 377.

7. Although Parabosco was hired as an organist, he was clearly a good salon singer (see n. 8 below). Londariti's surviving madrigals are negligible in number—four, plus two *napolitane*—though he produced a good deal more sacred music. See the brief entry "Londariti, Francesco," in *The New Grove* 11:142.

GIROLAMO PARABOSCO

"The rest of us are worth nothing. Who composes music? Parabosco. Who writes poetry? Parabosco. Who sings, who has a thousand talents? Parabosco. Pazienza!"[8]

So raves Parabosco's fictive rival Claudio Veggio in Doni's *Dialogo della musica* after the interlocutors have just sung three of Parabosco's pieces and then gone on to hear him recite some of his sonnets. At the time Doni wrote the *Dialogo,* the young Piacentine was only about twenty. He had learned keyboard from his father, organist at the cathedral of Brescia from 1536, before going to Venice to study composition with Willaert. Around the time he arrived in Venice a ricercar of his was published in Willaert's instrumental *Musica nova* of 1540, four years before the *Dialogo* appeared, and shortly thereafter he published his first madrigal, the three-voice *Ben madonna a che siamo,* in Constanzo Festa's *Primo libro de madrigali a tre voci . . . novamente ristampati* of 1541.[9] Yet *Ben madonna* is no new-styled setting but a diminutive madrigal on a text rhymed aABccDD that Parabosco rendered with almost childlike naïveté, outfitting it in a quasi-frottolistic dress suited to its simple complaint. In keeping with Festa's settings *a 3,* Parabosco's is largely homophonic, its voices pulling apart only occasionally in imitative or staggered entrances before moving into simultaneous, or near-simultaneous, cadences to end each verse. In this sense his reading is resolutely prosodic, matching single melodic phrases to each poetic line with little concern for syntax and even breaking syllables in mid-word in the way of light and parodistic genres ("ch'io mo-, ch'io mora").[10]

Parabosco may well have been the only one of Willaert's three main disciples who had already arrived in Venice by the late thirties to the early forties when Strozzi and Capponi were both encamped there, and who had begun by practicing a decidedly pre–*Musica nova* art. This may help explain why so much variety is found among his juvenilia from 1544, four in Doni's *Dialogo della musica* and one in Rore's *Secondo libro de madrigali a cinque voci.* Of these, two set poems by Petrarch (the octave from the sonnet *Giunto m'ha Amor fra belle e crude braccia,* no. 171, and stanza seven from the sestina *Nessun visse giamai più di me lieto,* no. 332); one the octave from a sonnet by the Florentine Lodovico Martelli (*Pur converrà ch'i miei martiri amore*);[11]

---

8. "Noi altri ci siam per nulla; chi compone i canti, Parabosco; chi fa versi, Parabosco; chi suona, chi ha mille virtù, Parabosco. Pazienza" (Antonfrancesco Doni, *Dialogo della musica,* ed. G. Francesco Malipiero and Virginio Fagotto [Vienna, 1965], p. 190). Another edition of the *Dialogo* is that of Anna Maria Monterosso Vacchelli, *L'opera musicale di Antonfrancesco Doni,* Instituta e monumenta, ser. 2, no. 1 (Cremona, 1969).

9. The latter work may have appeared even earlier since the Festa print is called "ristampato" on Gardane's title page, but the original edition is now lost (see Fenlon and Haar, *The Italian Madrigal,* p. 231). A mod. ed. of *Ben madonna* is included in Gerolamo Parabosco, *Composizioni a due, tre, quattro, cinque e sei voci,* ed. Francesco Bussi (Piacenza, 1961), pp. 5–6. For the ricercar see *Musica nova accommodata per cantar et sonar sopra organi,* ricercar "Da pacem," pp. 123–24. For further on Parabosco's biography see the citations in Chap. 1 n. 38 above.

10. For Zarlino's proscription against this see *Le istitutioni harmoniche* (Venice, 1558), p. 341.

11. For the Petrarch settings see the eds. in Doni, *Dialogo della musica,* pp. 64–69 and 123–28, respectively. For *Pur converrà* see idem, pp. 58–63, and Parabosco, *Composizioni,* pp. 7–11; for the poem see Lodovico Martelli, *Rime volgari* (Rome, 1533), fols. 20–20´.

one set a ballata by the Venetian Giovanni Brevio (*Cantai mentre ch'io arsi del mio foco*);[12] and the fifth—the one that appeared in Rore's collection—set a gloss on Petrarch's sonnet *Anima bella da quel nodo sciolta*.[13] These texts anticipate the predilection Parabosco, or his patrons, had for established poets. In his only printed madrigal collection, *Madrigali a cinque voci* of 1546, every poet can be named, save one, a distinction not shared by any of the other collections by Willaert's students (see Table 9). By 1544, in keeping with this high literary tone, Parabosco's madrigals also began to fashion themselves in response to Willaertian declamatory ideals: largely syllabic, carefully accentuated, complexly textured, ingeniously articulated, expressively colored, and newly sensitive to the subtleties of rhetoric.

Nevertheless, in altering or abridging a number of the texts he set, Parabosco eschewed the absolutist demands for perfect literary integrity that Willaert and Rore were making in the 1540s. His *Anima bella* irreverently tacks a newly written quatrain onto a quatrain by Petrarch. Another setting, *Niuna sconsolata* (in the *Madrigali a 5*), begins a thirteen-line madrigal by quoting the three-line *ripresa* from Boccaccio's ballata of the same incipit.[14] Such texts move between standard ploys of imitation and something more like revision. In line with the radical manipulations they work on preexistent verse, Parabosco's other settings often truncate poems, in some cases drastically. At other times, they extract stanzas from canzoni and sestine or take octaves from sonnets to set either in one part (as in *Giunto m'ha Amor*) or in two (as in *I' vo piangendo* from the *Madrigali a 5*). Truncations of extended lyrics were of course a typical corollary of the fairly freewheeling attitudes madrigalists across Italy often held about the texts they set, and it was precisely those attitudes that were called into question by the new reverence with which Venetians began treating vernacular poetry. Perhaps it is no surprise that a poet and brash, self-made man of culture like Parabosco would not fully have shared them.

Parabosco's music written for 1544 collections shows less sweeping affinities with Willaert's practice than that from 1546. The truncated *Giunto m'ha Amor* set *a 4* forms a case in point and a revealing basis for comparison with Parabosco's later work. *Giunto m'ha Amor* does not model itself on Willaert's five-voice setting from the *Musica nova* but unfolds in a series of Willaertian expositions on overlapping syntactic units.[15] Unlike Willaert, Parabosco balanced the claims of syntax against those of versification, rather than calibrating cadences strictly according to words' grammatical weight and order. The differences are notable in Willaert's and Parabosco's settings of vv. 2–3 of *Giunto m'ha Amor,* both of which are marked by

12. Modern eds. in Parabosco, *Composizioni*, pp. 12–24, and Doni, *Dialogo della musica*, pp. 176–88; for the poetic source see Table 6, no. 1.

13. Modern ed. in Einstein, *The Italian Madrigal* 3:151–54.

14. Cf. Boccaccio, *Decamerone*, ed. Mario Marti, 5th ed., 2 vols. (Milan, 1984), 1:262, and Girolamo Parabosco, *Il primo libro dei madrigali, 1551*, ed. Nicola Longo (Rome, 1987), p. 113.

15. Neither does Parabosco's setting show any relationship to Girolamo Scotto's setting of 1542, whose declamation is often oblivious to textual accent; see *Madrigali a quattro voci di Geronimo Scotto con alcuni alla misura breve, et altri a voce pari . . . Libro primo* (Venice, 1542), no. 20.

strong articulation owing to the deployment of three grammatical clauses over four poetic lines (as marked below in the version from Willaert's setting).

[1] Giunto m'ha Amor fra belle e crude braccia, Che m'ancidono à torto, [2] e s'io mi doglio Doppia 'l martir, [3] onde pur, com'io soglio, Il meglio è ch'io mi mora amando e taccia.

[1] Love has brought me within reach of lovely, cruel arms That unjustly kill me, [2] and if I complain he redoubles my torment; [3] thus still, as I am wont, it is better that I die loving and be silent.

In Petrarch's text all three syntactic parcels are effectively displaced from the versification, the first ending in the middle of v. 2 and the second in the middle of v. 3. For Willaert, these clauses determined the shape and layout of the syntactic counterpoint, as seen in the articulations he makes in the middles of those verses (See Ex. 33a beginning with v. 2). "E s'io mi doglio" and "onde pur" generate new *soggetti* (albeit internally varied ones) and, for the most part, new pitch planes. Willaert's setting separates each clause with rests, projecting the enjambments and practically effacing the poetic prosody. By contrast, Parabosco's setting virtually inverts Willaert's hierarchy of syntax and versification, closing off "Che m'ancidono a torto" with a simple cadence that is weak by comparison with the four-voice diminished *clausula in mi* ending "e s'io mi doglio" (Ex. 33b; compare mm. 8 and 10) and unfolding a separate exposition on "Dopp'il martir." Parabosco's ostensibly syntactic treatment thus masks what is really a poetic one, while Willaert treats the text almost as though it were prose.[16]

Put another way, Parabosco parsed text more like song than prose-based polyphony, consistent with his more lyric declamation. Not only are his melodies prone to free melismatic flights reminiscent of Rore's (see, for instance, the melisma in the tenor on "soglio," Ex. 33b, mm. 15–18), they are also more extended than Willaert would allow. Willaert, for example, set the *r*-, *o*-, and consonant-laden "e rompr'ogn'aspro scoglio" with unvaried austerity, reiterating a series of quarter notes (Ex. 34a), while Parabosco broke up the line to lyricize at least one voice (again, the tenor) with florid turns, graceful dotted notes, and leaps (Ex. 34b). In this sense Parabosco's *Giunto m'ha Amor,* and other settings of his from 1544, indicate he was under the sway of Rore's First Book. Given Veggio's suggestion that Parabosco was a fairly proficient singer—Veggio mentions it in a world in which virtually everyone could sing—and given his acquaintance with Ruberto Strozzi and the whole circle of those close to Willaert and Capponi, we can guess that Parabosco knew Rore's madrigals from having sung them in salons himself. Two of his madrigals can be located specifically within Rore's madrigalian production: *Anima bella,* the Petrarchan adaptation that had its debut in Rore's Second Book,

16. For further on Willaert's setting, see Howard Mayer Brown, "Words and Music: Willaert, the Chanson and the Madrigal about 1540," in *Florence and Venice, Comparisons and Relations: Acts of Two Conferences at Villa I Tatti in 1976–1977,* vol. 2, *Il Cinquecento,* ed. Christine Smith with Salvatore I. Camporeale (Florence, 1980), pp. 225–28.

Willaert, *Giunto m'ha Amor fra belle e crude braccia* (Petrarch, no. 171), mm. 9–24; *Musica nova* (Venice, 1559), no. 11.

Parabosco, *Giunto m'ha Amor fra belle e crude braccia* (Petrarch, no. 171), mm. 5–18; in Antonfrancesco Doni, *Dialogo della musica* (Venice, 1544), fol. 14 in cantus.

and the six-voice setting of Brevio's *Cantai mentre ch'io arsi*. The latter shows extensive similarities with the setting Rore had published at the head of his First Book, from the same signature and final (G mollis) and overall length (104 breves compared with Rore's 105) to numerous details of interpretation.

Cantai mentre ch'io arsi is a ballata, organized sonnetlike in fourteen hendecasyllabic verses, whose grammatical articulation coincides exactly with its formal scheme.[17]

17. I give the poem as it appears in Parabosco's setting. Bussi mistakes the poem for a sonnet and therefore presents a wayward analysis of Parabosco's setting (*Umanità e arte di Gerolamo Parabosco: madrigalista, organista, e poligrafo* [Piacenza, 1961], p. 127). The form of Brevio's ballata is exactly the same

EX. 34B. Parabosco, *Giunto m'ha Amor fra belle e crude braccia* (Petrarch, no. 171), mm. 29–36; in Antonfrancesco Doni, *Dialogo della musica* (Venice, 1544), fol. 14 in cantus.

Cantai, mentre ch'io arsi, del mio foco
La viva fiamma, ov'io morendo vissi,
Benchè quant'io cantai e quant'io scrissi
Di madonna e d'amor, fu nulla o poco.
    Ma se i begli occhi ond'il mio cor s'accese
Del lor chiaro divin almo splendore
Non m'havessero a torto fatto indegno,
Col canto havrei l'interno e grave ardore
Agl'orecchie di tal fatto palese,
Che pietà fora ove alberga ira e
    sdegno.

I sang while I burned from the living flame
Of my fire, whence I dying lived,
Although what I sang of and what I wrote
About my lady and love were nothing, or little.   4
    But if the lovely eyes from which my heart burned
Had not wrongly found me unworthy
Of their bright, divine, life-giving splendor,
With a song I would have made known
My grave inner passion to those ears,
So that there might be pity where anger and disdain
    now dwell.   10

as that of Petrarch's ballata no. 63, "Volgendo gli occhi al mio novo colore": a four-line *ripresa* (ABBA), a pair of three-line *mutazioni* (CDE/DCE), and a four-line *volta* (EFFA), all in *endecasillabi*.
    For Parabosco's complete setting, see the eds. cited in n. 12 above and for Rore's setting see his *Opera omnia,* ed. Bernhard Meier, Corpus mensurabilis musicae, no. 14, AIM, vol. 2 ([Rome], 1963), pp. 1–4.

Agl'amorosi strali fermo segno	I would be a sure mark for the
Sarei, pieno di dolce aspro martiro,	Amorous darts, full of bittersweet grief,
Ov'hora in libertà piango e sospiro:	Where now in freedom I weep and sigh:
Ahi, pace in cor d'amanti non ha loco.	Oh, peace has no place in the hearts of lovers! 14

The *ripresa* (vv. 1–4) encloses the ballata's life-death conceit in a single extended period, then elaborated in a complex if-then qualifier by the *mutazioni* (vv. 5–10). The *mutazioni* thereby culminate in the kind of rhetorical resolution usually reserved in a sonnet for the final verse, but typical at this point in a ballata. In the third and last clause the *volta* (vv. 11–14) provides by comparison more modest thematic closure through a distant trope on what has gone before, while still strengthening the poem's end by reintroducing the A rhyme that frames the *ripresa*.

Both Rore and Parabosco avoided dividing the ballata into two parts after the *ripresa* but marked its chief formal divisions with strong cadences. Like most of his other settings, Rore's is extensively articulated by means of cadences at every verse ending as well as at some of the internal caesurae (vv. 2 and 3). More strongly than Parabosco's setting Rore's reinforces the structural breaks at vv. 4 and 10 with two successive cadences for each (mm. 29 and 32 and mm. 61 and 64, respectively). Parabosco's setting, by contrast, uses few cadences. The first one, a major sixth to octave on C fortified with a descending fifth in the bass, appears only at the end of the *ripresa* (m. 31), with a similar one on B-flat (minor third to unison, now with a rising fourth in the bass) at the end of the *mutazioni* (m. 72).

While paying less attention to large formal divisions, Parabosco apparently emulated some of Rore's declamatory rhythms (as at the opening). What is more, he took over voicings and intervals from a striking contrapuntal passage on "dolce aspro martiro" from v. 12 that absorbs Brevio's Petrarchan oxymoron of bittersweet grief into successions of parallel sixths (Exx. 35a and 35b).[18] Especially noteworthy in connection with Parabosco's imitation is that Rore's setting deploys parallel six-three chords first in the upper voices (mm. 75–76), later shifting them to altus and bassus in staggered declamation and writing the last two intervals as major (mm. 79–80). In so doing Rore introduced dissonance in a mild way but accentuated it with the spiky major seventh struck on "aspro" (E-flat and d, m. 80—recall Zarlino's dicta on parallel motion and major intervals). Both passages resemble Willaert's exposition of the incipit "Aspro core e selvaggio, e cruda voglia" (Chap. 7, Ex. 16), which Parabosco himself imitated in a later setting (Ex. 38 below), as well as Rore's own apparent imitation of Willaert's exposition in setting the line "Sgombrino l'altre voglie aspr'e selvaggie" from *Sfrondate, o sacre dive* (Chap. 8, Ex. 32). Parabosco made similar use of parallel six-three chords in setting v. 12 from *Solo e pensoso*, "Ma pur sì aspre vie nè sì selvaggie," (*Madrigali a 5;* see Ex. 36). The entire complex of passages thus par-

---

18. On Willaert's use of the six-three chord and parallel sixths as mild dissonances, see Armen Carapetyan, "The *Musica Nova* of Adriano Willaert: With a Reference to the Humanistic Society of 16th-Century Venice" (Ph.D. diss., Harvard University, 1945), pp. 172–73 and passim.

EX. 35A.   Rore, *Cantai mentre ch'i arsi del mio foco* (Giovanni Brevio), mm. 74–82;
Madrigali a 5 (Venice, 1542), no. 1.

ticipates in a single musical topos that Venetian composers cultivated for expressions of harshness and wildness—a topos whose roots probably lie in Willaert's *Aspro core* and possibly in Rore's *Cantai mentre ch'i arsi* as well.[19]

The indebtedness of Parabosco's *Cantai mentre ch'io arsi* to Rore's setting is clearest at mm. 80–84, where it intermittently adopts Rore's parallel sixths and six-three chords when delivering "martiro" (Ex. 35b). Parabosco also adopted Rore's disposition of the text in semichoirs, high, then low (though his are more homorhythmic), and matched Rore's rhythmic declamation almost exactly (compare Rore's cantus at mm. 74–77 with Parabosco's at mm. 79–81). The only other

19. We could also add to this group the parallel-third-filled exordium of Rore's *Strane ruppi, aspri monti, alti tremanti* (see Ex. 15).

EX. 35B.   Parabosco, *Cantai mentre ch'io arsi del mio foco* (Giovanni Brevio), mm.
78–84; in Antonfrancesco Doni, *Dialogo della musica* (Venice, 1544), fol. 31 in cantus.

EX. 36.   Parabosco, *Solo e pensoso, i più deserti campi* (Petrarch, no. 35), mm. 91–92;
Madrigali a 5 (Venice, 1546), no. 4.

Rore, *Cantai mentre ch'i arsi del mio foco* (Giovanni Brevio), mm. 90–105; *Madrigali a 5* (Venice, 1542), no. 1.

Parabosco, *Cantai mentre ch'io arsi del mio foco* (Giovanni Brevio), mm. 92–104; in Antonfrancesco Doni, *Dialogo della musica* (Venice, 1544), fol. 31 in cantus.

passage that echoes Rore's so closely is the one setting the final aphorism, "Ahi, pace in cor d'amanti non ha loco" (compare Exx. 37a and 37b). Here the gasping "Ahi"s of both settings follow conventional practice, but Parabosco specifically emulated Rore in mm. 92–94 by staggering the vocal entrances in even semibreves over a B-flat in the bass.

––––––––––

Like Willaert's other students, Parabosco assembled his only madrigal collection, dedicated to Ruberto Strozzi, as a polyphonic miscellany.[20] All the poems in the *Madrigali a 5* align themselves with a literary vernacular and most explore the amorous, metaliterary tropes of courtly Petrarchan verse. Apart from these commonalities, the book embraces a wide variety of poetic forms and registers across the whole upper range of the Ciceronian spectrum, approaching the heterogeneity of a book like Rore's second by excluding only comic, low, and dialect verse. Given the ideals of Ciceronian propriety that (I have argued) demanded this exclusion, it is no surprise that Parabosco's *Madrigali a 5* bears little resemblance to his *Lettere amorose, Lettere famigliari, I diporti, Il viluppo,* or a host of other quasi-colloquial texts that he published between 1545 and his death in 1557. In most of these literary works Parabosco was openly eclectic, often droll, and at least a little subversive, evincing that self-serving blend of establishmentarianism and iconoclasm that defines the social climber in cosmopolitan Venice. Yet his one collection of madrigals was concertedly literary. None of Willaert's other students' books match Parabosco's in the amount of verse included that could also claim existence in literary venues. By concentrating on poems that carried enough cachet to have circulated with respectable lyric identities outside of music, Parabosco's collection could project a certain level of urbane sophistication. Perhaps to that end, the book avoids the provincial madrigalistic verse of his Piacentine countrymen Lodovico Domenichi, Bartolomeo Gottifredi, and even the wildly popular Luigi Cassola. It opens instead with two of Parabosco's own poems (a madrigal and a ballata-madrigal), then mixes in poems by more celebrated contemporaries—Baldassare Castiglione, Lodovico Martelli, Fortunio Spira, and Giovanni Mozzarello—among the many settings of Petrarch.

This chic vernacular eclecticism may explain why the book is built less on strictly high-styled, and especially "classical," sonnets than any of the other five-voice collections by Willaert's immediate pupils. Only six of its twenty numbers are complete sonnet settings (nos. 3, 4, 5, 7, 15, and 17), an additional two settings of sonnet octaves (nos. 13 and 14), as seen in Table 9. Of the nine Petrarchan settings (not counting *Anima bella*), only three are full sonnets, the rest partial sonnet settings (nos. 11 and 14) and stanzas drawn from canzoni (nos. 10 and 16) and sestine (nos. 9 and 12). About a third of the poems can be described as madrigals (nos. 1, 6, 8, 18, 19, and 20) or ballata-madrigals (no. 2).

20. For the dedication see Chap. 2 n. 65 above. There is no mod. ed. of the collection at present.

TABLE 9
Girolamo Parabosco, *Madrigali a 5* (1546)

Incipit; *Poetic Form; Poet and Poetic Source**	*System*	*Cleffing*	*Final*	*Modal Pair*
1. Chi vuol veder in un soggetto solo 15-line madr: ABB‖CDCEeFgGHhJJ Parabosco, *Il primo libro dei madrigali* (Rome, 1987), p. 93	b	g2c2c3c3F3	**G**	protus
2. Sì ch'io l'ho detto & dissi et diro sempre 15-line ballata-madr: ABB‖CDEDbFGAHaBB Parabosco, *Il primo libro dei madrigali* (Rome, 1987), p. 77	b	g2c2c3c3F3	**G**	
3. Aspro cor & selvaggia et cruda voglia ii. Vivo sol di speranza rimembrando sonnet Petrarch, no. 265	b b	c1c3c4c4F4 c1c3c4c4F4	D **GG**	
4. Solo e pensoso, in più deserti campi ii. Sì ch'io mi cred'homai che monti e piaggie sonnet Petrarch, no. 35	b b	c1c3c4c4F4 c1c3c4c4F4	AA **GG**	
5. Cantai mentre nel cor lieto fioria ii. Così un fosco pensier l'alm'ha in governo sonnet Baldassare Castiglione, in *Rime diverse . . .* *Libro primo*, p. 178 (Bussi, *Umanità e arte*, p. 142)	b b	c1c3c4c4F4 c1c3c4c4F4	C **FF**	tritus
6. Ultimi miei sospiri 10-line madr: aBaBcDeEDD Lodovico Martelli, *Rime volgari*, fol. 39	b	c1c3c4c4F4	**FF**	
7. Volgi, cor mio, il tuo pensier homai ii. Et a noi restarà fra sdegn' & ire sonnet Fortunio Spira, in *Rime diverse . . . Libro primo*, p. 195 (Bussi, *Umanità e arte*, p. 144)	b b	g2c2c3c3F3 g2c2c3c3F3	C **F**	
8. Beato sia quel punto 8-line madr: aBABCBDD Claudio Tolomei (Bussi, *Umanità e arte*, p. 145)	b	g2c2c3c3F3	**F**	
9. Mia benigna fortuna el viver lieto ii. Già mi fu col desir si dolc'il pianto sestina, stanzas 1 and 4 Petrarch, no. 332	— —	c1c3c4c4F4 c1c3c4c4F4	AA **EE**	deuterus
10. Amor, se voi ch'io torni al gioco antico canzone, stanza 1 Petrarch, no. 270	—	c1c3c4c4F4	**E**	

Table 9 *(continued)*

Incipit; *Poetic Form; Poet and Poetic Source**	System	Cleffing	Final	*Modal Pair*
11. Poiche la vista angelica & serena sonnet, octave only Petrarch, no. 276	—	c1c3c4c4F4	**EE**	
12. Nessun visse giamai più di me lieto sestina, stanza 7 Petrarch, no. 332 (cf. no. 9 above)	—	c2c4c4F3F4	**EE**	
13. Anima bella da quel nodo sciolta octave Petrarch, quatrain from no. 305, + Parabosco?	—	c1c3c4F3F4	**AA**	
14. I vo piangendo i miei passati tempi ii. Tu che vedi i miei mali indegni two quatrains from a sonnet Petrarch, no. 365	— —	c1c3c4c4F4 c1c3c4c4F4	AA **E**	
15. O desir di questi occhi, almo mio sole ii. O rose eterne, spars'infra le brine sonnet Giovanni Mozzarello, in *Rime diverse . . .* *Libro primo,* p. 80 (Bussi, *Umanità e arte,* p. 155)	— —	c1c3c4c4F4 c1c3c4c4F4	C **GG**	tetrardus
16. Vaghi pensier, che così passo passo canzone, stanza 3 Petrarch, no. 70	—	g2c2c3c3c4	**C**	
17. Gliocchi, di ch'io parlai sì caldamente ii. Et io pur vivo onde mi doglio e sdegno sonnet Petrarch, no. 292	— —	g2c2c3c3c4 g2c2c3c3c4	C **G**	
18. Niuna sconsolata 13-line madr: aBaCdEcffDGHH Parabosco (after Boccaccio), *Il primo libro dei madrigali,* p. 113	—	g2c2c3c3c4	**G**	
19. Non dispregiat'i miserelli amanti 7-line madr: AbAbBcC Lodovico Martelli (Fenlon and Haar, *The Italian Madrigal,* p. 318)	—	c1c2c3c3c4F4	**G**	
20. Se così fredda sete 7-line madr: aBCBbDD Anon.	—	g2c2c3c3c4	**G**	

N.B. Finals given in boldface, confinals in regular type.

*Table uses short-title references. For full citations see the Bibliography.

This idiosyncratic and rather paradoxical literary character—not conventionally elevated with a saturation of sonnets but nevertheless steeped in verse of recognizable pedigree—is matched by an equally unusual modal plan. Like many midcentury collections, the book is organized by cantus mollis and cantus durus as well as by final. The design that results seems to consist of four modal categories irregularly arranged without regard to ambitus: protus (nos. 1–4), tritus (nos. 5–8), deuterus (nos. 9–14), and tetrardus (nos. 15–20).[21]

Among the weightiest and surely the best-known setting in the *Madrigali a 5* is Parabosco's *Aspro cor*. Since Helga Meier's study of 1969, it has been widely recognized that Willaert's students at San Marco emulated some of his *Musica nova* settings with borrowings and citations in their resettings of the same texts.[22] Given that *Aspro cor* is the only one of Parabosco's settings to have done so directly, it is not surprising that it took over Willaert's decorum, gravity, careful rhetorical shaping, and many of his specific readings more completely than did any of Parabosco's other settings. (We will see that Parabosco's colleagues also followed Willaert's practices most closely when actually modeling their settings on his.) Indeed, Parabosco's imitation of Willaert is arguably even more striking than Meier made out.[23] It quotes almost literally the extraordinary conception Willaert imposed on the first verse, even while replacing Willaert's G-durus eighth mode with a G-mollis transposed second (Ex. 38; cf. Ex. 16). It also adopts the descending melodic profile of the main motive and, like Willaert's, introduces the vocal groups in a three-plus-three arrangement (v. 1; v. 1 repeated—though with Parabosco's reduction to five voices, one voice sings v. 1 twice). And, most important, it borrows the six-five and four-three suspensions, the parallel major thirds mentioned by Galilei, and the concentration of major imperfect intervals that makes Willaert's setting so distinctive.

Yet Parabosco's departures from Willaert's version reveal even more than his borrowings, for on the whole he alleviated the austerity of Willaert's reading despite the harsh character of the poem. The tenor voice that begins the exposition imitates Willaert's motive, but its effect is undermined by the syncopated entrance of the alto a minim later and a new syncopation introduced in the cantus in mm. 2–3. These syncopations lighten the overall ethos of the passage while slighting considerations of textual stress and sense: the word "e" invites syncopation and prolongation in the cantus not for its accentual position or textual meaning but only to allow a more sensuous surface. Willaert's rhythms, by comparison, initially spaced a semibreve apart and wholly bound to the tactus through v. 1, help fix and maintain a more

21. I take the tonal type ♮-g2-C to represent mode 7, after Pietro Aaron and the Italian tradition (see Powers, "Tonal Types and Modal Categories in Renaissance Polyphony," *JAMS* 34 [1981]: 466).

22. "Zur Chronologie der *Musica Nova* Adrian Willaerts," *Analecta musicologica* 12 (1973): 71–96.

23. For a mod. ed. of the madrigal see *Fünf Madrigale venezianischer Komponisten um Adrian Willaert zu 4–7 Stimmen,* ed. Helga Meier, *Das Chorwerk,* vol. 105 (Wolfenbüttel, 1969), pp. 14–22. See also Meier's discussion of the madrigal in the preface to the edition, p. iv, and in "Zur Chronologie der *Musica Nova,*" p. 78. In *Fünf Madrigale* Meier points out how Parabosco's setting of *Aspro core* and Donato's setting of *I vidi in terra angelici costumi* and *Liete e pensose* made explicit references to Willaert's models by placing citations in exposed positions at the beginnings or ends of one of the *parti*.

solemn pulse. The slow stepwise motion is hardly relieved by repeated minims, which do no more than fill in the basic semibreve structure.

In fact, Parabosco nearly reversed the role of metric stress and the discrete roles of tonic and agogic accents that Palisca found so striking a feature of Willaert's rendition, especially Willaert's staunch avoidance of syncopation in v. 1 and exploitation of it in v. 2; (see Chap. 7 n. 59). Furthermore, Parabosco's setting minimizes semantic contrasts between the verses by sprinkling the repetition of v. 1 with dotted semiminims while reducing the level of syncopation in v. 2. Despite the *sdrucciolosa* lilt in Petrarch's second verse, Parabosco had all the voices but the alto enter on the tactus. Similarly, he minimized the major-minor intervallic polarities that Palisca noted in Willaert's model by eliminating v. 2's emphasis on minor intervals. The only consistent way in which Parabosco realized these semantic dichotomies was through conventions that aligned textual meaning with melodic direction, moving largely downward for v. 1 and upward for v. 2.

In later passages Parabosco actually appropriated more completely Willaert's rhetorical delivery. At the beginning of v. 7, "Piango ad ogn'hor," for example, his setting exploits the same minor intervallic relationships with which Willaert's had personified the poet's weeping in the second quatrain (Exx. 39a and 39b).

Che quando nasce e mor fior erba e foglia,	For when the flowers, grass, and leaves are born or die,
Quando è 'l dì chiaro e quando è notte oscura,	When it is bright day and when it is dark night,
Piango ad ogni hor. Ben ò di mia ventura,	I weep at all times. From fate,
Di Madonna, e d'Amor onde mi doglia.	From my lady, and from Love I have much to grieve me. 8

Parabosco's setting concentrates on minor seconds and minor thirds, stressing the relationships B-flat/A and B-flat/G (cantus, tenor, quintus), as well as D/E-flat and E/F (altus). Beyond this, both settings take the beginning of v. 7 as a point of formal rupture by emphasizing the prosodic asymmetry it introduces into the quatrain. The nine and a half breves Willaert assigned to the first part of v. 7, "Piango ad ogn'hor" (as opposed to eight for all of v. 5 and seven for v. 6) magnify it rhetorically; Parabosco follows suit with eleven breves (compared with nine and eight and a half for vv. 5 and 6, respectively), and both set up its entrance with a perfect cadence and a registral shift to end v. 6 (aided in Willaert's case by a slowed surface motion).

Parabosco's setting continues to evoke the memorable textural, rhythmic, and tonal events that Willaert had deployed to mark the sonnet's major formal-expressive divisions in the sestet. But, here again, his setting mollified Willaert's effects. The voicing that opens Parabosco's *seconda parte*—three homophonic inner voices leading off, a fourth joining them after a semibreve, and the bass entering two and a half breves later—borrows from Willaert's, and the bass line in fifths comes from Willaert too (though Parabosco fails to sustain it beyond three chords). Parabosco

EX. 39A.   Willaert, *Aspro core e selvaggio e cruda voglia* (Petrarch, no. 265), mm. 48–58; *Musica nova* (Venice, 1559), no. 14.

used Willaert's rhetorical markers again at the beginning of the second tercet, "Non è sì duro cor che lagrimando," by isolating the first half of the verse, but here his motivic and tonal manipulations enervate the model even more (Exx. 40a and 40b). Willaert had started with a cross relation introduced by f-sharp in the sextus (third voice from the top, m. 103), which occurs within yet another brief circle-of-fifths progression, A to C, originating in the previous phrase. All but one of his approaches to "duro" hammers away in repetition figures that move up by major second. Parabosco treats the clause less uniformly, maximizing motivic and metric variety between parts where Willaert's setting pointedly avoids doing so, while underscoring Petrarch's verbal dissonance. His tenor leaps on "duro" to a mild minor sixth over the bassus (m. 105), resolving immediately to a perfect fifth. Three measures later (mm.

EX. 40A.   Willaert, *Aspro core e selvaggio e cruda voglia* (Petrarch, no. 265), mm. 103–10; *Musica nova* (Venice, 1559), no. 14.

EX. 40B.   Parabosco, *Aspro cor e selvaggio e cruda voglia* (Petrarch, no. 265), mm. 104–10; *Madrigali a 5* (Venice, 1546), no. 3.

108–9) suspended parallel sixths between outer voices invoke the madrigal's beginning.

Willaert's and Parabosco's treatments of the sonnet's final verse, "Ne sì freddo voler che non si scalde" (nor is there a will so cold that it cannot be warmed), resemble one another rhythmically but only confirm the sense that Parabosco largely refrained from riveting particular rhetorical effects to a single musical reading. In syncopating "freddo" with a dotted figure, Willaert's reading reinforced a level of

Parabosco, *Volgi, cor mio, il tuo pensier homai* (Fortunio Spira), mm. 1–6; *Madrigali a 5* (Venice, 1546), no. 7.

dissonance that Petrarch's poem achieves through consonantal clusters. The pompous energy of his syncopations captures rhythmically the spirit of the "cold will." By declaiming the word wholly in minims and thus misaccenting both syllables, Parabosco turned his back on Willaert's text-generated diction, giving up Willaert's semantic emphasis as well as the means to a stagier rhetorical climax.

Willaert's submission of all dimensions of his *Musica nova* madrigals to the rigors of a rhetorically determined declamation resulted in a speechlike musical oratory that his pupils generally pursued less adamantly than they did endearing local moments. The difference is evident even in Parabosco's sonnet settings, many of which (like *Aspro cor*) are less weighty than one might expect. We should recall in this regard that in midcentury Venice a preoccupation with Petrarch did not necessarily signal elitism or even imply de facto a preference for sonnets. Petrarch after all was the most widely disseminated poet in the marketplace of printed editions and commentaries, and the sonnet by far the most common genre of the mid-sixteenth century (as abundantly evident in the copious anthologies of the time). Not all of the modern sonnets Parabosco set were especially introspective, nor were his settings of them. Mozzarello's *O desir di questi occhi,* for one, is an untroubled series of apostrophes to the beloved ending with a vaguely erotic "Deh, sarà mai ch'io vi riveggia et oda?" (Ah, will I ever see and hear you again?) that Parabosco set lightly in a compact ninety-four breves.[24] Similarly, his cheerful fifth-mode setting of Spira's *Volgi, cor mio, il tuo pensier homai* depicts a spurned poet who makes a pact with his heart over a disdainful lady; for this Parabosco opened with a cantus-tenor duet in quixotic fourths and graceful syncopations (Ex. 41).

24. See the ed. in Bussi, *Composizioni,* pp. 38–50. It is not the only setting so brief; Parabosco's setting of Petrarch's *Gli occhi di ch'io parlai* is only eighty breves long.

Poems like these did not invite the expansively weighty style Parabosco used to set sonnets like *Aspro core, Solo e pensoso,* or *I' vo piangendo.*[25] Still further from these Petrarch sonnets—indeed at the opposite end of the spectrum—are settings like that of Martelli's madrigal *Ultimi miei sospiri.*

Ultimi miei sospiri,	My last breaths,
Che mi lasciate fred'e senza vita,	Which leave me cold and lifeless,
Contate i miei martiri	Recount my sufferings
A chi morir mi vede e non m'aita.	To one who sees me and does not help me.
Dite, o beltà infinita,	Speak, oh infinite beauty, 5
Dal tuo fidel ne caccia empio martire;	So that your faithful one may drive out bitter suffering;
Et se questo l'è grato,	And should this please her,
Gitene ratto in ciel', a miglior stato.	Go swiftly to Heaven, to a better state.
Ma se pietà gli porg'il vostro dire,	But if your speech arouses pity in her,
Tornat'a me, ch'io non vorrò morire.	Return to me, for I do not wish to die. 10

Since *settenari* appear equally with *endecasillabi* here, Parabosco turned out shorter melodies than he did for sonnets (see Ex. 42). Many of the phrases span a single *settenario* in the manner of earlier Italian secular music—an approach also evident in his canzone settings like the stanza from Petrarch's *Amor, se vuoi ch'io torni.* Unlike the motetlike expositions of Venetians' sonnet settings, *Ultimi miei sospiri* moves in fast surface rhythms right from the opening, with entrances driving at a buoyant minim rate instead of the standard semibreve. The playful rhythmic assonance of the exposition—accented "miei" against "-mi" and "spi-" against "so-," piling strong / weak accents amid waves of syncopations—sets the tone for the rest of the madrigal. Parabosco accentuates it with fragmentary divisions of the verse, breaking off "sospiri" from "ultimi miei" with the little gasp that precedes so many sixteenth-century sighs (and even a repetition of "ultimi miei" in the tenor part). Some of the strategies he uses resemble those of contemporaneous black-note madrigals, with their widely divergent note values. Note, for example, how sharply "Gitene ratto in ciel" (v. 8), spit out in groups of semiminims (mm. 44–52), contrasts with the calm apostrophe following the double bar, "Dite, o beltà infinita" (mm. 37ff.).[26]

25. In his setting of the two quatrains from *I' vo piangendo* Parabosco's extreme extension of the Venetian madrigal's new ideal of breadth seems almost like an exercise in one-upsmanship. By increasing dramatically the proportion of notes to words he virtually "used up" what he must have considered the allowable space for each *parte,* leaving no room for the sestet after 104 breves. A little arithmetic helps to clarify the point: had Parabosco set the complete sonnet with the same number of breves per verse as in the octave (on average thirteen), the entire madrigal would have expanded to 182 breves—an unheard-of size for a sonnet setting of the time. Rather than setting the sestet he merged two currently viable alternatives, the prototype of the extended sonnet setting developed by the Venetians and that of the truncated octave setting common in lighter madrigal repertories of the time.

26. "Volti subitamente," from v. 5 of the sestina *Mia benigna fortuna* (also included in the *Madrigali a 5*), is set similarly to "Gitene ratto in ciel."

Parabosco's use of tritus modes for setting poems like *Ultimi miei sospiri* and *Volgi, cor mio*—modes generally described by modal theorists as more joyful than deuterus or protus plagal—raises the question whether Parabosco tried to fulfill criteria of modal affect or modal structure. We have already seen that neither Willaert's settings, nor even those of Rore's modally ordered First Book, reveal clear links between mode and affect apart from some intriguing cases of Phrygian. Yet Parabosco's book, despite its unorthodox organization, presents some suggestive evidence to the contrary. The tritus works in F mollis all set facile poems, save perhaps the sonnet of Castiglione. The protus group, on the other hand, seems to divide affectively according to the traditional bifurcation of ambitus: the two poems by Parabosco may have been meant to represent first mode, the dark

Ex. 42. Parabosco, *Ultimi miei sospiri* (Lodovico Martelli), incl.; *Madrigali a 5* (Venice, 1546), no. 6.

(continued)

(continued)

Petrarchan sonnets *Aspro cor* and *Solo e pensoso* second mode. Most strikingly, *all* of the settings in the deuterus (Phrygian) category come from the "in morte" portion of Petrarch's *Canzoniere*—even the first four lines of the adapted *Anima bella*.

All of this jibes well with other knowledge of Parabosco. His debt to Rore's modally ordered *Primo libro* is clear at least in the case of *Cantai mentre ch'io arsi* and his book was dedicated to Rore's early patron Ruberto Strozzi. If modal issues occupied a place in the dialogues of Venetian salons, Parabosco would have been at the center of them, for he was as close to academic life there as any composer in the city.

PERISSONE CAMBIO: MADRIGALS FOR FIVE VOICES

FORESTIERO: And who have you got here in the way of noteworthy men?

VENETIAN: Starting with musicians, we have Messer Adrian Willaert, who is chapelmaster at San Marco, and you know what his fame is.

FORESTIERO: I've heard him called the Prince of Musicians.

VENETIAN: We also have Perissone, a soprano without equal who's been sought out by many princes but wouldn't exchange Venice for any other city.

FORESTIERO: It seems to me he's wise.[27]

Perissone Cambio was Willaert's most prolific disciple in the mid- to late 1540s. In addition to a book of *canzoni villanesche alla napolitana* dated 1545 he published three independent collections of madrigals, the two five-voice books of 1545 and 1550 and a four-voice book of 1547. All but the last were produced before Perissone even joined the roster at San Marco. Owing to a lack of positions or funds he entered the chapel only on 19 July 1548, before a real post had come available, and then, remarkably, on an unsalaried basis. Perissone owed his position to an unprecedented personal manoeuvre by doge Francesco Donà, who was effective in Perissone's being awarded the next valid opening seven months later, on 8 February 1549.[28] By that time Perissone may have developed connections with Rore as well as with Willaert, for Scotto's edition of Rore's Third Book of madrigals of 1548 (RISM 1548[9]) had included one of Perissone's works (as Rore's second book had done four years earlier) and Perissone's *Primo libro a quatro voci* offered first printings of three

---

27. For: E chi ci havete di huomini segnalati?

    Ven.   Cominciando dà Musici, noi ci habbiamo M. Adriano Vuigliaret, ilquale è Maestro di Capella di S. Marco, e voi sapete quale è la sua fama.

    For.   Lo ho sentito chiamar Principe de Musici.

    Ven.   Habbiamo similmente Perissone per Sorano senza alcun paro, ilquale desiderato da molti Principi, ma però non cambiarebbe Venetia per altra Città.

    For.   Mi par che sia savio.

From Francesco Sansovino, *Delle cose notabili che sono in Venetia. Libri due, ne quali ampiamente, e con ogni verità si contengono* (Venice, 1565) fol. 33; ded. 17 Sept. 1561. Il Venetiano goes on to name the other great musicians of that time: "il Salo Basso, il Zeffiro, il Franzese, Marc'Antonio, M. Angelo, Don Galeazzo da Pesaro, gentiliss. Spirito, Silvestro da Fontego, i Fauretti, Matteo dalla Viola, il Tromboncino, Annibale Organista, Claudio, Frate Armonio, e molti altri tutti eccellenti" (fols. 33–33').

28. Ongaro, "The Chapel of St. Mark's," pp. 127–28.

of Rore's madrigals. In addition, the printer Gardane appears to have exploited Perissone's connections with Rore by having him write the dedication to Gardane's edition of Rore's Third Book (RISM 1548[10]).

Francesco Donà numbered among several powerful Venetians who took an interest in Perissone's talents—a factor that was instrumental in building up his reputation as a singer and composer during the mid-forties. As we saw in Chapters 3 and 4, Perissone profited from the patronage of Gottardo Occagna, Antonio Zantani, and (most likely) Domenico Venier, and we can imagine him among the impressive performers Doni witnessed in Neri Capponi's salon too. Perissone was probably one of the showiest singers in the salons, a performer who repeatedly won plaudits in print for his singing, and, moreover, a singer of treble parts.[29]

Nothing precise is known of Perissone's origins or of the route that took him to Venice—only that he was Flemish, according to a privilege granted to him by the Senate.[30] By 1544 Perissone's five-voice setting of the anonymous sonnet *Che cosa al mondo far potea natura* appeared in Rore's *Secondo libro* and a four-voice setting of *Vivo sol di speranza, rimembrando* (the sestet of *Aspro core*) in Arcadelt's *Quinto libro*.[31] He made his first major appearance that same year in Doni's *Dialogo della musica*, where he was designated an interlocutor along with Parabosco, Veggio, and others.[32] Doni's text already places him within a group that pictures itself on the cutting edge of Venetian musical developments. After those assembled sing his setting of Bartolomeo Gottifredi's *Deh, perché com'è il vostro al nome mio*, one of the interlocutors praises Perissone as an "accomplished young man and commendable person" with a "beautiful voice" and fine compositional technique.[33] *Deh, perché* is one of two madrigals of Perissone's in the *Dialogo*'s Venetian second half, the other a six-voice setting of *Giunto m'ha Amor*.[34]

In this early repertory Perissone was already cultivating both stylistic poles of a dichotomy that has been emerging gradually in our discussions of Venetian madrigals—the dichotomy between a songlike polyphony generated directly out of lyric form and meter and a more declamatory, motetlike polyphony shaped by

29. Though the chapel rolls list Perissone as an alto, Francesco Sansovino's dialogue cited in n. 27 above suggests he must have taken the more difficult upper parts often enough to have been regarded popularly as a soprano, as Giulio Ongaro has argued ("The Chapel of St. Mark's," pp. 105 and 132). Ongaro notes that the term *soprano* was often used loosely, probably to designate anyone who sang the top line of a composition.

30. See n. 38 below.

31. The sestet had earlier been set by Arcadelt and published in his *Terzo libro* of 1539.

32. See James Haar, "Notes on the *Dialogo della musica* of Antonfrancesco Doni," *Music & Letters* 47 (1966): 198–224, and Chap. 1 above, n. 56.

33. The praise is initiated by the Piacentine Count Ottavio Landi: "Oh che belle parole, oh che bel canto! Perison certamente ha preso un modo dolce, fugato, chiaro e bellissimo." To this the female interlocutor Selvaggia responds, "Valente giovane e persona virtuosa non poteva far se non divinamente." Depicted here, like the other males in the dialogue, as an amorous courtier, Perissone responds by swearing fealty to Selvaggia (*Dialogo della musica*, p. 121).

34. Ibid., pp. 114–20 and pp. 232–42, respectively; in Malipiero's ed. *Giunto m'ha Amor* is wrongly attributed to Willaert. It reappeared in 1546 in *Madrigali di Verdelot et de altri autori a sei voci novamente con alcuni madrigali novi ristampati & corretti* [RISM 1546[19]].

rhetorical qualities and proselike diction. *Deh, perchè* and *Giunto m'ha Amor* mark the crystallization of this dichotomy. Gottifredi's poem concretizes the internalist poetics of Petrarch in playful, realistic, and sweetly erotic conceits, here encapsulated in the poet's plea that the beloved match his desire as her name does his.

Deh, perchè com'è il vostro al nome mio	Oh why, since your name
Parimente conforme	Conforms to mine
A mia voglia non è vostro desio?	Does not your desire to my longing?
Scaldat', oimè scaldate,	Warm, oh warm,
Donna gentil, nel mio amoroso ardore	Gentle lady, your frozen desires 5
Vostre voglie gelate,	In my loving ardor,
Che se qual esce fuore	For if, just as the same sound
De i nomi un suono stesso	Issues forth from our names,
Fosse par il voler nei cori impresso:	The same desire were only impressed in our hearts,
O che bell'union d'animi santi,	Oh what a lovely union of blessed souls, 10
O fortunati amanti!	Oh fortunate lovers!

Perissone's setting of *Deh, perchè* has nothing of the pious Willaertian sobriety and complexity Perissone aspired to (however partially) in sonnet settings. Instead it indulged in sweet cascading melody and light, airy counterpoint to create a clear formal exposition, notable in the way the cantus's opening bars lay out Gottifredi's first period (Ex. 43). Perissone's exordial cantus traces the poetic exposition (vv. 1–3) in a series of ascents that rise by successive steps, peaking on the confinal dd, dropping to a caesura on aa (and "mio"), then reascending for a more ecstatic reiteration of dd ("conform'a mia voglia non è") before the syncopated stepwise descent ("vostro desio"). His writing displays the skill of a great arioso melodist, with the cantus unbroken from start to finish, suspending a large melodic arc between two tonal axes. Unlike the recitational melodies and equal-voiced polyphony of Willaert's and Rore's madrigals, here poetic affect is projected mainly through melodious adornment of the text. With the G-mollis tonality, chiavette cleffing, and delicate coloration, Perissone fashions an engaging chiaroscuro in polyphonic accompaniment to the lyrical cantus. The profusion of cross relations that result (C/C-sharp, F/F-sharp, E/E-flat, and B/B-flat) were ones he continued to exploit in later madrigals.[35] In this lyric and coloristic ebullience, some of the words go breezily misaccented ("pa-**ri**-men-**te**") and in a way that resists the rigors of Willaert's sternly Bembist approach.

If the melodic style of *Deh, perchè* is pretty and tuneful, the six-voice setting of *Giunto m'ha Amor* shows that Perissone already knew something of the more severe idiom Willaert reserved for Petrarch's sonnets. *Giunto m'ha Amor* adheres closely to

---

35. On the matter of cross (or false) relations see James Haar, "False Relations and Chromaticism in Sixteenth-Century Music," *JAMS* 30 (1977): 391–418.

Ex. 43. Perissone, *Deh, perchè com'è il vostro al nome mio* (Bartolomeo Gottifredi), cantus, mm. 1–13; *Madrigali a 5* (Venice, 1545), no. 1.

the even pulse of Willaert's setting with only occasional syncopations. At the same time it exploits harmonic coloration almost as much as *Deh, perchè*. A single example may be seen in the sonorities at "Che m'ancidono a torto" (Ex. 44), where Perissone alternately strengthened the fifth motion of the bass from D to B-flat (mm. 14–17) or colored the text through the addition of accidentals.

Reminiscent of Parabosco's 1544 settings, Perissone's *Giunto m'ha Amor* set only lines 1 through 8. By the time his first collection, *Madrigali a cinque voci,* was published in 1545, however, Perissone had begun to treat texts more as literary artifacts. Much like Rore's First Book, the *Madrigali a 5* published twelve sonnet settings, all unabridged,[36] along with a few lighter settings including *Deh, perchè* at the head. This is the same mix seen in all the Venetian collections assembled principally for commercial markets, but the bibliographical history of Perissone's book explains more than most about the social context that helped generate it.

The *Madrigali a 5* is an unsigned print. According to Jane Bernstein, it was probably produced in the publishing house of Girolamo Scotto—head of a consortium of printers—and most likely printed by Ottaviano Scotto.[37] The venture was engineered by Perissone himself, as made clear enough from the survival of a privilege he applied for from the Venetian Senate in order to print it.[38] As his first publication, the *Madrigali a 5* thus represents Perissone's effort to make his name in Venice with a collection devoted exclusively to his own works (as I argued in Chapter 3). These circumstances are corroborated by its long and highly suggestive title page, which implies that the madrigals the book contains originated from a social setting much like the one depicted by Doni.

36. For my ed. of the book see Sixteenth-Century Madrigal, vol. 2 (New York, 1990).

37. "The Burning Salamander: Assigning a Printer to Some Sixteenth-Century Music Prints," *Music Library Association Notes* 42 (1985–86): 483–501, esp. pp. 493 and 497.

38. Perissone applied for the privilege in June 1545, granted with the description "La musica per lui composta de madrigali sopra li sonnetti del Petrarcha"; see Einstein, *The Italian Madrigal* 1:439, and Richard J. Agee, "The Privilege and Venetian Music Printing in the Sixteenth Century" (Ph.D. diss., Princeton University, 1982), pp. 95–96 and 179.

It might be of interest that the print has a fairly high number of errors; see the notes that accompany my ed. cited in n. 36 above.

EX. 44. Perissone, *Giunto m'ha Amor fra belle e crude braccia* (Petrarch, no. 164), mm. 12–19; in Antonfrancesco Doni, *Dialogo della musica* (Venice, 1544), fol. 38 in cantus.

Madrigals for five voices by the excellent musician Messer Perissone Cambio, composed for the pleasure of various friends of his and now brought to light at the request of the same, and corrected, revised, and arranged by the composer himself. Never before seen or printed. Five voices. Venice, 1545. With grace and privilege.

Notwithstanding the claim that none of the madrigals had been previously printed, the book does signal Perissone's first major step into the public eye and his first efforts as an entrepreneur. His avowal in the dedication to Occagna that he himself is "having a few of [his] . . . madrigals for five voices printed" tends to confirm this.[39]

To the Noble and Valorous Signor Gottardo Ochagna

My most honorable lord, your virtue, kindness, and courtesy, having obligated me as much as anyone else who considers and experiences them, I cannot but always wish to find a way whereby I might somehow show you some sign of the love that I bear to you, thanks to your divine qualities. Therefore, my lord, knowing that, among the many other such rare virtues in which my lordship delights, Music is one that pleases you exceedingly, I did not want to lose this opportunity. So, since I am having a few of my madrigals for five voices printed—however they may be—I make a gift of them to your lordship in order to give you a small sign of the great desire I have to serve you. Might you then deign to accept with your usual kindness my humble present, keeping ever in mind the affection in my heart. Your perpetual servant, Perissone Cambio

In turning for backing to an afficionado of vernacular letters as well as music, Perissone made visible the symbiotic threads of his inaugural book: its self-promotional origins, its involvement in the new Venetian vogue for setting Petrarch's sonnets, and its appeal to consciously styled literary tastes in the vernacular. Not all the madrigals in it are settings of Petrarch's sonnets (as the privilege implied), but sonnet settings do occupy nearly three-quarters of the book and over half of these are Petrarch's (see Table 10). The others include some novel literary choices: one by Petrarch's early fifteenth-century Florentine imitator, Buonaccorso da Montemagno (no. 8), one by the Neapolitan poet of the early sixteenth century Jacopo Sannazaro (no. 15), and one of mixed attribution, probably by the eminent sixteenth-century Petrarchan Vittoria Colonna (no. 11).[40] All of the sonnet settings, moreover, are complete—still a new practice in the mid-forties, the only real precedent (among printed works) for which was Rore's First Book.

39. See Chap. 3 above, nn. 13–14, and for the original title page and dedication Plates 9 and 10.
40. With the exception of Buonaccorso and Colonna, the identifications I make here are found in *Il nuovo Vogel* 1:304–5. In addition to the poetic source given in Table 10, Buonaccorso's sonnet is reprinted in *Poesia del quattrocento e del cinquecento,* ed. Carlo Muscetta and Daniele Ponchiroli, Parnaso italiano, no. 4 (Turin, 1959), p. 13. The text of no. 2 is attributed to Colonna in *Rime diverse, di molti ecc. autori . . . libro primo,* 2d ed. (Venice, 1546), p. 293, but Vogel names its author as Cottemanno, probably on the basis of its inclusion in Philippe de Monte's collection devoted to Cottemano's spiritual poems, *Primo libro de' madrigali spirituali a cinque voci* (Venice, 1581). The earlier attribution to Colonna seems more likely. The other sonnet settings, nos. 4 and 6, remain anonymous.

TABLE 10

Perissone Cambio, *Madrigali a 5* (1545)

Incipit; Poetic Form; Poet and Poetic Source*	System	Cleffing	Final	Mode
1. Deh, perchè com'il vostro nome al mio 10-line madr: AbAcDcdeEFf Bartolomeo Gottifredi, in *Rime diverse . . .* *Libro primo*, p. 234	b	g2c2c3c3F3	**G**	1
2. Se 'l breve suon che sol quest'aer frale ii. Che fia quand'udira con vivo zelo sonnet Vittoria Colonna, in *Rime diverse . . .* *Libro primo*, 2d ed. (1546), p. 293	b b	g2c2c3c3F3 g2c2c3c3F3	D **G**	1
3. Cantai, hor piango, et non men di dolcezza ii. Tengan dunque ver me l'usato stile sonnet Petrarch, no. 229	b b	g2c2c3c3F3 g2c2c3c3F3	D **G**	1
4. Che cosa al mondo far potea natura ii. Fu del fattor mirabil magistero sonnet Anon.	b b	c1c3c4c4F4 c1c3c4c4F4	A **GG**	2
5. Nova Diana con più vagha luce 8-line madr: ABAcDBeE Anon.	b	c1c3c4c4F4	**GG**	2
6. S'io potesse fermar'al mio desio ii. Et se talhor acquetto il mio desire sonnet Anon.	b b	c2c3c4c4F4 c2c3c4c4F4	D **GG**	2
7. Dir non poss'io man cara 12-line ballata-madr: aBBcDcDdEeBB Anon.	—	c1c3c4c4F4	**E**	3/4
8. Non mai sì belle luci o sì bel sole ii. Dal bel sguardo soave par che fiocchi sonnet Buonaccorso da Montemagno, in *Scelta di sonetti, prima parte*, p. 103	— —	c1c3c4c4F4 c1c3c4c4F4	A **E**	3/4
9. Pace non trovo et non ho da far guerra ii. Veggio senza occhi et non ho lingua et grido sonnet Petrarch, no. 134	b b	g2c2c3c3F3 g2c2c3c3F3	C **F**	5
10. Se 'l dolce sguardo di costei m'ancide ii. Però s'io tremo e vo col cor gelato sonnet Petrarch, no. 183	b b	g2c2c3c3F3 g2c2c3c3F3	C **F**	5
11. Non è sì chiaro il sol ne sì lucente ii. Com'io vidi l'altrier sott'al ner velo sonnet Anon.	b b	c1c3c3c4F4 c1c3c4c4F4	F **FF**	6

(continued)

TABLE 10 (*continued*)

Incipit; Poetic Form; Poet and Poetic Source*	System	Cleffing	Final	Mode
12. O invidia, nemica di virtute	b	c1c3c4c4F4	FF	6
ii. Ne però che con atti acerbi e rei	b	c1c3c4c4F4	**FF**	
sonnet				
Petrarch, no. 172				
13. Amor che nel pensier mio vive et regna	—	g2c2c3c3F3	D	7
ii. Ond'amor paventoso fug'al core	—	g2c2c3c3F3	**G**	
sonnet				
Petrarch, no. 140				
14. Non si vedrà giamai stancha ne satia	—	g2c2c3c3F3	**G**	7
canzone, stanza 1				
Pietro Bembo, *Gli asolani;* fol. [e vii′];				
Opere (1808) 1:108				
15. Simili a questi smisurati monti	—	c1c3c4c4F4	D	8
ii. Soffian spesso tra lor rabbiosi venti	—	c1c3c4c4F4	**GG**	
sonnet				
Sannazaro, *Opere volgari,* p. 227				
16. I piansi, hor canto, che 'l celeste lume	—	c1c3c4c4F4	D	8
ii. Sì profondo era et di si larga vena	—	c1c3c4c4F4	**GG**	
sonnet				
Petrarch, no. 330				

N.B. Nos. 6, 9, 12, and 14 are all in C time; all others are in cut time. Finals are given in boldface, confinals in regular type.
*Table uses short-title references. For full citations see the Bibliography.

Indeed, Perissone could well have gotten various ideas for his own collection from Rore's, including the idea of ordering the corpus by mode, with high-clef arrangements (chiavette) standing in for authentic modes, lower clefs for plagals. Rore's *Primo libro* may also have helped inspire Perissone's inclusion of several black-note madrigals using common time signatures (C), copious syncopation, and a wide range of rhythmic values (nos. 6, 9, 12, and 14).

Unlike Rore's, however, all of Perissone's sonnet settings divide (like Willaert's) after the octave, and none of them actually resets sonnets set by Rore. Instead, three of the six Petrarch sonnets (nos. 3, 12, and 16) were among those later published in the *Musica nova,* making the *Madrigali a 5* the first in the stream of books to imitate directly Willaert's madrigalian practice. Two of these, *Cantai, hor piango* and *I piansi, hor canto,* respond frankly to an implicit compositional challenge. In *Cantai, hor piango* Perissone adopted a characteristic imitative procedure from Willaert's exposition, compressed it, and simplified it thematically. (See the beginning of Willaert's setting in Ex. 45a and Perissone's imitation in Ex. 45b.) Following his model, Perissone introduced the downward- and upward-moving versions of the opening motive a semibreve apart but varied the whole texture less than Willaert had. He discarded the simple breve/semibreve motive that Willaert had assigned

EX. 45A. Willaert, *Cantai, hor piango, e non men di dolcezza* (Petrarch, no. 229), mm. 1–27; *Musica nova* (Venice, 1559), no. 17.

(continued)

EX. 45B.   Perissone, *Cantai, hor piango, e non men di dolcezza* (Petrarch, no. 229), mm. 15–18; *Madrigali a 5* (Venice, 1545), no. 3.

(continued)

to "cantai" in the outer parts and in place of Willaert's double-subject counterpoint
created a simpler single-subject point of imitation with every voice stating the lone
motive either in its original form or in inversion.

Perissone's opening also lacks the chiming multivoiced effect that Willaert
achieved by exploiting closely staggered inner parts. In Willaert's setting each of
these parts enters on the same note, a, the parts paired symmetrically with quintus
inverting tenor, then altus inverting sextus. The contrapuntal and motivic intricacies spread over twelve breves and more before v. 1 is played out by all voices, as
compared with seven in Perissone's setting. Perissone's smaller exposition is characteristic of his generally shorter-winded approach and the smaller proportions of his
work as a whole in comparison with Willaert's (53 and 57 measures, as compared
with 70 and 69 in Willaert's): the different sizes result from dissimilar ways of handling poetic and musical materials. Willaert's varied parsings often explore a variety

of syntactic divisions and groupings for a single excerpt of text, while Perissone reads more uniformly to produce terser settings overall.

Note, for instance, the array of alternatives Willaert searched out in parsing the first two verses of *Cantai, hor piango:*[41]

1. Cantus: Cantai / cantai / hor piango / e non men di dolcezza Del pianger prendo / che del canto presi / e non men di dolcezza del pianger prendo / che del canto presi

2. Quintus: Cantai / hor piango / e non men di dolcezza / Del pianger prendo / e non men di dolcezza del pianger prendo che del canto presi / che del canto presi

3. Altus: Cantai / hor piango / e non men di dolcezza / e non men di dolcezza Del pianger prendo che del canto presi / e non men di dolcezza del pianger prendo che del canto presi / che del canto presi

4. Tenor: Cantai / cantai / hor piango / e non men di dolcezza Del pianger prendo / e non men di dolcezza del pianger prendo che del canto presi che del canto presi

5. Sextus: Cantai / hor piango / e non men di dolcezza Del pianger prendo che del canto presi / e non men di dolcezza del pianger prendo che del canto presi

6. Bassus: Cantai / hor piango hor piango / e non men di dolcezza Del pianger prendo che del canto presi / che del canto presi

Each voice presents a different reading, stringing together various syntactic fragments freely and irregularly in a way that elevates variable syntax to the status of a musico-rhetorical ideal. By reading the same text identically in every part, Perissone's practice accords with many of Parabosco's text settings (the only exception is a repetition of "che del canto presi" by the quintus): "Cantai / hor piango / e non men di dolcezza Del pianger prendo che del canto presi / che del canto presi." Not surprisingly, Willaert required nine breves more than Perissone to set the same two lines in a manner that is weightier, broader, more complex and convoluted, but also less lucid and immediately winning than his student's.

Perissone must have taken Willaert's lead in building much of *Cantai* on harmonic motion by fifth, especially at the opening of the *seconda parte*. Willaert set the bass moving in circles of fifths a total of three times for the poet's proclamation "Tengan dunque ver me l'usato stile / Amor, Madonna, il mondo et mia fortuna" (Let them keep toward me their accustomed style, Love, my lady, the world, and my fortune): from an E-major triad to one on C-major; from E to C

41. These verses are not ambiguous in the way of v. 8 from *Pien d'un vago pensier,* however; see Chap. 7, pp. 246–49.

again at double the harmonic rhythm; and from A to F. Perissone began his *seconda parte* with fifth motion as well, initially from G to B-flat and (a little later) from A to C and D to F. The progressions and their particular locations differ, but the coloring and sense of drive are similar,[42] Perissone adopting Willaert's fifth motion to reinitiate the syntactic process after the octave break and propel the paratactic series forward at v. 10, "Amor, Madonna, il mondo et mia fortuna." Here it is worth recalling Einstein's observation that even in such polyphonic surroundings, this sort of writing can produce textures in which "the bass takes no part in the motivic structure but functions merely as a support," the four parts above it forming a sort of "concertante."[43]

In sum, Perissone's borrowings in *Cantai, hor piango* avoid literalism in favor of a free gloss. Comparison of these borrowings with those of *Cantai*'s companion sonnet *I piansi, hor canto* shows that Perissone's tendency to compress and simplify was habitual. Here too Willaert's model provided a complex exposition in double counterpoint (Ex. 46a), the first subject a three-note stepwise descent that generates harmonic suspensions, the second a fifth-leap followed by a downward step. At first both subjects move solely in breves. The two upper voices give out the opening subject, with the *comes* introducing suspensions over the *dux* as well as over lower voices that enter later. The second motive first emerges in the bass as a harmonic support (m. 2), resolving the harmonies set askew by the cantus, and only later takes flight as a melodic motive in its own right. Perissone's exposition (Ex. 46b), like the one in *Cantai,* is again substantially shorter than Willaert's (the words "I piansi" lasting through four and a half measures as opposed to ten in Willaert's), and his setting is more effulgent. Perissone appropriated Willaert's G-durus tonality but used it at a higher cleffing, replacing c1 with g2 in the cantus. As in *Cantai,* he smoothed out irregularities in Willaert's version by giving the syntactic readings a simpler, more homogeneous character. Instead of two motives of equal status, he employed just one, similar to the second of Willaert's two. He treated it in a regularized imitation, with each of the five voices entering at equal temporal intervals of a semibreve and moving straight through the rest of the verse ("hor canto che 'l celeste lume") after a single statement of "I piansi."

Along with the simplification and abbreviation that mark Perissone's imitation goes a general lightening of tone. Perissone did away with the descending motive of Willaert's exposition and its pervasive suspensions. Having eliminated the drooping minor second on "piansi," he reduced the number of suspensions to just one (m. 3), working neither of them back into Willaert's second motive—the one he did borrow.

---

42. For the scores see Willaert, *Opera omnia* 13:73–79, and Perissone, *Madrigali a cinque voci,* ed. Feldman, Sixteenth-Century Madrigal 2:24–40. There are a number of examples of this among Willaert's settings of sestets, e.g., *Mentre che 'l cor dagli amorosi vermi,* in Willaert, *Opera omnia,* ed. Hermann Zenck et al., Corpus mensurabilis musicae, no. 3, AIM ([Rome], 1950–), 13:32–36 (on which see Feldman, "Rore's 'selva selvaggia': The *Primo libro* of 1542," *JAMS* 42 [1989]: 558–60).
43. *The Italian Madrigal* 1:440.

Ex. 46A.   Willaert, *I piansi, hor canto, che 'l celeste lume* (Petrarch, no. 230), mm. 1–10; *Musica nova* (Venice, 1559), no. 16.

EX. 46B.   Perissone, *I piansi, hor canto che 'l celeste lume* (Petrarch, no. 230), mm. 1–5;
Madrigali a 5 (Venice, 1545), no. 16.

In the face of these modifications toward more appealing—and no doubt more
public—prototypes, we should not underestimate Perissone's participation in the
musical practices of Petrarchism that his teacher epitomized. Two further passages
from *I piansi* help make the point. First, Perissone's *I piansi* follows Willaert's model
in drawing the exposition of v. 5, "Onde suol trar di lagrime tal fiume" (Thus he
[Love] is wont to draw from me such a river of tears), over eleven breves. Also, like
Willaert, he introduced plaintive B-flat's at "lagrime" and later "pianger" (v. 10) to
produce minor seconds and thirds—a gesture that had by then become conventional.
Second, at the beginning of the final tercet, "Non lauro o palma, ma tranquilla
oliva / Pietà mi manda" (Pity sends me not a laurel or a palm, but the tranquil olive),
Perissone emulated Willaert's slowing of the composite rhythm to the semibreve. This
type of surface deceleration almost always marks moments of key rhetorical importance in Willaert's writing—a point of symbolic significance, a shift of grammatical
person or tense, or an important twist in meaning—especially in articulating structural divides. In the Petrarchan lexicon the words signify the crucial mirror relationship laurel-Laura, of course. Like Willaert, Perissone applied the device a second time
at the image of pity drying the poet's tears, "E 'l pianto asciuga" (v. 14),[44] a brief
reminder of the opening and one that helps bring the poem full circle.

———————

Perissone's second book *a 5* (and his last book of madrigals) continued to extend
directions taken up in the *Madrigali a 5*. Published by Antonio Gardane in 1550, it

44. In Willaert, mm. 116–18, and Perissone, mm. 111–12.

was given the title *Il segondo libro di madregali a cinque voci con tre dialoghi a otto voci & uno a sette voci novamente da lui composti & dati in luce* and affixed with a brief dedication to Domenego Roncalli.[45]

> To the noble and gentle young man, Mr. Domenego Roncalli, my most eminent lord.
>
> If your lordship will consider well your valor and kindness, you will surely believe without further ado that I have remained such a servant to you from the first day that I came to know you here in Venice; for an ardent desire was born in me to serve and honor you always. I dedicate to you, then, with all my powers, these madrigals of mine, which you might deign to accept not as a gift matched to your worth, but rather as a little sign of the great affection of my reverence, and I kiss your hands with all humility. From Venice on the 3rd of May. Loving servant, Pierisson Cambio.[46]

Domenego Roncalli is not a name that otherwise appears in connection with Venetian music. He may be the same as Giovanni Domenico Roncalli, descendant of a noble Bergamese family that was added in 1545 to the Consiglio Communale of Rovigo, a Venetian outpost. According to his recent biographer, this Roncalli spent a good deal of time at both Padua, where he had a house, and Venice, where in 1554 the doge Francesco Venier made him a cavalier of San Marco.[47] Intriguingly, he gained notoriety in the Veneto by founding an academy in Rovigo in 1553, the Accademia degli Addormentati (later condemned for Calvinist heresies) that was styled after the cultural academies of Venice but with a public aspect that prefigures Badoer's Accademia Veneziana.

Whether this Roncalli is the same as Perissone's dedicatee and what relation he might bear to the print unfortunately remain mysteries. It would be gratifying to connect the two, not least because the *Segondo libro* counts as yet another Venetian print to attempt some kind of modal ordering, though the least straightforwardly of Perissone's three madrigal books (see Table 11). Like Parabosco's collection, its works are arranged in modal groups without obvious distinctions of ambitus, but unlike Parabosco's they are given in the usual ascending order, protus, deuterus,

---

45. There is no mod. ed. of the book at present.

46. Al Nobile & Gentile Giovane Il Signor Domenego Roncalli Signor mio Osservandissimo.

> Se vostra signoria considerera bene il Valore & la gentilezza sua, ella senza piu credera bene ch'io le ristassi tanto servitore il primo giorno che qui in Vinegia la conobbi, che in me sia nasciuto ardente desiderio di sempre servirla, & honorarla. io le dedico adunque insieme con tutto il poter mio questi miei Madrigali: i quali ella si degnera d'accettare, non per presente conveniente al suo Valore: ma si bene per picciolo segno del grandissimo affetto della mia riverenza & a V.S. con ogni humilta bascio le mani. Di Vinegia alli 3 di Maggio. Amorevole Servitore Pierisson Cambio.

47. See Stefania Malavasi, "Giovanni Domenico Roncalli e l'Accademia degli Addormentati di Rovigo," *Archivio veneto,* 5th ser., 95 (1972): 47–58, and Gino Benzoni, "Aspetti della cultura urbana nella società veneta del' 5–600: le accademie," *Archivio veneto* 108 (1977): 114–15. My information relies on Malavasi, to which I can add only that a Giocan da Roncali fu Giovanni Domenico da Rovigo, apparently Roncalli's son, made his will in Venice on 25 May 1596 (I-Vas, Archivio Notarile, Testamenti, Atti Beni, b. 160, fol. 239).

TABLE 11
Perissone Cambio, *Segondo libro a 5* (1550)

Incipit; Poetic Form; Poet and Poetic Source*	System	Cleffing	Final	Mode/ Modal Pair
1. Come consenti amore 11-line madr: aBBAAccDdeE Anon.	b	g2c2c3c3F3	**G**	protus
2. Amor m'ha posto come segn'al strale ii. I pensier son saette al viso' un solo sonnet Petrarch, no. 133	— —	c1c1c3c4F4 c1c1c3c4F4	D D	
3. Son'io più quel che senza tema vissi ii. Non ch'io mi trov'amor presso al tuo laccio sonnet Anon.	— —	c1c3c4c4F4 c1c3c4c4F4	AA D	
4. I vidi'in terra angelici costumi ii. Amor, seno, valor, pietat'e doglia sonnet Petrarch, no. 156	b b	c1c3c4c4F4 c1c3c4c4F4	D **GG**	
5. Quando mai fin havranno 12-line ballata: aBB‖CdEDcEeBB Anon.	—	g2c2c3c3F3	D	
6. Amor se quei begli occhi 10-line ballata: aBB‖cDcDdBB Anon.	b	c1c3c4c4F4	**GG**	
7. Signor i vo che sappi in qual maniera ii. Qui canto dolcemente e qui s'assise sonnet Anon.	b b	c1c1c3c4F4 c1c1c3c4F4	AA **GG**	
8. Alma gentil s'in voi pietà fu mai 13-line madr: AbcA‖DbaEfEfGG Luigi Cassola, *Madrigali,* pp. 30–31	—	g2c2c3c3F3	D	
9. S'amor novo consiglio non n'apporta ii. Imaginata guida la conduce sonnet Petrarch, no. 277	— —	c1c3c4c4F4 c1c3c4c4F4	AA EE	deuterus
10. Del breve viver mio 14-line madr: abcabdcadeeaff Anon.	—	c1c3c4c4F4	E	
11. Poich'ogni ardir mi circonscriss'amore ii. Ch'io spererei de la pietat'ancora sonnet Bembo, *Opere in volgare,* pp. 457–58	— —	c1c3c4c4F4 c1c3c4c4F4	AA EE	
12. Hor vedi, Amor, che giovinetta donna trecento madr. Petrarch, no. 121	b	g2c2c3c3F3	**F**	tritus, 5

TABLE II   *(continued)*

Incipit; Poetic Form; Poet and Poetic Source*	System	Cleffing	Final	Mode/ Modal Pair
13. Amor, da che tu voi pur ch'io m'arischi	b	g2c2c3c3F3	C	
ii. Gentil coppia eccellente	b	g2c2c3c3F3	**F**	
16-line madr: AbacCDedE fggbfbA				
Anon.				
14. In qual parte del ciel, in qual idea	b	c1c3c4c4F4	GG	tritus, 6
ii. Per divina bellezz'in darno mira	b	c1c3c4c4F4	**FF**	
sonnet				
Petrarch, no. 159				
15. Ogni cos'al fin vola	b	c1c3c4c4F4	**FF**	
12-line madr: aBacdeeDffcC				
Anon.				
16. La pastorella mia	b	c1c3c3c4F4	**FF**	
7-line madr: abbcdCC				
Anon.				
17. Gionto m'h'Amor fra bell'e crude braccia	—	c1c3c3c4F4	D	tetrardus?
ii. Nulla posso levar io per mio' ingegno	—	c1c3c3c4F4	**GG**	
sonnet				
Petrarch, no. 171				
18. Son questi quei begliocchi in cui mirando	—	g2c2c3c3F3	G	
ii. Parmi veder nella tua front'amore	—	g2c2c3c3F3	C	
sonnet				
Bembo, *Opere in volgare,* p. 464				
19. Se pur fortun'a me sempre nemica	—	g2c2c3c3F3	G	
ii. Scarpello si vedrà di piomb'o lima	—	g2c2c3c3F3	C	
sonnet				
Ariosto, *Il nuovo Vogel* 1:306 (not confirmed by Ariosto, *Opere minori*)				
20. "Occhi piangete, accompagnate'il core"	—	c1c1c3c3c4c4F4F4	**E**	
dialogue sonnet				
Petrarch, no. 84				
21. "Liet'e pensose, accompagnat'e sole"	—	g2g2c2c2c3c3c4F3	**GG**	
dialogue sonnet				
Petrarch, no. 222				
22. "Che fai alma? Che pensi? Havren mai pace"	b	c1c1c3c3c4c4F4F4	**GG**	
dialogue sonnet				
Petrarch, no. 273				
23. "Quando nascesti, Amor? Quando la terra"	—	c1c2c3c4c4F3F4	**GG**	
dialogue sonnet				
Panfilo Sasso, *Il nuovo Vogel* 1:306				

N.B. No. 19 is in C time; all others are in cut time. Finals are given in boldface, confinals in regular type.
*Table uses short-title references. For full citations see the Bibliography.

tritus, and tetrardus, until the four dialogues at the end (nos. 20–23). Only the tritus-mode madrigals appear to distinguish unambiguously between authentics and plagals, ♭-g2-F madrigals representing authentic followed by ♭-c1-FF for plagal. The protus group is particularly obscure with respect to ambitus. It begins with the typical pitch system for transposed mode 1, ♭-g2-G (no. 1), and several ensuing transposed numbers in the protus group appear to represent mode 2 by means of a contrasting lower cleffing, ♭-c1-GG (nos. 4, 6, and 7). But interpolated between and after them are untransposed madrigals on D that reverse the order: lower cleffing followed by higher ♮-c1-D (no. 2 and 3), then ♮-g2-D (nos. 5 and 8). Alternatively, all the madrigals on D could have been meant to stand in for mode 2, so that only no. 1 represents mode 1, nos. 2 through 8 mode 2; or ambitus might have been intended to function in reverse for the D-durus madrigals, making nos. 1–3 mode 1 and nos. 4–8 mode 2, as Powers has found for Lasso's duos of 1577.[48] But again the three tetrardus madrigals defy traditional expectations for distinguishing modes 7 and 8: ♮-c1-GG (no. 17) is followed by ♮-g2-C (nos. 18 and 19), both of which could stand in for mode 7 but neither of which unambiguously represents either mode 7 or 8.[49] (The deuterus modes all share the same clefs and finals, with the exception of final EE for nos. 9 and 11 and final E for no. 10.)

Ambiguities like these confirm that the book's "modal" arrangement was made ex post facto, either by Perissone, who had made or collaborated on the modal ordering of his first five-voice book, or by Gardane in collaboration with Perissone. If I am right that modal ordering and sonnet setting were companion projects among Venetians, then the book's poetic contents show a commitment to sonnet setting about equal to its commitment to modal thinking (both of which were less than Perissone's had been in putting together his Rore-like First Book). Ten of the *Segondo libro*'s poems are Petrarch's, nine of them sonnets (three dialogues), and one a madrigal.[50] The book also contains two sonnets by Bembo and one possibly by Ariosto—poets represented by one poem each in Perissone's earlier two books. The only other poets identifiable at present are Luigi Cassola, author of the madrigal *Alma gentil, s'in voi pietà fu mai,* and Panfilo Sasso, the late-fifteenth-century Petrarchan poet whose dialogue *"Quando nascesti, Amor? Quando la terra"* was also included in Willaert's *Musica nova.* Eight poems remain anonymous.

In all, the *Segondo libro* contains a record seven settings of texts in the *Musica nova.*[51]

48. "Tonal Types and Modal Categories," pp. 451–52.

49. Powers notes that the type ♮-g2-C was extremely rare in modally ordered collections ("Tonal Types and Modal Categories," pp. 456–59), but it appears in two different books by Perissone, the *Segondo libro* and the *Primo libro de madrigali a quatro voci,* as nos. 16 and 18, respectively (see Tables 11 and 12).

50. One of these, the sonnet *Amor m'ha posto come segn'al strale,* had already been published in 1548 in Scotto's edition of Rore's *Terzo libro a 5,* RISM 1548⁹.

51. One other poem was previously set by Willaert, the anonymous *Amor, da che tu voi* (see Chap. 7 n. 40).

1. *I vid' in terra angelici costumi*

2. *In qual parte del ciel, in qual idea*

3. *Gionto m'ha Amor fra bell'e crude braccia*

4. *"Occhi piangete, accompagnate' il core"*

5. *"Liete e pensose, accompagnat'e sole"*

6. *"Che fai, alma? Che pensi? Havren mai pace?"*

7. *"Quando nascesti, Amor? Quando la terra"*

Helga Meier noted borrowings from Willaert's settings in five of these madrigals (as well as connections between Perissone's five-voice setting of the anonymous *Amor, da che tu voi pur ch'io m'arischi* and Willaert's four-voice *Amor, Fortuna, et la mia mente schiva*).[52] The *Musica nova*'s four dialogue sonnets make up four of the seven. They furnish yet another sign of how early the *Musica nova* had taken shape as a collection and represent through Perissone's placement of them at the end of his book a novel attempt to imitate something of the outer form of Willaert's collection.[53]

As in the *Madrigali a 5*, Perissone's Second Book's imitations showed a refined melodic flair and general brightening that resists Willaert's sternness. To cite a single example, he replaced the dark ♮-c2-E tonality (fourth mode in traditional numbering systems) and low F5 bass of Willaert's six-voice *In qual parte del ciel* with a brighter ♭-c1-F tonality (presumably sixth mode). (Perissone's four-voice setting of the same text used ♭-g2-F.) In Willaert's exposition, cantus, tenor, and sextus all explore the narrow species E to A with a solemn conjunct motive with cantus silent until m. 7 (Ex. 47a), while in Perissone's the cantus floats serenely above the other voices (Ex. 47b). Despite its being a sonnet setting, Perissone's lyricizing bent led him to write animated rhythms, rhythms of the sort Willaert had allowed himself only in madrigals destined for anthologies. With its nimble grace and arched treble, Perissone's cantus recalls his exposition for *Deh, perchè*. His homorhythmic shift to triple meter at v. 8 (Ex. 48), "Benchè la somm'è di mia morte rea," has an analogue in Willaert's setting of *Qual dolcezza giamai*, but none among Willaert's *Musica nova* settings.[54]

Nonetheless, Perissone's *In qual parte del ciel* offers a kind of ideal exemplar of emulation practice. Helga Meier pointed out two unambiguous references to Willaert's original: the circle of fifths imitating Willaert's characteristic opening of the *seconda parte* and its accompanying motivic-contrapuntal structure (Exx. 49a and 49b); and Willaert's *soggetto* for v. 4, "Mostrar qua giù quanto lassù potea"

---

52. The five related settings cited by Meier are: *I vidi in terra, In qual parte del ciel,* "*Liete e pensose,*" "*Che fai, alma?,*" and "*Quando nascesti, Amor?*" ("Zur Chronologie der *Musica Nova*," p. 76).

53. At least two other collections made a less sweeping attempt to do this: Donato's *Primo libro d'i madregali a 5 & a 6* of 1553 (discussed below) and the Paduan Francesco Portinaro's *Primo libro de madrigali a cinque voci* of 1550, with five six-voice settings and a seven-voice setting of "*Liete e pensose*" at the end.

54. Cf. the triple meter that starts the *seconda parte* of no. 11. For *Qual dolcezza giamai* see Willaert, *Opera omnia* 14:65–70, esp. mm. 64–69.

EX. 47A. Willaert, *In qual parte del ciel, in qual idea* (Petrarch, no. 159), mm. 1–13; *Musica nova* (Venice, 1559), no. 18.

EX. 47B.   Perissone, *In qual parte del ciel, in qual idea* (Petrarch, no. 159), mm. 1–13; *Segondo libro a 5* (Venice, 1550), no. 14.

(*continued*)

(compare the altus of each in Exx. 50a and 50b). In fact Perissone adopted Willaert's declamatory gestures even more extensively than this, borrowing the rhythm of Willaert's homorhythmic altus-tenor duet at v. 3 and taking over the four-note figure for "Chiome d'oro" of v. 6. Even so, he continued to avoid the obscuring intricacies of a pervasively varied motivic structure. In both of the cases just cited he turned Willaert's *soggetti* into unvaried rhythmic figures (or nearly so); Willaert's setting continually alters the rhythms applied to v. 3 by shifting stressed syllables between tonic and agogic accents and also adds small melismas, while Perissone's

Perissone, *In qual parte del ciel, in qual idea* (Petrarch, no. 159), mm. 51–62; *Segondo libro a 5* (Venice, 1550), no. 14.

retains the same rhythmic morphology for each entry (Exx. 51a and 51b). Likewise, Willaert made "Chiome d'oro" rhythmically fluid and metrically elusive: four of the six voices start with the syncopated figure and two others on the tactus, nearly transforming the motive into anonymity. Here again Perissone repeated Willaert's rhythm exactly at each of the five entrances—yet never with the precise rhetorical incentive Willaert seems to have had in those rare instances when he avoided motivic variation (see Ex. 15 and Chap. 7 n. 47).

Ex. 49B.   Perissone, *In qual parte del ciel, in qual idea* (Petrarch, no. 159), mm. 63–68;
Segondo libro a 5 (Venice, 1550), no. 14.

Ex. 50A.   Willaert, *In qual parte del ciel, in qual idea* (Petrarch, no. 159), altus, mm.
25–28; *Musica nova* (Venice, 1559), no. 18.

Ex. 50B.   Perissone, *In qual parte del ciel, in qual idea* (Petrarch, no. 159), altus, mm.
29–33; *Segondo libro a 5* (Venice, 1550), no. 14.

Ex. 51B.   Perissone, *In qual parte del ciel, in qual idea* (Petrarch, no. 159), mm. 17–21;
Segondo libro a 5 (Venice, 1550), no. 14.

PERISSONE CAMBIO: MADRIGALS FOR FOUR VOICES

In 1547 Perissone published with Gardane his *Primo libro di madrigali a quatro voci*—
as it turned out, the only four-voice madrigal book to be issued by any of Willaert's
immediate students.[55] Like Perissone's other books, the *Primo libro a 4* is arranged
in ascending modal order—at least through no. 22, the end of the consecutive block
of madrigals that are Perissone's own (see Table 12). The modal ordering extends to
distinctions between authentics and plagals (unlike the *Segondo libro a 5*), albeit with
a few anomalies.[56] Nothing else unites the book, however, and otherwise it is
Perissone's most diverse, merging in a single collection the widely disparate generic
traditions that attached to madrigals for four voices, on the one hand—chansonesque madrigals à la Verdelot and Arcadelt, madrigals for theater, madrigals
a note nere, madrigals related to frottole, and songs in the oral tradition—and the

55. I except the four-voice book of madrigals published by Nicola Vicentino of Vicenza (in the
Veneto) in 1546 because it bears so little relation to the style that Willaert's Venetian circle was pursuing
at the time; see *Del unico Adrian Willaerth discipulo don Nicola Vicentino madrigali a cinque voci per theorica et pratica da lui composti al nuovo modo dal celeberrimo suo maestro ritrovato. Libro primo* (Venice, 1546);
mod. ed. Nicola Vicentino, *Opera omnia,* ed. Henry W. Kaufmann, Corpus mensurabilis musicae, no.
26, AIM ([Rome], 1963), pp. 1–60.

56. First, the tonal makeup of no. 5, cantus durus on D with high clefs (chiavette), did not normally
signify plagal for protus modes. The architect of the print's modal ordering—whether printer, composer,
or both—may have conceived ♮-g2-D as plagal because of the way it contrasts with nos. 1 and 2, which
use both the standard transposition upward to G (cantus mollis) and high clefs, that is, ♭-g2-G. Second,
given that the only source of contrast among the tritus modes is that of cleffing, no. 11, with its low clefs
standing between two chiavette madrigals, is misplaced. This is probably a consequence of the printer's
effort to arrange the madrigals neatly on pages; since no. 13 needed a bit more than one side, it fit nicely
coming after no. 12, whose *secunda pars* left a little space at the bottom (no. 11, on the other hand,
required a full side). Finally, we should note the rather unusual use of cantus durus on C with high clefs
(nos. 16 and 18) to signify mode 7; see n. 49 above on its use in the *Segondo libro a 5*.

TABLE 12
Perissone Cambio, *Primo libro a 4* (1547)

Incipit; Poetic Form; Poet and Poetic Source*	System	Cleffing	Final	Mode

1. Io mi son bella e cruda
   8-line madr: aBBAccDD
   Anon. parody of Boccaccio's ballata
     Io mi son giovinetta
	b	g2c2c3F3	**G**	1

2. Vaga tranquilla e lieta
   6-line madr: ababCC
   Anon.
	b	g2c2c3F3	**G**	1

3. Io amai sempre & amo fort'ancora
   ii. Ma chi penso veder mai tutt'insieme
   sonnet
   Petrarch, no. 85
	b
	b
		c1c3c4F4
		c1c3c4F4
			D
			GG
				2

4. O perverso d'amor stato empio e rio
   ottava rima
   Anon.
	—	c1c3c4F4	**D**	2

5. Che giova posseder citad'e regni
   ottava rima
   Pietro Bembo, *Opere* (1808), 2:121
	—	g2c2c3F4	**D**	2?

6. Duo più potenti lumi
   6-line madr: abaCdD
   Anon.
	—	g2c2c3F4	**A**	3

7. Chi mett'il pie su l'amorosa pania
   ottava rima
   Ariosto, *Orlando furioso*, 24.1
	—	c1c3c4F4	**AA**	3/4

8. Chiara luce serena
   12-line madr: aBBCdEDf EgDD
   Anon.
	—	c3c3c4F4	**E**	4

9. Perchè la vit'è breve
   canzone, stanza 1, vv. 1–7
   Petrarch, no. 71
	—	c1c3c4F4	**E**	4

10. Se 'l ciel donna non vede
   8-line madr: abccabdD
   Anon.
	b	g2c2c3F3	**F**	5

11. Come potrò fidarmi
   12-line ballata: aBB CdEDcE eAA
   Anon.
	b	c1c3c4F4	**FF**	6

12. In qual parte del ciel, in qual idea
   ii. Per divina bellezza in darno mira
   sonnet
   Petrarch, no. 159
	b
	b
		g2c2c2c4
		g2c2c2c4
			C
			F
				5

13. Cantai mentre ch'i arsi del mio foco
   14-line ballata: ABBA CDEDCE EFFA
   Giovanni Brevio, *Rime e prose*, fol. B V
	b	c1c3c4F4	**FF**	6

TABLE 12 *(continued)*

Incipit; Poetic Form; Poet and Poetic Source*	System	Cleffing	Final	Mode
14. Più volte già dal bel sembiant'humano	b	c1c3c4F4	C	6
ii. Ond'io non puote mai formar parola	b	c1c3c4F4	**FF**	
sonnet				
Petrarch, no. 170				
15. Occhi leggiadri amorosetti & gravi	—	g2c2c3F3	**G**	7
7-line madr: AbAbacC				
Luigi Cassola, *Madrigali,* p. 28				
16. Nel partir del mio ben si part'amore	—	g2c2c3F3	**C**	7
8-line madr: ABaCBdEE				
Anon.				
17. Ove cols'amor lor'e di qual vena	—	g2c2c3F3	**D**	7
ii. Da quali angeli moss'e di qual spera	—	g2c2c3F3	**GG**	
sonnet				
Petrarch, no. 220				
18. Non di terrestre donna il chiaro viso	—	g2c2c3F3	**C**	7
8-line madr: ABCABCDD				
Anon.				
19. Se mai fu crud'a mei dolci pensieri	—	c1c3c3c4	**G**	8
ottava rima				
Anon.				
20. Sapete amanti perchè Amor è cieco	—	c1c3c4F4	**GG**	8
6-line madr: AbAbcC				
Anon.				
21. Pien d'un vago pensier che mi desvia	—	c1c3c4F4	**GG**	8
ii. Ben s'io non erro di pietat'un raggio	—	c1c3c4F4	**GG**	
sonnet				
Petrarch, no. 169				
22. Amor, da che tu voi pur ch'io m'arischi	—	c1c3c4F4	**D**	8
ii. Gentil coppia eccellente	—	c1c3c4F4	**GG**	
16-line madr: AbacCDedE fggbfbA				
Anon.				
23. Quel foco che tanti anni (Rore)	b	c2c3c4F4	**GG**	
9-line madr: aBBBACcDD				
Anon.				
24. Com'havrà fin le dolorose tempre (Rore)	—	c1c3c4F4	**E**	
7-line madr: ABbCcDD				
Anon.				
25. Anchor che col partire (Rore)	—	c1c3c4F4	**E**	
8-line madr: aaBbCCdD				
Alfonso d'Avalos, *Il nuovo Vogel* 1:304				
26. Fresch'herbe vaghi fiori ombre secrete	—	g2c2c4F3	**D**	
9-line madr: ABcdB?EBFF				
Anon.				

N.B. Nos. 4, 6, 14, 18–22, and 24–26 are in cut time; all others are in C time. Finals are given in boldface, confinals in regular type.

*Table uses short-title references. For full citations see the Bibliography.

generally more monolithic, learned traditions of five- and six-voice madrigals, especially of sonnet settings, on the other.

Perissone's book included sonnets, ballate, cinquecento madrigals, and ottave rime. Not all of these had lately been linked to *four*-voice settings and certainly not mixed in a single volume. Of the twenty-six numbers, the largest share (predictably) are settings of cinquecento madrigals, eleven of them by Perissone (nos. 1, 2, 6, 8, 10, 15, 16, 18, 20, 22, and 26) and three by Cipriano de Rore (nos. 23, 24, and 25).[57] Rore's contributions include the first publication of his setting of Alfonso d'Avalos's *Anchor che col partire,* one of the most often reprinted and imitated secular settings of the century. Einstein may have overstated the case in calling it the model for the whole collection,[58] but it has suggestive stylistic parallels with Perissone's many madrigal settings in the book.

Sonnet settings, by comparison, total only five—all Petrarch's and all complete (nos. 3, 12, 14, 17, and 21). This makes Perissone's emphasis on madrigals over sonnets an apparent emphasis of Rore's four-voice model over the four-voice madrigals in the *Musica nova*. Yet it is Perissone's sonnet settings that are newest and that introduce the single most significant dichotomy in the collection. Perissone was the only one of Willaert's disciples to write four-voice settings of Petrarch's sonnets in a style close to the *Musica nova*. Four of them in fact set *Musica nova* texts: *Io amai sempre & amo fort'ancora* (the only one also for four voices in Willaert's setting), *In qual parte del ciel, Più volte già dal bel sembiant'humano,* and *Pien d'un vago pensier.* We might add to the book's weightier sonnet side its two ballata settings, no. 11, *Come potrò fidarmi,* Brevio's *Cantai mentre ch'i arsi* (earlier published in settings by Rore and Parabosco), as well as the anonymous *Amor, da che tu voi* (no. 22), set in two parts (like Willaert's setting of 1548 and Perissone's of 1550).

None of the poems I have placed in this group is shorter than twelve lines long. By contrast, only one of the madrigal texts (apart from no. 22) is longer than nine lines (no. 8), including Rore's. These tiny poems generally concentrate on a single, concisely developed conceit. The slight literary status they claimed in musical prints may have been nil outside of music: except for those by Cassola (no. 15) and d'Avalos, all the madrigal texts are as yet anonymous.

To complete this sketch of the book's contents, the four remaining numbers are ottave rime. One of them is Bembo's (no. 5), another a stanza from Ariosto's *Orlando furioso,* 24.1 (no. 7), and the other two (nos. 4 and 19) again anonymous. Ottave rime are among the least common forms to appear in contemporary Venetian collections. With their lucid songlike textures and avoidance of contrapuntal artifice, they fall more on the madrigalian than the sonnet side of Venetian production. Their form—*endecasillabi* rhyming ABABABCC—was a long-standing

---

57. Perissone's setting of the first seven lines from Petrarch's canzone *Perchè la vit'è breve* (no. 9) might just as well be added to this group, as it functions similarly to the madrigals, extracting the *piedi* and the first line of the *sirima* from the opening stanza.

58. *The Italian Madrigal* 1:441.

vehicle of poet-improvisors in the oral tradition, the structural prototype shared by epic poetry and the lyric *strambotto,* as well as occasional stanzas. Thus their presence in the *Primo libro a 4* may signal yet again the enduring connection between settings of ottave rime and traditions of improvisatory song.[59]

This brings us to the dedication attached to the collection, made to the renowned Paduan poet Gaspara Stampa who was famed for her singing to the lute.

To the lovely and talented Signora Gasparina Stampa

Noble lady, well might I be reproved by the wise and learned composers of this sweet and admirable science—reproved in this science, yes, but no man in the world will ever be able to say that I have had little judgment in dedicating these notes of mine to your ladyship, however they may be. Because it is well known by now—and not only in this fortunate city, but almost everywhere—that no woman in the world loves music as much as you do, nor possesses it to such a rare degree. And thousands upon thousands of fine and noble spirits attest to this who, having heard your sweet harmonies, have given you the name of divine siren, remaining over time your most devoted servants, among whom I am as devoted as any. I come with this my little token and gift to refresh the memory of the love that I bear for your talent, begging that you deign to find me worthy to be placed where you place the innumerable throngs of those who adore and love your rare talents and beauties. And to your graces I commend and offer myself. Most devoted servant Pieresson Cambio.[60]

In Chapter 4, I suggested that a connection might exist between the kind of solo and at least quasi-improvisatory singing for which Stampa was acclaimed and the treble-dominated writing and periodic phraseology that pervades much of Perissone's four-voice book. Even though his published settings were suited to part singing, it is reasonable to imagine alternatively that at least some of them could have been adapted for solo singing to lute accompaniment or simply been performed by a solo treble singer to the accompaniment of viols or broken consort on the lower parts. Perissone's plea to be placed among Stampa's adoring throngs

---

59. On this matter and in connection with the discussion that follows see Chap. 4 nn. 68–80 above, esp. the literature cited in n. 75. See also James Haar, "Arie per cantar stanze ariotesche," in *L'Ariosto: la musica, i musicisti,* ed. Maria Antonella Balsano (Florence, 1981), pp. 31–46, and idem, *Essays on Italian Poetry and Music in the Renaissance, 1350–1600* (Berkeley and Los Angeles, 1986), pp. 92–99.

60. Alla bella et virtuosa Signora Gasparina Stampa

Valorosa signora, io potrò ben esser ripreso apresso ai saggi, & dotti compositori di questa dolce et mirabile scienza: in essa scienza ma no mi potra gia huomo del mondo dire giamai ch'io habbia havuto poco giuditio nel dedicare queste mie note, quale elle siano, alla S. V. perche si sa bene homai. & non pure in questa felice citta: ma quasi in ogni parte, niuna donna al mondo amar piu la Musica di quello che fate voi, ne altra piu raramente possederla, & di questo ne fanno fede i mille, & mille spirti gentili, & nobili: i quali udito havendo i dolci concenti vostri, v'hanno dato nome di divino sirena, restandovi per tempo devotissimi servi, fra i quali, io devoto quanto altro, vengo con questo mio picciolo segno & presente, a rinfrescarle nella memoria, lo amore ch'io porto alle sue virtu, pregandola che si degni, ch'io sia degno di esser posto dove ella pone la innumerabil turba di quei ch'adorano, & amano le sue rare virtu, & bellezze. & alla sua bona gratia mi raccomando & offero. Devotissimo servo Pieresson Cambio.

might be glossed as a hope that his songs will grace her repertory. It might also have been a way of insinuating himself as fellow singer in the elect circles of literary academists with which Stampa surrounded herself in various private homes, including her own. To say so is to suggest that a four-voice book of the 1540s might still have functioned at times as a sort of fakebook—as books of frottole had done—providing raw material to be freely adapted according to variable needs. One of its specific functions may have been that of a solo songbook (also like books of frottole), thus continuing the alliance of early madrigals with solo song made so patent by Willaert's intabulations of Verdelot's madrigals a decade earlier.[61]

Vestiges of recitational practice from unwritten traditions are embedded in Perissone's setting of Ariosto's stanza *Chi mett'il pie su l'amorosa pania* from *Orlando furioso*, the central textual repository for sixteenth-century *improvvisatori* (Ex. 52).

Chi mett'il pie su l'amorosa pania	May he who puts his foot in the loving birdlime
Cerchi ritrarlo e non inveschi l'ale,	Try to extract it and not catch his wing [in it],
Che non è in somm'Amor se non l'insania	For in the end Love is nothing but madness
A giuditio de savi universale;	In the universal opinion of wise men;
E se ben egualment'ogn'huom non smania,	And if everyone does not go raving about equally,
Suo furor mostrar'a qualch'altro segnale;	Its furor shows itself through other signs;
E qual è di pazzia segno più espresso	And what is a more telling sign of madness
Che per altri voler perder se stesso?	Than to lose your own self by desiring another?

Each of the stanza's eight lines is fitted to a distinct musical strain. None but the last receives a full repeat, and only the most minimal textual repetition occurs otherwise. Simultaneous declamation simulating accompanied solo singing plays a prominent role here, as it does in the other ottava settings, all but one of which begin in homorhythm. Homorhythm also helps articulate the couplets that organize the octave at the highest level: while cadences at line endings reinforce the sense of organization by melodic strains, the junctures between couplets are reinforced texturally by four-voice homophony (if only up to the cadence—compare mm. 8 and 14 with m. 18). At another level of formal articulation, Perissone's setting reproduces musically the effect of various textual rhymes by giving them similar cadences, like the ones ending vv. 3 and 5, "sania" / "smania" (mm. 10 and 16). Meanwhile, as in other ottava settings, the bass line moves much more harmonically than in Perissone's settings of other sorts of verse. This is not to underestimate Perissone's use of contrapuntal artifice or his exploitation of counterpoint to achieve cadences of varying weights: weakening the cadence of v. 1 (m. 3) by delaying the diminished suspension in the cantus, evading the cadences in mm. 13 and 14 for v. 4, or overlapping seams between vv. 7 and 8 (mm. 21–22). It is rather to point

61. *Intavolatura de li madrigali di Verdelotto da cantare et sonare nel lauto, intavolati per Messer Adriano* (Venice, 1536); Renaissance Music Prints, vol. 3, ed. Bernard Thomas (London, 1980); facs. ed. Archivum Musicum, Collana di testi rari, no. 36 (Florence, 1980).

Ex. 52. Perissone, *Chi mett'il pie su l'amorosa pania* (Ariosto), incl.; *Primo libro a 4* (Venice, 1547), no. 7.

(continued)

EX. 52 *(continued)*

(continued)

up the fortuitous merging of written contrapuntal with oral soloistic procedures that Perissone effects in settings like this.

Perissone's four-voice settings of madrigals avoid the signs of oral recitation that mark his ottava settings, though without aiming for a higher literary tone. Madrigals elicit more extensive text repetition and far more radical displacements of poetic lines between contrapuntal parts. (In no. 10, for example, the tenor is nearly three measures and fully one poetic line ahead of all three other voices by the end of m. 6.) Instead of playing a continuously harmonic role, bass lines in madrigal settings are inclined to alternate between two roles, that of harmonic support and that of equal participant in the imitative processes governing the whole texture.

Many of the madrigal texts are addressed directly to women in the form of serenades: *Vaga tranquilla e lieta* (no. 2, to a "Marina"), *Duo più potenti lumi* (no. 6), and *Chiara luce serena* (no. 8). Moving away from the sectionalizing strategy of the frottola, Perissone's settings give a continuous musical development to their amorous conceits, which invariably crest in a witty point at the end, rather than "[touching on] the principal motif . . . in the first line" or an opening *ripresa,* as happens in *barzellette.*[62] According to Parabosco (as he has Speroni declare in *I diporti*), both madrigals and *strambotti* resemble epigrams in sharing this sort of development.[63] Whereas Perissone's ottava settings reproduce the segmented techniques of solo recitation and rely on rhythmic energy for momentum, his madrigal settings mirror their poems' rhetorical trajectory by piling up voices, displaced in imitation, into a contrapuntal crescendo.

62. The quote is from Einstein, *The Italian Madrigal* 1:185.
63. "Above all else," he writes, "the madrigal and *strambotto* must have a lovely wit and invention, just like an epigram" (sopra ogni altra cosa, il madrigale e lo strambotto vuole andare vago d'arguzia e di invenzione, sì come apunto vuole apparire il motto); *I diporti* (Venice, [ca. 1550]; repr. in *Novellieri minori del cinquecento: G. Parabosco—S. Erizzo,* ed. Giuseppe Gigli and Fausto Nicolini [Bari, 1912]), p. 177; a longer excerpt, which includes this passage, is quoted and trans. in Einstein, *The Italian Madrigal* 1:184–85.

Both approaches could draw on aspects of madrigalistic repertories from the 1530s, though in different ways. By contrast, Perissone's sonnet settings *a 4* tend toward denser polyphony and more learned diction (if less so than his sonnets set *a 5*). While indebted to Willaert's settings, his sonnets *a 4* are less solemn and ample than Willaert's or Rore's settings *a 5 or 6*. Perissone's four-voice *In qual parte del ciel*, for instance, falls short of Willaert's for six voices by twenty-two breves. The *prima parte* of Willaert's six-voice *Pien d'un vago pensier* alone is longer than the *whole* of Perissone's four-voice setting of it (73 and 72 breves, respectively; Willaert's setting lasts 128 breves altogether).[64] Discrepancies like these are to be expected, given that contrapuntal complexities normally increase geometrically as voices are added. But differences also arise because Perissone tended to make his four-voice sonnet settings lighter, more condensed, and simpler in construction, with voices more frequently arranged in homophony or closely interwoven, and with somewhat less radically evaded cadences than Willaert did.[65]

Perissone's setting of the sonnet *Più volte già* (no. 14) embodies many of these differences. Like *In qual parte del ciel* and *Pien d'un vago pensier*, the setting is much shorter than Willaert's, with each line normally stated once, or at most repeated only partially. Whereas Willaert's exposition of *Più volte già* opened the *a*- and *o*-laden first verse in a languorous, irregular point of imitation, Perissone's opening ascends in chansonlike dactyllic tetrachords located in a regularized, efficient exposition (Exx. 53a and 53b). Willaert ambles through six breves before accelerating into a minim pace; Perissone establishes the minim as the basic declamatory pulse in the first measure. Perissone returned to this laconic style for the polysyndetonic vv. 6 and 7: (Exx. 54a and 54b): "Per ch'ogni mia fortuna, ogni mia sorte, / Mio ben, mio male, et mia vita et mia morte" (for all my fortune, all my destiny, my good, my ill,

64. Overall the four-voice settings in the *Musica nova* average about the same length as those for more voices and are about half again as long as the four-voice sonnet settings of Perissone.

65. On works in the *Primo libro a 4* that are modeled on settings in the *Musica nova*—*In qual parte del ciel* and *Amor, da che tu voi*—see Helga Meier, "Zur Chronologie der *Musica Nova*," pp. 84–87, and the preface to idem, ed., *Fünf Madrigale*, pp. iii–iv. The latter, she notes, is unique for borrowing its exposition (like Perissone's five-voice setting of the same poem, published in 1550) not from a setting by Willaert of the same text but rather from one that merely begins with the same word, *Amor, fortuna, et la mia mente*. Perissone's habit of modeling took a unique form in his four-voice setting of *In qual parte del ciel*, which borrowed extensively only *after* the exposition. Meier cites two of these borrowings, one in the motive at v. 3, "Quel bel viso leggiadro" (mm. 18–20; cf. Willaert, mm. 18–21), and the other in the latter half of v. 5, "in selva mai qual dea" (mm. 33–35; cf. Willaert mm. 36–47). In addition to emphasizing a C tonality, other correspondences may be cited as follows: Perissone's adoption of various aspects of Willaert's interpretation of v. 6, "Chiome d'oro sì fino a l'aura sciolse?" (Perissone, mm. 35–40; Willaert, mm. 45–52); the polymetric combination of tonic and agogic accents on the initial syllable "Chio-" of "Chiome d'oro"; and motivic similarities throughout the respective settings of vv. 12 and 13. The opening of the *seconda parte*, while not taken over as precisely in Perissone's version *a 4* as in that *a 5*, nonetheless borrows both the rhythm and general melodic direction of Willaert's original. Willaert's five opening sonorities—A-D-G-C-a—are also all present. Though Perissone reverses the order of the first two, he was apparently reconciling a harmonic imitation of Willaert's setting with the exigencies of his counterpoint, transposing A and D to permit a smooth transition from the *prima parte* and retain Willaert's colorful C-sharp on "divina" in the uppermost voice. This allowed him to adopt much of the sonority of Willaert's passage despite using a different mode. On the whole Perissone's setting is more tuneful and melodically more far-ranging than its model. In the exposition, for instance, where Willaert's opening is plain, full of repeated notes in small ambituses and devoid of rhythmic surprise, Perissone's lines sweep quickly over large areas of pitch space.

my life, and my death). Where Willaert had assigned a separate gesture to each rhetorical parcel, casting "mio ben/mio male" into a kind of dialogue (altus-tenor-quintus-bassus, mm. 47–49, answered by cantus-altus-tenor-quintus, mm. 49–51) and drawing out "e mia vita, e mia morte" in a madrigalistic rendering, Perissone set the same clause more plainly (mm. 38–41), phrasing the entire chain of possessives, save "mia fortuna," in a single, quasi-continuous gesture (mm. 31–41). Only the final verse broadens out through a series of textual repetitions marked by perfect cadences (mm. 76 and 84, as traditionally happens toward the end of a madrigal), and finally syncopated embellishment in the tenor.

It thus seems clear that Perissone's less expansive approach to sonnets reflects a continued tendency to view the four-voice madrigal as a qualitatively different

genre from madrigals for five or six voices or those for seven or eight. Yet his *Più volte già* also conforms to many other instances in which Willaert's disciples hesitated to embrace completely the restrictive seriousness that Willaert brought to *Musica nova* madrigals.

Although Perissone's career as chapel singer and freelancer continued to flourish in the 1550s,[66] no further collections devoted to his music have come down to us after that of 1550. A few of his works were anthologized up until 1576, but sometime during the 1560s Perissone passed away.[67] His death was mourned in Petrarchan tropes exchanged by two Venetian academists, Domenico Venier and Girolamo Fenaruolo: "The sound

66. See Jonathan Glixon, "A Musicians' Union in Sixteenth-Century Venice," *JAMS* 36 (1983): 409–10 n. 42, and Ongaro, "The Chapel of St. Mark's," pp. 140–41 and 145.

67. See the mentions of his death in documents from the Scuola di San Marco and the Scuola di Santa Maria della Carità reported by Glixon, "A Musicians' Union," pp. 409–10 n. 42. He may have died earlier than the late sixties, as suggested by his absence from the lists of singers at St. Mark's from 1562; see Ongaro, "The Chapel of St. Mark's," p. 165 n. 194, and Document 272.

EX. 54A.   Willaert, *Più volte già dal bel sembiante humano* (Petrarch, no. 170), mm. 41–50; *Musica nova* (Venice, 1559), no. 6.

EX. 54B. Perissone, *Più volte già dal bel sembiant'humano* (Petrarch, no. 170), mm. 31–41; *Primo libro a 4* (Venice, 1547), no. 14.

of his sweet tones stopped / the waves in the sea, the wind in the air, / burned ice, moved mountains, and made serene the clouded sky."[68]

BALDASSARE DONATO, MADRIGALS TO 1553

We have already glimpsed Baldassare Donato several times in previous chapters—Donato the maturing choirboy who gained favor in the salons of Venice, was made right-hand man to Willaert, and informant to the Procuratori. Donato's beginnings are in some respects an inverse reflection of Perissone's. Whereas Perissone entered San Marco only in 1548 after several years of scrambling to publish and to perform under private aegises, Donato was already mounting the chapel hierarchy at a comfortable pace by 1545–46, in his mid- to late teens. Yet neither of the prints that unveiled the Venetian school in 1544—Doni's au courant *Dialogo della musica* or Rore's *Secondo libro*—showed any sign of him. Donato's first published work appeared only with Scotto's edition of Rore's *Terzo libro* of 1548 when Donato was about eighteen to twenty-two years old—still young but hardly precocious by the standards of a Parabosco.[69] Unlike Perissone's compositional career, then, Donato's seems to have been hatched directly from his breeding in the chapel.

Donato's first published madrigal was a setting of Petrarch's sonnet *S'una fed'amorosa, un cor non finto* (no. 224) that showed him already adept in the diction and counterpoint reserved for sonnets.[70] Petrarch's poem, compounded of seven conditional clauses resolved only in the final verse, deploys a rhetorical strategy ready-made for the continuously woven polyphony and slight motivic variation developed by Willaert. The entire sonnet consists of a large paratactic chain, reinforced by anaphora and structured by linking together in additive series several of its ubiquitous "if" clauses. Since the verb of the main clause is postponed all the way until v. 13, the poem's essential form can be gleaned from the opening and closing lines (1–4 and 12–14):

S'una fed'amorosa, un cor non finto,	If faithfulness in love, an undeceiving heart,
Un languir dolce, un desiar cortese,	A sweet languishing, a courteous desire,
S'honeste voglie in gentil fuoc'accese,	If virtuous longings kindled in a noble fire,
S'un lungh'error in cieco laberinto . . . ,	If a long wandering in a blind labyrinth . . . ,
. . . .	. . . .
S'arder da lunge et agghiacciar da presso,	If to burn from afar and freeze close by
Son le cagion ch'amand'io mi distempre,	Are the reasons that I untune myself with love,
Vostro, Donn', è 'l peccato et mio fia il danno.	Yours is the wrong, Lady, and mine may be the loss.

68. The words are Venier's; see the Appendix to this chap.
69. On Donato's age I follow Ongaro, "The Chapel of St. Mark's," who thinks he was probably on the younger side of the four-year span given.
70. For a full transcription see my "Venice and the Madrigal in the Mid-Sixteenth Century," 2 vols. (Ph.D. diss., University of Pennsylvania, 1987), 2:656–67.

In setting this sonnet Donato appealed to the plainest possible motivic idiom, avoiding individual semantic emphasis in favor of a language that would play up the poem's local syntactic and rhetorical differentiations while still countering any pull toward articulation. The setting's dearth of syncopation or sustained progressions by fifth and its proliferation of two-note declamatory groups help check the possibility of any forceful approaches to cadence. The entire setting uses only one diminished cadence: it takes place at the end of the first couplet, but with textual and contrapuntal cadences displaced from one another (see mm. 14–16 in Ex. 55) and only the cantus's noncadential bb-flat sharing the text with the cadencing contratenor. The only other cadences in the first quatrain fall at the end of v. 4, both simple cadences, the first (mm. 26–27) emphasized with an f-sharp in the cantus, the second with an undiminished half cadence (mm. 31–32).

All of this contrasts greatly with Donato's madrigalian settings from his first solo collection of 1550, a medley of light madrigals for four voices and *canzoni villanesche alla napolitana* published as *Le napolitane, et alcuni madrigali a quattro voci*.[71] *Le napolitane* points up the loose affinity of *villanesche* with lighter four-voice madrigals, both of which profited from Donato's natural gifts for vivid, animated rhythms and sharply etched melodies. None of the madrigals in it are sonnet settings. Indeed the opening number, *Vaghi pensier che così passo passo,* setting the third stanza from Petrarch's canzone no. 70, serves as a reminder that single canzone stanzas—even Petrarch's—were thought of by composers in a way more akin to poetic madrigals than to weightier sonnets (as poets conceived them).

Vaghi pensier is a compact mix of *endecasillabi* and *settenari*. With its emblematic lament on the stony lady culminating in the famous incipit from Dante's *Rime petrose,* it must have made good capital with literary-minded book buyers. (The stanza had already been singled out for musical treatment by Parabosco four years earlier; see Table 9, no. 16.)

Vaghi pensier che così passo passo	Yearning thoughts, which thus step by step
Scorto ma'havet'a ragionar tant'alto;	Have led me to such high speech:
Vedete che madonna ha 'l cor di smalto	You see that my lady has a heart of such hard
Sì forte ch'io per me dentro no 'l passo.	Stone that I cannot by myself pass within it.
Ella non degna di mirar sì basso	She does not deign to look so low 5
Che di nostre parole	As to care about our words,
Curi, che 'l ciel non vuole,	For the heavens do not wish it,
Al qual pur contrastand'io son già lasso;	And resisting them I am already weary;
Onde come nel cor m'induro e 'naspro,	Therefore as in my heart I become sad and bitter,
"Così nel mio parlar vogli'esser aspro."	"So in my speech I wish to become harsh." 10

---

71. The print also included *villotte* by Perissone. The last three numbers in it are Donato's settings of Venier's stanzas in praise of Venice (see Chap. 4 nn. 78–79).

Between publications of *S'una fed'amorosa* in 1548 and *Le napolitane* in 1550 Donato published a single ottava setting, *O felice colui ch'al suo volere,* in Scotto's *Fantesie, et recerchari a tre voci, accomodate da cantare et sonare . . . con la giunta di alcuni altri Recerchari, et Madrigali a tre voci* of 1549 (1549³⁴), a print that includes works by Willaert, Rore, and others. (Einstein's statement that this was the first appearance of Donato's music in print is of course incorrect; *The Italian Madrigal* 1:448.)

EX. 55.   Donato, *S'una fed'amorosa, un cor non finto* (Petrarch, no. 224), mm. 1–32; in Cipriano de Rore, *Terzo libro a 5* (Venice, 1548) (RISM 1548⁹), p. 13.

(continued)

Donato's style here so much avoids the heavier manner of Willaert's and Perissone's sonnet settings that Einstein likened it to that of the young Palestrina.[72] Sealing off the four lines of *piedi* with a sectional break, Donato recognized the stanza's segmented character, as earlier madrigalists had done in setting canzoni and ballata-madrigals, and also (like them) built his setting out of crisp, short phrases and a metrically uniform imitative technique. Cadences like the ones in Ex. 56 assemble the voices in homorhythmic declamation (mm. 38, 43, and 48), or else they converge successively by pairs.

Donato's generally careful declamation helped project the stanza formally, rather than elaborating it rhetorically, but he also embellished the text in line with the lighter traditions that especially suited his natural gifts. Thus, for example, the end of v. 3 ignores declamatory demands altogether, applying a graceful decorative melisma in the manner of chansonesque madrigals. Following the lead of Rore's recent *Vergine bella* setting (and unlike Willaert's madrigals), voices do not always sing the complete stanza, but often drop out to reduce textures epigrammatically without reinstating omitted text. Donato lingers only for formal reasons, like the standard reiteration of the last line. This is one place, at Petrarch's deft elision into Dante's text, where a more arduous rhetoric might be expected, but Donato ventures nothing but a few consecutive six-three chords on "aspro" and a single four-three appoggiatura. If Donato's *S'una fed'amorosa* avoided semantic intensity in favor of sober recitation, *Vaghi pensier* avoids it to preserve an air of light lyricism.

---

72. *The Italian Madrigal* 1:452. For a complete transcription see Feldman, "Venice and the Madrigal," 2:668–76.

EX. 56. Donato, *Vaghi pensier, che così passo passo* (Petrarch, no. 70, stanza 3), mm. 32–48; *Le napolitane, et alcuni madrigali a 4* (Venice, 1550), p. 1.

Donato's first full-fledged print of madrigals was not issued until 1553, under the title *Il primo libro d'i madregali a cinque & a sei voci, con tre dialoghi a sette.*[73] The book bore a mysterious and intriguing dedication to one Cardinal of Sant'Angelo, whom Donato called his "sole benefactor."

> To the most Illustrious and Reverend Monsignor, Cardinal of Sant'Angelo, my sole Lord and Benefactor. Baldassara Donato.
>
> Most Illustrious and Reverend Monsignor, my most honorable patron: Two symbols used to be specially assigned by the ancients to the sun, the bow and the lyre—the bow because with the arrows of its rays it [both] strikes and gives life to everything; the lyre because, placed in the midst of all the other planets, almost as the norm and temperament of all the others, it guides the softest and the grandest celestial harmony. But we, owing to our disproportioned senses, fail to hear it. It is fitting that the moderns should give the same to Your Most Illustrious and Reverend Lordship, sun and ornament of this age—you who with the rays of your many virtues and with your splendor and that of your ancestors manifest and kindle everything and who with your lyre of internal reasoning and prudence so well harmonize the affects of your soul in the midst of the other princes that both in great fortunes past and in the glory of the present one could barely discern which was greater in you, grandeur or charm, happiness or humanity, forcefulness or mildness. Beyond this it will suit you when the time comes to you, taking the place of your most blessed forefathers, to temper amongst all the other princes the harmony of the Christian Republic. Owing to this renown, then, the dedications of works in all fields are due to the name of your Most Illustrious and Reverend Lordship. But those of music are most due to you. My having therefore collected some of my efforts in this science I consecrate them to you, as to their true and appropriate recipient, considering that the virtue of your sacred name must make the harmony of my labors sweeter and more welcome to whomever will hear them. Kissing your sacred hands with this, I pray for you a happiness equal to your merit.[74]

---

73. A complete ed. may be found in Sixteenth-Century Madrigal, vol. 10, ed. Martha Feldman (New York, 1991).

74. ALL'ILLUSTRISSIMO ET REVERENDISSIMO Monsignor, Il Cardinale di Santo Angelo, Signor & Benefattore unico. Baldassara Donato.

> Illustrissimo & Reverendissimo Monsignore, Patrone Colendissimo. Due insegne si solevano da gli antichi spetialmente dar al sole l'arco et la cetra: L'arco perche con le saette de suo raggi ferisce & vivifica ogni cosa. La cetra perche posto in mezzo di tutti gli altri pianeti quasi norma et temperamento de gli altri guida la celeste armonia soavissima et grandissima. Ma da noi per la sproportion del nostro senso non udita: L'istesso conviene che moderni dieno a Vostro Illustrissima et Reverendissima .S. Sole & ornamento di questa età, Il quale co raggi di tante virtu vostre, & dello splendore Avito & proprio illustrate, & infiammate ogni cosa, & con la cetra dell'interna ragione & prudenza accordate in mezzo a gli altri Principi cosi bene gli affetti del vostro animo, che nella maggior fortuna passata et nella grande d'hora mal s'e possuto scorgere qual sia stata maggiore la grandezza, o la piacevolezza, la felicita, o l'humanita, l'amplitudine o la mansuetudine, Oltre che a voi converrà, quando per l'eta vi sarà concesso occupando il luogo del vostro Santissimo Avo temperare fra tutti gli altri Principi l'armonia della Christiana Republica: Per questo nome dunque le dedicationi de componimenti in ogni scientia sono dovute al nome di Vostra Illustrissima & Reverendissima .S. Ma quelle della Musica le sono dovutissime: Havendo io per tanto raccolte alcune mie fatiche in questa scienza le consacro a lei come ad obietto loro proprio et adequato: Considerando che la virtu del vostro sacro nome dovra render piu dolce & piu aggradevole l'armonia di queste mie fatiche a chiunque le udira, & basciandole con questo le sacre mano le prego felicita eguale al suo merito.

Though signed by the composer, Donato probably could not have crafted such an extended Neoplatonic conceit without the aid of an acquaintance or house editor versed in letters (if indeed he authored it at all). The language seems designed to complement august aspects of the book itself, with its full panoply of five-, six-, and seven-voice works (twenty-six in all), its sumptuous stylistic and topical variety, and its several ceremonious dedicatory works.

Given this, it is fitting to realize that the Cardinal of Sant'Angelo is identical to Ranuccio Farnese (1530–1565), member of the powerful Farnese family who ruled Parma from 1545. Remembered today especially for the famous portrait of him painted by Titian in 1542 (Plate 20), Ranuccio was the son of Parma's first duke Pierluigi Farnese, grandson of Alessandro Farnese (better known as Pope Paul III) and a cardinal from the age of fifteen.[75] Corroboration of his identity comes in the print's inaugural piece, which gives his Christian name in the variant Rinuccio, together with various allusions to the family's history and the fleur-de-lis on its coat of arms.[76]

Mentre quest'alme et honorate rive	While you make these life-giving
Co' tuoi purpurei gigli	And honored shores bloom
Fai fiorir d'ogn'intorno,	All about with your purple lilies,
Rinuccio, de le cose al mondo Dive,	Rinuccio, divine among the things of the world,
Odo il tuo Tebro e 'l sacro Vaticano,	I hear your Tiber and your sacred Vatican 5
Quasi un de suoi più chiari et degni figli,	Sighing for you, almost as one of their
Sospirarti lontano,	Worthiest and most eminent sons, far away,
Pur attendendo il dì del tuo ritorno,	And still awaiting the day of your return,
Sperando l'un le sponde	Hoping to see fertile again,
L'altro le sue pendici	The one its banks, the other its slopes, 10
D'Olive et palme riveder feconde,	With olives and palms,
Quai le fer già le tue sante radici,	As your holy roots already make them,
Et de tuoi gigli tutta Italia et Roma	And all of Italy and Rome [hoping]
Ornarsi anchor la gloriosa chioma.	To crown themselves gloriously with your lilies.[77]

Nothing is known of Ranuccio's relationship to Donato and the *Primo libro a 5 & a 6* apart from this book. Perhaps Donato came to the attention of the Farnese family through Willaert, whose setting of the sonnet *Mentre al bel lett'ove dormia Phetonte,*

75. See the genealogy in Emilio Nasalli Rocca, *I Farnese* (Varese, 1969), Table II and p. 108, which explains that Ranuccio came to be called "Sant'Angelo" for the name of his church. See also the Table in Edoardo del Vecchio, *I Farnese,* Istituto di Studi Romani (Città di Castello, 1972), and on Ranuccio, pp. 107ff. On Titian's portrait and its subject see Harold E. Wethey, *The Paintings of Titian: Complete Edition,* 2 vols. (New York, 1971), vol. 2, *The Portraits,* pp. 98–99, and Plates 109 and 111–14, including details. See also Georg Gronau, "Zwei Tizianische Bildnisse der Berliner Galerie: I, Das Bildnis des Ranuccio Farnese; II, Das Bildnis der Tochter des Roberto Strozzi," *Jahrbuch der königlich preuszischen Kunstsammlungen* 27 (1906): 3–12.

76. For a description of the Farnese arms see G. B. di Crollalanza, *Dizionario storico-blasonico delle famiglie nobili e notabili italiane estinte e fiorente,* 3 vols. (Pisa, 1886–90; repr. Bologna, 1965), 1:392, and for the arms showing the lilies described in the poem, Lina Balestrieri, *Feste e spettacoli alla corte di Farnese,* Quaderni parmigiani, no. 6 (Parma, 1981), front matter.

77. My translations of this poem and the dedication were much aided by advice from Linda Armao.

20. Titian, *Portrait of Ranuccio Farnese,* 1542. Photo courtesy of the Gemäldegalerie, Staatliche Museen Preussischer Kulturbesitz, Berlin.

published in 1548, appears to celebrate the heroics of Ranuccio's father, Pierluigi, on the occasion of the Farnese's takeover of Parma and Pierluigi's assumption of Parma's dukedom in September and October 1545.[78] Other texts in Donato's book celebrating famous families may form part of a complex of tributes to the Farnese (though none of these has the positive markers of *Mentre quest'alme*). The ottava rima *Pianta beata,*

---

78. The setting was published in Rore's *Terzo libro a 5* (RISM 1548⁹). The identification of the poem's probable occasion and dedicatee was made by Helga Meier in her edition of Willaert, *Opera omnia,* vol. 14, *Madrigali e Canzoni Villanesche,* AIM (Neuhausen-Stuttgart, 1977), p. x.

che già fosti degna (no. 18), in particular, exalts the "Fronde de vincitor felice insegna / A cui fan sempre i più bei spirti honore" (branch of the victor, happy insignia, to which the most beautiful spirits always pay homage). Later it calls up the "Rami sacri felici almi'et beati" (sacred branches, happy, life-giving, and blessed) as part of a final two-verse acclamation that occupies nearly half the length of Donato's setting. The final dialogue, *"Ahi miserelle, ahi sventurate noi,"* celebrating Pluto, Proserpina, and Hymen, probably evolved as an *intermedio* that formed part of a staged wedding celebration. Only Italy's wealthiest families, like the Farnese, typically produced such celebrations, but no positive clues of a connection to them exist.[79]

Following roughly the form of the *Musica nova,* Donato's *Primo libro a 5 & a 6* contains seventeen five-voice madrigals, six six-voice madrigals, and three seven-voice dialogues, in no traditional modal order (see Table 13). Surely the desire to position the dedicatory madrigal at the book's opening and order its madrigals by numbers of voices superseded modal concerns. Nevertheless, like nearly all Gardane's prints, Donato's book groups works with like pitch systems—hence nos. 4–6 are all in cantus durus on E, nos. 10–13 all share the type ♭-c1-GG, and so forth.[80]

The *Primo libro a 5 & a 6* stresses sonnets, but not to the exclusion of other poems. Half of the book's twenty-six numbers are sonnet settings, only ten of them complete. All but one of the complete settings divide after the octave; the single exception, set continuously, is no. 10, on a light May Day text. Otherwise only the dialogues dispense with this two-part arrangement, two of them resetting texts from the *Musica nova* (nos. 24 and 25). The remaining thirteen works divide between cinquecento poetic madrigals (nos. 1, 11, 15, 19, and 26), ottave rime (nos. 4, 12, 13, 14, and 18), a canzone stanza by Petrarch (no. 3), and two ballata-madrigals (nos. 16 and 23). In addition to somewhat older poets like the Venetians Andrea Navagero and Pietro Bembo, the book makes notable use of a younger group of poets who were intimates of Domenico Venier's literary salon: Giovanni Battista Amalteo, Lodovico Dolce, and Fortunio Spira. Donato, as we saw in Chapter 4, may have gotten to know Venier when he set his three patriotic stanzas for a public festival in the city (the settings were published as the final three numbers in Donato's *Napolitane* of 1550), and the sonnet setting no. 9 almost surely celebrated one of Venier's noble academists, Lorenzo Contarini (see n. 79).

Donato's first book shows a facility for counterpoint and melody as endearing as Perissone's and just as fit to win admirers and freelance work from wealthy patrons.

---

79. On *Ahi miserelle* see Einstein, *The Italian Madrigal* 1:452–53.
   One other setting, no. 9, *Angelico intelletto hor che nel seno,* on a sonnet lamenting the death of one "Contareno," eulogizes another nobleman, a member of the prominent Venetian family also called Contarini. The sonnet's emphasis on the deceased's intellect leads me to think that it referred to Lorenzo Contarini, the philosopher, Latin scholar, and member of Venier's circle, included as interlocutor in Parabosco's *I diporti,* who died on 8 November 1552; see A. Venturi, "Contarini, Lorenzo," in *Dizionario biografico degli italiani,* vol. 28 (Rome, 1983), pp. 231–33.
   80. On Gardane's practice of grouping works by some combination of system, ambitus, and/or final see Mary S. Lewis, "Antonio Gardane and His Publications of Sacred Music 1538–55" (Ph.D. diss, Brandeis University, 1979), pp. 184–91. For the argument that Gardane was arranging by tonal type and not mode see Powers, "Tonal Types and Modal Categories," esp. p. 461.

TABLE 13

Baldassare Donato, *Primo libro a 5 & a 6* (1553)

Incipit; Poetic Form; Poet and Poetic Source*	System	Cleffing	Final
1. Mentre quest'alme et honorate rive 14-line madr: AbcADBdCefEFGG Anon.	b	c1c3c4c4F4	**FF**
2. Stiamo'Amor a veder la gloria nostra	b	c1c3c4c4F4	C
ii. L'herbetta verde ei fior di color mille sonnet Petrarch, no. 192	b	c1c3c4c4F4	**FF**
3. Se 'l pensier che mi strugge canzone, stanza 1 Petrarch, no. 125	b	c1c3c4c4F4	**C**
4. Lasso, se tanto pianto e tant'ardore ottava rima Anon.	—	c3c4c4F3F5	**EE**
5. I vo piangendo i miei passati tempi	—	c4c4F3F4F5	A
ii. Sì che s'io viss'in guerra et in tempesta sonnet Petrarch, no. 365	—	c4c4F3F4F5	**EE**
6. O viva fiamma, O miei sospiri ardenti	—	c1c3c4c4F4	A

ii. O gloriosi allori, O verdi mirti
sonnet
Giovanni Andrea Gesualdo, in
    Rime diverse . . . Libro primo (Venice, 1545),
    p. 34
	—	c1c2c3c4F4	**E**

7. Quasi vaghe Sirene in mezz'a l'onde	b	g2c2c3c3F3	d
ii. O soavi leggiadre alte parole sonnet Giovanni Battista Amalteo, in *Libro terzo delle rime di diversi,* fol. 177′	b	g2c2c3c3F3	**a**
8. Da que' bei crin che tanto più sempr'amo sonnet, octave only Bembo, *Opere in volgare,* pp. 458–59	—	c1c3c4c4F4	**A**
9. Angelico intelletto, hor che nel seno	b	c1c3c4c4F4	C
ii. La cagion de le cose hor dei sapere sonnet Anon.	b	c1c3c4c4F4	**FF**
10. Il primo dì del bel fiorito Maggio sonnet Anon.	b	c1c3c4c4F4	**GG**
11. Sarra, vostra beltate è tanta e tale 12-line madr: AbbCCDEEffgG Anon.	b	c1c3c4c4F4	**GG**
12. Laura, le selve'et le campagne apriche ottava rima Anon.	b	c1c3c4c4F4	**GG**

TABLE 13   (continued)

Incipit; Poetic Form; Poet and Poetic Source*	System	Cleffing	Final
13. Altro non è languir ch'odiar se stesso ottava rima Lodovico Martelli, *Rime volgari,* fol. 107′	b	c1c3c4c4F4	**GG**
14. Qual sera mai sì miserabil pianto ottava rima Anon.	b	g2c2c3c3F3	**D**
15. Vivo mio ghiaccio et colorita neve 10-line madr: ABCCbaDdEE Anon.	b	g2c2c3c3F3	**G**
16. Da duo occhi lucenti 12-line ballata-madr: aBB CdEDcE eBB Lodovico Martelli, *Rime volgari,* fol. 17	—	g2c2c3c3F4	**G**
17. Cantai un tempo, et se fu dolce il canto sonnet, octave only Bembo, *Opere in volgare,* p. 476	—	c1c3c4c4F4	**GG**
18. Pianta beata, che già fosti degna ottava rima Anon.	—	c1c3c3c4c4F4	**D**
19. Fiamm'amorosa et bella 12-line madr: aBCACBBDdEDE Andrea Navagero, in *Rime diverse . . . Libro primo* (Venice, 1545), p. 101	b	c1c3c4c4F3F4	**GG**
20. Quel rossignuol che sì soave piagne sonnet, octave only Petrarch, no. 311	—	c1c2c3c4F4F5	**A**
21. Scalda, Signor, il mio gelato core ii. Tu sempre mi consola, Et quella voce sonnet Lodovico Dolce, in *Rime di diversi . . . Libro secondo,* fol. 179	b b	c1c3c3c4c4F4 c1c3c3c4c4F4	A **GG**
22. I vidi in terra angelici costumi ii. Amor, senno, valor, pietate e doglia sonnet Petrarch, no. 156	b b	c1c3c4c4F3F4 c1c3c4c4F3F4	A **FF**
23. Non è, lasso, martire 10-line ballata-madr: aABb cCDd aA Fortunio Spira, in *Rime diverse . . . Libro primo* (Venice, 1545), p. 200	—	c1c2c4c4c4F4	**EE**
24. "Liete e pensose, accompagnat'e sole" dialogue sonnet Petrarch, no. 222	—	c1c1c3c3c4c4F4	**GG**
25. "Che fai alma, che pensi havrem mai pace" dialogue sonnet Petrarch, no. 150	b	c1c1c3c3c4c4F4	**FF**
26. "Ahi miserelle, ahi sventurati noi" 14-line dialogue madr: AbCbD+C-efgFgEHH Anon.	—	c1c3c3c4c4c4F4	**D**

N.B. Finals are given in boldface, confinals in regular type.
*Table uses short-title references. For full citations see the Bibliography.

Only rarely, as in his fourth-mode setting of Petrarch's spiritual sonnet *I vo piangendo,* scored for low male voices, did Donato essay the same dark effects as Willaert. More often his work followed that of other disciples at San Marco in reconciling Willaert's rhetorical lessons with a lighter style, approximating Bembist ideals without clinging to such introverted declamation as Willaert's.

Indeed Donato did so while borrowing from Willaert in less concealed ways than Perissone. His setting of *I vidi in terra* employs the same tonal type as Willaert's, ♭-CI-FF, and scatters obvious citations and adaptations from Willaert's model throughout. Since Donato followed Willaert's music so closely, his resettings of *Musica nova* texts tend to exhibit more Willaertian irregularity than Perissone's—the sort of metrical, imitative, and motivic asymmetries seen in Chapter 7. Thus, where Perissone's *I vidi in terra* introduces each voice at the same temporal interval, Donato's employs the less predictable timing of vocal entries found in Willaert's setting (cf. Exx. 57 a–c). Both Willaert's and Donato's settings introduce motivic variations right from the outset, whereas Perissone was apt to deploy motives unchanged. Because of this, and because each uses the same tonal type, their melodies resemble one another more than they do Perissone's: compare, for example, the altus in Donato's version (mm. 1–2) with the cantus in Willaert's (mm. 3–4), or the first appearance of the bassus in both. Declamation is the only common ground among all three settings, and here again Donato's rhythmic similarities to Willaert are pervasive:[81] the dotted figure on "angelici" of v. 1 (bassus, m. 8); the highly distinctive syncopation and semiminim declamation on "udi sospirando" of v. 7 in mm. 42–44 (also notable in Perissone's setting); and the dotted figure on "Che farian gir i monti" of v. 8 that immediately follows (mm. 46–48), along with, in essence, all the declamation to the end of the *prima parte.* The rhythmic relationship of Donato's *prima parte* to Willaert's is too extensive to be coincidental.

But the most striking borrowing comes at the beginning of the *seconda parte,* where Donato adopted almost every facet of Willaert's composition (cf. Ex. 58a below with Ex. 58b)—the lengthy movement by fifths, the pacing and development of the declamatory rhythm, and even much of the voicing and many of the individual motives. The passage is little more than a rescoring of Willaert's original. Here Donato's imitative practice verges on the kind of submissive reverence contemporary Venetian literati exhorted for imitating Petrarch.[82] The same can be said of both his other resettings of *Musica nova* texts, the two dialogues *"Liete e pensose"* and *"Che fai alma,"* which (again) mimic Willaert in ways that are less camouflaged than Perissone's. For *"Che fai alma,"* in fact, Donato closely adapted the polyphony of Willaert's entire exposition.[83]

81. To follow a complete score, see my ed., pp. 214–21.

82. On this matter see Chap. 5 above and Thomas M. Greene, *The Light in Troy: Imitation and Discovery in Renaissance Poetry* (New Haven, 1982).

83. See H. Meier, "Zur Chronologie der *Musica Nova,*" p. 78. On the concision that typically marks Donato's adaptations see David Alan Nutter, "The Italian Polyphonic Dialogue of the Sixteenth Century," 2 vols. (Ph.D. diss., University of Nottingham, 1978), p. 107.

EX. 57A. Willaert, *I vidi in terra angelici costumi* (Petrarch, no. 156), mm. 1–6; *Musica nova* (Venice, 1559), no. 19.

EX. 57B. Perissone, *I' vid'in terra angelici costumi* (Petrarch, no. 156), mm. 1–7; *Segondo libro a 5* (Venice, 1550), p. 6.

EX. 57C.   Donato, *I vidi in terra angelici costumi* (Petrarch, no. 156), mm. 1–8; *Primo libro a 5 & a 6* (Venice, 1560), p. 28.

EX. 58A.   Willaert, *I vidi in terra angelici costumi* (Petrarch, no. 156), mm. 72–83; *Musica nova* (Venice, 1559), no. 19.

Donato, *I vidi in terra angelici costumi* (Petrarch, no. 156), mm. 60–68; *Primo libro a 5 & a 6* (Venice, 1560), p. 28.

These are not the sorts of furtive borrowings to thread the counterpoint with witty glosses, perceptible only to the canniest observers. They are servile acts of praise, readily identified by any listener well acquainted with the model. Given Donato's relation to Willaert as both close collaborator and subordinate, it comes as no surprise that his imitations took the form of public homage.

By their simultaneous gestures of overt tribute and self-display, imitations of this kind allow us privileged scrutiny of the public debts disciples paid their masters at the same time as they paradoxically illuminate disciples' styles in nonemulatory works. Donato's setting of Dolce's *Scalda, Signor, il mio gelato core* (no. 21) forms a case in point. As a spiritual sonnet, *Scalda, Signor* aligned itself with a pious Petrarchan rhetoric through direct supplications to God, calling for a somber diction as naturally as Petrarch's secular sonnets did. Donato set *Scalda, Signor* with the same proportions as *Musica nova* settings, yet asserted his own voice by fashioning a more melodious and metrical exemplar of the spiritual style. Such lyricism is even more surprising in Donato's other spiritual madrigal, on Petrarch's *I vo piangendo,* a text that he might have set more like *Scalda, Signor. I vo piangendo* lacked a model in either Willaert or Rore but had a direct antecedent in Parabosco's setting of its octave, published in 1546. Donato's madrigal shows no relation to Parabosco's, except that both use Phrygian mode and avoid chiavette (in fact Donato's dips into the lowest possible tessituras with the cleffing c4c4F3F4F5, as compared with Parabosco's c1c3c4c4F4; cf. Table 9, no. 14 with Table 13, no. 5). In other respects Donato's setting forms a virtual antitype to Parabosco's, collapsing the entire sonnet into a scant 89 breves as against the 104 Parabosco used for the octave.[84]

Once outside the imposing domain of Petrarchan sonnets and close cousins like *Scalda, Signor,* Donato's knack for pithy execution, distinctive motives, and melodic grace led him to author wonderfully fresh madrigals. In his settings of poetic madrigals, in particular, Donato's stylishness, lyricism, and wit went unsurpassed by his contemporaries. A good example of these melodic gifts is the anonymous *Sarra, vostra beltate è tanta e tale* (no. 11), an encomium to the Sarra apostrophized in the incipit, where Donato's cantus sparkles its way through the plagal octave d to dd, with semiminims lighting down by thirds (mm. 14–15), before reaching the final g (Ex. 59). Another madrigal, Lodovico Martelli's *Da duo occhi lucenti* (no. 16), unveils the opening conceit on the beloved's "two eyes" with a tongue-in-cheek musical icon: two lone voices in homorhythm. Still other settings—*Il primo dì del bel fiorito maggio* (no. 10) and the octave of Bembo's *Cantai un tempo, et se fu dolce il canto* (no. 17)—turn to breezy triple meters and sprightly melismas (note the rhapsodic example of the latter in Ex. 60).

With this playful melodic bent, Donato must have been a great hit in the salons of Venice. Yet not all his 1553 settings of lighter texts are so insouciant—most notably his setting of Spira's ballata-madrigal, *Non è, lasso, martire* (no. 23).

---

84. See Einstein's description, *The Italian Madrigal* 1:452.

EX. 59. Donato, *Sarra, vostra beltate è tante e tale*, cantus, mm. 5–18; *Primo libro a 5 & a 6* (Venice, 1560), p. 16.

EX. 60. Donato, *Cantai un tempo, e se fu dolce il canto* (Pietro Bembo), cantus, mm. 30–37; *Primo libro a 5 & a 6* (Venice, 1560), p. 22.

Non è, lasso, martire	It is not, alas, a martyrdom
Il convenir per voi, Donna, morire,	To agree for you, Lady, to die,
Se la cagion de la mia mort'è tale	If the cause of death is such
Che fa lieve ogni male;	That it lessens every suffering.
Ma quel che mi tormenta	But what torments me
È che del mio morir sete contenta,	Is that my death contents you,
E ch'al primo veder d'altro amadore	And that at the first sight of another admirer
Cangiaste 'l vostro core.	You changed your heart.
Non è, dunque, martire,	Is it not, then, a martyrdom
Il convenir per voi, Donna, morire?	To agree for you, Lady, to die?

(with line numbers 5 and 10 marked at right)

Already in 1545, when Spira's text was published in the first of the *Rime diverse* series, its form was a throwback to the old madrigal-with-refrain popular with poets like Lodovico Martelli and Dragonetto Bonifazio in the twenties and thirties. Like Bonifazio's *Amor mi fa morire* (see Chap. 7 nn. 18–19), Spira's poem elides the *ripresa*'s return by means of a slight rhetorical transformation. In keeping with the poetic device, the music that begins the madrigal returns to end it (mm. 54–72), neatly joined by means of an expressive cross relation, C-sharp/C. However old the setting was in 1553 (it could well have been newly written, or as old as eight or

Ex. 61.   Donato, *Mentre quest'alme et honorate rive*, mm. 1–4; *Primo libro a 5 & a 6*
(Venice, 1560), p. 1.

ten years), it resembles Verdelot's six-voice madrigals on similar texts[85]—not only their form but their calm, graceful rhythms. *Non è, lasso, martire* begins with a chansonesque dactyllic figure and disposes the opening verse with a minimum of fuss, avoiding any syncopation until the cadential figure occurs after eight bars. The metrical regularity of the opening endures throughout, with balanced, lucid expositions introducing each new line of text. Choirs of voices often deliver the text in consort, with even-paced counterpoint declaimed in semiminims (like that setting v. 4), adding a chansonesque metric feel. Apart from the cross relation noted earlier, these steady rhythms accompany a pervasive diatonicism.

Such tonal-rhythmic simplicity is shared by Donato's several celebratory settings, which were probably recent creations. The dedication piece *Mentre quest'alme* begins with a similar dactyllic figure but in a triadic form appropriate to the enunciatory rhetoric of celebration; and the same figure later opens out more spaciously in the invocation to the dedicatee "Rinuccio" (Exx. 61 and 62). Another occasional piece, *Pianta beata*, realizes this style of choral celebration more fully through its quick triadic exchanges and clear registral shifts. Like those of *Non è, lasso, martire*, the rhythmic motives of *Pianta beata* are simple and square and its soundscape diatonic as well. Yet as an ottava rima, *Pianta beata*'s formal-tonal organization is based on the distich principle. The conjunction of simple diatonicism, motivic simplicity, and ottava form is natural, since historically the form was aligned with declamatory song. Even though, as a six-voice setting, *Pianta beata* has a fair share of imitative

---

85. I refer to those published in the collection of 1541 and reprinted in 1546 [RISM 1546¹⁹]. See also Verdelot's *Madonna, qual certeça* on a ballata-madrigal by Bonifazio, in H. Colin Slim, ed., *A Gift of Madrigals and Motets*, 2 vols. (Chicago, 1972), pp. 379–81, with the text on p. 446.

EX. 62.   Donato, *Mentre quest'alme et honorate rive*, mm. 13–17; *Primo libro a 5 & a 6*
(Venice, 1560), p. 1.

counterpoint, each one of its couplets finishes with a strongly marked cadence
joined by at least five of the six voices.

Pianta beata is one of five ottave rime in the *Primo libro a 5 & a 6,* a higher number than found in any other print in the Venetian repertory. Ottave rime are more at
home in Perissone's *Primo libro a 4* (the only other print I have dealt with in these
chapters to include them, not counting Venier's stanzas in Donato's *Napolitane*),
since Perissone's four-voice book straddles the fence that separates song from
polyphony. By contrast, none of the ottave Donato set in the *Primo libro a 5 & a 6,*
save *Pianta beata,* looks formally or stylistically different from his madrigals: indeed
some seem to merge the rhythmic vivacity of the madrigals with the polyphonic
complexity of larger forms. *Laura, le selv'et le campagne apriche* (no. 12), a games-
manly series of wordplays on the Laura-*l'aura* homonym, is such an ottava setting,
gamboling in widely displaced points of imitation and ebullient declamation.

———————

Unlike any of his peers' collections, Donato's *Primo libro* was reprinted twice, in
1557 and in 1560. By that time the Willaertian madrigal was already on the wane, and
Donato himself published no new books until his first for four voices of 1568. In
later years Donato's prestige in the chapel continued to rise as he repeatedly found
success in the administrative ranks of San Marco. In addition to regular salary
increases, he was made maestro of a newly formed *cappella piccola* at St. Mark's in
1562,[86] and in 1590 finally became maestro di cappella—a position in which he died

———————

86. See Ongaro, "The Chapel of St. Mark's," pp. 153–56 and Document 259, on the formation of the
cappella piccola, and on Donato's raises in salary, passim.

in 1603, succeeded by the local musician Giovanni Croce. Donato thus takes his place in a neat line of succession from Willaert, Rore, and Zarlino to Monteverdi, who eventually replaced Croce's successor in 1612. His turn toward administration corresponds to the creative trajectory of the madrigal, which had already begun to move out of Venice shortly after Donato published his book. By the mid- to late 1550s exciting transformations of Willaert's style were no longer ventured by composers in Venice but by Rore in Ferrara and, later on, by his students Giaches de Wert and Luzzasco Luzzaschi in Ferrara and Mantua through the 1590s. It is in their works, as well as in those of Luca Marenzio and others, that the lineage of multi-voice madrigals from midcentury can be followed, culminating in Monteverdi's provocative madrigal collections from the turn of the century.

APPENDIX: SONNETS ON THE DEATH OF PERISSONE CAMBIO[87]

Del Sig. Domenico Veniero In morte di M. Perison Cambio Musico Eccell.

Ben perì suon, qual suona il nome stesso	The sound that sounds the same angelic and
Di cui piangemo, angelico, e divino	Divine name for whom we weep perished down there
Qua giuso il dì, che 'l tolse empio destino	The day that bitter fate took him away,
E perì tutto il nostro ben con esso.	And all our good perished with him. 4
Sol fu per gratia un tempo à noi concesso	Such a rare, choice, and uncommon spirit
Sì raro spirto, eletto, e pellegrino,	Was only granted us by grace for a time,
Ma troppo hebbe al principio il fin vicino	But the end was too close to the beginning
Del viver suo da morte invida oppresso.	Of his life, oppressed by envious death. 8
Fermò l'onde nel mar, ne l'aria i venti,	The sound of his sweet tones stopped
Arse il gel, mosse i monti, e 'l ciel turbato	The waves in the sea, the wind in the air,
Serenò 'l suon de' suoi soavi accenti.	Burned ice, moved mountains, and made serene
	the clouded sky. 11
Quando egual cambio in cambio à noi fia dato	When is an equal change given to us in exchange
Di sì gran Cambio? in van speran le genti,	For such a great Cambio? In vain do people hope
Che piu tal dono a lor conceda il Fato.	That fate will award them again such a gift. 14

Risposta di Mons. Fenarolo.

Sì mi sento ne l'alma il suono impresso	I so hear in my soul the sound made
Di lui, che verso il ciel prese il camino,	By him that has taken the path toward Heaven
Che mel par di veder sempre da presso,	That I seem to see him always close by,
E fermo il passo, e 'l dolce canto inchino.	And I hold my step and bend toward the sweet song. 4

87. From *Rime di Mons. Girolamo Fenaruolo* (Venice, 1574), fol. [38].

Poscia avveduto del mio inganno espresso
Allargo a gli occhi il pianto, e 'l viso chino,
E grido; ahi Cigno gloria di Permesso
Perche lasciarmi qui solo, e meschino?

In un punto però suon sì preghiato,
E 'n sua vece mandò tristi lamenti,
(Duro Cambio,) il mar d'Adria in ogni lato.

Però, se meco piangi, e ti lamenti,
Fai ciò, che chiede il nostro acerbo stato,
E la fera cagion de' miei tormenti.

Then realizing my express mistake
I widen my eyes to the tears and bow down my face;
And I cry, "Oh swan, glory of Permessus,
Why do you leave me here alone and wretched?"   8

In one moment the sound so esteemed perished,
And in its place the sea of Hadrian from every side
(In bitter exchange) sent sad laments.   11

But if you weep and lament with me,
You do what our bitter state
And the fierce cause of my torments asks.   14

Chapter 10 · EPILOGUE
"SOPRA LE STANZE DEL PETRARCA IN LAUDE DELLA MADONNA"
Rore's Vergine Cycle of 1548

In proposing ways to read large lyric forms from start to finish Venetian madrigalists took on one of the principal challenges to cinquecento polyphony. The new mood of lingering meditation that pervaded their madrigals in the 1540s was chiefly sustained by adapting the imitative strategies of sacred polyphony to the long lines and formal units of whole sonnets. But imitative polyphony, especially as embodied in sacred form, made a strange match for lyric verse. Lurking in those vast, cerebral settings was something that contradicted the deepest lyric principles of concision, melodiousness, and spontaneity.

To be sure, a composer like Rore could turn these expansive proportions to rich expressive account, even while working within the general confines of a Ciceronian poetics that placed decorum at its aesthetic core. From this centrist position, Rore's expressivity continually pressed against boundaries that guarded the way to more eccentric idioms. By the time of his *Quattro libro a 5* and *Secondo libro a 4,* both published in 1557, the rhetorical lessons of Venetian madrigals had been absorbed into tighter, more emotional settings—shorter in the main, more direct, and more extreme. Rore's ponderous early madrigals contrast sharply with the pithy style he sought in these later ones; but the extravagance of his late style nonetheless grew out of gestures he was cultivating from the start. In this last chapter I locate Rore's stylistic shift within his *Vergine* cycle, his setting of Petrarch's final canzone (no. 366), first printed in 1548–49.

Rore's *Vergine* sits at a crossroads between his early and late manners, representing the consummation of the old and beginning of the new. On the one hand, the cycle was his last major contribution to the repertory of Venetian-styled madrigals and to the ideals of Venetian Petrarchism, epitomizing propensities toward elegiac breadth and introspection that were the fountainhead of his Italian style. Its polyphony remains largely imitative and continuous, and its harmony coolly diatonic. At the same time, its wealth of animated declamation, flexible speech rhythms, sharply pitted homorhythmic duets and trios, overt madrigalisms, and sudden shifts of pace and texture betoken deep shifts beneath the surface that make it a pivotal work not only in Rore's development but in the whole development of lyric part singing in Italy. With these techniques Rore rearranged the basic textual components of vocal polyphonic architecture that had ensured Venetian madrigals their measured flow. His *Vergine* questions Venetian norms through a new form of poetic reading—a reading that enlarges the relatively minor rift between Rore's earliest efforts and the *Musica nova* into a major aesthetic gulf.

Let me begin by expanding slightly some bibliographical details of the *Vergine*'s publication that I first broached in Chapter 3.[1] Rore set the *Vergine* canzone as a cycle of eleven madrigals, one on each of the poem's stanzas. Around April 1548, when Rore had already been chapelmaster at Ferrara for at least two years, the first editions of his *Terzo libro a 5* by Scotto and Gardane printed stanzas one through six. In this fragmentary state the cycle was decidedly incomplete and quite likely had been issued without Rore's approval. Furthermore, neither the dedication of the Scotto edition to Gottardo Occagna nor of the Gardane edition to the poet-cleric Giovanni della Casa was made by Rore himself, and neither dedication claimed to have Rore's blessing. Not long after the initial editions appeared, and probably in 1549 as Mary Lewis has argued, both printing houses issued supplements to their respective editions appending the last five stanzas along with three additional madrigals.[2] This made the cycle complete, but Rore must still have wanted it revised: in 1552 the whole was reissued by Gardane in a complete edition containing substantial alterations to the original printed versions.[3] Gardane's revised edition can be taken as the final bibliographical bit of a compositional puzzle whose first pieces were set in place by mid-1547, by which time at least the first six stanzas must have existed in draft.[4]

I will bring my account of midcentury Venetian madrigals to a close by suggesting that musical aspects of the work's two sections—stanzas 1 to 6 and 7 to 11—reveal a work stratified in its compositional genesis as well as its dissemination. Each section seems to represent not merely different stages at which printers acquired portions of the cycle but different compositional layers, hence stages, in Rore's approach to setting text. Taken in sum, discrepancies between the two layers offer a remarkable lens through which to view Rore's refocusing of the Venetian

---

1. For more details see Chap. 3 nn. 31–35.

2. These supplements appear in fewer than a handful of copies of the *Terzo libro;* for a listing see Mary S. Lewis, "Rore's Setting of Petrarch's *Vergine bella:* A History of Its Composition and Early Transmission," *Journal of Musicology* 4 (1985–86): 366–67, Tables 1 and 2. It was only the altus part book of Gardane's supplement that actually carried the dedication to della Casa.

3. This is the version reflected in the edition of Bernhard Meier and the one from which I will cite. No substantive revisions from the earlier editions appear in the examples shown in this chapter. For the complete cycle see Cipriani Rore, *Opera Omnia,* ed. Bernhard Meier, Corpus mensurabilis musicae, no. 14, AIM, vol. 3 ([Rome], 1961), pp. 1–33.

4. Cf. Chap. 8 above, n. 1.

idiom, without contradicting evidence that Rore intended a cyclic conception at the macrolevel. There can be no doubt that the cycle's final form displays signs of unification by consistently using five voices, a single cleffing arrangement (c1-c3-c4-c4-F4), alla breve time signatures, and even the same signature and final for the first and last stanzas.[5]

More than all this, Rore unified the cycle by invariably intensifying the invocations to the Virgin that occur twice each strophe at vv. 1 and 9 while also shaping the equally regular rhythmic articulations between *piedi* and *sirima* that come between vv. 6 and 7. In so doing, Rore recognized the dual articulative scheme basic to Petrarch's stanzaic construction, as seen in stanza one.

A	Vergine bella, che si sol vestita,	Lovely Virgin who, clothed with the sun and	
B	Coronata di stelle, al sommo Sole	Crowned with stars, so pleased	
C	Piacesti sì che 'n te sua luce ascose:	The highest Sun that He hid his light in you:	
B	Amor mi spinge a dir di te parole,	Love drives me to say words about you,	
A	Ma non so 'ncominciar senza tua aita	But I know not how to start without your aid	
C	Et di colui ch'amando in te si pose.	And that of Him who loving placed Himself in you.	6
C	Invoco lei che ben sempre rispose	I invoke her who has always answered	
d	Chi la chiamò con fede,	Whoever called on her with faith.	
d	Vergine, s'a mercede	Virgin, if extreme misery	
C	Miseria estrema de l'umane cose	Of human things ever turned you	10
E	Giamai ti volse, al mio prego t'inchina,	To mercy, bend to my prayer,	
f	Soccorri a la mia guerra	Give succor to my war,	
(f) E	Ben ch'i' sia terra et tu del Ciel regina.	Though I am earth and you are queen of Heaven.	13

Indeed, the rhythmic-rhetorical counterpoint is even more complex than this. The shared rhymes C-C, which smooth the auditory transition between *piedi* and *sirima*, have a parallel in the rhythmic kinship of vv. 8 and 9 (d-d), rhymed *settenari* that straddle the second invocation. (The so-called *unità*—the rhyme that links the *piedi* and the *sirima*—is standard to canzoni, but the rhyme scheme of the *sirima* itself is idiosyncratic among those of Petrarch. More typical would be CDEEDFF or some variant thereof.) As a constant accompaniment to the invocatory structure, the rhymed pair elides v. 9, giving the invocation a *ripresa*-like character almost reminiscent of a ballata—an effect made strongest when the *sirime* do not coincide with a significant syntactic pause, as in stanzas 2 and 3.

A quick sampling of some of Rore's invocation settings will show what diversity he brought to them, especially in the way of rhetorical articulations. What matters here is not just the immediate counterpoint applied to any one fragment of text but

5. Meier has proposed a modal design consisting of five pairs, but the reasoning to me seems contrived and unsupported by the musico-rhetorical design. See *The Modes of Classical Vocal Polyphony Described according to the Sources,* trans. Ellen S. Beebe, rev. ed. (New York, 1988), pp. 392–94, and Rore, *Opera omnia* 3:i–ii.

E X . 6 3 . Rore, *Vergine bella, che di sol vestita* (Petrarch, no. 366, stanza 1), mm. 41–51; *Terzo libro a 5* (Venice, 1552), p. 1.

the whole musico-rhetorical context in which each invocation lies. In the passage excerpted in Ex. 63 from stanza 1, the second invocation of v. 9, "Vergine, s'a mercede," gains its presence in relation to the rhymed mate that precedes it (always a source of rhythmic elision), "Chi la chiamò con fede" (v. 8). In Rore's presentation v. 8 is all motion and clarity—the ubiquitous octave leaps, recurrent moves toward cadence, and consistently metric patterning of the declamation. By contrast, the "Vergine" of v. 9 is invoked in a series of plain calls fixed within a static space. Their entrances coincide with the end of the brief circle-of-fifths progression, A-D-G-C, that begins with the cadence of v. 8 (mm. 46–47) and closes in the pile-up of "Vergine" cries at m. 48. Rather than drawing the whole of v. 9's plea into the continuing circular motion, Rore truncates the circle, using its major harmonies to

Ex. 64. Rore, *Vergine santa, d'ogni gratia piena* (Petrarch, no. 366, stanza 4), cantus, mm. 1–5; *Terzo libro a 5* (Venice, 1552), p. 4.

Ex. 65. Rore, *Vergine santa, d'ogni gratia piena* (Petrarch, no. 366, stanza 4), mm. 45–48; *Terzo libro a 5* (Venice, 1552), p. 4.

adumbrate and irradiate the Virgin's name. Thus in the cadential m. 47 the invocation is highlighted even as it emerges from the shadowed inner voices whose cadence it shares. In all of this, Rore fuses the demands of a viscous Willaertian polyphony with a newer urge to articulate the separate parts.

Stanza one represents the Virgin in one of her conventional guises as the embodiment of noble simplicity. As set in stanza four, where a lovely "Vergine santa" floats through a minor sixth in the cantus to open the stanza, delicate and untethered in its Phrygian otherworldliness, the invocation calls up more ethereal images (Ex. 64). Here the polyphony too is elusively vague, with uneven entries and whimsical curves. But at v. 9 Rore made the second invocation, "Vergine gloriosa," into a choral acclamation that counterbalances the first (Ex. 65). In the brief space of a semibreve each of the voices is crowded into a thick homophony, with the echoing *o*'s of "gloriosa" resounding in communal exaltation against the cantus's top-of-the-register dd.

Junctures like these are Rore's rhetorical bread and butter. He handled them in sharper, more striking ways beginning at the sixth stanza (and they were to become far more dramatic still in stanza seven). A passage that occurs at the beginning of the *sirima,* is especially revealing since its invocation takes place—most unusually, and problematically, for a musical setting—within a continuous grammatical process.

Ma pur in te l'anima mia si fida,	But still my soul relies on you—
Peccatrice, io no 'l nego,	A sinful one, I do not deny,
Vergine, ma ti prego	Virgin—but I beg you
Ch'el tuo nemico del mio mal non rida.	That your enemy not laugh at my harm. 10

Rore's challenge was to project both the invocation and the continuities of rhetorical detail in which it is embedded. To meet it his setting extracts the full measure of rhetorical contrast from the passage with no fewer than four distinct declamatory styles of polyphony (Ex. 66). It may be useful to review them in turn. First, both the end of the *piedi* and the end of v. 7 are tied off with cadences that enclose the syncopated cross rhythms adopted for the conditional thought at the beginning of the *sirima*. Two different vocal groupings—cantus, altus, and tenor imitating quintus and bassus—trade a buoyant melody between them as expressive foil for the quasi-parenthetical "Peccatrice, io no 'l nego, / Vergine" that follows. With these words the madrigal opens into a second declamatory style, a series of near-homorhythmic blocks that carry the text along in speech rhythms—an upper-voice trio on "Peccatrice" dovetailing the lower-voice duet "io no 'l nego, Vergine," with *cadenze semplici* serving as caesurae at mm. 41 and 43. The invocation thus keeps its proper grammatical place, but the full pause that punctuates it supplies retrospectively the sort of structural definition that Rore's rhetorical conception requires. A fuller complement of low voices extends equally speechlike rhythms to the prayer "ma ti prego,"[6] and as it echoes in the lone cantus, a third kind of declamation resonates beneath. This is the sort of spare recitation in overlapping counterpoint common to Willaert's works—and increasingly rare in Rore's. Why "tuo nemico" (your enemy) should elicit such semantic neutrality can only be answered by the need to clear expressive space for the avant-garde flourishes Rore next fashioned for "rida." They count as the fourth distinct textural-declamatory entity to appear in the few bars that compress vv. 7–10. A frenetic kind of mid-cinquecento *ars subtilior,* these flourishes reduce the rhythmic pulse from the half-note value (minim) to the quarter-note (semiminim), bizarrely and radically dividing the semiminims from the moment the quintus executes a straight suspension cadence in m. 48.

The excerpt shown in Ex. 66 raises several issues that will be central to my consideration of stanza seven. The passage is the first in the cycle in which various voices omit to present the entire poem, as Willaert's madrigals had invariably done. Rore's willingness not to make each part bear the full text marks a critical shift in his thinking about how words and music were to be consolidated. Its implications for the singers' encounter with the poem are profound. And it carries far-reaching

6. Such speech rhythms reappear in stanza seven (as noted below) and stanza ten, mm. 26–33.

E x . 6 6 .   Rore, *Vergine chiara e stabil'in eterno* (Petrarch, no. 366, stanza 6), mm. 35–53; *Terzo libro a 5* (Venice, 1552), p. 6.

(continued)

ramifications for texture, ones that are more familiar from the late madrigals of Marenzio, Wert, and Monteverdi.

Once the lyric text was scattered through several parts whose aggregate is needed to enable an integral reading, the linear and individual representation of the poetry by separate voices was sacrificed in favor of the composite, corporate one of the "score." Rather than directing the poetic experience inward toward the sense and intellect of each singer and the communal experience each of them shares, this new approach implies an audience of listeners *outside,* who are necessary now to construct the poem in its totality. The new approach thus implies *projection* outward too, with an attendant shift in the statuses of singers (now extroverted performers) and auditors (now passive appreciators). Potentially, at least, the two were more sharply separated than ever before, with professional church singers and female vocalists made indispensable in the parlor room and the relations to them of amateurs dramatically altered.[7]

A crucial corollary of these shifts and ruptures is that if madrigals were now to be sung for auditors, real or implied, they needed to be diverting to hear. A reading projected out of a performative frame, as opposed to a silent or communal one, wants a showier veneer, and those performing it are in turn the showmen and -women rather than mutual participants in an inner experience. This situation ushers in another change hinted at in the passage I quoted from stanza six—a more virtuosic persona. The florid writing on "rida" is harder to sing, harder to count, and harder to coordinate than most anything in earlier madrigals. Its closest kin are

---

7. James Haar makes a related point about the new staginess of late-sixteenth-century madrigals at the conclusion of his *Essays on Italian Poetry and Music in the Renaissance, 1350–1600* (Berkeley and Los Angeles, 1986), esp. p. 147.

some of the madrigals in the black-note anthologies published by Gardane, to which Rore's first book is obliquely related.[8] With poetic coherence dependent on a dynamic yet well-coordinated performing body, fast shifts of tempo, texture, and vocal style become part of the rhetorical hardware. The whole surface turns more mercurial, more temperamental: Rore's *Vergine,* though usually serene, at times seems to foreshadow the quixotic stylization of late-sixteenth-century Ferrarese madrigals.

All of these factors come together in Rore's rendering of stanza seven. The single group of words omitted in the texting of stanza six is a mere foretaste of more rampant textual omissions here. In all, four verses receive partial texting, as shown in italics below: v. 1 is given in a homophonic exordium, but only by cantus, altus, and quintus; v. 5 is omitted by the altus; the first part of v. 7 by the cantus and tenor; and v. 12 by the quintus and bassus. (As discussed below, v. 11 also omits its latter part from the repetition made by cantus and altus.) Consequently, the whole poem is delivered with more than usual dispatch.

Vergine, quante lagrim'ho già sparte,	Virgin, how many tears have I already scattered,	
Quante lusinghe e quanti pregh'indarno,	How many pleadings and how many prayers in vain,	
Pur per mia pena e per mio grave danno!	Only to my pain and my heavy loss!	
Da poi ch'io nacqu'in su la riva d'Arno,	Since I was born on the bank of the Arno,	
Cercand'hor quest'et hor quell'altra parte,	Searching in this, now that other direction,	
Non è stata mia vit'altro ch'affanno.	My life has been nothing but troubles.	6
Mortal bellezza, atti e parole m'hanno	Mortal beauty, acts, and words have	
Tutt'ingombrata l'alma.	Burdened all my soul.	
Vergine sacr'et alma,	Holy and life-giving Virgin,	
Non tardar, ch'io son fors'all'ultim'anno;	Do not delay, for I am perhaps in my last year;	10
I dì miei più correnti che saetta,	My days, more swift than an arrow	
Fra miserie e peccati,	Amid wretchedness and sin,	
Son se n'andati e sol morte n'aspetta.	Have gone away and only Death awaits me.	13

Rore's setting of stanza seven evinces an extraordinary turn in his compositional thinking. His freer disposition of text is linked to a more outspoken rhetoric and a new polyphonic architecture that this rhetoric commanded. The rhythmic and textural diversity and strenuous changes of declamatory tempo with which Rore handled the passage I focused on from stanza six now pervade the entire setting (see Ex. 67). The stanza moves regularly into patter declamation ("in su la riva d'Arno," "atti e parole," "più correnti che saetta," "Son se n'andati"—mm. 36–38, 51–54, 57–58), much of it arrayed in duets or trios with an out-and-out homorhythm of the sort Willaert avoided almost completely in the *Musica nova*. In place of Willaertian

8. For a mod. ed. of them see Don Harrán, ed., *The Anthologies of Black-Note Madrigals,* Corpus mensurabilis musicae, no. 73, AIM, 5 vols. (Neuhausen-Stuttgart, 1978), and on Rore's black-note madrigals idem, "Rore and the *Madrigale Cromatico,*" *Music Review* 34 (1973): 66–81.

EX. 67.   Rore, *Vergine, quante lagrim'ho già sparte* (Petrarch, no. 366, stanza 7), incl.; *Terzo libro a 5* (Venice, 1552), p. 7.

(continued)

EX. 67 *(continued)*

Ex. 67 (continued)

(continued)

expansion this technique substitutes brevity and concision. (Not by coincidence, stanza seven lasts only 65 breves, five fewer than the next shortest stanza).[9]

The combined effect of these novelties is most pronounced in Rore's setting of the rhetorical point of vv. 11–13 (mm. 49 to the end), a proto-Monteverdian passage without precedent in his earlier canon and one to which we will shortly turn. Up to that point his articulative techniques are in part, at least, still conventional. The first nine to ten verses make a number of traditional suspension cadences, despite some patter rhythms and homophonic textures: a perfect cadence at m. 12 ending v. 2 (c/C, altus and quintus), another at m. 20 ending v. 3 (c/C, altus and quintus), an evaded cadence at m. 34 ending the *piedi* of v. 6 (aa/F, cantus and tenor), a perfect

9. Further, the average length of stanzas seven, eight, nine, and ten is six breves less than that of the first six—just over 71 breves as opposed to just over 77.

cadence at m. 36 setting off the "Mortal bellezza" of v. 7 (f/F, altus and bassus), and perfect cadences at mm. 41 and 44 preceding and closing the invocation of v. 9 (b-flat/B-flat, tenor and bassus; f/f, cantus and altus). In mm. 13–16 Rore also made expressive use of two unusual suspension cadences on "pena"—close to what Zarlino would later call *cadenze stravaganti*. Their resolutions in parallel fifths (between cantus and tenor, mm. 13–14, then quintus and bassus, mm. 15–16) are indeed irregular, yet their contrapuntal techniques remain canonical.

Not all the contrapuntal articulation in the first nine verses is even as straightforward as these examples. With text now omissible from various voices, textures can easily be reduced to two parts or otherwise dissolved for expressive ends. Something approaching what Anthony Newcomb has dubbed the "evaporated cadence" marks off v. 5 (mm. 28–29):[10] the quintus drops to cadence followed a minim later by a suspension-staggered cantus, while the altus that would normally be part of this upper-voice group is denied the verse altogether. Nonetheless the syntactic principles still in force here do not admit a full caesura between vv. 5 and 6. Thus the altus returns with v. 6 at the start of m. 29, overlapping the seam just as the surrounding voices come to rest.

More often than not, however—and this crucial point holds throughout the cycle—suspension cadences, when they do occur, are far more lucid than the ones in the *Musica nova*. Rore's proclivity toward strong articulation is an enabling factor in the new musical rhetoric that emerges in these later *Vergine* stanzas. Many of the cadences are perfect, often with the same text ending in both voices, and a good number involve three, four, or all five voices.[11] Even in passages of patter-style duets and trios, Rore fashioned legitimate contrapuntal cadences in a way that brings the chattering homorhythm simultaneously into harmonic and rhetorical focus. The undiminished articulations to aa/a at m. 37 and a/A at m. 38 on "atti e parole," for example, meet quite unproblematically Zarlino's guidelines for "simple" cadences.

By comparison, the cadential constructs of traditional counterpoint fall away almost entirely after the invocation of v. 9, replaced by new modes of articulation—speech rhythms, fast-shifting choral groups, and flashes of textual-motivic fragments—much of it moving by parallel thirds and six-three chords. The setting opens onto this new terrain with two sharply drawn motivic gestures, the pithy head motive on the nominative "I dì miei" offset by a run of semiminims for the comparative "più correnti che saetta." From this lopsided opposition (three syllables vs. eight) Rore drew forth contrasting sounds and rhythms that help distill the semantic essence of each, working them, in the manner of fugal subject and countersubject, into a dynamic multiple counterpoint. The head motives, stolidly equalized in conjunct minim ascents (e.g., cantus: c-d-e, rest, f-g-aa, mm. 49–50), are neutralized metrically by their open-ended linearity and avoidance of downbeat.

---

10. See *The Madrigal at Ferrara, 1579–1597*, 2 vols. (Princeton, 1980), 1:120 n. 16.
11. Cf. the discussion of *Per mezz'i boschi*, Chap. 8 above, n. 20 and Table 7.

This equalization increases the sonorous parity between vowels of the first phrase ("i," "i," and "iei") well beyond the level of spoken prosody. The rushing tail motive, usually anchored to consecutive downbeats equal in status on an implied metric grid (e.g., mm. 51–52), brings out only vowels regarded as *piacevole* by contemporaneous literati—the two "e" sounds on "correnti" and "saetta." From mm. 49–52 the cantus traces an arc from c to cc and back, with two statements of the head motive, one of the tail. Motivically, the two motives stand in a bipolar relationship: with the tail inverting the melodic direction and doubling the declamatory speed, they form antitheses—of up vs. down, ametric to metric, "i"/"iei" to "e," and slow vs. fast.

The larger goal of this motivic polarization is a flexible multiple counterpoint that embodies text as a virtual physical presence. No sooner is the consequent broached in m. 51 than the head motive enters beneath it in the role of bass line (mm. 51–52). The two form a pseudo-villanella texture as the upper voices turn quickly into parallel thirds ("che saetta") against the slower bass line. This is the same sort of villanella-like texture that proliferates in the pastoral madrigals of Andrea Gabrieli and Luca Marenzio and the later assimilations of their styles by Wert, Monteverdi, and others.[12]

In subsequent measures these same motives continue searching out new and varied scorings, transposing the consequent back to the lower register and arraying the parallel thirds anew. Rore's textual omissions allow him some delightfully unforeseen turns. As the cantus-altus duo falls unexpectedly mute after m. 53, the way is cleared for their languorous trio with the tenor of mm. 55–57—a two-breve interlude on the miseries and sins of v. 12. This passage transforms the earlier parallel-third motion by expanding it into a doleful plaint of fauxbourdon.[13] At the next rescoring it is bassus and quintus, silent since v. 11, who come (for the first time) to the fore. Cadencing as part of a C-major triad with "Son se n'andati" (m. 58),[14] they restore the previous contrapuntal climate—root-position harmony along with imitative duets, chipper canzonetta homorhythms, and parallel thirds.

One event thus vanishes as quickly as the next. The final poetic turn to the poet's anticipation of death, "e sol morte n'aspetta," brings a last shift of texture, pace, and tonality as evanescent as any. It flips the tonal orbit suddenly backward to the flat side and introduces an unsettling string of intervals spanning minor sevenths (quin-

12. According to Gary Tomlinson, Monteverdi borrowed the device from Marenzio's *Non vidi mai dopo notturno pioggia* (see Marenzio, *Madrigali a quattro voci* of 1585), to use in his *Non si levava ancor l'alba novella,* printed in Monteverdi's *Secondo libro a 5* of 1590; see *Monteverdi and the End of the Renaissance* (Berkeley and Los Angeles, 1987), pp. 42–44.

13. The technique was picked up by Wert. For an early instance of it see Wert's setting of Petrarch's *Voi ch'ascoltate in rime sparse 'l suono,* mm. 24–29, from his *Madrigali del fiore, libro secondo* (Venice, 1561); mod. ed. in *Collected Works,* ed. Carol MacClintock with Melvin Bernstein, Corpus mensurabilis musicae, no. 24, AIM ([Rome], 1962) 2:5. Verdelot sometimes wrote similar counterpoint, but melismatically.

14. The cadence to e in the cantus of m. 57 is strange in the context of the apparent mode 6—a *clausula peregrina,* as Meier calls it (*The Modes,* p. 252). But must we view it in such modal terms? The effect is that of a half-cadence, an actual dominant in this case. One senses a moving away from modal principles in the setting of vv. 11–13.

tus, bassus, cantus) and ninths (cantus, mm. 61–65) in a move of unprecedented dramatic force before dissipating in the ethereal cadences of the final measures.

———————

These transformations of Venetian style raise profound questions about how and why Rore now reads text so differently from the way he had before. His writing here rejects the staid introspection, balance, and temperance that *Musica nova*–styled madrigals made all-important. In their place it proposes something almost gleefully hedonistic. The flood of motives is so thick and fast that few affective-semantic entities stay in place long enough to sink in. The vivid contrasts that unfold so rapidly in parts of the *Vergine* setting leave the auditor no chance — indeed no *time* — to enter a meditative state. Radically disjunct, they are often abandoned before the listener can ever begin to legitimize them.

Rore's now extreme iconic interpretations are inevitably fragmenting even in semantic terms. They destabilize lyrics by focusing on the single word and on isolated word groups. The startling verbal disembodiments that result are not just grammatical, hence formal, ones. In Rore's rendition, phrases like "più correnti che saetta" and "son se n'andati" could have been found in the most secular contexts, depicting the wiles of Cupid or the woes of a forsaken lover, rather than in a confessional prayer on life's sins and a presage of death.[15] Even the last and most explicit iteration of this confession, "e sol Morte n'aspetta," undercuts the anticipation of death to which Petrarch's words point by winding them voice to voice in a sumptuous stream of melismas.

Here Rore flirts with unabashed showmanship and flagrant sensuality.[16] His novelties do not, after all, simply "raise" music's level to meet abstract ideals of rhetorical sophistication — something we might impute to more conventional Willaertian madrigals — but confront the most performative aspect of Petrarch's poetics, his lyric bravura, with a new contrapuntal prowess. Neither Rore nor Willaert, nor anyone attempting to hear rhetoric in so close a way as they, would have been deaf to Petrarch's tremendous formal virtuosity, its signifying power, and the contradictions it poses with Petrarchan thematics. As Robert M. Durling has put it, the "self-conscious technical mastery" that Petrarch flaunts and worries time and again is "integral to his expressiveness."[17] It is this linguistic virtuosity, this formal gamesmanship in Petrarch's lyric achievement, that Rore's new readings isolate and elevate.

Indeed his is arguably a reading admitted within this seemingly most pious of canzoni, the *Vergine* poem itself. Petrarch's wily poetics, his nearly subversive formal

15. For other words and phrases taken out of context see stanza three, "in allegrezza torni" (mm. 51–55), a reference to the Virgin's effect on the tears of Eve, and stanza four, "il Sol che rasserena" (mm. 27–30), to the brightening power of the sun.

16. Similar melismas occur in stanza two, "chiara lampa" (mm. 17ff.) and "fortuna" (mm. 32ff.), and in stanza eight, "Tu ved'il tutto" (mm. 52ff.).

17. *Petrarch's Lyric Poems: The "Rime sparse" and Other Lyrics* (Cambridge, Mass., 1976), p. 12.

manipulations, at times call the fundamental seriousness—or at least sacredness—of the whole poem into question, and with a measure of metaliterary distance that permeates the entire *Canzoniere*. An almost reckless instance of this comes in the middle of stanza eight, as Petrarch problematizes his always ambiguous address to the Virgin.

Hor tu, Donna del ciel, tu nostra Dea,	Now you, Lady of Heaven, you our Goddess
Se dir lic'e conviensi,	(If it is permitted and fitting to say it),
Vergine d'alti sensi,	Virgin of deep wisdom:
Tu ved'il tutto, e quel che non potea	You see all, and what another could not 10
Far altri è null'a la tua gran virtute.	Do is nothing to your great power:
Pon fin al mio dolore,	Put an end to my sorrow,
Ch'a te honore et a me fia salute.	Which to you would be honor and to me salvation.

Petrarch's ambivalent "Vergine" is never entirely distinct in his *Canzoniere* from the virginal Laura (nor Laura from Her). Here She is a pagan goddess, "Donna del ciel, tu nostra Dea." Petrarch's obsequious bowing and scraping in v. 8 ("se dir lic'e conviensi") only draws attention to the audacity of his address and the forever unresolved and partial status of his faith, so necessary to sustaining his poetic design.[18]

Rore picks up Petrarch's cue in mm. 47–63 (see Ex. 68). After a full pause marks off v. 8, She becomes the "Vergine d'alti sensi," as lightly told in a choral exchange of lower and upper voices. She sees all ("Tu ved'il tutto"), they continue, jauntily weaving fast-dotted melismas between them until their dissolution in m. 54.[19] Thereafter a shift to triple meter, the first of two such in the last few stanzas of the cycle,[20] leads to a cheerful course of florid parallel tenths (cantus and bassus, mm. 60–61) in celebration of her "gran virtute."[21]

This passage seems unabashedly flippant but in a way that becomes typical of the last five stanzas.[22] Rore's reading moves decidedly away from the patriarchal and Ciceronian orientation of Willaert's settings.[23] To be sure, it extends directions

18. Note too the presumptuous conclusion, where the consolatory function that she plays toward him becomes a source of her honor.

19. The same sorts of dotted melismas can be seen in stanza five, altus, m. 41, on "gioconda."

20. The other occurs in stanza ten, mm. 62–63.

21. Simultaneous melismas of this sort do not appear in the *Musica nova*. Other examples in the *Vergine* cycle may be found in stanza two, mm. 60–61 (with parallel sixths between the upper voices), stanza four, m. 71 (parallel thirds between quintus and tenor), and stanza ten, mm. 65–66 (parallel sixths between cantus and tenor).

22. Earlier stanzas toy with a similarly brazen rhetoric, though to a lesser extent. In stanza one, mm. 59–66, for instance, as Petrarch beseeches the Virgin to turn to his prayer and aid in his war ("al mio prego t'inchina; / Soccorri a la mia guerra," vv. 11b–12), Rore launches the first of his dotted-note melismas and syncopated minim/semiminim cross rhythms. Once the poet declares himself but earth beside her heavenly reign ("bench'io sia terra et tu del ciel Regina," v. 13, with its internal rhyme to "guerra"), his fawnings begin to look like a thin excuse for bravura paradox. For this Rore makes a dip into his lowest tessitura and drollest affective regions. (Another example of the cross rhythms found here crops up in stanza six, "Di questo tempestoso mare stella," mm. 11–15.)

23. My thinking here has been influenced by William J. Kennedy's interpretations of Petrarchan commentaries like Bernardino Daniello's *Sonetti, canzoni, e triomphi di Messer Francesco Petrarca con la spositione* (1541; Venice, 1549) that emerged from the Venetian milieu during the third to fifth decades. Kennedy's forthcoming book on sixteenth-century Petrarchan commentaries promises fascinating new insights into relationships between civic and personal identities and modes of reading.

Ex. 68.   Rore, *Vergine, tal è terra e post'ha in doglia* (Petrarch, no. 366, stanza 8), mm. 47–63; *Terzo libro a 5* (Venice, 1552), p. 8.

anticipated in his first two books of madrigals, which ruffled Willaert's smooth Ciceronian surfaces by periodically disrupting the placid and continuous polyphonic flow. Already in a Dantean madrigal like *Strane ruppi* Rore maximized gestures of destabilizing discontinuity: consecutive leaps, fast, vaulting melismas, constant voice crossings, strings of inverted triads, textural evaporations, suspended dissonances, and tone clusters generated out of anticipated notes of resolution.[24] Where Willaert mainly stuck to verbal projection through linguistic structure—syntax—Rore balanced syntactic with semantic considerations. It is no surprise that Rore's early books continued to be reprinted into the 1590s.[25]

All of this we might view as underpinning his later *seconda pratica* style, if not actually broaching its harmonic experiments. To see in the madrigals of Rore's Books 1–3 a monolithic repertory, therefore, all falling under the rubric "Venetian," is to miss the new stirrings in Book 3 and even Rore's earlier books. It was the *Vergine* cycle that explicitly enunciated rhythmic and textural procedures that were essential to Rore's late compositional techniques. Far more than the early sonnet settings I have discussed, the *Vergine* forms a link between the classic Venetian style of the early forties and the late madrigalistic idioms of the north Italian courts, Ferrara and Mantua. It looks at once backward over the monumental style of the 1540s and forward to various quixotic strategies of the late 1550s and beyond, strategies at once iconic and iconoclastic.

I am tempted to propose, finally, that Rore's *Vergine* theatricalized text in a way that post-Ciceronian poetics encouraged. Aristotelian notions of imitation that were just then beginning to supplant Ciceronian ones bedazzled practitioners of mimetic arts with their vivid iconic promise and possibilities for imitating directly natural human speech and action. Rore's demonstrative imitations of textual events resonate in sympathy with this representational mimetic model. In making them he put at risk Venice's Ciceronian supertrope, its trope of tropes, decorum, pushing it from its dominant space at the center of discursive practice to a marginal position outside.

24. See Chap. 8 above, pp. 285–93, for a discussion of the madrigal.
25. On Rore's legacy see Meier's foreword to the *Opera omnia* 2:i–ii.

APPENDIX:
DOCUMENTS CITED IN CHAPTER 3

A. Will of Gottardo Occagna, I-Vas, Archivio Notarile, Testamenti, Atti bianchi, notaio Francesco Bianco, b. 125, fol. 349, 19 February 1547 [m.v.; =1548 n.s.]

Die dominico decimanona *mensis* febr*uarij* 1547 Ind*ictione* sesta R*ivoal*ti.

Cum vite sue et terminis etc.: La qual cosa considerando al presente Io gottardo di Ochagna fiol. che fu del q*uondam* mis*ier* Alfonso de Benites & al presente residente qui in la cita di Venetia in casa della habitatione del mag*nifi*co mis*ier* Zuanagostino de marini gentilomo genovese in la contra de San moyse, ben sano della mente ma molto infermo del corpo et vollendo ordinare delli mei beni: Io ho fatto chiamare et venir da me pre franc*esc*o bianco nodaro di venetia, il qualle presente li testimonij infrascripti. Ho pregatto che scrivi & noti di sua mano il presente mio ordine et lo ultimo mio voler & testamento. Il qualle volgio che sia vallido & fermo p*er* ogni millgior modo. Et in cadauno loco: et tempo: Da poi la mia morte etiam io ordino chel sia rellevato autentico & in p*ub*lica forma p*er* il modo di venetia consuete et cum tute le clausule: cassando et annullando ogni altro testamento p*er* ava*n*ti p*er* mi o dito o scripto o vero ordinato: ma dico che questo sia exequito p*er* lo infrascripto mio sollo co*m*missario. lo quale etiam io p*er* il presente mio ordine instituisco. et volgio che sia il molto mag*nifi*co misier Ioan*n*e Agostino de marini et sollo exequtore et administrator della presente mia co*m*missaria et heredita. Et etiam de tuti et cadauni mei beni, in cadauno loco posti. Et dove che si ritrovasseno spettante et a me p*er*tine*n*te. Lasso alla scolla de madona Sancta Maria della Carita di Venetia della qualle io ne son fratello duc*ati* vinti / 20: azioche vengano li fratelli come et sollito a compagnar el mio corpo alla sepoltura: Lasso allo hospedal delli Incurabilli duc*ati* diese et altri duc*ati* diese io lasso al hospedal de San Zuane Paulo p*er* l'anima mia. doma*n*dato delli altri lochi p*er* il nodaro si come lui se obligato: R*is*po*n*do no*n* voler altro ordinar de quelli. Item lasso al mio carissimo fratello mis*ier* fra Anto*n*io dalla Croce, de lo ordine de Sancto dominico delli observanti duc*ati* Cento / 100. in segno di fraternal amore et azioche lui se aricordi di pregar Dio p*er* me. Item lasso a madona Suor Maria di San B*er*nardo monacha del monastario di sibillia chiamado Sancta Maria di gratia mia honorandissima madre duc*ati* cento / 100. zoe duc*ati* cento correnti a *lire* 6 *soldi* 4 p*er* duc*ato* azioche lei si degni p*er* lo amor fillial e o vero materno de p*re*gar Dio in le sue

oratione p*er* lanima mia: Item lasso al fidellissimo servitor Zuan Piero da zandin ducati quaranta: Simelmente correnti a *lire* 6 *soldi* 4 p*er* duc*ato* de moneta venetiana. Item lasso a
Alberto Restagno de la Niella scudi dodese doro, et alla sua consorte paula altri scudi cinque
che sono in tuto scudi disisette p*er* l'anima mia. Item lasso a mis*ier* Lorenzo Sansone genovese da Savona fiol de mis*ier* Raymondo mio carissimo, la mia casaca et la mia bereta nova
di villuto negro con la sua medalgia in segno di bon amore; et il restante de tute le altre mie
robbe et panni io volgio che per il sopradeto mis*ier* Ioa*n*ne agostino siano vendute, et il tratto
di quelle siano poste al monte del mio residuo. Item ancora lasso al sopradeto mis*ier* Lorenzo
la mia spada con il suo fodro di villuto, et il mio pugnalle in segno di p*er*fetto amore. Item
lasso a Alleandro Donati, fiol di mis*ier* piero Donati mio cordiallissimo amico, il mio zaco di
malgia. Il qualle se ritrova esser in sua mano e cosi io gello dono per benivolentia stata fra
noi. Lasso a valleria putina, la qualle io facto arlevare da dona Anzola barcharolla moier de
Sier hier*oni*mo che Sta a San barnaba. barcharolo dico del mag*nifi*co ambasiatore di francia
duc*ati* vinti correnti ut supra p*er* il suo maridar o vero monegar, et p*er* l'anima mia: Item io
ordino et volgio che se forse p*er* domenticanza se trovasse qualche p*er*sona che iuridicamente
monstrassano de dover haver alguna cosa da mi tuti siano sattisfati come porta la iustitia.
Item dechiaro et volgio che siano dilligentemente visti tuti et cadauni mei conti a me p*er*ti-
nenti. In ogni loco et tempo et che con cadauno sia tirato in resto, et che siano ben saldati real
et iuxtamente, et qua*n*to che me trovassano restare creditore. Tuto sia posto in mio nome et
in la presente mia comissaria et nel mio residuo el qual residuo de tuti & qualunque mei beni
mobilli stabilli presente futuri caduchi desordenati et prono*n*scripti si existenti qui in venetia
come in spagna et in ogni altro loco, tuto io lasso, et liberamente dono et volgio che sia del
mio molto carissimo, et honorandissimo mis*ier* Ioanne Agostino de marini *soprascritt*o mio
sollo co*m*missario et exequtore di questo mio ordine il quale io certamente instituisco mio
sollo et unico et universal herede, senza alguna diminution overo contradiction, et questo io
volgio che sia vallido, si p*er* via del presente mio testamento, come etiam p*er* via de codicillo,
o, vero de donatione, et etiam p*er* ogni modo milgiore che si possa di raggione. Item volgio
ancora che p*er* il deto herede et co*m*missario mio siano dispensati duc*ati* vinti p*er* lanima mia
tra li poveri vergognosi de questa contra de Sancto moyse tam*en* con lo intervento dil pio-
vano o vero di altro che sia della p*re*dicta chiesia: p*er* lanima mia: Item lasso p*er* la fabrica
della chiesia de sancto moyse zoe p*er* far il corro di essa chiesia duc*ati* cinque p*er* lanima mia.
Et al nodaro dil presente mio testamento sia dat*a* la sua mercede consueta delli *soprascritt*i
mei beni come e sollito preterea plenissima*m* virtutem et potestatem Do tribuo atq*ue* con-
ferro *soprascript*o meo sollo co*m*missario et unico post obitum meum presentem meum co*m*-
missariam intromitendi administrandi serviendi et per complendi. Item petendi exigendi et
recipiendi omne id et totum de quicquid habere deberem hic et ubiq*ue* a cunctis michi dare
debenti*bus*. Item quietandi solvendi petendi respondendi In iuditio comparendi omnia allia
in premissis opportuna negociandi p*r*out egomet vivens facere possem statuens firmum et
Innapellabile. Si quis igitur. [formula] signum.

[Witnesses]

Io Zuanne morello [?] fo de m*isier* lorenzo fuj testimonio p*re*gado e zurado

Io An*toni*o paniza spicial al carro in contra d*i Sanc*to moiese fui testimone pregato et
zurato

Io Pompeo gonfalonero [added: milanese] fui testimonio pregato et giurato

Io Ioa*n*ne savonese fui testimonio pregato et zurato

[On the outside]

Test*amentu*m D*omini* gottardi de Ochagna filij q*uondam* D*omini* Alfonsi de Benetes de confinio S. Moysi

Obiijt die vigesima septima m*ensi*s martij et fuit publicat*um* die 30 dicti mensis 1567. R*ogatum* ad meu*m* cancellu*m* intrascripto D*omino* Ioanni augustino de marini comissario

B. Girolamo Parabosco, *I quattro libri delle lettere amorose* (Venice, 1561), fols. 103′–105′

[**fol. 103′**] Aggiunta, Al valoroso Signor Gotta[r]do Occagna.

Se i dolci comandamenti vostri, Signor Gottardo, cosi mi facessero sapiente, a satisfarvi, come mi fanno ardente ad obedirvi, certamente V. S. sarebbe molto meglio da me, che da qual altro si sia, risoluta del bellissimo dubbio, che ella mi move circa i tre amori: de iquali, benche mal volentieri, per non esserne molto esperto, parlerò; poi che da voi mi è comandato. E quanto al primo, dico, che è cosa da saggio il guardar di non inciamparvi dentro, per la molta fatica, che conviensi haver prima, che pervenir si possa ad alcuna risolutione, della qual fatica non ragionerò per haverne parlato assai in un'altra mia, che V. S. potrà veder nel presente libro, scritta al virtuoso M. Horatio Brunetto. Quanto poi al secondo, a me veramente pare, che sia un dolce amore; perche amando [**fol. 104**] una tale, non solamente non si patisce la fatica, che nel primo patir si suole; ma spesse fiate ella la toglie a chi ama di pensare, come pervenir possa al desiderato fine. Quante ne sono state, che in sì fatti casi hanno in un punto trovato rimedij, che in mille anni non harebbono imaginato i piu acuti huomini del mondo? O felicità grande di uno amante; a cui sia concesso veder per sublime ingegno della sua Donna, quasi al dispetto di fortuna, posto ottimo fine al suo desiderio: chi potrà considerar la dolcezza, che all'hora sente quel fortunato, che ad un tempo si certifica dell'amore dell'amata, & di amar cosa di grandissimo valore, poi che non men gli si scopre l'ingegno, che l'affettione di chi egli ama? Oltra ciò, essendo caldo l'huomo di questo secondo ardore, puo egli sempre haver più speranza di conseguir l'intento suo, che in ogni altro: & non men per le coperte, che hanno queste tali Donne alla sua pietà, che per la commodità, che similmente hanno di usarla. queste non hanno poi [**fol. 104′**] bisogno che si gli dimostri quale, & quanta dolcezza ben amando gustar si suole: perche elleno ne sono chiarissime, o almanco n'hanno una grandissima arra. onde sono quasi sempre disposte a ricever l'amoroso foco. Si che Signor mio, non mi spiace, anzi mi rallegro, qual hor io veggo uno amico mio darsi in preda allo amare per simil suggetto, del qual non dirò altro perch'io so, che V. S. sa molto meglio di me la dolcezza, che se ne trahe. Circa poi il terzo, io in tanta riverenza, & cosi degno santo & dolce amor le tengo, che quasi non ardisco parlarne; temendo pure di scemar le sue lode, come veramente farò parlandone. Questo è quello ardore, che sempre aumenta nel petto di chi amor degna accenderlo, come per infiniti essempi d'huomini valorosi appare. i quali sempre fino la morte hanno amato estremamente senza mai credere, che piu felice vita si potesse goder quà giù. Questo è quello amore, che solo si possiede senza timore, che si gode senza gelosia. O dolci sguardi, [**fol. 105**] o dolci risi, o dolci parole, che dolci sono ben veramente più che l'ambrosia delli Dei. poscia che considerando chi le dice, non si puo temere, che artificiosamente dette siano, onde si godono poi quei favori perfettamente; il che non lice in altro patto godere. Forse che chi ama persone tali; puo dubitar di non esser sempre tenuto caro, o se a sorte, ilche non puo avenire, gli nascesse timore, che altro gli fosse compagno, non se ne chiarirebbe al primo tratto, senza mille anni portare nel petto l'inferno, come interviene a chi non sa fare cosi sicura, & degna elettione. Che dirò poi di quella santa commodità, che s'ha da ragionare ad ogni hora con chi s'adora? laqual cosa è troppo a far felice un'huomo. ilquale sarebbe degno d'infinita pena, se havendo cotal commodità non rompesse un diamante, o non infiammasse un ghiaccio. Infinite sono le ragioni, per lequali io potrei chiaramente far conoscere la felicità di questo amore, superare tutte l'altre: ma voglio, che mi bastino queste po- [**fol. 105ʹ**] che; poi ch'io so, ch'elle saranno a bastanza per farvi conoscere l'animo mio. Fra tanto V. S. mi tenga nella sua gratia, & mi comandi.

C. Will of Antonio Zantani, I-Vas, Archivio Notarile, Testamenti, Vettor Maffei, b. 657, fol. 72, 19 June 1559

Anno Ab incarnatione *domini nostri* Jesu Ch*risti* 1559. Ind*ictio*ne 2ᵈᵃ die vero lune XIX mensis Junij R*ivoalti*

Considerando quanto sij fragile la vita humana Io Antonio Zantani [inserted: conte et cavalier] fu del cl*arissi*mo m*esser* marco del confin di *santa* margarita Et *che* cosa alcuna piu certa no*n* habbiamo della morte et niente lhora di questa essendo al *present*e *per* gra*tia* d'Iddio sano *del* mente et inteleto benche alquanto infermo di corpo et jacendo nel leto ho fato venir da me vetor maphei notarijo di Venetia qual ho *pre*gado acio li beni mei inordinati no*n* remanghino *che* scriver debbi questo mio testame*n*to et q*ue*llo doppo la morte mia publicar et compir co*n* le clausule opportune secundo il stil d*i* Venetia. et quando allo altissimo mio creator piacera a se chiamarmi li arricomando et alla madre sua gloriosa Vergene maria et alla [?] sua corte celestial la*n*i*m*a mia. *primo* lasso p*er*mei comissarie et executrice di questo mio testame*n*to la m*agnifi*ca madonna Thomasina mia honorandis*sim*a madre et la mia car*issi*ma consorte Helena quale *pre*go ch*e* venendo il caso d*el*la morte mia voglino exeguir quanto p*er* questo mio testamento ordino. voglio ch*e*l mio corpo sii sepulto *per* il piovan solo d*el*la mia contra. et quando lui no*n* volesse o non potesse venire d*e*bbi mandare uno altro sacerdote in suo loco. Et voglio p*er*ho sij data la elemosina *per* il capitolo d*el*la contra secondo il co*n*sueto et sij sepulto il mio corpo al corpus domini in un deposito ch*e* voglio sij fato in deta chiesa sopra la parte [?] di mezo ch*e* e p*er* mezo lo altar d*el*la mado*n*na, qual loco ci è stato comesso *per* le monache che capitular mente. lasso ducati diese al anno inp*er*petuo alla sacristia di essa chiesa d*el* corpus domini *per* haverli cosi *pro*messo altempo che le R*everen*de monache mi concessero detto loco. voglio p*er*ho ch*e* li ducati 10 ch*e* ogni p*as*qua [?] soglio dar a suor colomba in deto monache in deto monasterio ch*e* doppo la morte di essa suor colomba rimanghino ad esso monasterio in loco delli deti ducati 10 al anno. dichiaro oltra cio ch*e* la mia sepultura seu deposito sij fato secondo il modello ch*e* si atrova in charta azura in la mia cassetta con il [?] di mercado fato con il taiapiera beretino da Verona. il quale taiapiera anco lui ha uno simile dissegno—et *pre*gho dete mie comissarie a no*n* mancare d*i* hexeguire quanto desopra ordino come credo no*n* mancherano. et *per*ch*e* mi atrovo in due scole cioe la misericordia et S. Thodaro et prima intrai in S. Thodaro avanti la fusse levata in scola grande *per*ho acio non naschi controversia tra dete scolle, voglio essere accompagnato da ambedue esse scole. ma voglio il mio corpo sii levato *per* la scolla d*i* S. Thodaro. et voglio le habbino ducati 50 *per* cadauna del mio. et voglio ch*e* in loco d*i* *pre*ti ch*e* essi accompagnino alla sepultura siino tolti 100 poveri d*el*li piu poveri si possino atrovare alli quali sij dato un torzo *per*uno. et compagnato che mi haverano li torzi siino sui liberi. Alla mia carissima consorte Helena lasso tutta la sua dote integra et tutti li sui vestimenti denari [inserted: ori] et zoie ch*e* lei si ritrova. voglio p*er*ho ch*e* della sua dote la si debbi pagare sopra la possessio*n* di sesto. Alla mia Honora*n*dissima madre madonna Thomasina lasso ch*e* doppoi che lei si havera pagata d*el*la sua dote la sii donna et mado*n*na d'ogni cosa sino la vive. et doppo la sua morte voglio il mio residuo sij d*el* ospedal d*el*la pieta di Venetia. It*em* lasso la casa di portoguer fornida et conza come la si ritrova a m*esser* Thoma[s] donado mio zerman [inserted: p*er* segno damor]. et no*n* fazando quel tutto che io ordino voglio ch*e* deta mia madre et consorte restino prive di quanto li lasso et il tutto vadi nel hospedal d*el*la pieta *pre*det*o*. Et [word deleted] prego detta mia car*issi*ma consorte et cosi la exorto ch*e* la si vogl*i*j maridare. et fra

tanto la prego stij in compagnia della magnifica mia madre. Item lasso a sebastian mio servitor la barca fornida come la sta, et voglio il sia vestido per una volta tantum. Item a nicolo mio
servitor lasso ducati X. et sii vestido per una volta tantum Dimandado dal nodaro delli altri
loci pietosi della cita ha risposto cosi no non voler altro ordinare salvo che lasso al nodaro
ducati diesi. [Latin formula follows]

[Witnesses:]

Io Antonio di Zuanpiero mazzer a santa malgarita fui testimonio pregado et zurado

Io marchio condan bernardo boter asanta malgarita fui stestimonio pregado et surado

[On the outside:]

19 Junij 1559. Testamentum clarissimi domini Antonij Zantani
comitis et equitis

D. Will of Elena Barozza Zantani, I-Vas, Archivio Notarile, Testamenti, notaio Cesare Ziliol,
b. 1257, fol. 321, 22 January 1580 [m.v.; =1581 n.s.]; notarized 11 April 1581

In nome del nostro signor Dio, et della Gloriosa Vergene Maria, ritrovandomi io Helena
Zantana relita di messer Antonio del K. per gratia di Dio sana della mente, ne mi parendo di
tardar piu mi son messa a scriver di mia mano questo mio testamento et ultima volonta.
prima ricomando lanema mia al nostro Signor Dio il qual priego, che fino che li piacera di
chiamarmi a se vogli darmi gratia di fare quello che si conviene a una bona sua serva, come
desiderio di esser io, et poi al suo tempo acetare ditta anima mia come sua creatura nel suo
santo paradiso presso di se. el mio corpo voglio che el sia sepulto al corpus domini nel arca,
che fece fare mio suocero dove lui he et el quondam mio marido senza alcuna pompa nel
modo che parera a mei comessari vestita pero del ordine delle munege del corpus domini.
voglio che in anti, che sia sepulta, siano fatte le elimosine in fra scritte. prima siano ditte messe
30 in la mia contra et 30 al corpus domini per lanema mia, et siano depensati ducati 100 in
questo modo: al ospedal dincurabili ducati 10, a quello di san zanepolo ducati 10, alli
presonieri della forte ducati 10, alle incovertide ducati 10, alle munege del corpus domini
ducati 10, a quelle di santa maria Mazor ducati 10, a quele di miracoli ducati 10, a san servolo
ducati 10, santa chiara di muran ducati 10, alla croce [+] di venetia ducati 10. comessari et esecutori di questo mio testamento lasso messer Anzolo Barozzi mio carissimo fratello, monsignor [?] suo fiollo mio nepotte, messer Carlo di Garzoni mio nepote, et Helena sua consorte
mia nezza, quali tutti 4 priego, per le visere di Jesu cristo, acordarsi con amorevolezza et dar
esecusione in tutto di questo mio testamento et ultima volonta sopra el cargo delle aneme
sue. et si per sorte non si trovasse in casa al tempo della mia morte tanti dinari di bastase a fare
le sopra scritte spese prego li mei comessari con ogni sorte di afeto a trovarli, et poi rimbor-
sarsi con li primi, che si cavera di biave o vini se ne sera o qui, o a sesto, o col trato di mobili
come ordinero qui soto. a madonna iustina zantana mia Carissima parente et compagnia
lasso ducati 24 al anno fino che la vivera, cioè ducati 12 a mesi sei da poi la mia morte, et cosi
ogni mesi sei la sua rata. et questo per segno di amore si ben conoso, che la merita molto piu,
per lamorevolezza che lha usato sempre verso di me. ma so che la non ha bisogno essendo
obligati li eriedi del K. mio marido a farli le spese, et vestirla fina, che la vivera, come si contiene nel suo testamento. et si li dovese dar dinari, che molte volte mi servo del suo, come al
presente. voglio che la sia satisfatta del tutto et si vedera sul mio libro rouan dove tegno conto
con lei, et si la ne havese insalvo nel mio scrigno dove la i tiene voglio subito averto ditto
scrigno che li siano datti quelli, che lei dira esser sui, che la conoso Dona di anima, che la non
tora si non li sui. et cosi tutta la sua roba, che he, per casa insieme con la mia che lei dira esser

sua volgio che la li sia datta senza contradition alcuna, essendo sicura, che la non tora si no el s[ua]. a mia cugnada lasso la mia vesta di saga, et a Helena mia neza, per segno di amore 12 delle mie camise, et 24 fazoletti, che la cerna di ditte mie cose quelle, che piu li piazera. lasso [**fol. 1′**] alle mie altre 3 nezze munege ducati 3 al anno per cadauna, che sia datti dalli miei eriedi da Nadale fino che le viverano. a zuane dalle Gambarare servitore stando con mi al tempo della mia morte ducati 20 per una volta, et non altro, al macere che mi servira ducati 2 comise delle mie 2 per cadauna. a cornelia che mi serve al presente ducati 10 al suo maritate, a Margarita, fiolla si Anzolo Sartora ducati 10 al suo maritar, a Giulia fiolla di Laura del quondam Gasparo Zantani ducati 10 al suo maritar. tutti di quelli, che ho da maritar donzele come sera dichiarito qui sotto, priego mia cugnada insieme con Helena mia nezza a despensar tutti li mei drapi di doso di lana, et di pelle per lanema mia tra nostre parente povere si ne sarana, et le fiolle del quondam Gasparo Zantani, et Anzola Sartora, al mio fattor [sartor] si el sera vivo ducati 10 alli mei massari ducati 5 per masaria di quelli che si trovera star su le mie possession, che siano disfalcati di sui debiti chi havera con mi, et per che la magior parte del mobile, chio quello? he di comessaria. voglio, che si veda nel prencipio del mio primo libro che le/ he notado [?] el mio propio. voglio, che el sia venduto, et da poi fatto li legati sopraditti, et a preso li dinari che si cavera di vini et biave si ne sarano a sesto tutti siano di messer Carlo di Garzoni mio nepote a conto di ducati 1000, che li ho promesso in contrato. qual prego a contentarse a tuorli [?] in questo modo: quelli che restera al sal, per quello, che i valera a quel tempo, quelli che si trovera al novissimo in mio nome, per quello, che i valera li cent [?] ducati [?] si ne sarano, et poi per finirse da satisfar ho di mei livelli propii in frial a 7 per cento ho vero con le mie preme intrade con questo, che li mei eriedi siano obligati a darli ducati 6 per cento per suo utile a rason di anno del suo eredito che li manchera fino sia satisfato del tutto, et possi lui tuor qual partido di sopraditi per esser satisfato, che piu li piacera, et per che lano 1571 non fu eseguido el legato del quondam mio marido non essendo reduto el giorno di Santo Antonio el gran conseglio, voglio per discargo de lanima mia, che delle mie intrade siano maridate tante donzele si che siano despensati ducati 103 havendone io fino a questo giorno dispensati ducati 5 di quali dinari voglio, che siano datti ducati 30 alle 3 sopra scritte donzele. resto voglio che siano in 3 anni in maritar tante donzele dispensati li sopraditti dinari, et si in el tempo di ditti 3 anni si maritase una de le tre fiolle del quondam Gasparo zantani voglio, che tutti li dinari di questo rason, che si trovera in mano di mei eriedi siano della ditta fiolla, che si maritase ecetuando li ducati 30 de le 3 sopra nominate. et si io ne maritase qualche una ho facese alcuno di legati soprascriti farò notta sul mio libro, perche non voglio, che i siano fatti piu di una volta ne parera stranio ad alcuno che io perla mi sia risolta a maritar ditte donzele essendo questo cargo di comessari di quel tempo del quondam mio marido, et mio insieme. quello ho fatto, per esser certa, che altri che io non si havera mai veduto a far questo effetto, onde il fato in vita, ho. voglio che li mei eriedi siano obligati a farlo sopra el cargo delle anime sue essendo io sola la debitora. questo voglio che sia fatto per descargo de lanema mia, et della mia consientia. voglio che sia fatta una mansionaria perpetua nella iesia del corpus domini alla qual sia eletto un sacerdote per capelano, per messer Anzolo Barozzi mio fratello fino che lui vivera, et da poi, per el primogenito di sui fiolli mei nepoti et cosi di un in l'altro fino, che ne sara di quella linia da ca Barozzi li qual maniando o mentre che viverano non elegendo in termine di un mese da poi la mia morte, overo da poi la morte del capelano eleto o dal primo da sucesori. voglio, che sia questo cargo della Reverenda Abadessa del monasterio del corpus domini che el suo capitolo, elegere il qual capelano habbi a dir messa tre volte alle settimana, per lanema mia in ditta iesia et mancando el ditto senza legitima causa di malatia per giorni 15 da dir le 3 messe sopradite chi tochera a eleger debia sopra el cargo de lanema sua elegere un altro in loco suo per elimosina. voglio che habbi ditto capella [obscured] anno tutto el pro che si cavera che ducati 450 di civedale di monte novisimo di angarie pagade, che gia ho fatto scriver dal mio nome a quello del monasterio del corpus domini. mio eriede universale di tutti i beni che mi atrovo, et che per alcun tempo mi potese per venire lasso messer Anzolo Barozzi mio carissimo fratello, et da poi lui sui fiolli mascoli mei Carissimi nepoti, ei sui fioli si ne haverano ma nasciti di legitimo matrimonio si, che siano abili andar a consegio avertendo che voglio che le mie possession da sesto romagna condicionata, che non si possa ne vender ne impiegar ne in alcun modo o via alienar ne partir. et questo perche conoso, che così unita la he belissima non et val qualche cosa che a parirla la valeria poco po la lasso alli mascoli soli fiolli che mei nepoti nasciti come ho ditto che di sopra, et non havendo mascoli che Dio non el voglia a suo fiolle femine legitime et non havendo ne mascoli ne femine voglio, che ditta possession vada in Helena di Garzoni mia nezza, et sui fiolli mascoli si ne haverano et non havendo mascoli alle fiolle femine ne si maraveglia alcuno si io lasso le possession condicionate per che desidero, che cosi unita la resta in ca Barozzi, per che i cavera onesto utile, che a parirla essendo cosi lontana si caveria poco. et voglio, che li possesori di ditte possessioni siano obligati pagar le angarie et tenir li coperti in conzo et in colmo come si conviene et questo sopra el cargo de le anime sue. et prego Dio che le lassi galdar alli mei eriedi in gratia sua laus Deo. Helena Zantana.

[On the outside]
1581 Indictione nona mensis Aprilis da undecima Rivoaltj in domo habitationis clarissimae Dominae Helena Barotio relicta quondam clarissimi Domini Antonij Zantani juilis sua, ut dixit, manu propria scriptum, presentantum mihi Caesar Ziliolo Aulae Serenissimi Populi Venetiani Cancellari per me servandum, et quando occurrerit in publicam formam elevandum etc.: Et Interrogatus de his respondit o quello, che mi hà parso etc.

[Witnesses]
1582 In mense octobris iuxta? Aiutalem obijt Reverendissima
Intus vero testamenti tenor talis est de verbo ad verbum
Hic finis Testamentum preterra

Iutus verò Testamentum mortalis est De verbis ad verbum   Hic finis est Testamenti

E. Orazio Toscanella, *I nomi antichi, e moderni delle provincie, regioni, città, castella, monti, laghi, fiumi, mari, golfi, porti, & isole dell'Europa, dell'Africa, & dell'Asia; con le graduationi loro in lunghezza, e larghezza & un abreve descrittione delle suddette parti del mondo . . .* (Venice, 1567), fols. [2]–[3′]

[fol. {2}] Al Clarissimo M. Antonio Zantani Conte, & Cavaliero. Oratio Toscanella.
Viddero alcuni belli ingegni Clariss. Sig. che la lettura dei nomi antichi dava molto travaglio alli studiosi de i tempi nostri, perche le Provincie, & gli altri luochi con nomi differentissimi hoggidì si chiamano; però si diedero a porre di rimpetto a gli antichi, quei che a'nostri tempi s'usano. Con questa consideratione il dottissimo RUSSELLI fece il suo Tolomeo, & il valorosissimo CASTALDI alcune carte, & altri pellegrini spiriti, altre cose in questo proposito tutte utili, & degne. A questo medesimamente considerando M. BOLOGNIN ZALTIERI, che sempre pensa di giovare a' letterati à tutto poter suo, diede carico a me in particolare di raccorre per ordine d'Alfabeto i Nomi antichi, & moderni, accioche i lettori non solo sapessero, come adesso si chiamano; ma à un tratto ordinatissimamente gli sapessero. Cosi feci adunque; ma perche io solo non potea far questa impresa; trovò una persona intendentissima di questa professione, aquale volentieri nominarei sel suo nome sapessi, che non puo essere altro, che hororatissimo [sic]: & fece, ch'ella supplì à quello, che io non haveva potuto fare, & cosi s'è fatto questo volume di Nomi antichi, & moderni delle Pro-[fol. {2′}]vincie, regioni, città, monti, laghi, fiumi, mari, golfi, porti, & isole di tutto il mondo, picciolo di corpo certo,

ma di utilità grandissimo. Et perche egli se ne viene a farsi vedere dalla luce del mondo, ho voluto dedicarlo a V. S. C. laquale prende maraviglioso piacere delle cose di Cosmografia, & di Geografia, anzi d'ogni sorte di dottrine, & d'arti onorate. E pur notissimo, ch'ella s'è di Musica in guisa dilettata, che lungo tempo pagò la compagnia de'Fabretti, & de'Fruttaruoli cantatori, & sonatori eccellentissimi, iquali facevano in casa di lei Musiche rarissime, & tenne anco pagato à questo effetto GIULIO dal Pistrino Sonator di Liuto senza pari. Ove concorrevano Girolamo Parabosco, Annibal organista di S. Marco, Claudio da Correggio Organista di S. Marco, Baldassare Donato, Perissone, Francesco Londarit, detto il Greco, & altri Musici di fama immortale. Si sà ottimamente che V. C. S. ha fatto fare compositioni preciose, & Stampar Madrigali, intitolati Corona di diversi. Non è nascoso ancora, che S. S. C. dipinge, riccama, & intaglia sopra ogni credenza bene. Quanto poi si diletti d'anticaglie quel bellissimo libro, intitolato, Le Imagini, con tutti i Riversi trovati, & le vite de gli Imperatori, tratte dalle Medaglie, & dalle istorie degli antichi, lo fa chiarissimate conoscere, & lo fara anco meglio l'altro lib. di Medaglie, che adesso và componendo. Si diletta somigliantemente di Architettura tanto, che ha fatto diverse belle cose, & tra le altre, il modello della chiesa dell'ospitale de gl'Incurabili, ilquale le reca non minor laude di quello, che si sa lo essere ella stata inventrice di detta chiesa, & lo essersi mossa per zelo di carità fino ad accattar per Dio con lunghe & dure fatiche, accio [**fol. {3}**] che detta fabrica ad onor della Maestà divina si faccia. E in oltre così cortese, & fautrice & larga benefatrice dei virtuosi, che se fosse un' Alessandro, ò un' Augusto fiorirebbono più che mai tutte le scienze, & discipline, & arti. Ultimamente è tanto affettionata alla sua patria, che arde in desiderio di spendere in suo servigio la robba, & il sangue, & da à conoscere al sicuro, che le fù padre il Clarissimo M. Marco fu del Clariss. M. Antonio Zantani, ilquale per le fatiche durate in prò della Patria, d'uno in altro grado salendo, arrivò à Consigliere, & in quella dignità ci fu molte volte. Che dirò io della buona memoria del Clarissimo M. Antonio Zantani? dirò ch'essendo Rettore à Modone nell'assedio del Turco, per non volersi rendere, fu segato vivo fra duo tavole, & patì prima che morisse tanta fame, che tutti nella terra furono constretti à mangiar cavalli, cani, gatti, & simili animali, & a partir quel poco licor, che havevano coi fondi delle scodelle. Per la gloriosa morte di cosi gran gentilhuomo i Zantani, che successero, onde haveano prima per Cimiero un leopordo [*sic*] in un siepe legato ad un pino, levarono poscia sopra l'elmo una corona d'oro, che ha dentro un braccio armato, et una Scimitara, che passa il braccio, con una palma per banda del detto braccio. La corona, & la palma significano, che fu coronato del martirio, & la Scimitara, la morte, con un breve che dice PRO DEO ET PATRIA, perche era morto per Dio, cioè per la fede, et per la patria. Di quì nacque principalmente, che il santiss. Pontifice Giulio III. Si mosse ad ornare V. M. C. del titolo di Conte, & cavaliero, con un privilegio tanto ampio, ch'io non sò, se vedessi mai il piu ampio à miei giorni. S'io [**fol. {3'}**] volessi raccontar come casa sua è ripiena di Medaglie d'alto prezzo, di Quadri fatti per mano di pittori illustri, & d'altre anticaglie ricche di Maestà, s'io volessi dire, che fa l'Ascendenza, & Discendenza di tutta la Nobiltà Vinitiana, & che tesse tuttavia una bellissima Historia; non verrei mai à fine di questa lettera. Però lasciando da canto il gran numero de' suoi meriti, vengo a pregarla che non si sdegni, ch'io le habbia dedicata questa opera; ma l'accetti con allegro core, che Iddio le dia lunga vita, & felicità. Di Venetia ai xxii. Agosto. M.D.LXVII.

SELECTIVE BIBLIOGRAPHY

PRIMARY SOURCES

Manuscript

Bologna, Civico Museo Bibliografico Musicale
    MS Q 19 ("Rusconi Codex")
    MS Q 21
    MS R 141 (*See Libro primo de la fortuna*)
    MS B. 107, 1–3
Brussels, Bibliothèque du Conservatoire Royal de Musique
    MS 27.731
Chicago, Newberry Library
    Case MS-VM 1578.M91 ("Newberry Partbooks")
    Strozzi MS 6A 11, no. XXV, "Vita di Filippo Strozzi Gentilhuomo fiorentino."
Florence, Archivio di Stato di Firenze
    Carte Strozziane, ser. III and V
——, Biblioteca del Conservatorio di Musica Luigi Cherubini
    MS Basevi 2440
    MS Basevi 2442 ("Strozzi Chansonnier")
——, Biblioteca Medicea-Laurenziana
    MS Acquisti e doni 666 ("Medici Codex")
London, British Library (olim British Museum)
    MS Add. 12.197. "Sonetti e poema in italiano di Benedetto Corner e di Domenico Venier di
        Venezia—Corretti da altra mano piu tardi."
    MS Add. 16557. "Sonetti madrigali e canzoni di Messer Lodovico Domenichi scritte da suo
        proprio mano d'anno 1535."
Padua, Biblioteca Capitolare
    MS A 17
Rome, Biblioteca Vallicelliana
    MS S¹ 35–40 (olim Inc. 107bis, S. Borromeo E. II.55–60; "Vallicelliana manuscript")
Vatican City, Biblioteca Apostolica Vaticana
    MS C.S. 16
    MS Vat. lat. 5318. (Letters of Pietro Aaron, Giovanni Spataro, Giovanni del Lago, et al.)
    MS Vat. lat. 5385

Venice, Archivio di Stato di Venezia
  Avogaria di Comun, Contratti di nozze
  Dieci savi alle decime, Condizioni
  Notarile
    Atti
    Testamenti
  Raccolta dei Consegi
  Segretario alle voci
    Elezioni del Maggior Consiglio
    Elezioni del Senato
———, Biblioteca Nazionale Marciana
  MSS It. Cl. VII, 152 (8045): "Libro di tutti li nobili, che vanno in Maggior Consiglio, con
    tutte le nozze, e parentadi dal 1480 circa al 1595 circa."
  MSS It. Cl. VII, 227 (7609), fols. 1–20: "Lettera 'Al Mag.ᶜᵒ M. Francesco Longo del Clar.ᵐᵒ M.
    Antonio.'"
  MSS It. Cl. VII, 313–314 (8809–8810): "Patrizie veneziane." Apostolo Zeno. Alberi genealogici
    di famiglie. 2 vols.
  MSS It. Cl. IX, 173 (6282): "Rime in lingua veneziana di diversi . . ." (including sonnets
    between Venier and Corner).
  MSS It. Cl. IX, 248 (7071): "Domenico Venier Rime, con altre di altri Autori del suo tempo,
    che sono Pietro Aretino, Luigi Alemanni, Giulio Camillo, Niccolò Delfino, Cipriano
    Fortebraccio, Veronica Gambara, e Claudio Tolomei."
  MSS It. Cl. IX, 589 (9765): [Domenico Venier], "Frammento di canzoniere autografo."
  MSS It. Cl. X, 1 (6394): "Istoria delle vite de' poeti italiani, di Alessandro Zilioli veneziano."
  MSS It. Cl. X, 23 (6526): "Lettere inedite di Pietro Gradenigo patrizio veneto scritte a diversi."
  MSS It. Cl. X, 81 (7105): "Leges Accademie Venete." Apostolo Zeno. "Zibaldone di accademie
    italiane."
  MSS It. Cl. X, 89 (6431). Girolamo Muzio. "Lettere 172, trascritte da un codice Ms. della
    Biblioteca Riccardiana di Firenze."
  MSS It. Cl. X, 95 (6565): Domenico Gisberto di Murano. "Notizie delle accademie."
  MSS It. Cl. XI, 25 (6671): "Testamento originale e lettere autografe del Cardinale Pietro
    Bembo."
———, Museo Civico Correr
  Cod. Cic. 770. Bernardino Tomitano. "Lettera a Francesco Longo."
  Cod. Cic. 818. (Collected poetry of the sixteenth century.)
  Cod. Cic. 906. Petrus Gaetanus. "Oratio & origine et dignitate musices."
  Cod. Cic. 1099, fols. 70–92. Girolamo Molino. "Difesa di se stessa al Consiglio dei X."
  MS Correr 355. (Collected poetry of the sixteenth century.)
  MS Gradenigo 81. [Genealogy.]
  MS Gradenigo 83: "Notizie su cittadini veneziani."
  MS Gradenigo 181: "Accademie in Venezia."
  MS P.D. 308-c/IX: "Sentimenti giocosi havuti in Parnaso per L'Academia degl'Unisoni."
  MS P.D. 509-c/I: "Conto de M. Francesco di Prioli presentato contra la heredità dei Q M
    Girolamo da Molin, et la commissaria del Q Mag. M. Pietro da Molin del M. D. LV. al
    petition."
  33.D.76: "Cittadini veneziani."
  Toderini, Teodoro. "Genealogie delle famiglie Venete ascritte alla cittidinanza originaria."
Wolfenbüttel, Herzog August Bibliothek
  MS Codex Guelf 293

Printed (Including Modern Editions)

Aaron, Pietro. *Lucidario in musica*. Venice, 1545. Facs. ed. BMB, ser. 2, no. 12. Bologna, 1969.
———. *Toscanello in musica*. 2d ed. Venice, 1529. Facs. ed. BMB, ser. 2, no. 10. Ed. Willem Elders.
  Bologna, 1969.

———. *Trattato della natura et cognitione di tutti gli tuoni di canto figurato.* Venice, 1525. Facs. ed. BMB, ser. 2, no. 9. Bologna, 1970.

Accademici della Crusca. *Vocabolario degli Accademici della Crusca, con tre indici delle voci, locuzioni, proverbi Latini, e Greci, posti per entro l'Opera.* Venice, 1612.

Agricola, Martin. *Rudimenta musices.* Wittemberg, 1539. Facs. ed. New York, 1966.

Alberici, Giacomo. *Catalogo breve de gl'illustri et famosi scrittori venetiani, quali tutti hanno dato in luce qualche opera, conforme alla loro professione particolare.* Bologna, 1605.

Antico, Andrea, ed. *Motetti novi e chanzoni franciose.* Venice, 1520.

Aragona, Tullia. *Rime della Signora Tullia di Aragona; et di diversi a lei.* Venice, 1547.

Arcadelt, Jacobi. *Opera omnia.* Ed. Albert Seay. Corpus mensurabilis musicae, no. 31. AIM. 10 vols. [Rome], 1965–71.

Aretino, Pietro. *Lettere di M. Pietro Aretino.* 6 vols. Paris, 1609.

———. *Lettere sull'arte di Pietro Aretino.* Commentary by Fidenzio Pertile. Ed. Ettore Camesasca. 3 vols. in 4. Milan, 1957–60.

———. *The Letters of Pietro Aretino.* Trans. Thomas Caldecot Chubb. Baskerville, 1967.

———. *Il primo libro delle lettere.* Ed. Fausto Nicolini. Bari, 1913.

———. *Ragionamenti nel quale M. Pietro Aretino figura quattro suoi amici che favellano delle corti del mondo e di quella di cielo.* Venice, [1538] 1539.

———. *Tutte le commedie.* Ed. G. B. De Sanctis. Milan, 1968.

———. *The Works of Aretino: Letters and Sonnets.* Ed. Samuel Putnam. New York, 1933.

Ariosto, Ludovico. *Opere.* Ed. Adriano Seroni. Milan, n.d.

———. *Opere minori.* Ed. Cesare Segre. La letteratura italiana: storia e testi, vol. 20. Milan and Naples, 1954.

Aristotle. *"Art" of Rhetoric.* Trans. John Henry Freese. The Loeb Classical Library, vol. 193. Cambridge, Mass., 1926.

———. *Poetics.* Trans. Gerald F. Else. Ann Arbor, 1967.

[Arrivabene, Andrea, ed.] *Il sesto libro. Delle rime di diversi eccellenti autori, nuovamente raccolte, et mandate in luce. Con un discorso di Girolamo Ruscelli.* Venice, 1553.

———. *See also Libro terzo delle rime di diversi; Rime di diversi*

Atanagi, Dionigi, ed. *De le rime di diversi nobili poeti toscani, raccolte da M. Dionigi Atanagi, libro secondo, con una nuova tavola del medesimo. . . .* Venice, 1565.

———, ed. *Rime di diversi nobilissimi, et eccellentissimi autori, in morte della Signora Irene delle Signore di Spilimbergo. Alle quali si sono aggiunti versi Latini di diversi egregij Poeti, in morte della medesima Signora.* Venice, 1561.

Baldacci, Luigi, ed. *Lirici del cinquecento.* 2d ed. Milan, 1975.

Barbaro, Daniele. *Della eloquenza dialogo.* Pref. by Girolamo Ruscelli. Venice, 1557. [Comp. Padua, ca. 1535]. Mod. ed. in Weinberg, *Trattati* 2:335–451.

Bardi, Giovanni de'. "Discorso mandato . . . a Giulio Caccini detto Romano sopra la musica antica, e 'l cantar bene." In Gio. Batista Doni, *La lyra barberina amphichordos.* Vol. 2, *De' trattati di musica.* Ed. Antonio Francesco Gori and Giovanni Battista Martini, pp. 233–48. Florence, 1763.

Bardi, Girolamo. *Delle cose notabili della città di Venetia libri III.* Venice, 1587.

Barges, Antonio. *Di Antonino Barges maestro di cappella alla Casa grande di Venetia il primo libro de villotte a quatro voci con un'altra canzon della galina novamente da lui composte & date in luce.* Venice, 1550.

Barré, Antonio. *Primo libro delle muse, a quattro voci. Madrigali ariosi di Ant. Barre et altri diversi autori, nuovamente stampati.* Rome, 1555.

Bembo, Pietro. *Gli asolani di Messer Pietro Bembo.* Venice, 1505.

———. *Delle lettere di M. Pietro Bembo . . . di nuovo riveduto et corretto da Francesco Sansovino.* 2 vols. Venice, 1560.

———. *Opere del Cardinale Pietro Bembo, ora per la prima volta tutte in un corpo unite.* Venice, 1729.

———. *Opere di M. Pietro Bembo.* Classici italiani, nos. 55–56. Vol. 2, *Rime.* Milan, 1808.

———. *Opere in volgare.* Ed. Mario Marti. Florence, 1961.

———, commentator. *Il Petrarca con dichiaratione non piu stampate, insieme alcune belle annotazioni, tratte dalle dottissime Prose di Monsignor Bembo, cose sommamente utili, à chi di rimare leggiadramente, & senza volere i segni del Petrarca passare, si prenda cura. . . .* Lyons, 1558.

———. *Prose della volgar lingua*. Ed. Mario Marti. Padua, 1967.

———. *Prose e rime*. Ed. Carlo Dionisotti. Turin, 1960.

———. *Prose della volgar lingua, Gli asolani, Rime*. Ed. Carlo Dionisotti. Turin, 1966.

Berchem, Jachet. *Madrigali a cinque voci . . . novamente da lui composti et posti in luce. Libro primo*. . . . Venice, 1546. Mod. ed. Jessie Ann Owens. Sixteenth-Century Madrigal, vol. 1. New York, 1993.

Berni, Francesco. *Rime*. Ed. Giorgio Barberi Squarotti. Turin, 1969.

Bernstein, Lawrence F., ed. *La couronne et fleur des chansons a troys*. 2 pts. Masters and Monuments of the Renaissance, vol. 3. New York, 1984.

Blackburn, Bonnie J., Edward E. Lowinsky, and Clement A. Miller, eds. *A Correspondence of Renaissance Musicians*. Oxford, 1991.

Boccaccio, Giovanni. *Decamerone*. Ed. Mario Marti. 5th ed. 2 vols. Milan, 1984.

Bossinensis, Franciscus. *Le frottole per canto e liuto intabulate da Franciscus Bossinensis*. Ed. Benvenuto Disertori. Istituzioni e monumenti dell'arte musicale italiana, new ser., vol. 3. Milan, 1964.

———. *20 ricercari da sonar laùto dall'unicum di Brera (Libro II, Petrucci, Fossombrone, 1511)*. Ed. Benvenuto Disertori. Milan, 1954.

———. *Tenori e contrabassi intabulati col sopran in canto figurato per cantar e sonar col lauto: libro secundo*. Venice, 1511. Repr. Geneva, 1982.

[Bottrigaro, Hercole, ed]. *Libro quarto delle rime di diversi eccellentiss. autori nella lingua volgare. Novamente raccolte*. Bologna, 1551.

———. See also *Rime di diversi*.

Brevio, Giovanni. *Rime et prose volgari di M. Giovanni Brevio*. Rome, 1545.

Calmeta, Vincenzo. *Prose e lettere edite e inedite*. Ed. Cecil Grayson. Bologna, 1959.

Calmo, Andrea. *Le bizzarre, faconde, et ingeniose rime pescatorie nelle quali si contengono sonetti, stanze, capitoli, madrigali, epitaphij, disperate, e canzoni*. Venice, 1553.

———. *Delle lettere di M. Andrea Calmo libro terzo. Nel quale si contiene varij, & ingeniosi discorsi filosofici, in lingua Veneta composti*. 4 vols. Venice, 1572.

Cambio, Perissone. *Canzone villanesche alla napolitana a quatro voci di Perissone novamente poste in luce*. . . . Venice, 1545.

———. *Madrigali a cinque voci*. Venice, 1545. Mod. ed. Martha Feldman. Sixteenth-Century Madrigal, vol. 2. New York, 1990.

———. *Il primo libro di madrigali a quatro voci*. Venice, 1547. Mod. ed. Martha Feldman. Sixteenth-Century Madrigal, vol. 3. New York, 1989. [RISM 1547[14]].

———. *Il secondo libro di madregali a cinque voci con tre dialoghi a otto voci & uno a sette voci novamente da lui composti & dati in luce*. Venice, 1550.

Capilupi, Lelio. *Rime del S. Lelio, e fratelli de Capilupi*. Mantua, 1585.

Cappello, Bernardo. *Rime di M. Bernardo Cappello corrette, illustrate, e accresciute colla vita dell' autore scritta dall'Abate Pierantonio Serassi, e le annotazioni di Agamiro Pelopideo*. Ed. Pierantonio Serassi. Bergamo, 1753.

Cardamone, Donna G., ed. *Adrian Willaert and His Circle: Canzone Villanesche alla Napolitana and Villotte*. Recent Researches in the Music of the Renaissance, vol. 30. Madison, 1978.

Caro, Annibale. *Delle lettere famigliari del Commendatore Annibale Caro*. Padua, 1742.

Cassola, Luigi. *Madrigali del magnifico Signor Cavallier Luigi Cassola Piacentino*. Venice, 1544.

Castellino, Alvise [il Varoter]. *Il primo libro delle villotte di Alvise Castellino chiamato il Varoter venetiano da lui composti li versi et il canto*. Venice, 1541.

Castelvetro, Lodovico. *Le rime del Petrarca brevemente sposte per Lodovico Castelvetro*. . . . Basel, 1582.

Castiglione, Baldassarre. *The Book of the Courtier*. Trans. George Bull. Harmondsworth, 1967.

———. *Il libro del cortegiano*. Ed. Ettore Bonora. 2d ed. Milan, 1976.

Cicero, Marcus Tullius. *Brutus and Orator*. Trans. G[eorge] L[incoln] Hendrickson and H[arry] M[ortimer] Hubbell. Loeb Classical Library, vol. 342. Rev. ed. Cambridge, Mass., 1971.

———. *De Oratore*. Trans. H[arry] Rackham and E[dward] W[illiam] Sutton. Loeb Classical Library, vols. 348–49. 2 vols. Cambridge, Mass., 1942.

Colonna, Vittoria. *Le rime spirituali della illustrissima Signora Vittoria Colonna Marchesana di Pescara*. Venice, 1548.

Contarini, Gasparo. *De magistratibus et republica Venetorum libri quinque*. Venice, 1551. Trans. Lewes Lewkenor as *The Commonwealth and Government of Venice*. London, 1599.

Conti, Vicenzo, ed. *Rime di diversi autori eccellentiss. Libro nono*. Cremona, 1560.

Corso, Anton Giacomo. *Le rime di M. Anton Giacomo Corso*. Venice, 1550.

Coryat, Thomas. *Coryat's Crudities*. 2 vols. 1611. Repr. Glasgow, 1905.

Crescimbeni, Giovan Mario. *Istorie della volgar poesia*. 2 vols. Venice, 1730.

Crispolti, Cesare. "Lezione del sonetto: lezione recitata publicamente nell'Accademia Insensata. . . ." Mod. ed. in Weinberg, *Trattati* 4:193–206.

Dalla Viola. *See* Viola, Alfonso dalla.

Daniello, Bernardino. *La poetica*. Venice, 1536. Facs. ed. in the series Poetiken des Cinquecento. Ed. Bernhard Fabian. Vol. 2. Munich, 1968. Mod. ed. in Weinberg, *Trattati* 1:227–318.

——. *Sonetti, canzoni, e triomphi di Messer Francesco Petrarca con la spositione di Bernardino Daniello da Lucca*. Venice, 1541.

Dante Alighieri. *The Divine Comedy*. Ed. and trans. Charles S. Singleton. 3 vols. Princeton, 1970–75.

——. *The Divine Comedy of Dante Alighieri: Inferno*. Trans. John D. Sinclair. Oxford, 1939. Repr. New York, 1980.

De diversi autori il quarto libro de madrigali a quattro voci a note bianche novamente dato in luce. Venice, 1554. [Vogel/Einstein 1554¹; RISM 1554²⁸].

Del Lago, Giovanni. *Breve introduttione di musica misurata, composta per il venerabile Pre Giovanni del Lago Venetiano: scritta al Magnifico Lorenzo Moresino patricio Venetiano patron suo honorendissimo*. Venice, 1540. Facs. ed. BMB, ser. 2, no. 17. Bologna, 1969.

Della nuova scielta di lettere di diversi nobilissimi huomini, et eccell. ingegni, scritte in diverse materie, fatta da tutti i libri sin'hora stampati, libro primo [-e secondo]. Venice, 1574.

Delle rime di diversi nobili huomini eccellenti poeti nel la lingua thoscana. Nuovamente ristampate. Libro secondo. [2d ed.] Venice, 1548.

Delle rime scelte di diversi autori, di nuovo corrette e ristampate. Venice, 1587.

Delminio, Giulio Camillo. *Della imitazione*. [Comp. ca. 1530]. Mod. ed. in Weinberg, *Trattati* 1:159–85.

——. *Trattato delle materie che possono venir sotto lo stile dell'eloquente*. [Comp. ca. 1540]. Mod. ed. in Weinberg, *Trattati* 1:319–56.

Dolce, Lodovico. *Opere morali di Marco Tullio Cicerone: cioè tre libri de gli uffici, due dialoghi, l'uno dell'amicitia, l'altro della vecchiezza, sei paradossi secondo l'openione de gli storici*. Trans. Francesco Vendramin. Venice, 1563.

——. *Osservationi nella volgar lingua. Di M. Lodovico Dolce divise in quattro libri*. Venice, 1550.

——, ed. *Il Petrarca novissimamente revisto e corretto da Messer Lodovico Dolce. Con alcuni dottiss. avertimenti di M. Giulio Camillo, et Indici del Dolce de' concetti, e delle parole, che nel Poeta si trovano. . . .* Venice, 1554.

——, trans. *La poetica d'Horatio*. Venice, 1535.

[——], ed. *Prima parte delle stanze di diversi illust. poeti raccolte da M. Lodovico Dolce. . . .* Venice, 1580.

[——], ed. *Rime di diversi signori napolitani, e d'altri. Nuovamente raccolte et impresse. Libro settimo*. Venice, 1556.

——. See also *Libro quinto delle rime di diversi; Rime di diversi*.

Domenichi, Lodovico. *La nobiltà delle donne . . . Corretta, & di nuovo ristampata*. Venice, 1551.

Donato, Baldassare. *Baldissara Donato musico e cantor in santo Marco, le napolitane, et alcuni madrigali a quattro voci da lui novamente composte, corrette, & misse in luce*. Venice, 1550.

——. *Il primo libro d'i madregali a cinque & a sei voci*. Venice, 1553; 1560. Mod. ed. Martha Feldman. Sixteenth-Century Madrigal, vol. 10. New York, 1991.

Doni, Antonfrancesco. *Dialogo della musica*. Venice, 1544. Ed. G. Francesco Malipiero and Virginio Fagotto. Collana di musiche veneziane inedite e rare, no. 7. Vienna, 1964.

——. *Lettere d'Antonfrancesco Doni*. Venice, 1544.

——. *La libraria*. Venice, 1550. Facs. ed. BMB, ser. 1, no. 13. Bologna, 1979.

——. *I marmi*. Mod. ed. Ezio Chiorboli. 2 vols. Bari, 1928.

——. *Inferni del Doni Accademico Pellegrino. Libro secondo de mondi*. Venice, 1553.

——. *Pistolotti amorosi del Doni, con alcune altre lettere d'amore di diversi autori, ingegni mirabili et nobilissimi.* Venice, 1552.

——. *La seconda libraria.* Venice, 1551.

——. *Tre libri di lettere del Doni e i termini della lingua toscana.* Venice, 1552.

Le dotte. See Verdelot, Philippe.

Fano, Giovambattista Dragoncino da. *Lode delle nobildonne vinitiane del secolo moderno.* N.p., 1547.

Fantasie recercari contrapunti a tre voci di M. adriano & da altri autori appropriati per cantare & sonare d'ogni sorte di stromenti, con dui regina celi, l'uno di M. adriano & l'altro di M. cipriano, sopra uno medesimo canto fermo, novamente dati in luce. Venice, 1551. [RISM 1551¹⁶].

Fenaruolo, Girolamo. *Rime di Mons. Girolamo Fenaruolo.* Venice, 1574.

Ferroni, Giulio, ed. *Poesia italiana del cinquecento.* Milan, 1978.

Festa, Constanzo. *Primo libro de madrigali a tre voci con la gionta de quaranta madrigali di Jhan Gero, novamente ristampato. . . .* Venice, 1541.

Ficino, Marsilio. *Marsilio Ficino fiorentino filosofo eccellentissimo de le tre vite.* Trans. Lucio Fauno [Giovanni Tarcagnota]. Venice, 1548.

Finck, Hermann. *Practica musica.* Wittemberg, 1556. Facs. ed. BMB, ser. 2, no. 21. Bologna, 1969.

Fiorino, Gasparo. *Libro secondo canzonelle a tre e a quatro voci.* Venice, 1574.

Fortunio, Giovanni Francesco. *Regole grammaticali della volgar lingua.* Ancona, 1516.

——. *Regole grammaticali della volgar lingua . . . nuovamente reviste, et con somma diligentia corrette.* Venice, 1545.

Franco, Niccolò. *Dialoghi piacevoli.* Venice, 1545.

——. *Il Petrarchista, dialogo . . . nel quale si scuoprono nuovi secreti sopra il Petrarca.* Venice, 1539. Mod. ed. Roberto L. Bruni. Exeter, 1979.

——. *La Philena . . . Historia amorosa ultimamente composta. . . .* Mantua, 1547.

——. *Le pistole vulgari di M. Nicolo Franco.* Venice, 1539.

Franco, Veronica. *Gaspara Stampa–Veronica Franco: Rime.* Ed. Abdelkader Salza. Bari, 1913.

——. *Lettere familiari a diversi.* Venice, 1580. Mod. ed. *Lettere dall'unica edizione del MDLXXX.* Ed. Benedetto Croce. Naples, 1949.

Frangipane, Cornelio. *Saggio di rime e prose.* Ed. Lorenzo Cosatti. Milan, 1812.

Gabrieli, Andrea and Giovanni. *Concerti di Andrea e di Gio: Gabrieli . . . primo libro e secondo.* Venice, 1587.

Gaffurius, Franchinus. *Practica musice.* Milan, 1496. Ed. and trans. Clement A. Miller as *Practica musicae.* Musicological Studies and Documents, no. 20. AIM. [Rome], 1968.

Galilei, Vincenzo. *Dialogo della musica antica, et della moderna.* Florence, 1581. Facs. ed. New York, 1967.

——. *Fronimo dialogo, nel quale si contengono le vere, et necessarie regole del intavolare la musica nel liuto.* Venice, 1568. Facs. of 1584 ed. BMB, ser. 2, no. 22. Bologna, 1969.

Ganassi dal Fontego, Silvestro. *Lettione seconda pur della prattica di sonare il violone d'arco da tasti.* Venice, 1543. Facs. ed. BMB, ser. 2, no. 18b. Bologna, 1970.

——. *Regola rubertina.* Venice, 1542. Facs. ed. BMB, ser. 2, no. 18a. Bologna, 1976.

——. *Regola rubertina, First and Second Part: A Manual of Playing the Viola da Gamba and of the Playing the Lute, Venice, 1542 and 1543.* Trans. Hildemarie Peter from the German ed. of Daphne and Stephen Silvester. Berlin-Lichterfelde, 1972.

Garzoni da Bugnacavallo, Tommaso. *La piazza universale di tutte le professioni del mondo, e nobili et ignobili.* Rev. ed. Venice, 1585.

Gelli, Giovanni Battista. *Tutte le lettioni di Giovan Battista Gelli, fatte da lui nella Accademia fiorentina.* Florence, 1551.

Gero, Jhan. *Il secondo libro di madrigali a tre voci.* 2d ed. Venice, 1556.

Giambullari, Pierfrancesco. *Lettioni sopra Dante.* In *Lettioni d'Accademici Fiorentini sopra Dante, libro primo,* pp. 53–68, 83–96. Florence, 1547.

Giannotti, Donato. *Lettere italiane (1526–1571).* Ed. Furio Diaz. Vol. 2. Milan, 1974.

——. *Libro della republica de' vinitiani.* [Venice], 1540.

——. See also *Secondary Sources,* Starn, Rudolph.

Gigli, Giuseppe, and Fausto Nicolini, eds. *Novellieri minori del cinquecento: G. Parabosco—S. Erizzo.* Bari, 1912.

Giraldi, Lilio Gregorio. [*De poetica et poetarum dialogus* I.] In *Historiae poetarum tam graecorum quam latinorum dialogi decem . . .* , pp. 1–123. Basel, 1545.

Glareanus, Henricus. *Dodecachordon.* Basel, 1547. Facs. ed. Monuments of Music and Music Literature, 2d ser., no. 65. New York, 1967.

Glaser, Victoria, ed. *Three Italian Partsongs.* Boston, 1983.

Habiti d'huomeni e donne venetiane con la processione della ser.^{ma} *signoria et altri particolari. . . .* Venice, 1570.

Harrán, Don, ed. *The Anthologies of Black-Note Madrigals.* Corpus mensurabilis musicae, no. 73. AIM. 5 vols. Neuhausen-Stuttgart, 1978.

Heyden, Sebald. *De arte canendi.* Nuremberg, 1540. Ed. and trans. Clement A. Miller. Musicological Studies and Documents, no. 26. AIM. [Rome], 1972.

Horace. *Satires, Epistles, and Ars Poetica.* Trans. H. Rushton Fairclough. Loeb Classical Library, vol. 194. Rev. ed. Cambridge, Mass., 1929.

Jhan, Maitre. *Il primo libro de i madrigali, di Maistre Ihan, maestro di capella, dello eccellentissimo Signor Duca di Ferrara, & di altri eccellentissimi auttori. Novamente posto in luce.* Venice, 1541.

[Landi, Ortensio]. *Paradossi cioè, sententie fuori del comun parare, novellamente venute in luce, opra non men dotta, che piacevole, & in due parti separata.* Lyons, 1543.

[———]. *Quattro libri de dubbi con le solutioni a ciascun dubbio accommodate.* Venice, 1552.

[———]. *Sette libri de cathaloghi a' varie cose appartenenti, non solo antiche, ma anche moderne: opera utile molto alla historia, et da cui prender si po materia di favellare d'ogni proposto che si occorra.* Venice, 1552; colophon 1553.

[Lanfranco], Giovanni Maria da Terenzo. *Scintille di musica.* Brescia, 1533. Facs. ed. BMB, ser. 2, no. 15. Bologna, 1970.

Lenzoni, Carlo. *In difesa della lingua fiorentina, e di Dante. Con le regole da far bella et numerosa la prosa.* Florence, 1556.

Levi, Eugenia, ed. *Lirica italiana nel cinquecento e nel seicento fino all'Arcadia. . . .* Florence, 1909.

Libro primo de la fortuna. N.p., n.d. [I-Bc R 141; RISM {c. 1530}¹ {recte c. 1526}].

Libro primo de la serena. See Madrigali novi.

Libro quarto delle rime di diversi eccellentiss. autori nella lingua volgare. Novamente raccolte. [Ed. Hercole Bottrigaro]. Bologna, 1551.

Libro quinto delle rime di diversi illustri signori napoletani, e d'altri nobilissimi ingegni. Nuovamente raccolte, e con nova additione ristampate. [Ed. Lodovico Dolce.] [2d ed.] Venice, 1555.

Libro terzo delle rime di diversi nobilissimi et eccellentissimi autori nuovamente raccolte. [Ed. Andrea Arrivabene]. Venice, 1550.

Liburnio, Niccolò. *Le tre fontane . . . in tre libbri divise, sopra la grammatica, et eloquenza di Dante, Petrarcha, et Boccaccio.* Venice, 1526.

———. *Le vulgari elegantie di Messer Nicolao Liburnio.* Venice, 1521.

Lowinsky, Edward E., ed. *The Medici Codex of 1518: A Choirbook of Motets Dedicated to Lorenzo de' Medici, Duke of Urbino.* Monuments of Renaissance Music, vols. 3–5. 3 vols. Chicago, 1968.

Machiavelli, Niccolò. *Discorso o dialogo intorno alla nostra lingua.* Ed. Bortolo Tommaso Sozzi. Turin, 1976.

Madrigali novi de diversi excellentissimi musici libro primo de la serena. Rome, 1530; 1533. [RISM 1530²; 1534¹⁵].

Magno, Celio. *Canzone in morte del clarissimo M. Domenico Veniero.* N.p., n.d. [ca. 1582].

———. *Rime di Celio Magno et Orsatto Giustiniano.* Venice, 1600.

Manutio, Paolo, ed. *Lettere volgari di diversi nobilissimi huomini, et eccellentissimi ingegni scritte in diverse materie.* Venice, 1542.

Manuzio il giovane, Aldo. *Il perfetto gentiluomo.* Venice, 1584.

Marcellino, Marco Valerio. *Il diamerone di m. Valerio, ove con vive ragioni si mostra, la morte non esser qual male, che 'l senso si persuade. Con una dotta e giudiciosa lettera, over discorso intorno alla lingua volgare.* Venice, 1564.

Marenzio, Luca. *Opera Omnia.* Ed. Bernhard Meier and Roland Jackson. Corpus mensurabilis musicae, no. 72. AIM. 6 vols. to date. Neuhausen-Stuttgart, 1976–.

———. *Sämtliche Werke.* Ed. Alfred Einstein. Publikationen älterer Musik. 2 vols. Vol. 4, pt. 1; vol. 6. Leipzig, 1929; 1931.

Marot, Clement. *Les Epistres: Edition critique*. Ed. C. A. Mayer. London, 1958.

Martelli, Lodovico. *Opere di Lodovico Martelli corrette et, con diligentia ristampata. Aggiuntovi il quarto di Vergilio, tradotto del medesimo*. Florence, 1548.

———. *Rime di Lodovico Martelli fiorentino*. 3d printing. Lucca, 1730.

———. *Rime volgari di Lodovico di Lorenzo Martelli. . . .* Rome, 1533.

Mei, Girolamo. *See* Palisca, *Letters of Girolamo Mei*.

Meier, Helga, ed. *Fünf Madrigale venezianischer Komponisten um Adrian Willaert zu 4–7 Stimmen*. Das Chorwerk, vol. 105. Wolfenbüttel, 1969.

Messa motetti canzonni novamente stampate libro primo. N.p., [1526].

[Michiel, Marcantonio]. *The Anonimo: Notes on Pictures and Works of Art in Italy Made by an Anonymous Writer in the Sixteenth Century*. Trans. Paolo Mussi. Ed. George C. Williamson. London, 1903.

Molino, Antonio. *I dilettevoli madrigali a quatro voci . . . Libro primo*. Venice, 1568.

Molino, Girolamo. *Rime di M. Girolamo Molino nuovamente venute in luce*. Venice, 1573. With a biography by Giovan Mario Verdizzotti.

Montaigne, Michel de. *Oeuvres complètes*. Ed. Pléiade. [Paris], 1962.

Monte, Philippe de. *Primo libro de' madrigali spirituali a cinque voci*. Venice, 1581.

Monteverdi, Claudio. *Tutte le opere*. Ed. G. Francesco Malipiero. 17 vols. Asolo, 1926–42; Venice, 1966.

Muscetta, Carlo, and Daniele Ponchiroli, eds. *Poesia del quattrocento e del cinquecento*. Parnaso italiano, no. 4. Turin, 1959.

Muzio, Girolamo. *Dell'arte poetica*. Mod. ed. in Weinberg, *Trattati* 2:163–209.

———. *Battaglie di Hieronimo Mutio Giustinopolitano per la diffesa dell'italica lingua, con alcune lettere . . . annotationi sopra il Petrarca*. Venice, 1582.

———. *Il duello del Mutio Justinopolitano*. Venice, 1550.

———. *Il gentiluomo . . . In questo volume distinto in tre dialoghi si tratta la materia della nobilità: & si mostra quante ne siano origine; come si acquisti; come si conservi; e come si perda. . . .* Venice, 1571.

———. *Lettere del Mutio iustinopolitano*. Venice, 1551. Mod. ed. L. Borsetto. Bologna, 1985.

———. *Rime diverse del Mutio Iustino Politano* [including the *Arte poetica*]. Venice, 1551. Mod. ed. Weinberg, *Trattati* 2:163–209.

———. *La Varchina*. [Venice, 1573.] Repr. in *L'ercolano; dialogo di Benedetto Varchi . . . con . . . La Varchina di Muzio. . . .* Ed. Pietro dal Rio. Florence, 1846.

Naich, Hubert. *Exercitium seraficum. Madrigali di M. Hubert Naich a quattro & a cinque voci, tutte cose nove & non piu viste in stampa da persona*. Rome, [ca. 1540].

Nardi, Jacopo. *Istorie della città di Firenze*. Ed. Agenore Gelli. 2 vols. Florence, 1858.

Nasco, Giovanni. *Madrigali di Giovanni Nasco a cinque voci maestro de la nobile et virtuosa Accademia d'i signori Filarmonici veronesi*. Venice, 1548.

Novello, Lodovico. *Mascherate . . . di piu sorte et varii soggetti appropriati al carnevale nuovamente da lui composte . . . libro primo a quatro voci*. Venice, 1546.

Nuova scelta di rime di diversi begli ingegni; frà le quali ne sono molte del Tansillo non più per l'adietro impresse, e pur' hora date in luce. Genoa, 1573.

Nuova scelta di rime di molti elevati ingegni dell'eta nostra, nella quale sono leggiadramente spiegati vari concetti d'Amore. . . . Pavia, 1593.

Owens, Jessie Ann, gen. ed. *Sixteenth-Century Madrigal*. 30 vols. New York, 1987–.

Palisca, Claude V. *Girolamo Mei (1519–1594): Letters on Ancient and Modern Music to Vincenzo Galilei and Giovanni Bardi*. Musicological Studies and Documents, no. 3. AIM. [Rome], 1960. 2d ed. 1977.

Parabosco, Girolamo. *Composizione a due, tre, quattro, cinque e sei voci*. Ed. Francesco Bussi. Piacenza, 1961.

———. *I diporti*. Venice, [ca. 1550]. Repr. in *Novellieri minori del cinquecento: G. Parabosco—S. Erizzo*. Ed. Giuseppe Gigli and Fausto Nicolini, pp. 1–199. Bari, 1912.

———. *Libro primo [-al quarto] delle lettere amorose di M. Girolamo Parabosco*. 4 vols. Venice, 1573.

———. *Madrigali a cinque voci di Girolamo Parabosco discipulo di M. Adriano novamente da lui composti et posti in luce*. Venice, 1546.

———. *La notte*. Venice, 1546.

——. *Il primo libro dei madrigali, 1551.* Ed. Nicola Longo. "Europa delle Corti." Centro studi sulle società di antico regime. Biblioteca del Cinquecento, no. 37. Rome, 1987.

——. *Il primo libro delle lettere famigliari . . . et il primo libro de' suoi madrigali.* Venice, 1551.

——. *I quattro libri delle lettere amorose.* Ed. Thomaso Porcacchi. Venice, 1561. Rev. ed. 1607.

——. *Rime di M. Girolamo Parabosco.* Venice, 1547.

——. *La seconda parte delle rime di M. Girolamo Parabosco.* Venice, 1555.

Parthenio, Bernardino. *Della imitatione poetica.* Venice, 1560. Mod. ed. of the "Libro Primo," Weinberg, *Trattati* 2:519–58.

Perissone. *See* Cambio, Perissone.

Petrarca, Francesco. *Canzoniere.* Ed. Gianfranco Contini and Daniele Ponchiroli. Turin, 1964.

——. *Letters from Petrarch.* Trans. Morris Bishop. Bloomington, 1966.

——. *Petrarch's Lyric Poems: The "Rime sparse" and Other Lyrics.* Ed. and trans. Robert M. Durling. Cambridge, Mass., 1976.

——. *Letters on Familiar Matters: Rerum familiarum libri.* Trans. Aldo S. Bernardo. Baltimore and London, 1985.

——. *Le "Rime sparse."* Ed. Ezio Chiòrboli. Milan, 1924.

Petrucci, Ottaviano. *Frottole, Buch I und IV: Nach dem Erstlingsdrucken von 1504 und 1505 (?).* Ed. Rudolf Schwartz. Publikationen älterer Musik, vol. 8. Leipzig, 1935. Repr. Hildesheim, 1967.

Ponchiroli, Daniele, ed. *Lirici del cinquecento.* Turin, 1958.

Portinaro, Francesco. *Primo libro de madrigali a cinque voci novamente da lui composti et dati in luce. . . .* Venice, 1550.

——. *Il primo libro . . . a quatro voci . . . con due madrigali a sei voci.* Venice, 1563.

Pozzi, Mario, ed. *Trattatisti del cinquecento.* Vol. 1, *Bembo, Speroni e Gelli.* Milan and Naples, 1978.

Quadrio, Francesco Saverio. *Della storia e ragione d'ogni poesia, volumi quattro. . . .* Bologna and Milan, 1739–44.

Quintilian. *The Institutio oratoria.* Trans. H.E. Butler, 4 vols. Loeb Classical Library, vols. 124–27. Cambridge, Mass., 1920.

Raccolta di prose fiorentine: tomo quinto contenente lettere. Venice, 1735.

Raccolta ferrarese di opuscoli. Vol. 17. Venice, 1785.

Rime de' piu illustri poeti italiani scelte dall'abbate Antonini. Parte prima. Ed. Annibale Antonini. Paris, 1731.

Rime di diversi illustri signori napoletani, et d'altri nobiliss. ingegni. Nuovamente raccolte, et con nuova additione ristampate. Libro quinto. [Ed. Lodovico Dolce]. Venice, 1552.

Rime di diversi nobili huomini et eccellenti poeti nella lingua thoscana. Libro secondo. Venice, 1547.

Rime di diversi signori napoletani e d'altri. Nuovamente raccolte et impresse. Libro settimo. [Ed. Lodovico Dolce]. Venice, 1556.

Rime diverse di molti eccellentiss. auttori nuovamente raccolte. Libro primo. [Ed. Lodovico Domenichi]. Venice, 1545.

Rime diverse di molti eccellentiss. auttori nuovamente raccolte. Libro primo, con nuova additione ristampato. [Ed. Lodovico Domenichi.] 2d ed. Venice, 1546.

Rore, Cipriano de. *Di Cipriano il secondo libro de madregali a cinque voci insieme alcuni di M. Adriano et altri autori a misura comune novamente posti in luce a cinque voci. Venetijs apud Antonium Gardane. 1544.* [RISM 1544[17]].

——. *Di Cipriano Rore et di altri eccellentissimi musici il terzo libro di madrigali a cinque voci novamente da lui composti et non piu posti in luce. Con diligentia stampati. Musica nova & rara come a quelli che la canteranno & udiranno sara palese. Venetijs 1548 apresso Hieronimo Scotto.* [RISM 1548[9]].

——. *Di Cipriano Rore il terzo libro de madrigali a cinque voci dove si contengono le Vergine, et altri madrigali novamente con ogni diligentia ristampato. A cinque voci.* Venice, 1552.

——. *Di Cipriano Rore i madrigali a cinque voci, nuovamente posti in luce. Venetijs apud Hieronymum Scotum. 1542.* [Primo libro, 1st ed.].

——. *Di Cipriano Rore i madrigali a cinque voci, nuovamente ristampati, et con ogni diligentia corretti con la gionta. Venetiis apud Hieronymum Scotum. 1544.* [Primo libro, repr. ed.].

——. *Musica di Cipriano Rore sopra le stanze del Petrarcha in laude della Madonna, et altri madrigali a cinque voci, con cinque madrigali di due parte l'uno del medesimo autore bellissimi non piu veduti, insieme quatro madrigali nuovi a cinque di Messer Adriano. Libro terzo.* [Cantus] *In Venetia appresso di Antonio Gardane. M.D.XLVIII.* [RISM 1548[10]].

———. *Opera omnia*. Ed. Bernhard Meier. Corpus mensurabilis musicae, no. 14. AIM. 8 vols. Rome and Neuhausen-Stuttgart, 1959–77.

Ruscelli, Girolamo. *Del modo de comporre in versi, nella lingua italiana*. Venice, 1559.

———. "Discorso secondo nel quale si discorrono molte cose, intorno all'Osservationi della lingua volgare." In *Tre discorsi di Girolamo Ruscelli, a M. Lodovico Dolce . . .*, pp. 45–82. Venice, 1553.

———, ed. *I fiori delle rime de' poeti illustri, nuovamente raccolti et ordinati da Girolamo Ruscelli. Con alcune annotationi del medesimo, sopra i luoghi, che le ricercano per l'intendimento delle sentenze, ò per le regole & precetti della lingua, & dell'ornamento*. Venice, 1558.

———, ed. *Il Petrarca, nuovamente con la perfetta ortografia della lingua volgare, corretto da Girolamo Ruscelli. Con alcune annotationi, & un pieno Vocabolario del medesimo, sopra tutte le voci, che nel libro si contengono, bisognose di dichiaratione, d'avvertimento, & di regola, et con uno utilissimo rimario di M. Lanfranco Parmegiano, & un raccolto di tutti gli Epiteti usati dall'autore*. Venice, 1554.

Sannazaro, Iacobo. *Opere volgari*. Ed. Alfredo Mauro. Bari, 1961.

Sansovino, Francesco. *L'arte oratoria secondo i modi della lingua volgare, di Francesco Sansovino divisa in tre libri. Ne quali si ragiona tutto quello ch'all'artificio appartiene, cosi del poeta come dell'oratore, con l'autorità de i nostri scrittori*. Venice, 1546.

[———]. *Delle cose notabili che sono in Venetia. Libri due, ne quali ampiamente, e con ogni verità si contengono*. Venice, 1565.

———. "La retorica." Mod. ed. in Weinberg, *Trattati* 1:451–67.

———. *Sette libri di satire di Lodovico Ariosto, Hercole Bentivoglio, Luigi Alamanni, Pietro Nelli, Antonio Vinciguerra, Francesco Sansovino, e d'altri scrittori . . . Con un discorso in materia della satira. Di nuovo raccolti per Francesco Sansovino*. 1560; Venice, 1573. Mod. ed. of the "Discorso in materia della satira" in Weinberg, *Trattati* 1:513–18.

———. *Venezia città nobilissima et singolare descritta in XIII. libri da Francesco Sansovino. . . .* Venice, 1581. Rev. ed. Giustiniano Martinoni. Venice, 1663.

———, ed. *Diversi oratoni volgarmente scritte da gli huomini illustri de tempi nostri*. Venice, 1561.

[Sansovino, Francesco, adaptation of Bernardino Tomitano]. *Dialogo del gentilhuomo veneziano cioè institutione nella quale si discorre quali hanno a essere i costumi del nobile di questa città, per acquistare gloria & honore*. Venice, 1566.

Sanudo il giovane, Marin. *De origine, situ et magistratibus urbis venetae, ovvero La città di Venetia (1493–1530)*. Ed. Angela Caracciolo Aricò. Milan, 1980.

Sanuto, Marino. *I diarii*. Ed. Rinaldo Fulin et al. 58 vols. Venice, 1879–1903.

Scelta di sonetti e canzoni de' più eccellenti rimatori d'ogni secolo. Parte prima, che contiene i rimatori antichi del 1400., e del 1500. fino al 1550. 2d ed. Bologna, 1718.

Scotto, Girolamo. *Madrigali a quatro voci di Geronimo Scotto con alcuni alla misura breve, et altri a voce pari. . . . Libro primo*. Venice, 1542.

Segni, Bernardo. *Istorie fiorentine dall'anno MDXXVII al MDLV*. Ed. G. Gargani. Florence, 1857.

Slim, H. Colin, ed. *A Gift of Madrigals and Motets*. 2 vols. Chicago, 1972. Original altus parts publ. as *Ten Altus Parts at Oscott College Sutton Coldfield*. Ed. H. Colin Slim. Printed privately by the editor, n.d.

———. *Musica nova accommodata per cantar et sonar sopra organi; et altri strumenti, composta per diversi eccellentissimi musici. In Venetia, MDXL*. Foreword by Edward E. Lowinsky. Monuments of Renaissance Music, vol. 1. Chicago, 1964.

Spathafora, Bartolomeo. *Quattro orationi di M. Bartolomeo Spathafora di Moncata, gentil'huomo venetiano l'una in morte del serenissimo Marc'Antonio Trivisano. . . .* Venice, 1554.

Speroni, Sperone. *Dialogo delle lingue*. Venice, 1544. Repr. ed. in *Les sources italiennes de la "Deffense et illustration de la langue françoise."* Ed. Pierre Villey, pp. 111–46.

———. *Opere di M. Sperone Speroni degli Alvarotti, tratte da' mss. originali*. 5 vols. Venice, 1740.

Stampa, Gaspara. *Rime*. Ed. Maria Bellonci and Rodolfo Ceriello. 2d ed. Milan, 1976.

———. *Rime di Madonna Gaspara Stampa*. Venice, 1554.

Stoquerus, Gaspar. *De musica verbali, libro duo: Two Books on Verbal Music*. [ca. 1570]. Trans. and ed. Albert C. Rotola, S.J. Greek and Latin Music Theory. Lincoln, Nebr., and London, 1988.

Strozzi, Lorenzo. *Le vite degli uomini illustri della casa Strozzi; commentario di Lorenzo di Filippo Strozzi ora intieramente publicato con un ragionamento inedito di Francesco Zeffi sopra la vita dell'autore*. Ed. Pietro Stromboli. Florence, 1892.

Strunk, Oliver, ed. *Source Readings in Music History: From Classical Antiquity through the Romantic Era.* New York, 1950.

Tansillo, Luigi. *Poesie liriche edite ed inedite di Luigi Tansillo con prefazione e note.* Ed. F[rancesco] Fiorentino. Naples, 1882.

———. *Il canzoniere edito ed inedito secondo una copia dell'autografo ed altri manoscritti e stampe.* Vol. 1, *Poesie amorose, pastorali e pescatorie, personali, famigliari e religiose.* Ed. Erasmo Pèrcopo. Naples, 1926.

Tasso, Bernardo. *Delle lettere di M. Bernardo Tasso.* 3 vols. in 2. Padua, 1733–51.

———. *Il ragionamento della poesia.* In *Delle lettere,* vol. 2. Mod. ed. in Weinberg, *Trattati* 2:567–84.

Tasso, Torquato. *Discorsi del Signor Torquato Tasso dell'arte poetica; et in particolare del poema heroico.* Venice, 1587.

———. *Lezione recitata nell'Accademia Ferrarese sopra il sonetto "Questa vita mortal" ecc. di monsignor della Casa.* [comp. ca. 1565–72].

———. *Le prose diverse di Torquato Tasso.* Ed. Cesare Guasti. 2 vols. Florence, 1875.

Tassoni, Alessandro, Girolamo Muzio, and Lodovico Antonio Muratori, eds. *Le rime di Francesco Petrarca riscontrate co i testi a penna della Libreria Estense e co i fragmenti dell'originale d'esso poeta. S'aggiungono d'Alessandro Tassoni, e le osservazioni di Lodovico Antonio Muratori Bibliotecario del Sereniss. Sig. Duca di Modena.* 3d ed. Venice, 1759.

Tebaldeo, Antonio. *Rime di M. Antonio Tibaldeo Ferrarese.* Modena, 1499.

Tempo, Antonio da. *De ritimis vulgaribus, videlicet de sonetis: de balatis: de cantionibus extensis: de rotondellis: madrigalibus: de serventesiis. . . .* Venice, 1509.

Tiburtino, Giuliano. *Fantesie, et recerchari a tre voci, accomodate da cantare et sonare per ogni instrumento, composte da M. Giuliano Tiburtino da Tievoli, musico eccellentiss. con la giunta di alcuni altri recerchari, et madrigali a tre voce, composti da lo eccellentiss. Adriano Vuigliart, et Cipriano Rore suo discepolo. . . .* Venice, 1549. [RISM 1549³⁴].

Tinctoris, Johannes. *The Art of Counterpoint (Liber de arte contrapuncti).* Trans. and ed. Albert Seay. AIM. [Rome], 1961.

Tomitano, Bernardino. *Lettera di M. Bernardino Tomitano al Magnifico M. Francesco Longo del Clarissimo M. Antonio.* [n.p., n.d.]

———. *Oratione di M. Bernardino Tomitano, recitata per nome de lo studio de le arti padovano, ne la creatione del serenissimo principe di Vinetia M. Marcantonio Trivisano.* Venice, 1554.

———. *Ragionamenti della lingua toscana di M. Bernardin Tomitano. I precetti della rhetorica secondo l'artificio d'Aristotile & Cicerone nel fine del secondo libro nuovamente aggionti.* Venice, 1546. Orig. ed. 1545, in 2 vols., without the addition at the end of Book 2.

Toralto, Vincenzo. *La Veronica, o del sonetto.* Genoa, 1589.

Toscanella, Orazio. *I nomi antichi, e moderni delle provincie, regioni, città, castella, monti, laghi, fiumi, mari, golfi, porti, & isole dell'Europa, dell'Africa, & dell'Asia; con le graduationi loro in lunghezza, e larghezza & un abreve descrittione delle suddette parti del mondo. . . .* Venice, 1567.

———. *Precetti necessarie.* Venice, 1562. Mod. ed. in Weinberg, *Trattati* 2:559–66.

Trissino, Giovan Giorgio. *La poetica di M. Giovan Giorgio Trissino.* Pts. 1–4, Vicenza, 1529; pts. 5–6, Vicenza, 1562. Facs. ed. in the series *Poetiken des Cinquecento.* Ed. Bernhard Fabian. Vol. 24. Munich, 1969. Mod. ed. in Weinberg, *Trattati* 1:28–158; 2:5–90.

Vander Straeten, Edmond, ed. *La musique aux Pays-Bas avant le XIXe siècle: Documents inédits et annotés. Compositeurs, virtuoses, théoriciens, luthiers; opéras, motets, airs nationaux, académies, maîtresses, livres, portraits, etc. avec planches de musique et table alphabétique.* 8 vols. Brussels, 1882. Repr. in 4 vols. with an intro. by Edward E. Lowinsky. New York, 1969.

Vanneo, Stefano. *Recanetum de musica aurea.* Rome, 1533. Facs. ed. BMB, ser. 2, no. 16. Bologna, 1969.

Varchi, Benedetto. *L'Hercolano dialogo di Messer Benedetto Varchi, nelqual si ragiona generalmente delle lingue, & in particolare della Toscana, e della fiorentina. Composto da lui sulla occasione della disputa occorsa tra 'l Commendator Caro, e M. Lodovico Castelvetro.* Venice, 1570.

———. *Storia fiorentina.* 2 vols. Florence, 1963.

———. *Storia fiorentina.* Ed. Gaetano Milanesi. 3 vols. Florence, 1857.

Vasari, Giorgio. *Il libro delle ricordanze di Giorgio Vasari.* Ed. Alessandro del Vita. Rome, 1938.

Veggio, Claudio. *Madrigali a quattro voci di Messer Claudio Veggio, con la gionta di sei altri di Arcadelth della misura a breve.* Venice, 1540.

Venier, Domenico. *Rime di Domenico Veniero senatore viniziano raccolte ora per la prima volta ed illustrate.* Ed. Pierantonio Serassi. Bergamo, 1751.

Verdelot, Philippe. *De i madrigali di Verdelotto et de altri eccellentissimi auttori a cinque voci, libro secondo.* [Venice], 1537. [RISM 1538²¹].

——. *Di Verdelotto tutti i madrigali del primo, et secondo libro a quatro voci. Con la gionta de i madrigali del medesmo auttore, non piu stampati. Aggiontovi anchora altri madrigali novamente composti da Messer Adriano, & da altri eccellentissimi musici.* Venice, 1540. [RISM 1540²⁰].

——. *Le dotte, et eccellente compositioni de i madrigali a cinque voci da diversi perfettissimi musici fatte. Novamente raccolte, & con ogni diligentia stampate. Auttori. Di Adriano Vuillaert, & di Leonardo Barri suo discipulo. Di Verdelotto. Di Constantio Festa. Di Archadelt. Di Corteggia. Di Jachet Berchem. De Yvo, & di Nolet.* Venice, 1540. [RISM 1540¹⁸].

——. *Intavolatura de li madrigali di Verdelotto da cantare et sonare nel lauto, 1536.* Renaissance Music Prints, vol. 3. Ed. Bernard Thomas. London, 1980. Facs. ed. Archivum Musicum, Collana di testi rari, no. 36. Florence, 1980.

——. *Madrigali di Verdelot et de altri autori a sei voci novamente con alcuni madrigali novi ristampati & corretti.* Venice, 1546. [RISM 1546¹⁹].

——. *La piu divina, et piu bella musica, che se udisse giamai delli presenti madrigali, a sei voci. Composti per lo eccellentissimo Verdelot. Et d'altri musici.* . . . Venice, 1541. [RISM 1541¹⁶].

——. *Il secondo libro di Verdelot insieme con altri bellissimi madrigali di Adriano, et di Constantio Festa. Nuovamente stampati.* . . . [Venice], 1536. [RISM 1536⁷].

Vicentino, Nicola. *L'antica musica ridotta alla moderna prattica.* Rome, 1555. Facs. ed. Edward E. Lowinsky. Documenta musicologica, ser. 1. Druckschriften-Faksimiles, no. 17. Kassel, 1959.

——. *Del unico Adrian Willaerth discipulo don Nicola Vicentino madrigali a cinque voci per theorica e pratica da lui composti al nuovo modo dal celeberrimo suo maestro ritrovato. Libro primo.* Venice, 1546.

——. *Opera omnia.* Ed. Henry W. Kaufmann. Corpus mensurabilis musicae, no. 26. AIM. [Rome], 1963.

Vico, Enea. *Discorsi . . . sopra le medaglie de gli antichi divisi in due libri.* Venice, 1558.

Villey [Desmeserets], Pierre. *Les sources italiennes de la "Deffense et illustration de la langue françoise" de Joachim du Bellay.* Bibliothèque litteraire de la renaissance, ser. 1, vol. 9. Paris, 1969.

Viola, Alfonso dalla. *Primo libro di madrigali d'Alfonso dalla Viola novamente stampato.* Ferrara, 1539.

——. *Il secondo libro di madrigali de M. Alfonso dalla Viola novamente stampato.* Ferrara, 1540.

"Vita di Benedetto Varchi." In Benedetto Varchi, *Storia fiorentina.* Ed. Gaetano Milanesi, 1:21–31. 3 vols. Florence, 1857.

Weinberg, Bernard, ed. *Trattati di poetica e retorica del cinquecento.* 4 vols. Bari, 1970–74.

Wert, Giaches de. *Collected Works.* Ed. Carol MacClintock with Melvin Bernstein. Corpus mensurabilis musicae, no. 24. AIM. [Rome], 1962.

——. *Di Giaches de Wert l'ottavo libro de madrigali a cinque voci, novamente composto e dato in luce.* Venice, 1586.

——. *Madrigali del fiore, libro secondo.* Venice, 1561.

Willaert, Adrian. *Musica nova di Adriano Willaert all'illustrissimo et eccellentissimo signor il signor donno Alfonso d'Este prencipe di Ferrara.* Venice, 1559.

——. *Opera omnia.* Ed. Hermann Zenck, Walter Gerstenberg, and Helga Meier. Corpus mensurabilis musicae, no. 3. AIM. [Rome], 1950–.

Zane, Giacomo. *Rime.* Venice, 1562.

[Zantani, Antonio]. *Le imagini con tutti i riversi trovati et le vite de gli imperatori tratte dalle medaglie et dalle historie de gli antichi. Libro primo.* [Venice], 1548.

[——]. *Omnium caesarum verissime imagines ex antiquis numismatis desumptae.* [Venice], 1553.

[Zantani, Antonio], and Zuan Iacomo Zorzi, eds. *La eletta di tutta la musica intitolata corona de diversi novamente stampate libro primo.* Venice, 1569.

Zarlino, Gioseffo. *The Art of Counterpoint: Part Three of "Le istitutioni harmoniche," 1558.* Trans. Guy A. Marco and Claude V. Palisca. New York, 1976.

——. *Dimostrationi harmoniche.* Venice, 1571. Facs. ed. Ridgewood, N.J., 1966.

——. *"Le istitutioni harmoniche": A Facsimile of the 1558 Edition.* New York, 1965.

———. *Le istitutioni harmoniche di M. Gioseffo Zarlino da Chioggia; nelle quali; oltra le materie appartenenti alla musica; si trovano dichiarati molti luoghi di poeti, d'historici, & di filosofi; si come nel leggerle si potrà chiaramente vedere. Con privilegio dell'Illustriss. Signoria di Venetia, per anni X.* Venice, 1558.

———. *Le istitutioni harmoniche del Rev. Messere Gioseffo Zarlino da Chioggia.* 2d ed. Venice, 1573. Facs. ed. Ridgewood, N.J., 1966.

———. *Musici moduli liber primus.* Venice, 1549.

———. *Nove madrigali a cinque voci.* Collana di musiche veneziane inedite e rare, no. 3. Venice, [1963].

———. *On the Modes: Part Four of "Le Istitutioni Harmoniche," 1558.* Trans. Vered Cohen and ed. with an introduction by Claude V. Palisca. New Haven, 1983.

———. *Sopplimenti musicali.* Venice, 1588. Facs. ed. Ridgewood, N.J., 1966.

SECONDARY SOURCES

Abrams, M. H. *The Mirror and the Lamp: Romantic Theory and the Critical Tradition.* Oxford, 1953.

Adler, Sara Marie. "Veronica Franco's Petrarchan *Terze Rime:* Subverting the Master's Plan." *Italica* 65 (1988): 213–33.

Agee, Richard J. "Filippo Strozzi and the Early Madrigal." *JAMS* 38 (1985): 227–37.

———. "The Privilege and Venetian Music Printing in the Sixteenth Century." Ph.D. diss. Princeton University, 1982.

———. "Ruberto Strozzi and the Early Madrigal." *JAMS* 36 (1983): 1–17.

———. "The Venetian Privilege and Music-Printing in the Sixteenth Century." *Early Music History* 3 (1983): 1–42.

Agee, Richard J., and Jessie Ann Owens. "La stampa della *Musica nova* di Willaert." *Rivista italiana di musicologia* 24 (1989): 219–305.

Agostini Nordio, Tiziana. "Poesie dialettali di Domenico Venier." *Quaderni veneti* 14 (1991): 33–56.

Aikema, Bernard, and Dulcia Meijers. *Nel regno dei poveri: arte e storia dei grandi ospedali veneziani in età moderna, 1474–1797.* Venice, 1989.

Alonso, Dámaso. "La poesia del Petrarca e il petrarchismo (mondo estetico della pluralità)." *Studi petrarcheschi* 7 (1961): 73–120.

Alonso, Dámaso, and Carlos Bousoño. *Seis calas en la expresión literaria española (prosa, poesía, teatro).* 4th ed. Madrid, 1970.

Appadurai, Arjun. "Introduction: Commodities and the Politics of Value." In *The Social Life of Things: Commodities in Cultural Perspective.* Ed. Arjun Appadurai, pp. 3–63. Cambridge, 1986.

Aquilecchia, Giovanni. "Pietro Bembo e altri poligrafi a Venezia." In *Storia della cultura veneta: dal primo quattrocento al concilio di Trenta.* Vol. 3, pt. 2. Ed. Girolamo Arnaldi and Manlio Pastore Stocchi, pp. 61–98. Vicenza, 1980.

Ascoli, Albert Russell. "Petrarch's Middle Age: Memory, Imagination, History, and the 'Ascent of Mount Ventoux.'" *Stanford Italian Review* 10 (1992): 5–43.

Bakhtin, M[ikhail] M. *The Dialogic Imagination: Four Essays.* Ed. Michael Holquist. Trans. Michael Holquist and Caryl Emerson. Austin, 1981.

———. *Rabelais and His World.* Trans. Hélène Iswolsky. Bloomington, 1984.

Baldacci, Luigi. *Il petrarchismo italiano nel cinquecento.* Rev. ed. Padua, 1974.

Baldauf-Berdes, Jane L. *Women Musicians of Venice: Musical Foundations, 1525–1855.* Oxford, 1993.

Balduino, Armando. "Le esperienze nella poesia volgare." In *Storia della cultura veneta: dal primo quattrocento al Concilio di Trenta.* Vol. 3, pt. 1. Ed. Girolamo Arnaldi and Manlio Pastore Stocchi, pp. 265–367. Vicenza, 1980.

———. "Petrarchismo veneto e tradizione manoscritta." In *Petrarca, Venezia e il Veneto.* Ed. Giorgio Padoan, pp. 243–70. Civiltà veneziana, Saggi 21. Florence, 1976.

Balestrieri, Lina. *Feste e spettacoli alla corte di Farnese.* Quaderni parmigiani, no. 6. Parma, 1981.

Bandini, Fernando. "La letteratura pavana dopo il Ruzzante tra il manierismo e barocco." In *Storia della cultura veneta: il seicento.* Vol. 4, pt. 1. Ed. Girolamo Arnaldi and Manlio Pastore Stocchi, pp. 327–62. Vicenza, 1983.

Barbi, Michele. *Della fortuna di Dante nel secolo XVI*. Pisa, 1890.

Barblan, Guglielmo. "Aspetti e figure del cinquecento musicale veneziano." In *La civiltà veneziana del rinascimento,* pp. 57–80. Fondazione Giorgio Cini, Centro di Cultura e Civiltà. Florence, 1958.

Barzaghi, Antonio. *Donne o cortegiane? la prostituzione a Venezia: documenti di costume dal XVI al XVIII secolo*. Verona, 1980.

Bassanese, Fiora A. *Gaspara Stampa*. Boston, 1982.

———. "Gaspara Stampa's Poetics of Negativity." *Italica* 61 (1984): 355–46.

Battagia, Michele. *Delle accademie veneziane: dissertazione storica*. Venice, 1826.

Baxandall, Michael. *Giotto and the Orators: Humanist Observers of Painting in the Renaissance and the Discovery of Pictorial Composition*. Oxford, 1971.

Beck, Hans-Georg, Manoussos Manoussacas, and Agostino Pertusi, eds. *Venezia centro di mediazione tra oriente e occidente (secoli XV–XVI): aspetti e problemi*. Fondazione Giorgio Cini, Centro di Cultura e Civiltà. 2 vols. Florence, 1977.

Beck, Hermann. "Grundlagen des venezianischen Stils bei Adrian Willaert und Cyprian de Rore." In *Renaissance-Muziek, 1400–1600: Donum natalicum René Bernard Lenaerts*. Ed. Jozef Robijns, pp. 39–50. Louvain, 1969.

———. *Die venezianischer Musikschule im 16. Jahrhundert*. Wilhelmshaven, 1968.

Bella, Valeria, and Piero Bella, eds. *Cartografia rara: antiche carte geografiche, topografiche e storiche della collezione Franco Novacco*. Milan, [1986].

Bent, Margaret. "*Resfacta* and *Cantare Super Librum*." *JAMS* 36 (1983): 371–91.

Benzoni, Gino. "Le accademie." In *Storia della cultura veneta: il seicento*. Vol. 4, pt. 1. Ed. Girolamo Arnaldi and Manlio Pastore Stocchi, pp. 131–62. Vicenza, 1983.

———. "L'accademia: appunti e spunti per un profilo." *Ateneo veneto* 26 (1988): 37–58.

———. *Gli affanni della cultura: intelletuali e potere nell'Italia della Controriforma e barocca*. Milan, 1978.

———. "Aspetti della cultura urbana nella società veneta del '5–'600: le accademie." *Archivio Veneto* 108 (1977): 87–159.

———, ed. *I dogi*. Milan, 1982.

Berger, Karol. *Musica ficta: Theories of Accidental Inflections in Vocal Polyphony from Marchetto da Padova to Gioseffo Zarlino*. Cambridge, 1987.

———. *Theories of Chromatic and Enharmonic Music in Late 16th Century Italy*. Ann Arbor, 1976.

Bergin, Thomas G. *Petrarch*. New York, 1970.

Bergquist, Ed Peter, Jr. "The Theoretical Writings of Pietro Aaron." Ph.D. diss. Columbia University, 1964.

Bernstein, Jane A. "The Burning Salamander: Assigning a Printer to Some Sixteenth-Century Music Prints." *Music Library Association Notes* 42 (1985–86): 483–501.

———. "Financial Arrangements and the Role of Printer and Composer in Sixteenth-Century Italian Music Printing." *Acta musicologica* 62 (1990): 39–56.

Bernstein, Lawrence F. " 'La couronne et fleur des chansons a troys': A Mirror of the French Chanson in Italy in the Years between Ottaviano Petrucci and Antonio Gardano." *JAMS* 26 (1973): 1–68.

Bever, Ad[olphe] van, and Ed[mond] Sansot-Orland. *Oeuvres galantes des conteurs italiens*. 2d ser., 4th ed. Paris, 1907.

Bianchini, Giuseppe. *Girolamo Parabosco: scrittore e organista del secolo XVI*. Miscellanea di Storia Veneta, ser. 2, vol. 6, pp. 207–486. Venice, 1899.

Bianconi, Lorenzo, and Antonio Vassalli. "Circolazione letteraria e circolazione musicale del madrigale: il caso G. B. Strozzi." In *Il madrigale tra cinque e seicento*. Ed. Paolo Fabbri, pp. 123–38. Bologna, 1988.

Black, Christopher F. *Italian Confraternities in the Sixteenth Century*. Cambridge, 1989.

Blanc, Pierre. "Pétrarque lecteur de Cicéron: les scolies pétrarquiennes du *De Oratore* et de l'*Orator*." *Studi petrarcheschi* 9 (1978): 109–66.

Bolzoni, Lina. "L'Accademia Veneziana: splendore e decadenza di una utopia enciclopedica." In *Università, accademie e società scientifiche in Italia e in Germania dal cinquecento al settecento*. Ed. Laetitia Boehm and Ezio Raimondi, pp. 117–67. Annali dell'Istituto Storico Italo-Germanico, no. 9. Bologna, 1981.

Bombi, A. "Sul ruolo dei ritmi nel procedimento compositivo del madrigale." *Rivista italiana di musicologia* 26 (1991): 173–204.

Bongi, Salvatore. *Annali di Gabriel Giolito de' Ferrari.* 2 vols. Rome, 1890–97. Repr. Rome, n.d.

Boorman, Stanley. "Some Non-Conflicting Attributions, and Some Newly Anonymous Compositions, from the Early Sixteenth Century." *Early Music History* 6 (1986): 109–57.

———. "What Bibliography Can Do: Music Printing and the Early Madrigal." *Music & Letters* 72 (1991): 236–58.

Borsellino, Nino. *Gli anticlassicisti del cinquecento.* Rome, 1973.

Borsellino, Nino, and Marcello Aurigemma. *Il cinquecento dal rinascimento alla controriforma.* La letteratura italiana: Storia e testi, vol. 4. 2 vols. Rome, 1973.

Bosco, Umberto. "Il linguaggio lirico del Petrarca tra Dante e il Bembo." *Studi petrarcheschi* 7 (1961): 121–32.

Bossuyt, Ignace. *Adriaan Willaert (ca. 1490–1562): Leven en werk, stil en genres.* Louvain, 1985.

Bourdieu, Pierre. *Outline of a Theory of Practice.* Trans. Richard Nice. Cambridge, 1977.

Bouwsma, William J. *Venice and the Defense of Republican Liberty: Renaissance Values in the Age of the Counter Reformation.* Berkeley and Los Angeles, 1968.

Branca, Vittore. "Ermolao Barbaro and Late *Quattrocento* Venetian Humanism." In *Renaissance Venice.* Ed. John R. Hale, pp. 218–43. London, 1973.

———, ed. *Rinascimento europeo e rinascimento veneziano.* Civiltà europea e civiltà veneziana: aspetti e problemi, vol. 3. Fondazione Giorgio Cini, Centro di Cultura e Civiltà. Florence, 1967.

———, ed. *Umanesimo europeo e umanesimo veneziano.* Civiltà europea e civiltà veneziana: aspetti e problemi, vol. 2. Fondazione Giorgio Cini, Centro di Cultura e Civiltà. Florence, 1963.

Bridges, Thomas W. "The Publishing of Arcadelt's First Book of Madrigals." 2 vols. Ph.D. diss. Harvard University, 1982.

Brown, Howard Mayer. "Bossinensis, Willaert and Verdelot: Pitch and the Conventions of Transcribing Music for Lute and Voice in Italy in the Early Sixteenth Century." *Revue de musicologie* 75 (1989): 25–46.

———. "Chansons for the Pleasure of a Florentine Patrician: Florence, Biblioteca del Conservatorio di Musica, MS Basevi 2442." In *Aspects of Medieval and Renaissance Music: A Birthday Offering in Honor of Gustave Reese,* ed. Jan LaRue et al., pp. 56–66. New York, 1966. Repr. New York, 1978.

———. "A Cook's Tour of Ferrara in 1529." *Rivista italiana di musicologia* 10 (1975): 216–41.

———. "Emulation, Competition, and Homage: Imitation and Theories of Imitation in the Renaissance." *JAMS* 35 (1982): 1–48.

———. *Instrumental Music Printed before 1600: A Bibliography.* Cambridge, Mass., 1965.

———. *Music in the Renaissance.* Englewood Cliffs, N.J., 1976.

———. "The Music of the Strozzi Chansonnier (Florence, Biblioteca del Conservatorio di Musica, MS Basevi 2442)." *Acta musicologica* 40 (1968): 115–29.

———. *Sixteenth-Century Instrumentation: The Music for the Florentine Intermedi.* Musicological Studies and Documents, no. 30. [Rome], 1973.

———. "Verso una definizione dell'armonia nel sedicesimo secolo: sui 'madrigali ariosi' di Antonio Barré." *Rivista italiana di musicologia* 25 (1990): 18–60.

———. "Words and Music: Willaert, the Chanson, and the Madrigal about 1540." In *Florence and Venice, Comparisons and Relations: Acts of Two Conferences at Villa I Tatti in 1976–1977.* Vol. 2, *Il Cinquecento.* Ed. Christine Smith with Salvatore I. Camporeale, pp. 217–66. Florence, 1980.

Brucker, Gene A. *Renaissance Florence.* New York, 1969.

Brunelli, Bruno. "Due accademie padovane del cinquecento." *Atti e memorie della R. Accademia di scienze, lettere, ed arte in Padova,* pp. 43–57. Padua, 1920.

Bruni, Francesco. "Sperone Speroni e l'Accademia degli Infiammati." *Filologia e letteratura* 13 (1967): 24–71.

Bullard, Melissa Meriam. *Filippo Strozzi and the Medici: Favour and Finance in Sixteenth-Century Florence and Rome.* Cambridge, 1980.

———. "Marriage Politics and the Family in Renaissance Florence: The Strozzi-Medici Alliance in 1508." *American Historical Review* 74 (1979): 51–71.

Burke, Peter. *Culture and Society in Renaissance Italy, 1420–1540.* London, 1972.

Bussi, Francesco. *Umanità e arte di Gerolamo Parabosco: madrigalista, organista e poligrafo.* Piacenza, 1961.

Butchart, David S. " 'La Pecorina' at Mantua, *Musica Nova* at Florence." *Early Music* 13 (1985): 358–66.

Caanitz, Mechtild. *Petrarca in der Geschichte der Musik.* Freiburg im Breisgau, 1969.

Caffi, Francesco. *Storia della musica sacra nella già cappella ducale di San Marco in Venezia dal 1318 al 1797: riedizione annotata con aggiornamenti bibliograW (al 1984).* Ed. Elvidio Surian. 2 vols. Venice, 1854. Rev. ed. Florence, 1987.

Cairns, Christopher. *Pietro Aretino and the Republic of Venice: Researches on Aretino and His Circle in Venice, 1527–1556.* Biblioteca dell' "Archivum Romanicum." Ser. 1, vol. 194. Florence, 1985.

Cambier, A. "De grootste roem van de stad Ronse: De komponist Cypriaan De Ro[de]re, 'omnium musicorum princeps.' " *Annalen Geschieden Oudheidkundige Kring van Ronse en het Tenement van Inde* 30 (1981): 5–56.

———. "Meer gegevens over de Ronsische komponist Cypriaan De Rore." *Annalen Geschieden Oudheidkundige Kring van Ronse en het Tenement van Inde* 31 (1982): 91–97.

Carapetyan, Armen. "The *Musica Nova* of Adriano Willaert." *Journal of Renaissance and Baroque Music* 1 (1946–47): 200–221.

———. "The *Musica Nova* of Adriano Willaert: With a Special Reference to the Humanistic Society of 16th-Century Venice." Ph.D. diss. Harvard University, 1945.

Cardamone, Donna G. *The "Canzone villanesca alla napolitana" and Related Forms, 1537–1570.* 2 vols. Ann Arbor, 1981.

Carlson, Catherine Allen. "Gaspara Stampa and Cinquecento Petrarchism: Innovations in the Transposition of Convention." Ph.D. diss. Yale University, 1978.

Carroll, Linda L. "Carnival Rites as Vehicles of Protest in Renaissance Venice." *The Sixteenth Century Journal* 16 (1985): 487–502.

Casagrande di Villaviera, Rita. *Le cortigiane veneziane del cinquecento.* Milan, 1968.

Casimiri, Raffaele. "Il codice Vatic. 5318: carteggio musicale autografo tra teorici e musici del sec. XVI dall'anno 1517 al 1543." *Note d'Archivio per la Storia Musicale* 16 (1939): 109–31.

Cassimatis, Gregorio. "L'Humanisme dans la société vénetienne au XVe siècle." In *Venezia, centro di mediazione tra oriente e occidente (secoli XV–XVI): aspetti e problemi.* Ed. Hans-Georg Beck et al., 1:359–68. 2 vols. Florence, 1977.

Castelli, Pierfilippo. *La vita di Giovangiorgio Trissino, oratore, e poeta.* Venice, 1753.

Cattin, Giulio. "Formazione e attività delle cappelle polifoniche nelle cattedrali: La musica nelle città." In *Storia della cultura veneta: dal primo quattrocento al Concilio di Trenta.* Vol. 3, pt. 3. Ed. Girolamo Arnaldi and Manlio Pastore Stocchi, pp. 267–96. Vicenza, 1981.

Cerretta, Florindo [V.]. *Alessandro Piccolomini: letterato e filosofo senese del cinquecento.* Siena, 1960.

———. "An Account of the Early Life of the Accademia degli Infiammati in the Letters of Alessandro Piccolomini to Benedetto Varchi." *Romanic Review* 48 (1957): 249–64.

Cesari, Gaetano. "Le origini del madrigale cinquecentesco." *Rivista musicale italiana* 19 (1912): 1–34 and 380–428.

Chambers, D. S. *The Imperial Age of Venice, 1380–1580.* London, 1970.

Chambers, David, and Brian Pullan, eds., with Jennifer Fletcher. *Venice: A Documentary History, 1450–1630.* Oxford, 1992.

Charteris, Richard, ed. *Essays on Italian Music in the Cinquecento.* Altro Polo. Sydney, 1990.

Chartier, Roger. *The Cultural Uses of Print in Early Modern France.* Trans. Lydia G. Cochrane. Princeton, 1987.

———, ed. *The Culture of Print: Power and Uses of Print in Early Modern Europe.* Trans. Lydia G. Cochrane. Princeton, 1989.

Chiappelli, Fredi. "An Analysis of Structuration in Petrarch's Poetry." In *Francis Petrarch, Six Centuries Later: A Symposium.* Ed. Aldo Scaglione, pp. 105–16. North Carolina Studies in the Romance Languages and Literature: Symposia, no. 3. Chapel Hill and Chicago, 1975.

———. *Studi sul linguaggio del Petrarca: la canzone delle visioni.* Florence, 1971.

Chojnacki, Stanley. "Dowries and Kinsmen in Early Renaissance Venice." *Journal of Interdisciplinary History* 5 (1975): 571–600.

———. "In Search of the Venetian Patriciate: Families and Factions in the Fourteenth Century." In *Renaissance Venice*, pp. 47–90. Ed. John R. Hale. London, 1973.

——. "Kinship Ties and Young Patricians in Fifteenth-Century Venice." *RQ* 38 (1985): 240–70.

——. "Patrician Women in Early Renaissance Venice." *Studies in the Renaissance* 21 (1974): 176–203.

——. "La posizione della donna a Venezia nel cinquecento." In *Tiziano e Venezia: Convegno Internazionale di Studi, Venezia, 1976.* Ed. Neri Pozza et al., pp. 65–70. Vicenza, 1980.

Cicogna, Emmanuele A. *Delle inscrizioni veneziane.* 6 vols. Venice, 1834–61.

Clubb, Louise George. "Castiglione's Humanistic Art and Renaissance Drama." In *Castiglione: The Ideal and the Real in Renaissance Culture.* Ed. Robert W. Hanning and David Rosand, pp. 191–208. New Haven, 1983.

Cobban, Alan B. *The Medieval Universities: Their Development and Organization.* London, 1975.

Cochrane, Eric. *Florence in the Forgotten Centuries, 1527–1800: A History of Florence and the Florentines in the Age of the Grand Dukes.* Chicago and London, 1973.

Contini, Gianfranco. "Preliminari sulla lingua del Petrarca." In *Varianti e altra linguistica: una raccolta di saggi (1938–1968),* pp. 169–92. Turin, 1970.

Cortelazzo, Manlio. "Uso, vitalità e espansione del dialetto." In *Storia della cultura veneta: il seicento.* Vol. 4, pt. 1. Ed. Girolamo Arnaldi and Manlio Pastore Stocchi, pp. 363–79. Vicenza, 1983.

Cox, Virginia. *The Renaissance Dialogue: Literary Dialogue in Its Social and Political Contexts, Castiglione to Galileo.* Cambridge, 1993.

Crane, Thomas Frederick. *Italian Social Customs of the Sixteenth Century and Their Influence on the Literatures of Europe.* New Haven, 1920.

Crawford, David. "A Review of Costanza Festa's Biography." *JAMS* 28 (1975): 102–11.

Croce, Benedetto. *Poeti e scrittori del pieno e del tardo rinascimento.* 2d ed. 3 vols. Bari, 1945–52.

Crollalanza, G. B. di. *Dizionario storico-blasonico delle famiglie nobili e notabili italiane estinte e fiorenti.* 3 vols. Pisa, 1886–90. Repr. Bologna, 1965.

Cumming, Julie E. "Music for the Doge in Early Renaissance Venice." *Speculum* 67 (1992): 324–64.

D'Accone, Frank A. "Alessandro Coppini and Bartolomeo degli Organi: Two Florentine Composers of the Renaissance." *Analecta musicologica* 4 (1967): 38–76.

——. "Bernardo Pisano: An Introduction to His Life and Works." *Musica disciplina* 17 (1963): 115–35.

——. "Transitional Text Forms and Settings in an Early 16th-Century Florentine Manuscript." In *Words and Music—The Scholar's View: A Medley of Problems and Solutions Compiled in Honor of A. Tillman Merritt by Sundry Hands.* Ed. Laurence Berman, pp. 29–58. Cambridge, Mass., 1972.

Dahlhaus, Carl. *Untersuchungen über die Entstehung der harmonischen Tonalität.* Kassel, 1968. Trans. Robert O. Gjerdigen as *Studies on the Origin of Harmonic Tonality.* Princeton, 1990.

——. "War Zarlino Dualist?" *Musikforschung* 10 (1957): 286–90.

Da Mosto, Andrea. *L'Archivio di Stato di Venezia: indice generale, storico descrittivo e analittico.* Bibliothèque des "Annales Institutorum," vol. 5. 2 vols. Rome, 1937–40.

——. *I dogi di Venezia nella vita pubblica e privata.* Repr. Florence, 1977.

Davis, James Cushman. *The Decline of the Venetian Nobility as a Ruling Class.* Baltimore, 1962.

Davis, Natalie Zemon. *Society and Culture in Early Modern France.* Stanford, 1975.

Debenedetti, Santorre. *Gli studi provenzali in Italia nel cinquecento.* Turin, 1911.

De Gramatica, M. R. "Daniello, Bernardino." *Dizionario biografico degli italiani* 32:608–10. Rome, 1986.

Della Neva, JoAnn. "Reflecting Lesser Lights: The Imitation of Minor Writers in the Renaissance." *RQ* 42 (1989): 449–79.

Desroussilles, François Dupruigrenet. "L'Università di Padova dal 1405 al Concilio di Trenta." In *Storia della cultura veneta: dal primo quattrocento al Concilio di Trenta.* Vol. 3, pt. 2. Ed. Girolamo Arnaldi and Manlio Pastore Stocchi, pp. 607–47. Vicenza, 1980.

Dionisotti, Carlo. "Bembo, Pietro." *Dizionario biografico degli italiani,* 8:133–51. Rome, 1966.

——. *Geografia e storia della letteratura italiana.* Turin, 1967.

——. "Niccolò Liburnio e la letteratura cortigiana." *Lettere italiane* 14 (1962): 33–58.

——. *Gli umanisti e il volgare fra quattro e cinquecento.* Florence, 1968.

Dizionario biografico degli italiani. Ed. Instituto della Enciclopedico Italiana. 39 vols. to date. Rome, 1960–.

Dizionario enciclopedico della letteratura italiana. Ed. Giuseppe Petronio. 6 vols. Palermo, 1966–70.

Dobbins, Frank. *Music in Renaissance Lyons.* Oxford, 1992.

Doglio, Maria Luisa. "La letteratura ufficiale e l'oratoria celebrativa." In *Storia della cultura veneta: il seicento.* Vol. 4, pt. 1. Ed. Girolamo Arnaldi and Manlio Pastore Stocchi, pp. 163–87. Vicenza, 1983.

Dorosao, Renzo. "Moralità e giustitia a Venezia nel '500–'600: gli Esecutori contro la bestemmia." In *Stato, società, e giustitia nella repubblica veneta (sec. XV–XVIII).* Ed. Gaetano Cozzi, pp. 431–528. Rome, 1980.

Dürr, Walther. "Zum Verhältnis von Wort und Ton im Rhythmus des Cinquecento-Madrigals." *Archiv für Musikwissenschaft* 15 (1958): 89–100.

Edwards, Rebecca A. "Claudio Merulo: Servant of the State and Musical Entrepreneur in Later Sixteenth-Century Venice." Ph.D. diss. Princeton University, 1990.

Einstein, Alfred. *The Italian Madrigal.* Trans. Alexander H. Knappe, Roger H. Sessions, and Oliver Strunk. 3 vols. Princeton, 1949. Repr. Princeton, 1971.

Eisenstein, Elizabeth L. *The Printing Press as an Agent of Change: Communications and Cultural Transformations in Early Modern Europe.* 2 vols. Cambridge, 1979.

——. *The Printing Revolution in Early Modern Europe.* Cambridge, 1983.

Eitner, Robert. "Zwei Briefe von Georg Wytzel." *Monatshefte für Musik-Geschichte* 8, no. 11 (1876): 157–59.

Elwert, W. Theodor. "L'importanza letteraria di Venezia." In *Studi di letteratura veneziana,* pp. 1–52. Fondazione Giorgio Cini, Centro di Cultura e Civiltà. Venice, 1958.

——. "Pietro Bembo e la vita letteraria del suo tempo." In *La civiltà veneziana del rinascimento,* pp. 125–76. Fondazione Giorgio Cini, Centro di Cultura e Civiltà. Florence, 1958.

——. *Studi di letteratura veneziana.* Fondazione Giorgio Cini, Centro di Cultura e Civiltà. Venice, 1958.

——. *Versificazione italiana dalle origini ai giorni nostri.* Bibliotechina del saggiatore, no. 36. Florence, 1973.

Erspamer, Francesco. "Petrarchismo e manierismo nella lirica del secondo cinquecento." In *Storia della cultura veneta: il seicento.* Vol. 4, pt. 1. Ed. Girolamo Arnaldi and Manlio Pastore Stocchi, pp. 189–222. Vicenza, 1983.

Faithfull, R. G. "On the Concept of 'Living Language' in Cinquecento Italian Philology." *Modern Language Review* 48 (1953): 278–92.

Favretti, Elvira. "Una raccolta di rime del cinquecento." *Giornale storico della letteratura italiana* 158 (1981): 543–72.

Febvre, Lucien, and Henri-Jean Martin. *The Coming of the Book: The Impact of Printing, 1450–1800.* Trans. David Gerard. Ed. Geoffrey Nowell-Smith and David Wootton. 1958; London, 1976.

Fedi, Roberto. *La memoria della poesia: canzonieri, lirici e libri d'amore nel rinascimento.* Rome, 1990.

Fehl, Philipp P. *Decorum and Wit, the Poetry of Venetian Painting: Studies in the History of the Classical Tradition.* Vienna, 1992.

Feldman, Martha. "The Academy of Domenico Venier, Music's Literary Muse in Mid-Cinquecento Venice." *RQ* 44 (1991): 476–512.

——. "The Composer as Exegete: Interpretations of Petrarchan Syntax in the Venetian Madrigal." *Studi musicali* 18 (1989): 203–38.

——. "In Defense of Campion: A New Look at His Ayres and *Observations.*" *Journal of Musicology* 5 (1987): 226–56.

——. "Petrarchizing the Patron in *Cinquecento* Venice." In International Musicological Society, *Report of the 15th Congress, Madrid, 1992.* In press.

——. "Rore's 'selva selvaggia': The *Primo libro* of 1542." *JAMS* 42 (1989): 547–603.

——. "Venice and the Madrigal in the Mid-Sixteenth Century." 2 vols. Ph.D. diss. University of Pennsylvania, 1987.

Fenlon, Iain. "Fiorino, Gasparo." *The New Grove* 6:601–2.

——. "Lepanto: The Arts of Celebration in Renaissance Venice." *Proceedings of the British Academy* 73 (1987): 201–36.

——. "Venice: Theatre of the World." In *Man and Music: The Renaissance from the 1470s to the End of the 16th Century.* Ed. Iain Fenlon, pp. 102–32. Englewood Cliffs, N.J., 1989.

Fenlon, Iain, and James Haar. *The Italian Madrigal in the Early Sixteenth Century: Sources and Interpretation*. Cambridge, 1988.

Ferrai, L[uigi] A[lberto]. *Lorenzino de' Medici e la società cortigiana del cinquecento*. Milan, 1891.

Ferroni, Giulio, and Amedeo Quondam. *La locuzione artificiosa: teoria ed esperienza della lirica a Napoli nell'età del manierismo*. Rome, 1973.

Field, Arthur. *The Origins of the Platonic Academy of Florence*. Princeton, 1988.

Finlay, Robert. *Politics in Renaissance Venice*. London, 1980.

Flamini, Francesco. *Storia letteraria d'Italia: il cinquecento*. Milan, 1901.

Flora, Francesco. *Storia della letteratura italiana*. Vol. 2, pt. 1, *Il cinquecento*. Verona, 1948.

Floriani, Piero. "Grammatici e teorici della letteratura volgare." In *Storia della cultura veneta: dal primo quattrocento al concilio di Trenta*. Vol. 3, pt. 2. Ed. Girolamo Arnaldi and Manlio Pastore Stocchi, pp. 139–81. Vicenza, 1980.

Forster, Leonard. *The Icy Fire: Five Studies in European Petrarchism*. Cambridge, 1969.

Franzoni, Lanfranco. "Antiquari e collezionisti nel cinquecento." In *Storia della cultura veneta: dal primo quattrocento al Concilio di Trenta*. Vol. 3, pt. 3. Ed. Girolamo Arnaldi and Manlio Pastore Stocchi, pp. 207–66. Vicenza, 1981.

Freccero, John. *Dante: The Poetics of Conversion*. Ed. Rachel Jacoff. Cambridge, Mass., 1986.

——. "The Fig Tree and the Laurel: Petrarch's Poetics." *Diacritics* 5 (1975): 34–40.

Fromson, Michele. "Imitation and Innovation in the North Italian Motet, 1560–1605." Ph.D. diss. University of Pennsylvania, 1988.

Gaeta, Franco. "Alcune considerazioni sul mito di Venezia." *Bibliothèque d'Humanisme et Renaissance* 23 (1961): 58–75.

Gallo, F. Alberto. "Citazioni di teorici medievali nelle lettere di Giovanni del Lago." *Quadrivium* 14 (1973): 171–77.

——. "La trattatistica musicale." In *Storia della cultura veneta: dal primo quattrocento al concilio di Trenta*. Vol. 3, pt. 3. Ed. Girolamo Arnaldi and Manlio Pastore Stocchi, pp. 297–314. Vicenza, 1981.

Gerstenberg, Walter. "Um der Begriff einer venezianischen Schule." *Renaissance-muziek 1400–1600: Donum natalicium René Lenaerts*. Ed. Jozef Robijns, pp. 131–42. Louvain, 1969.

Giazotto, Remo. *Harmonici concenti in aere veneto*. Rome, 1954.

Gilbert, Creighton. "When Did a Man in the Renaissance Grow Old?" *Studies in the Renaissance* 14 (1967): 7–32.

Gilbert, Felix. *The Pope, His Banker, and Venice*. Cambridge, Mass., 1980.

——. "Venice in the Crisis of the League of Cambrai." In *Renaissance Venice*. Ed. John R. Hale, pp. 274–92. Totowa, N.J., 1973.

Glixon, Jonathan. "Music at the Venetian *Scuole Grandi*, 1440–1540." Ph.D. diss. Princeton University, 1979.

——. "Music at the Venetian Scuole Grandi, 1440–1540." In *Music in Medieval and Early Modern Europe: Patronage, Sources, and Texts*. Ed. Iain Fenlon, pp. 193–208. Cambridge, 1981.

——. "A Musicians' Union in Sixteenth-Century Venice." *JAMS* 36 (1983): 392–421.

Goldsmith, Elizabeth C. *Exclusive Conversations: The Art of Interaction in Seventeenth-Century France*. Philadelphia, 1988.

——, ed. *Writing the Female Voice: Essays on Epistolary Literature*. Boston, 1989.

Goldthwaite, Richard A. *Private Wealth in Renaissance Florence: A Study of Four Families*. Princeton, 1968.

Grafton, Anthony, and Lisa Jardine. *From Humanism to the Humanities: Education and the Liberal Arts in Fifteenth- and Sixteenth-Century Europe*. London, 1986.

Gray, Hanna H. "Renaissance Humanism: The Pursuit of Eloquence." In *Renaissance Essays from the Journal of the History of Ideas*. Ed. Paul Oskar Kristeller and Philip P. Weiner, pp. 199–216. New York, 1968. Orig. publ. in *Journal of the History of Ideas* 24 (1963): 497–514.

Greenblatt, Stephen. *Marvelous Possessions: The Wonder of the New World*. Chicago, 1991.

——. *Renaissance Self-Fashioning: From More to Shakespeare*. Chicago, 1980.

——. *Shakespearean Negotiations: The Circulation of Social Energy in Renaissance England*. Berkeley and Los Angeles, 1988.

Greene, Roland. *Post-Petrarchism: Origins and Innovations of the Western Lyric Sequence*. Princeton, 1991.

Greene, Thomas M. "*Il Cortegiano* and the Choice of a Game." In *Castiglione: The Ideal and the Real in Renaissance Culture*. Ed. Robert W. Hanning and David Rosand, pp. 1–15. New Haven, 1983.

——. "The Flexibility of the Self in Renaissance Literature." In *The Disciplines of Criticism: Essays in Literary Theory, Interpretation, and History*. Ed. Peter Demetz, Thomas Greene, and Lowry Nelson, Jr., pp. 241–64. New Haven, 1968.

——. *The Light in Troy: Imitation and Discovery in Renaissance Poetry*. New Haven, 1982.

Greggio, Elisa. "Girolamo da Molino." 2 pts. Ser. 18, vol. 2, pp. 188–202 and 255–323. *Ateneo veneto*. Venice, 1894.

Grendler, Paul F. *Critics of the Italian World, 1530–1560: Anton Francesco Doni, Nicolò Franco, & Ortensio Lando*. Madison, 1969.

——. "Francesco Sansovino and Italian Popular History, 1560–1600." *Studies in the Renaissance* 16 (1969): 139–80.

——. *The Roman Inquisition and the Venetian Press, 1540–1605*. Princeton, 1977.

——. *Schooling in Renaissance Italy: Literacy and Learning, 1300–1600*. Baltimore, 1989.

Gronau, Georg. "Zwei Tizianische Bildnisse der Berliner Galerie: I, Das Bildnis des Ranuccio Farnese; II, Das Bildnis der Tochter des Roberto Strozzi." *Jahrbuch der königlich preuszischen Kunstsammlungen* 27 (1906): 3–12.

Grubb, James S. "When Myths Lose Power: Four Decades of Venetian Historiography." *Journal of Modern History* 58 (1986): 43–94.

Haar, James. "Arie per cantar stanze ariotesche." In *L'Ariosto: la musica, i musicisti*. Ed. Maria Antonella Balsano, pp. 31–46. Florence, 1981.

——. "Cambio, Perissone." *The New Grove* 14:535.

——. "The *Capriccio* of Giachet Berchem: A Study in Modal Organization." *Musica disciplina* 42 (1988): 129–56.

——. "The Courtier as Musician: Castiglione's View of the Science and Art of Music." In *Castiglione: The Ideal and the Real in Renaissance Culture*. Ed. Robert W. Hanning and David Rosand, pp. 165–89. New Haven, 1983.

——. "The Early Madrigal: A Re-appraisal of Its Sources and Its Character." In *Music in Medieval and Early Modern Europe: Patronage, Sources, and Texts*. Ed. Iain Fenlon, pp. 163–92. Cambridge, 1981.

——. *Essays on Italian Poetry and Music in the Renaissance, 1350–1600*. Berkeley and Los Angeles, 1986.

——. "False Relations and Chromaticism in Sixteenth-Century Music." *JAMS* 30 (1977): 391–418.

——. "The *Libraria* of Antonfrancesco Doni." *Musica disciplina* 24 (1970): 101–25.

——. "The *Madrigale Arioso*: A Mid-Century Development in the Cinquecento Madrigal." *Studi musicali* 12 (1983): 203–19.

——. "Music in 16th-Century Florence and Venice: Some Points of Comparison and Contrast." In *Florence and Venice, Comparisons and Relations: Acts of Two Conferences at Villa I Tatti in 1976–1977*. Vol. 2, *Il cinquecento*. Ed. Christine Smith with Salvatore I. Camporeale, pp. 267–84. Florence, 1980.

——. "The *Note Nere* Madrigal." *JAMS* 18 (1965): 22–41.

——. "Notes on the *Dialogo della musica* of Antonfrancesco Doni." *Music & Letters* 47 (1966): 198–224.

——. "*Pace non trovo*: A Study in Literary and Musical Parody." *Musica disciplina* 20 (1966): 95–148.

——. "Self-Consciousness about Style, Form, and Genre in 16th-Century Music." *Studi musicali* 3 (1974): 219–31.

——. "Towards a Chronology of the Madrigals of Arcadelt." *Journal of Musicology* 5 (1987): 28–54.

——. "Zarlino's Definition of Fugue and Imitation." *JAMS* 24 (1971): 226–54.

Hainsworth, Peter. *Petrarch the Poet: An Introduction to the "Rerum vulgarium fragmenta."* London, 1988.

Hale, John R., ed. *Renaissance Venice*. London, 1973.

Hall, Dale Emerson. "The Italian Secular Works of Jacquet Berchem." Ph.D. diss. The Ohio State University, 1973.

Hall, Robert A., Jr. *The Italian "Questione della lingua:" An Interpretative Essay*. University of North Carolina Studies in the Romance Languages and Literature, no. 4. Chapel Hill, 1942.

Hanning, Robert W., and David Rosand, eds. *Castiglione: The Ideal and the Real in Renaissance Culture*. New Haven, 1983.

Harrán, Don. "Elegance as a Concept in Sixteenth-Century Music Criticism." *RQ* 41 (1988): 413–38.

———. "Hubert Naich, Musicien, Académicien." *Fontes artes musicae* 28 (1981): 177–94.

———. *In Search of Harmony: Hebrew and Humanistic Elements in Sixteenth-Century Musical Thought*. Musicological Studies and Documents, no. 42. AIM. Neuhausen-Stuttgart, 1988.

———. "New Light on the Question of Text Underlay prior to Zarlino." *Acta musicologica* 45 (1973): 24–56.

———. "Rore and the *Madrigale Cromatico*." *Music Review* 34 (1973): 66–81.

———. "The Theorist Giovanni del Lago: A New View of the Man and His Writings." *Musica disciplina* 27 (1973): 107–51.

———. "Verse Types in the Early Madrigal." *JAMS* 22 (1969): 27–53.

———. *Word-Tone Relations in Musical Thought: From Antiquity to the Seventeenth Century*. Musicological Studies and Documents, no. 40. AIM. Neuhausen-Stuttgart, 1986.

———, ed. *"Maniera" e il madrigale: una raccolta di poesie musicali del cinquecento*. Biblioteca dell' "Archivum Romanicum," vol. 158. Florence, 1980.

Hathaway, Baxter. *The Age of Criticism: The Late Renaissance in Italy*. Ithaca, 1962.

———. *Marvels and Commonplaces: Renaissance Literary Criticism*. New York, 1968.

Hay, Denys. *The Italian Renaissance in Its Historical Background*. 2d ed. Cambridge, 1977.

Herczeg, Giulio. "La struttura della frase nei versi del Petrarca." *Studi petrarcheschi* 8 (1976): 169–96.

———. "La struttura delle antitesi nel *Canzoniere* petrarchesco." *Studi petrarcheschi* 7 (1961): 195–208.

Hermelink, Siegfried. *Dispositiones modorum: Die Tonarten in der Musik Palestrinas und seiner Zeitgenossen*. Tutzing, 1960.

———. "Über Zarlinos Kadenzbegriff." In *Scritti in onore di Luigi Ronga*, pp. 253–73. Milan, 1973.

Herrick, Marvin T. *The Fusion of Horatian and Aristotelian Literary Criticism, 1531–1555*. Illinois Studies in Language and Literature, vol. 32, no. 1. Urbana, Ill., 1946.

Hersh, Donald Lee [Don Harrán]. "Philippe Verdelot and the Early Madrigal." Ph.D. diss. University of California at Berkeley, 1963.

Hertzmann, Erich. *Adrian Willaert in der weltlichen Vokalmusik seiner Zeit: Ein Beitrag zur Entwicklungsgeschichte der niederländisch-französischen und italienischen Liedformen in der ersten Hälfte des 16. Jahrhunderts*. Leipzig, 1931.

Hindman, Sandra L., ed. *Printing the Written Word: The Social History of Books, Circa 1450–1520*. Ithaca, 1991.

Hofer, P. "Early Book Illustration in the Intaglio Medium." *The Print Collector's Quarterly* 21 (1934): 203–27; 295–316.

Hol, J. C. "Cipriano de Rore." In *Festschrift für Karl Nef zum 60. Geburtstag (22. August 1933)*, pp. 134–49. Zurich, 1933.

Howard, Deborah. *The Architectural History of Venice*. London, 1980.

———. *Jacopo Sansovino: Architecture and Patronage in Renaissance Venice*. New Haven, 1975.

Inventari dei manoscritti delle biblioteche d'Italia. Ed. Giuseppe Mazzatinti et al. 106 vols. Vol. 1: Turin, 1887; vols. 2–106: Forli and Florence, 1890–1990.

Javitch, Daniel. "Self-Justifying Norms in the Genre Theories of Italian Renaissance Poets." *Philological Quarterly* 67 (1988): 195–217.

Jeppesen, Knud. "Eine musiktheoretische Korrespondenz des früheren Cinquecento." *Acta musicologica* 12 (1940): 3–39.

———. *La frottola*. 3 vols. Copenhagen, 1968.

Johnson, Alvin H. "The 1548 Editions of Cipriano de Rore's Third Book of Madrigals." *Studies in Musicology in Honor of Otto E. Albrecht*. Ed. John Walter Hill, pp. 110–24. Kassel, 1980.

———. "The Liturgical Music of Cipriano de Rore." Ph.D. diss. Yale University, 1954.

———. "Rore, Cipriano de." *The New Grove* 16:185–90.

Jones, Ann Rosalind. "City Women and Their Audiences: Louise Labé and Veronica Franco." In *Rewriting the Renaissance: The Discourses of Sexual Difference in Early Modern Europe*. Ed. Margaret W. Ferguson, Maureen Quilligan, and Nancy J. Vickers, pp. 299–316 and 390–92. Chicago, 1986.

——. *The Currency of Eros: Women's Love Lyric in Europe, 1540–1620*. Indianapolis, 1990.

——. "Surprising Fame: Renaissance Gender Ideologies and Women's Lyric." In *The Poetics of Gender*. Ed. Nancy K. Miller, pp. 74–95. New York, 1986.

Jonnson, Ritva, and Leo Treitler. "Medieval Music and Language: A Reconsideration of the Relationship." In *Music and Language*, pp. 1–23. Studies in the History of Music, vol. 1. New York, 1983.

Jordan, Constance. *Renaissance Feminism: Literary Texts and Political Models*. Ithaca, 1990.

Kaufmann, Henry William. *The Life and Works of Nicola Vicentino (1511–c.1576)*. Musicological Studies and Documents, no. 11. AIM. Rome, 1966.

Kennedy, William J. *Rhetorical Norms in Renaissance Literature*. New Haven, 1978.

——. "Petrarchan Audiences and Print Technology." *Journal of Medieval and Renaissance Studies* 14 (1984): 1–20.

——. "Petrarchan Textuality: Commentaries and Gender Revisions." In *Discourses of Authority in Medieval and Renaissance Literature*. Ed. Kevin Brownlee and Walter Stephens, pp. 151–68 and 277. Hanover and London, 1989.

Kent, Francis William. *Household and Lineage in Renaissance Florence: The Family Life of the Capponi, Ginori, and Rucellai*. Princeton, 1977.

King, Margaret L. *Venetian Humanism in an Age of Patrician Dominance*. Princeton, 1986.

Kirkendale, Warren. "Ciceronians versus Aristotelians on the Ricercar as Exordium, from Bembo to Bach." *JAMS* 32 (1979): 1–44.

Kleinhenz, Christoph. "The Art of the Sonnet." In *Francis Petrarch, Six Centuries Later: A Symposium*. Ed. Aldo Scaglione, pp. 177–91. North Carolina Studies in the Romance Languages and Literature, Symposia, no. 3. Chapel Hill and Chicago, 1975.

Kristeller, Paul Oskar. "Music and Learning in the Early Italian Renaissance." *Journal of Renaissance and Baroque Music* 1 (1947): 255–74.

——. *The Philosophy of Marsilio Ficino*. Trans. Virginia Conant. Gloucester, Mass., 1964.

——. *Renaissance Thought and Its Sources*. Ed. Michael Mooney. New York, 1979.

——. *Renaissance Thought: The Classic, Scholastic, and Humanist Strains*. New York, 1961. Rev. and enlarged ed. of *The Classics and Renaissance Thought*. Cambridge, Mass., 1955.

Kroyer, Theodor. *Die Anfänge der Chromatik im italienischen Madrigal des XVI. Jahrhunderts*. Publikationen der Internationalen Musikgesellschaft, vol. 4. Leipzig, 1902.

Labalme, Patricia H. *Bernardo Giustiniani: A Venetian of the Quattrocento*. Uomini e dottrini, no. 13. Rome, 1969.

——. "Personality and Politics in Venice: Pietro Aretino." In *Titian: His World and His Legacy*, ed. David Rosand. pp. 119–32. New York, 1982.

Labande-Jeanroy, Thérèse. *La question de la langue en Italie*. Strasbourg and Paris, 1925.

Lane, Frederic C. *Venice: A Maritime Republic*. Baltimore, 1973.

Lanza, Alfonso. *La lirica amorosa veneziana del secolo XVI*. Verona, 1938.

La Via, Stefano. "Cipriano de Rore as Reader and as Read: A Literary Study of Madrigals from Rore's Later Collections (1557–1566)." Ph.D. diss. Princeton University, 1991.

——. "*Madrigale* e rapporto fra poesia e musica nella critica letteraria del cinquecento." *Studi musicali* 19 (1990): 33–70.

Lawner, Lynne. *Lives of the Courtesans: Portraits of the Renaissance*. New York, 1987.

Lazzarini, Lino. "Francesco Petrarca e il primo umanesimo a Venezia." In *Umanesimo europeo e umanesimo veneziano*. Ed. Vittore Branca, pp. 63–92. Fondazione Giorgio Cini, Centro di Cultura e Civiltà. Florence, 1963.

Lenaerts, René. "La Chapelle de Sainte-Marc à Venise sous Adriaen Willaert (1527–1562): Documents inédits." *Bulletin de l'Institut Historique Belge de Rome* 19 (1938): 205–55.

——. "Notes sur Adrien Willaert maître de chapelle de Saint Marc à Venise de 1527 à 1562." *Bulletin de l'Institut Historique Belge de Rome* 15 (1935): 107–17.

——. "Voor de biographie van Adriaen Willaert." In *Hommage à Charles van den Borren: Mélanges*. Ed. Suzanne Clercx and Albert vander Linden, pp. 205–15. Antwerp, 1945.

Lester, Libby J. "Venetian History and Political Thought after 1509." *Studies in the Renaissance* 20 (1973): 7–45.

Lewis, Douglas. "Jacopo Sansovino, Sculptor of Venice." In *Titian: His World and His Legacy.* Ed. David Rosand, pp. 133–90. New York, 1982.

Lewis, Mary S. "Antonio Gardane and His Publications of Sacred Music, 1538–55." Ph.D. diss. Brandeis University, 1979.

——. *Antonio Gardane, Venetian Music Printer, 1538–1569: A Descriptive Bibliography and Historical Study.* Vol. 1, *1538–49.* New York, 1988.

——. "Antonio Gardane's Early Connections with the Willaert Circle." In *Music in Medieval and Early Modern Europe: Patronage, Sources and Texts.* Ed. Iain Fenlon, pp. 209–26. Cambridge, 1981.

——. "Rore's Setting of Petrarch's *Vergine bella:* A History of Its Composition and Early Transmission." *Journal of Musicology* 4 (1985–86): 365–409.

——. "Zarlino's Theories of Text Underlay as Illustrated in His Motet Book of 1549." *Music Library Association Notes* 42 (1985–86): 239–67.

Litta, Pompeo, ed. *Le famiglie celebri italiane.* 15 vols. Milan, 1819–1902.

Llorens, Josephus M. *Cappellae Sixtinae codices, musicis notis instructi sive manu scripti sive praelo excussi.* Studi e testi, no. 202. Vatican City, 1960.

Lockwood, Lewis. "Adrian Willaert and Cardinal Ippolito I d'Este: New Light on Willaert's Early Career in Italy, 1515–21." *Early Music History* 5 (1985): 85–112.

——. *The Counter-Reformation and the Masses of Vincenzo Ruffo.* Vienna, 1970.

——. "Jean Mouton and Jean Michel: French Music and Musicians in Italy, 1505–1520." *JAMS* 32 (1979): 191–246.

——. "Josquin at Ferrara: New Documents and Letters." *Josquin des Prez: Proceedings of the International Josquin Festival-Conference, New York, 21–25 June 1971.* Ed. Edward E. Lowinsky and Bonnie J. Blackburn, pp. 103–37. London, 1976.

Lockwood, Lewis, and Jessie Ann Owens. "Willaert, Adrian." *The New Grove* 20:421–28.

Logan, Oliver. *Culture and Society in Venice, 1470–1790: The Renaissance and Its Heritage.* New York, 1972.

"Londariti, Francesco." *The New Grove* 11:142.

Long, Joan Anne. "The Motets, Psalms, and Hymns of Adrian Willaert: A Liturgico-Musical Study." Ph.D. diss. Columbia University, 1971.

Lowinsky, Edward E. "A Newly Discovered Sixteenth-Century Motet Manuscript at the Biblioteca Vallicelliana in Rome." *JAMS* 3 (1950): 173–232. Rev. version in his *Music in the Culture of the Renaissance* 2:433–82.

——. "A Treatise on Text Underlay by a German Disciple of Francisco de Salinas." In *Festschrift Heinrich Besseler zum sechzigsten Geburtstag,* pp. 231–51. Leipzig, 1962. Repr. in his *Music in the Culture of the Renaissance* 2:868–83.

——. "*Calami sonum ferentes:* A New Interpretation." In his *Music in the Culture of the Renaissance* 2:595–626.

——. *Cipriano de Rore's Venus Motet: Its Poetic and Pictorial Sources.* Provo, Utah, 1986. Repr. in his *Music in the Culture of the Renaissance* 2:575–94.

——. "Humanism in the Music of the Renaissance." *Medieval and Renaissance Studies* 9. *Proceedings of the Southeastern Institute of Medieval and Renaissance Studies, Summer, 1978.* Ed. Frank Tirro. Durham, N.C., 1982. Repr. in his *Music in the Culture of the Renaissance* 1:154–218.

——. *Music in the Culture of the Renaissance and Other Essays.* Ed. Bonnie J. Blackburn. 2 vols. Chicago, 1989.

——. "Orlando di Lasso's Antwerp Motet Book and Its Relationship to the Contemporary Netherlandish Motet." In his *Music in the Culture of the Renaissance* 1:433–82. Orig. published as *Das Antwerpener Motettenbuch Orlando di Lassos und seine Beziehungen zum Motettenschaffen der niederländischen Zeitgenossen.* The Hague, 1937.

——. "The Problem of Mannerism in Music: An Attempt at a Definition." *Studi musicali* 3 (1974): 131–218. Repr. in his *Music in the Culture of the Renaissance* 1:106–53.

——. "Problems in Adrian Willaert's Iconography." In *Aspects of Medieval and Renaissance Music: A Birthday Offering to Gustave Reese.* Ed. Jan La Rue et al., pp. 576–94. New York, 1966. Repr. in his *Music in the Culture of the Renaissance* 1:267–77.

——. "Rore's New Year's Gift for Albrecht V of Bavaria." In his *Music in the Culture of the Renaissance* 2:636–43.

———. "Zur Frage der Deklamationsrhythmik in der a-capella Musik des 16. Jahrhunderts." *Acta musicologica* 7 (1935): 62–67.

Lowry, Martin. *The World of Aldus Manutius: Business and Scholarship in Renaissance Venice.* Ithaca, 1979.

Lucchetta, Giuliano. "Viaggiatori e racconti di viaggi nel cinquecento." In *Storia della cultura veneta: dal primo quattrocento al concilio di Trenta.* Vol. 3, pt. 2. Ed. Girolamo Arnaldi and Manlio Pastore Stocchi, pp. 433–89. Vicenza, 1980.

Luoma, Robert G. "Relationships between Music and Poetry (Cipriano de Rore's *Quando signor lasciaste*)." *Musica disciplina* 31 (1977): 135–54.

Mace, Dean T. "Pietro Bembo and the Literary Origins of the Italian Madrigal." *The Musical Quarterly* 55 (1969): 65–86.

MacLuhan, Marshall. *The Gutenberg Galaxy: The Making of Typographic Man.* Toronto, 1962.

Malavasi, Stefania. "Giovanni Domenico Roncalli e l'Accademia degli Addormentati di Rovigo." *Archivio veneto,* 5th ser., 95 (1972): 47–58.

Maniates, Maria Rika. *Mannerism in Italian Music and Culture, 1530–1630.* Chapel Hill, 1979.

Marsh, David. *The Quattrocento Dialogue: Classical Tradition and Humanist Innovation.* Cambridge, Mass., 1980.

Marsili-Libelli, C. Ricottini. *Anton Francesco Doni, scrittore e stampatore.* Florence, 1960.

Martines, Lauro. "The Gentleman in Renaissance Italy: Strains of Isolation in the Body Politic." In *The Darker Vision of the Renaissance: Beyond the Fields of Reason.* Ed. Robert S. Kinsman, pp. 77–93. UCLA Center for Medieval and Renaissance Studies, Contributions, no. 6. Berkeley and Los Angeles, 1974.

———. *Power and Imagination: City-States in Renaissance Italy.* New York, 1979.

Mason, Kevin. "Per cantare e sonare: Lute Song Arrangements of Italian Vocal Polyphony at the End of the Renaissance." In *Playing Lute, Guitar, and Vihuela: Historical Practice and Modern Interpretation.* Ed. Victor Coelho. Cambridge, forthcoming.

Masson, Georgina. *Courtesans of the Italian Renaissance.* New York, 1975.

Maylender, Michele. *Storia delle accademie d'Italia.* 5 vols. Bologna, 1926–30.

Mazzacurati, Giancarlo. *Misure del classicismo rinascimentale.* Naples, 1967.

———. "Pietro Bembo." In *Storia della cultura veneta: dal primo quattrocento al concilio di Trenta.* Vol. 3, pt. 2. Ed. Girolamo Arnaldi and Manlio Pastore Stocchi, pp. 1–59. Vicenza, 1980.

Mazzotta, Giuseppe. "The *Canzoniere* and the Language of the Self." *Studies in Philology* 75 (1978): 271–96.

Medin, Antonio. "Il culto del Petrarca nel Veneto fino alla dittatura del Bembo." *Archivio veneto* 8 (1904): 421–65.

Meier, Bernhard. *The Modes of Classical Vocal Polyphony Described according to the Sources.* Trans. Ellen S. Beebe. Rev. ed. New York, 1988. Orig. published as *Die Tonarten der klassischen Vokalpolyphonie.* Utrecht, 1974.

———. "Rhetorical Aspects of Renaissance Modes." *Journal of the Royal Musical Association* 115 (1990): 182–90.

———. "Zur Modalität der *ad equales* disponierten Werke klassischer Vokalpolyphonie." In *Festschrift Georg von Dadelsen zum 60. Geburtstag.* Ed. Thomas Kohlhase and Volker Scherliess, pp. 230–39. Neuhausen-Stuttgart, 1978.

Meier, Helga. "Zur Chronologie der *Musica Nova* Adrian Willaerts." *Analecta musicologica* 12 (1973): 71–96.

Migliorini, Bruno. *The Italian Language.* Abridg., recast, and rev. T. Gwynfor Griffith. London, 1984.

Miller, Jonathan Marcus. "Word-Sound and Musical Texture in the Mid-Sixteenth-Century Venetian Madrigal." Ph.D. diss. University of North Carolina at Chapel Hill, 1991.

Molmenti, Pompeo. *La storia di Venezia nella vita privata dalle origini alla caduta della repubblica.* 7th ed. 3 vols. Bergamo, 1928.

Monterosso, Raffaello. "L'estetica di Gioseffo Zarlino." *Chigiana: Rassegna annuale di studi musicologici* 24 (1967): 13–28.

———. "Strutture ritmiche nel madrigale cinquecentesco." *Studi musicali* 3 (1974): 287–311.

Monterosso Vacchelli, Anna Maria. *L'opera musicale di Antonfrancesco Doni.* Instituta e monumenta, ser. 2, no. 1. Cremona, 1969.

Moore, James H. "Venezia favorita da Maria: Music for the Madonna Nicopeia and Santa Maria della Salute." *JAMS* 37 (1984): 299–355.

Morando di Custoza, Eugenio. *Libro d'arme di Venezia.* Verona, 1979.

Morelli, Jacopo, ed. *Operette.* Vol. 3. Venice, 1820.

Mortimer, Ruth. *Harvard College Library, Department of Printing and Graphic Arts: Catalogue of Books and Manuscripts.* Pt. 2: *Italian Sixteenth-Century Books.* 2 vols. Cambridge, Mass., 1974.

Moschini, l'Abbé. *Itineraire de la ville de Venise et des îles circonvoisines.* Venice, 1819.

Muir, Edward. *Civic Ritual in Renaissance Venice.* Princeton, 1981.

Muir, Edward, and Ronald F. E. Weissman. "Social and Symbolic Places in Renaissance Venice and Florence." In *The Power of Place: Bringing Together Geographical and Sociological Imaginations.* Ed. John A. Agnew and James S. Duncan, pp. 81–103. Boston, 1989.

Muraro, Maria Teresa. "La festa a Venezia e le sue manifestazioni rappresentative: La Compagnie della Calza e le *Momarie.*" In *Storia della cultura veneta: dal primo quattrocento al concilio di Trenta.* Vol. 3, pt. 3. Ed. Girolamo Arnaldi and Manlio Pastore Stocchi, pp. 315–41. Vicenza, 1981.

Muraro, Michelangelo. *Il "libro secondo" di Francesco e Jacopo dal Ponte.* Bassano and Florence, 1992.

Murphy, James J., ed. *Renaissance Eloquence: Studies in the Theory and Practice of Renaissance Rhetoric,* pp. 303–30. Berkeley and Los Angeles, 1983.

Die Musik in Geschichte und Gegenwart: Allgemeine Enzyklopädie der Musik. Ed. Friedrich Blume. 17 vols. Kassel, 1949–70. Index, 2 vols. Kassel, 1986.

Newcomb, Anthony. "Courtesans, Muses, or Musicians? Professional Women Musicians in Sixteenth-Century Italy." In *Women Making Music: The Western Art Tradition, 1150–1950.* Ed. Jane Bowers and Judith Tick, pp. 90–115. Urbana and Chicago, 1986.

——. "Editions of Willaert's *Musica Nova:* New Evidence, New Speculations." *JAMS* 26 (1973): 132–45.

——. *The Madrigal at Ferrara, 1579–1597.* 2 vols. Princeton, 1980.

Niccolini, G[iovanni].-B[attista]. *Filippo Strozzi, tragedia.* Florence, 1847.

Nuernberger, Louis Dean. "The Five-Voice Madrigals of Cipriano de Rore." Ph.D. diss. University of Michigan, 1963.

Nugent, George. "The Jacquet Motets and Their Authors." Ph.D. diss. Princeton University, 1973.

Nutter, David Alan. "The Italian Polyphonic Dialogue of the Sixteenth Century." 2 vols. Ph.D. diss. University of Nottingham, 1978.

Olivieri, Achille. "L'intellettuale e le accademie fra '500 e '600: Verona e Venezia." *Archivio veneto,* 5th ser., 130 (1988): 31–56.

Ong, Walter J. *Ramus, Method, and the Decay of Dialogue: From the Art of Discourse to the Art of Reason.* Cambridge, Mass., 1958.

Ongaro, Giulio Maria. "The Chapel of St. Mark's at the Time of Adrian Willaert (1527–1562): A Documentary Study." Ph.D. diss. University of North Carolina at Chapel Hill, 1986.

——. "Willaert, Gritti e Luppato: miti e realtà." *Studi musicali* 17 (1988): 55–70.

Ossola, Carlo. *Dal "Cortegiano" al' "Uomo di mondo": storia di un libro e di un modello sociale.* Turin, 1987.

Osthoff, Wolfgang. *Theatergesang und darstellende Musik in der italienischen Renaissance.* 2 vols. Tutzing, 1969.

Owens, Jessie Ann. "The Milan Partbooks: Evidence of Cipriano de Rore's Compositional Process." *JAMS* 37 (1984): 270–98.

——. "Mode in the Madrigals of Cipriano de Rore." In *Essays in Italian Music in the Cinquecento.* Altro Polo. Ed. Richard Charteris, pp. 1–15. Sydney, 1990.

——. "Music and Meaning in Cipriano de Rore's Setting of *Donec gratus eram tibi.*" In *Music and Language,* pp. 95–117. Studies in the History of Music, vol. 1. New York, 1983.

——. Review of Bonnie J. Blackburn, Edward E. Lowinsky, and Clement A. Miller, eds., *A Correspondence of Renaissance Musicians* (Oxford, 1991). In *JAMS* 46 (1993): 313–18.

Padley, G. A. *Grammatical Theory in Western Europe, 1500–1700: Trends in Vernacular Grammar II.* Cambridge, 1988.

Padoan, Giorgio. *Momenti del rinascimento veneto.* Padua, 1978.

———, ed. *Petrarca, Venezia e il Veneto*. Civiltà veneziana, Saggi, vol. 21. Fondazione Giorgio Cini, Centro di Cultura e Civiltà. Florence, 1976.

Pagan, Pietro. "Sulla Accademia 'Venetiana' o della 'Fama.'" *Atti dell'Istituto Veneto di Scienze, Lettere ed Arti* 132 (1973–74): 359–92.

Palisca, Claude V. *Humanism in Italian Renaissance Musical Thought*. New Haven, 1985.

———. "The Musical Humanism of Giovanni Bardi." In *Poesia e musica nell'estetica del XVI e XVII secolo, 3–10 maggio 1976*. Ed. Hagop Meyvalian, pp. 45–72. Florence, 1979.

Pappi, Lionello. "La teoria artistica nel cinquecento." In *Storia della cultura veneta: dal primo quattrocento al concilio di Trenta*. Vol. 3, pt. 3. Ed. Girolamo Arnaldi and Manlio Pastore Stocchi, pp. 173–92. Vicenza, 1981.

Parker, Deborah. *Commentary and Ideology: Dante in the Renaissance*. Durham, 1993.

Patterson, Annabel M. *Hermogenes and the Renaissance: Seven Ideas of Style*. Princeton, 1970.

Percival, Keith W. "Deep and Surface Structure Concepts in Renaissance and Medieval Syntactic Theory." In *History of Linguistic Thought and Contemporary Linguistics*. Ed. Herman Parret, pp. 238–53. Berlin and New York, 1976.

———. "Grammar and Rhetoric in the Renaissance." In *Renaissance Eloquence: Studies in the Theory and Practice of Renaissance Rhetoric*. Ed. James J. Murphy, pp. 303–30. Berkeley and Los Angeles, 1983.

Percopo, E[rasmo]. "Dragonetto Bonifacio, marchese d'Orio: rimatore napolitano del sec. XVI." *Giornale storico della letteratura italiana* 10 (1887): 197–233.

Perkins, Leeman L. Review of Edward E. Lowinsky, *The Medici Codex of 1518: A Choirbook of Motets Dedicated to Lorenzo de' Medici, Duke of Urbino* (Monuments of Renaissance Music, vols. 3–5 [Chicago, 1968]). In *The Musical Quarterly* 55 (1969): 255–69.

Pesenti, Tiziana. "Stampatori e letterati nell'industria editoriale a Venezia e in terraferma." In *Storia della cultura veneta: il seicento*. Vol. 4, pt. 1. Ed. Girolamo Arnaldi and Manlio Pastore Stocchi, pp. 93–129. Vicenza, 1983.

Petrie, Jennifer. *Petrarch: The Augustan Poets, the Italian Tradition and the Canzoniere*. Dublin, 1983.

Petrocchi, Giorgio. *La dottrina linguistica del Bembo*. Messina, 1959.

Phillippy, Patricia. "Gaspara Stampa's *Rime*: Replication and Retraction." *Philological Quarterly* 68 (1989): 1–24.

Pigman, G. W., III. "Versions of Imitation in the Renaissance." *RQ* 33 (1980): 1–32.

Pilot, Antonio. "Gli ordini dell'Accademia Veneziana degli Uniti 1551." *Ateneo veneto* 35 (1912): 193–207.

———. *Un peccataccio di Domenico Venier*. Repr. Rome, 1906.

Pincus, Debra. *The Arco Foscari: The Building of a Triumphal Gateway in Fifteenth-Century Venice*. New York, 1976.

Pirotti, Umberto. "Benedetto Varchi e la questione della lingua." *Convivium* 28 (1960): 524–52.

Pirrotta, Nino. *Music and Culture in Italy from the Middle Ages to the Baroque: A Collection of Essays*. Cambridge, Mass., 1984.

———. "Musiche intorno a Tiziano." In *Tiziano e Venezia: Convegno Internazionale di Studi, Venezia, 1976*. Ed. Neri Pozza et al., pp. 29–34. Vicenza, 1980.

———. "The Oral and Written Traditions of Music." In his *Music and Culture*, pp. 72–79.

———. "*Ricercare* and Variations on *O rosa bella*." In his *Music and Culture*, pp. 145–58.

———. "Willaert and the *Canzone villanesca*." In his *Music and Culture*, pp. 175–97.

Pirrotta, Nino, and Elena Povoledo. *Music and Theatre from Poliziano to Monteverdi*. Trans. Karen Eales. Cambridge, 1982.

Plumb, J. H. *The Italian Renaissance: A Concise Survey of Its History and Culture*. New York, 1965.

Poulakos, Takis, ed. *Rethinking the History of Rhetoric: Multidisciplinary Essays on the Rhetorical Tradition*. Boulder, 1993.

Powers, Harold S. "Is Mode Real? Pietro Aron, the Octenary System, and Polyphony." *Basler Jahrbuch für historische Musikpraxis* 16 (1992): 9–52.

———. "The Modality of *Vestiva i colli*." In *Studies in Renaissance and Baroque Music in Honor of Arthur Mendel*, pp. 31–46. Kassel, 1974.

———. "Mode." *The New Grove* 12:376–450.

———. "Tonal Types and Modal Categories in Renaissance Polyphony." *JAMS* 34 (1981): 428–70.

Princeton Encyclopedia of Poetry and Poetics. Ed. Alex Preminger; Frank J. Warnke and O. B. Hardison, Jr., assoc. eds. Enlarged ed. Princeton, 1974.

Prizer, William F. "The Frottola and the Unwritten Tradition." *Studi musicali* 15 (1986): 3–37.
———. "Games of Venus: Secular Vocal Music in the Late Quattrocento and Early Cinquecento." *Journal of Musicology* 9 (1991): 3–56.
Pullan, Brian. "The Occupations and Investments of the Venetian Nobility in the Middle and Late Sixteenth Century." In *Renaissance Venice*. Ed. John R. Hale, pp. 379–408. London, 1973.
———. *Rich and Poor in Renaissance Venice: The Social Institutions of a Catholic State to 1620.* Oxford, 1971.
———, ed. *Crisis and Change in the Venetian Economy in the Sixteenth and Seventeenth Centuries.* London, 1958.
Queller, Donald E. *The Venetian Patriciate: Reality versus Myth.* Urbana and Chicago, 1986.
Queller, Donald E., and Thomas F. Madden. "Father of the Bride: Fathers, Daughters, and Dowries in Late Medieval and Early Renaissance Venice." *RQ* 46 (1993): 685–711.
Quilligan, Maureen. "Sidney and His Queen." In *The Historical Renaissance*. Ed. Heather Dubrow and Richard Strier, pp. 171–96. Chicago, 1989.
Quondam, Amedeo. *Le "carte messaggiere": retorica e modelli di comunicazione epistolare, per un indice dei libri di lettere del cinquecento.* Rome, 1981.
———. *Petrarchismo mediato: per una critica della forma antologia.* Rome, 1974.
Raimondi, Ezio. "Bernardo Daniello, lettore di poesia." In *Rinascimento inquieto,* pp. 23–69. Palermo, 1965.
———. *Poesia come retorica.* Florence, 1980.
Rashdall, Hastings. *The Universities in the Middle Ages.* Rev. ed. F. M. Powicke and A. B. Emden. 3 vols. Vol. 1, *Salerno—Bologna—Paris.* Oxford, 1936.
Rebhorn, Wayne A. *Courtly Performances: Masking and Festivity in Castiglione's "Book of the Courtier."* Detroit, 1978.
Reese, Gustave. *Music in the Renaissance.* Rev. ed. New York, 1959.
Richter, Bodo L. O. "Petrarchism and Anti-Petrarchism among the Veniers." *Forum italicum* 3 (1969): 20–42.
Rizzi, Fortunato. "La moda lirica del cinquecento: le forme e i gradi del petrarchismo." *La rassegna nazionale* 49 (1928): 178–85.
Rocca, Emilio Nasalli. *I Farnese.* Varese, 1969.
Roche, Jerome. *The Madrigal.* Oxford, 1972. 2d ed. 1990.
Romano, Dennis. "Aspects of Patronage in Fifteenth- and Sixteenth-Century Venice." *RQ* 46 (1993): 712–33.
———. *Patricians and "Popolani": The Social Foundations of the Venetian Renaissance State.* Baltimore, 1987.
Rosand, David. *Painting in Cinquecento Venice: Titian, Veronese, Tintoretto.* New Haven, 1982.
———. "So-and-So Reclining on Her Couch." In *Titian: 500.* Ed. Joseph Manca. Studies in the History of Art. Washington, D.C., 1994.
———. "Titian and the Critical Tradition." In *Titian: His World and His Legacy.* Ed. David Rosand, pp. 1–39. New York, 1982.
———. "Venereal Hermeneutics: Reading Titian's *Venus of Urbino.*" In *Renaissance Society and Culture: Essays in Honor of Eugene F. Rice, Jr.* Ed. John Monfasani and Ronald G. Musto, pp. 263–80. New York, 1991.
———. "*Venetia figurata:* The Iconography of a Myth." In *Interpretazioni veneziane: studi di storia dell'arte in onore di Michelangelo Muraro,* pp. 177–96. Ed. David Rosand. Venice, 1984.
Rosand, Ellen. "Barbara Strozzi, *virtuosissima cantatrice:* The Composer's Voice." *JAMS* 31 (1978): 241–81.
———. "Music in the Myth of Venice." *RQ* 30 (1977): 511–37.
———. *Opera in Seventeenth-Century Venice: The Creation of a Genre.* Berkeley and Los Angeles, 1991.
Rose, Paul Lawrence. "The *Accademia Venetiana:* Science and Culture in Renaissance Venice." *Studi veneziani* 11 (1969): 191–242.
Rosenthal, Margaret F. *The Honest Courtesan: Veronica Franco, Citizen and Writer in Sixteenth-Century Venice.* Chicago, 1992.
———. "Veronica Franco: The Courtesan as Poet in the Sixteenth Century." Ph.D. diss. Yale University, 1985.

———. "Veronica Franco's *Terze Rime:* The Venetian Courtesan's Defense." *RQ* 42 (1989): 227–57.

Ross, James Bruce. "Venetian Schools and Teachers, Fourteenth to Early Sixteenth Century: A Survey and a Study of Giovanni Battista Egnazio." *RQ* 29 (1976): 521–60.

Rossi, Vittorio. "Appunti per la storia della musica alla corte di Francesco Maria e di Guidobaldo della Rovere." *Rassegna emiliana* 1 (1888): 453–69.

Rubsamen, Walter H. "From Frottola to Madrigal: The Changing Pattern of Secular Italian Vocal Music." In *Chanson & Madrigal, 1480–1530: Studies in Comparison and Contrast.* Isham Memorial Library, 13–14 September 1961. Ed. James Haar, pp. 51–87. Cambridge, Mass., 1964.

Rudmann, Valnea. "Lettura della canzone per la peste di Venezia di Maffio Venier." *Atti dell'Istituto Veneto di Scienze, Lettere ed Arti* 121 (1962–63): 599–641.

Ruggiero, Guido. *The Boundaries of Eros: Sex Crime and Sexuality in Renaissance Venice.* Oxford, 1985.

Sagredo, Agostino. "Statuti della Fraternità e Compagnia dei Fiorentini in Venezia dell'anno MDLVI dati in luce per cura e preceduti da un discorso." *Archivio storico italiano,* App. 9 (1853): 441–97.

Salza, Abdelkader. "Madonna Gasparina Stampa, secondo nuove indagini." *Giornale storico della letteratura italiana* 62 (1913): 1–101.

———. "Madonna Gasparina Stampa e la società veneziana del suo tempo (nuove discussioni)." *Giornale storico della letteratura italiana* 66 (1917): 217–306.

Santangelo, Giorgio. *Le epistole "De imitatione" di Giovanfrancesco Pico della Mirandola e di Pietro Bembo.* Florence, 1954.

———. *Il petrarchismo del Bembo e di altri poeti del '500.* Rome, 1967.

Saviotti, Alfredo. "Un'artista del cinquecento: Virginia Vagnoli." *Bulletino senese di storia patria* 26 (1919): 105–34.

Scaglione, Aldo, ed. *Francis Petrarch, Six Centuries Later: A Symposium.* North Carolina Studies in the Romance Languages and Literature, Symposia, no. 3. Chapel Hill and Chicago, 1975.

Schulz, Juergen. "Jacobo de' Barbari's *View of Venice:* Map Making, City Views, and Moralized Geography before the Year 1500." *Art Bulletin* 60, no. 31 (1978): 425–74.

———. *The Printed Plans and Panoramic Views of Venice (1486–1797).* Saggi e memorie di storia dell'arte, no. 7. Venice, 1970.

Schulz-Buschhaus, Ulrich. *Das Madrigal: Zur Stilgeschichte der italienischen Lyrik zwischen Renaissance und Barock.* Bad Homburg, 1969.

Schutte, Anne Jacobson. "Commemorators of Irene di Spilimbergo." *RQ* 45 (1992): 524–36.

———. "Irene di Spilimbergo: The Image of a Creative Woman in Late Renaissance Italy." *RQ* 44 (1991): 42–61.

———. "The *Lettere Volgari* and the Crisis of Evangelism in Italy." *RQ* 28 (1975): 639–88.

Scoppa, M. Ant. *Rapport présenté au nom de la Section de Musique, et adopté par la Classe des Beaux-Arts de L'Institut Impérial de France, dans ses séances du 18 avril et des 2 et 9 mai 1812, sur un ouvrage intitulé: Les Vrais Principes de la versification, développés par un examen comparatif entre les langues italienne et française, etc.* Paris, 1812.

Scott, Izora. *Controversies over the Imitation of Cicero in the Renaissance.* 1910; Davis, Calif., 1991.

Scrivano, Riccardo. "Cultura e letteratura in Sperone Speroni." In *Cultura e letteratura nel cinque-cento,* pp. 117–42. Rome, 1966.

———. *La norma e lo scarto: proposte per il cinquecento letterario italiano.* Rome, 1980.

———. "La poetessa Veronica Franco." In *Cultura e letteratura nel cinquecento,* pp. 195–228. Rome, 1966.

Seigel, Jerrold. *Rhetoric and Philosophy in Renaissance Humanism: The Union of Eloquence and Wisdom, Petrarch to Valla.* Princeton, 1968.

Selfridge-Field, Eleanor. *Venetian Instrumental Music from Gabrieli to Vivaldi.* New York, 1975.

Sherr, Richard. "Verdelot in Florence, Coppini in Rome, and the Singer 'La Fiore'." *JAMS* 37 (1984): 402–11.

Simone, Raffaele. "Sperone Speroni et l'idée de diachronie dans la linguistique de la Renaissance italienne." In *History of Linguistic Thought and Contemporary Linguistics.* Ed. Herman Parret, pp. 302–16. New York, 1976.

Slim, H. Colin. "An Iconographical Echo of the Unwritten Tradition." *Studi musicali* 17 (1988): 33–54.

———. "Parabosco, Girolamo." *The New Grove* 14:173–77.

———. "A Royal Treasure at Sutton Coldfield." *Early Music* 6 (1978): 57–74.

———. "Verdelot, Philippe." *The New Grove* 19:631–35.

Smarr, Janet L. "Gaspara Stampa's Poetry for Performance." *Journal of the Rocky Mountain Medieval and Renaissance Association* 12 (1991): 61–84.

Smith, Barbara Herrnstein. *Poetic Closure: A Study of How Poems End.* Chicago, 1968.

Snyder, Jon R. *Writing the Scene of Speaking: Theories of Dialogue in the Late Italian Renaissance.* Stanford, 1989.

Spingarn, Joel E. *Literary Criticism in the Renaissance.* Repr. with introduction by Bernard Weinberg. 1899; New York, 1963.

Starn, Randolph. *Contrary Commonwealth: The Theme of Exile in Medieval and Renaissance Italy.* Berkeley and Los Angeles, 1982.

———. *Donato Giannotti and His "Epistolae": Biblioteca Universitaria Alessandrina, Rome, M. 107.* Travaux d'humanisme et renaissance, 97. Geneva, 1968.

Stocchi, Manlio Pastore. "Scuola e cultura umanistica fra due secoli." In *Storia della cultura veneta: dal primo quattrocento al concilio di Trenta.* Vol. 3, pt. 1. Ed. Girolamo Arnaldi and Manlio Pastore Stocchi, pp. 93–121. Vicenza, 1980.

Sybrandy, Henry. "Abondante, Giulio." *The New Grove* 1:20.

Taddeo, Edoardo. *Il manierismo letterario e i lirici veneziani del tardo cinquecento.* Rome, 1974.

Tagliavini, Luigi F. "Abondante, Giulio." *Dizionario biografico degli italiani,* 1:55–56.

Tanturli, Giuliano. "Il disprezzo per Dante dal Petrarca al Bruni." *Rinascimento,* 2d ser., 25 (1985): 199–220.

Tassini, Giuseppe. *Alcuni palazzi ed antichi edifichi di Venezia storicamente illustrati con annotazioni.* Venice, 1879.

———. *Curiosità veneziane, ovvero origini delle denominazioni stradali di Venezia.* 4th ed. Venice, 1887. Rev. ed. Lino Moretti. Venice, 1988.

Tenenti, Alberto. "The Sense of Space and Time in the Venetian World of the Fifteenth and Sixteenth Centuries." In *Renaissance Venice.* Ed. John R. Hale, pp. 17–46. London, 1973.

Tigerstedt, E. N. "Observations on the Reception of the Aristotelian *Poetics* in the Latin West." *Studies in the Renaissance* 15 (1968): 7–24.

Tiraboschi, Girolamo. *Storia della letteratura italiana.* Vol. 7, 4 pts. Milan, 1824.

Todorov, Tzvetan. *Mikhail Bakhtin: The Dialogical Principle.* Trans. Wlad Godzich. Minneapolis, 1984.

Toffanin, Giuseppe. *Storia della letteratura d'Italia: il cinquecento.* 3d ed. Milan, 1945.

Tomlinson, Gary. "Madrigal, Monody, and Monteverdi's *via naturale alla immitatione.*" *JAMS* 34 (1981): 60–108.

———. *Monteverdi and the End of the Renaissance.* Berkeley and Los Angeles, 1987.

———. *Music in Renaissance Magic: Toward a Historiography of Others.* Chicago, 1993.

———. "Rinuccini, Peri, Monteverdi, and the Humanist Heritage of Opera." Ph.D. diss. University of California at Berkeley, 1979.

Trinkaus, Charles. *The Poet as Philosopher: Petrarch and the Formation of Renaissance Consciousness.* New Haven, 1979.

Tripet, Arnaud. *Pétrarque, ou la connaissance de soi.* Geneva, 1967.

Trovato, Paolo. *Dante in Petrarca: per un inventario dei dantismi nei "Rerum vulgarium fragmenta."* Florence, 1979.

Tucci, Ugo. "Il patrizio veneziano mercante e umanista." In *Venezia centro di mediazione tra oriente e occidente (secoli XV–XVI): aspetti e problemi.* 2 vols. Ed. Hans-Georg Beck et al., 1:335–58. Fondazione Giorgio Cini. Florence, 1977.

———. "The Psychology of the Venetian Merchant in the Sixteenth Century." In *Renaissance Venice.* Ed. John R. Hale, pp. 346–78. London, 1973.

Turrini, Giuseppe. *L'Accademia Filarmonica di Verona dalla fondazione (maggio 1543) al 1600 e il suo patrimonio musicale antico.* Atti e memorie della Accademia di Agricoltura, Scienze e Lettere di Verona, no. 18. Verona, 1941.

———. *Catalogo delle opere musicali: città di Verona, Biblioteca della Società Accademia Filarmonica di Verona.* BMB, ser. 1, no. 18. Bologna, 1983.

Tyson, Gerald P., and Sylvia S. Wagonheim, eds. *Print and Culture in the Renaissance: Essays on the Advent of Printing in Europe.* Newark, Del., 1986.

Vallone, Aldo. "Di alcuni aspetti del petrarchismo napoletano (con inediti di Scipione Ammirato)." *Studi petrarcheschi* 7 (1961): 355–75.

Vasoli, Cesare. *Marsilio Ficino e il ritorno di Platone.* Ed. Gian Carlo Garfagnini. Studi e documenti. 2 vols. Florence, 1986.

Vecchio, Edoardo del. *I Farnese.* Istituto di Studi Romani. Città di Castello, 1972.

Venezia e d'intorni. Guida d'Italia del Touring Club Italiano. 2d ed. Milan, 1969.

Ventura, A. "Contarini, Lorenzo." *Dizionario biografico degli italiani,* 28:231–33. Rome, 1983.

Vianello, Valerio. *Il letterato, l'accademia, il libro: contributi sulla cultura veneta del cinquecento.* Biblioteca Veneta, no. 6. Padua, 1988.

——. "Tra Firenze e Venezia: il fenomeno del fuoruscitismo." In *Il letterato, l'accademia, il libro: contributi sulla cultura veneta del cinquecento,* pp. 17–46. Biblioteca Veneta, no. 6. Padua, 1988.

Vickers, Nancy J. "Diana Described: Scattered Woman and Scattered Rhyme." In *Writing and Sexual Difference.* Ed. Elizabeth Abel, pp. 95–109. Chicago, 1982.

——. "Vital Signs: Petrarch and Popular Culture." *Romanic Review* 79 (1988): 184–95.

Villas, James. "The Petrarchan Topos *Bel Piede:* Generative Footsteps." *Romance Notes* 11 (1969–70): 167–73.

Vinciguerra, Mario. *Interpretazione del petrarchismo.* Turin, 1926.

Vogel, Emil. *Bibliografia della musica italiana profana nuova ed. interamente rifatta e aumentata con gli indici dei musicisti, poeti, cantanti, dedicatari e dei capoversi dei testi letterari.* [*Il nuovo Vogel.*] Rev. ed. François Lesure and Claudio Sartori. 3 vols. Pomezia, 1977.

——. *Bibliothek der gedruckten weltlichen Vocalmusik Italiens, aus den Jahren 1500 bis 1700.* Berlin, 1892. Rev., enlarged ed. Alfred Einstein. Hildesheim, 1962. Repr. from *Music Library Association Notes* 2–4 (1944–48).

Waisman, Leonardo Julio. "The Ferrarese Madrigal in the Mid-Sixteenth Century." 4 vols. Ph.D. diss. The University of Chicago, 1988.

Walker, D. P. *Music, Spirit, and Language in the Renaissance.* Ed. Penelope Gouk. London, 1985.

——. *Spiritual and Demonic Magic from Ficino to Campanella.* Notre Dame, Ind., 1975.

Waller, Marguerite R. *Petrarch's Poetics and Literary History.* Amherst, 1980.

Ward, John O. "Commentators on Ciceronian Rhetoric in the Renaissance." In *Renaissance Eloquence: Studies in the Theory and Practice of Renaissance Rhetoric.* Ed. James J. Murphy, pp. 126–73. Berkeley, 1983.

Weinberg, Bernard. *A History of Literary Criticism in the Italian Renaissance.* 2 vols. Chicago, 1961.

Wethey, Harold E. *The Paintings of Titian: Complete Edition.* 2 vols. New York, 1971.

Weyler, Walter. "Documenten betreffende de muziekkapel aan het hof van Ferrara." *Vlaamsch Jaarboek voor Muziekgeschiedenis* 1 (1939): 81–113.

Whigham, Frank. *Ambition and Privilege: The Social Tropes of Elizabethan Courtesy Poetry.* Berkeley and Los Angeles, 1984.

Wienpahl, Robert W. "Zarlino, the Senario, and Tonality." *JAMS* 12 (1959): 27–41.

Wilkins, Ernest Hatch. *A History of Italian Literature.* Rev. ed. Thomas Bergin. Cambridge, Mass., 1974.

——. *The Making of the "Canzoniere" and Other Petrarchan Studies.* Storia e Letteratura, Raccolta di Studi e Testi, no. 38. Rome, 1951.

Williams, Ralph C. "The Originality of Daniello." *Romanic Review* 15 (1924): 121–22.

Woodhouse, J. R. *Baldesar Castiglione: A Reassessment of "The Courtier."* Edinburgh, 1978.

Zancan, Marina. "L'intellettualità femminile nel primo cinquecento: Maria Savorgnan e Gaspara Stampa." In *Women's Voices in Italian Literature.* Ed. Rebecca West and Dino Cervigni. *Annali d'italianistica* 7 (1989): 42–65.

Zenck, Hermann. "Zarlinos *Istitutioni harmoniche* als Quelle zur Musikanschauung der italienischen Renaissance." *Zeitschrift für Musikwissenschaft* 12 (1929–30): 540–78.

Zimmerman, Susan, and Ronald F. E. Weissman, eds. *Urban Life in the Renaissance.* Newark, Del., 1989.

Zingarelli, Nicolò. *Le rime di Francesco Petrarca.* Bologna, 1963.

Zorzi, Alvise. *Cortigiana veneziana: Veronica Franco e i suoi poeti.* Milan, 1986.

——. *Venezia scomparsa.* 2d ed. Milan, 1984.

Zorzi, Marino, ed. *Collezioni di antichità a Venezia nei secoli della repubblica (dai libri e documenti della Biblioteca Marciana).* Rome, 1988.

Music examples and plates are designated *(ex.)* or *(exx.)* and *(pl.)* or *(plates)* following the page number.

Compositor: Impressions
Music setter: Thomas Bauman
Text: 10/14 Galliard
Display: Galliard
Printer: Edwards Brothers, Inc.
Binder: Edwards Brothers, Inc.

VENETIA ex Aereis Formis BOLOGNINI ZALTERII.

AL SIG. GIROLAMO MVRARI,
Paolo Forlani Veronese.

VENETIA Città marauiglioso, Magnifico Signor mio, da tutto l'vniuerso per fama, et antichità, et celebrata antichità di molti honorati Gentil huomini con non poca mia diligenza è stata da me intagliata inseme in questa commoda, et picciola forma, accio che cadauno puossi sopra di questa carta intheramente considerarla; hauendo io, il maggior inftruttione segnate le numeriche sorti più notabili leuata da esse ricontrada dimostrano tutte le particolarità, che l'huomo dinderà di sapere.